Little Lulu's Pal *Pal* TUBBY™

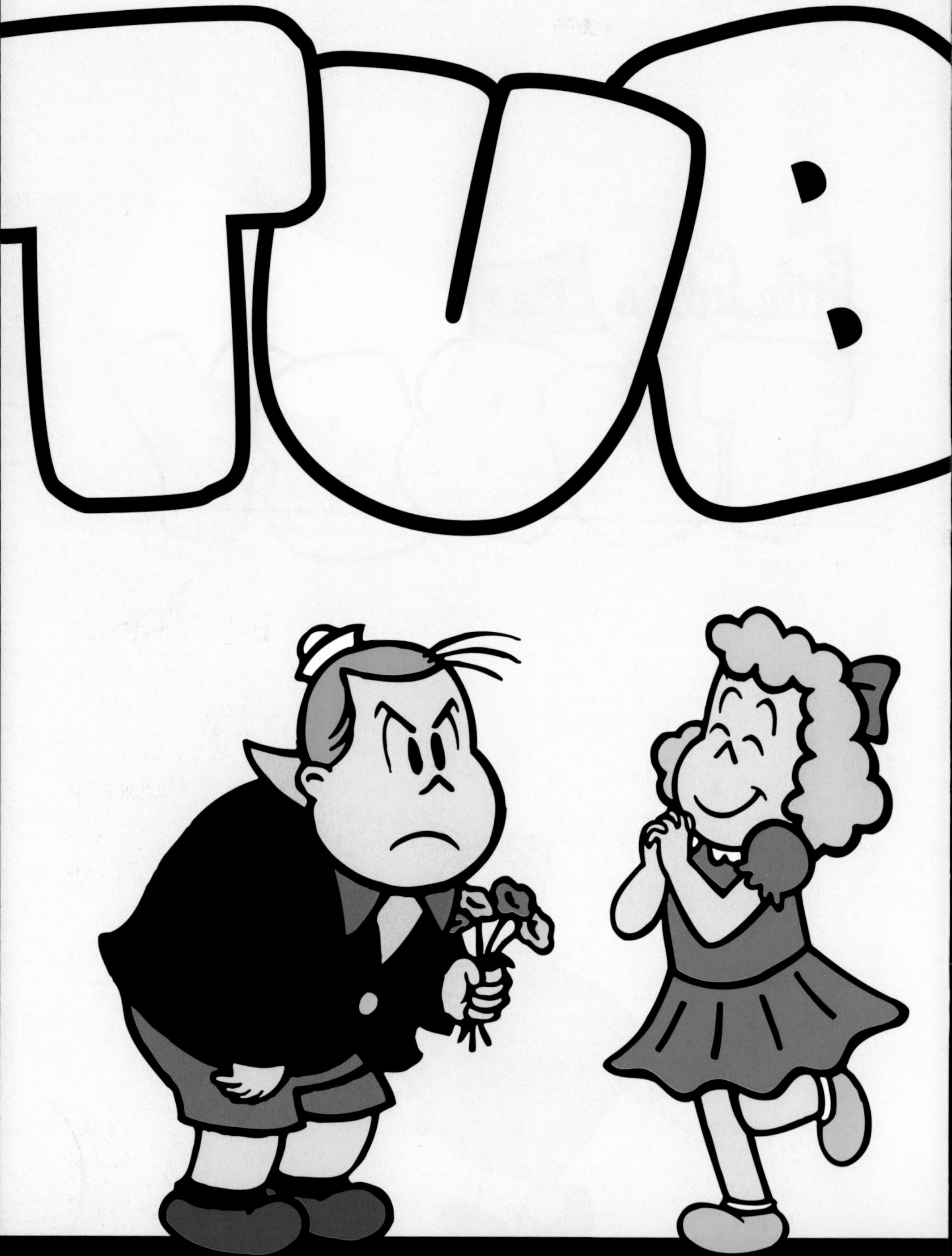
TUB

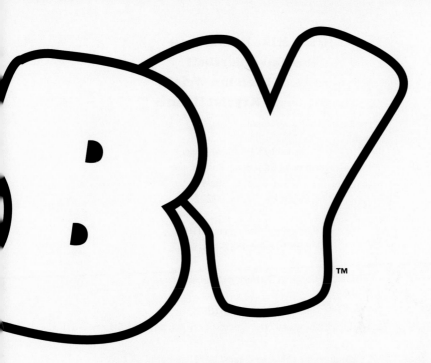

™

The Castaway and Other Stories

Story and art by
John Stanley

Finishes on *Four Color Comics* #381
Irving Tripp

Based on the character created by
Marge Buell

Dark Horse Books®

Publisher **Mike Richardson**

Editor **Dave Marshall**

Assistant Editor **Brendan Wright**

Collection Designer **Krystal Hennes**

Published by Dark Horse Books

A division of Dark Horse Comics, Inc.

10956 SE Main Street

Milwaukie, Oregon 97222

First edition: September 2010

ISBN 978-1-59582-421-9

Library of Congress Cataloging-in-Publication Data

Stanley, John, 1914-1993.

Little Lulu's pal Tubby : the castaway and other stories / story and art, John Stanley. -- 1st ed.

p. cm.

"Based on the character created by Marge Buell."

ISBN 978-1-59582-421-9

I. Title.

PN6727.S656L58 2010

741.5'973--dc22

2010006180

Little Lulu's Pal Tubby™ Vol. 1: The Castaway and Other Stories

This volume contains every comic from *Four Color Comics* issues #381, #430, #444, and #461, and issues #5–#6 of *Marge's Tubby*, all originally published by Dell Comics from March 1952 to October 1953.

Mike Richardson, President and Publisher • Neil Hankerson, Executive Vice President • Tom Weddle, Chief Financial Officer • Randy Stradley, Vice President of Publishing • Michael Martens, Vice President of Business Development • Anita Nelson, Vice President of Marketing, Sales, and Licensing • David Scroggy, Vice President of Product Development • Dale LaFountain, Vice President of Information Technology • Darlene Vogel, Director of Purchasing • Ken Lizzi, General Counsel • Davey Estrada, Editorial Director • Scott Allie, Senior Managing Editor • Chris Warner, Senior Books Editor • Diana Schutz, Executive Editor • Cary Grazzini, Director of Design and Production • Lia Ribacchi, Art Director • Cara Niece, Director of Scheduling

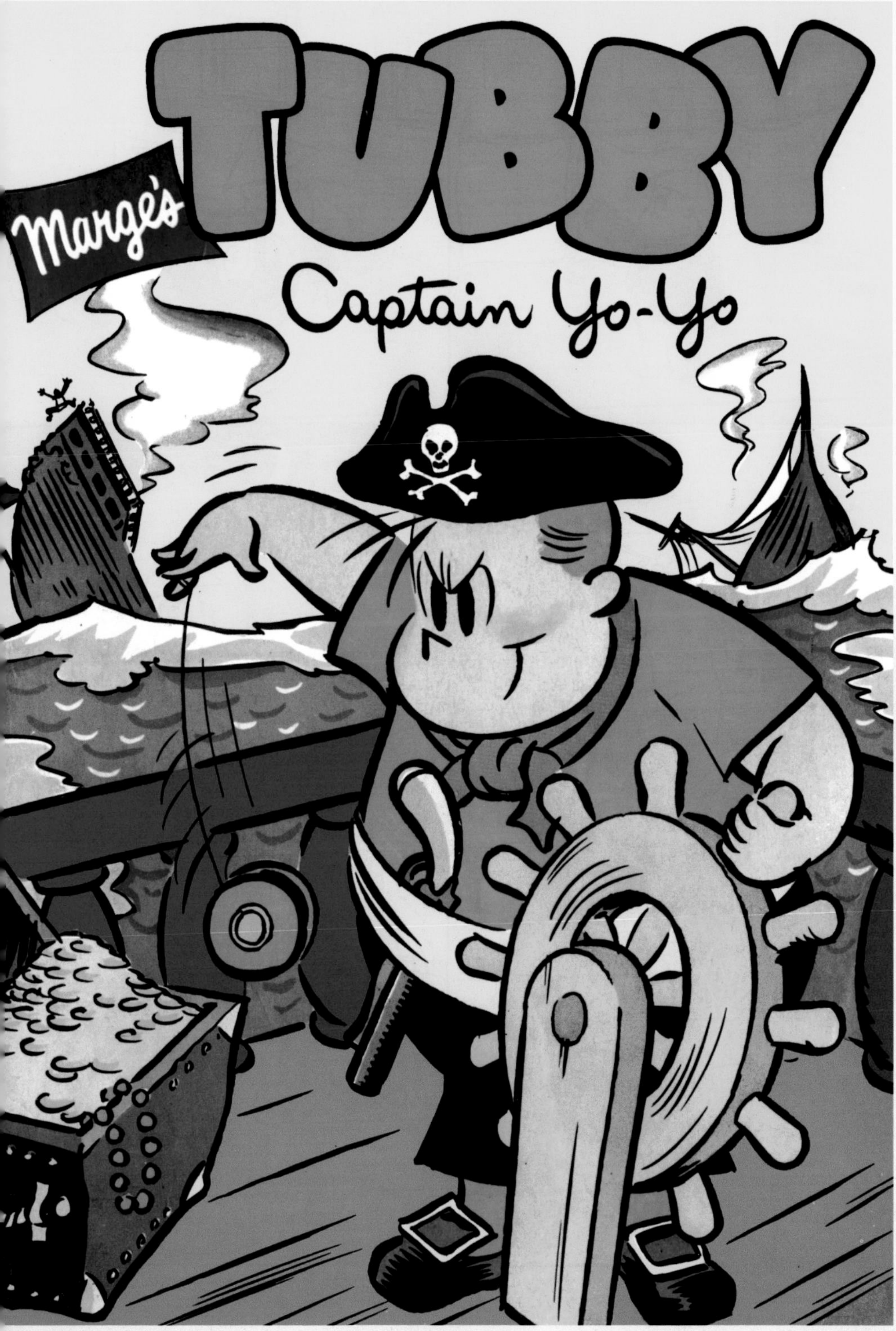
Marge's
TUBBY
Captain Yo-Yo

TUBBY

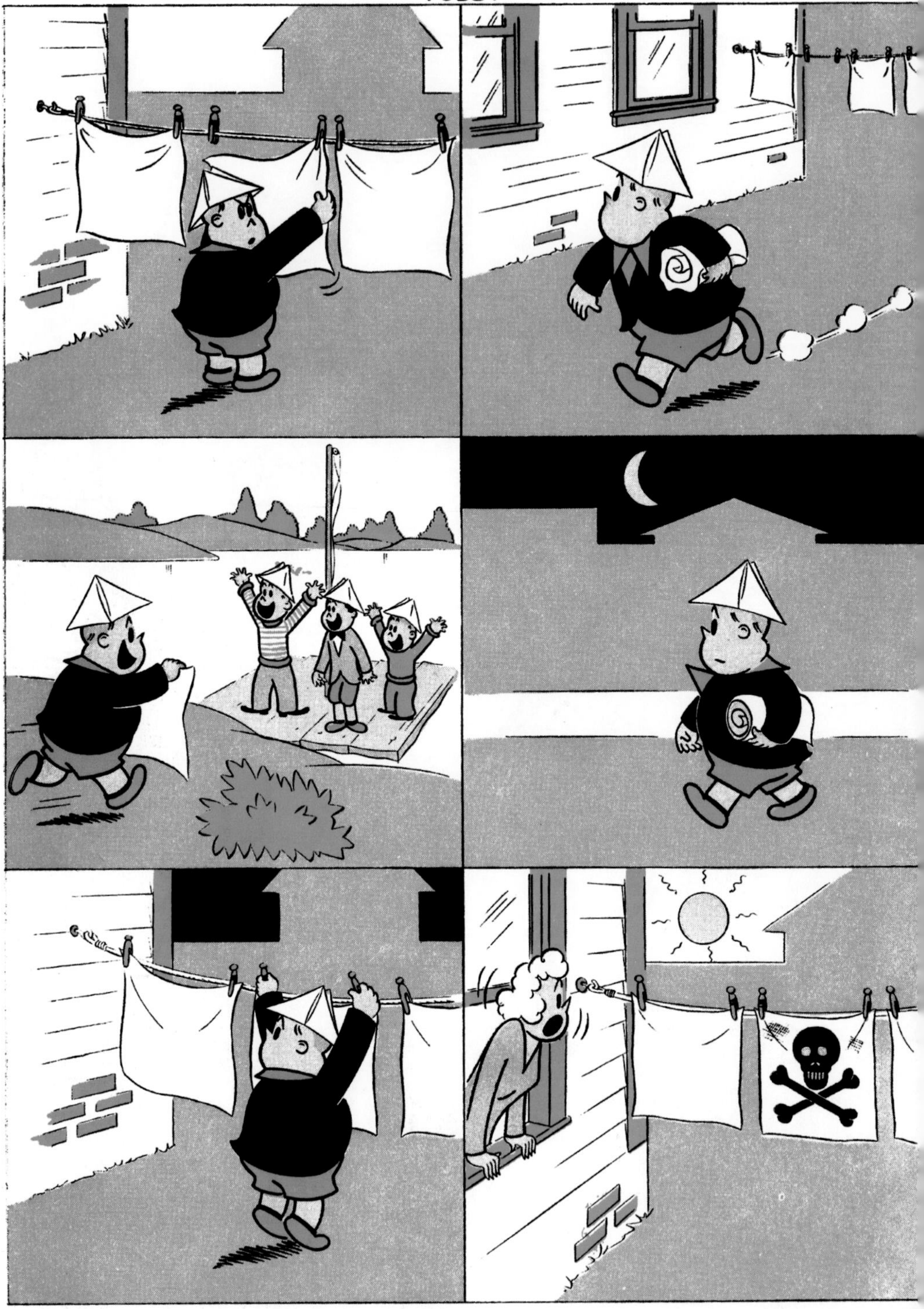

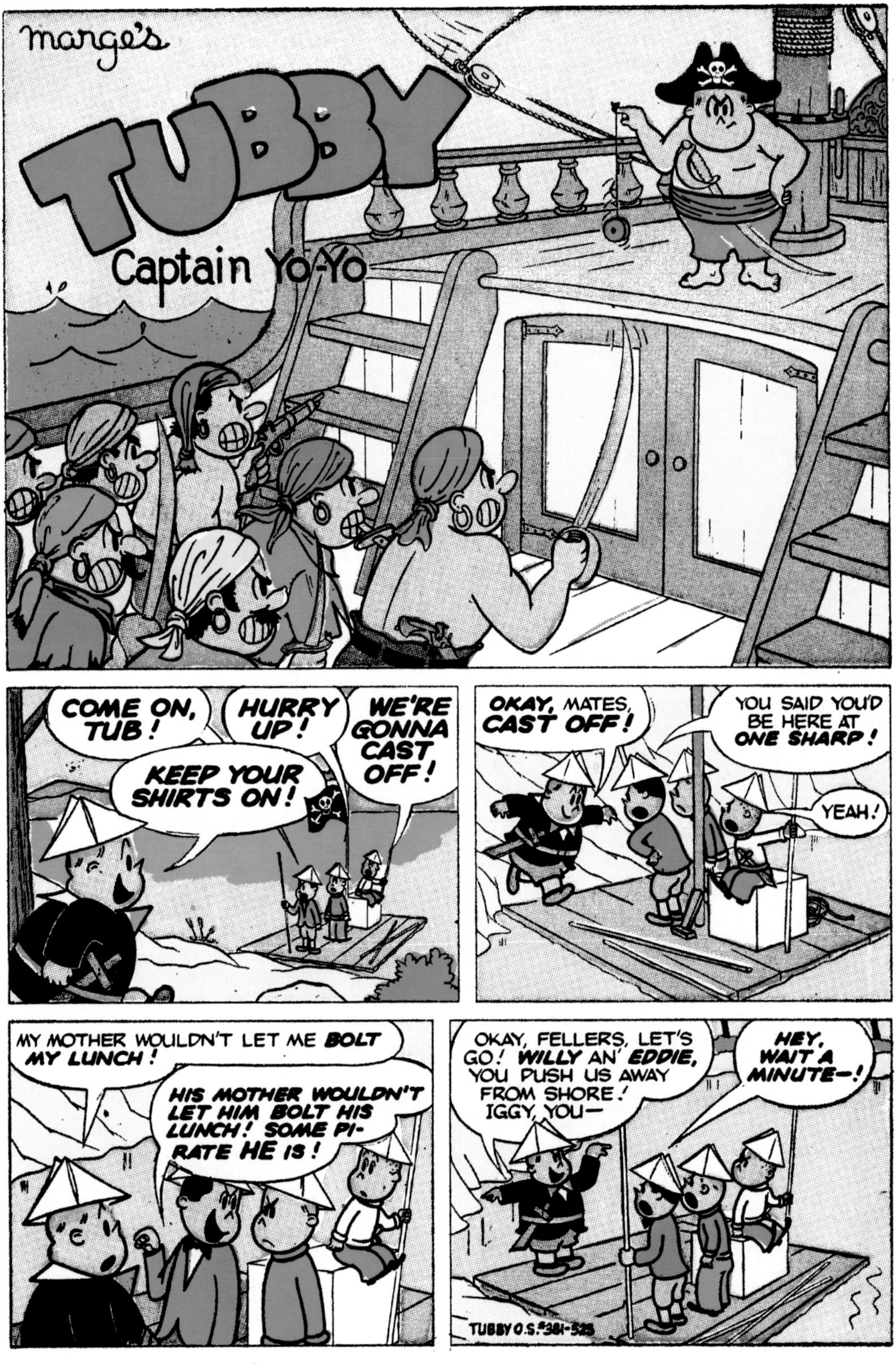

marge's
TUBBY
Captain Yo-Yo
COME ON, TUB!
HURRY UP!
WE'RE GONNA CAST OFF!
KEEP YOUR SHIRTS ON!
OKAY, MATES, CAST OFF!
YOU SAID YOU'D BE HERE AT ONE SHARP!
YEAH!
MY MOTHER WOULDN'T LET ME BOLT MY LUNCH!
HIS MOTHER WOULDN'T LET HIM BOLT HIS LUNCH! SOME PI-RATE HE IS!
OKAY, FELLERS, LET'S GO! WILLY AN' EDDIE, YOU PUSH US AWAY FROM SHORE! IGGY, YOU—
HEY, WAIT A MINUTE—!
TUBBY O.S. #381-525

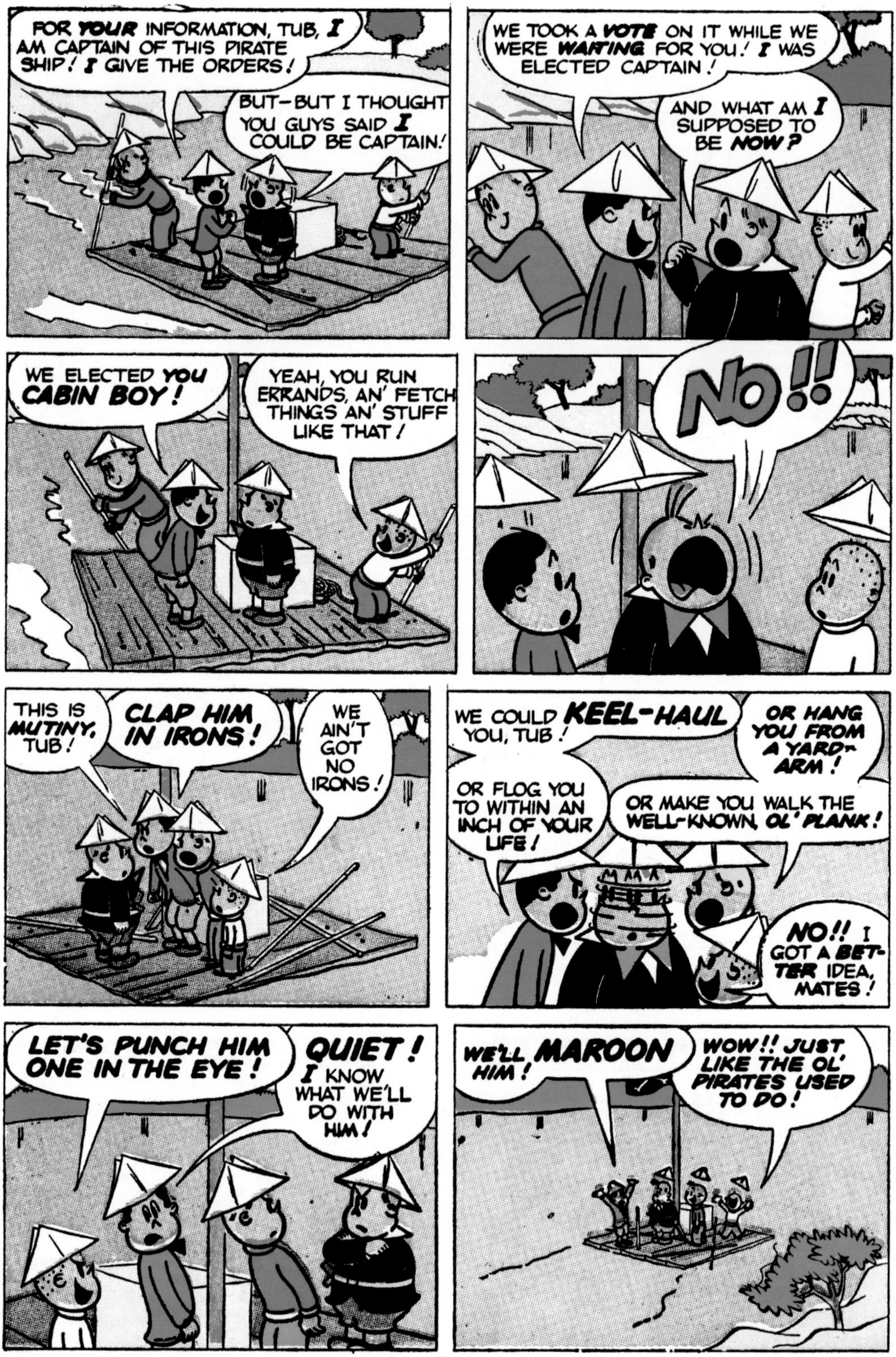
FOR YOUR INFORMATION, TUB, I AM CAPTAIN OF THIS PIRATE SHIP! I GIVE THE ORDERS!
BUT-BUT I THOUGHT YOU GUYS SAID I COULD BE CAPTAIN!
WE TOOK A VOTE ON IT WHILE WE WERE WAITING FOR YOU! I WAS ELECTED CAPTAIN!
AND WHAT AM I SUPPOSED TO BE NOW?
WE ELECTED YOU CABIN BOY!
YEAH, YOU RUN ERRANDS, AN' FETCH THINGS AN' STUFF LIKE THAT!
NO!!
THIS IS MUTINY, TUB!
CLAP HIM IN IRONS!
WE AIN'T GOT NO IRONS!
WE COULD KEEL-HAUL YOU, TUB!
OR HANG YOU FROM A YARD-ARM!
OR FLOG YOU TO WITHIN AN INCH OF YOUR LIFE!
OR MAKE YOU WALK THE WELL-KNOWN OL' PLANK!
NO!! I GOT A BETTER IDEA, MATES!
LET'S PUNCH HIM ONE IN THE EYE!
QUIET! I KNOW WHAT WE'LL DO WITH HIM!
WE'LL MAROON HIM!
WOW!! JUST LIKE THE OL' PIRATES USED TO DO!

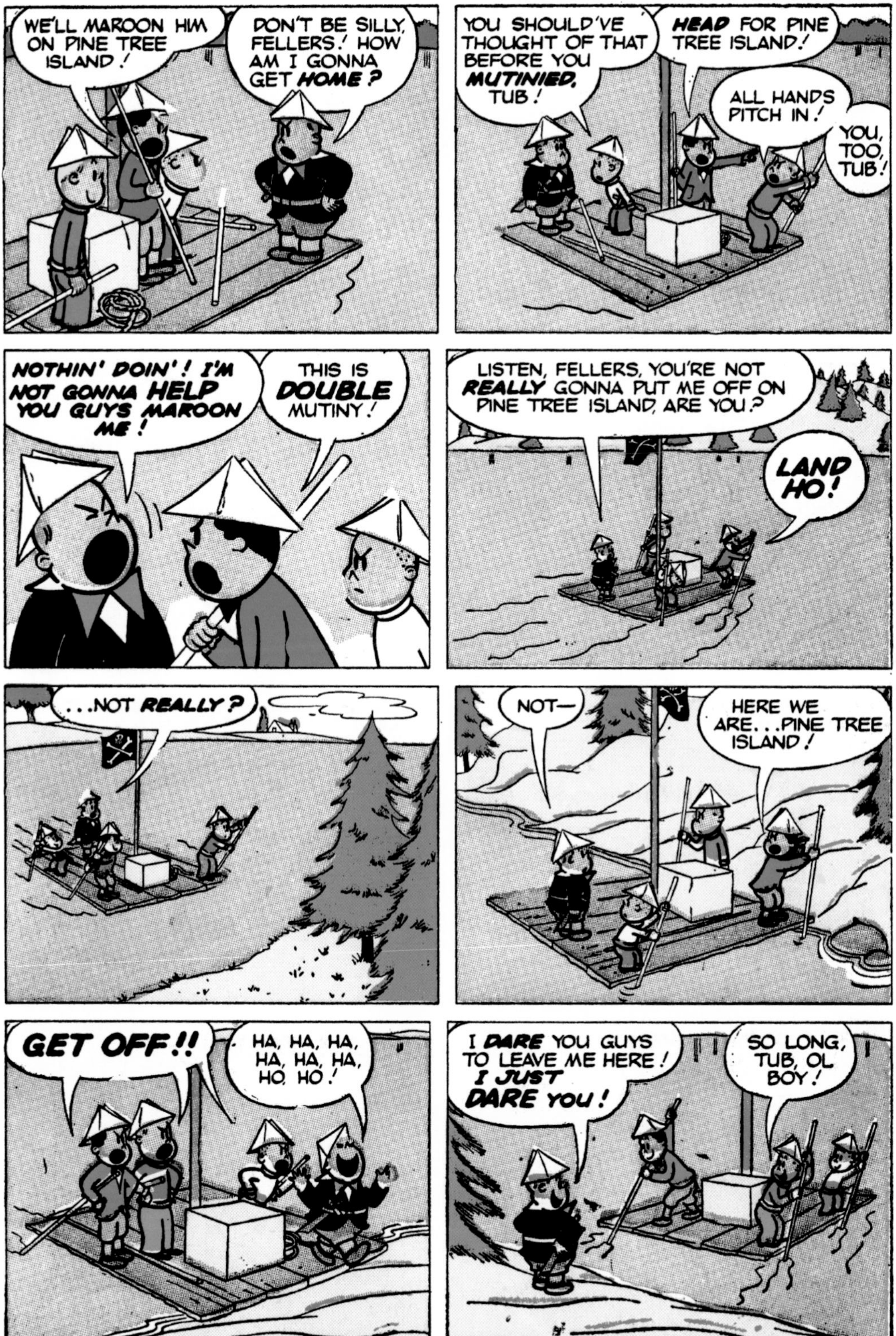

WE'LL MAROON HIM ON PINE TREE ISLAND!
DON'T BE SILLY, FELLERS! HOW AM I GONNA GET HOME?
YOU SHOULD'VE THOUGHT OF THAT BEFORE YOU MUTINIED, TUB!
HEAD FOR PINE TREE ISLAND!
ALL HANDS PITCH IN!
YOU, TOO, TUB!
NOTHIN' DOIN'! I'M NOT GONNA HELP YOU GUYS MAROON ME!
THIS IS DOUBLE MUTINY!
LISTEN, FELLERS, YOU'RE NOT REALLY GONNA PUT ME OFF ON PINE TREE ISLAND, ARE YOU?
LAND HO!
...NOT REALLY?
NOT—
HERE WE ARE...PINE TREE ISLAND!
GET OFF!!
HA, HA, HA, HA, HA, HA, HO, HO!
I DARE YOU GUYS TO LEAVE ME HERE! I JUST DARE YOU!
SO LONG, TUB, OL BOY!

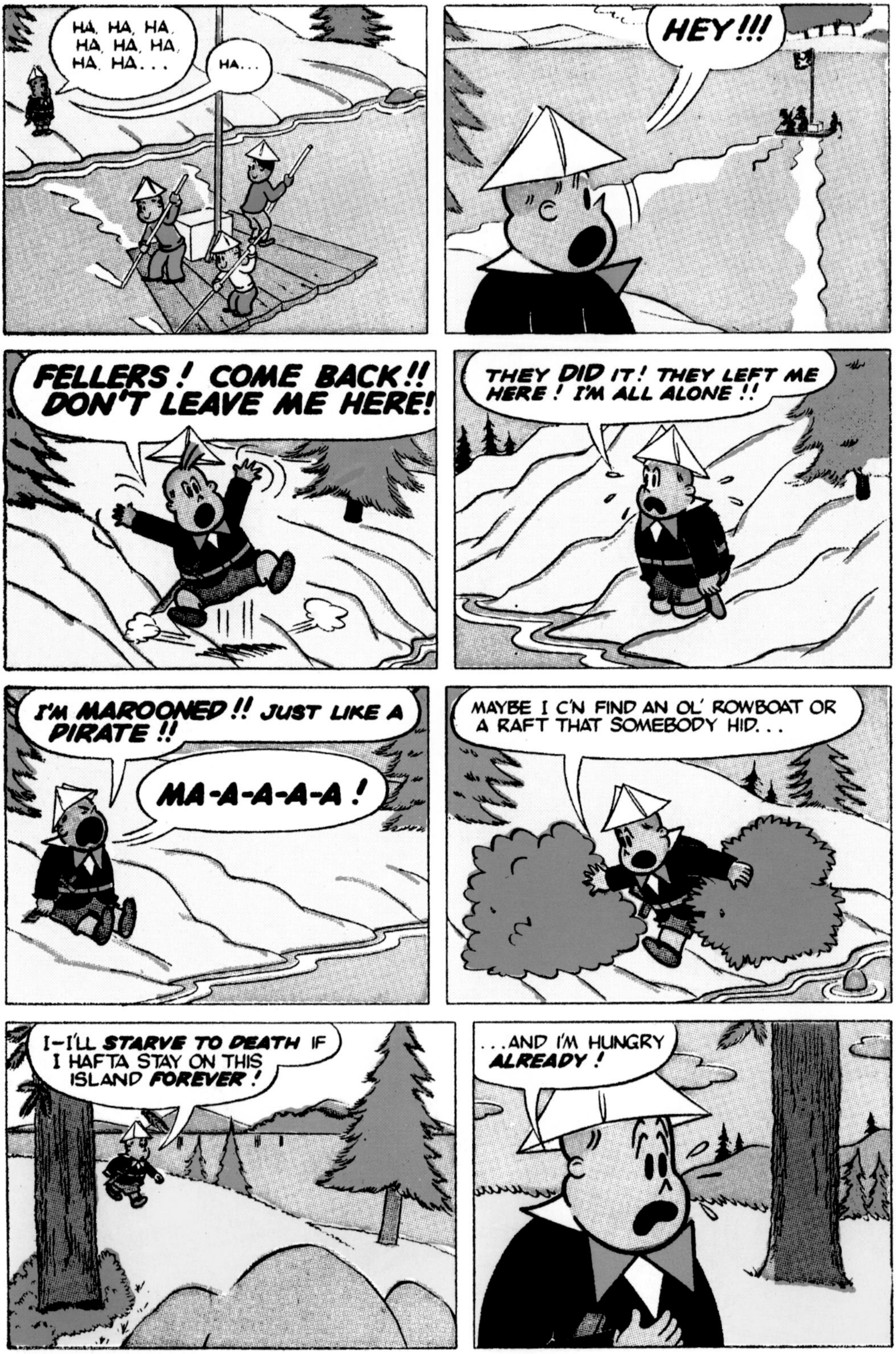
HA, HA, HA, HA, HA, HA, HA, HA...
HA...
HEY!!!
FELLERS! COME BACK!! DON'T LEAVE ME HERE!
THEY DID IT! THEY LEFT ME HERE! I'M ALL ALONE!!
I'M MAROONED!! JUST LIKE A PIRATE!!
MA-A-A-A-A!
MAYBE I C'N FIND AN OL' ROWBOAT OR A RAFT THAT SOMEBODY HID...
I–I'LL STARVE TO DEATH IF I HAFTA STAY ON THIS ISLAND FOREVER!
...AND I'M HUNGRY ALREADY!

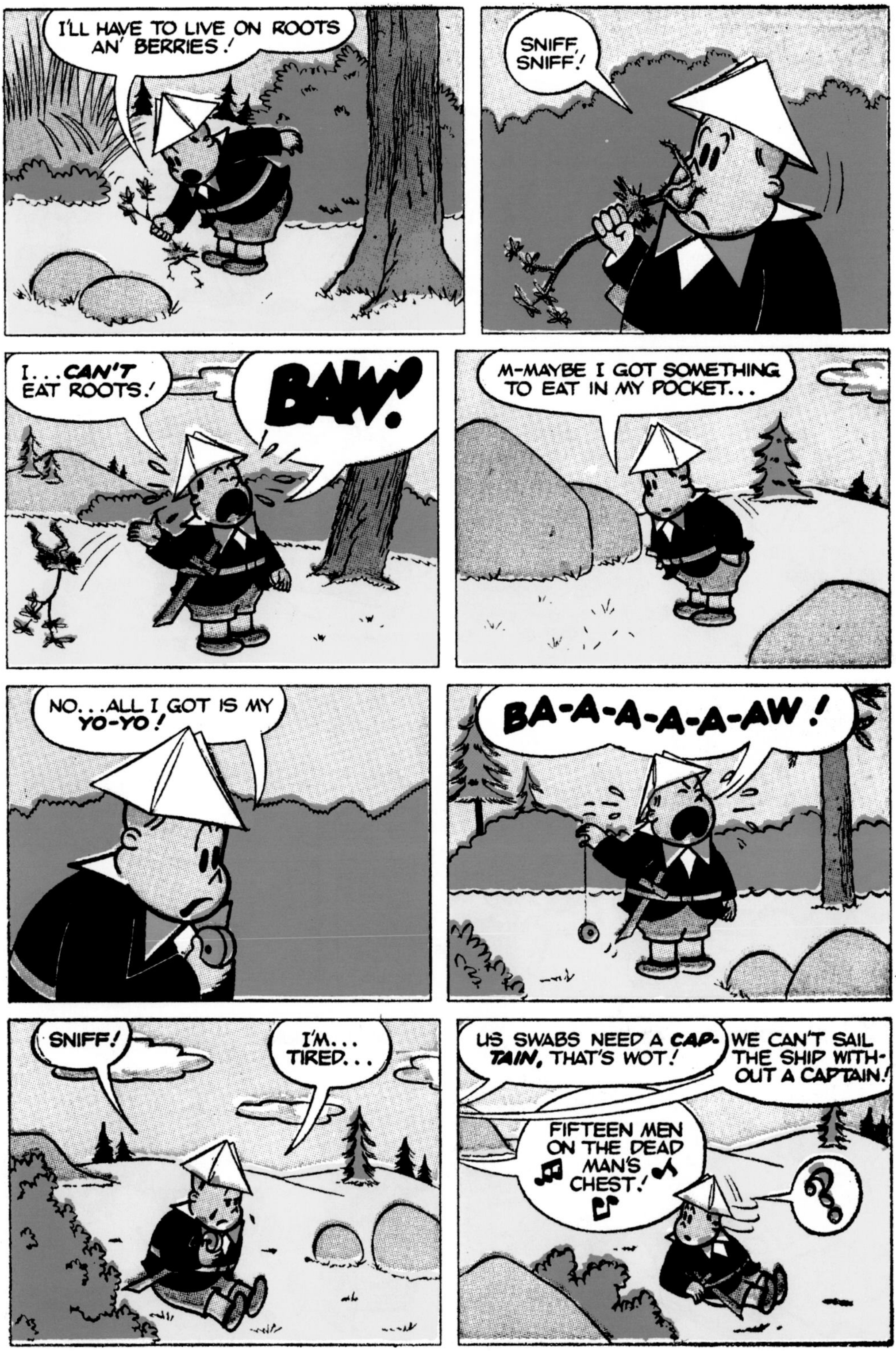
I'LL HAVE TO LIVE ON ROOTS AN' BERRIES!
SNIFF SNIFF!
I...CAN'T EAT ROOTS!
BAW!
M-MAYBE I GOT SOMETHING TO EAT IN MY POCKET...
NO...ALL I GOT IS MY YO-YO!
BA-A-A-A-A-AW!
SNIFF!
I'M... TIRED...
US SWABS NEED A CAPTAIN, THAT'S WOT!
WE CAN'T SAIL THE SHIP WITHOUT A CAPTAIN!
FIFTEEN MEN ON THE DEAD MAN'S CHEST!
?

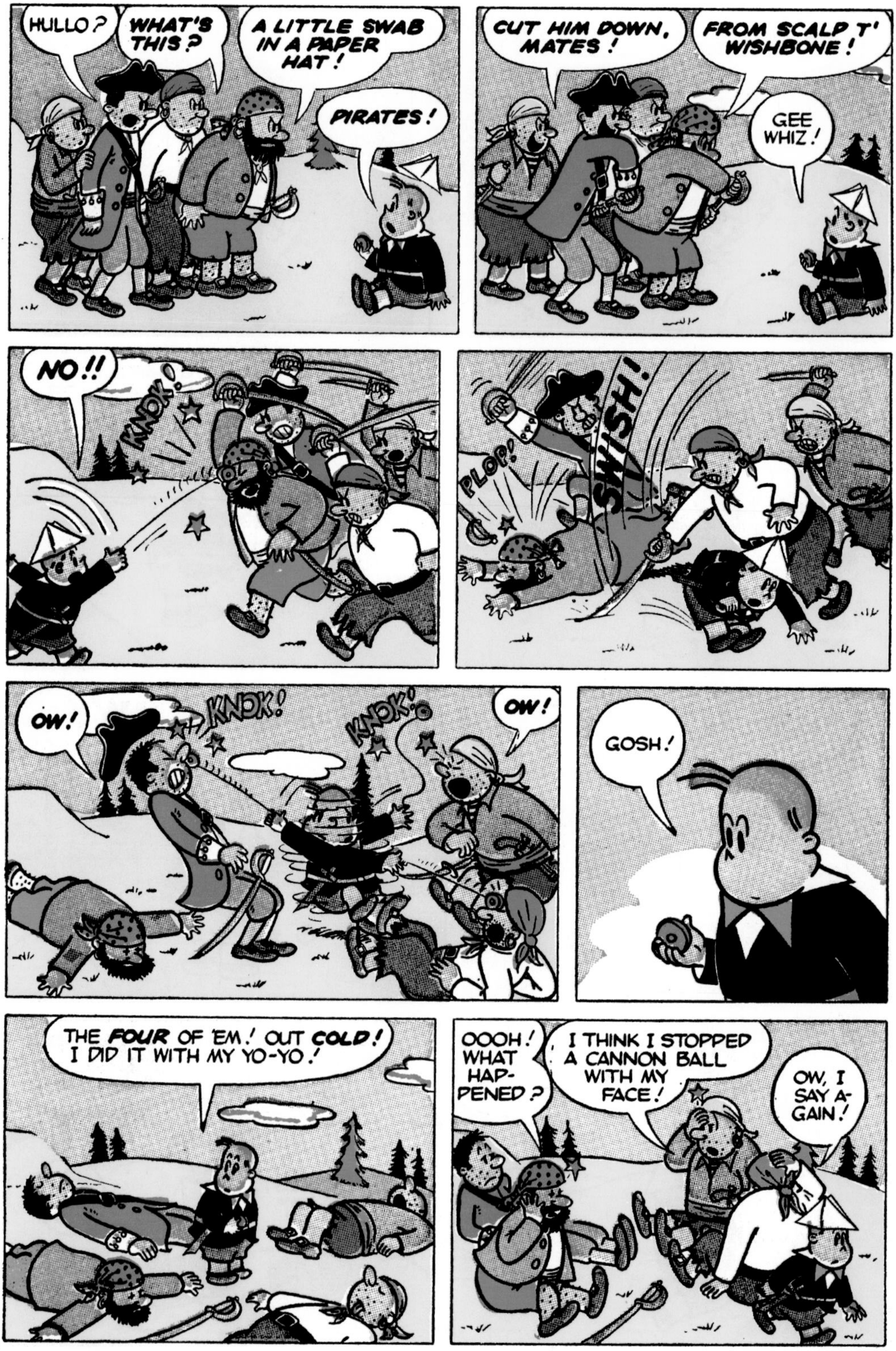
HULLO?
WHAT'S THIS?
A LITTLE SWAB IN A PAPER HAT!
PIRATES!
CUT HIM DOWN, MATES!
FROM SCALP T' WISHBONE!
GEE WHIZ!
NO!!
KNOK!
PLOP!
SWISH!
OW!
KNOK!
KNOK!
OW!
GOSH!
THE FOUR OF 'EM! OUT COLD! I DID IT WITH MY YO-YO!
OOOH! WHAT HAP-PENED?
I THINK I STOPPED A CANNON BALL WITH MY FACE!
OW, I SAY A-GAIN!

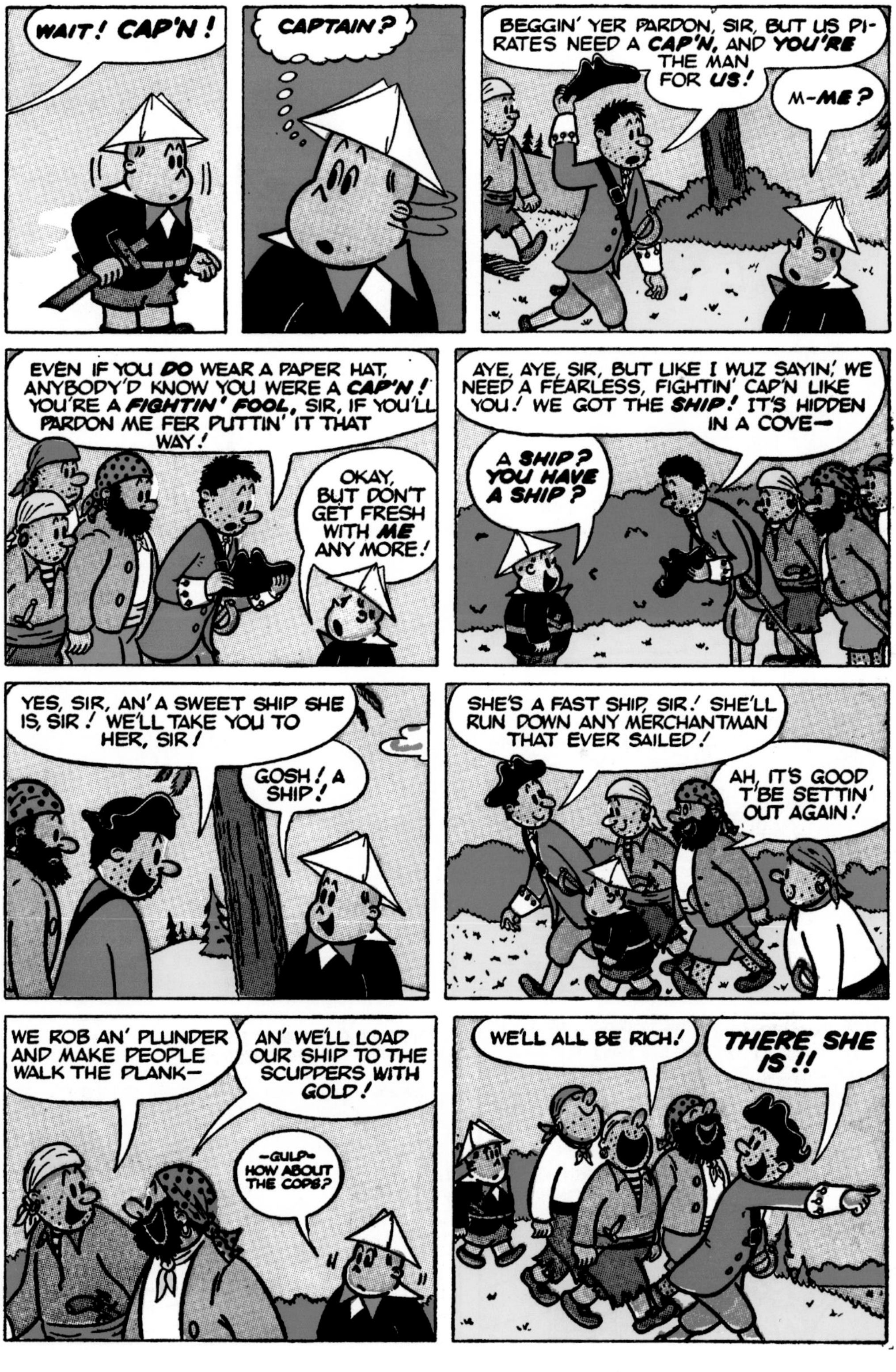

WAIT! CAP'N!
CAPTAIN?
BEGGIN' YER PARDON, SIR, BUT US PI-RATES NEED A CAP'N, AND YOU'RE THE MAN FOR US!
M-ME?
EVEN IF YOU DO WEAR A PAPER HAT, ANYBODY'D KNOW YOU WERE A CAP'N! YOU'RE A FIGHTIN' FOOL, SIR, IF YOU'LL PARDON ME FER PUTTIN' IT THAT WAY!
OKAY, BUT DON'T GET FRESH WITH ME ANY MORE!
AYE, AYE, SIR, BUT LIKE I WUZ SAYIN,' WE NEED A FEARLESS, FIGHTIN' CAP'N LIKE YOU! WE GOT THE SHIP! IT'S HIDDEN IN A COVE—
A SHIP? YOU HAVE A SHIP?
YES, SIR, AN' A SWEET SHIP SHE IS, SIR! WE'LL TAKE YOU TO HER, SIR!
GOSH! A SHIP!
SHE'S A FAST SHIP, SIR! SHE'LL RUN DOWN ANY MERCHANTMAN THAT EVER SAILED!
AH, IT'S GOOD T'BE SETTIN' OUT AGAIN!
WE ROB AN' PLUNDER AND MAKE PEOPLE WALK THE PLANK—
AN' WE'LL LOAD OUR SHIP TO THE SCUPPERS WITH GOLD!
—GULP— HOW ABOUT THE COPS?
WE'LL ALL BE RICH!
THERE SHE IS!!

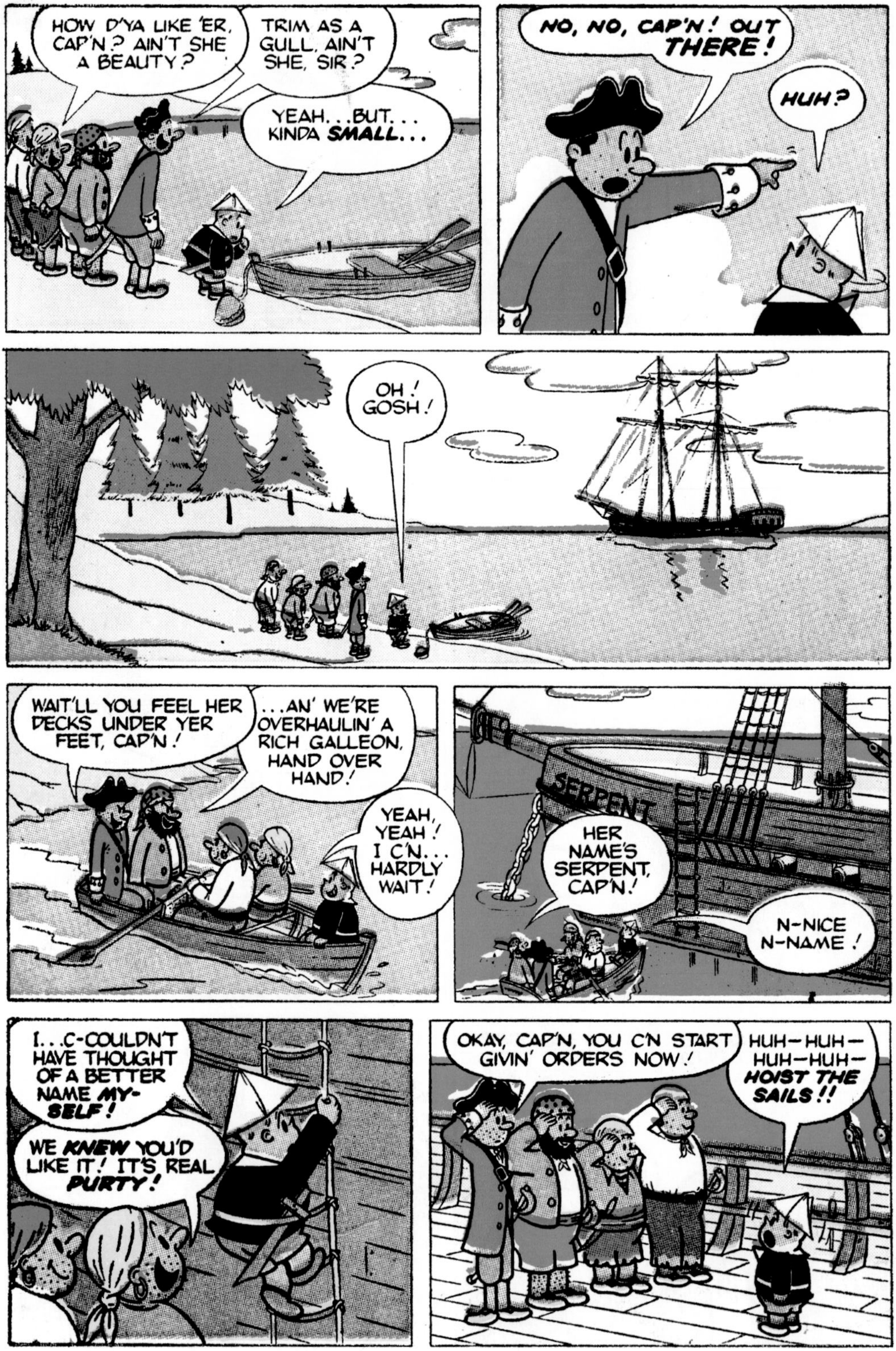
HOW D'YA LIKE 'ER, CAP'N? AIN'T SHE A BEAUTY?
TRIM AS A GULL, AIN'T SHE, SIR?
YEAH...BUT... KINDA SMALL...
NO, NO, CAP'N! OUT THERE!
HUH?
OH! GOSH!
WAIT'LL YOU FEEL HER DECKS UNDER YER FEET, CAP'N!
...AN' WE'RE OVERHAULIN' A RICH GALLEON, HAND OVER HAND!
YEAH, YEAH! I C'N... HARDLY WAIT!
SERPENT
HER NAME'S SERPENT, CAP'N!
N-NICE N-NAME!
I...C-COULDN'T HAVE THOUGHT OF A BETTER NAME MY-SELF!
WE KNEW YOU'D LIKE IT! IT'S REAL PURTY!
OKAY, CAP'N, YOU C'N START GIVIN' ORDERS NOW!
HUH—HUH—HUH—HUH—HOIST THE SAILS!!

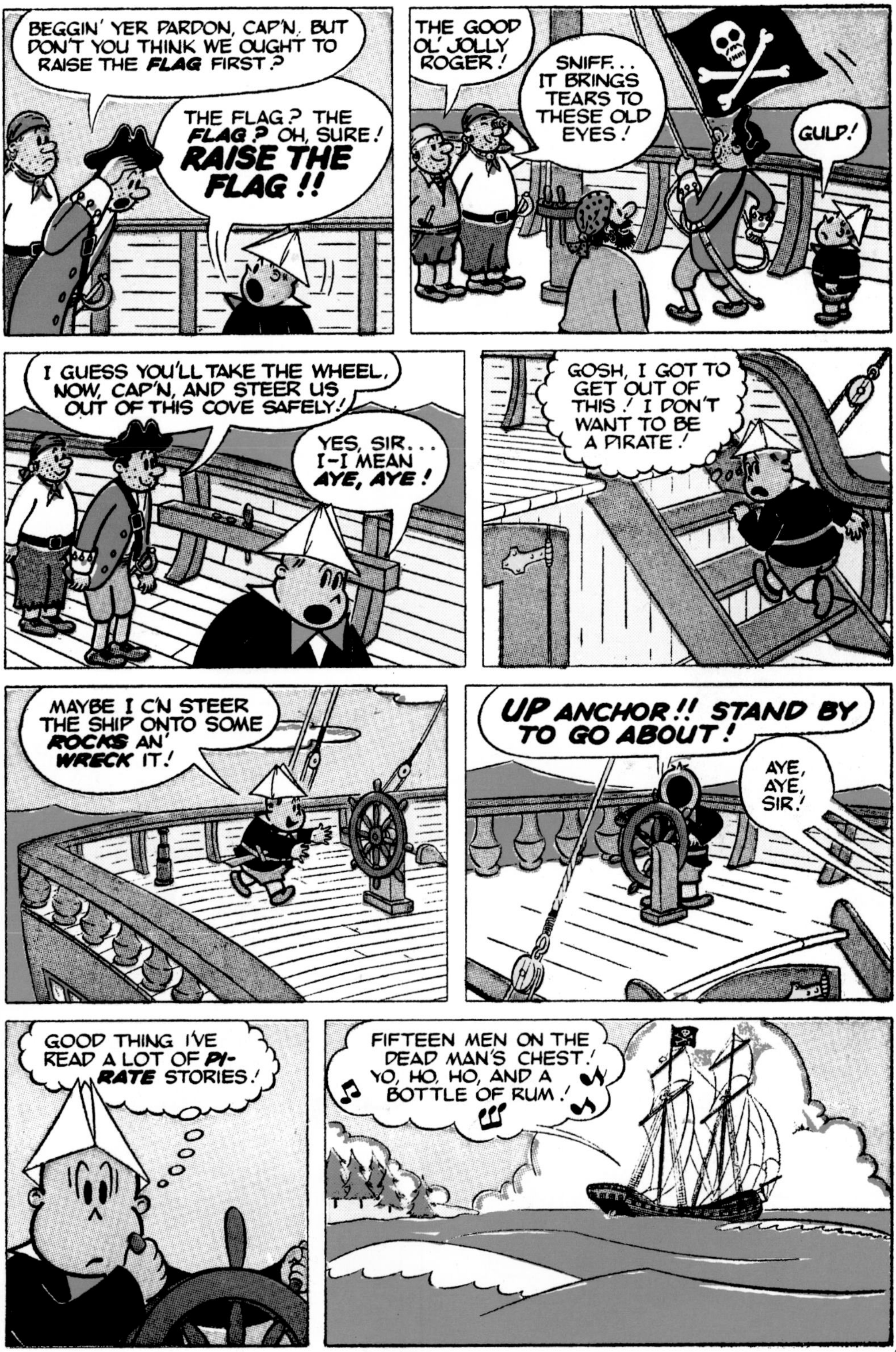
BEGGIN' YER PARDON, CAP'N, BUT DON'T YOU THINK WE OUGHT TO RAISE THE FLAG FIRST?
THE FLAG? THE FLAG? OH, SURE! RAISE THE FLAG!!
THE GOOD OL' JOLLY ROGER!
SNIFF... IT BRINGS TEARS TO THESE OLD EYES!
GULP!
I GUESS YOU'LL TAKE THE WHEEL, NOW, CAP'N, AND STEER US OUT OF THIS COVE SAFELY!
YES, SIR... I-I MEAN AYE, AYE!
GOSH, I GOT TO GET OUT OF THIS! I DON'T WANT TO BE A PIRATE!
MAYBE I C'N STEER THE SHIP ONTO SOME ROCKS AN' WRECK IT!
UP ANCHOR!! STAND BY TO GO ABOUT!
AYE, AYE, SIR!
GOOD THING I'VE READ A LOT OF PI-RATE STORIES!
FIFTEEN MEN ON THE DEAD MAN'S CHEST! YO, HO, HO, AND A BOTTLE OF RUM!

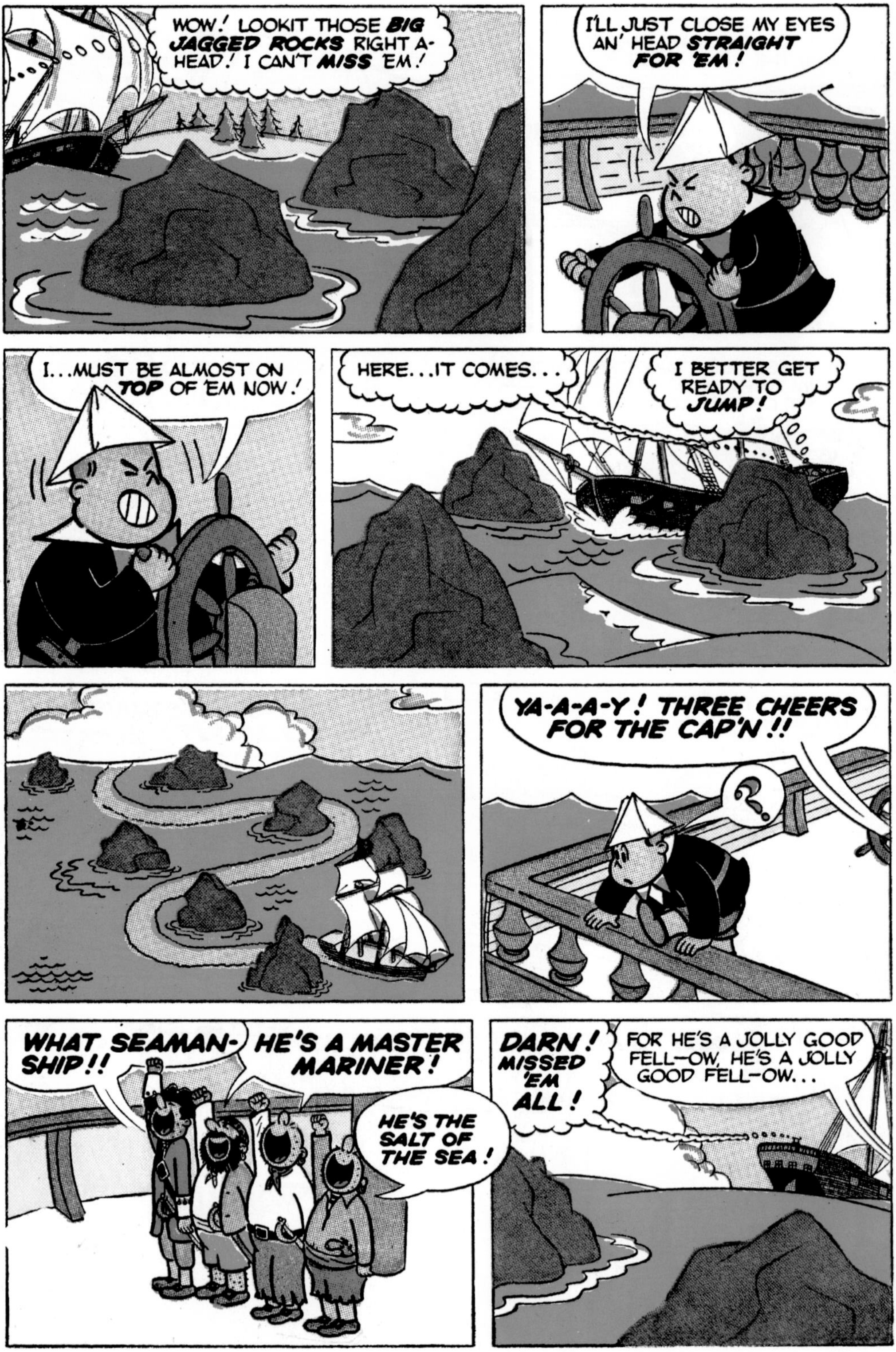
WOW! LOOKIT THOSE BIG JAGGED ROCKS RIGHT A-HEAD! I CAN'T MISS 'EM!
I'LL JUST CLOSE MY EYES AN' HEAD STRAIGHT FOR 'EM!
I...MUST BE ALMOST ON TOP OF 'EM NOW!
HERE...IT COMES...
I BETTER GET READY TO JUMP!
YA-A-A-Y! THREE CHEERS FOR THE CAP'N!!
WHAT SEAMAN-SHIP!!
HE'S A MASTER MARINER!
HE'S THE SALT OF THE SEA!
DARN! MISSED 'EM ALL!
FOR HE'S A JOLLY GOOD FELL-OW, HE'S A JOLLY GOOD FELL-OW...

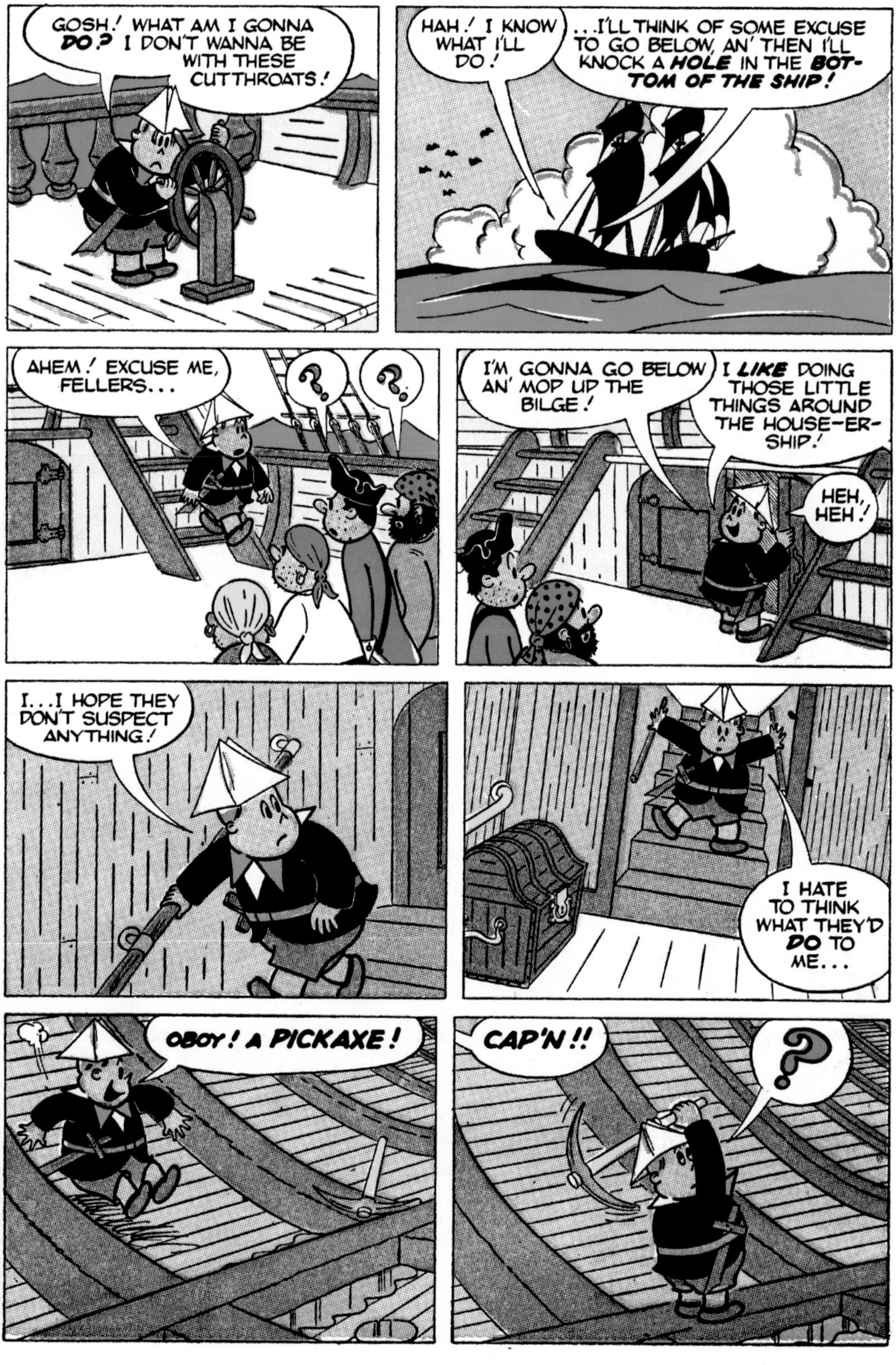
GOSH! WHAT AM I GONNA DO? I DON'T WANNA BE WITH THESE CUTTHROATS!
HAH! I KNOW WHAT I'LL DO!
...I'LL THINK OF SOME EXCUSE TO GO BELOW, AN' THEN I'LL KNOCK A HOLE IN THE BOTTOM OF THE SHIP!
AHEM! EXCUSE ME, FELLERS...
?
?
I'M GONNA GO BELOW AN' MOP UP THE BILGE!
I LIKE DOING THOSE LITTLE THINGS AROUND THE HOUSE–ER–SHIP!
HEH, HEH!
I...I HOPE THEY DON'T SUSPECT ANYTHING!
I HATE TO THINK WHAT THEY'D DO TO ME...
OBOY! A PICKAXE!
CAP'N!!
?

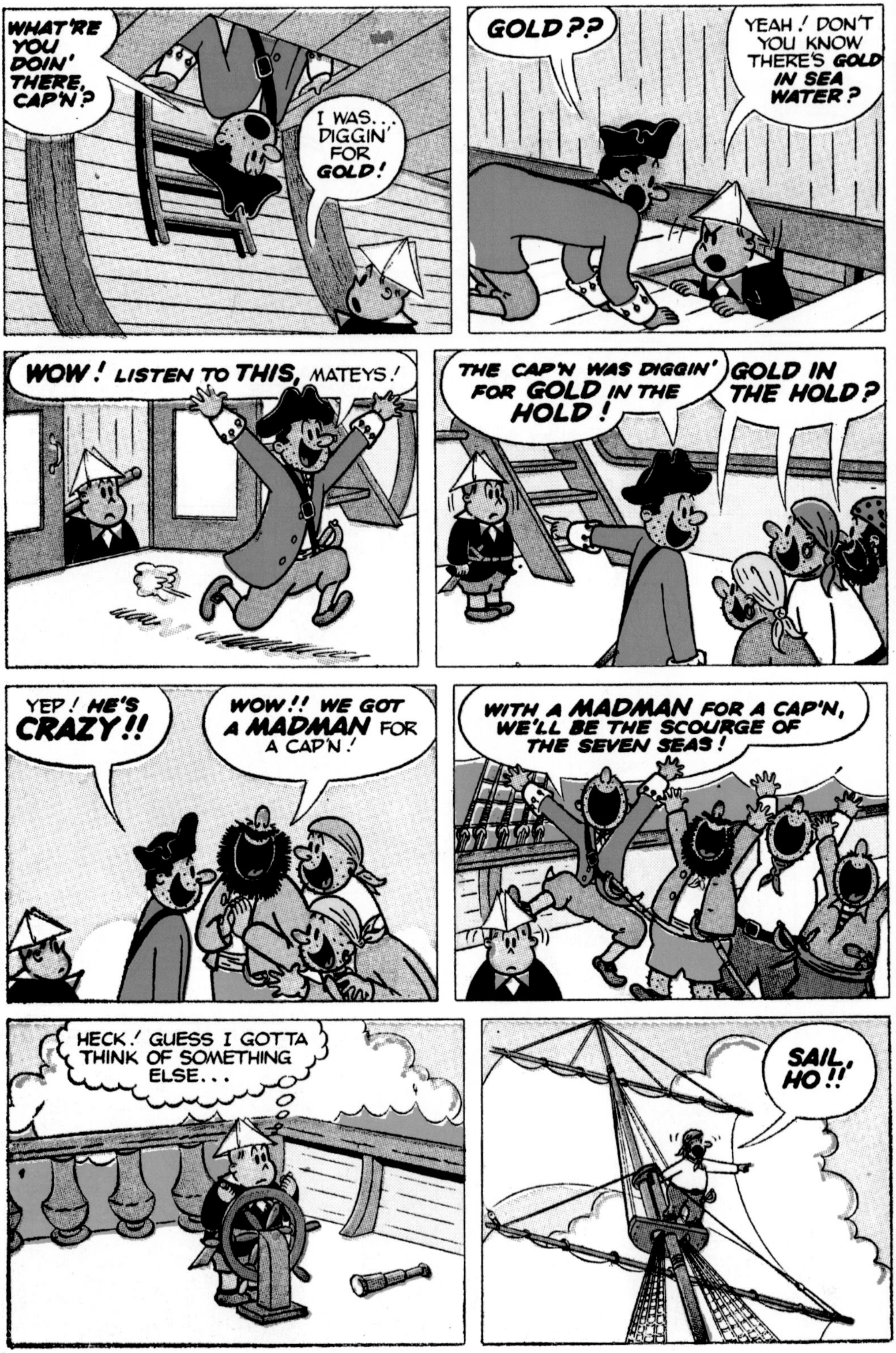
WHAT'RE YOU DOIN' THERE, CAP'N?
I WAS... DIGGIN' FOR GOLD!
GOLD??
YEAH! DON'T YOU KNOW THERE'S GOLD IN SEA WATER?
WOW! LISTEN TO THIS, MATEYS!
THE CAP'N WAS DIGGIN' FOR GOLD IN THE HOLD!
GOLD IN THE HOLD?
YEP! HE'S CRAZY!!
WOW!! WE GOT A MADMAN FOR A CAP'N!
WITH A MADMAN FOR A CAP'N, WE'LL BE THE SCOURGE OF THE SEVEN SEAS!
HECK! GUESS I GOTTA THINK OF SOMETHING ELSE...
SAIL, HO!!

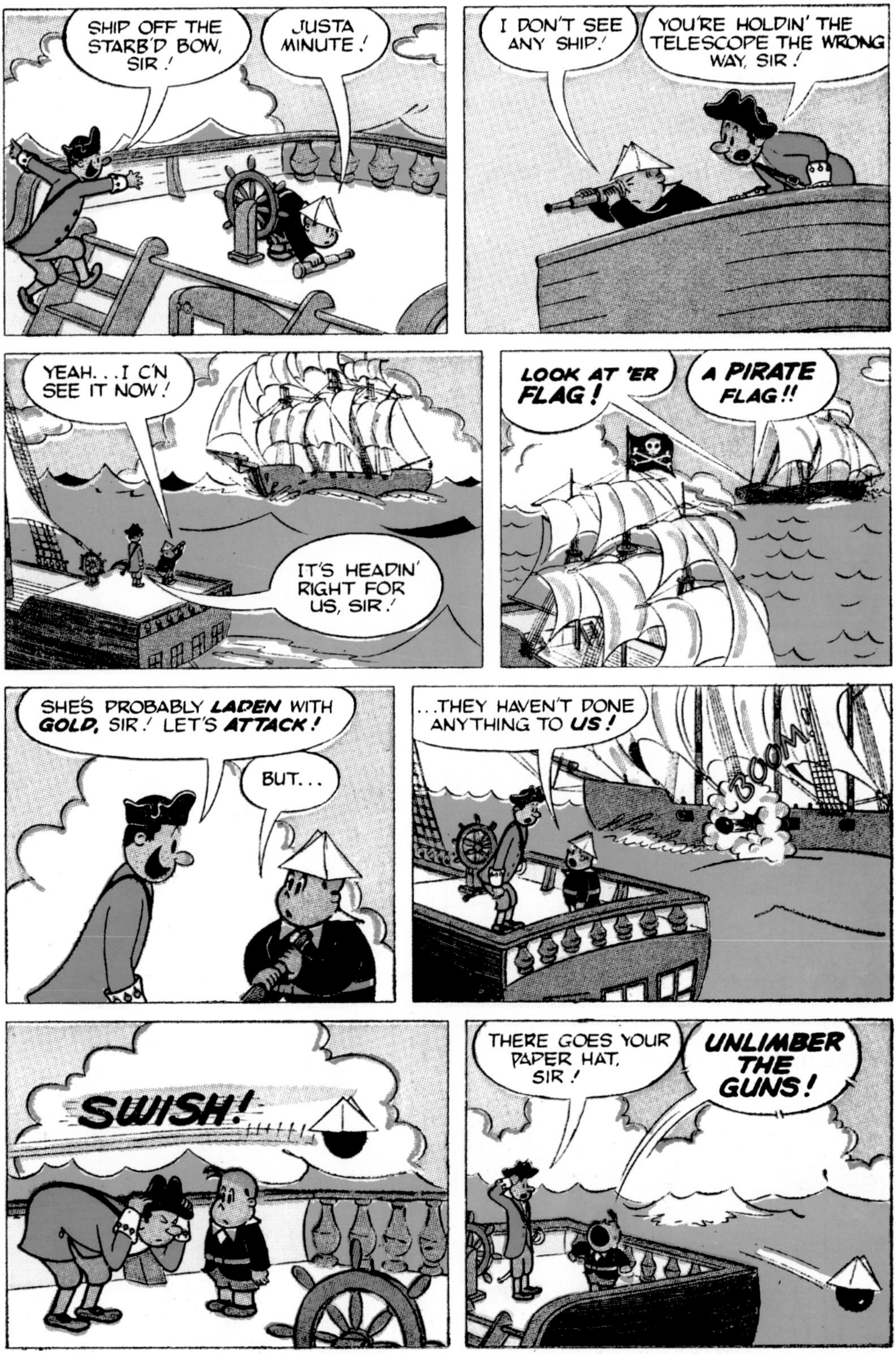
SHIP OFF THE STARB'D BOW, SIR!
JUSTA MINUTE!
I DON'T SEE ANY SHIP!
YOU'RE HOLDIN' THE TELESCOPE THE WRONG WAY, SIR!
YEAH...I C'N SEE IT NOW!
IT'S HEADIN' RIGHT FOR US, SIR!
LOOK AT 'ER FLAG!
A PIRATE FLAG!!
SHE'S PROBABLY LADEN WITH GOLD, SIR! LET'S ATTACK!
BUT...
...THEY HAVEN'T DONE ANYTHING TO US!
BOOM!
SWISH!
THERE GOES YOUR PAPER HAT, SIR!
UNLIMBER THE GUNS!

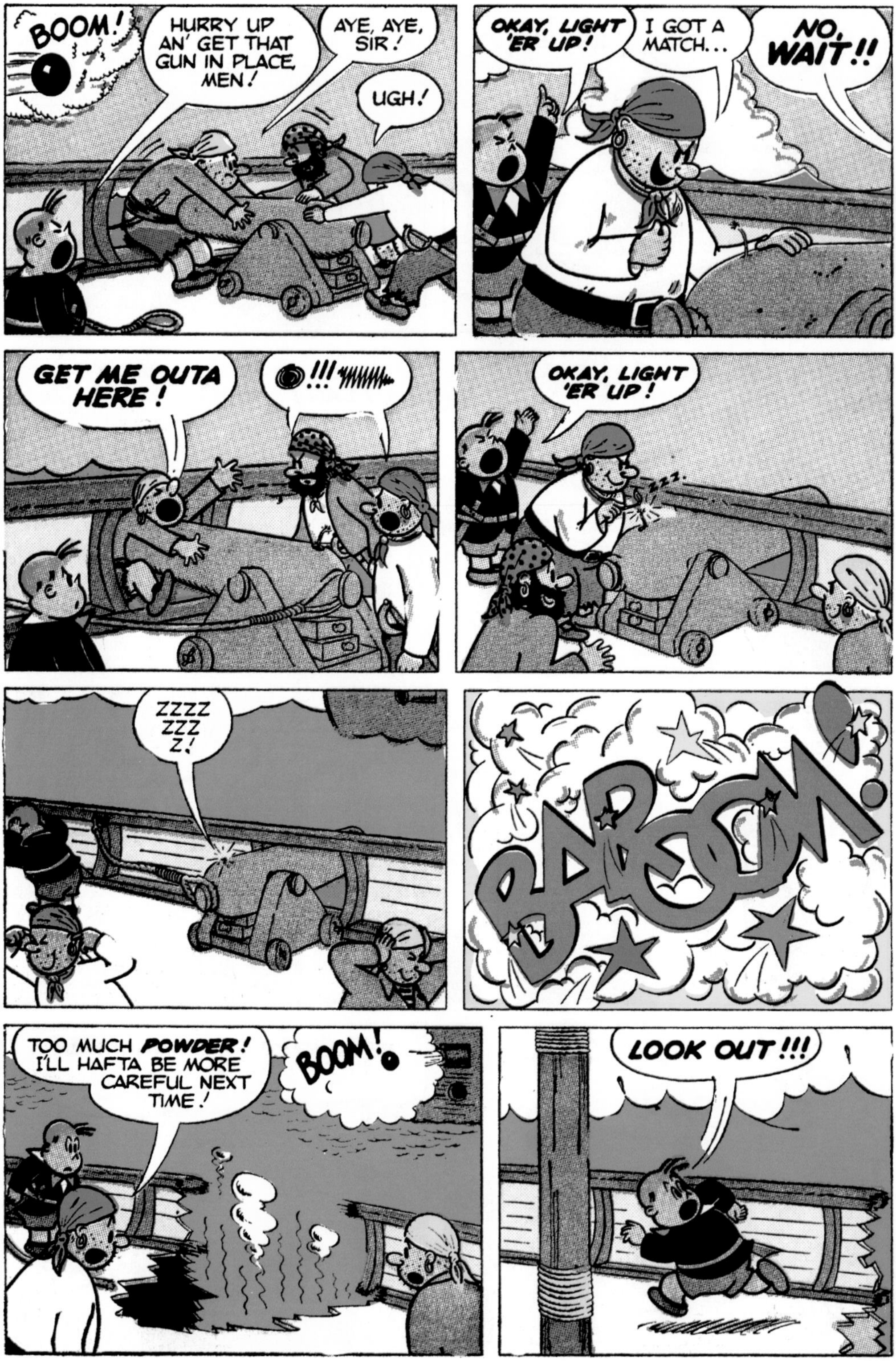
BOOM!
HURRY UP AN' GET THAT GUN IN PLACE, MEN!
AYE, AYE, SIR!
UGH!
OKAY, LIGHT 'ER UP!
I GOT A MATCH...
NO, WAIT!!
GET ME OUTA HERE!
!!!
OKAY, LIGHT 'ER UP!
ZZZ.
ZZZZ ZZZ Z!
BABOOM!
TOO MUCH POWDER! I'LL HAFTA BE MORE CAREFUL NEXT TIME!
BOOM!
LOOK OUT!!!

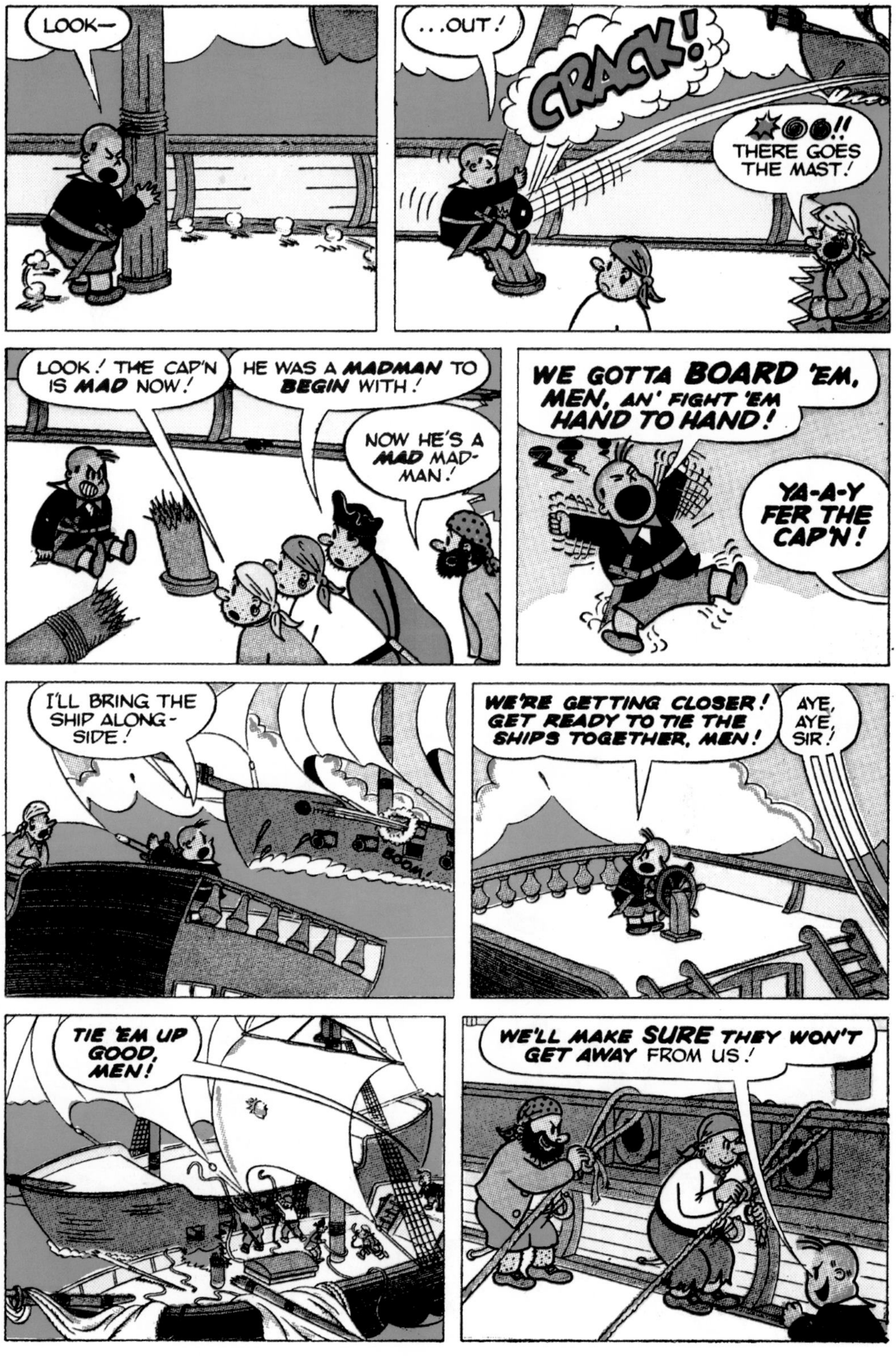
LOOK—
...OUT!
CRACK!
THERE GOES THE MAST!
LOOK! THE CAP'N IS MAD NOW!
HE WAS A MADMAN TO BEGIN WITH!
NOW HE'S A MAD MAD-MAN!
WE GOTTA BOARD 'EM, MEN, AN' FIGHT 'EM HAND TO HAND!
YA-A-Y FER THE CAP'N!
I'LL BRING THE SHIP ALONG-SIDE!
BOOM!
WE'RE GETTING CLOSER! GET READY TO TIE THE SHIPS TOGETHER, MEN!
AYE, AYE, SIR!
TIE 'EM UP GOOD, MEN!
WE'LL MAKE SURE THEY WON'T GET AWAY FROM US!

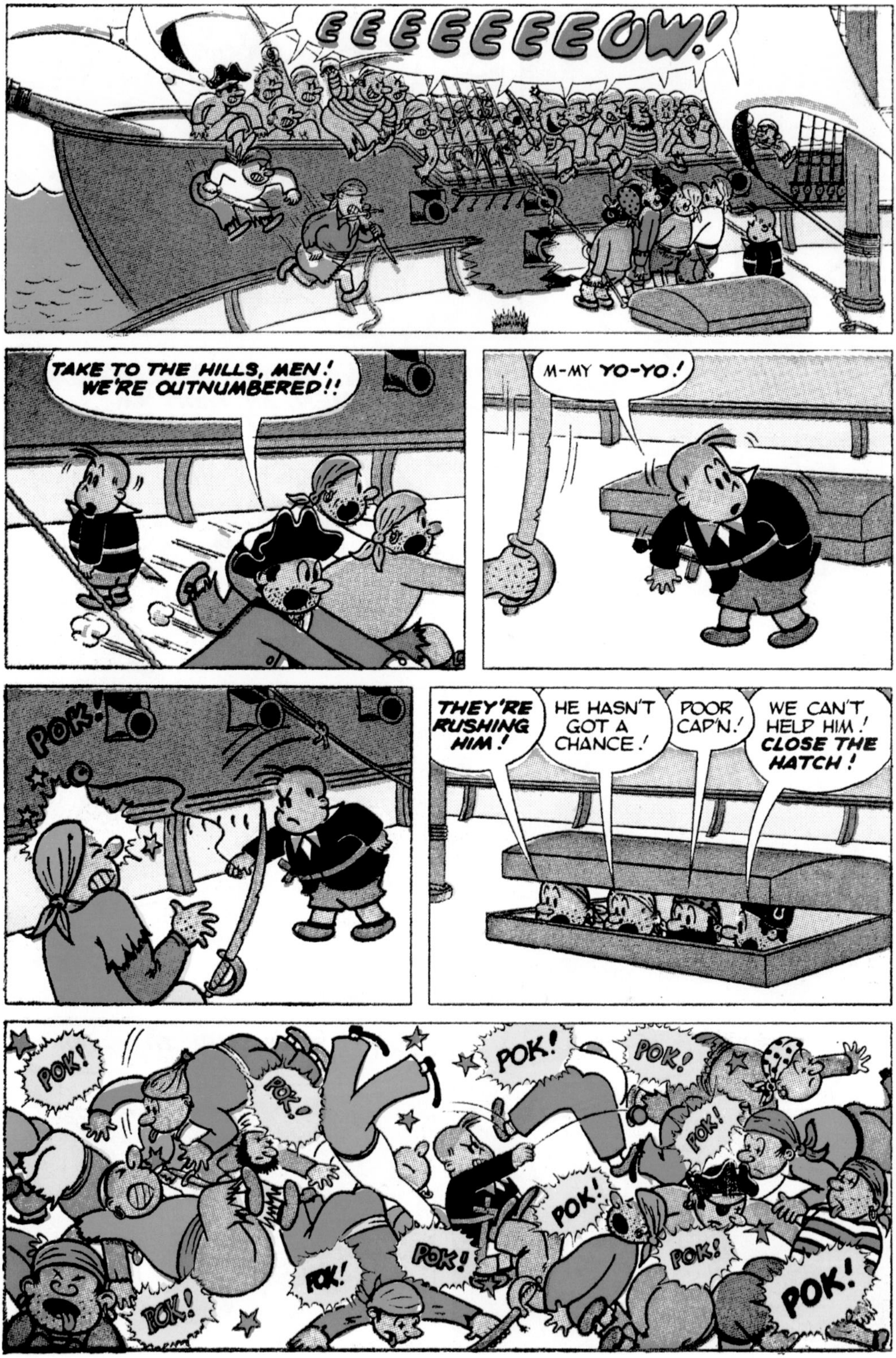
EEEEEEEEOW!
TAKE TO THE HILLS, MEN! WE'RE OUTNUMBERED!!
M-MY YO-YO!
POK!
THEY'RE RUSHING HIM!
HE HASN'T GOT A CHANCE!
POOR CAP'N.!
WE CAN'T HELP HIM! CLOSE THE HATCH!
POK!
POK!
POK!
POK!
POK!
POK!
POK!
POK!
POK!
POK!
POK!

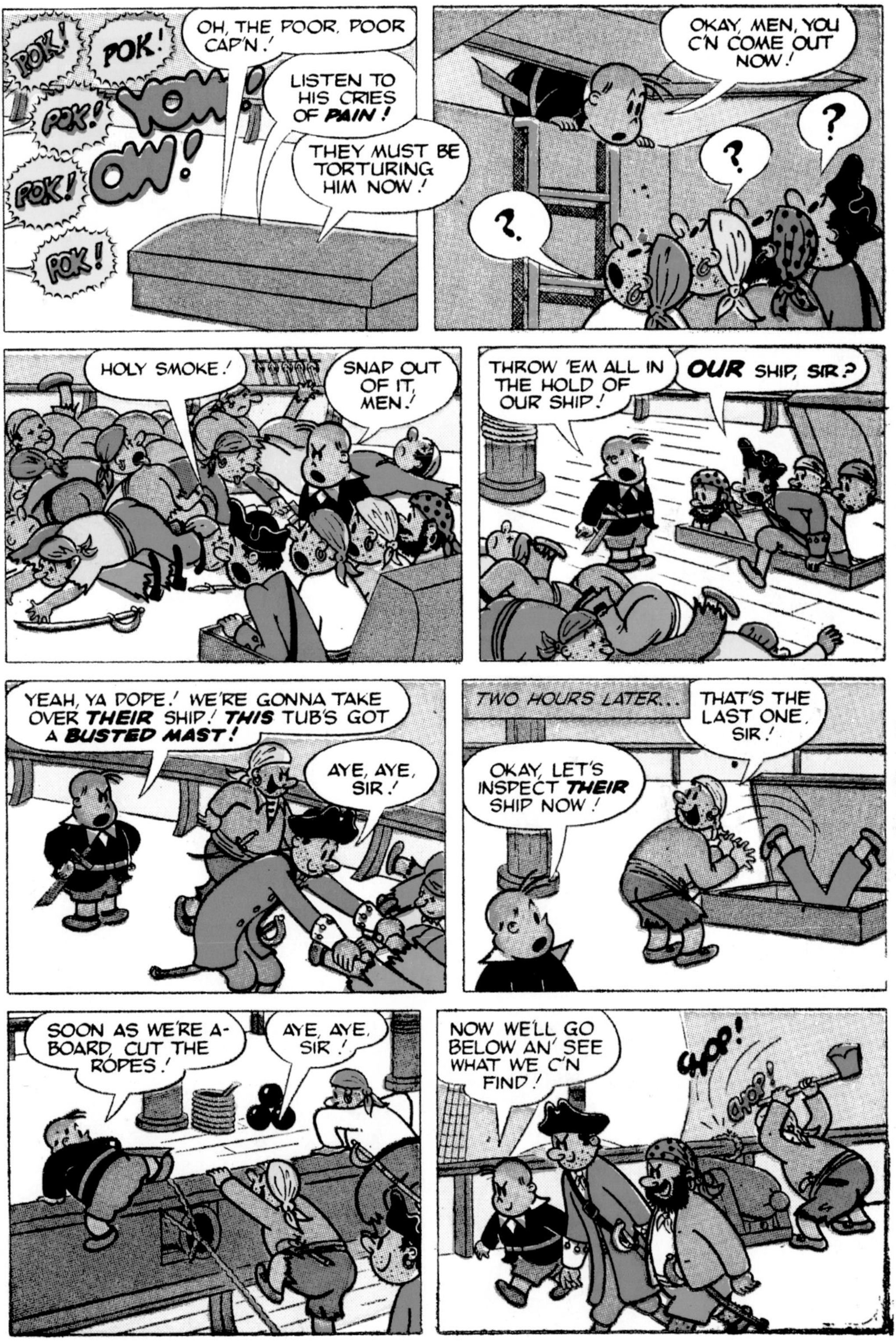
POK!
POK!
POK!
POK!
POK!
YOW!
OW!
OH, THE POOR, POOR CAP'N!
LISTEN TO HIS CRIES OF PAIN!
THEY MUST BE TORTURING HIM NOW!
OKAY, MEN, YOU C'N COME OUT NOW!
?
?
?
HOLY SMOKE!
SNAP OUT OF IT, MEN!
THROW 'EM ALL IN THE HOLD OF OUR SHIP!
OUR SHIP, SIR?
YEAH, YA DOPE! WE'RE GONNA TAKE OVER THEIR SHIP! THIS TUB'S GOT A BUSTED MAST!
AYE, AYE, SIR!
TWO HOURS LATER...
THAT'S THE LAST ONE, SIR!
OKAY, LET'S INSPECT THEIR SHIP NOW!
SOON AS WE'RE ABOARD, CUT THE ROPES!
AYE, AYE, SIR!
NOW WE'LL GO BELOW AN' SEE WHAT WE C'N FIND!
CHOP!
CHOP!

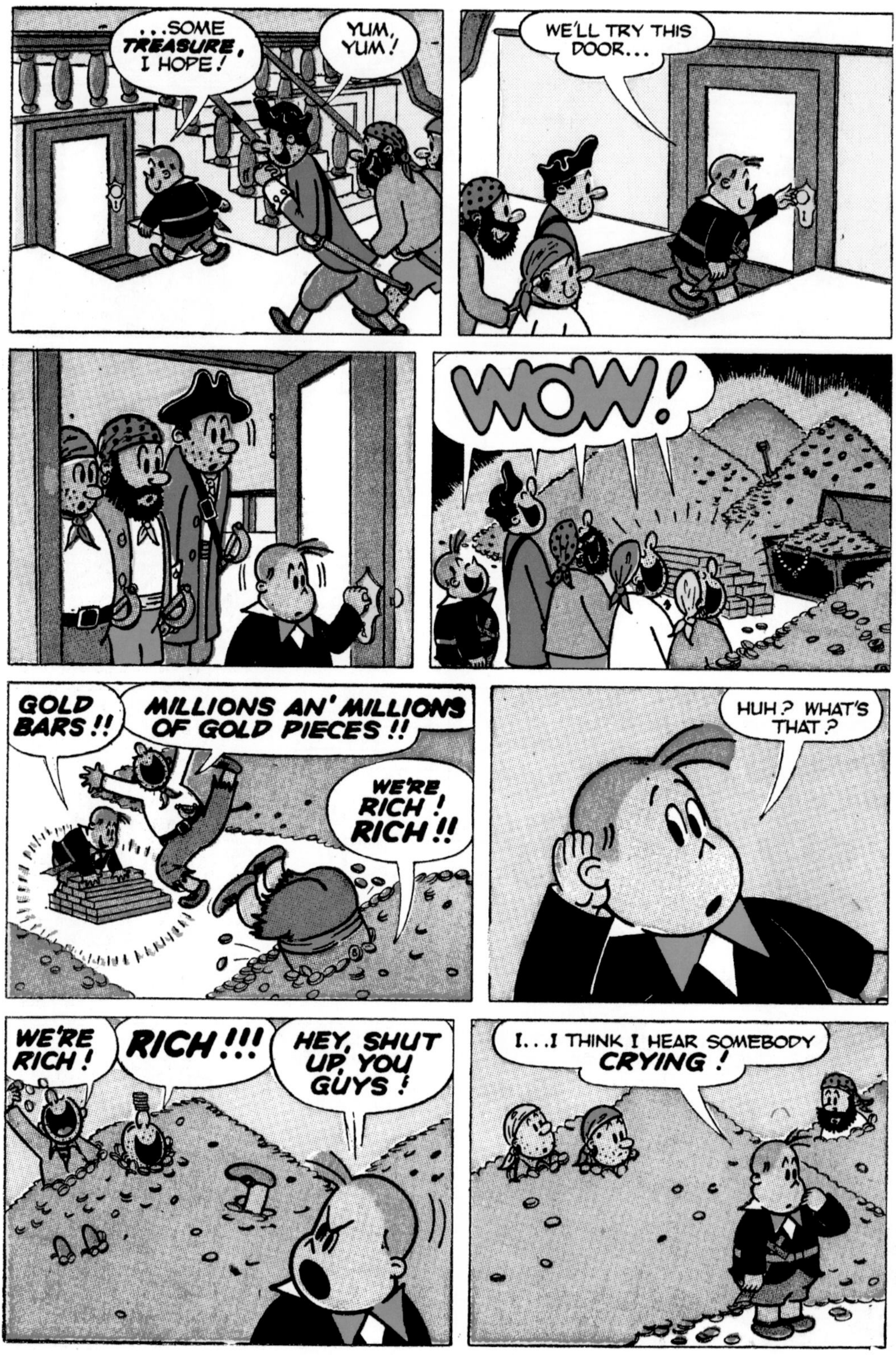
...SOME TREASURE, I HOPE!
YUM, YUM!
WE'LL TRY THIS DOOR...
WOW!
GOLD BARS!!
MILLIONS AN' MILLIONS OF GOLD PIECES!!
WE'RE RICH! RICH!!
HUH? WHAT'S THAT?
WE'RE RICH!
RICH!!!
HEY, SHUT UP, YOU GUYS!
I...I THINK I HEAR SOMEBODY CRYING!

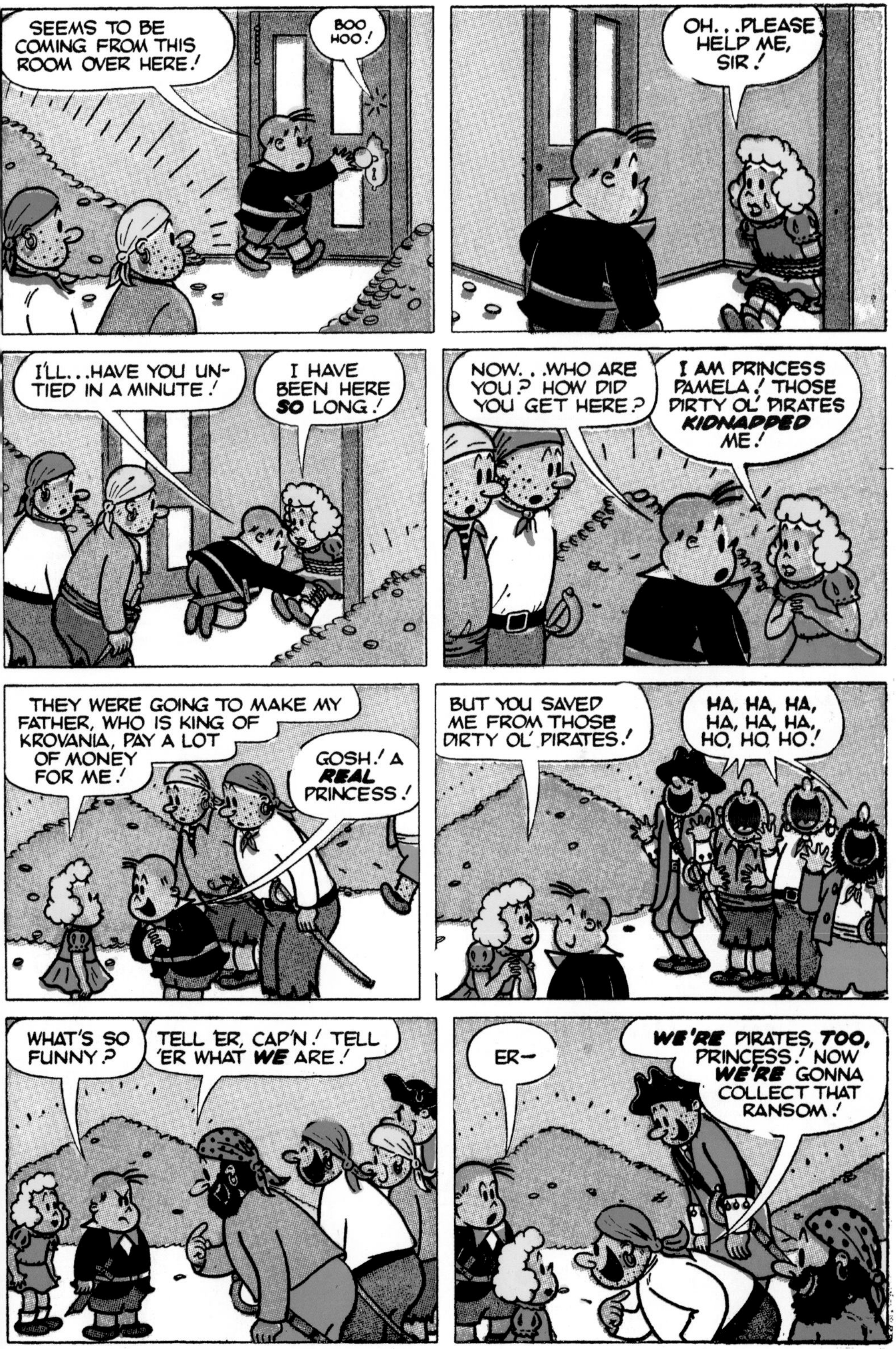
SEEMS TO BE COMING FROM THIS ROOM OVER HERE!
BOO HOO!
OH...PLEASE HELP ME, SIR!
I'LL...HAVE YOU UN-TIED IN A MINUTE!
I HAVE BEEN HERE SO LONG!
NOW...WHO ARE YOU? HOW DID YOU GET HERE?
I AM PRINCESS PAMELA! THOSE DIRTY OL' PIRATES KIDNAPPED ME!
THEY WERE GOING TO MAKE MY FATHER, WHO IS KING OF KROVANIA, PAY A LOT OF MONEY FOR ME!
GOSH! A REAL PRINCESS!
BUT YOU SAVED ME FROM THOSE DIRTY OL' PIRATES!
HA, HA, HA, HA, HA, HA, HO, HO, HO!
WHAT'S SO FUNNY?
TELL 'ER, CAP'N! TELL 'ER WHAT WE ARE!
ER—
WE'RE PIRATES, TOO, PRINCESS! NOW WE'RE GONNA COLLECT THAT RANSOM!

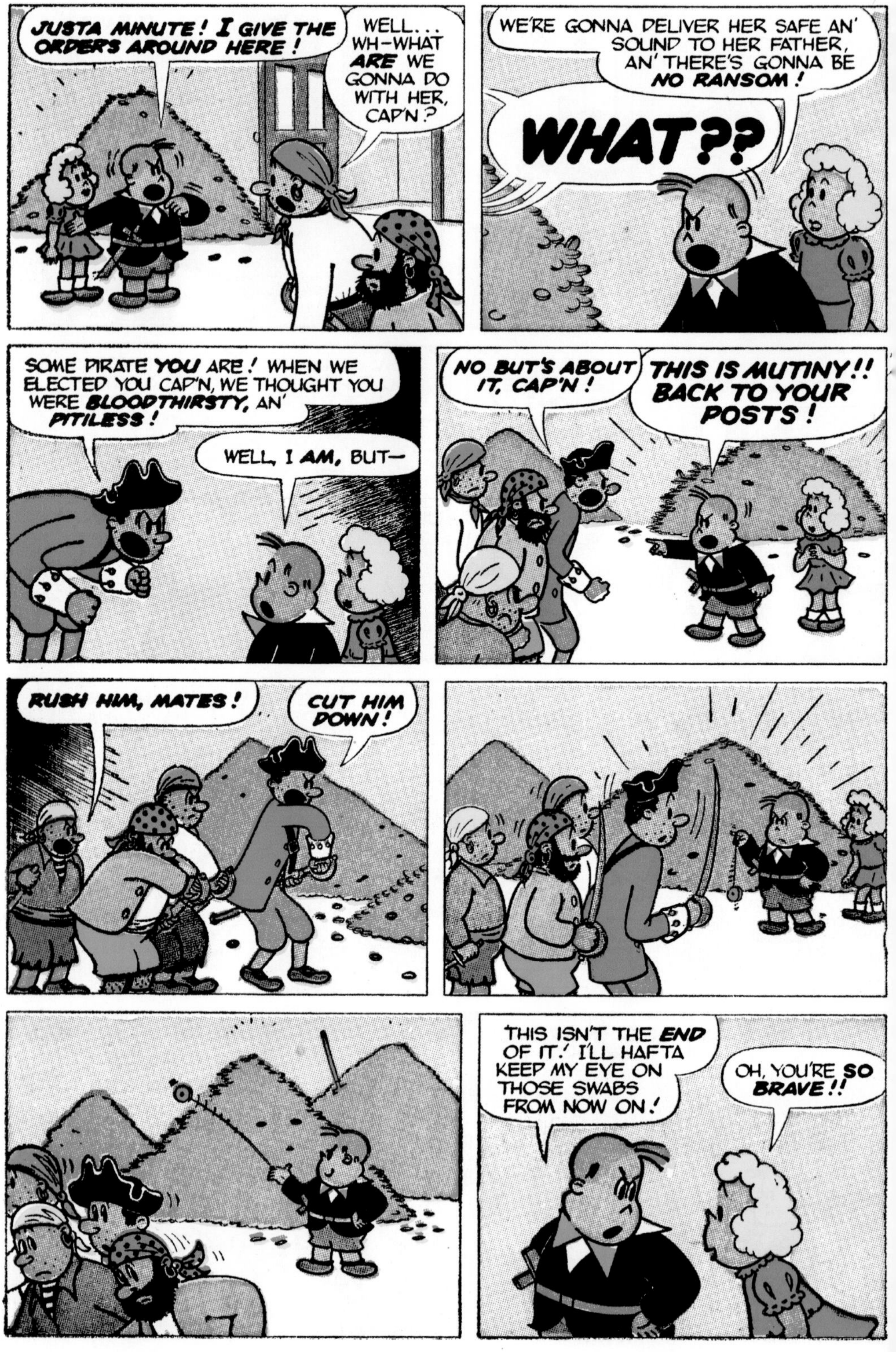
JUSTA MINUTE! I GIVE THE ORDERS AROUND HERE!
WELL... WH-WHAT ARE WE GONNA DO WITH HER, CAP'N?
WE'RE GONNA DELIVER HER SAFE AN' SOUND TO HER FATHER, AN' THERE'S GONNA BE NO RANSOM!
WHAT??
SOME PIRATE YOU ARE! WHEN WE ELECTED YOU CAP'N, WE THOUGHT YOU WERE BLOODTHIRSTY, AN' PITILESS!
WELL, I AM, BUT—
NO BUT'S ABOUT IT, CAP'N!
THIS IS MUTINY!! BACK TO YOUR POSTS!
RUSH HIM, MATES!
CUT HIM DOWN!
THIS ISN'T THE END OF IT! I'LL HAFTA KEEP MY EYE ON THOSE SWABS FROM NOW ON!
OH, YOU'RE SO BRAVE!!

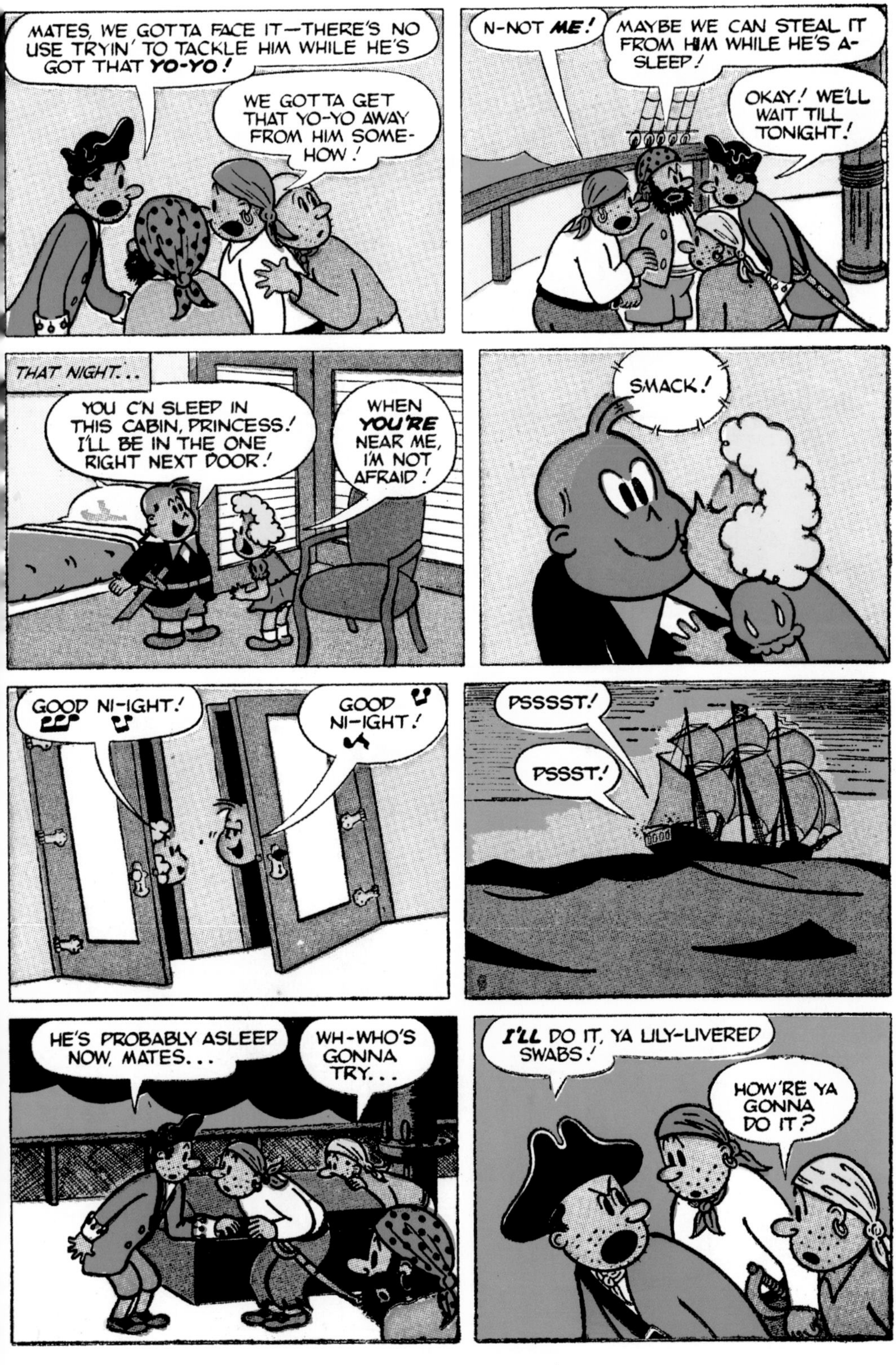
MATES, WE GOTTA FACE IT—THERE'S NO USE TRYIN' TO TACKLE HIM WHILE HE'S GOT THAT YO-YO!
WE GOTTA GET THAT YO-YO AWAY FROM HIM SOMEHOW!
N-NOT ME!
MAYBE WE CAN STEAL IT FROM HIM WHILE HE'S A-SLEEP!
OKAY! WE'LL WAIT TILL TONIGHT!
THAT NIGHT...
YOU C'N SLEEP IN THIS CABIN, PRINCESS! I'LL BE IN THE ONE RIGHT NEXT DOOR!
WHEN YOU'RE NEAR ME, I'M NOT AFRAID!
SMACK!
GOOD NI-IGHT!
GOOD NI-IGHT!
PSSSST!
PSSST!
HE'S PROBABLY ASLEEP NOW, MATES...
WH-WHO'S GONNA TRY...
I'LL DO IT, YA LILY-LIVERED SWABS!
HOW'RE YA GONNA DO IT?

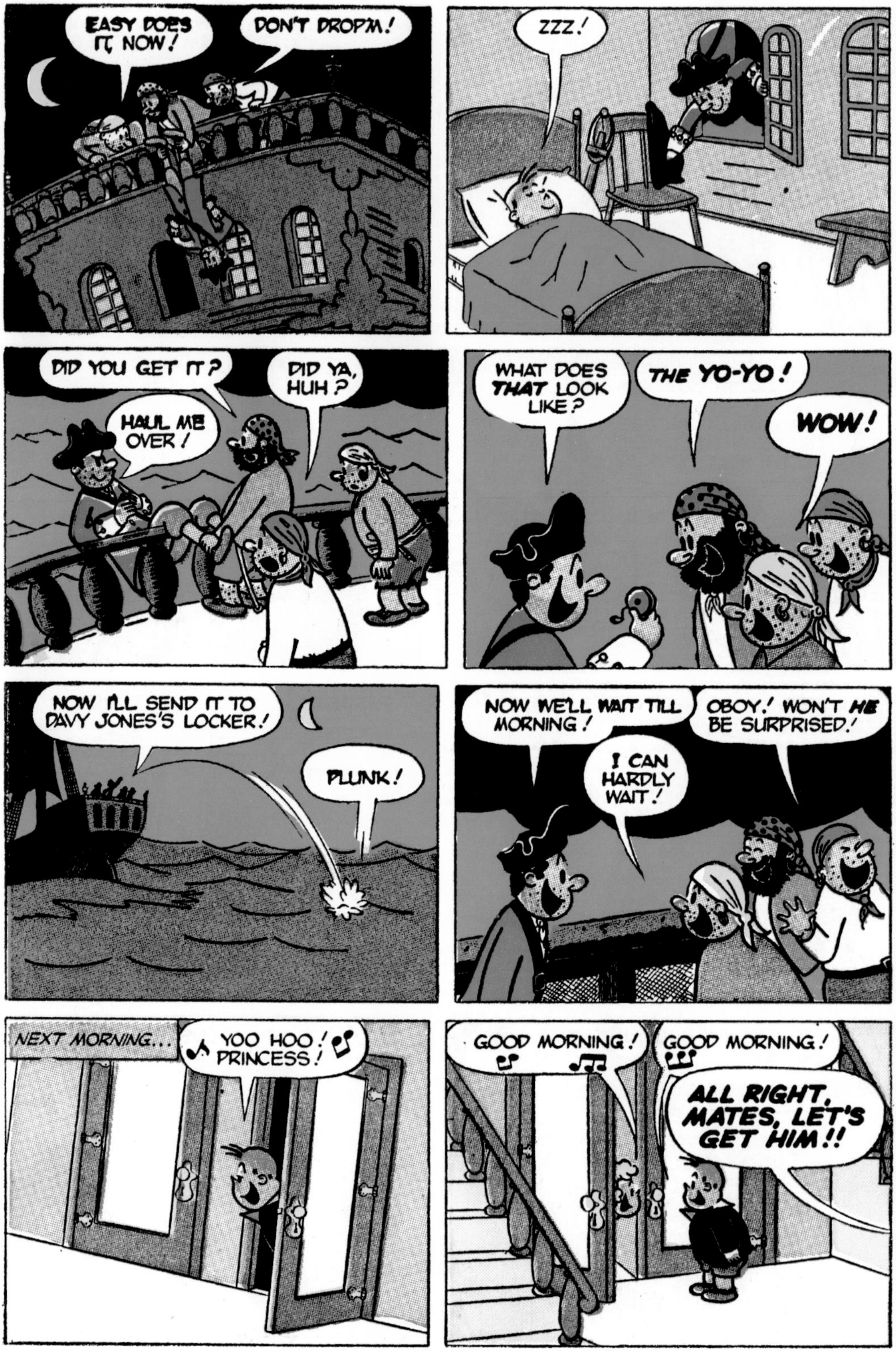
EASY DOES IT, NOW!
DON'T DROP'M!
ZZZ!
DID YOU GET IT?
HAUL ME OVER!
DID YA, HUH?
WHAT DOES THAT LOOK LIKE?
THE YO-YO!
WOW!
NOW I'LL SEND IT TO DAVY JONES'S LOCKER!
PLUNK!
NOW WE'LL WAIT TILL MORNING!
I CAN HARDLY WAIT!
OBOY! WON'T HE BE SURPRISED!
NEXT MORNING...
YOO HOO PRINCESS!
GOOD MORNING!
GOOD MORNING!
ALL RIGHT, MATES, LET'S GET HIM!!

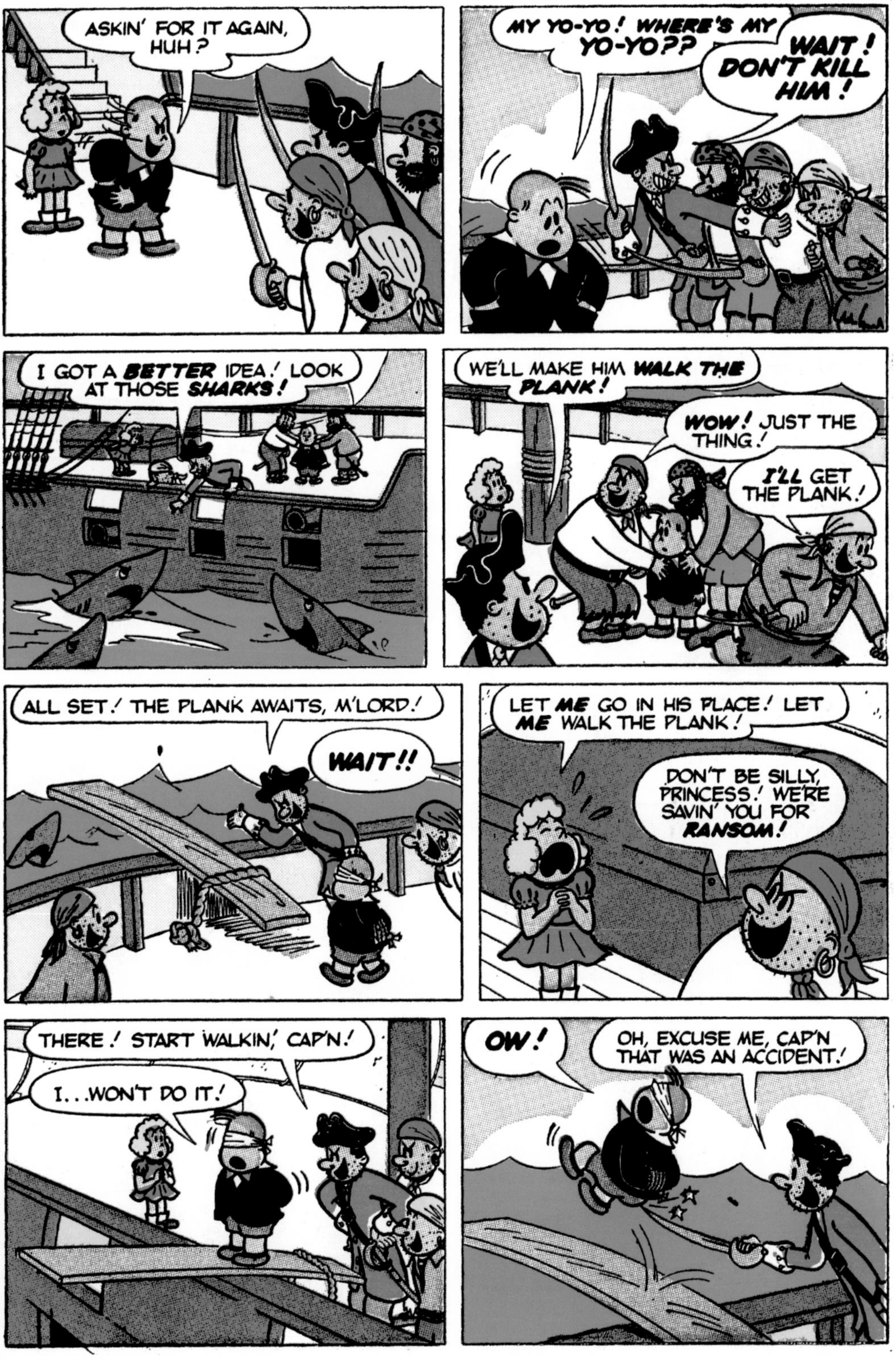
ASKIN' FOR IT AGAIN, HUH?
MY YO-YO! WHERE'S MY YO-YO??
WAIT! DON'T KILL HIM!
I GOT A BETTER IDEA! LOOK AT THOSE SHARKS!
WE'LL MAKE HIM WALK THE PLANK!
WOW! JUST THE THING!
I'LL GET THE PLANK!
ALL SET! THE PLANK AWAITS, M'LORD!
WAIT!!
LET ME GO IN HIS PLACE! LET ME WALK THE PLANK!
DON'T BE SILLY, PRINCESS! WE'RE SAVIN' YOU FOR RANSOM!
THERE! START WALKIN', CAP'N!
I...WON'T DO IT!
OW!
OH, EXCUSE ME, CAP'N THAT WAS AN ACCIDENT!

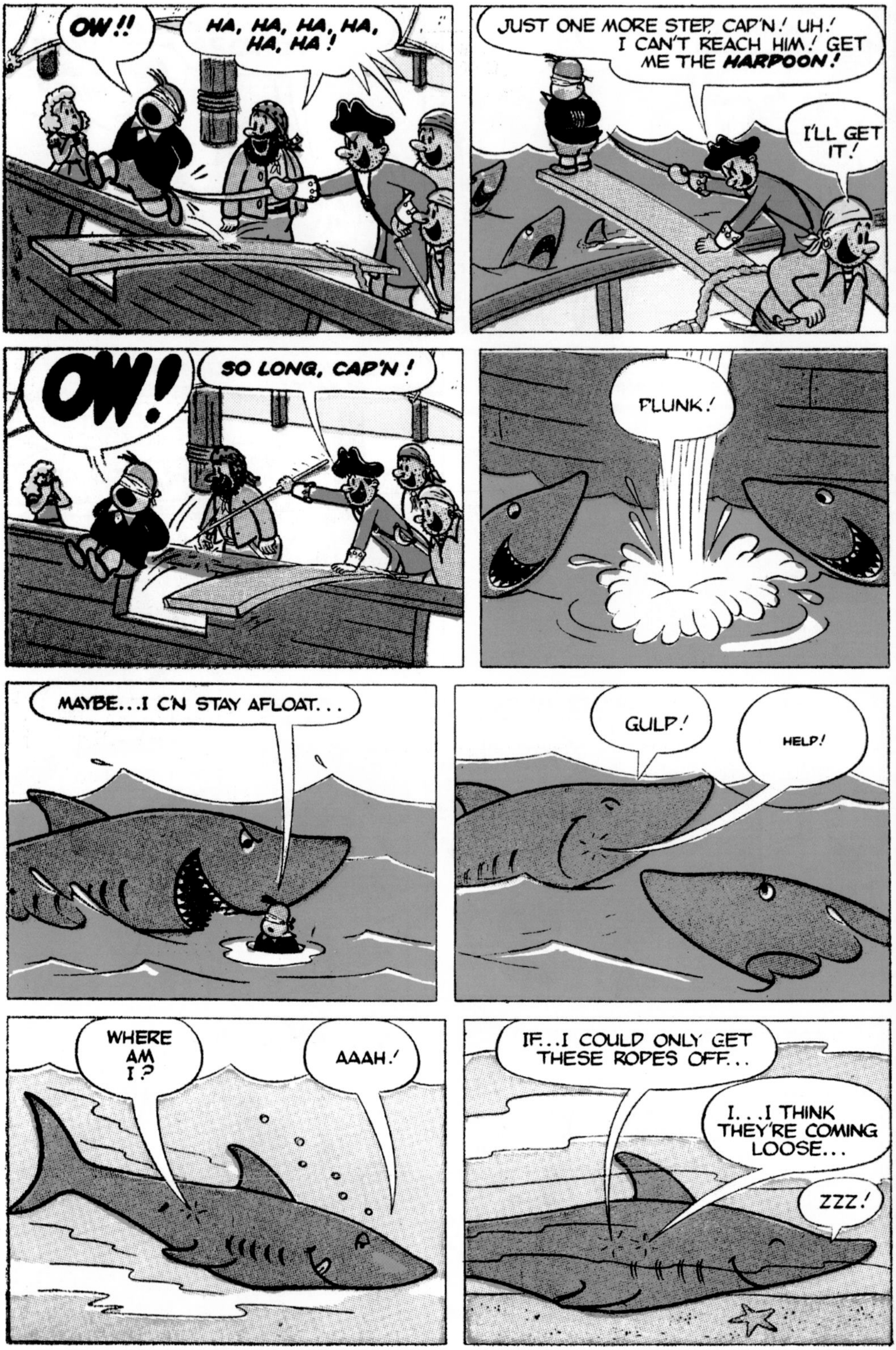
OW!!
HA, HA, HA, HA,
HA, HA!
JUST ONE MORE STEP, CAP'N.! UH.! I CAN'T REACH HIM.! GET ME THE HARPOON!
I'LL GET IT.!
OW!
SO LONG, CAP'N!
PLUNK.!
MAYBE...I C'N STAY AFLOAT...
GULP.!
HELP!
WHERE AM I?
AAAH.!
IF...I COULD ONLY GET THESE ROPES OFF...
I...I THINK THEY'RE COMING LOOSE...
ZZZ.!

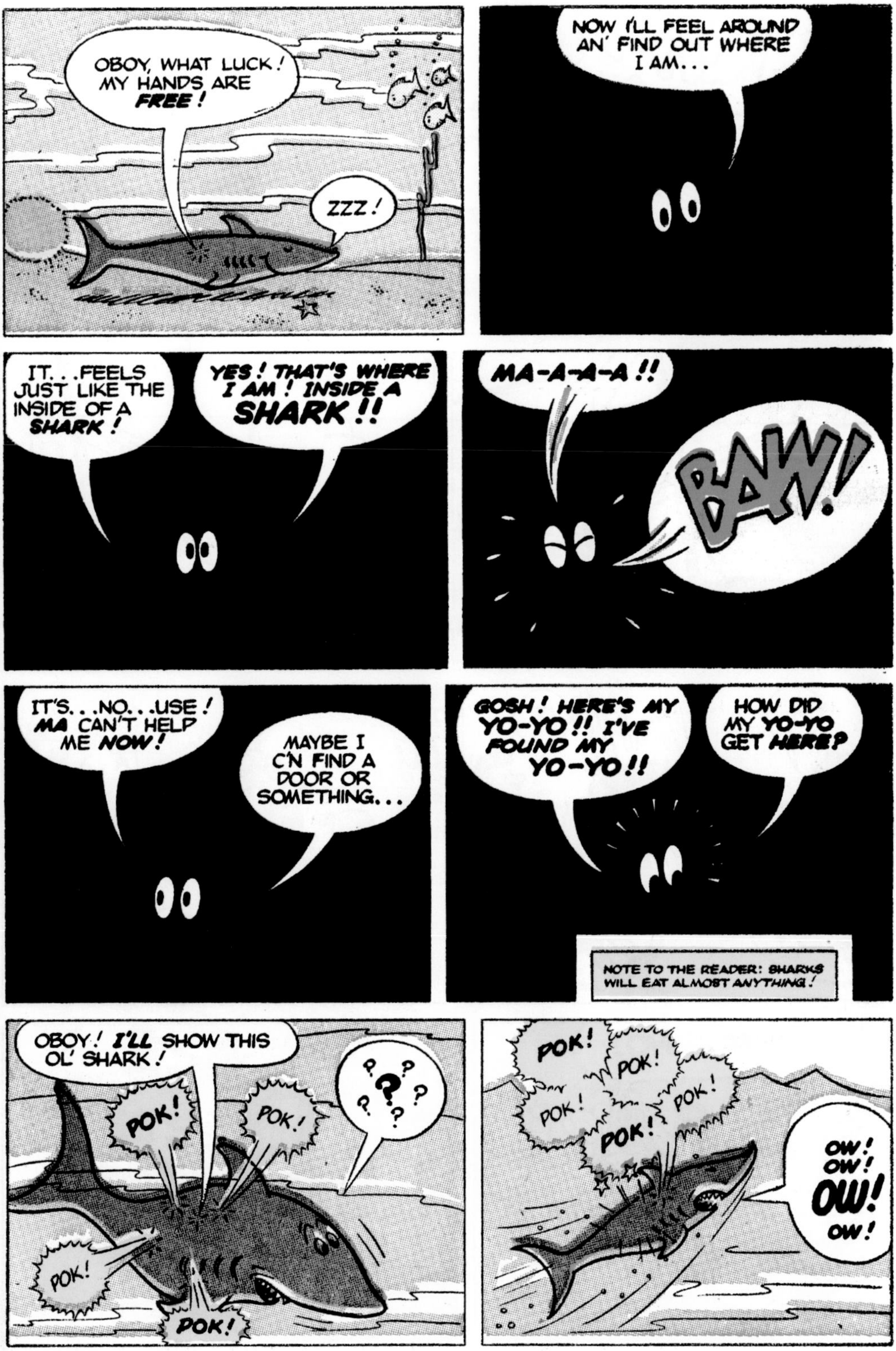
OBOY, WHAT LUCK! MY HANDS ARE FREE!
ZZZ!
NOW I'LL FEEL AROUND AN' FIND OUT WHERE I AM...
IT...FEELS JUST LIKE THE INSIDE OF A SHARK!
YES! THAT'S WHERE I AM! INSIDE A SHARK!!
MA-A-A-A!!
BAW!
IT'S...NO...USE! MA CAN'T HELP ME NOW!
MAYBE I C'N FIND A DOOR OR SOMETHING...
GOSH! HERE'S MY YO-YO!! I'VE FOUND MY YO-YO!!
HOW DID MY YO-YO GET HERE?
NOTE TO THE READER: SHARKS WILL EAT ALMOST ANYTHING!
OBOY! I'LL SHOW THIS OL' SHARK!
POK!
POK!
?
POK!
POK!
POK!
POK!
POK!
POK!
POK!
OW! OW! OW! OW!

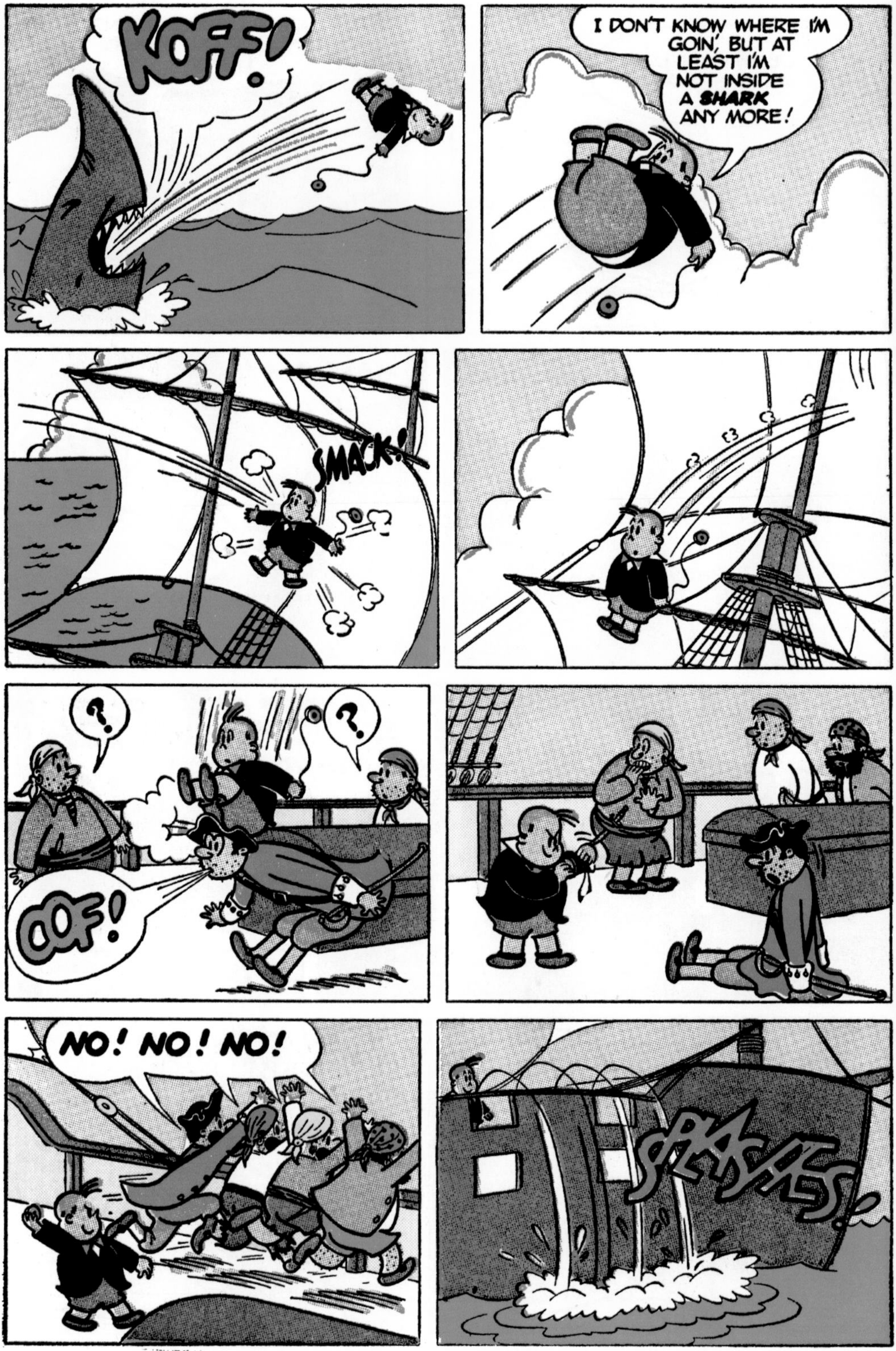
KOFF!
I DON'T KNOW WHERE I'M GOIN', BUT AT LEAST I'M NOT INSIDE A SHARK ANY MORE!
SMACK!
?
?
OOF!
NO! NO! NO!
SPLASHES!

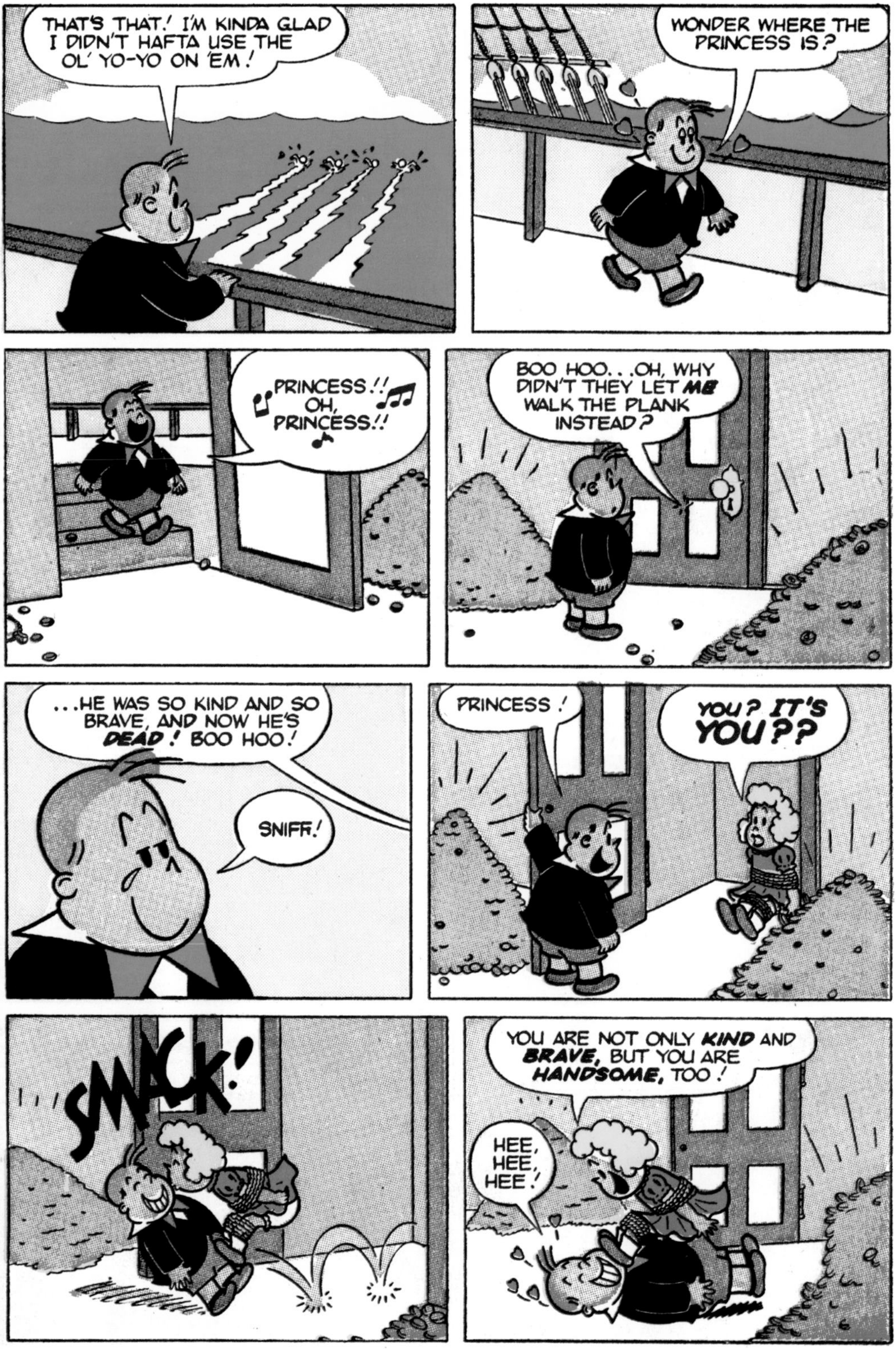
THAT'S THAT.! I'M KINDA GLAD I DIDN'T HAFTA USE THE OL' YO-YO ON 'EM.!
WONDER WHERE THE PRINCESS IS?
PRINCESS.!! OH, PRINCESS.!!
BOO HOO...OH, WHY DIDN'T THEY LET ME WALK THE PLANK INSTEAD?
...HE WAS SO KIND AND SO BRAVE, AND NOW HE'S DEAD.! BOO HOO.!
SNIFF.!
PRINCESS.!
YOU? IT'S YOU??
SMACK!
YOU ARE NOT ONLY KIND AND BRAVE, BUT YOU ARE HANDSOME, TOO.!
HEE, HEE, HEE.!

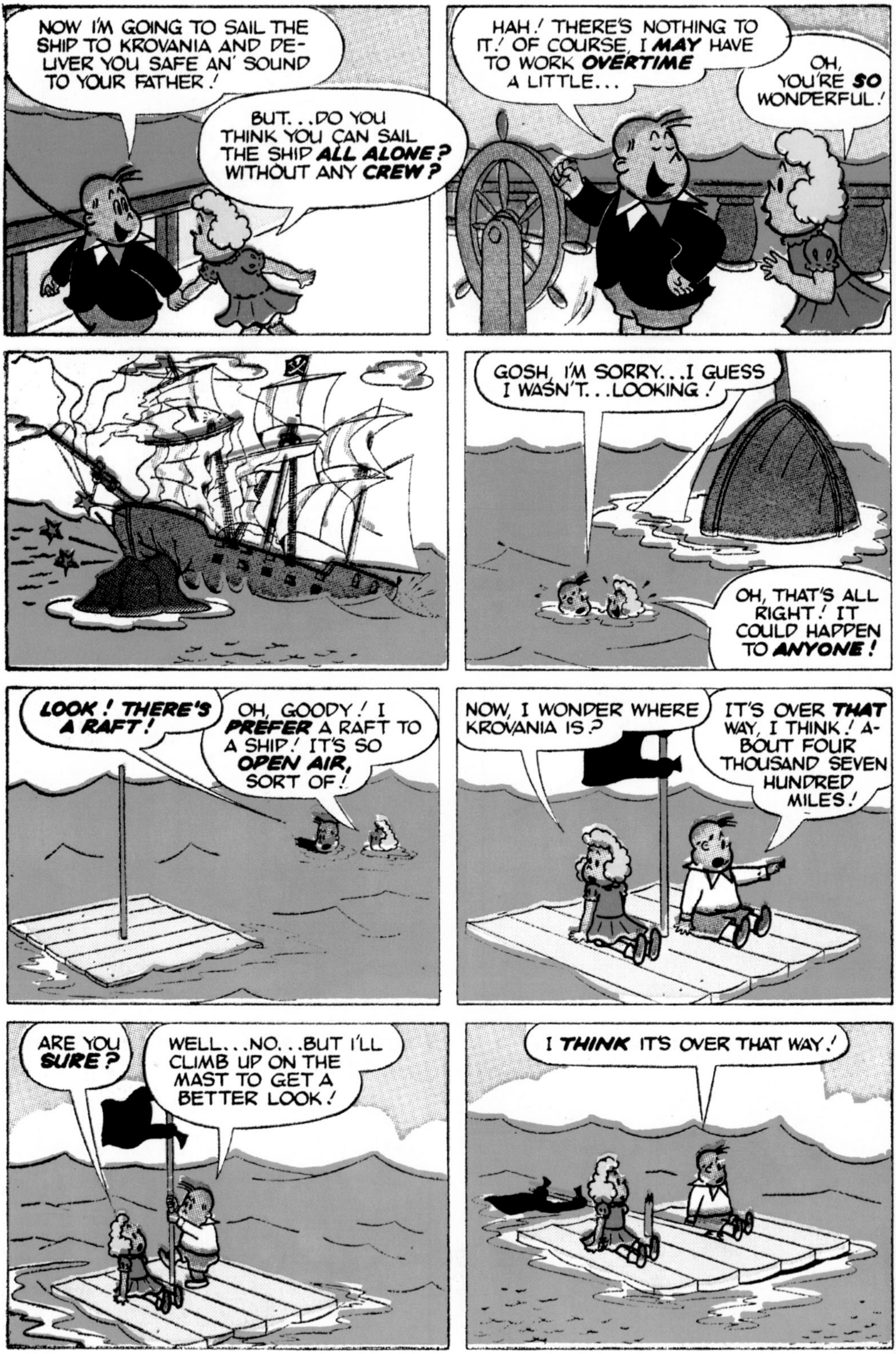
NOW I'M GOING TO SAIL THE SHIP TO KROVANIA AND DELIVER YOU SAFE AN' SOUND TO YOUR FATHER!
BUT...DO YOU THINK YOU CAN SAIL THE SHIP ALL ALONE? WITHOUT ANY CREW?
HAH! THERE'S NOTHING TO IT! OF COURSE, I MAY HAVE TO WORK OVERTIME A LITTLE...
OH, YOU'RE SO WONDERFUL!
GOSH, I'M SORRY...I GUESS I WASN'T...LOOKING!
OH, THAT'S ALL RIGHT! IT COULD HAPPEN TO ANYONE!
LOOK! THERE'S A RAFT!
OH, GOODY! I PREFER A RAFT TO A SHIP! IT'S SO OPEN AIR, SORT OF!
NOW, I WONDER WHERE KROVANIA IS?
IT'S OVER THAT WAY, I THINK! ABOUT FOUR THOUSAND SEVEN HUNDRED MILES!
ARE YOU SURE?
WELL...NO...BUT I'LL CLIMB UP ON THE MAST TO GET A BETTER LOOK!
I THINK IT'S OVER THAT WAY!

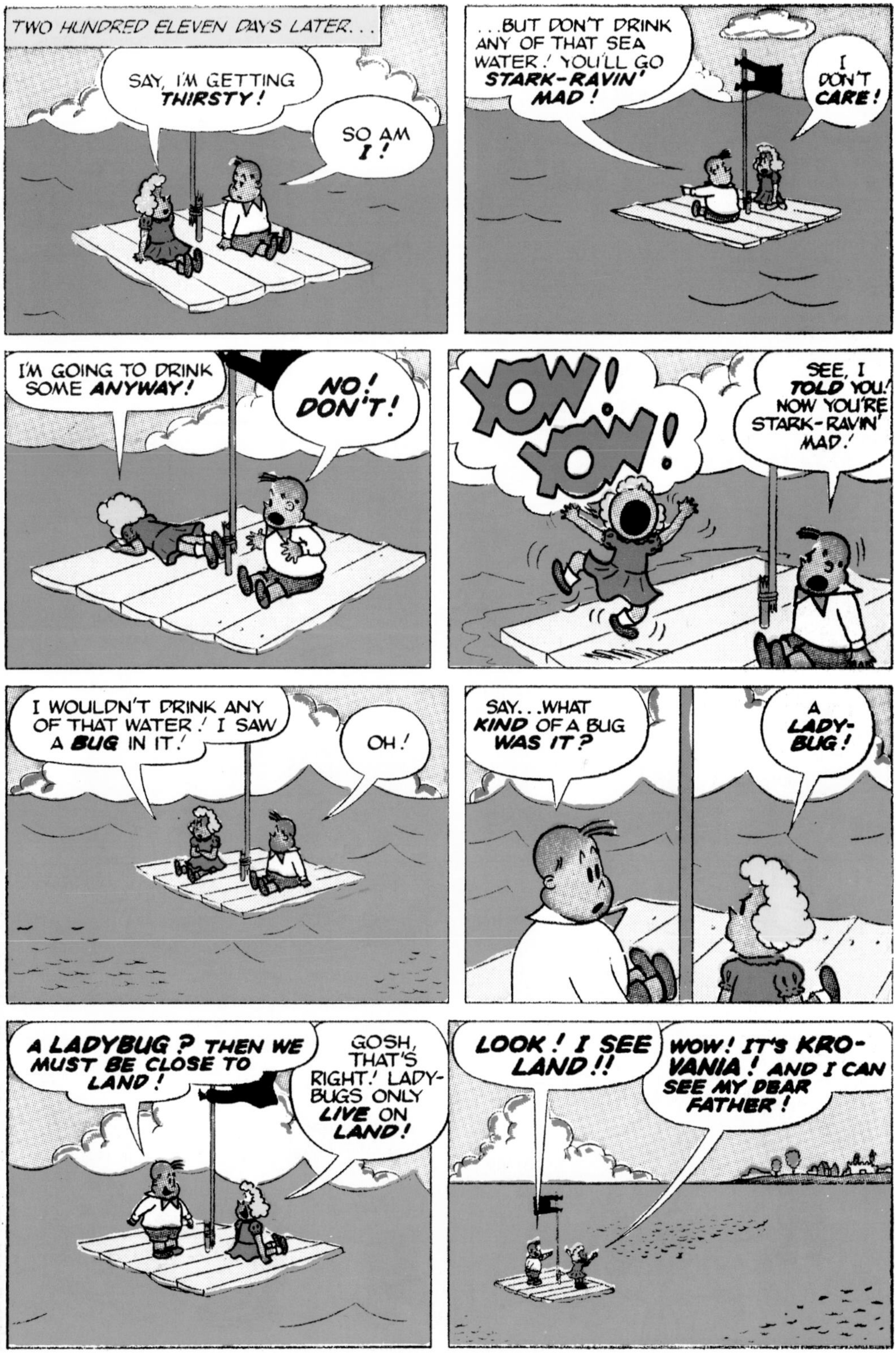
TWO HUNDRED ELEVEN DAYS LATER...
SAY, I'M GETTING THIRSTY!
SO AM I!
...BUT DON'T DRINK ANY OF THAT SEA WATER! YOU'LL GO STARK-RAVIN' MAD!
I DON'T CARE!
I'M GOING TO DRINK SOME ANYWAY!
NO! DON'T!
YOW! YOW!
SEE, I TOLD YOU! NOW YOU'RE STARK-RAVIN' MAD!
I WOULDN'T DRINK ANY OF THAT WATER! I SAW A BUG IN IT!
OH!
SAY...WHAT KIND OF A BUG WAS IT?
A LADY-BUG!
A LADYBUG? THEN WE MUST BE CLOSE TO LAND!
GOSH, THAT'S RIGHT! LADY-BUGS ONLY LIVE ON LAND!
LOOK! I SEE LAND!!
WOW! IT'S KRO-VANIA! AND I CAN SEE MY DEAR FATHER!

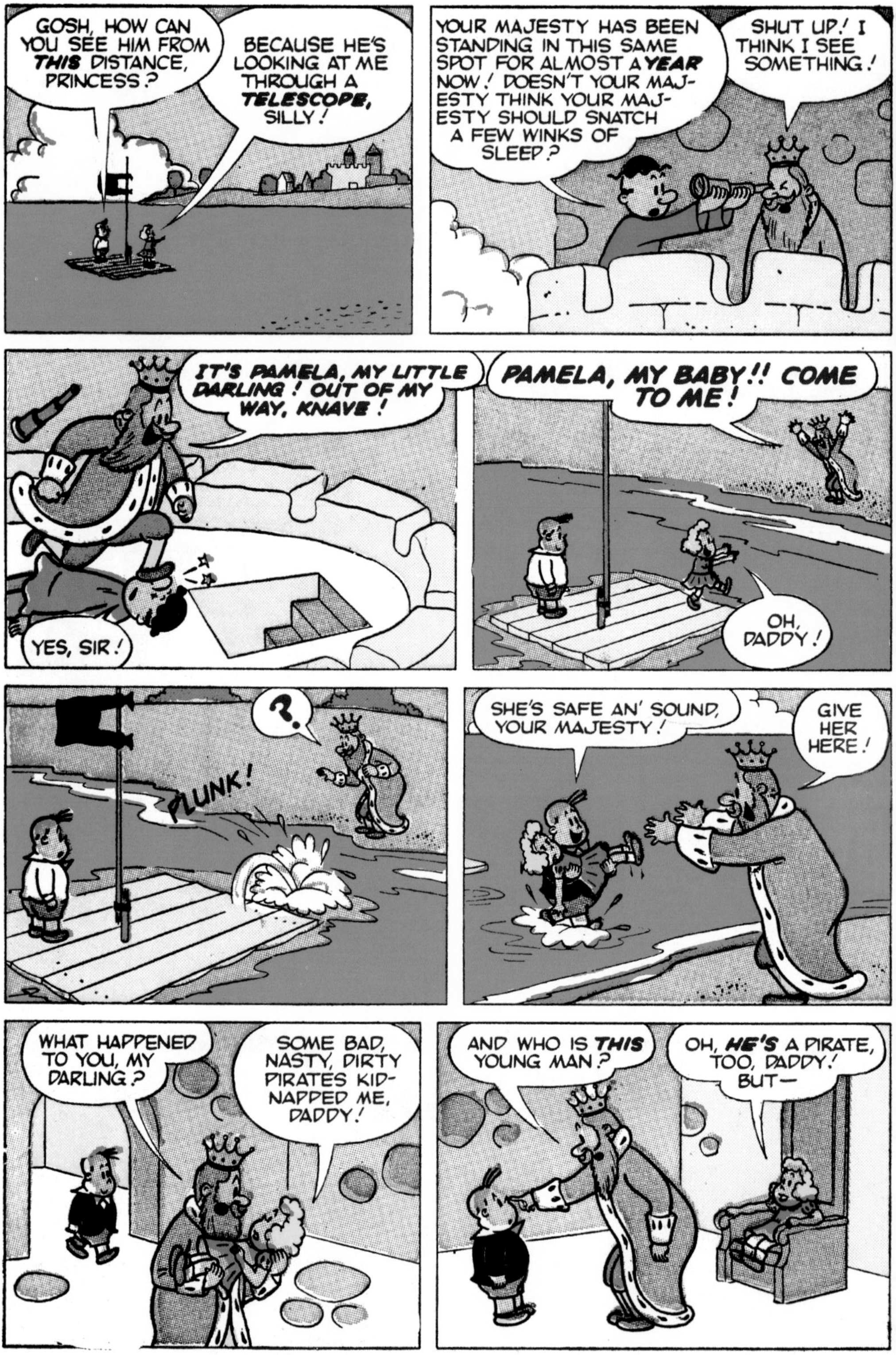
GOSH, HOW CAN YOU SEE HIM FROM THIS DISTANCE, PRINCESS?
BECAUSE HE'S LOOKING AT ME THROUGH A TELESCOPE, SILLY!
YOUR MAJESTY HAS BEEN STANDING IN THIS SAME SPOT FOR ALMOST A YEAR NOW! DOESN'T YOUR MAJESTY THINK YOUR MAJESTY SHOULD SNATCH A FEW WINKS OF SLEEP?
SHUT UP! I THINK I SEE SOMETHING!
IT'S PAMELA, MY LITTLE DARLING! OUT OF MY WAY, KNAVE!
YES, SIR!
PAMELA, MY BABY!! COME TO ME!
OH, DADDY!
?
PLUNK!
SHE'S SAFE AN' SOUND, YOUR MAJESTY!
GIVE HER HERE!
WHAT HAPPENED TO YOU, MY DARLING?
SOME BAD, NASTY, DIRTY PIRATES KIDNAPPED ME, DADDY!
AND WHO IS THIS YOUNG MAN?
OH, HE'S A PIRATE, TOO, DADDY! BUT—

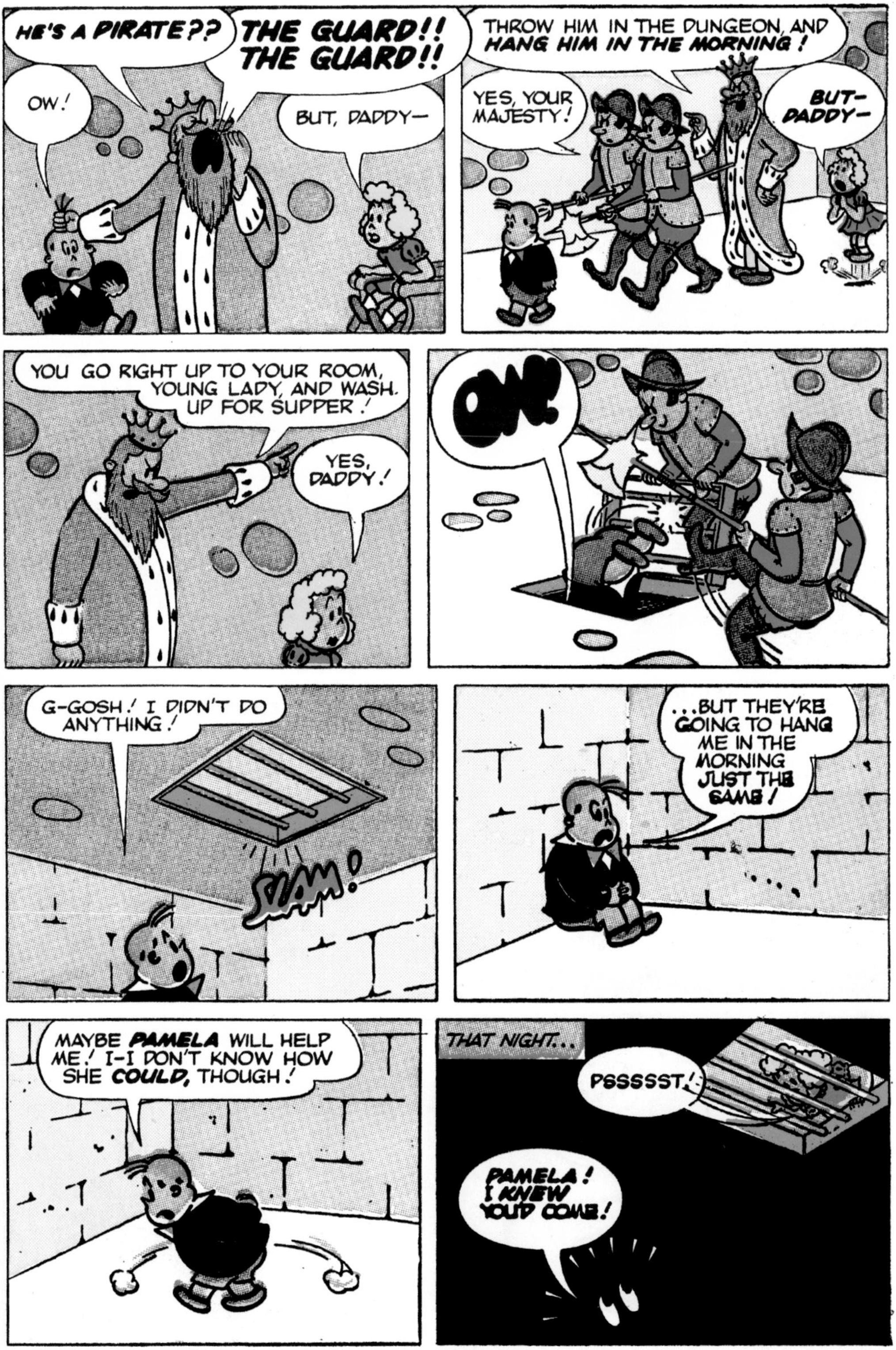
HE'S A PIRATE??
THE GUARD!! THE GUARD!!
OW!
BUT, DADDY—
THROW HIM IN THE DUNGEON, AND HANG HIM IN THE MORNING!
YES, YOUR MAJESTY!
BUT—DADDY—
YOU GO RIGHT UP TO YOUR ROOM, YOUNG LADY, AND WASH UP FOR SUPPER!
YES, DADDY!
OW!
G-GOSH! I DIDN'T DO ANYTHING!
SLAM!
...BUT THEY'RE GOING TO HANG ME IN THE MORNING JUST THE SAME!
MAYBE PAMELA WILL HELP ME! I-I DON'T KNOW HOW SHE COULD, THOUGH!
THAT NIGHT...
PSSSSST!
PAMELA! I KNEW YOU'D COME!

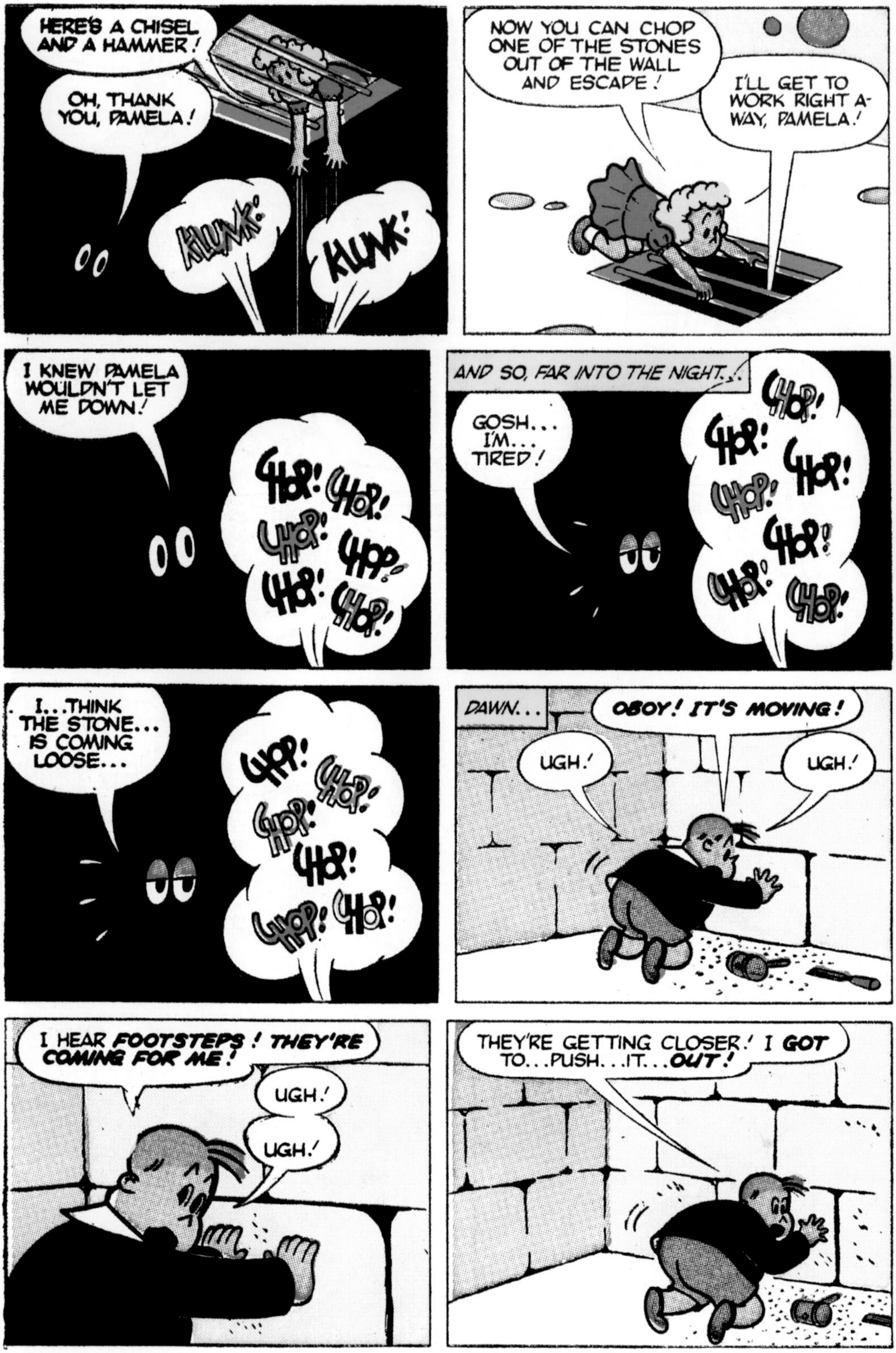
HERE'S A CHISEL AND A HAMMER!
OH, THANK YOU, PAMELA!
KLUNK!
KLUNK!
NOW YOU CAN CHOP ONE OF THE STONES OUT OF THE WALL AND ESCAPE!
I'LL GET TO WORK RIGHT A-WAY, PAMELA!
I KNEW PAMELA WOULDN'T LET ME DOWN!
CHOP! CHOP! CHOP! CHOP! CHOP! CHOP!
AND SO, FAR INTO THE NIGHT...
GOSH... I'M... TIRED!
CHOP! CHOP! CHOP! CHOP! CHOP! CHOP! CHOP!
I...THINK THE STONE... IS COMING LOOSE...
CHOP! CHOP! CHOP! CHOP! CHOP! CHOP!
DAWN...
OBOY! IT'S MOVING!
UGH!
UGH!
I HEAR FOOTSTEPS! THEY'RE COMING FOR ME!
UGH!
UGH!
THEY'RE GETTING CLOSER! I GOT TO...PUSH...IT...OUT!

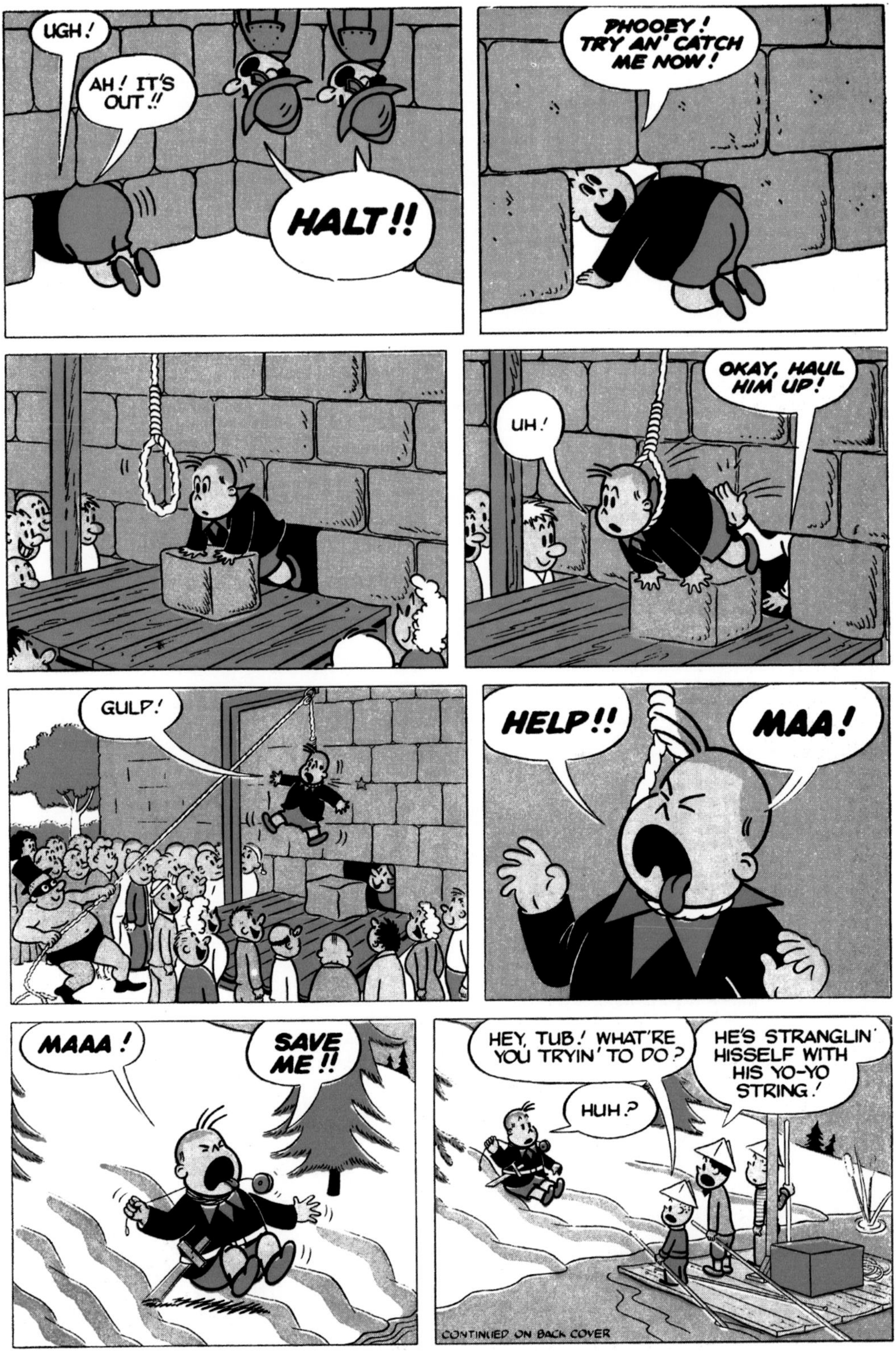
UGH!
AH! IT'S OUT!!
HALT!!
PHOOEY! TRY AN' CATCH ME NOW!
UH!
OKAY, HAUL HIM UP!
GULP!
HELP!!
MAA!
MAAA!
SAVE ME!!
HEY, TUB! WHAT'RE YOU TRYIN' TO DO?
HUH?
HE'S STRANGLIN' HISSELF WITH HIS YO-YO STRING!
CONTINUED ON BACK COVER

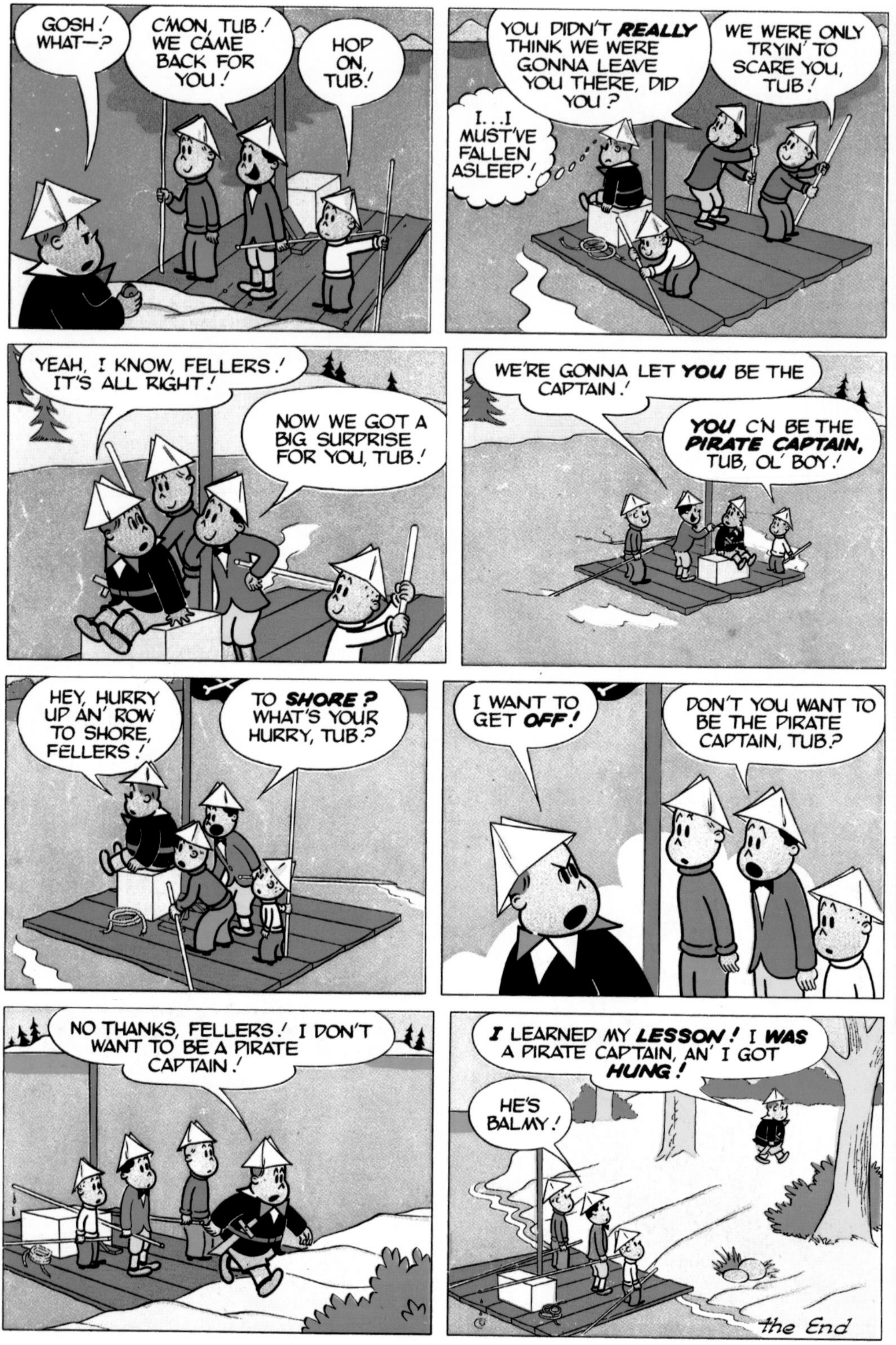
GOSH! WHAT—?
C'MON, TUB! WE CAME BACK FOR YOU!
HOP ON, TUB!
YOU DIDN'T REALLY THINK WE WERE GONNA LEAVE YOU THERE, DID YOU?
WE WERE ONLY TRYIN' TO SCARE YOU, TUB!
I...I MUST'VE FALLEN ASLEEP!
YEAH, I KNOW, FELLERS! IT'S ALL RIGHT!
NOW WE GOT A BIG SURPRISE FOR YOU, TUB!
WE'RE GONNA LET YOU BE THE CAPTAIN!
YOU C'N BE THE PIRATE CAPTAIN, TUB, OL' BOY!
HEY, HURRY UP AN' ROW TO SHORE, FELLERS!
TO SHORE? WHAT'S YOUR HURRY, TUB?
I WANT TO GET OFF!
DON'T YOU WANT TO BE THE PIRATE CAPTAIN, TUB?
NO THANKS, FELLERS! I DON'T WANT TO BE A PIRATE CAPTAIN!
I LEARNED MY LESSON! I WAS A PIRATE CAPTAIN, AN' I GOT HUNG!
HE'S BALMY!
the End

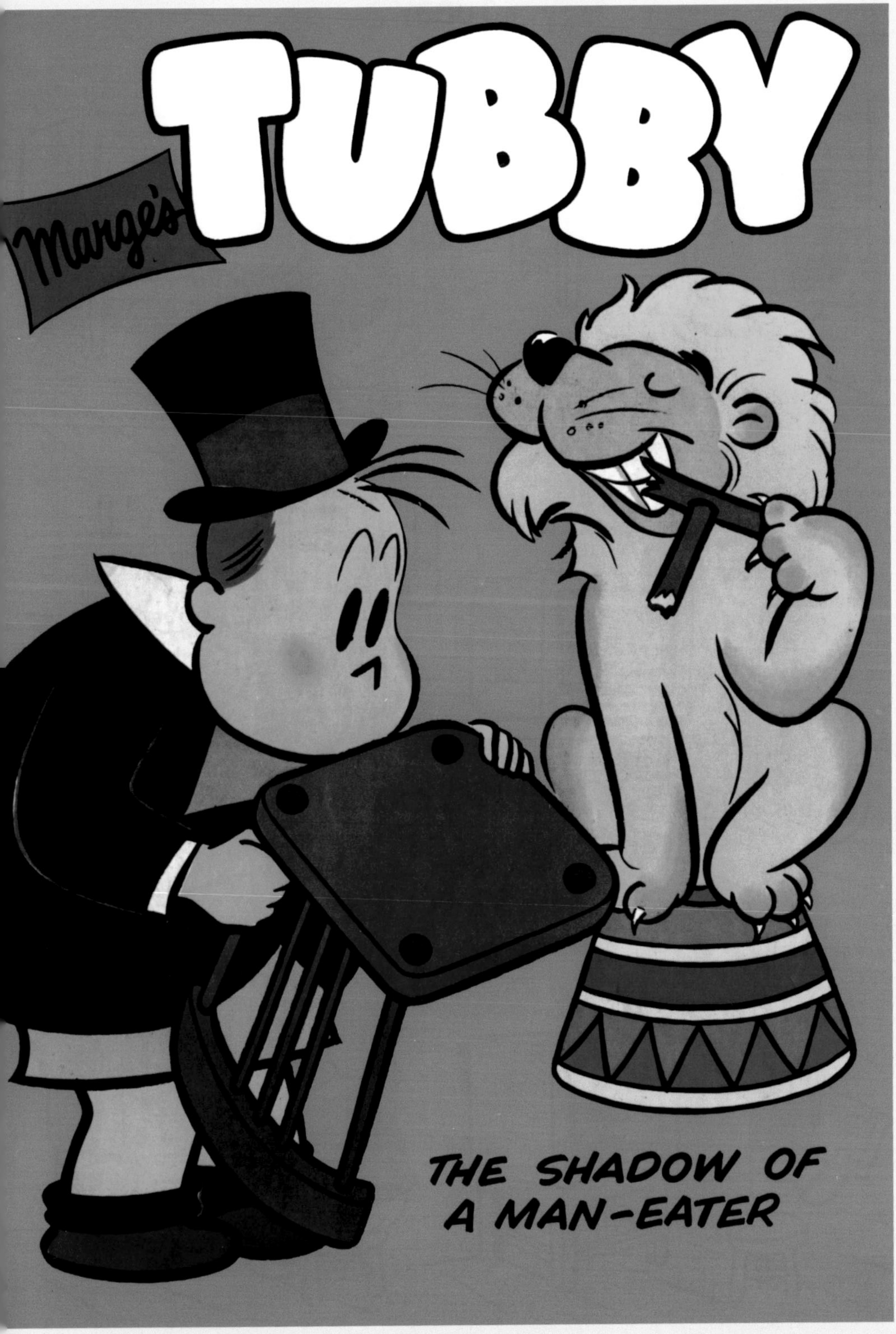
Marge's
TUBBY
THE SHADOW OF
A MAN-EATER

TUBBY

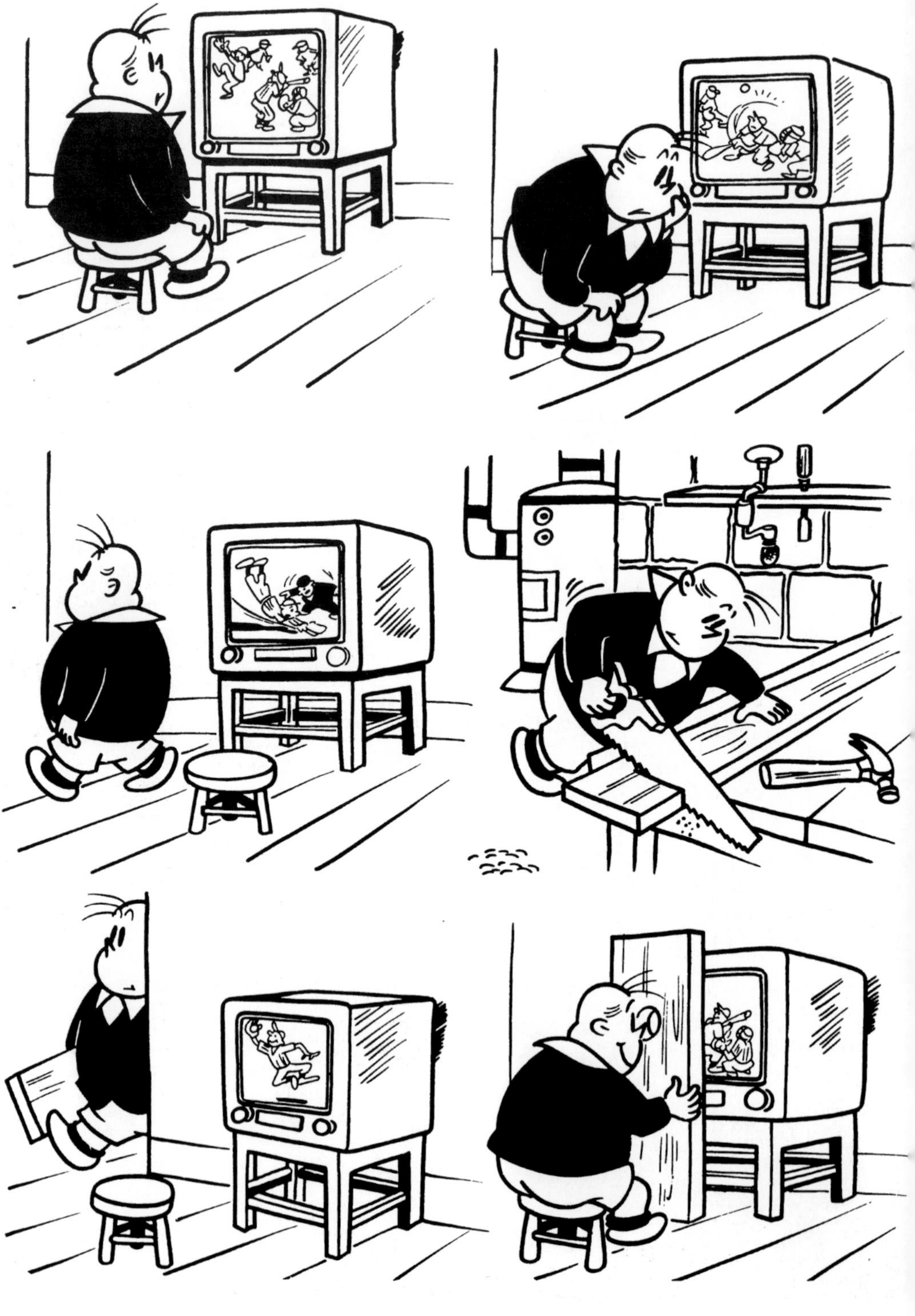

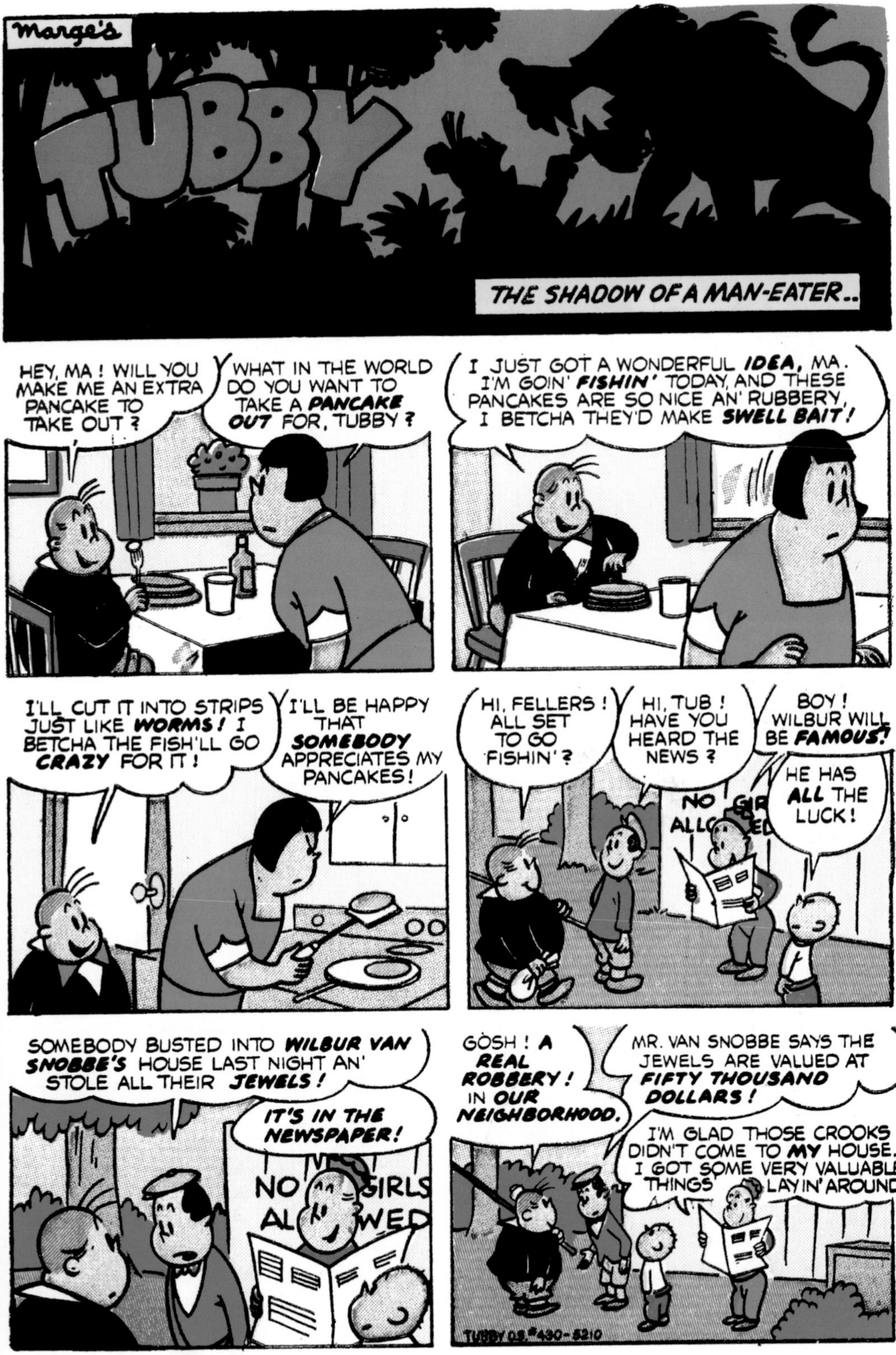
Marge's
TUBBY
THE SHADOW OF A MAN-EATER..
HEY, MA ! WILL YOU MAKE ME AN EXTRA PANCAKE TO TAKE OUT ?
WHAT IN THE WORLD DO YOU WANT TO TAKE A PANCAKE OUT FOR, TUBBY ?
I JUST GOT A WONDERFUL IDEA, MA. I'M GOIN' FISHIN' TODAY, AND THESE PANCAKES ARE SO NICE AN' RUBBERY, I BETCHA THEY'D MAKE SWELL BAIT !
I'LL CUT IT INTO STRIPS JUST LIKE WORMS ! I BETCHA THE FISH'LL GO CRAZY FOR IT !
I'LL BE HAPPY THAT SOMEBODY APPRECIATES MY PANCAKES !
HI, FELLERS ! ALL SET TO GO FISHIN' ?
HI, TUB ! HAVE YOU HEARD THE NEWS ?
BOY ! WILBUR WILL BE FAMOUS !
HE HAS ALL THE LUCK !
SOMEBODY BUSTED INTO WILBUR VAN SNOBBE'S HOUSE LAST NIGHT AN' STOLE ALL THEIR JEWELS !
IT'S IN THE NEWSPAPER !
NO GIRLS AL WED
GOSH ! A REAL ROBBERY ! IN OUR NEIGHBORHOOD.
MR. VAN SNOBBE SAYS THE JEWELS ARE VALUED AT FIFTY THOUSAND DOLLARS !
I'M GLAD THOSE CROOKS DIDN'T COME TO MY HOUSE. I GOT SOME VERY VALUABLE THINGS LAYIN' AROUND.
TUBBY O.S. #430-5210

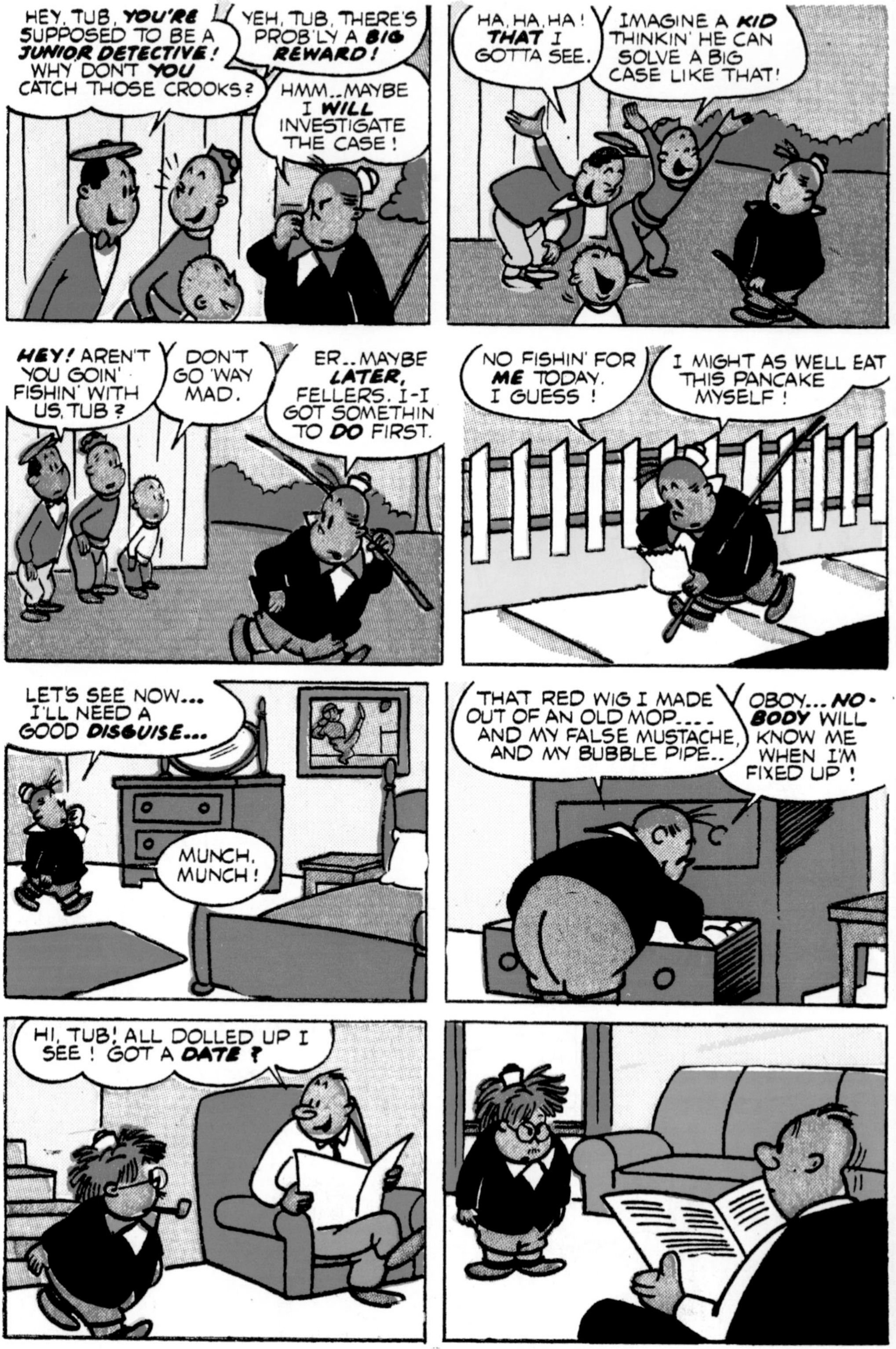
HEY, TUB, YOU'RE SUPPOSED TO BE A JUNIOR DETECTIVE! WHY DON'T YOU CATCH THOSE CROOKS?
YEH, TUB, THERE'S PROB'LY A BIG REWARD!
HMM..MAYBE I WILL INVESTIGATE THE CASE!
HA, HA, HA! THAT I GOTTA SEE.
IMAGINE A KID THINKIN' HE CAN SOLVE A BIG CASE LIKE THAT!
HEY! AREN'T YOU GOIN' FISHIN' WITH US, TUB?
DON'T GO 'WAY MAD.
ER..MAYBE LATER, FELLERS. I-I GOT SOMETHIN TO DO FIRST.
NO FISHIN' FOR ME TODAY, I GUESS!
I MIGHT AS WELL EAT THIS PANCAKE MYSELF!
LET'S SEE NOW... I'LL NEED A GOOD DISGUISE...
MUNCH, MUNCH!
THAT RED WIG I MADE OUT OF AN OLD MOP.... AND MY FALSE MUSTACHE, AND MY BUBBLE PIPE..
OBOY... NOBODY WILL KNOW ME WHEN I'M FIXED UP!
HI, TUB! ALL DOLLED UP I SEE! GOT A DATE?

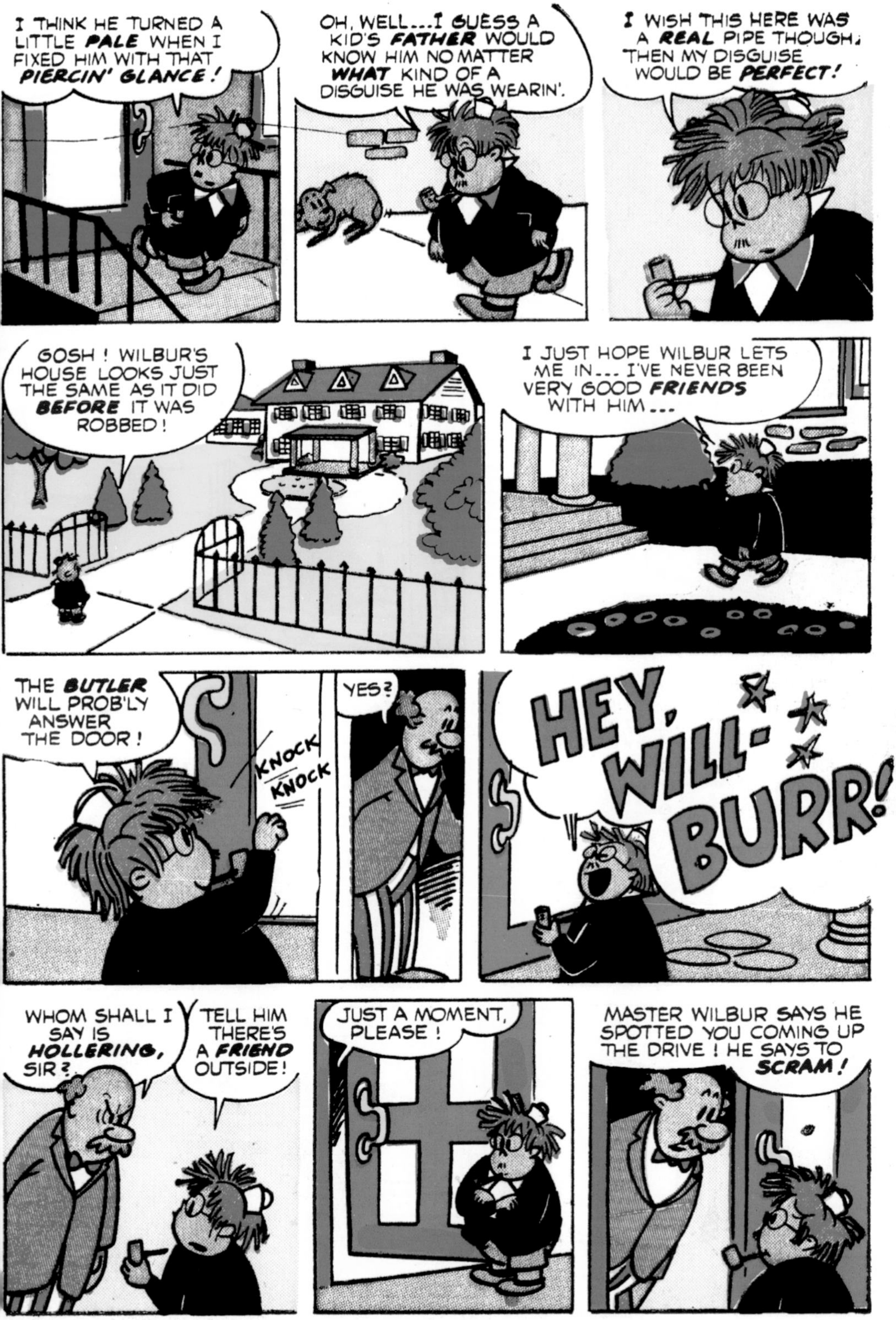
I THINK HE TURNED A LITTLE PALE WHEN I FIXED HIM WITH THAT PIERCIN' GLANCE!
OH, WELL...I GUESS A KID'S FATHER WOULD KNOW HIM NO MATTER WHAT KIND OF A DISGUISE HE WAS WEARIN'.
I WISH THIS HERE WAS A REAL PIPE THOUGH. THEN MY DISGUISE WOULD BE PERFECT!
GOSH! WILBUR'S HOUSE LOOKS JUST THE SAME AS IT DID BEFORE IT WAS ROBBED!
I JUST HOPE WILBUR LETS ME IN... I'VE NEVER BEEN VERY GOOD FRIENDS WITH HIM...
THE BUTLER WILL PROB'LY ANSWER THE DOOR!
KNOCK
KNOCK
YES?
HEY, WILL-BURR!
WHOM SHALL I SAY IS HOLLERING, SIR?
TELL HIM THERE'S A FRIEND OUTSIDE!
JUST A MOMENT, PLEASE!
MASTER WILBUR SAYS HE SPOTTED YOU COMING UP THE DRIVE! HE SAYS TO SCRAM!

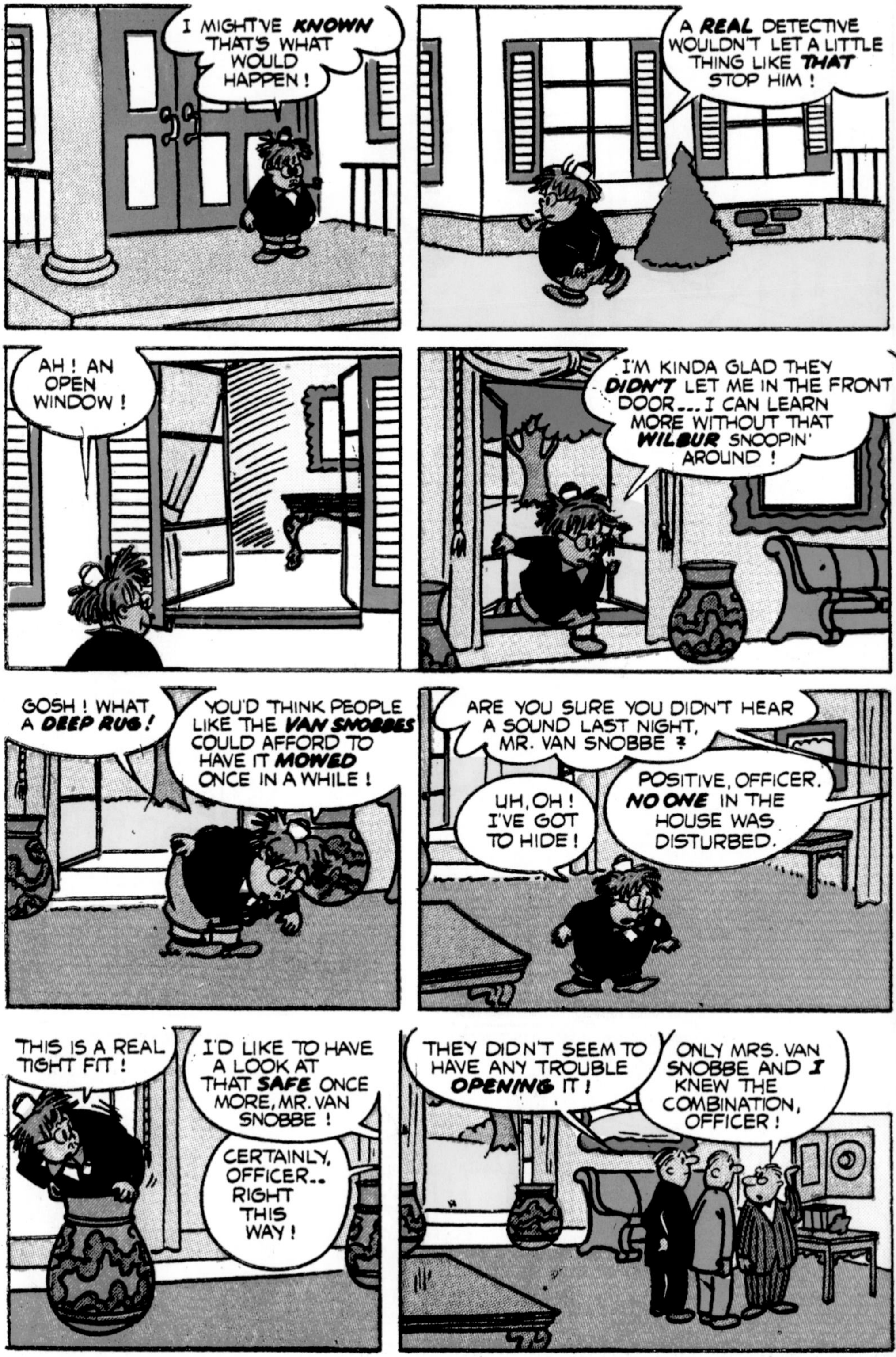
I MIGHT'VE KNOWN THAT'S WHAT WOULD HAPPEN !
A REAL DETECTIVE WOULDN'T LET A LITTLE THING LIKE THAT STOP HIM !
AH ! AN OPEN WINDOW !
I'M KINDA GLAD THEY DIDN'T LET ME IN THE FRONT DOOR... I CAN LEARN MORE WITHOUT THAT WILBUR SNOOPIN' AROUND !
GOSH ! WHAT A DEEP RUG !
YOU'D THINK PEOPLE LIKE THE VAN SNOBBES COULD AFFORD TO HAVE IT MOWED ONCE IN A WHILE !
ARE YOU SURE YOU DIDN'T HEAR A SOUND LAST NIGHT, MR. VAN SNOBBE ?
UH, OH ! I'VE GOT TO HIDE !
POSITIVE, OFFICER. NO ONE IN THE HOUSE WAS DISTURBED.
THIS IS A REAL TIGHT FIT !
I'D LIKE TO HAVE A LOOK AT THAT SAFE ONCE MORE, MR. VAN SNOBBE !
CERTAINLY, OFFICER.. RIGHT THIS WAY !
THEY DIDN'T SEEM TO HAVE ANY TROUBLE OPENING IT !
ONLY MRS. VAN SNOBBE AND I KNEW THE COMBINATION, OFFICER !

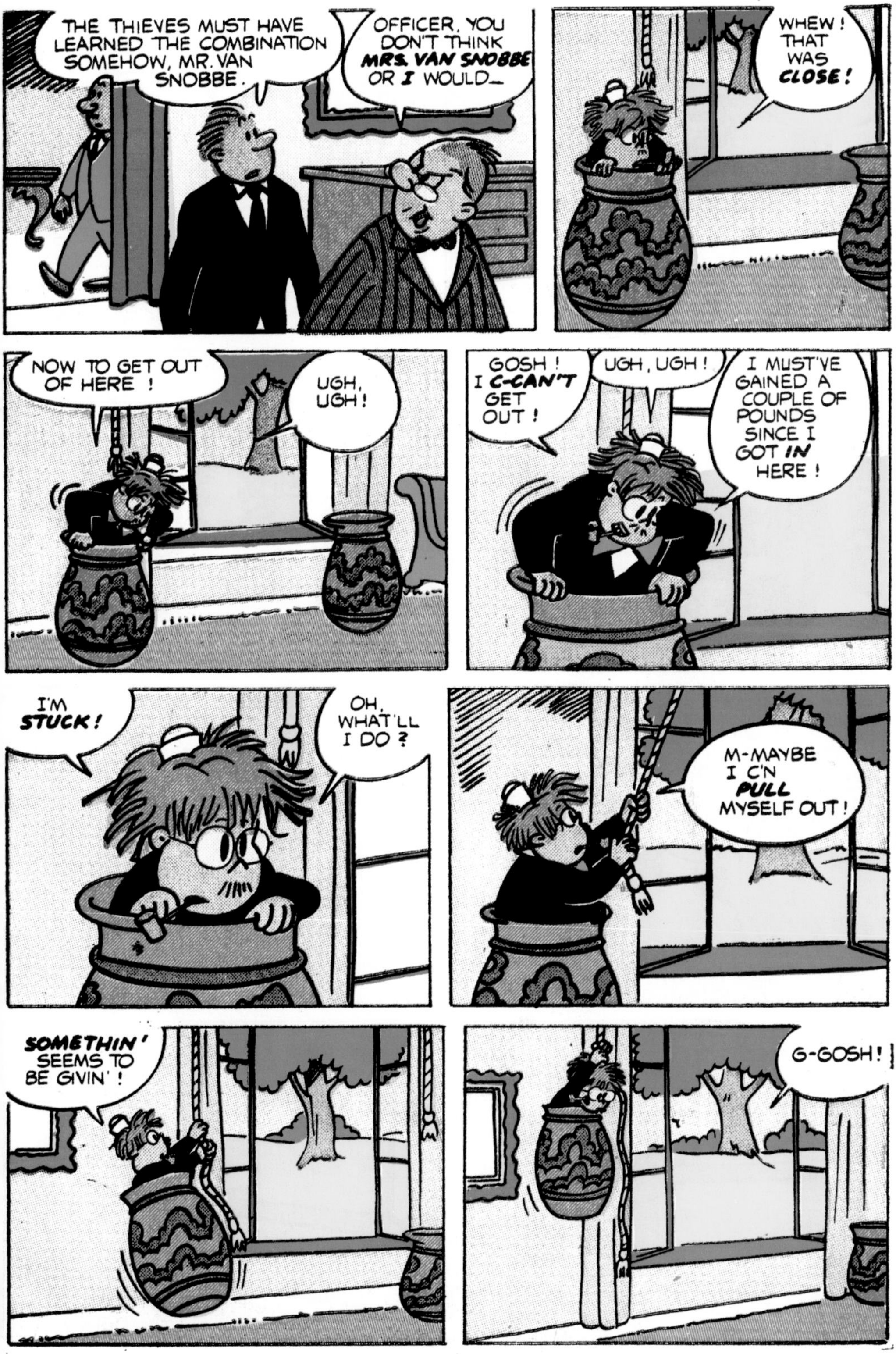
THE THIEVES MUST HAVE LEARNED THE COMBINATION SOMEHOW, MR. VAN SNOBBE.
OFFICER, YOU DON'T THINK MRS. VAN SNOBBE OR I WOULD—
WHEW! THAT WAS CLOSE!
NOW TO GET OUT OF HERE!
UGH, UGH!
GOSH! I C-CAN'T GET OUT!
UGH, UGH!
I MUST'VE GAINED A COUPLE OF POUNDS SINCE I GOT IN HERE!
I'M STUCK!
OH, WHAT'LL I DO?
M-MAYBE I C'N PULL MYSELF OUT!
SOMETHIN' SEEMS TO BE GIVIN'!
G-GOSH!

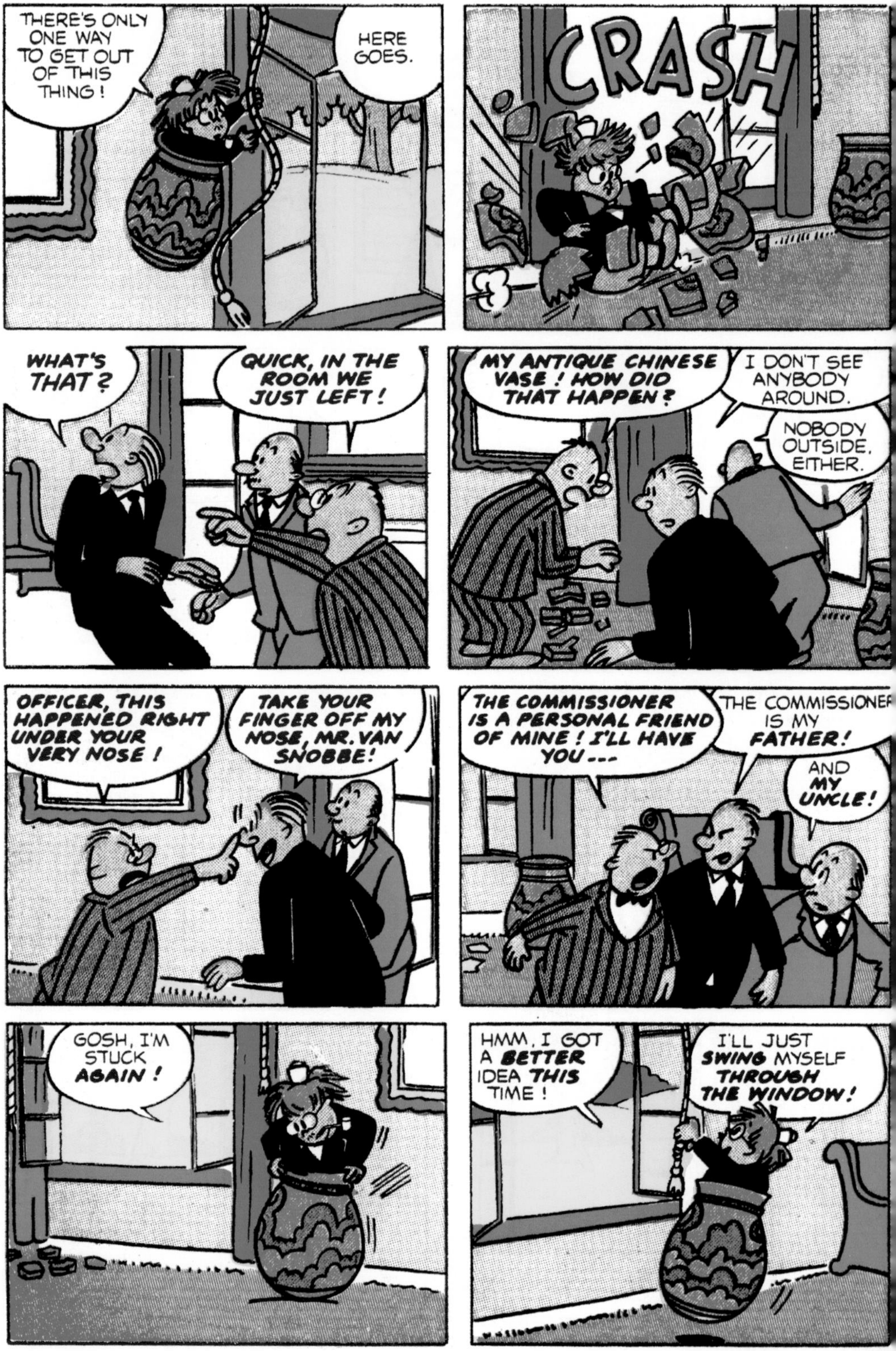
THERE'S ONLY ONE WAY TO GET OUT OF THIS THING!
HERE GOES.
CRASH
WHAT'S THAT?
QUICK, IN THE ROOM WE JUST LEFT!
MY ANTIQUE CHINESE VASE! HOW DID THAT HAPPEN?
I DON'T SEE ANYBODY AROUND.
NOBODY OUTSIDE, EITHER.
OFFICER, THIS HAPPENED RIGHT UNDER YOUR VERY NOSE!
TAKE YOUR FINGER OFF MY NOSE, MR. VAN SNOBBE!
THE COMMISSIONER IS A PERSONAL FRIEND OF MINE! I'LL HAVE YOU---
THE COMMISSIONER IS MY FATHER!
AND MY UNCLE!
GOSH, I'M STUCK AGAIN!
HMM, I GOT A BETTER IDEA THIS TIME!
I'LL JUST SWING MYSELF THROUGH THE WINDOW!

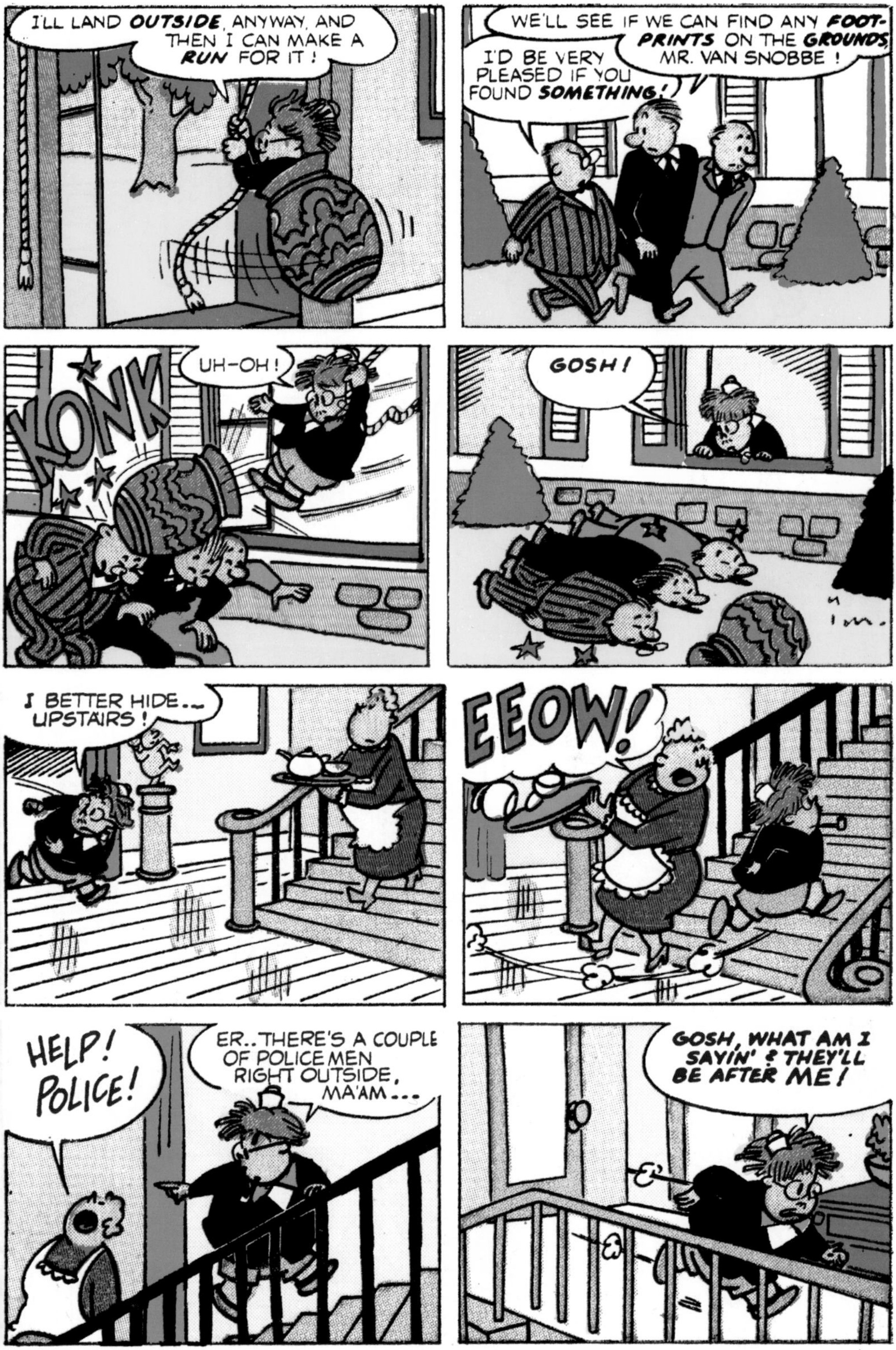
I'LL LAND OUTSIDE, ANYWAY, AND THEN I CAN MAKE A RUN FOR IT!
WE'LL SEE IF WE CAN FIND ANY FOOT-PRINTS ON THE GROUNDS, MR. VAN SNOBBE!
I'D BE VERY PLEASED IF YOU FOUND SOMETHING!
KONK
UH-OH!
GOSH!
I BETTER HIDE... UPSTAIRS!
EEOW!
HELP! POLICE!
ER..THERE'S A COUPLE OF POLICEMEN RIGHT OUTSIDE, MA'AM...
GOSH, WHAT AM I SAYIN'? THEY'LL BE AFTER ME!

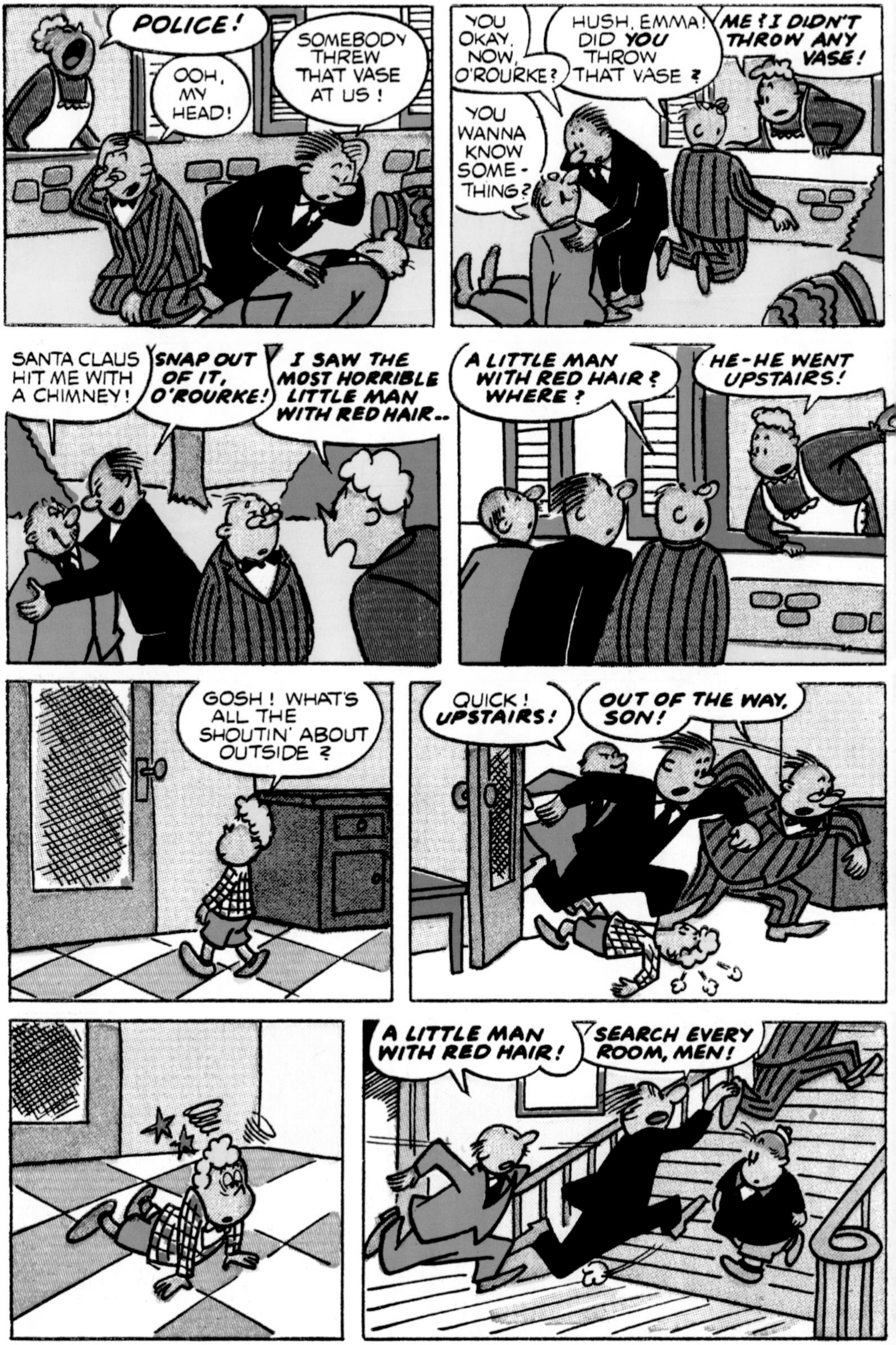
POLICE!
OOH, MY HEAD!
SOMEBODY THREW THAT VASE AT US!
YOU OKAY, NOW, O'ROURKE?
HUSH, EMMA! DID YOU THROW THAT VASE?
ME? I DIDN'T THROW ANY VASE!
YOU WANNA KNOW SOME-THING?
SANTA CLAUS HIT ME WITH A CHIMNEY!
SNAP OUT OF IT, O'ROURKE!
I SAW THE MOST HORRIBLE LITTLE MAN WITH RED HAIR..
A LITTLE MAN WITH RED HAIR? WHERE?
HE-HE WENT UPSTAIRS!
GOSH! WHAT'S ALL THE SHOUTIN' ABOUT OUTSIDE?
QUICK! UPSTAIRS!
OUT OF THE WAY, SON!
A LITTLE MAN WITH RED HAIR!
SEARCH EVERY ROOM, MEN!

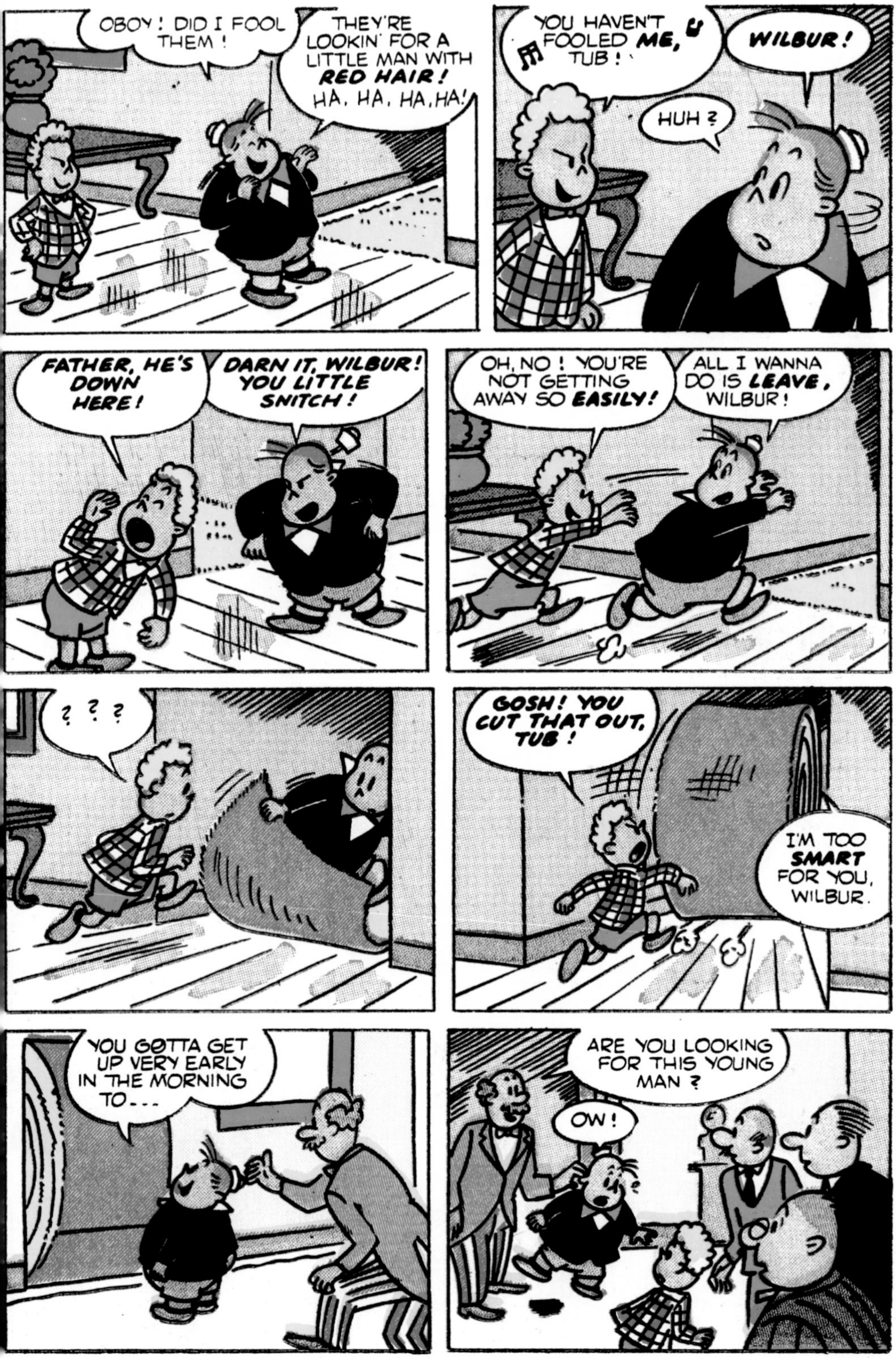
OBOY! DID I FOOL THEM!
THEY'RE LOOKIN' FOR A LITTLE MAN WITH RED HAIR! HA. HA. HA. HA!
YOU HAVEN'T FOOLED ME, TUB!
WILBUR!
HUH?
FATHER, HE'S DOWN HERE!
DARN IT, WILBUR! YOU LITTLE SNITCH!
OH, NO! YOU'RE NOT GETTING AWAY SO EASILY!
ALL I WANNA DO IS LEAVE, WILBUR!
? ? ?
GOSH! YOU CUT THAT OUT, TUB!
I'M TOO SMART FOR YOU, WILBUR.
YOU GOTTA GET UP VERY EARLY IN THE MORNING TO...
ARE YOU LOOKING FOR THIS YOUNG MAN?
OW!

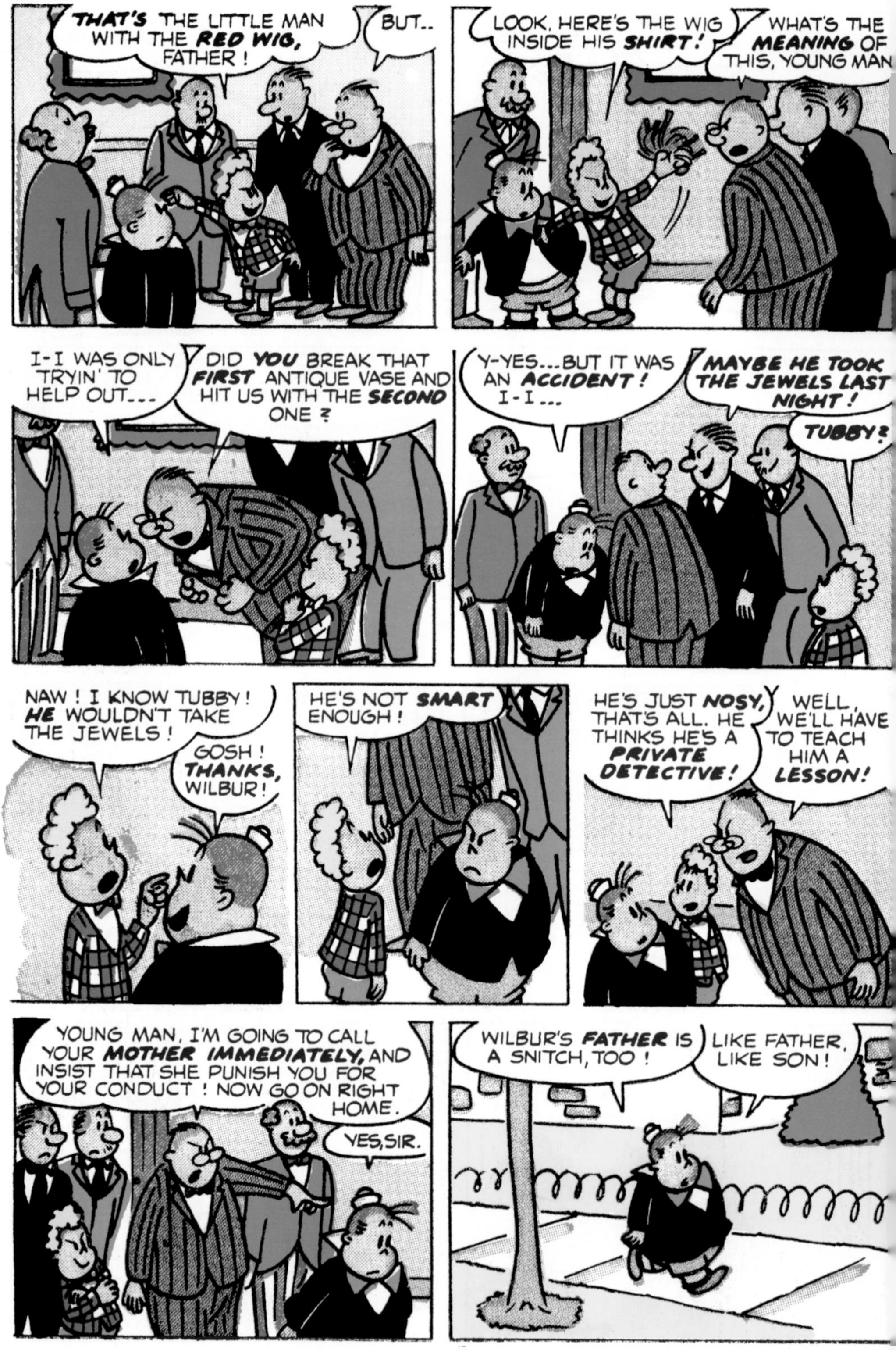
THAT'S THE LITTLE MAN WITH THE RED WIG, FATHER!
BUT..
LOOK, HERE'S THE WIG INSIDE HIS SHIRT!
WHAT'S THE MEANING OF THIS, YOUNG MAN
I-I WAS ONLY TRYIN' TO HELP OUT...
DID YOU BREAK THAT FIRST ANTIQUE VASE AND HIT US WITH THE SECOND ONE ?
Y-YES...BUT IT WAS AN ACCIDENT! I-I...
MAYBE HE TOOK THE JEWELS LAST NIGHT!
TUBBY?
NAW! I KNOW TUBBY! HE WOULDN'T TAKE THE JEWELS!
GOSH! THANKS, WILBUR!
HE'S NOT SMART ENOUGH!
HE'S JUST NOSY, THAT'S ALL. HE THINKS HE'S A PRIVATE DETECTIVE!
WELL, WE'LL HAVE TO TEACH HIM A LESSON!
YOUNG MAN, I'M GOING TO CALL YOUR MOTHER IMMEDIATELY, AND INSIST THAT SHE PUNISH YOU FOR YOUR CONDUCT! NOW GO ON RIGHT HOME.
YES, SIR.
WILBUR'S FATHER IS A SNITCH, TOO!
LIKE FATHER, LIKE SON!

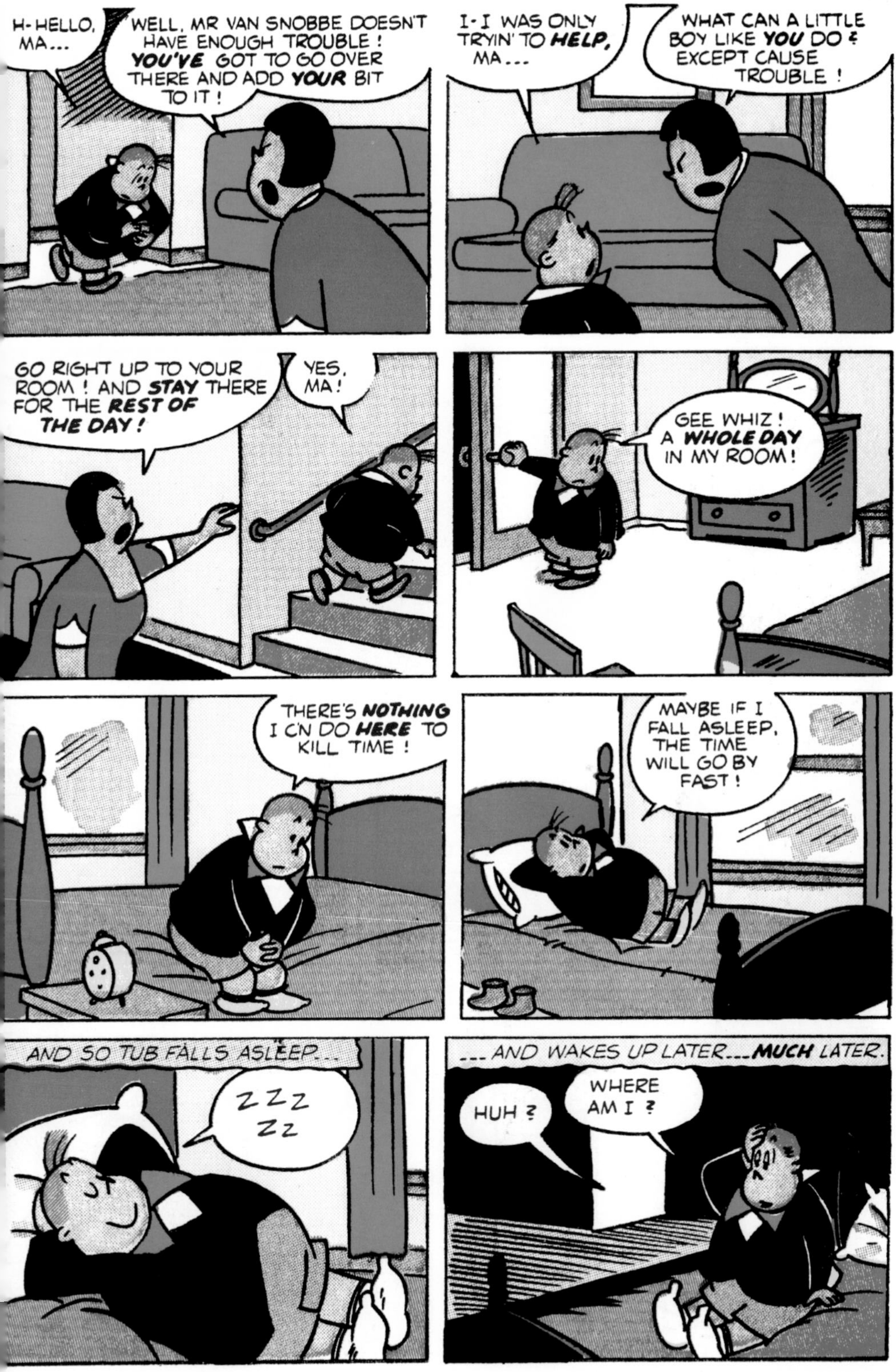
H-HELLO, MA...
WELL, MR VAN SNOBBE DOESN'T HAVE ENOUGH TROUBLE! **YOU'VE** GOT TO GO OVER THERE AND ADD **YOUR** BIT TO IT!
I-I WAS ONLY TRYIN' TO **HELP,** MA...
WHAT CAN A LITTLE BOY LIKE **YOU** DO? EXCEPT CAUSE TROUBLE!
GO RIGHT UP TO YOUR ROOM! AND **STAY** THERE FOR THE **REST OF THE DAY!**
YES, MA!
GEE WHIZ! A **WHOLE DAY** IN MY ROOM!
THERE'S **NOTHING** I C'N DO **HERE** TO KILL TIME!
MAYBE IF I FALL ASLEEP, THE TIME WILL GO BY FAST!
AND SO TUB FALLS ASLEEP...
ZZZ ZZ
...AND WAKES UP LATER...**MUCH** LATER.
HUH?
WHERE AM I?

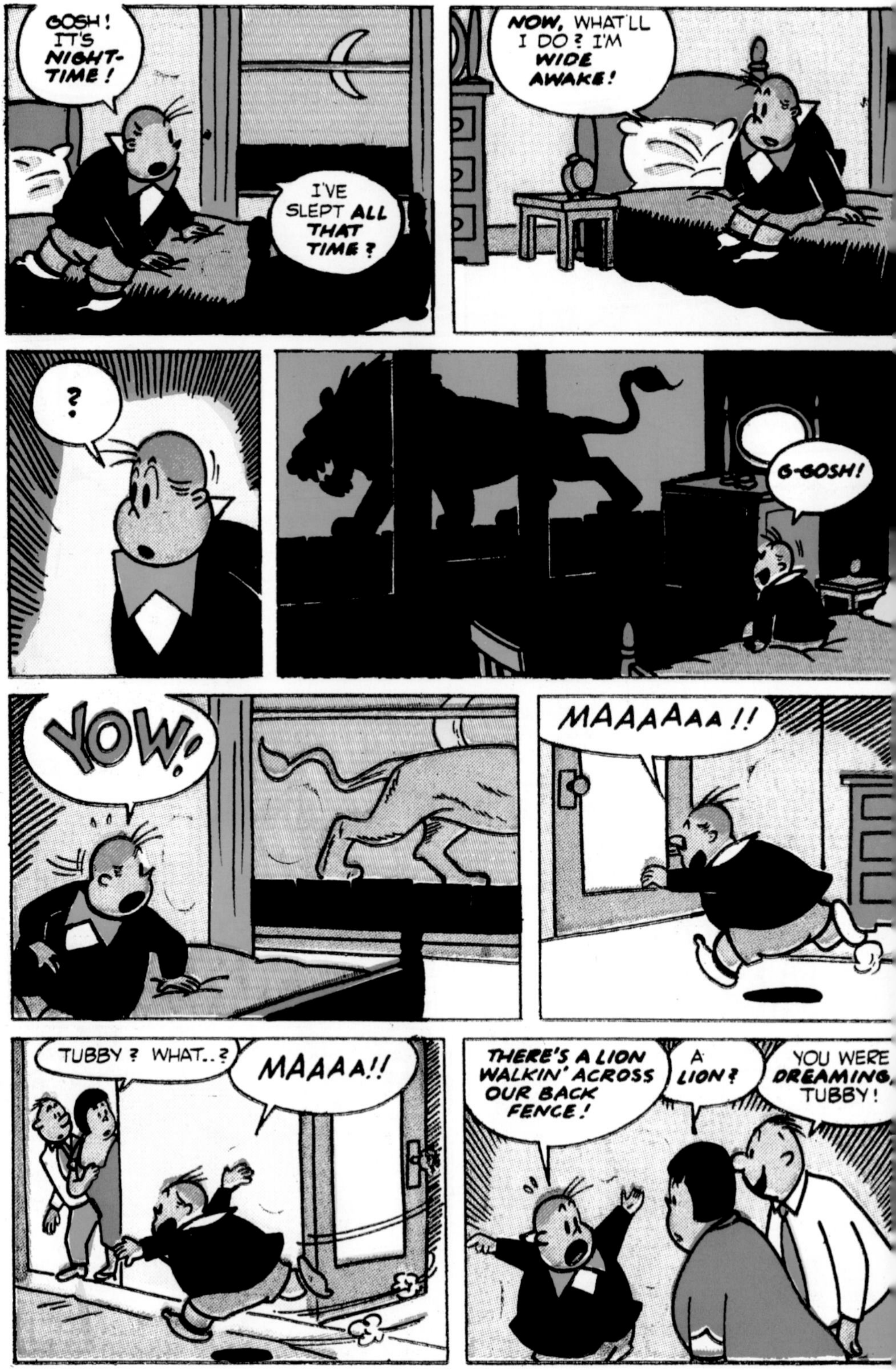
GOSH! IT'S NIGHT-TIME!
I'VE SLEPT ALL THAT TIME?
NOW, WHAT'LL I DO? I'M WIDE AWAKE!
?
G-GOSH!
YOW!
MAAAAAA!!
TUBBY? WHAT..?
MAAAA!!
THERE'S A LION WALKIN' ACROSS OUR BACK FENCE!
A LION?
YOU WERE DREAMING, TUBBY!

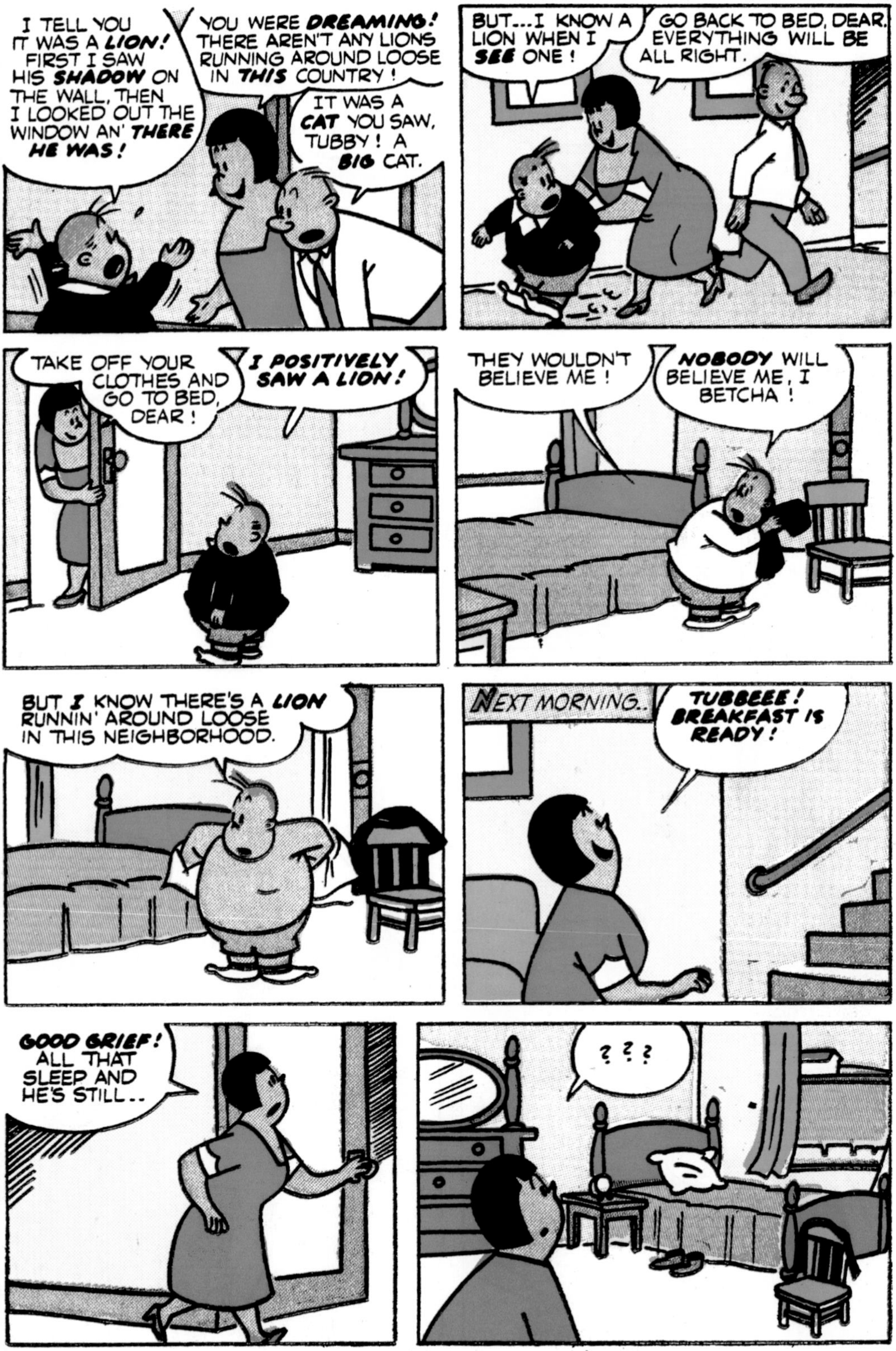
I TELL YOU IT WAS A LION! FIRST I SAW HIS SHADOW ON THE WALL, THEN I LOOKED OUT THE WINDOW AN' THERE HE WAS!
YOU WERE DREAMING! THERE AREN'T ANY LIONS RUNNING AROUND LOOSE IN THIS COUNTRY!
IT WAS A CAT YOU SAW, TUBBY! A BIG CAT.
BUT... I KNOW A LION WHEN I SEE ONE!
GO BACK TO BED, DEAR. EVERYTHING WILL BE ALL RIGHT.
TAKE OFF YOUR CLOTHES AND GO TO BED, DEAR!
I POSITIVELY SAW A LION!
THEY WOULDN'T BELIEVE ME!
NOBODY WILL BELIEVE ME, I BETCHA!
BUT I KNOW THERE'S A LION RUNNIN' AROUND LOOSE IN THIS NEIGHBORHOOD.
NEXT MORNING..
TUBBEEE! BREAKFAST IS READY!
GOOD GRIEF! ALL THAT SLEEP AND HE'S STILL..
???

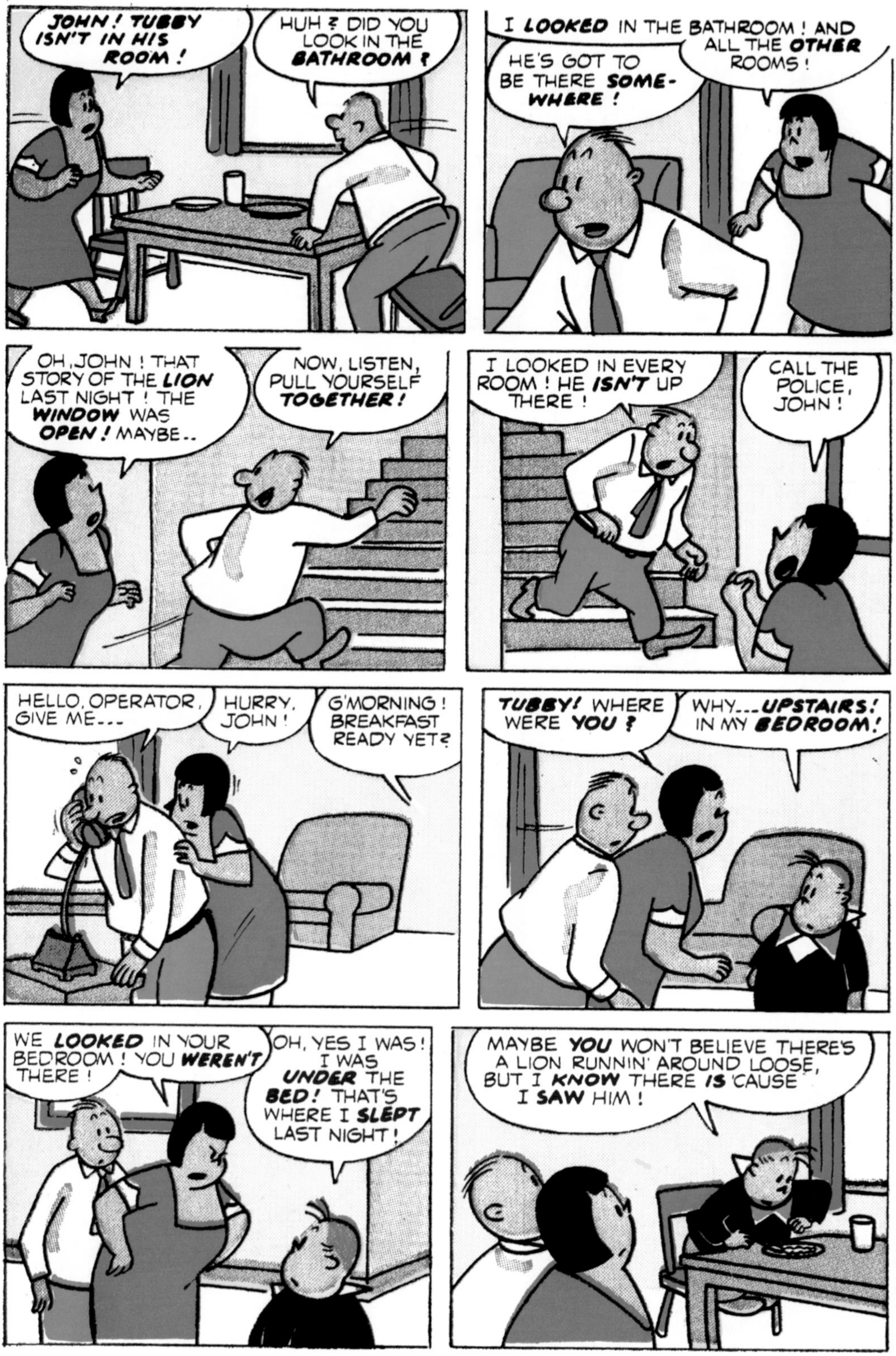
JOHN! TUBBY ISN'T IN HIS ROOM!
HUH? DID YOU LOOK IN THE BATHROOM?
I LOOKED IN THE BATHROOM! AND ALL THE OTHER ROOMS!
HE'S GOT TO BE THERE SOME-WHERE!
OH, JOHN! THAT STORY OF THE LION LAST NIGHT! THE WINDOW WAS OPEN! MAYBE..
NOW, LISTEN, PULL YOURSELF TOGETHER!
I LOOKED IN EVERY ROOM! HE ISN'T UP THERE!
CALL THE POLICE, JOHN!
HELLO, OPERATOR, GIVE ME---
HURRY, JOHN!
G'MORNING! BREAKFAST READY YET?
TUBBY! WHERE WERE YOU?
WHY...UPSTAIRS! IN MY BEDROOM!
WE LOOKED IN YOUR BEDROOM! YOU WEREN'T THERE!
OH, YES I WAS! I WAS UNDER THE BED! THAT'S WHERE I SLEPT LAST NIGHT!
MAYBE YOU WON'T BELIEVE THERE'S A LION RUNNIN' AROUND LOOSE, BUT I KNOW THERE IS 'CAUSE I SAW HIM!

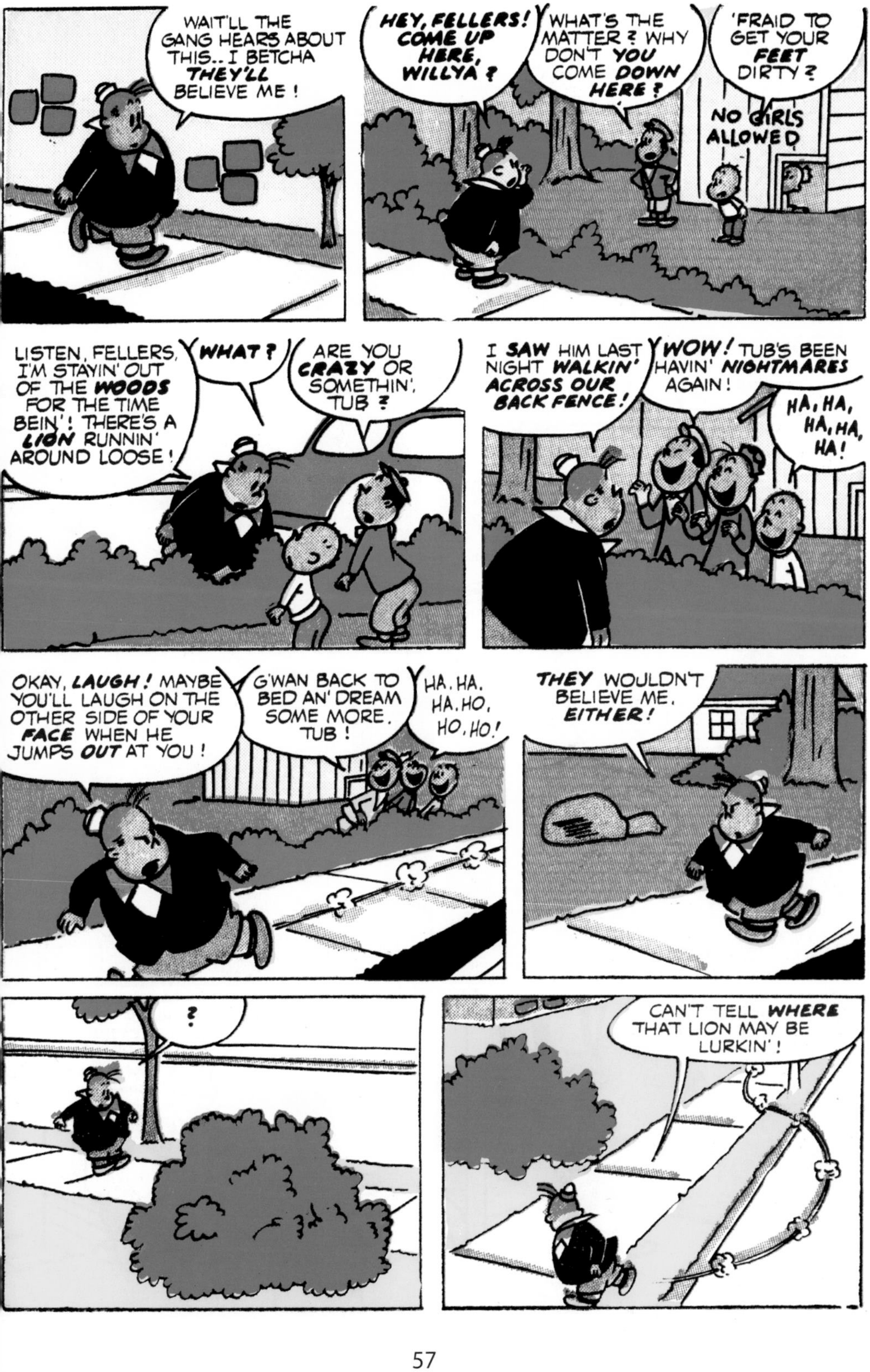
WAIT'LL THE GANG HEARS ABOUT THIS.. I BETCHA THEY'LL BELIEVE ME!
HEY, FELLERS! COME UP HERE, WILLYA?
WHAT'S THE MATTER? WHY DON'T YOU COME DOWN HERE?
'FRAID TO GET YOUR FEET DIRTY?
NO GIRLS ALLOWED
LISTEN, FELLERS, I'M STAYIN' OUT OF THE WOODS FOR THE TIME BEIN'! THERE'S A LION RUNNIN' AROUND LOOSE!
WHAT?
ARE YOU CRAZY OR SOMETHIN', TUB?
I SAW HIM LAST NIGHT WALKIN' ACROSS OUR BACK FENCE!
WOW! TUB'S BEEN HAVIN' NIGHTMARES AGAIN!
HA, HA, HA, HA, HA!
OKAY, LAUGH! MAYBE YOU'LL LAUGH ON THE OTHER SIDE OF YOUR FACE WHEN HE JUMPS OUT AT YOU!
G'WAN BACK TO BED AN' DREAM SOME MORE, TUB!
HA. HA. HA. HO. HO. HO!
THEY WOULDN'T BELIEVE ME, EITHER!
?
CAN'T TELL WHERE THAT LION MAY BE LURKIN'!

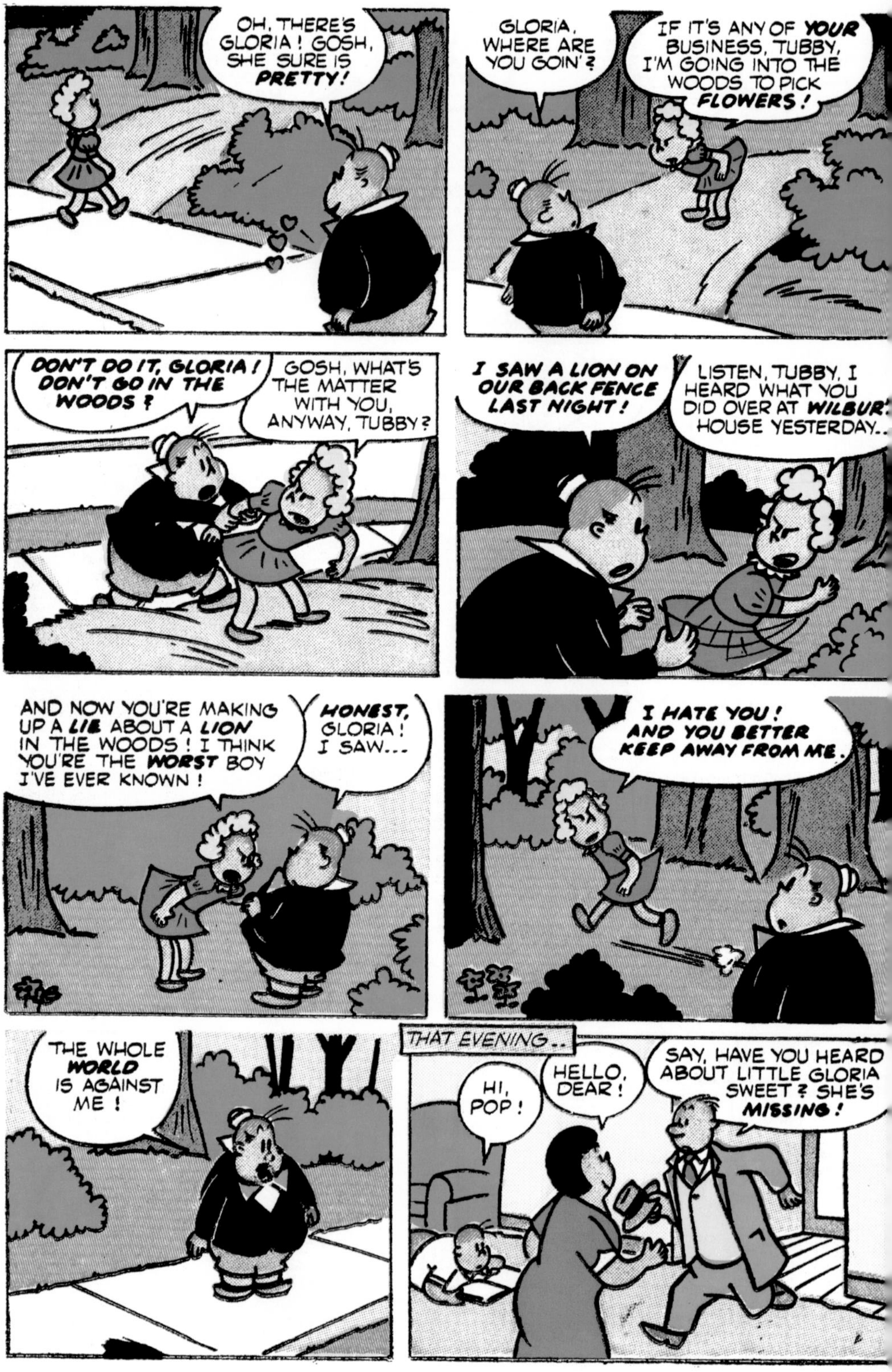
OH, THERE'S GLORIA! GOSH, SHE SURE IS PRETTY!
GLORIA, WHERE ARE YOU GOIN'?
IF IT'S ANY OF YOUR BUSINESS, TUBBY, I'M GOING INTO THE WOODS TO PICK FLOWERS!
DON'T DO IT, GLORIA! DON'T GO IN THE WOODS!
GOSH, WHAT'S THE MATTER WITH YOU, ANYWAY, TUBBY?
I SAW A LION ON OUR BACK FENCE LAST NIGHT!
LISTEN, TUBBY, I HEARD WHAT YOU DID OVER AT WILBUR'S HOUSE YESTERDAY...
AND NOW YOU'RE MAKING UP A LIE ABOUT A LION IN THE WOODS! I THINK YOU'RE THE WORST BOY I'VE EVER KNOWN!
HONEST, GLORIA! I SAW...
I HATE YOU! AND YOU BETTER KEEP AWAY FROM ME.
THE WHOLE WORLD IS AGAINST ME!
THAT EVENING...
HI, POP!
HELLO, DEAR!
SAY, HAVE YOU HEARD ABOUT LITTLE GLORIA SWEET? SHE'S MISSING!

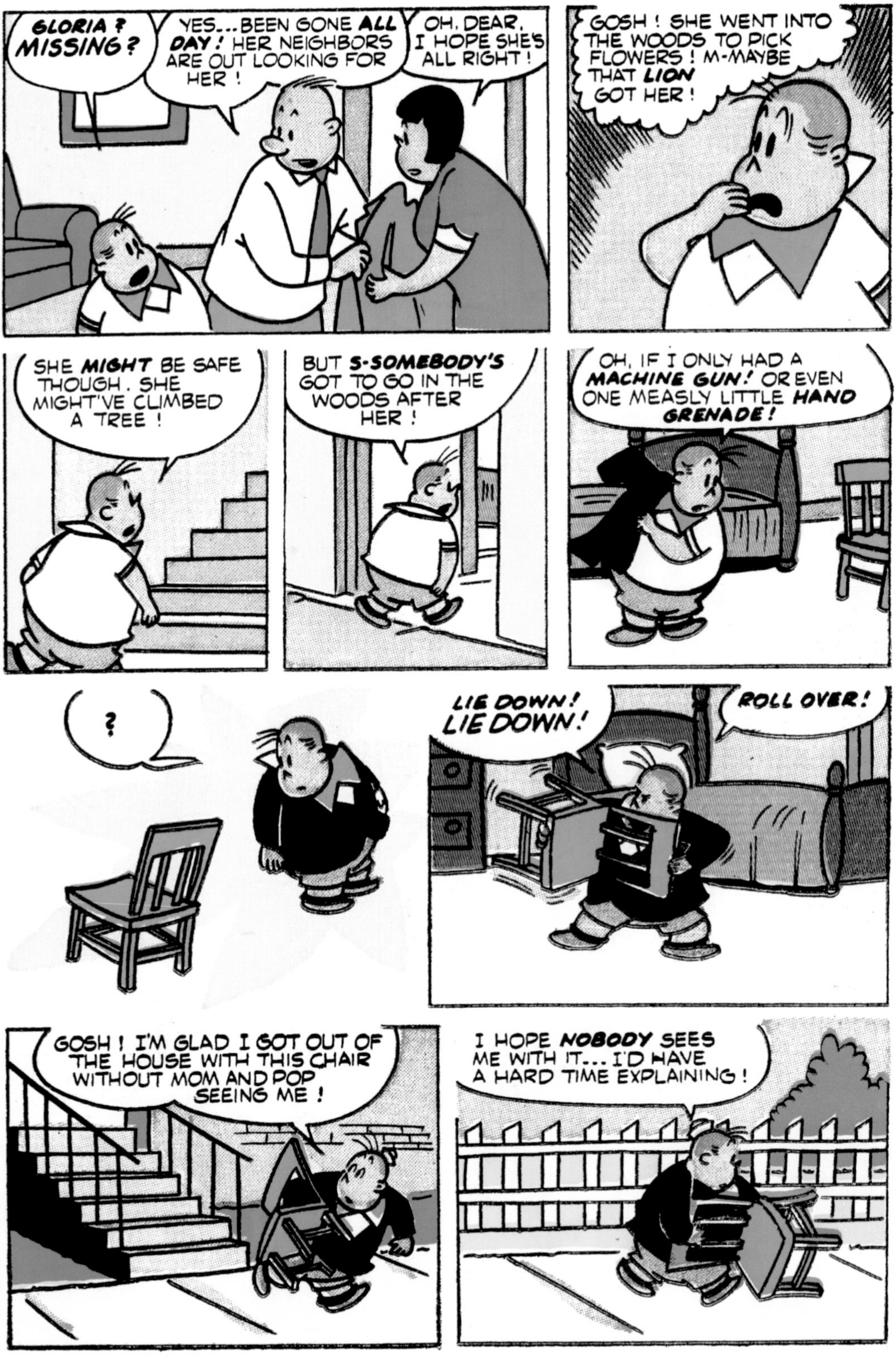
GLORIA? MISSING?
YES... BEEN GONE ALL DAY! HER NEIGHBORS ARE OUT LOOKING FOR HER!
OH, DEAR, I HOPE SHE'S ALL RIGHT!
GOSH! SHE WENT INTO THE WOODS TO PICK FLOWERS! M-MAYBE THAT LION GOT HER!
SHE MIGHT BE SAFE THOUGH. SHE MIGHT'VE CLIMBED A TREE!
BUT S-SOMEBODY'S GOT TO GO IN THE WOODS AFTER HER!
OH, IF I ONLY HAD A MACHINE GUN! OR EVEN ONE MEASLY LITTLE HAND GRENADE!
?
LIE DOWN! LIE DOWN!
ROLL OVER!
GOSH! I'M GLAD I GOT OUT OF THE HOUSE WITH THIS CHAIR WITHOUT MOM AND POP SEEING ME!
I HOPE NOBODY SEES ME WITH IT... I'D HAVE A HARD TIME EXPLAINING!

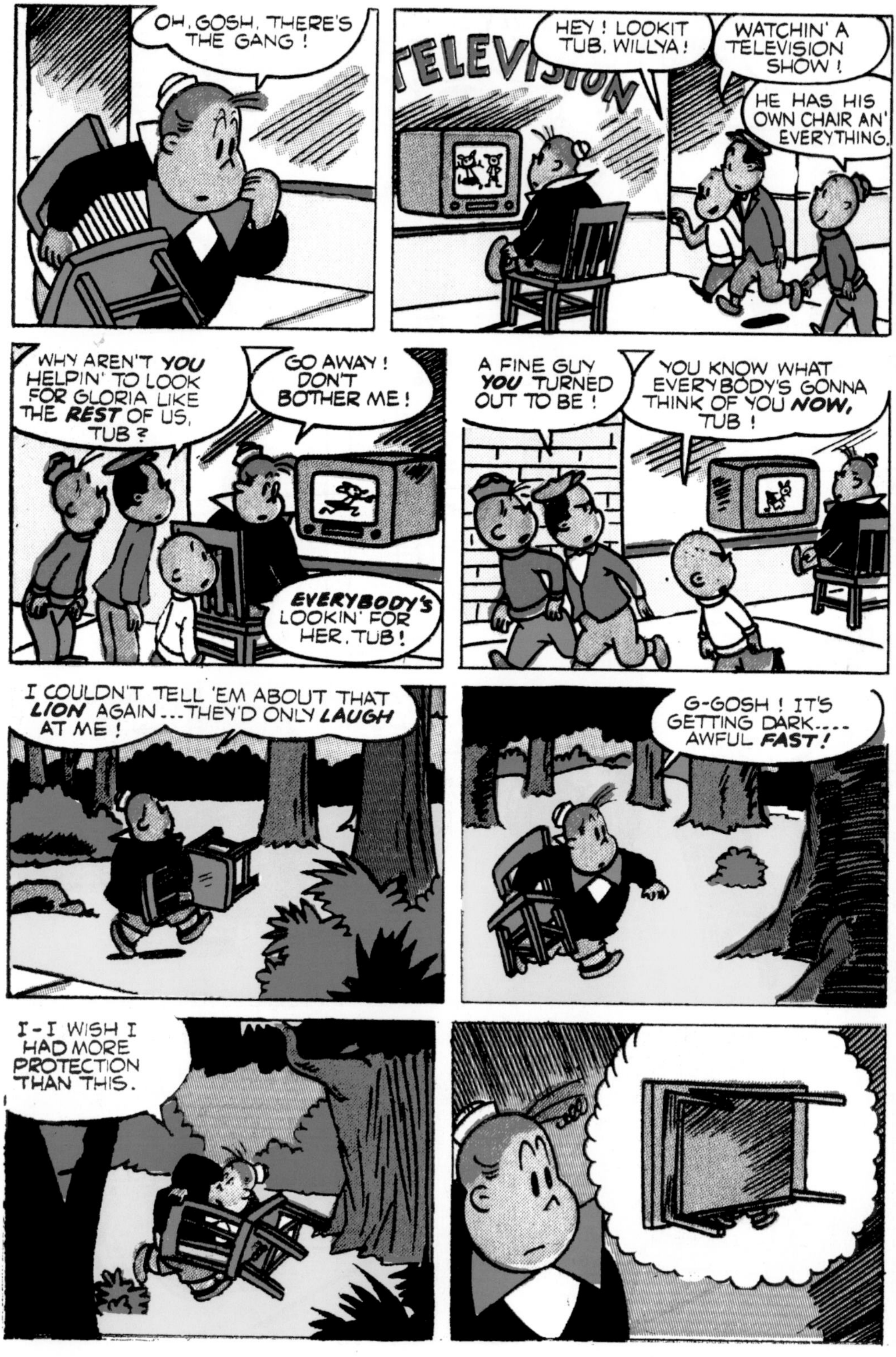
OH, GOSH, THERE'S THE GANG !
HEY ! LOOKIT TUB, WILLYA !
WATCHIN' A TELEVISION SHOW !
HE HAS HIS OWN CHAIR AN' EVERYTHING.
TELEVISION
WHY AREN'T YOU HELPIN' TO LOOK FOR GLORIA LIKE THE REST OF US, TUB ?
GO AWAY ! DON'T BOTHER ME !
EVERYBODY'S LOOKIN' FOR HER, TUB !
A FINE GUY YOU TURNED OUT TO BE !
YOU KNOW WHAT EVERYBODY'S GONNA THINK OF YOU NOW, TUB !
I COULDN'T TELL 'EM ABOUT THAT LION AGAIN ... THEY'D ONLY LAUGH AT ME !
G-GOSH ! IT'S GETTING DARK.... AWFUL FAST !
I-I WISH I HAD MORE PROTECTION THAN THIS.

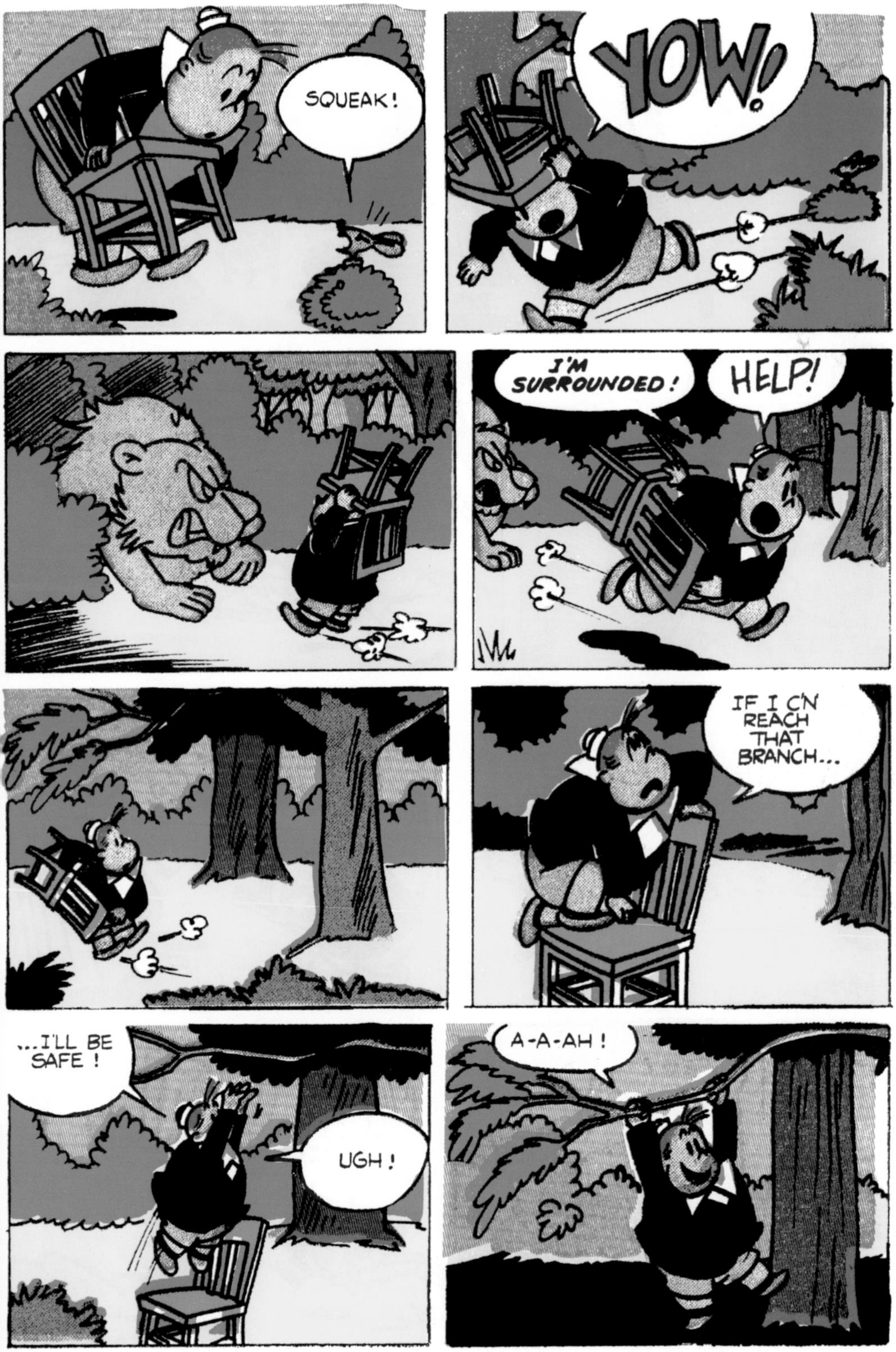
SQUEAK!
YOW!
I'M SURROUNDED!
HELP!
IF I C'N REACH THAT BRANCH...
...I'LL BE SAFE!
UGH!
A-A-AH!

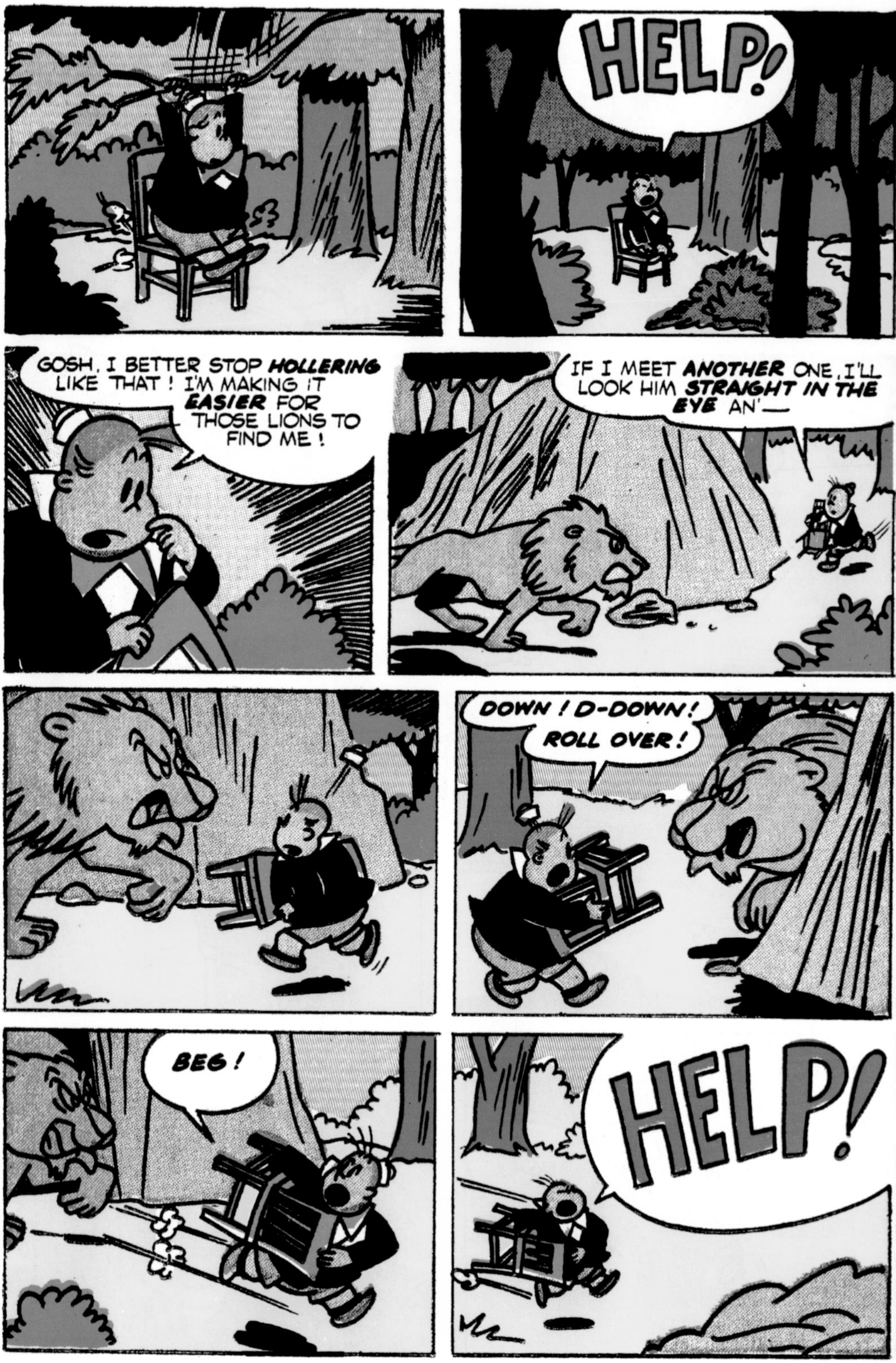
HELP!
GOSH, I BETTER STOP HOLLERING LIKE THAT! I'M MAKING IT EASIER FOR THOSE LIONS TO FIND ME!
IF I MEET ANOTHER ONE, I'LL LOOK HIM STRAIGHT IN THE EYE AN'—
DOWN! D-DOWN! ROLL OVER!
BEG!
HELP!

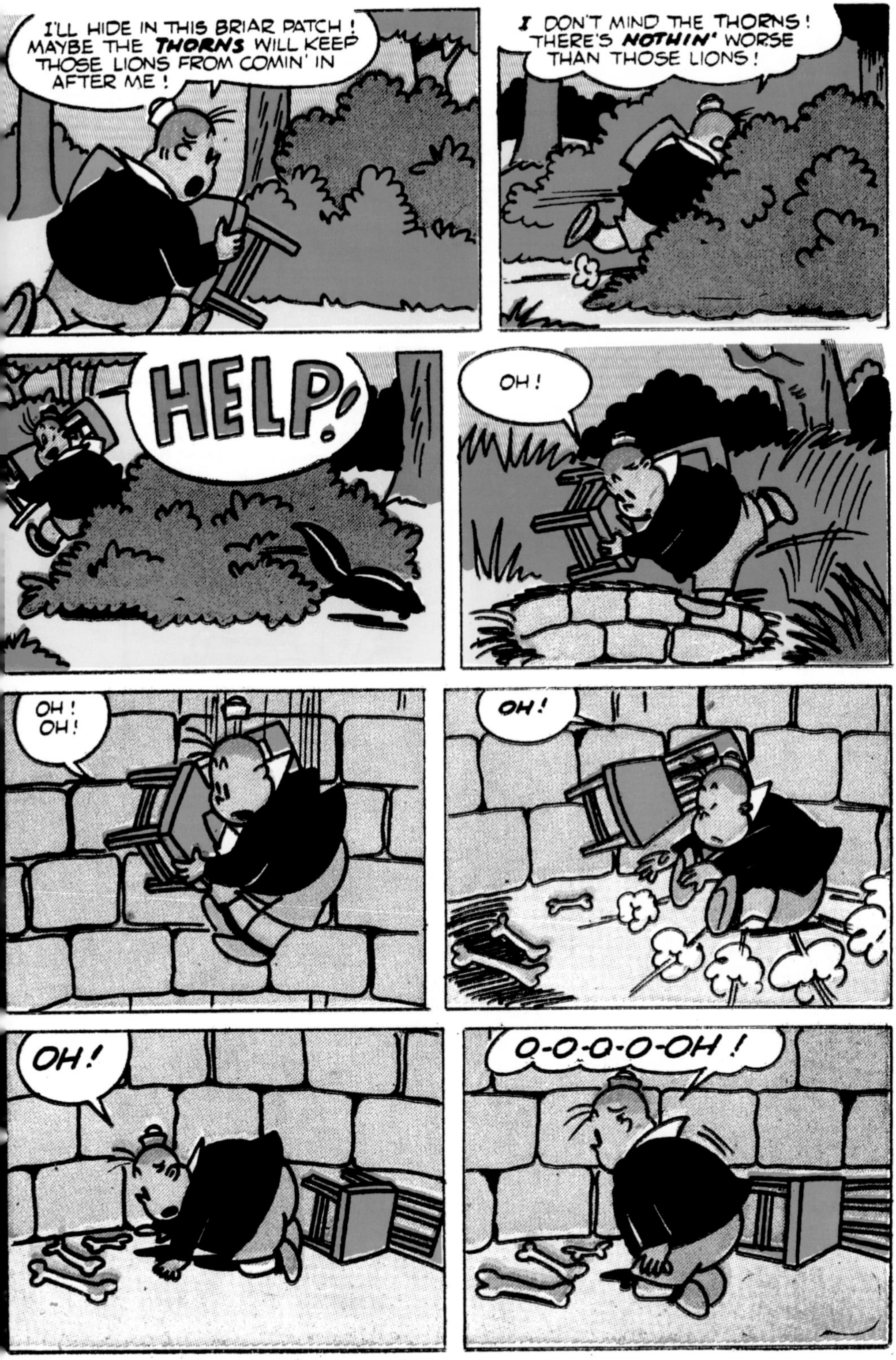
I'LL HIDE IN THIS BRIAR PATCH! MAYBE THE THORNS WILL KEEP THOSE LIONS FROM COMIN' IN AFTER ME!
I DON'T MIND THE THORNS! THERE'S NOTHIN' WORSE THAN THOSE LIONS!
HELP!
OH!
OH! OH!
OH!
OH!
O-O-O-O-OH!

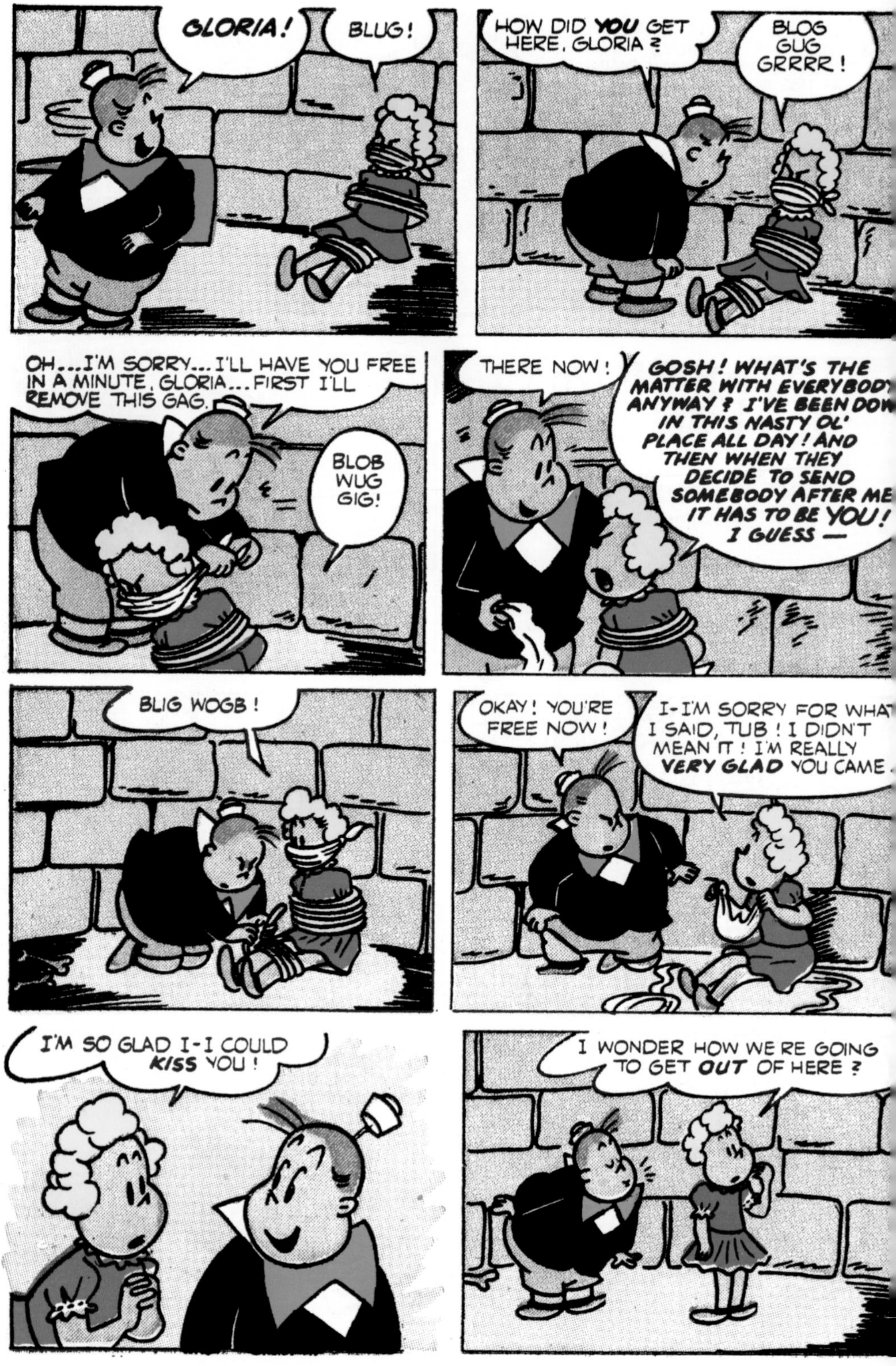
GLORIA!
BLUG!
HOW DID YOU GET HERE, GLORIA?
BLOG GUG GRRRR!
OH...I'M SORRY...I'LL HAVE YOU FREE IN A MINUTE, GLORIA...FIRST I'LL REMOVE THIS GAG.
BLOB WUG GIG!
THERE NOW!
GOSH! WHAT'S THE MATTER WITH EVERYBOD ANYWAY? I'VE BEEN DOW IN THIS NASTY OL' PLACE ALL DAY! AND THEN WHEN THEY DECIDE TO SEND SOMEBODY AFTER ME IT HAS TO BE YOU! I GUESS —
BLIG WOGB!
OKAY! YOU'RE FREE NOW!
I-I'M SORRY FOR WHA I SAID, TUB! I DIDN'T MEAN IT! I'M REALLY VERY GLAD YOU CAME.
I'M SO GLAD I-I COULD KISS YOU!
I WONDER HOW WE'RE GOING TO GET OUT OF HERE?

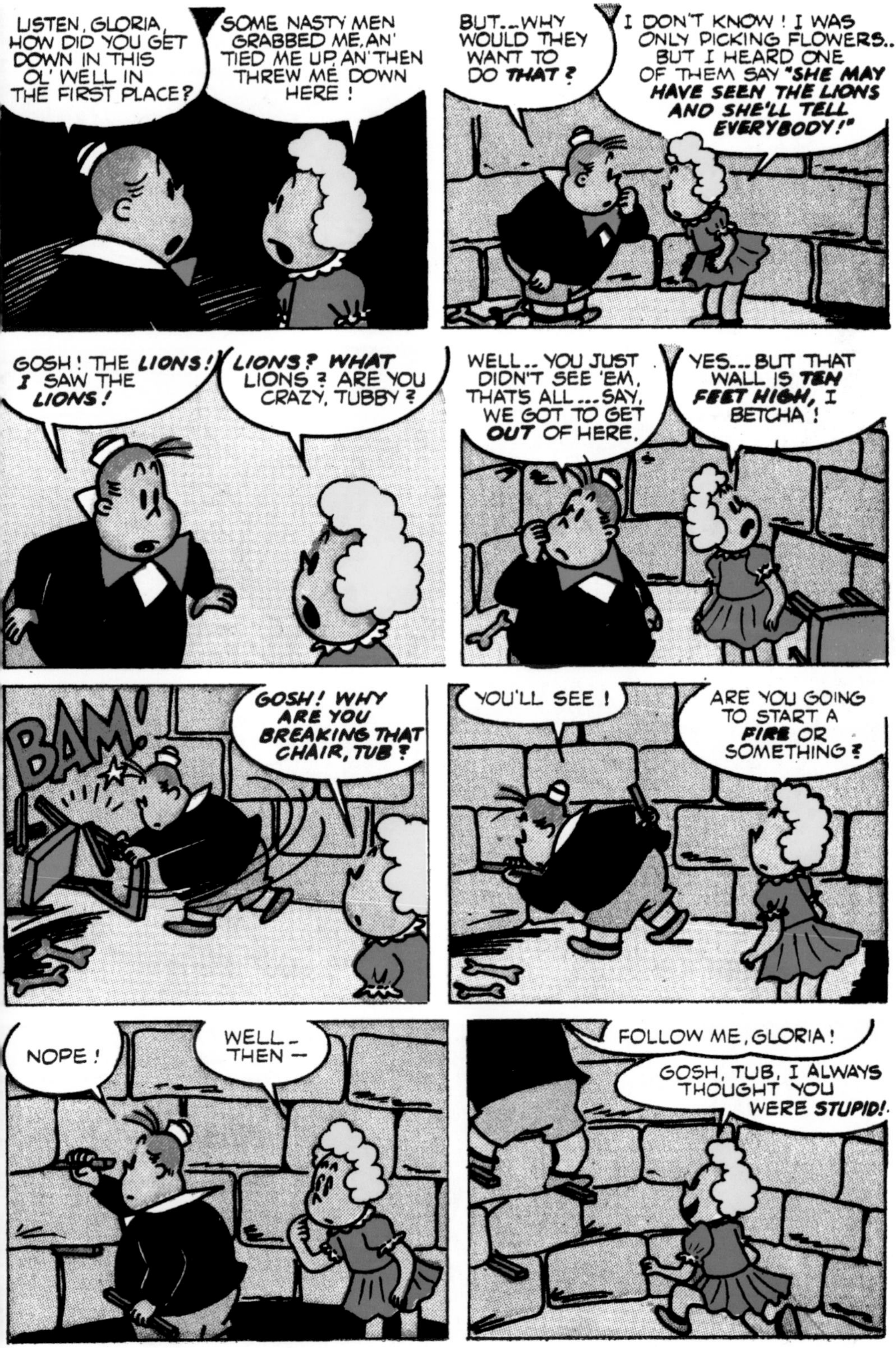
LISTEN, GLORIA, HOW DID YOU GET DOWN IN THIS OL' WELL IN THE FIRST PLACE?
SOME NASTY MEN GRABBED ME, AN' TIED ME UP, AN' THEN THREW ME DOWN HERE!
BUT...WHY WOULD THEY WANT TO DO THAT?
I DON'T KNOW! I WAS ONLY PICKING FLOWERS.. BUT I HEARD ONE OF THEM SAY "SHE MAY HAVE SEEN THE LIONS AND SHE'LL TELL EVERYBODY!"
GOSH! THE LIONS! I SAW THE LIONS!
LIONS? WHAT LIONS? ARE YOU CRAZY, TUBBY?
WELL.. YOU JUST DIDN'T SEE 'EM, THAT'S ALL...SAY, WE GOT TO GET OUT OF HERE.
YES... BUT THAT WALL IS TEN FEET HIGH, I BETCHA!
BAM!
GOSH! WHY ARE YOU BREAKING THAT CHAIR, TUB?
YOU'LL SEE!
ARE YOU GOING TO START A FIRE OR SOMETHING?
NOPE!
WELL- THEN --
FOLLOW ME, GLORIA!
GOSH, TUB, I ALWAYS THOUGHT YOU WERE STUPID!

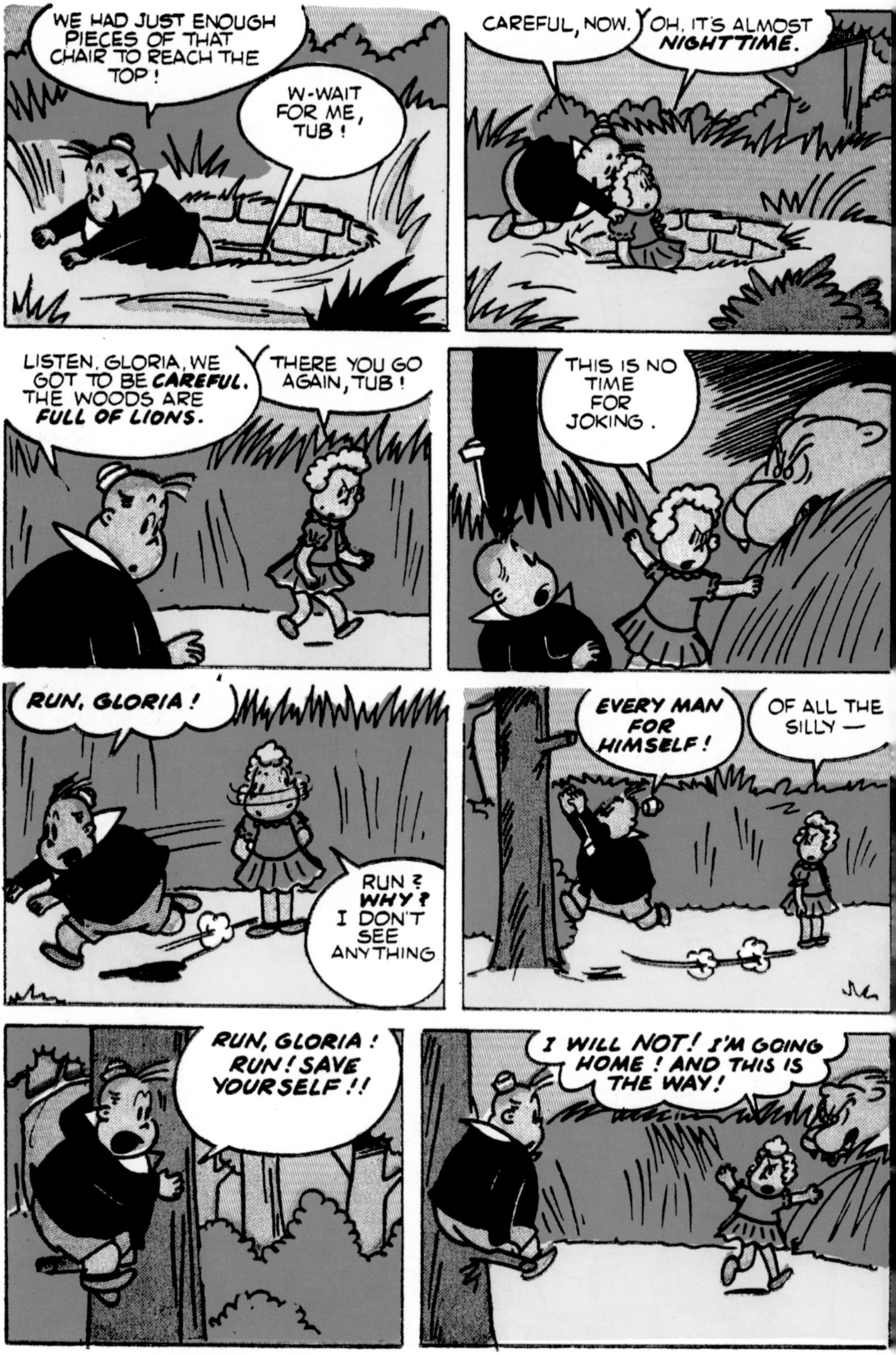
WE HAD JUST ENOUGH PIECES OF THAT CHAIR TO REACH THE TOP!
W-WAIT FOR ME, TUB!
CAREFUL, NOW.
OH, IT'S ALMOST NIGHTTIME.
LISTEN, GLORIA, WE GOT TO BE CAREFUL. THE WOODS ARE FULL OF LIONS.
THERE YOU GO AGAIN, TUB!
THIS IS NO TIME FOR JOKING.
RUN, GLORIA!
RUN? WHY? I DON'T SEE ANYTHING
EVERY MAN FOR HIMSELF!
OF ALL THE SILLY —
RUN, GLORIA! RUN! SAVE YOURSELF!!
I WILL NOT! I'M GOING HOME! AND THIS IS THE WAY!

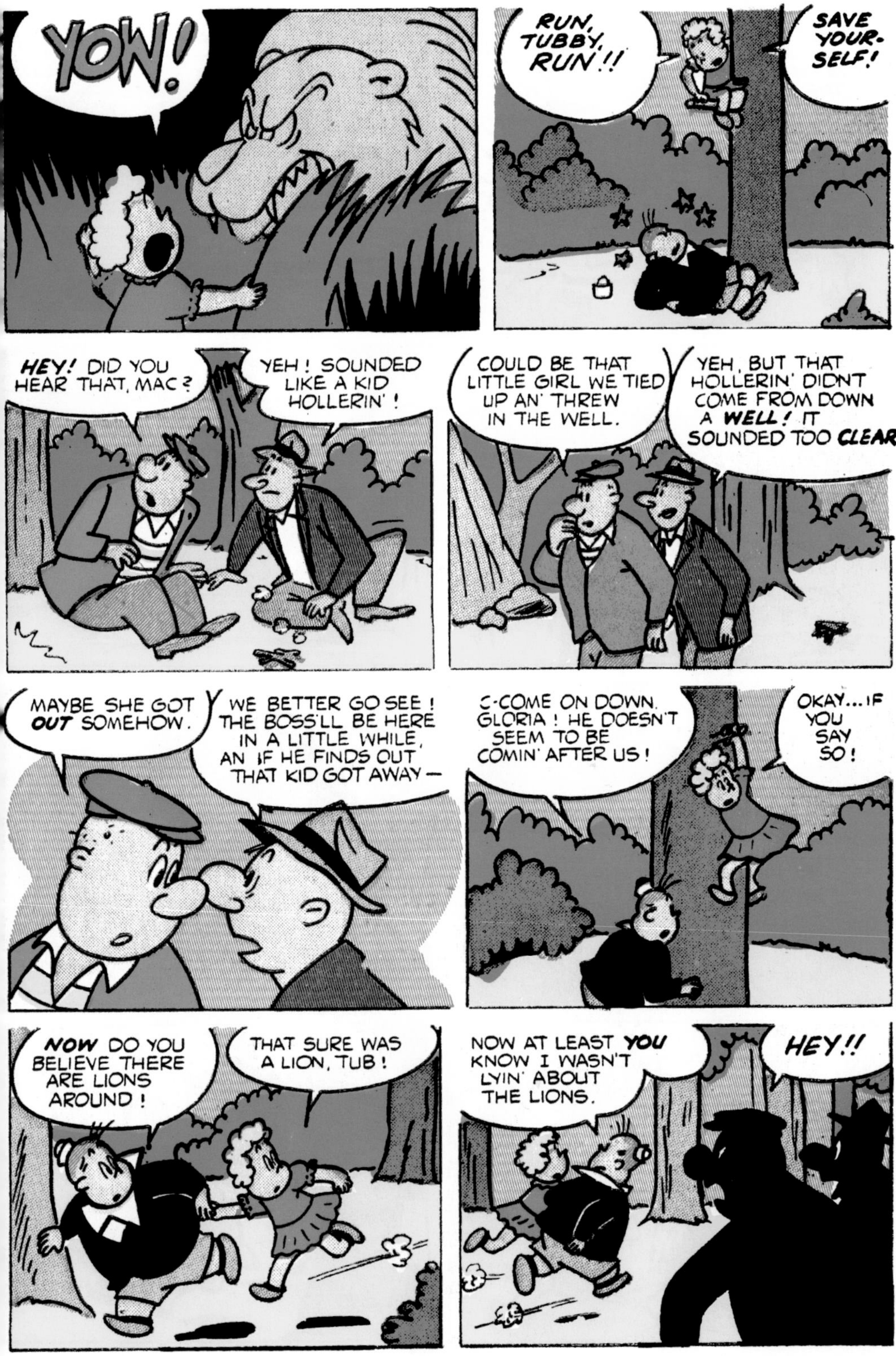
YOW!
RUN, TUBBY, RUN!!
SAVE YOURSELF!
HEY! DID YOU HEAR THAT, MAC?
YEH! SOUNDED LIKE A KID HOLLERIN'!
COULD BE THAT LITTLE GIRL WE TIED UP AN' THREW IN THE WELL.
YEH, BUT THAT HOLLERIN' DIDN'T COME FROM DOWN A WELL! IT SOUNDED TOO CLEAR.
MAYBE SHE GOT OUT SOMEHOW.
WE BETTER GO SEE! THE BOSS'LL BE HERE IN A LITTLE WHILE, AN' IF HE FINDS OUT THAT KID GOT AWAY—
C-COME ON DOWN, GLORIA! HE DOESN'T SEEM TO BE COMIN' AFTER US!
OKAY... IF YOU SAY SO!
NOW DO YOU BELIEVE THERE ARE LIONS AROUND!
THAT SURE WAS A LION, TUB!
NOW AT LEAST YOU KNOW I WASN'T LYIN' ABOUT THE LIONS.
HEY!!

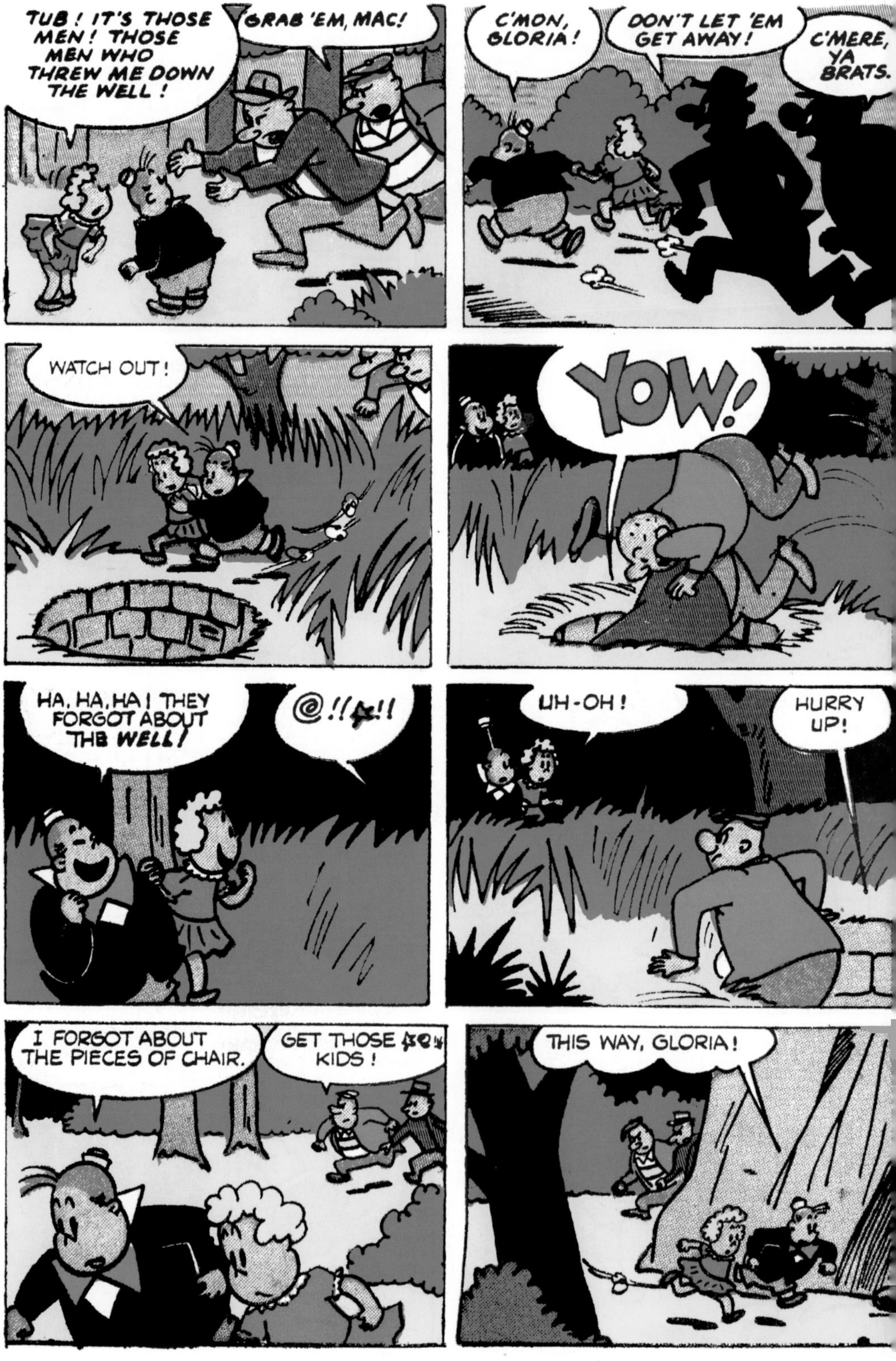
TUB! IT'S THOSE MEN! THOSE MEN WHO THREW ME DOWN THE WELL!
GRAB 'EM, MAC!
C'MON, GLORIA!
DON'T LET 'EM GET AWAY!
C'MERE, YA BRATS.
WATCH OUT!
YOW!
HA, HA, HA! THEY FORGOT ABOUT THE WELL!
UH-OH!
HURRY UP!
I FORGOT ABOUT THE PIECES OF CHAIR.
GET THOSE KIDS!
THIS WAY, GLORIA!

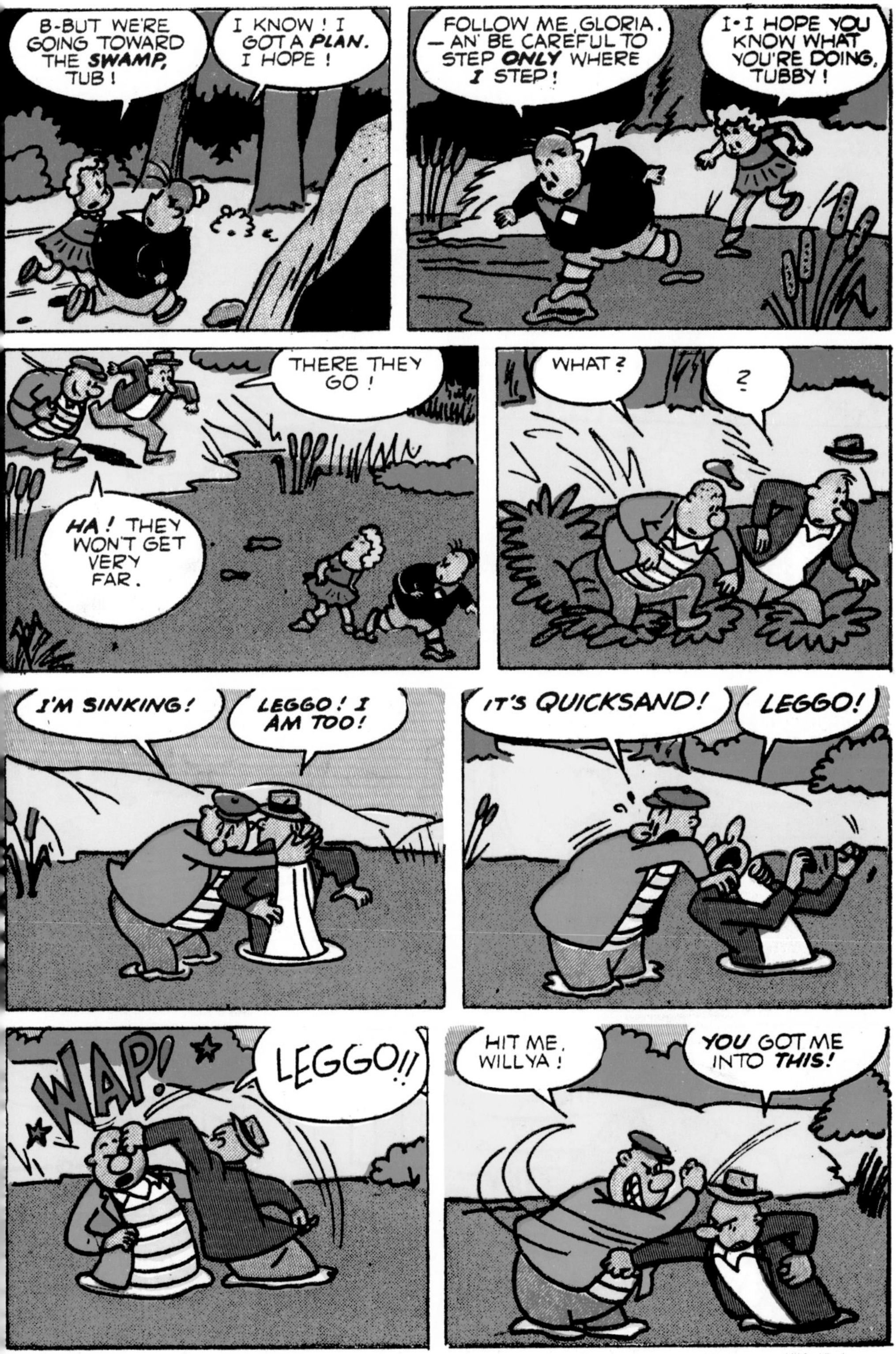
B-BUT WE'RE GOING TOWARD THE SWAMP, TUB!
I KNOW! I GOT A PLAN. I HOPE!
FOLLOW ME, GLORIA. —AN' BE CAREFUL TO STEP ONLY WHERE I STEP!
I-I HOPE YOU KNOW WHAT YOU'RE DOING, TUBBY!
THERE THEY GO!
HA! THEY WON'T GET VERY FAR.
WHAT?
?
I'M SINKING!
LEGGO! I AM TOO!
IT'S QUICKSAND!
LEGGO!
WAP!
LEGGO!!
HIT ME, WILLYA!
YOU GOT ME INTO THIS!

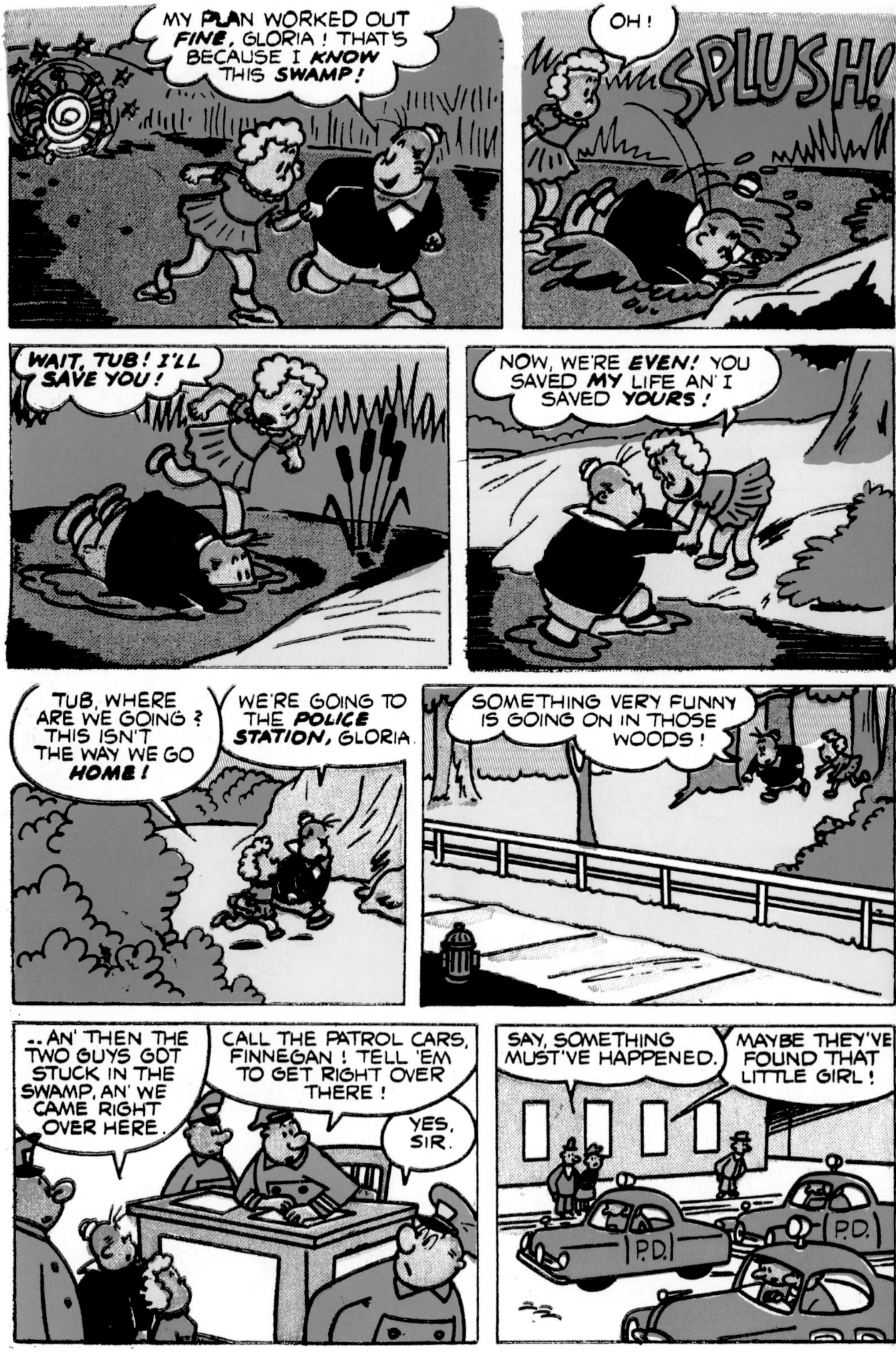
MY PLAN WORKED OUT FINE, GLORIA! THAT'S BECAUSE I KNOW THIS SWAMP!
OH!
SPLUSH!
WAIT, TUB! I'LL SAVE YOU!
NOW, WE'RE EVEN! YOU SAVED MY LIFE AN' I SAVED YOURS!
TUB, WHERE ARE WE GOING? THIS ISN'T THE WAY WE GO HOME!
WE'RE GOING TO THE POLICE STATION, GLORIA.
SOMETHING VERY FUNNY IS GOING ON IN THOSE WOODS!
..AN' THEN THE TWO GUYS GOT STUCK IN THE SWAMP, AN' WE CAME RIGHT OVER HERE.
CALL THE PATROL CARS, FINNEGAN! TELL 'EM TO GET RIGHT OVER THERE!
YES, SIR.
SAY, SOMETHING MUST'VE HAPPENED.
MAYBE THEY'VE FOUND THAT LITTLE GIRL!
P.D.
P.D.

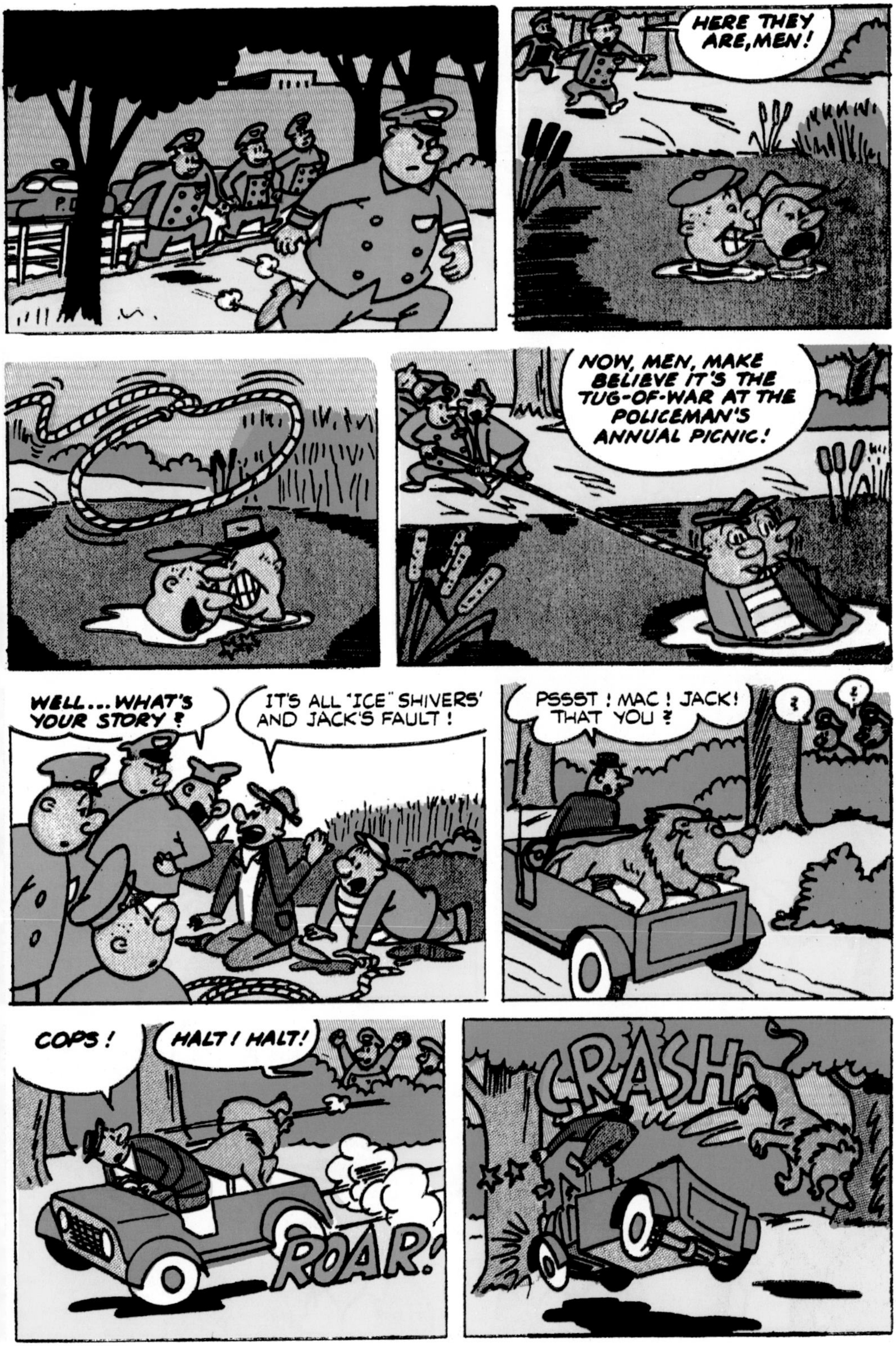
HERE THEY ARE, MEN!
NOW, MEN, MAKE BELIEVE IT'S THE TUG-OF-WAR AT THE POLICEMAN'S ANNUAL PICNIC!
WELL... WHAT'S YOUR STORY ?
IT'S ALL "ICE" SHIVERS' AND JACK'S FAULT !
PSSST ! MAC ! JACK! THAT YOU ?
COPS !
HALT ! HALT!
ROAR!
CRASH

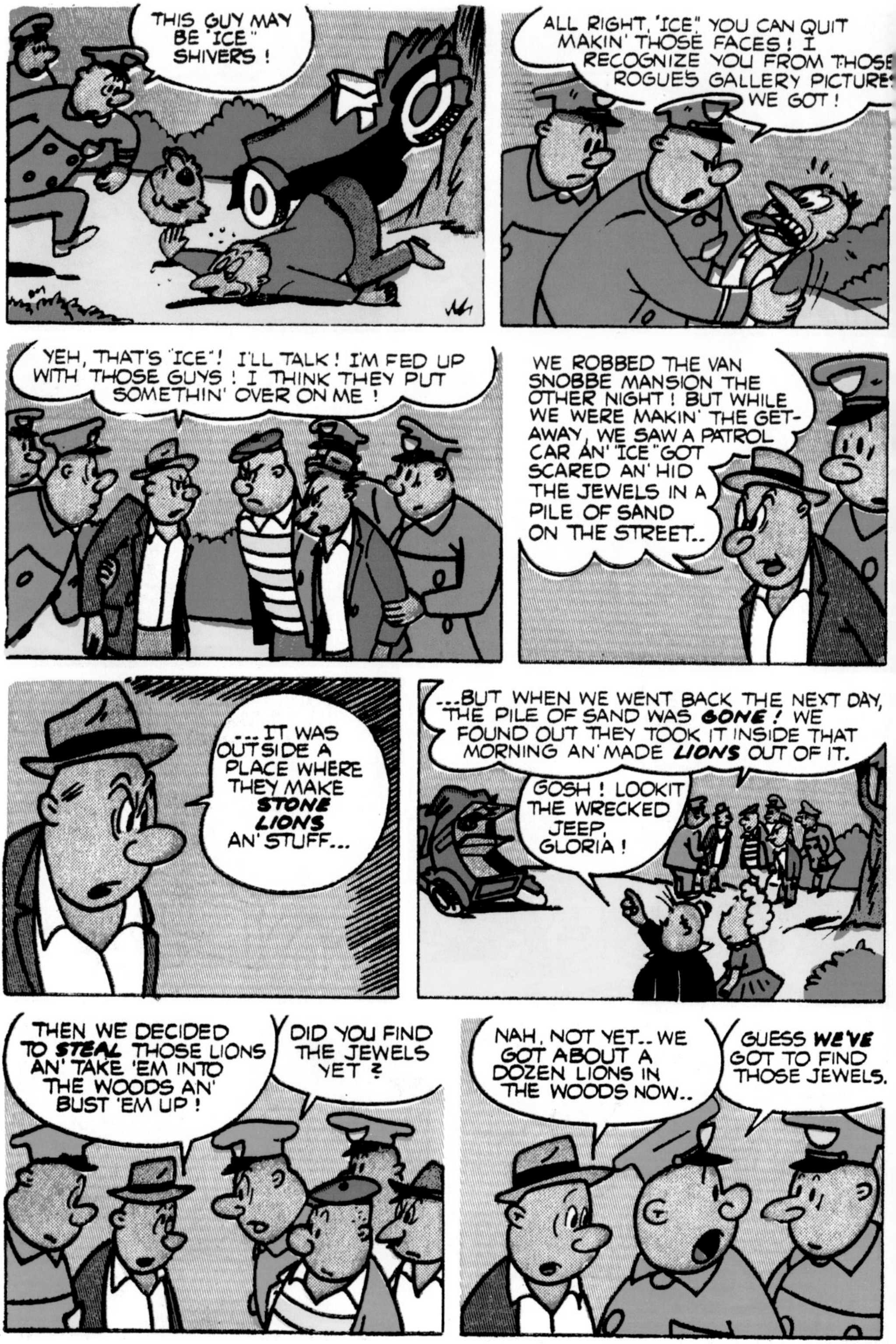

THIS GUY MAY BE "ICE" SHIVERS !
ALL RIGHT, "ICE," YOU CAN QUIT MAKIN' THOSE FACES ! I RECOGNIZE YOU FROM THOSE ROGUES GALLERY PICTURES WE GOT !
YEH, THAT'S "ICE" ! I'LL TALK ! I'M FED UP WITH THOSE GUYS ! I THINK THEY PUT SOMETHIN' OVER ON ME !
WE ROBBED THE VAN SNOBBE MANSION THE OTHER NIGHT ! BUT WHILE WE WERE MAKIN' THE GET-AWAY, WE SAW A PATROL CAR AN' "ICE" GOT SCARED AN' HID THE JEWELS IN A PILE OF SAND ON THE STREET..
... IT WAS OUTSIDE A PLACE WHERE THEY MAKE STONE LIONS AN' STUFF...
...BUT WHEN WE WENT BACK THE NEXT DAY, THE PILE OF SAND WAS GONE ! WE FOUND OUT THEY TOOK IT INSIDE THAT MORNING AN' MADE LIONS OUT OF IT.
GOSH ! LOOKIT THE WRECKED JEEP, GLORIA !
THEN WE DECIDED TO STEAL THOSE LIONS AN' TAKE 'EM INTO THE WOODS AN' BUST 'EM UP !
DID YOU FIND THE JEWELS YET ?
NAH, NOT YET.. WE GOT ABOUT A DOZEN LIONS IN THE WOODS NOW..
GUESS WE'VE GOT TO FIND THOSE JEWELS.

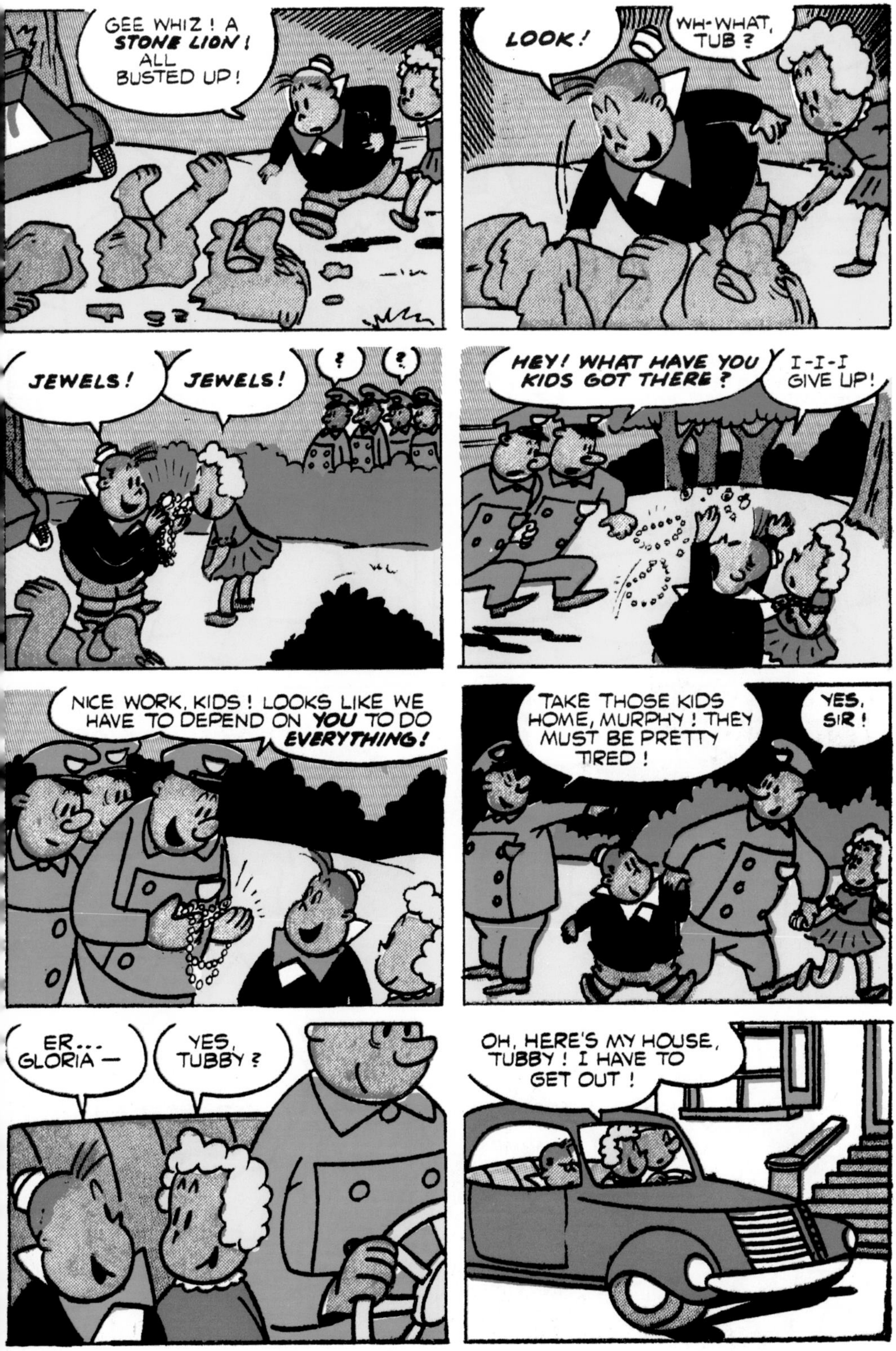
GEE WHIZ! A STONE LION! ALL BUSTED UP!
LOOK!
WH-WHAT, TUB?
JEWELS!
JEWELS!
?
?
HEY! WHAT HAVE YOU KIDS GOT THERE?
I-I-I GIVE UP!
NICE WORK, KIDS! LOOKS LIKE WE HAVE TO DEPEND ON YOU TO DO EVERYTHING!
TAKE THOSE KIDS HOME, MURPHY! THEY MUST BE PRETTY TIRED!
YES, SIR!
ER... GLORIA —
YES, TUBBY?
OH, HERE'S MY HOUSE, TUBBY! I HAVE TO GET OUT!

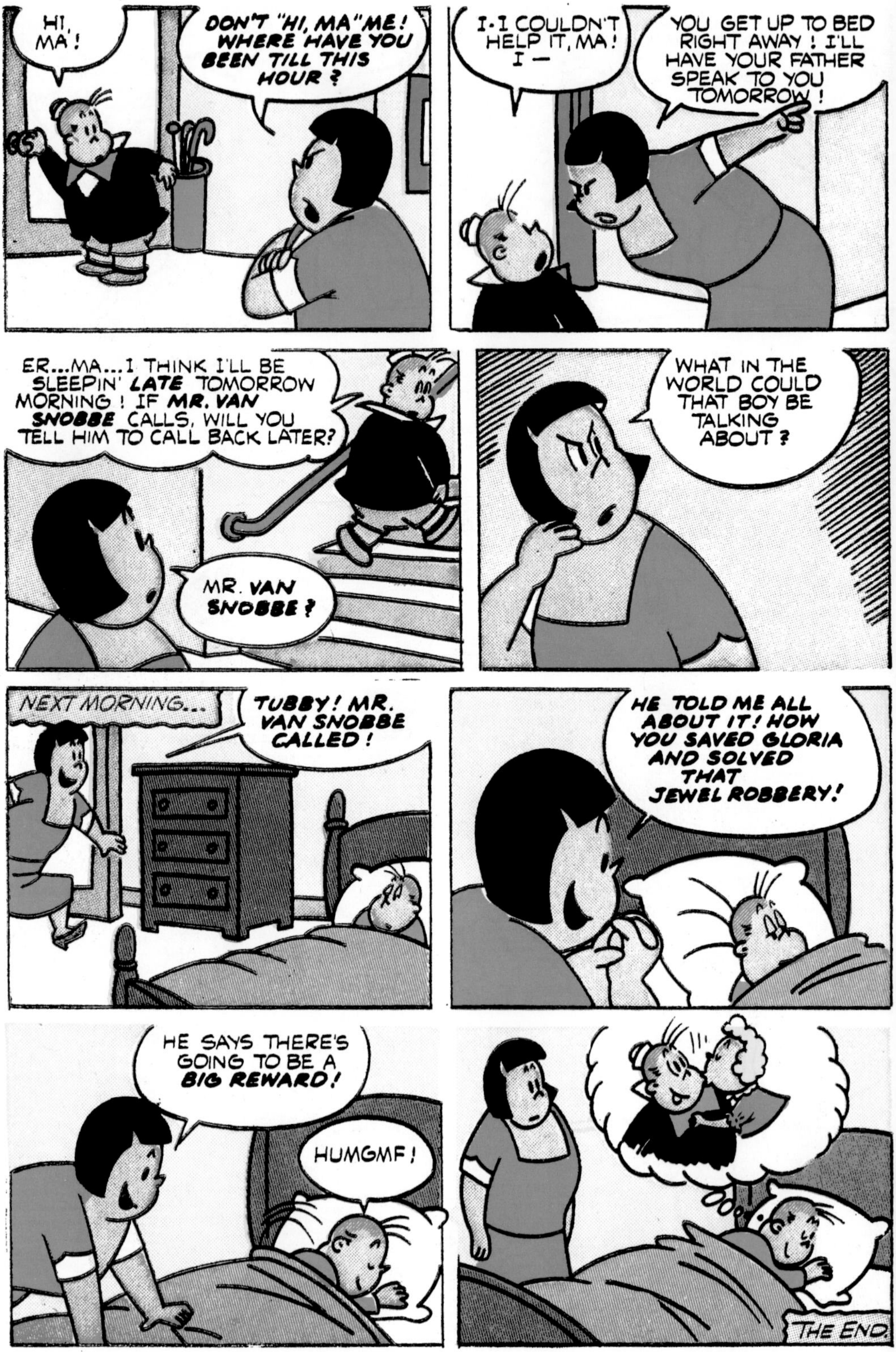

HI, MA!
DON'T "HI, MA" ME! WHERE HAVE YOU BEEN TILL THIS HOUR?
I-I COULDN'T HELP IT, MA! I —
YOU GET UP TO BED RIGHT AWAY! I'LL HAVE YOUR FATHER SPEAK TO YOU TOMORROW!
ER...MA...I THINK I'LL BE SLEEPIN' LATE TOMORROW MORNING! IF MR. VAN SNOBBE CALLS, WILL YOU TELL HIM TO CALL BACK LATER?
MR. VAN SNOBBE?
WHAT IN THE WORLD COULD THAT BOY BE TALKING ABOUT?
NEXT MORNING...
TUBBY! MR. VAN SNOBBE CALLED!
HE TOLD ME ALL ABOUT IT! HOW YOU SAVED GLORIA AND SOLVED THAT JEWEL ROBBERY!
HE SAYS THERE'S GOING TO BE A BIG REWARD!
HUMGMF!
THE END

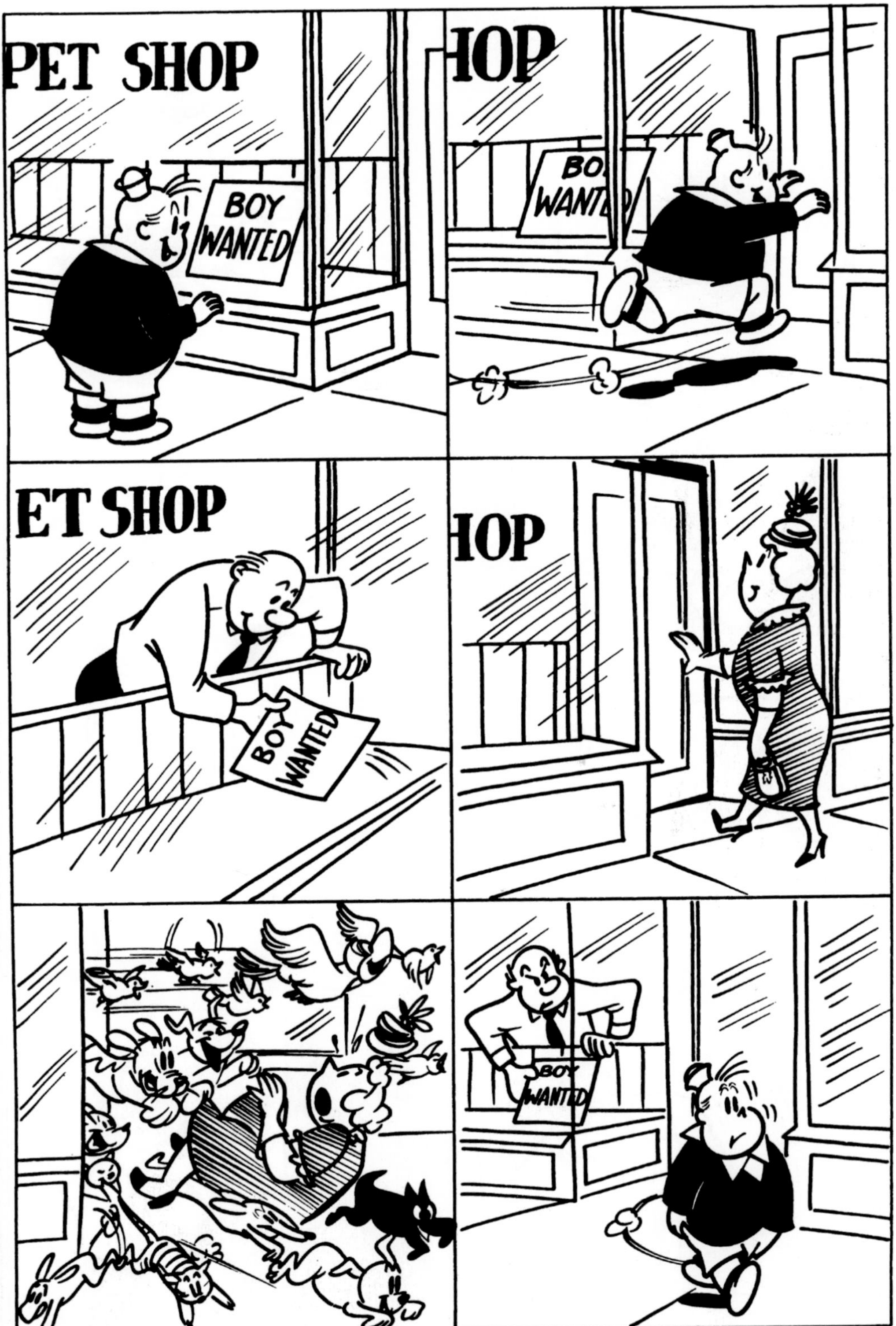
PET SHOP
BOY WANTED
HOP
BOY WANTED
ET SHOP
BOY WANTED
HOP
BOY WANTED

TUBBY

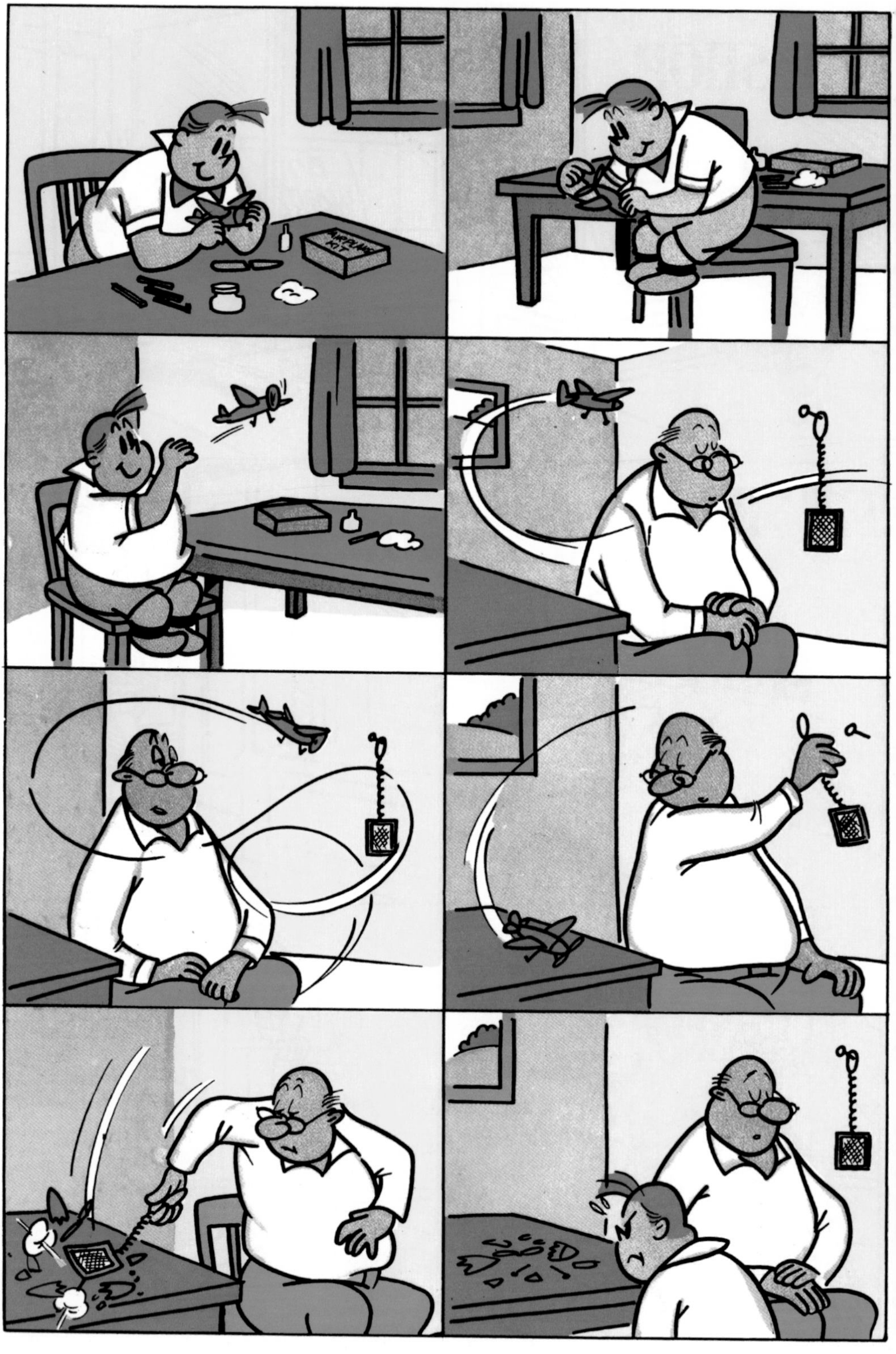
AIRPLANE KIT

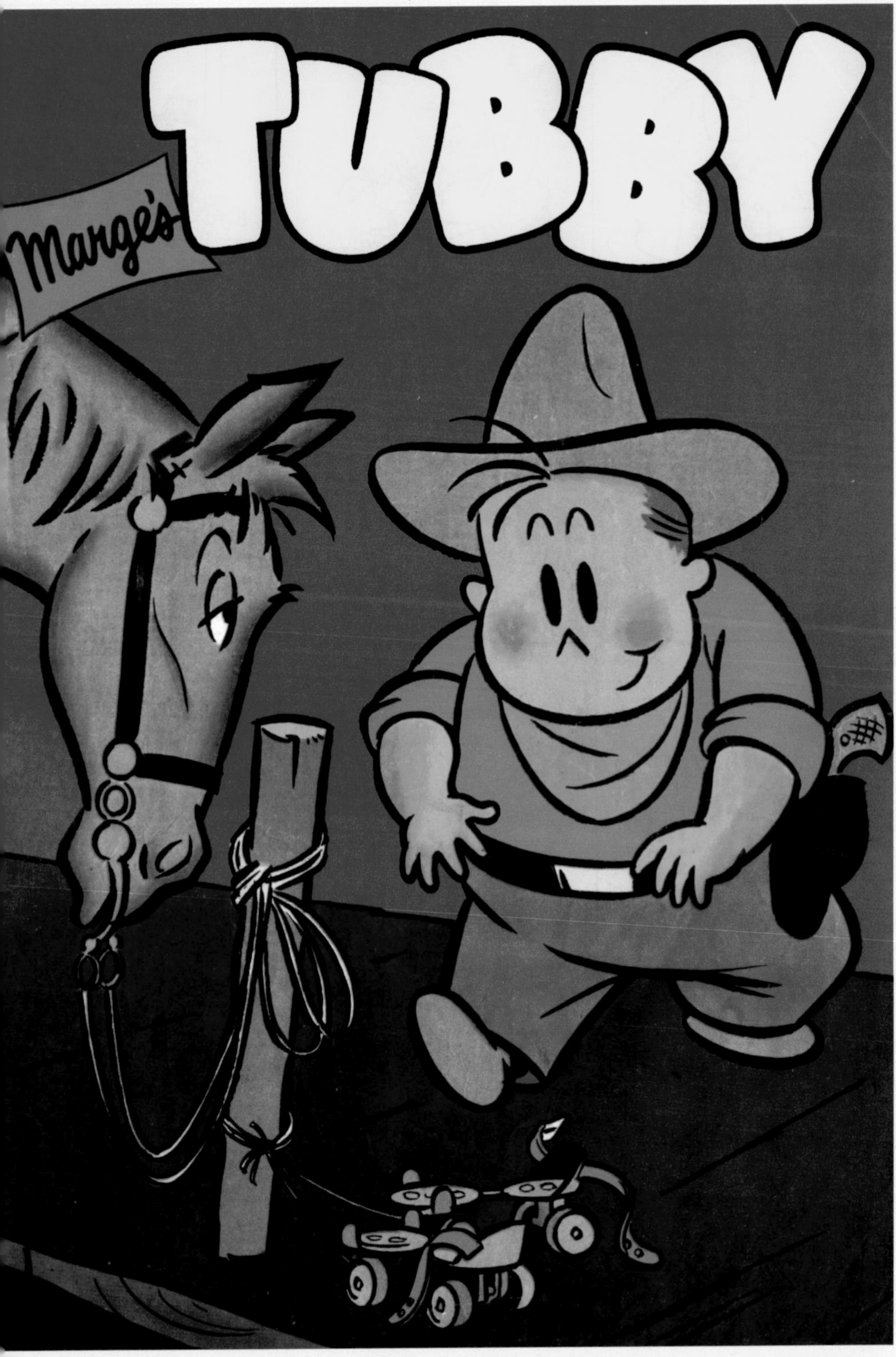
Marge's
TUBBY

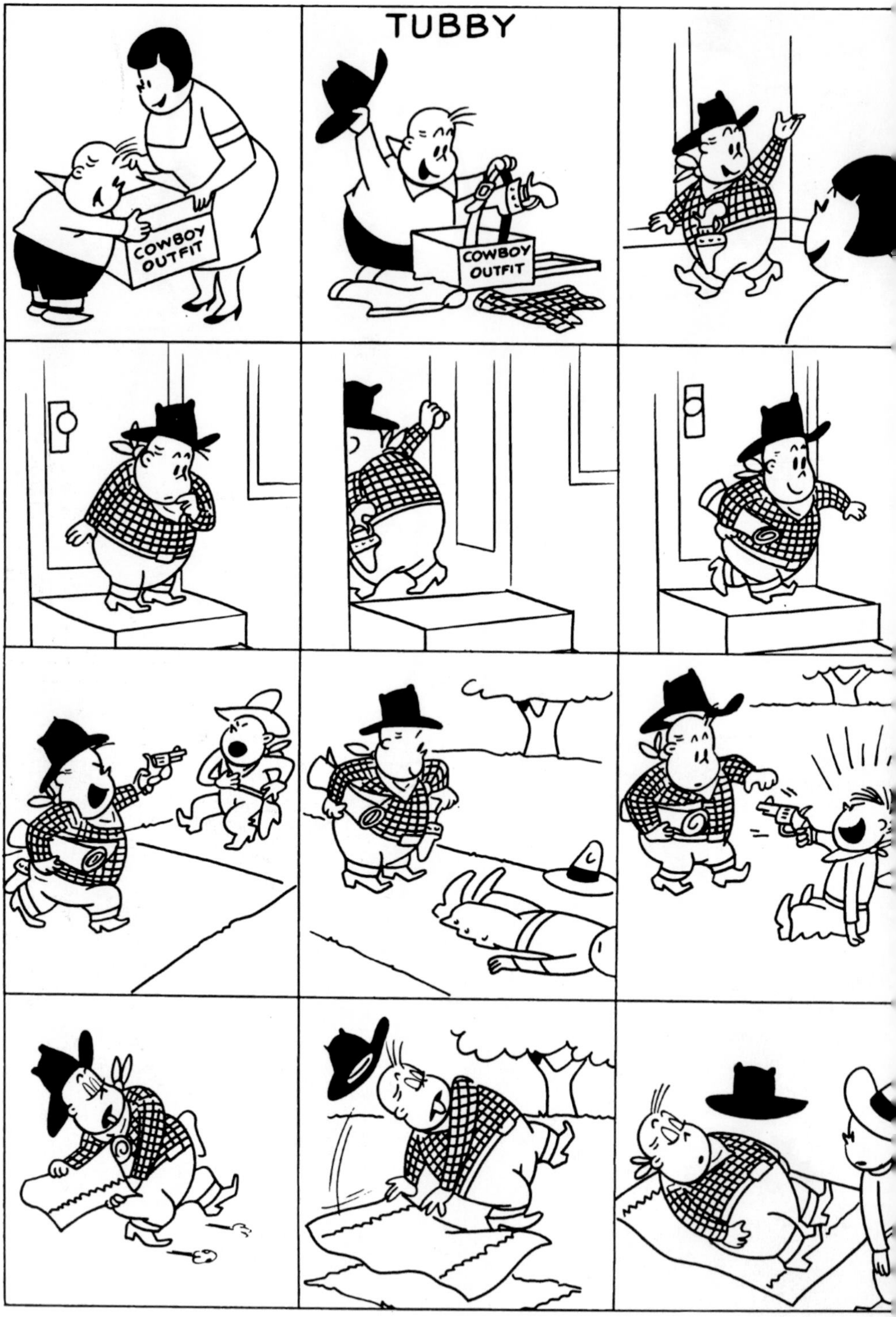
COWBOY OUTFIT
TUBBY
COWBOY OUTFIT

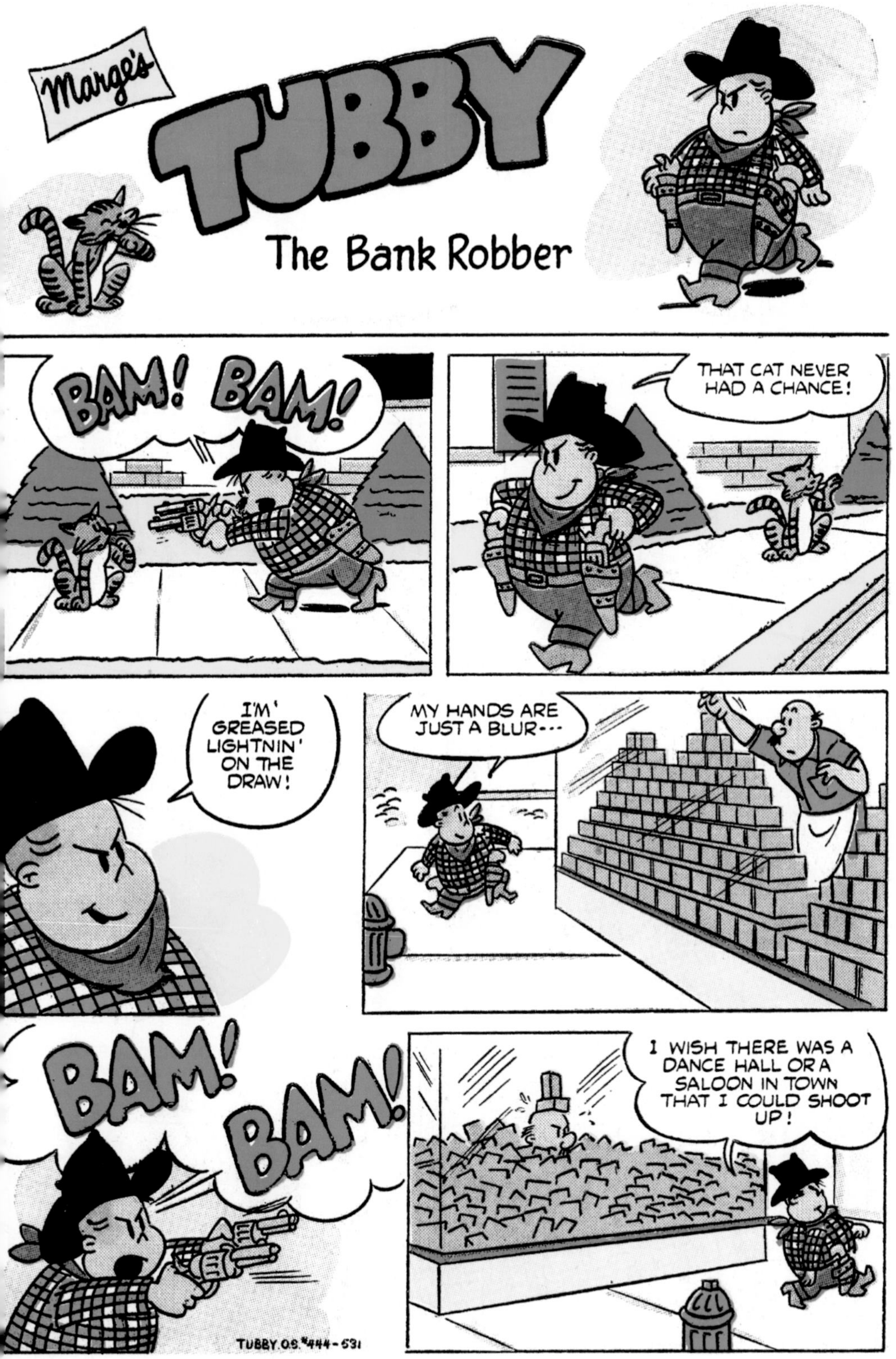
Marge's
TUBBY
The Bank Robber
BAM! BAM!
THAT CAT NEVER HAD A CHANCE!
I'M GREASED LIGHTNIN' ON THE DRAW!
MY HANDS ARE JUST A BLUR---
BAM! BAM!
I WISH THERE WAS A DANCE HALL OR A SALOON IN TOWN THAT I COULD SHOOT UP!
TUBBY O.S. #444-531

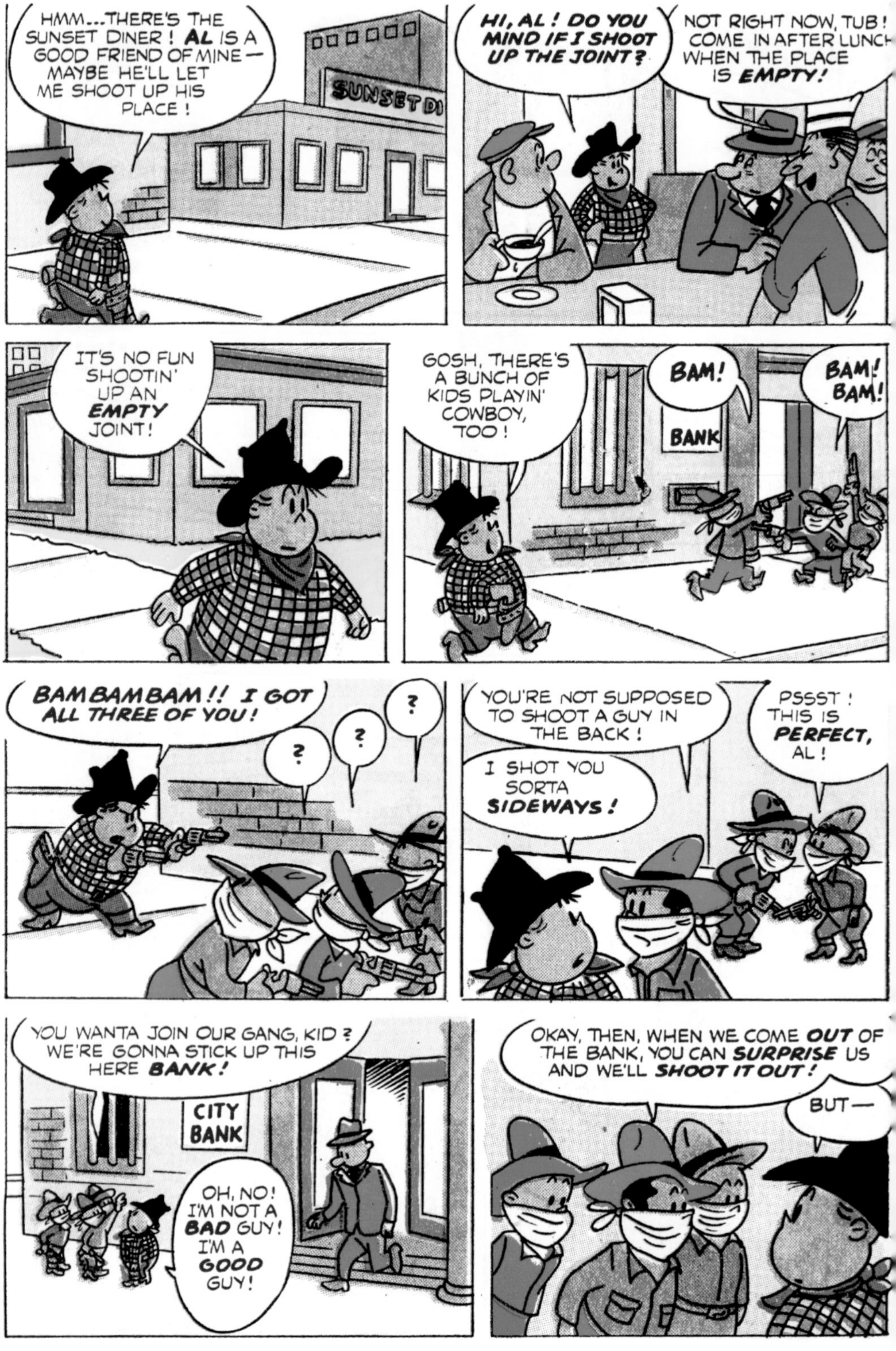
HMM...THERE'S THE SUNSET DINER! AL IS A GOOD FRIEND OF MINE — MAYBE HE'LL LET ME SHOOT UP HIS PLACE!
SUNSET DI
HI, AL! DO YOU MIND IF I SHOOT UP THE JOINT?
NOT RIGHT NOW, TUB! COME IN AFTER LUNCH WHEN THE PLACE IS EMPTY!
IT'S NO FUN SHOOTIN' UP AN EMPTY JOINT!
GOSH, THERE'S A BUNCH OF KIDS PLAYIN' COWBOY, TOO!
BAM!
BAM! BAM!
BANK
BAM BAM BAM!! I GOT ALL THREE OF YOU!
?
?
?
YOU'RE NOT SUPPOSED TO SHOOT A GUY IN THE BACK!
I SHOT YOU SORTA SIDEWAYS!
PSSST! THIS IS PERFECT, AL!
YOU WANTA JOIN OUR GANG, KID? WE'RE GONNA STICK UP THIS HERE BANK!
CITY BANK
OH, NO! I'M NOT A BAD GUY! I'M A GOOD GUY!
OKAY, THEN, WHEN WE COME OUT OF THE BANK, YOU CAN SURPRISE US AND WE'LL SHOOT IT OUT!
BUT—

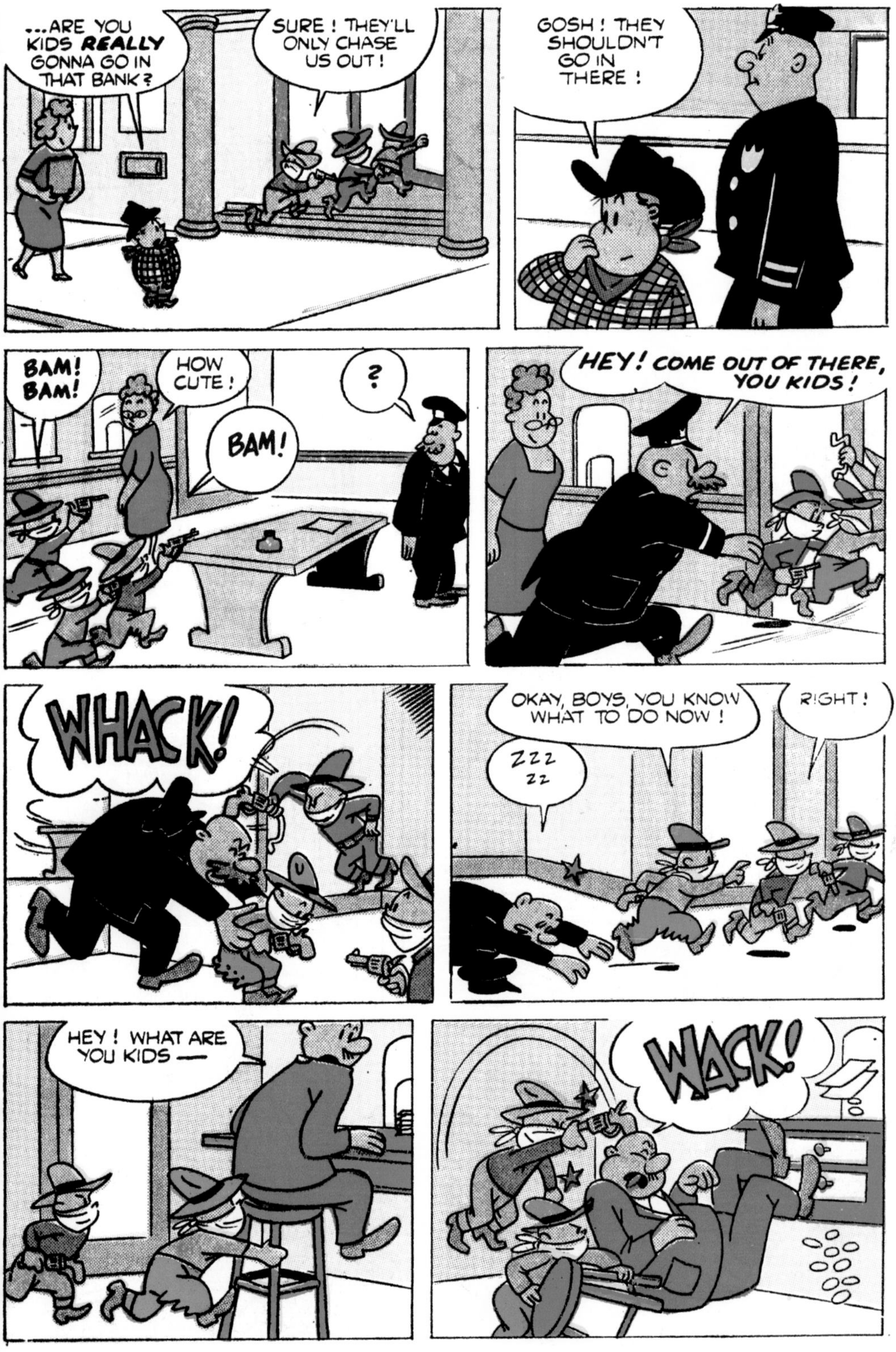
...ARE YOU KIDS REALLY GONNA GO IN THAT BANK?
SURE! THEY'LL ONLY CHASE US OUT!
GOSH! THEY SHOULDN'T GO IN THERE!
BAM! BAM!
HOW CUTE!
BAM!
?
HEY! COME OUT OF THERE, YOU KIDS!
WHACK!
OKAY, BOYS, YOU KNOW WHAT TO DO NOW!
RIGHT!
ZZZ ZZ
HEY! WHAT ARE YOU KIDS —
WACK!

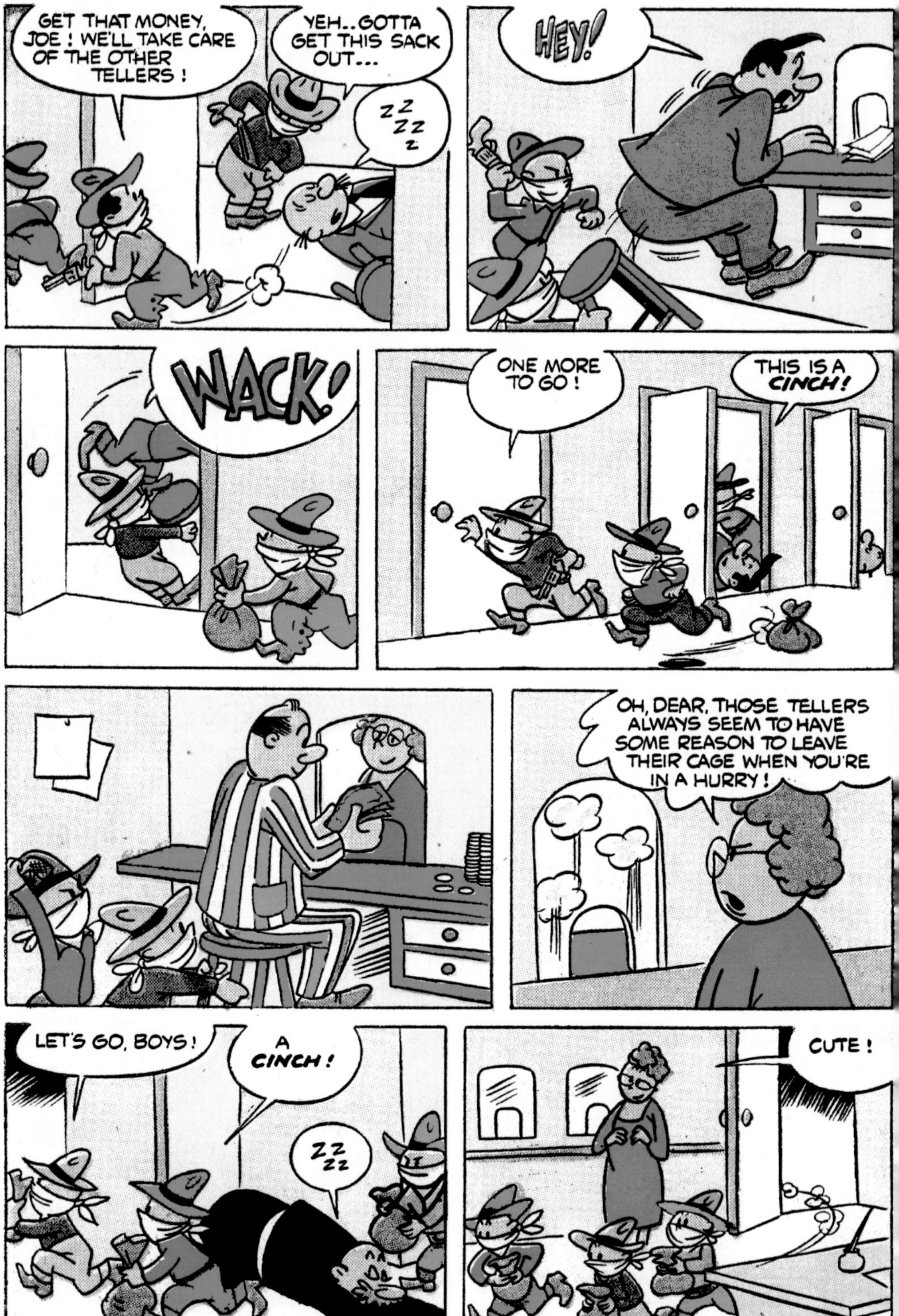
GET THAT MONEY, JOE! WE'LL TAKE CARE OF THE OTHER TELLERS!
YEH..GOTTA GET THIS SACK OUT...
Z Z Z Z Z
HEY!
WACK!
ONE MORE TO GO!
THIS IS A CINCH!
OH, DEAR, THOSE TELLERS ALWAYS SEEM TO HAVE SOME REASON TO LEAVE THEIR CAGE WHEN YOU'RE IN A HURRY!
LET'S GO, BOYS!
A CINCH!
Z Z Z Z
CUTE!

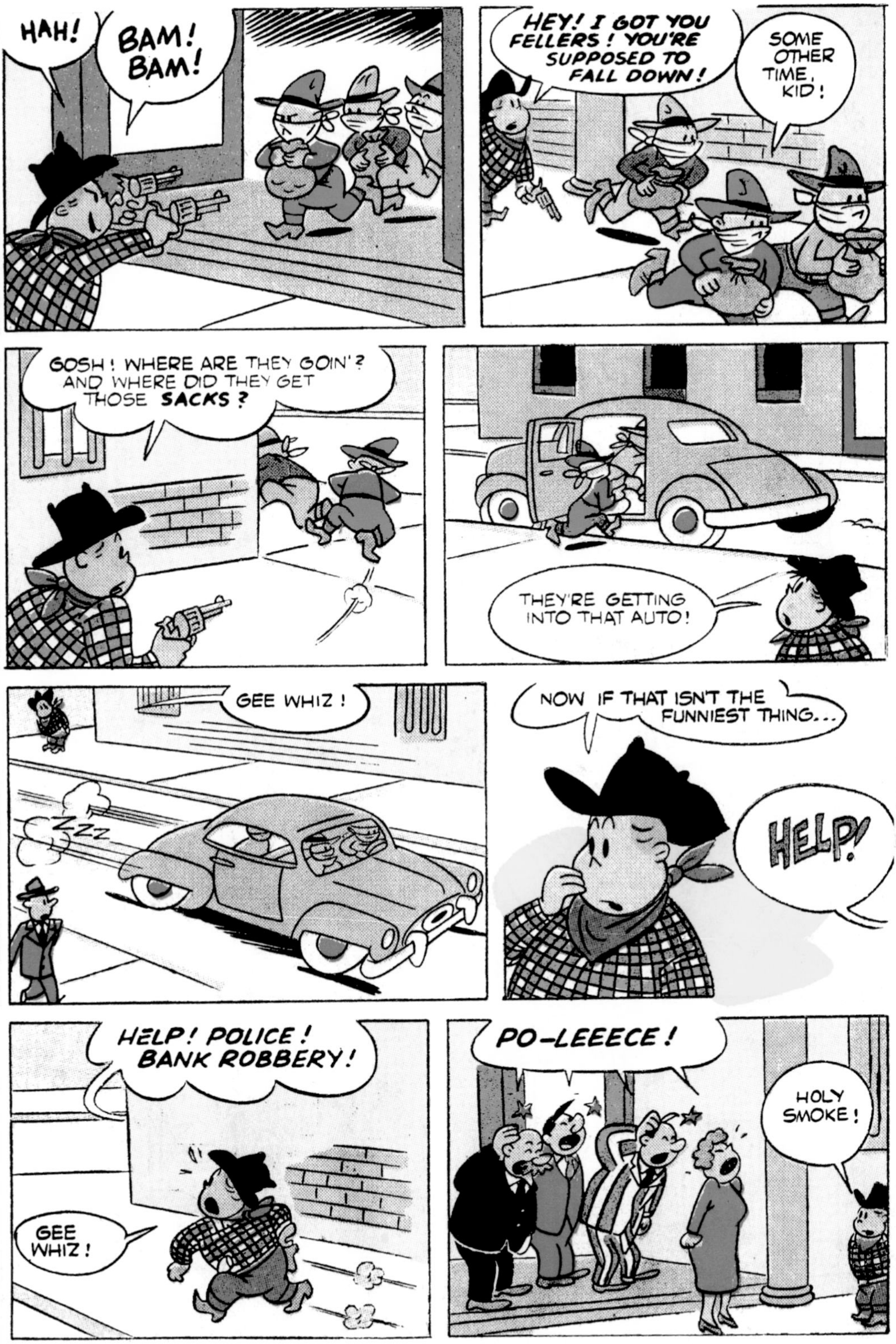
HAH!
BAM! BAM!
HEY! I GOT YOU FELLERS! YOU'RE SUPPOSED TO FALL DOWN!
SOME OTHER TIME, KID!
GOSH! WHERE ARE THEY GOIN'? AND WHERE DID THEY GET THOSE SACKS?
THEY'RE GETTING INTO THAT AUTO!
GEE WHIZ!
ZZZ
NOW IF THAT ISN'T THE FUNNIEST THING...
HELP!
HELP! POLICE! BANK ROBBERY!
GEE WHIZ!
PO-LEEECE!
HOLY SMOKE!

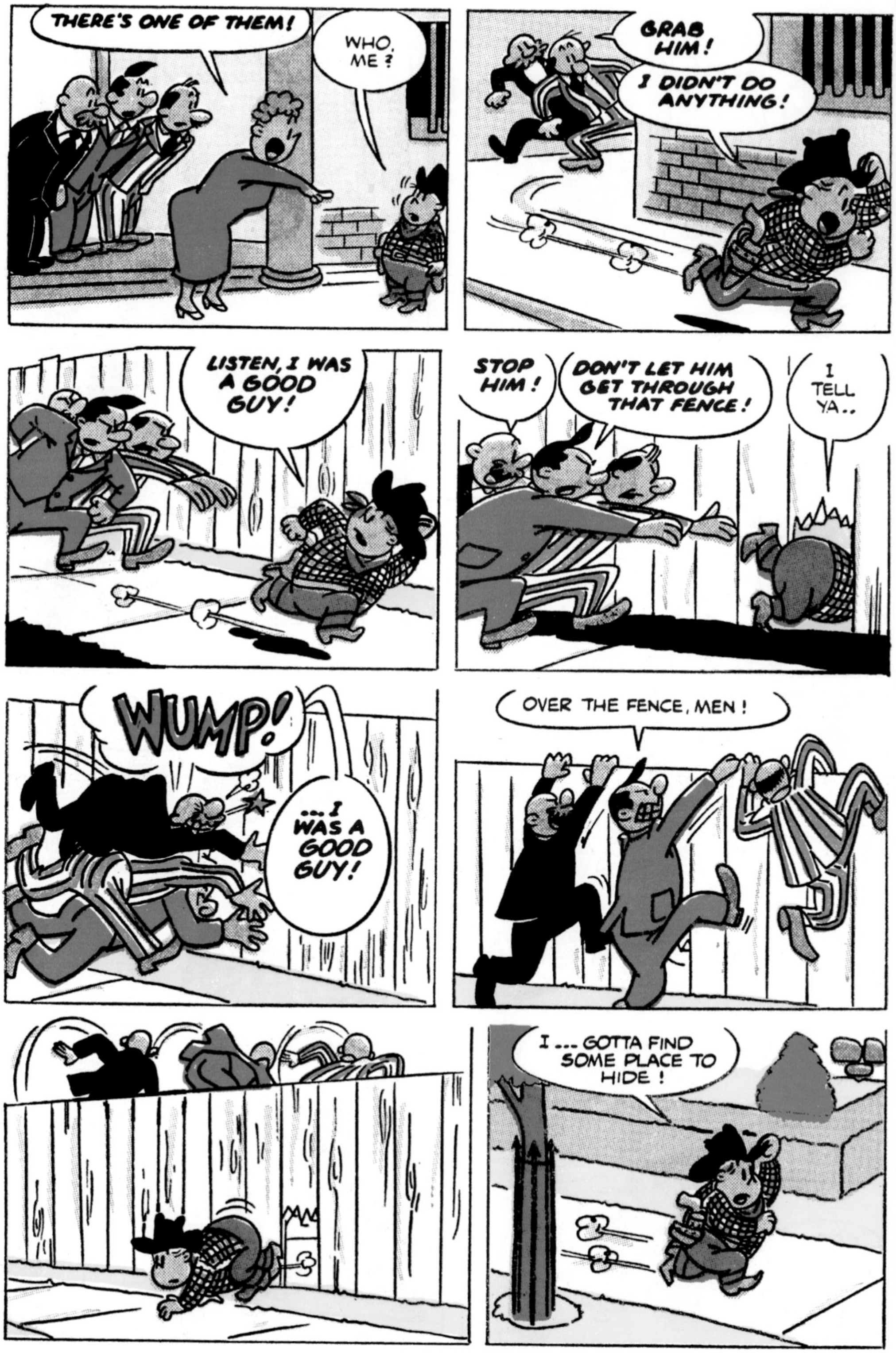
THERE'S ONE OF THEM!
WHO, ME?
GRAB HIM!
I DIDN'T DO ANYTHING!
LISTEN, I WAS A GOOD GUY!
STOP HIM!
DON'T LET HIM GET THROUGH THAT FENCE!
I TELL YA..
WUMP!
...I WAS A GOOD GUY!
OVER THE FENCE, MEN!
I ... GOTTA FIND SOME PLACE TO HIDE!

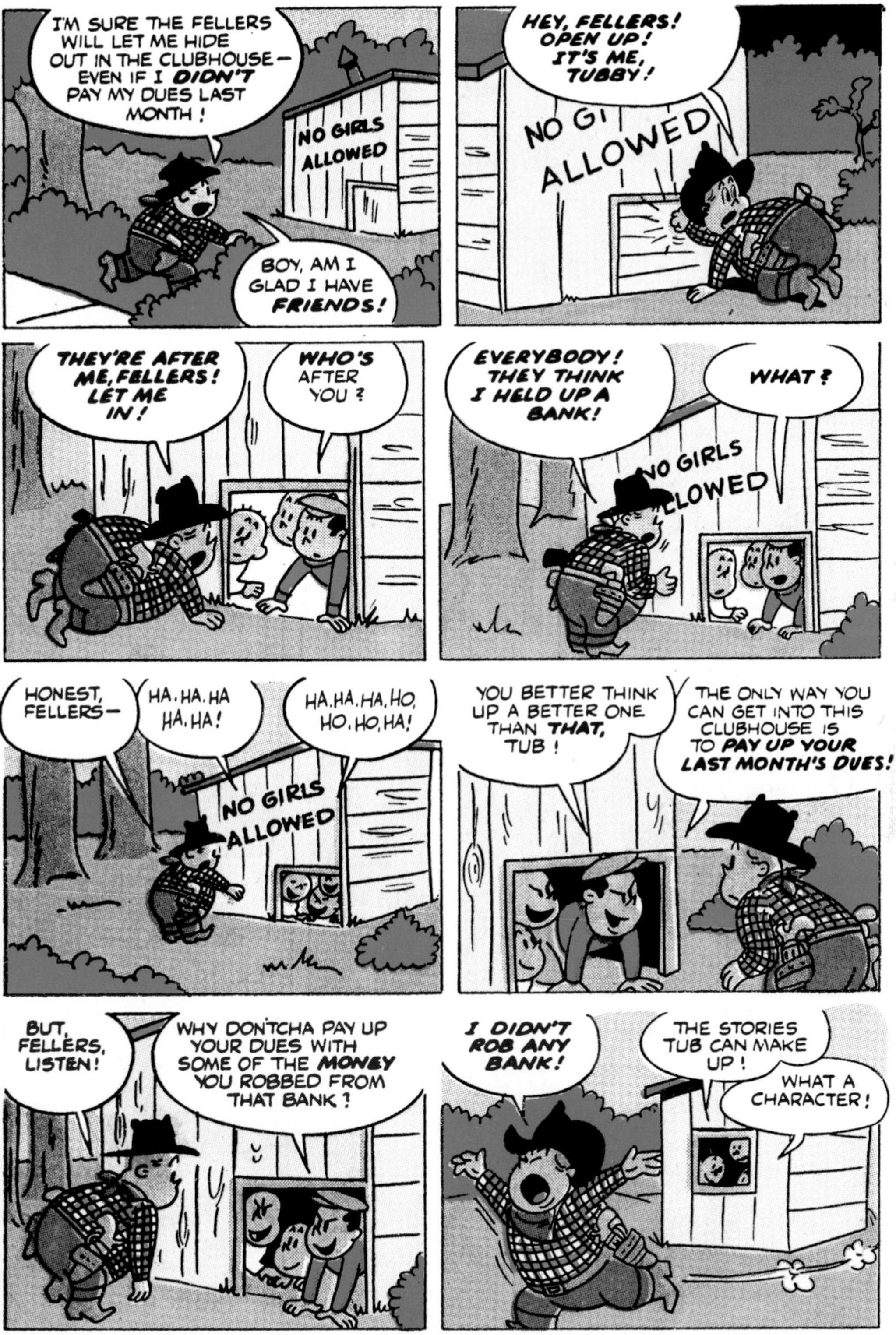
I'M SURE THE FELLERS WILL LET ME HIDE OUT IN THE CLUBHOUSE— EVEN IF I DIDN'T PAY MY DUES LAST MONTH!
NO GIRLS ALLOWED
BOY, AM I GLAD I HAVE FRIENDS!
HEY, FELLERS! OPEN UP! IT'S ME, TUBBY!
NO GI ALLOWED
THEY'RE AFTER ME, FELLERS! LET ME IN!
WHO'S AFTER YOU?
EVERYBODY! THEY THINK I HELD UP A BANK!
WHAT?
NO GIRLS ALLOWED
HONEST, FELLERS—
HA. HA. HA HA. HA!
HA. HA. HA. HO. HO. HO. HA!
NO GIRLS ALLOWED
YOU BETTER THINK UP A BETTER ONE THAN THAT, TUB!
THE ONLY WAY YOU CAN GET INTO THIS CLUBHOUSE IS TO PAY UP YOUR LAST MONTH'S DUES!
BUT, FELLERS, LISTEN!
WHY DON'TCHA PAY UP YOUR DUES WITH SOME OF THE MONEY YOU ROBBED FROM THAT BANK?
I DIDN'T ROB ANY BANK!
THE STORIES TUB CAN MAKE UP!
WHAT A CHARACTER!

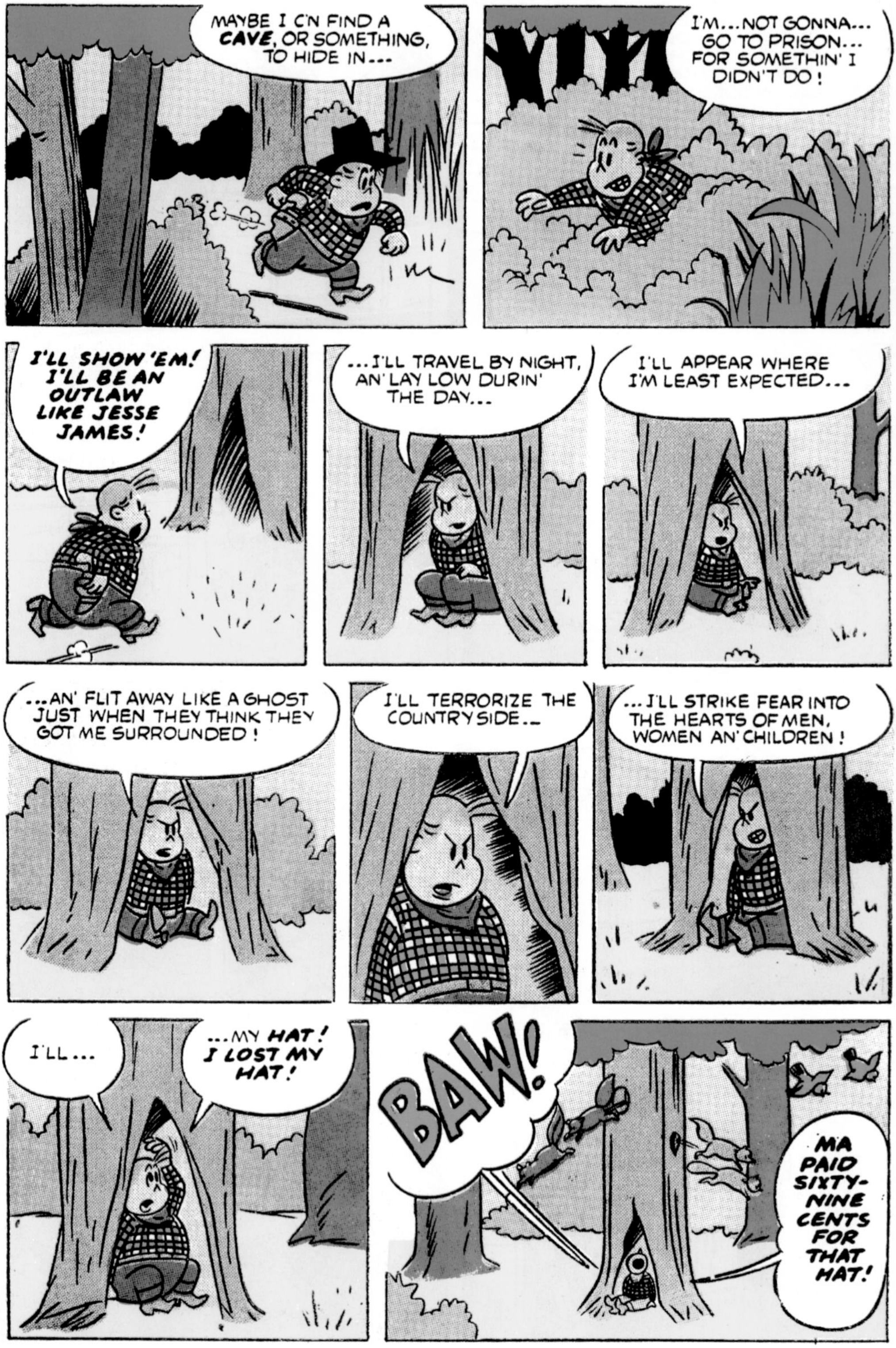
MAYBE I C'N FIND A CAVE, OR SOMETHING, TO HIDE IN...
I'M...NOT GONNA... GO TO PRISON... FOR SOMETHIN' I DIDN'T DO!
I'LL SHOW 'EM! I'LL BE AN OUTLAW LIKE JESSE JAMES!
...I'LL TRAVEL BY NIGHT, AN' LAY LOW DURIN' THE DAY...
I'LL APPEAR WHERE I'M LEAST EXPECTED...
...AN' FLIT AWAY LIKE A GHOST JUST WHEN THEY THINK THEY GOT ME SURROUNDED!
I'LL TERRORIZE THE COUNTRYSIDE...
...I'LL STRIKE FEAR INTO THE HEARTS OF MEN, WOMEN AN' CHILDREN!
I'LL...
...MY HAT! I LOST MY HAT!
BAW!
MA PAID SIXTY-NINE CENTS FOR THAT HAT!

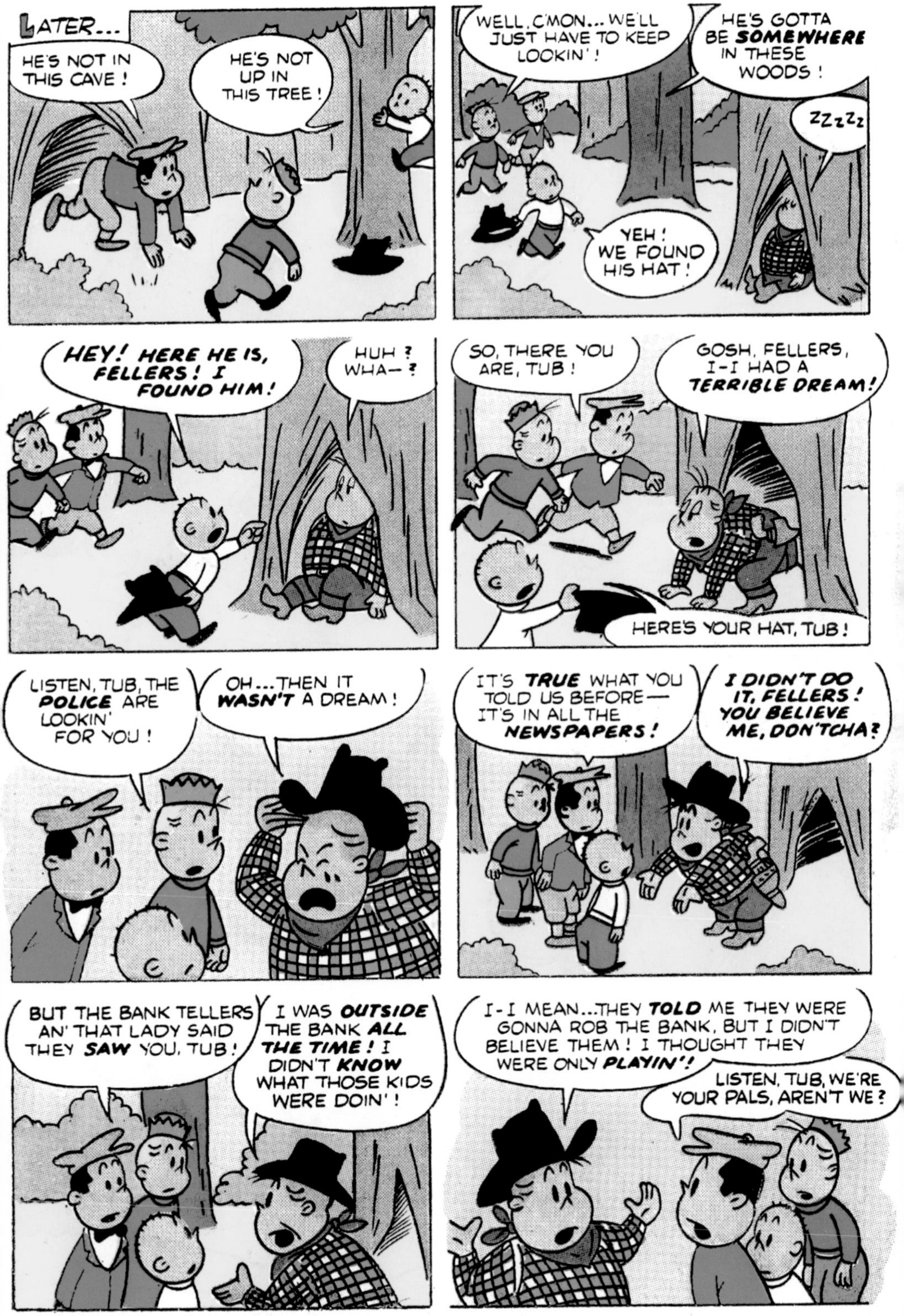
LATER...
HE'S NOT IN THIS CAVE!
HE'S NOT UP IN THIS TREE!
WELL, C'MON... WE'LL JUST HAVE TO KEEP LOOKIN'!
HE'S GOTTA BE SOMEWHERE IN THESE WOODS!
ZZzzZz
YEH! WE FOUND HIS HAT!
HEY! HERE HE IS, FELLERS! I FOUND HIM!
HUH? WHA—?
SO, THERE YOU ARE, TUB!
GOSH, FELLERS, I-I HAD A TERRIBLE DREAM!
HERE'S YOUR HAT, TUB!
LISTEN, TUB, THE POLICE ARE LOOKIN' FOR YOU!
OH... THEN IT WASN'T A DREAM!
IT'S TRUE WHAT YOU TOLD US BEFORE— IT'S IN ALL THE NEWSPAPERS!
I DIDN'T DO IT, FELLERS! YOU BELIEVE ME, DON'TCHA?
BUT THE BANK TELLERS AN' THAT LADY SAID THEY SAW YOU, TUB!
I WAS OUTSIDE THE BANK ALL THE TIME! I DIDN'T KNOW WHAT THOSE KIDS WERE DOIN'!
I-I MEAN... THEY TOLD ME THEY WERE GONNA ROB THE BANK, BUT I DIDN'T BELIEVE THEM! I THOUGHT THEY WERE ONLY PLAYIN'!
LISTEN, TUB, WE'RE YOUR PALS, AREN'T WE?

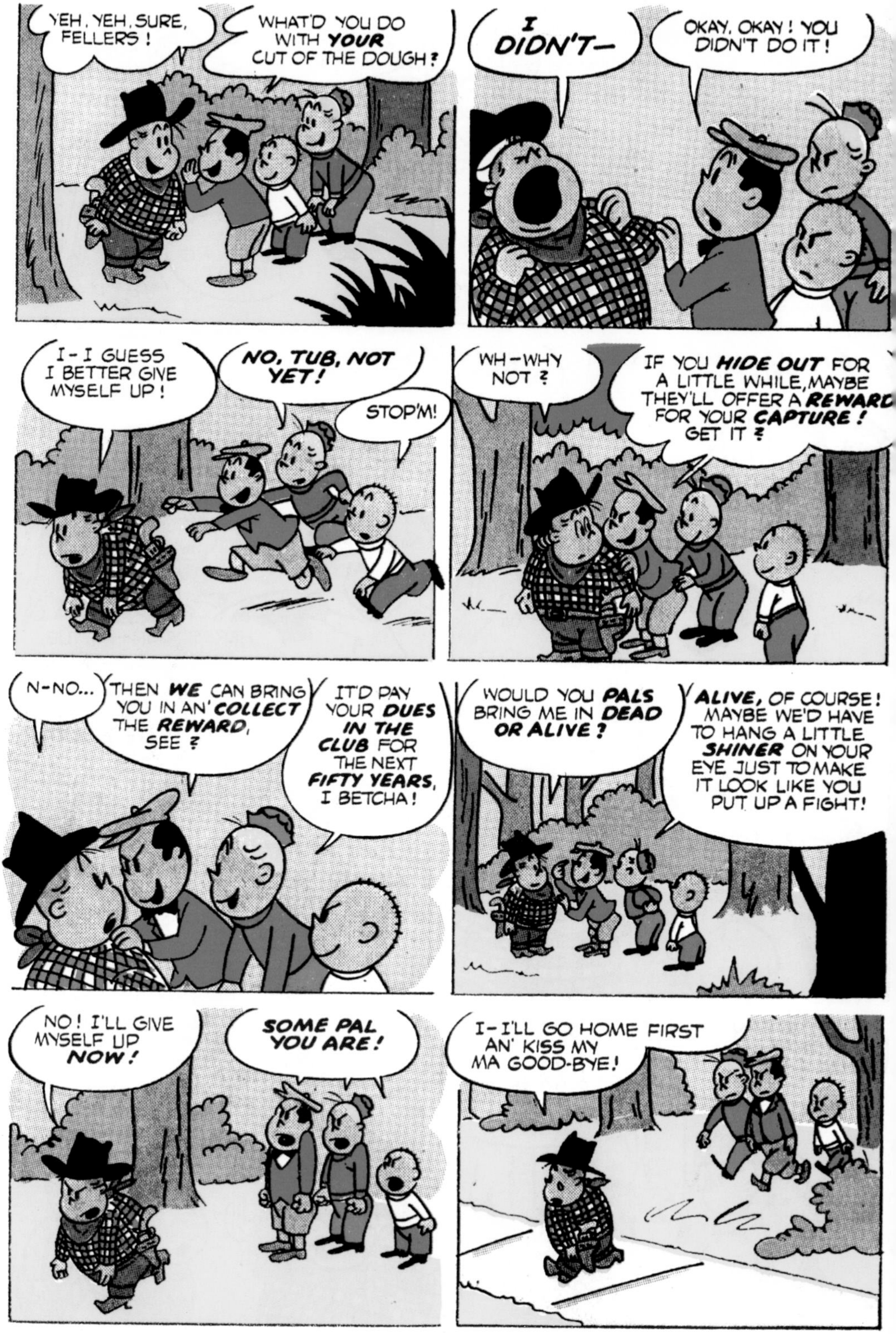
YEH, YEH, SURE, FELLERS!
WHAT'D YOU DO WITH YOUR CUT OF THE DOUGH?
I DIDN'T—
OKAY, OKAY! YOU DIDN'T DO IT!
I-I GUESS I BETTER GIVE MYSELF UP!
NO, TUB, NOT YET!
STOP'M!
WH-WHY NOT?
IF YOU HIDE OUT FOR A LITTLE WHILE, MAYBE THEY'LL OFFER A REWARD FOR YOUR CAPTURE! GET IT?
N-NO...
THEN WE CAN BRING YOU IN AN' COLLECT THE REWARD, SEE?
IT'D PAY YOUR DUES IN THE CLUB FOR THE NEXT FIFTY YEARS, I BETCHA!
WOULD YOU PALS BRING ME IN DEAD OR ALIVE?
ALIVE, OF COURSE! MAYBE WE'D HAVE TO HANG A LITTLE SHINER ON YOUR EYE JUST TO MAKE IT LOOK LIKE YOU PUT UP A FIGHT!
NO! I'LL GIVE MYSELF UP NOW!
SOME PAL YOU ARE!
I-I'LL GO HOME FIRST AN' KISS MY MA GOOD-BYE!

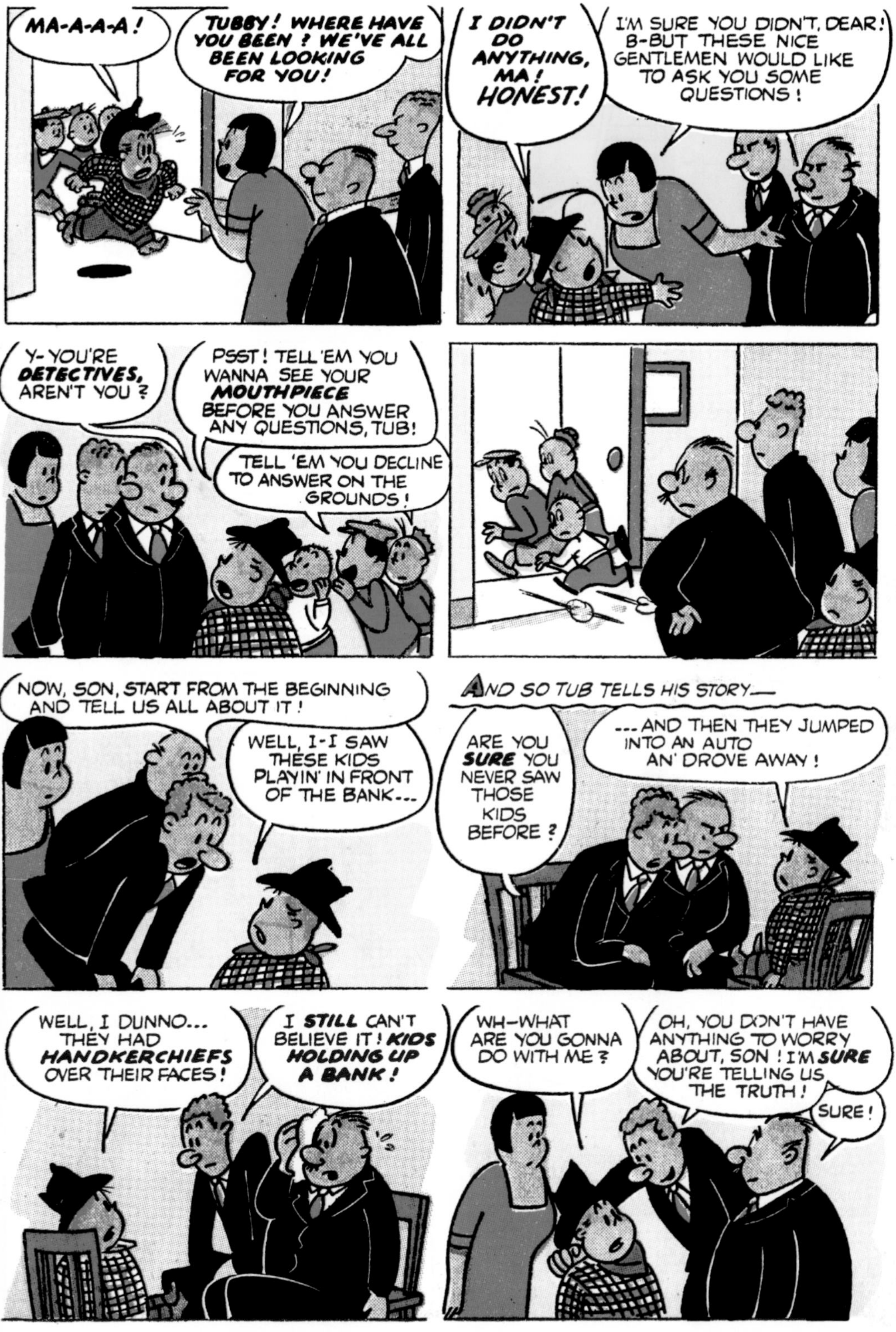
MA-A-A-A!
TUBBY! WHERE HAVE YOU BEEN? WE'VE ALL BEEN LOOKING FOR YOU!
I DIDN'T DO ANYTHING, MA! HONEST!
I'M SURE YOU DIDN'T, DEAR! B-BUT THESE NICE GENTLEMEN WOULD LIKE TO ASK YOU SOME QUESTIONS!
Y-YOU'RE DETECTIVES, AREN'T YOU?
PSST! TELL 'EM YOU WANNA SEE YOUR MOUTHPIECE BEFORE YOU ANSWER ANY QUESTIONS, TUB!
TELL 'EM YOU DECLINE TO ANSWER ON THE GROUNDS!
NOW, SON, START FROM THE BEGINNING AND TELL US ALL ABOUT IT!
WELL, I-I SAW THESE KIDS PLAYIN' IN FRONT OF THE BANK...
AND SO TUB TELLS HIS STORY—
ARE YOU SURE YOU NEVER SAW THOSE KIDS BEFORE?
...AND THEN THEY JUMPED INTO AN AUTO AN' DROVE AWAY!
WELL, I DUNNO... THEY HAD HANDKERCHIEFS OVER THEIR FACES!
I STILL CAN'T BELIEVE IT! KIDS HOLDING UP A BANK!
WH-WHAT ARE YOU GONNA DO WITH ME?
OH, YOU DON'T HAVE ANYTHING TO WORRY ABOUT, SON! I'M SURE YOU'RE TELLING US THE TRUTH!
SURE!

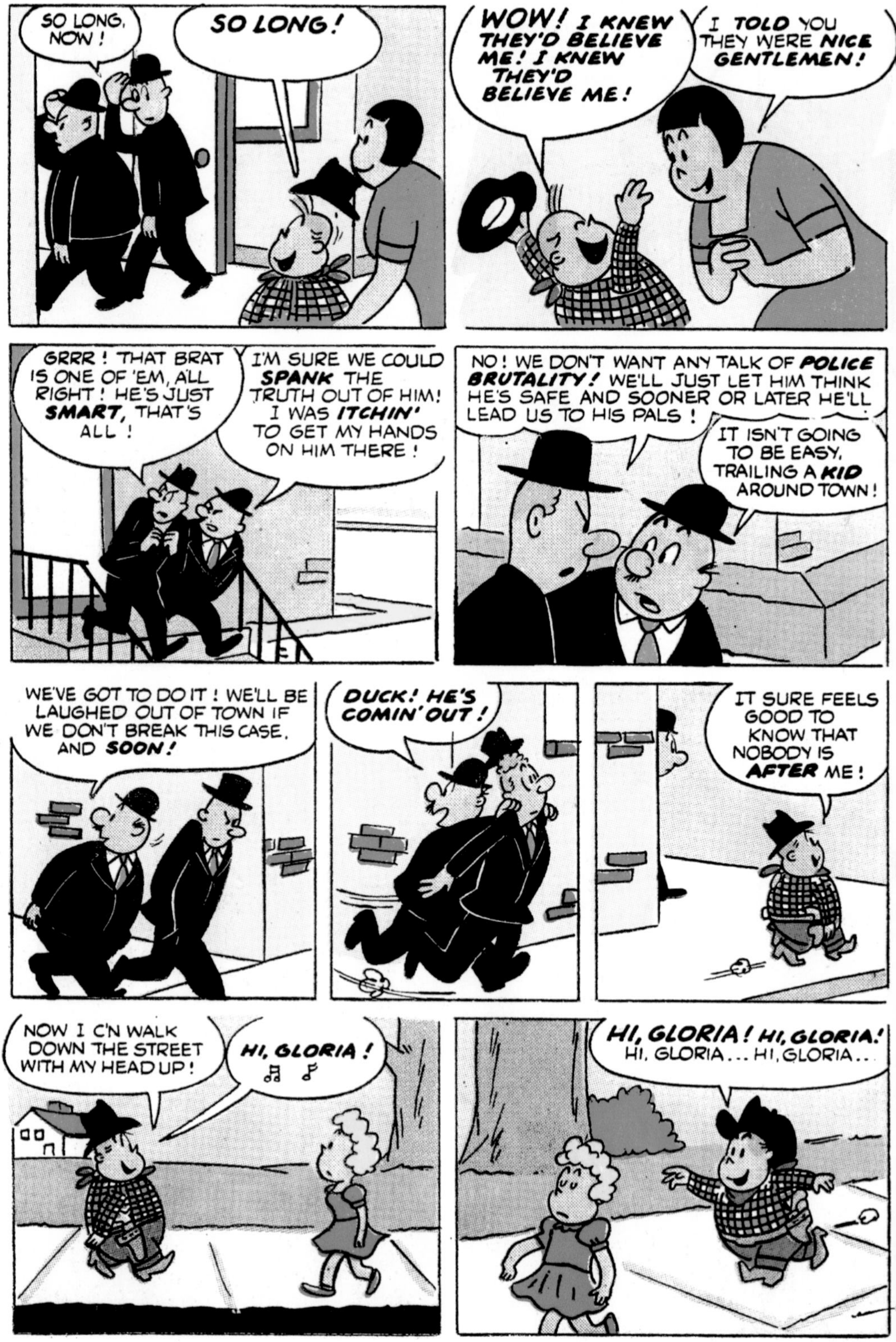
SO LONG, NOW !
SO LONG!
WOW! I KNEW THEY'D BELIEVE ME! I KNEW THEY'D BELIEVE ME!
I TOLD YOU THEY WERE NICE GENTLEMEN!
GRRR ! THAT BRAT IS ONE OF 'EM, ALL RIGHT ! HE'S JUST SMART, THAT'S ALL !
I'M SURE WE COULD SPANK THE TRUTH OUT OF HIM! I WAS ITCHIN' TO GET MY HANDS ON HIM THERE !
NO ! WE DON'T WANT ANY TALK OF POLICE BRUTALITY! WE'LL JUST LET HIM THINK HE'S SAFE AND SOONER OR LATER HE'LL LEAD US TO HIS PALS !
IT ISN'T GOING TO BE EASY, TRAILING A KID AROUND TOWN!
WE'VE GOT TO DO IT ! WE'LL BE LAUGHED OUT OF TOWN IF WE DON'T BREAK THIS CASE, AND SOON!
DUCK! HE'S COMIN' OUT !
IT SURE FEELS GOOD TO KNOW THAT NOBODY IS AFTER ME !
NOW I C'N WALK DOWN THE STREET WITH MY HEAD UP !
HI, GLORIA !
HI, GLORIA! HI, GLORIA! HI, GLORIA... HI, GLORIA...

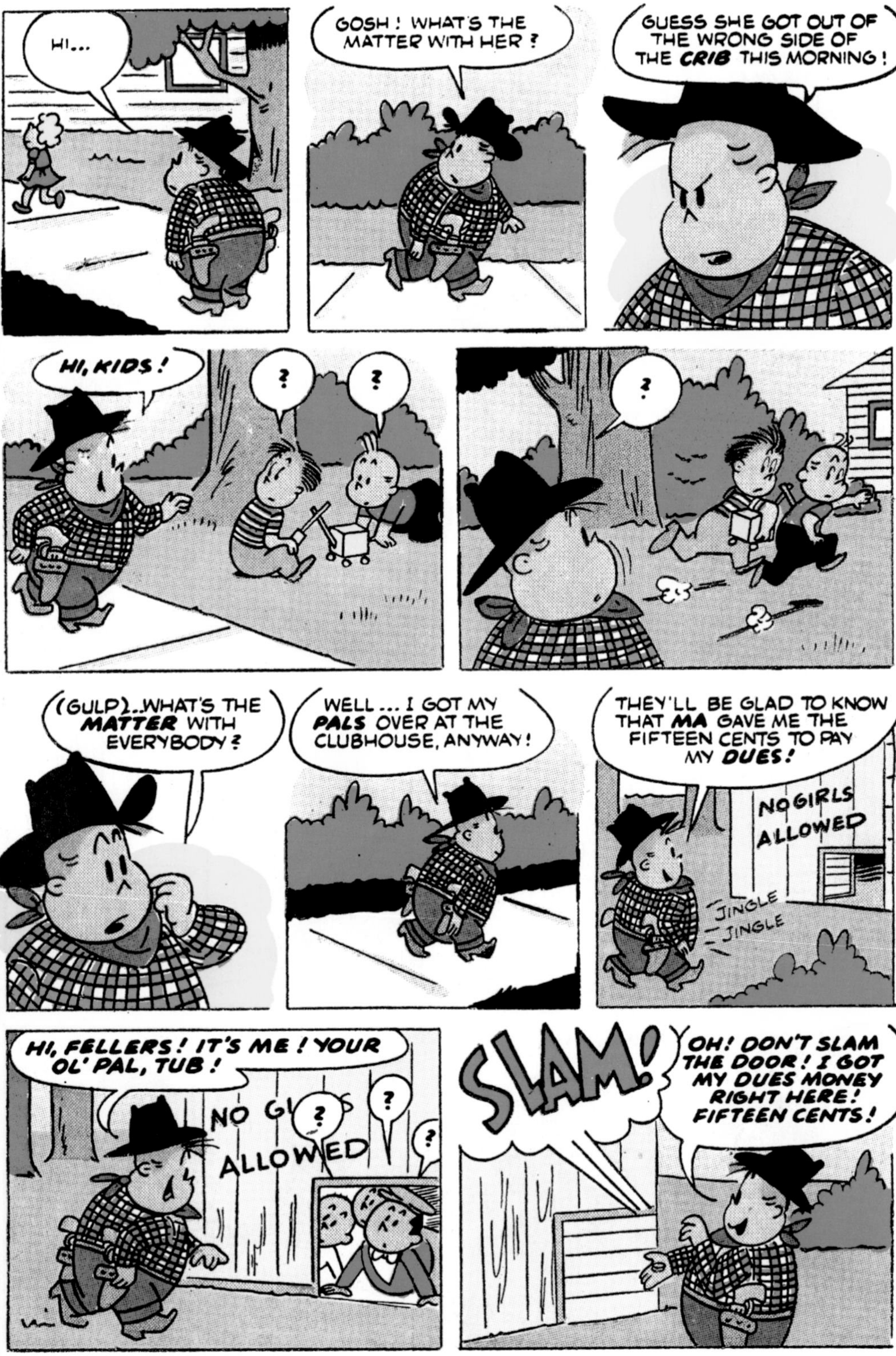
HI...
GOSH! WHAT'S THE MATTER WITH HER?
GUESS SHE GOT OUT OF THE WRONG SIDE OF THE CRIB THIS MORNING!
HI, KIDS!
?
?
?
(GULP)..WHAT'S THE MATTER WITH EVERYBODY?
WELL... I GOT MY PALS OVER AT THE CLUBHOUSE, ANYWAY!
THEY'LL BE GLAD TO KNOW THAT MA GAVE ME THE FIFTEEN CENTS TO PAY MY DUES!
NO GIRLS ALLOWED
JINGLE JINGLE
HI, FELLERS! IT'S ME! YOUR OL' PAL, TUB!
?
?
?
SLAM!
OH! DON'T SLAM THE DOOR! I GOT MY DUES MONEY RIGHT HERE! FIFTEEN CENTS!

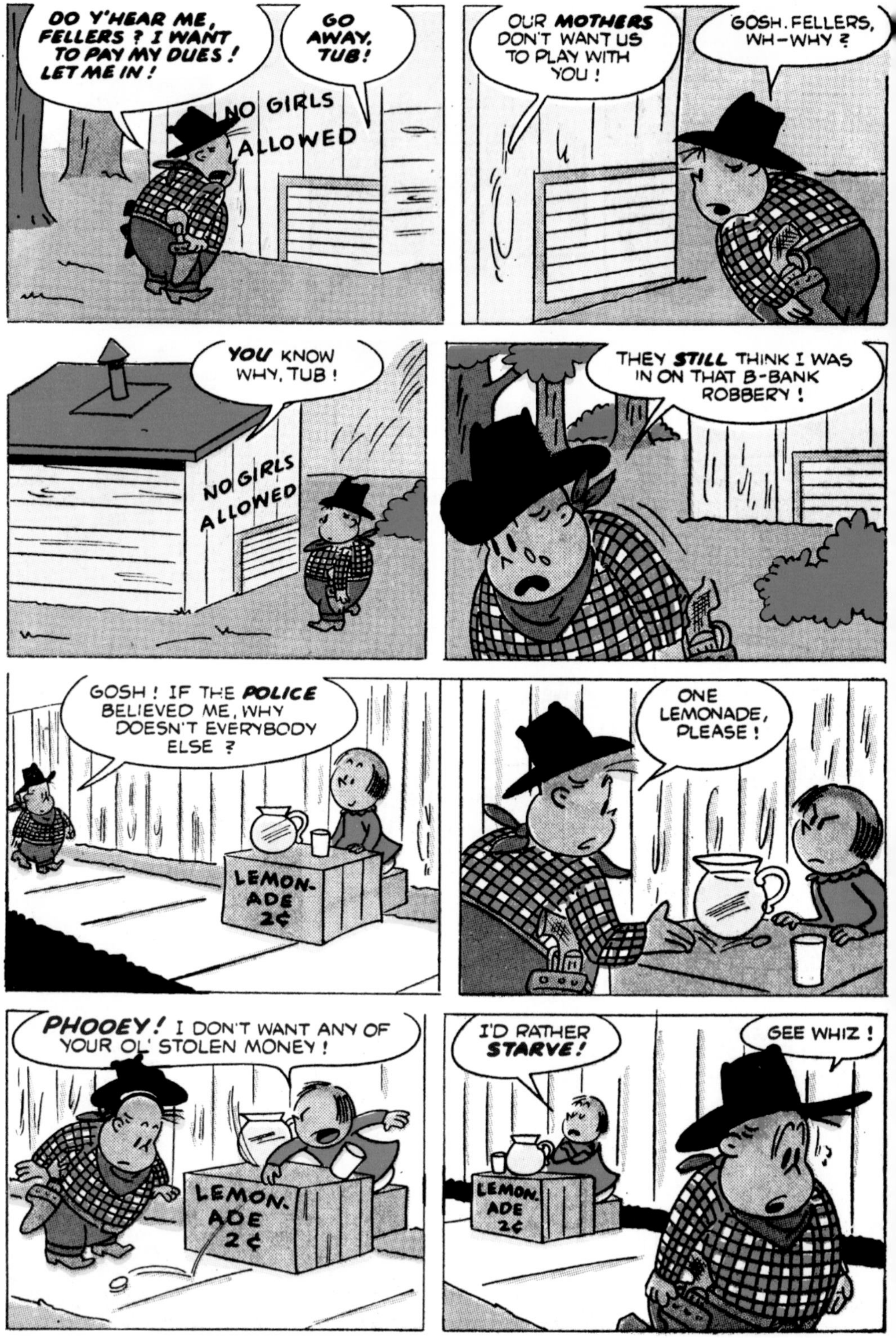
DO Y'HEAR ME, FELLERS ? I WANT TO PAY MY DUES ! LET ME IN !
GO AWAY, TUB!
NO GIRLS ALLOWED
OUR MOTHERS DON'T WANT US TO PLAY WITH YOU !
GOSH. FELLERS, WH-WHY ?
YOU KNOW WHY, TUB !
NO GIRLS ALLOWED
THEY STILL THINK I WAS IN ON THAT B-BANK ROBBERY !
GOSH ! IF THE POLICE BELIEVED ME, WHY DOESN'T EVERYBODY ELSE ?
LEMON-ADE 2¢
ONE LEMONADE, PLEASE !
PHOOEY! I DON'T WANT ANY OF YOUR OL' STOLEN MONEY !
LEMON-ADE 2¢
I'D RATHER STARVE!
GEE WHIZ !
LEMON-ADE 2¢

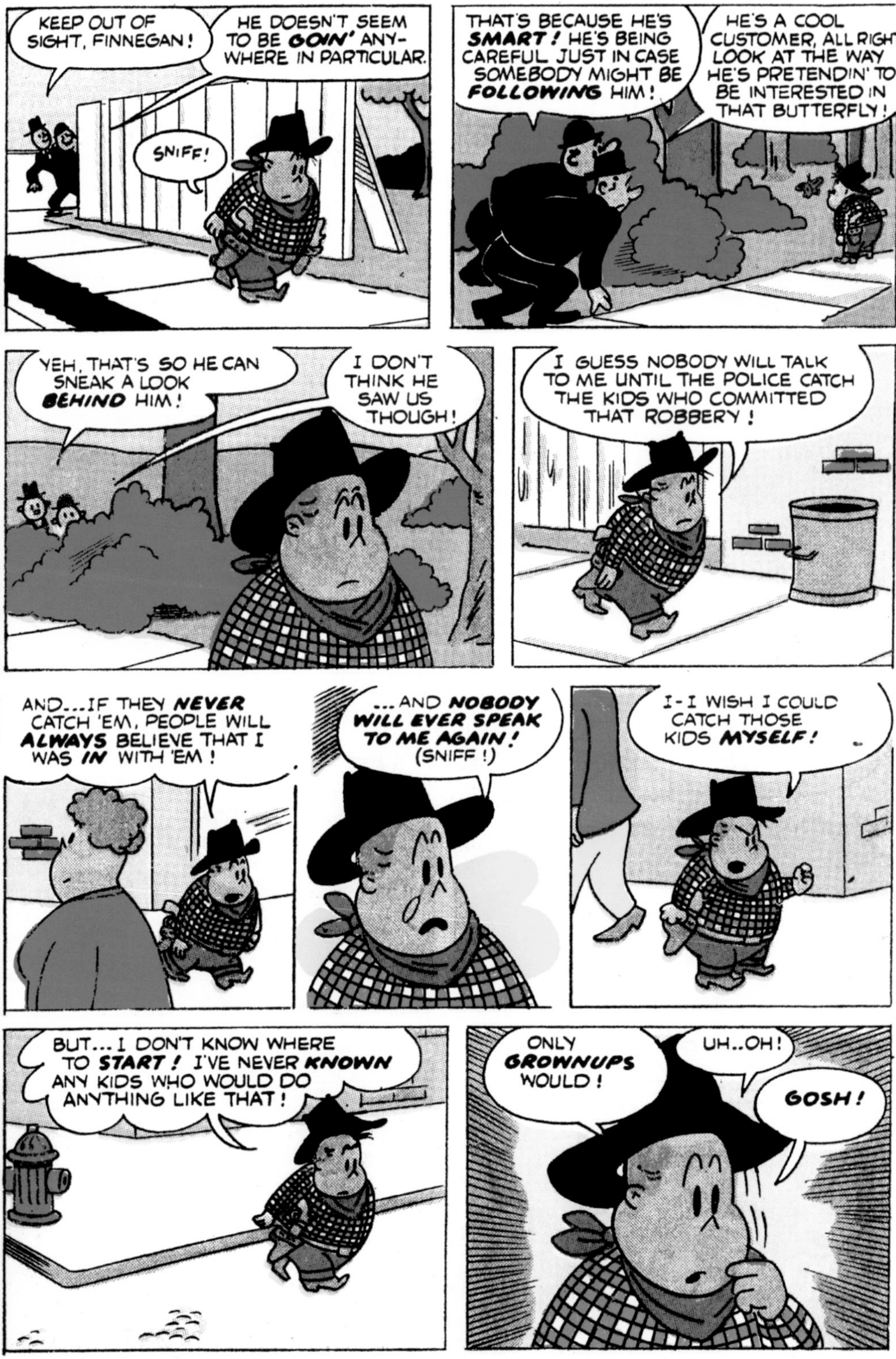
KEEP OUT OF SIGHT, FINNEGAN!
HE DOESN'T SEEM TO BE GOIN' ANYWHERE IN PARTICULAR.
SNIFF!
THAT'S BECAUSE HE'S SMART! HE'S BEING CAREFUL JUST IN CASE SOMEBODY MIGHT BE FOLLOWING HIM!
HE'S A COOL CUSTOMER, ALL RIGHT! LOOK AT THE WAY HE'S PRETENDIN' TO BE INTERESTED IN THAT BUTTERFLY!
YEH, THAT'S SO HE CAN SNEAK A LOOK BEHIND HIM!
I DON'T THINK HE SAW US THOUGH!
I GUESS NOBODY WILL TALK TO ME UNTIL THE POLICE CATCH THE KIDS WHO COMMITTED THAT ROBBERY!
AND...IF THEY NEVER CATCH 'EM, PEOPLE WILL ALWAYS BELIEVE THAT I WAS IN WITH 'EM!
...AND NOBODY WILL EVER SPEAK TO ME AGAIN! (SNIFF!)
I-I WISH I COULD CATCH THOSE KIDS MYSELF!
BUT... I DON'T KNOW WHERE TO START! I'VE NEVER KNOWN ANY KIDS WHO WOULD DO ANYTHING LIKE THAT!
ONLY GROWNUPS WOULD!
UH..OH!
GOSH!

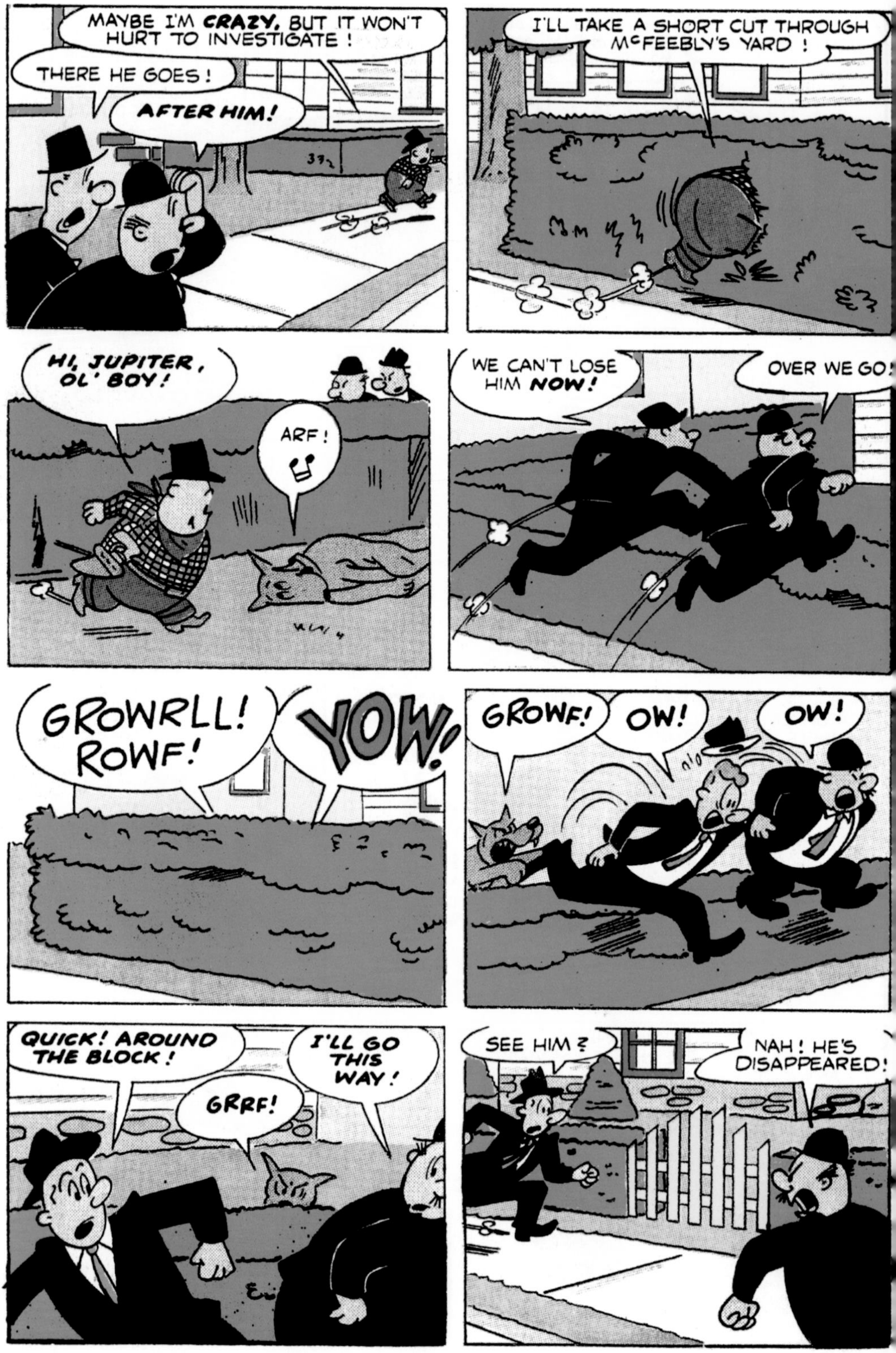
MAYBE I'M CRAZY, BUT IT WON'T HURT TO INVESTIGATE!
THERE HE GOES!
AFTER HIM!
I'LL TAKE A SHORT CUT THROUGH McFEEBLY'S YARD!
HI, JUPITER, OL' BOY!
ARF!
WE CAN'T LOSE HIM NOW!
OVER WE GO!
GROWRLL! ROWF!
YOW!
GROWF!
OW!
OW!
QUICK! AROUND THE BLOCK!
GRRF!
I'LL GO THIS WAY!
SEE HIM?
NAH! HE'S DISAPPEARED!

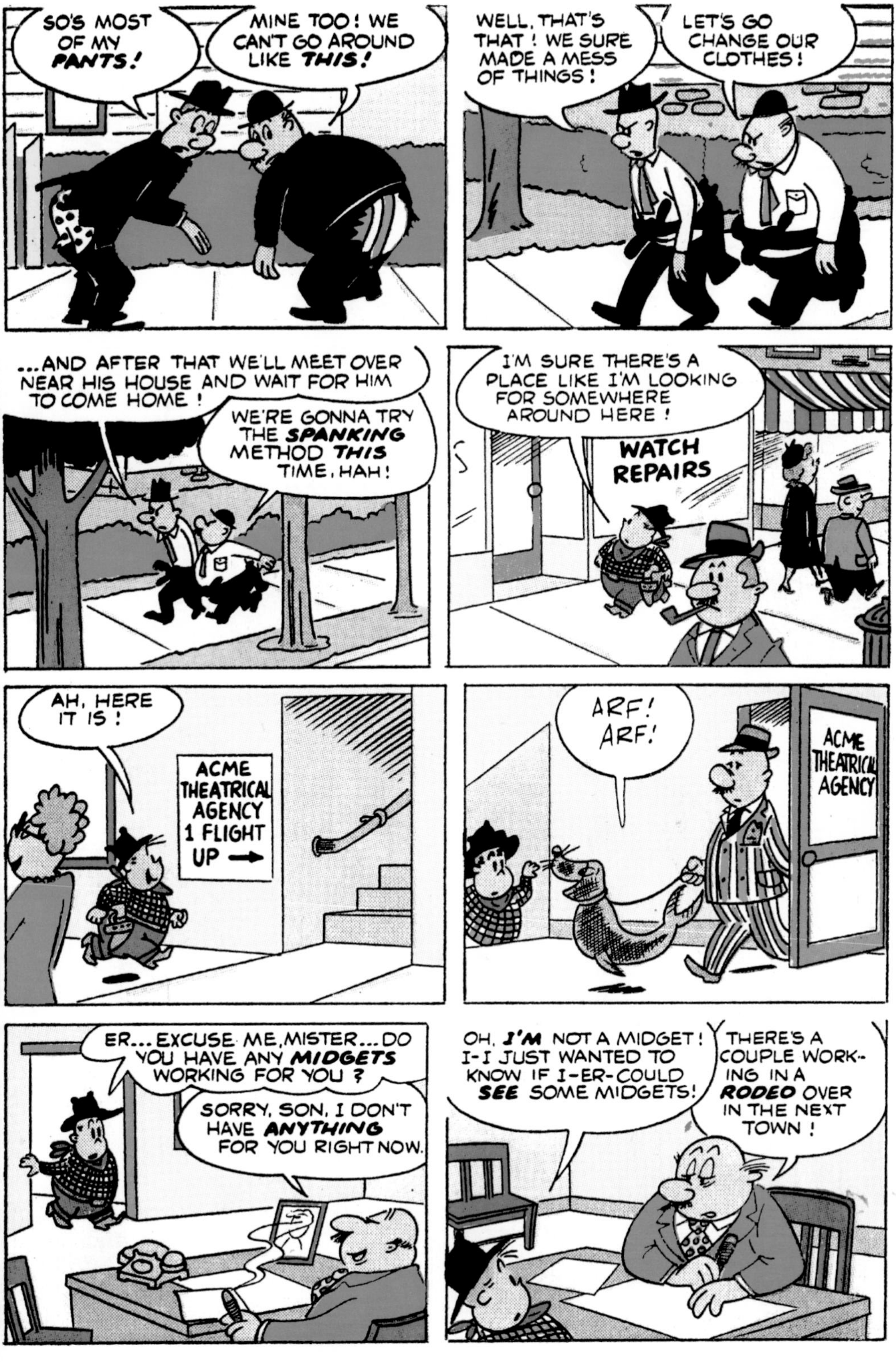
SO'S MOST OF MY PANTS!
MINE TOO! WE CAN'T GO AROUND LIKE THIS!
WELL, THAT'S THAT! WE SURE MADE A MESS OF THINGS!
LET'S GO CHANGE OUR CLOTHES!
...AND AFTER THAT WE'LL MEET OVER NEAR HIS HOUSE AND WAIT FOR HIM TO COME HOME!
WE'RE GONNA TRY THE SPANKING METHOD THIS TIME, HAH!
I'M SURE THERE'S A PLACE LIKE I'M LOOKING FOR SOMEWHERE AROUND HERE!
WATCH REPAIRS
AH, HERE IT IS!
ACME THEATRICAL AGENCY 1 FLIGHT UP →
ARF! ARF!
ACME THEATRICAL AGENCY
ER... EXCUSE ME, MISTER... DO YOU HAVE ANY MIDGETS WORKING FOR YOU?
SORRY, SON, I DON'T HAVE ANYTHING FOR YOU RIGHT NOW.
OH, I'M NOT A MIDGET! I-I JUST WANTED TO KNOW IF I-ER-COULD SEE SOME MIDGETS!
THERE'S A COUPLE WORK-ING IN A RODEO OVER IN THE NEXT TOWN!

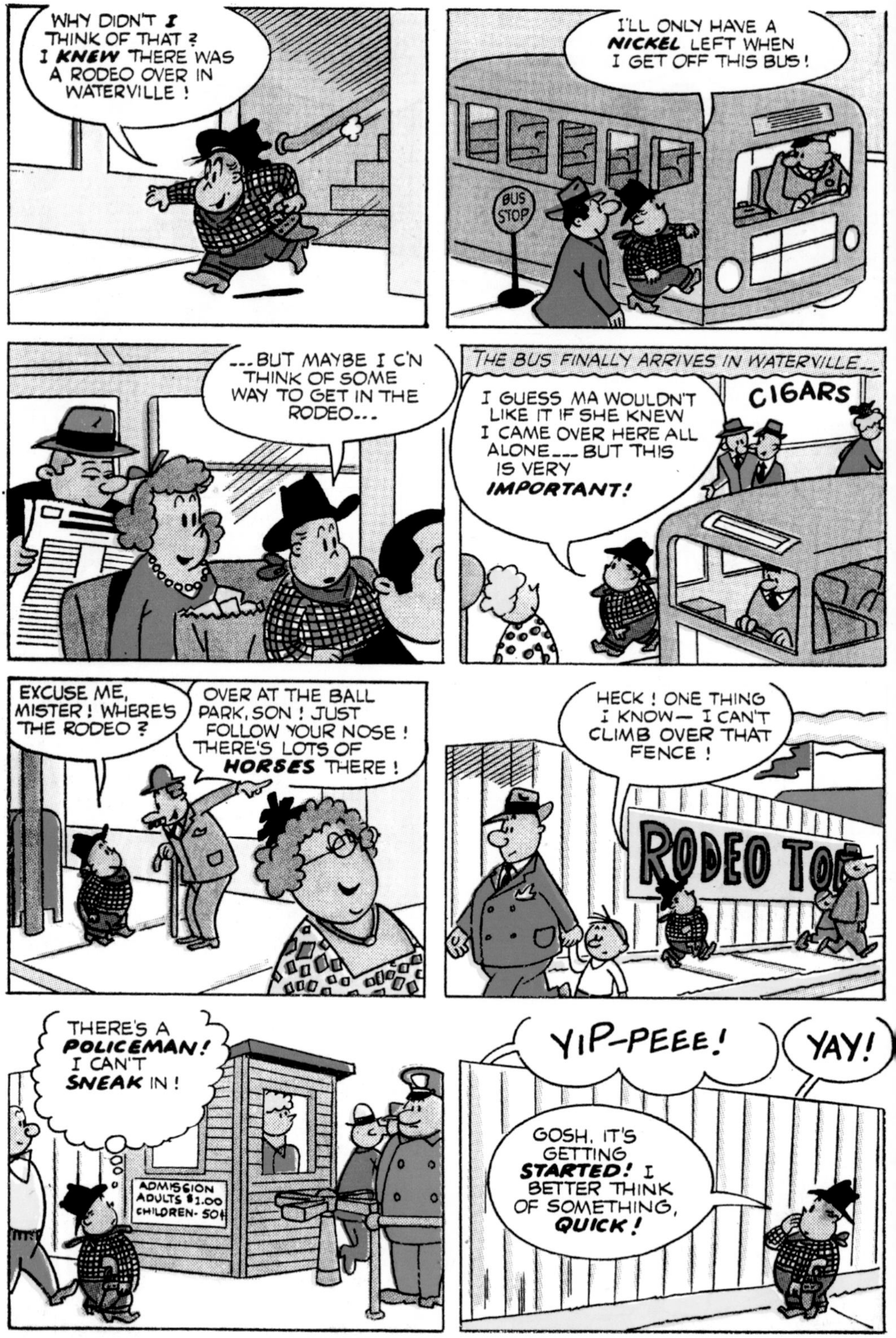
WHY DIDN'T I THINK OF THAT ? I KNEW THERE WAS A RODEO OVER IN WATERVILLE !
I'LL ONLY HAVE A NICKEL LEFT WHEN I GET OFF THIS BUS !
BUS STOP
---BUT MAYBE I C'N THINK OF SOME WAY TO GET IN THE RODEO---
THE BUS FINALLY ARRIVES IN WATERVILLE---
CIGARS
I GUESS MA WOULDN'T LIKE IT IF SHE KNEW I CAME OVER HERE ALL ALONE--- BUT THIS IS VERY IMPORTANT!
EXCUSE ME, MISTER ! WHERE'S THE RODEO ?
OVER AT THE BALL PARK, SON ! JUST FOLLOW YOUR NOSE ! THERE'S LOTS OF HORSES THERE !
HECK ! ONE THING I KNOW— I CAN'T CLIMB OVER THAT FENCE !
RODEO TO
THERE'S A POLICEMAN! I CAN'T SNEAK IN !
ADMISSION ADULTS $1.00 CHILDREN- 50¢
YIP-PEEE!
YAY!
GOSH, IT'S GETTING STARTED! I BETTER THINK OF SOMETHING, QUICK !

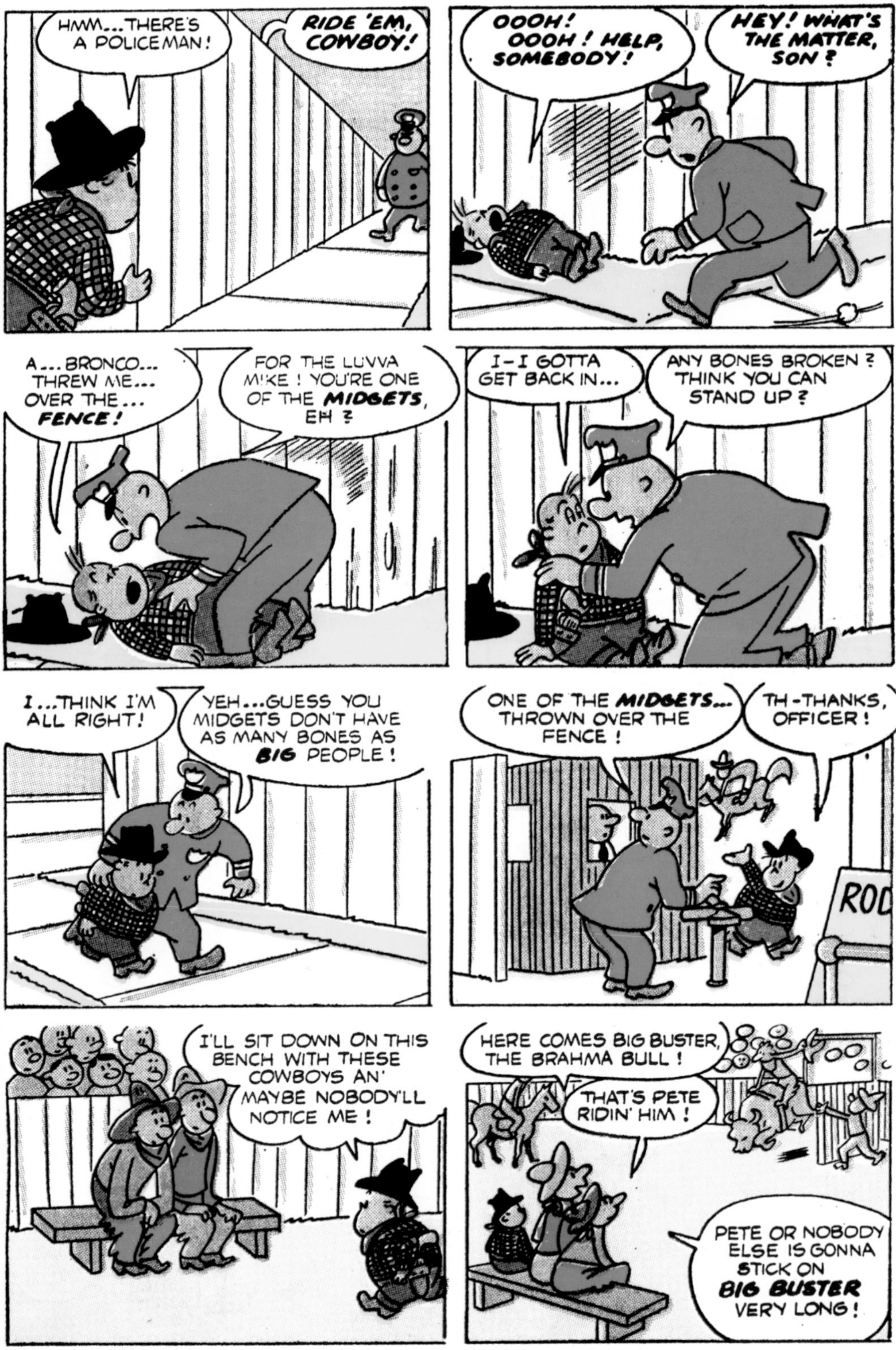
HMM...THERE'S A POLICEMAN!
RIDE 'EM, COWBOY!
OOOH! OOOH! HELP, SOMEBODY!
HEY! WHAT'S THE MATTER, SON?
A...BRONCO... THREW ME... OVER THE... FENCE!
FOR THE LUVVA MIKE! YOU'RE ONE OF THE MIDGETS, EH?
I-I GOTTA GET BACK IN...
ANY BONES BROKEN? THINK YOU CAN STAND UP?
I...THINK I'M ALL RIGHT!
YEH...GUESS YOU MIDGETS DON'T HAVE AS MANY BONES AS BIG PEOPLE!
ONE OF THE MIDGETS... THROWN OVER THE FENCE!
TH-THANKS, OFFICER!
ROD
I'LL SIT DOWN ON THIS BENCH WITH THESE COWBOYS AN' MAYBE NOBODY'LL NOTICE ME!
HERE COMES BIG BUSTER, THE BRAHMA BULL!
THAT'S PETE RIDIN' HIM!
PETE OR NOBODY ELSE IS GONNA STICK ON BIG BUSTER VERY LONG!

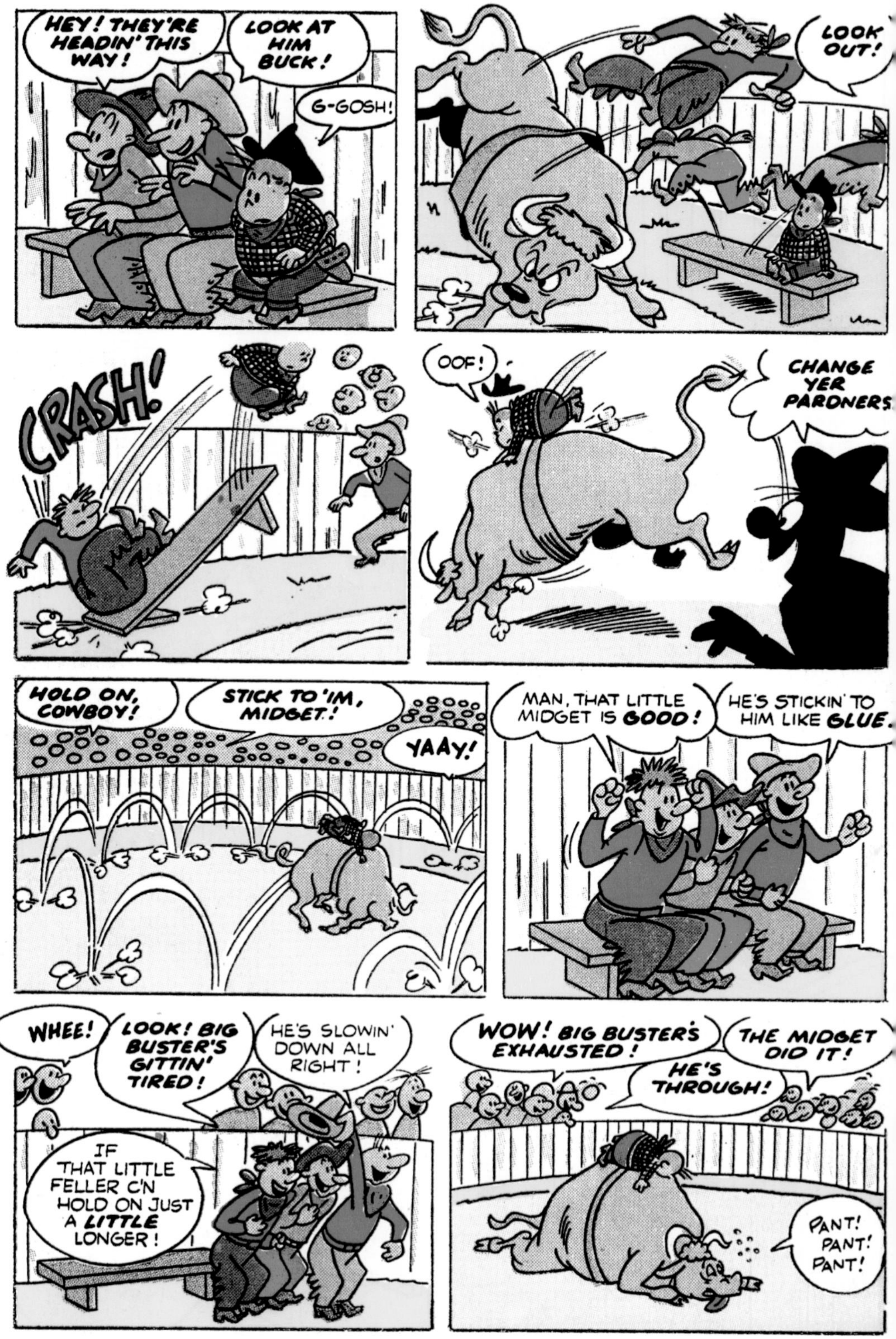
HEY! THEY'RE HEADIN' THIS WAY!
LOOK AT HIM BUCK!
G-GOSH!
LOOK OUT!
CRASH!
OOF!
CHANGE YER PARDNERS
HOLD ON, COWBOY!
STICK TO 'IM, MIDGET!
YAAY!
MAN, THAT LITTLE MIDGET IS GOOD!
HE'S STICKIN' TO HIM LIKE GLUE.
WHEE!
LOOK! BIG BUSTER'S GITTIN' TIRED!
HE'S SLOWIN' DOWN ALL RIGHT!
IF THAT LITTLE FELLER C'N HOLD ON JUST A LITTLE LONGER!
WOW! BIG BUSTER'S EXHAUSTED!
THE MIDGET DID IT!
HE'S THROUGH!
PANT! PANT! PANT!

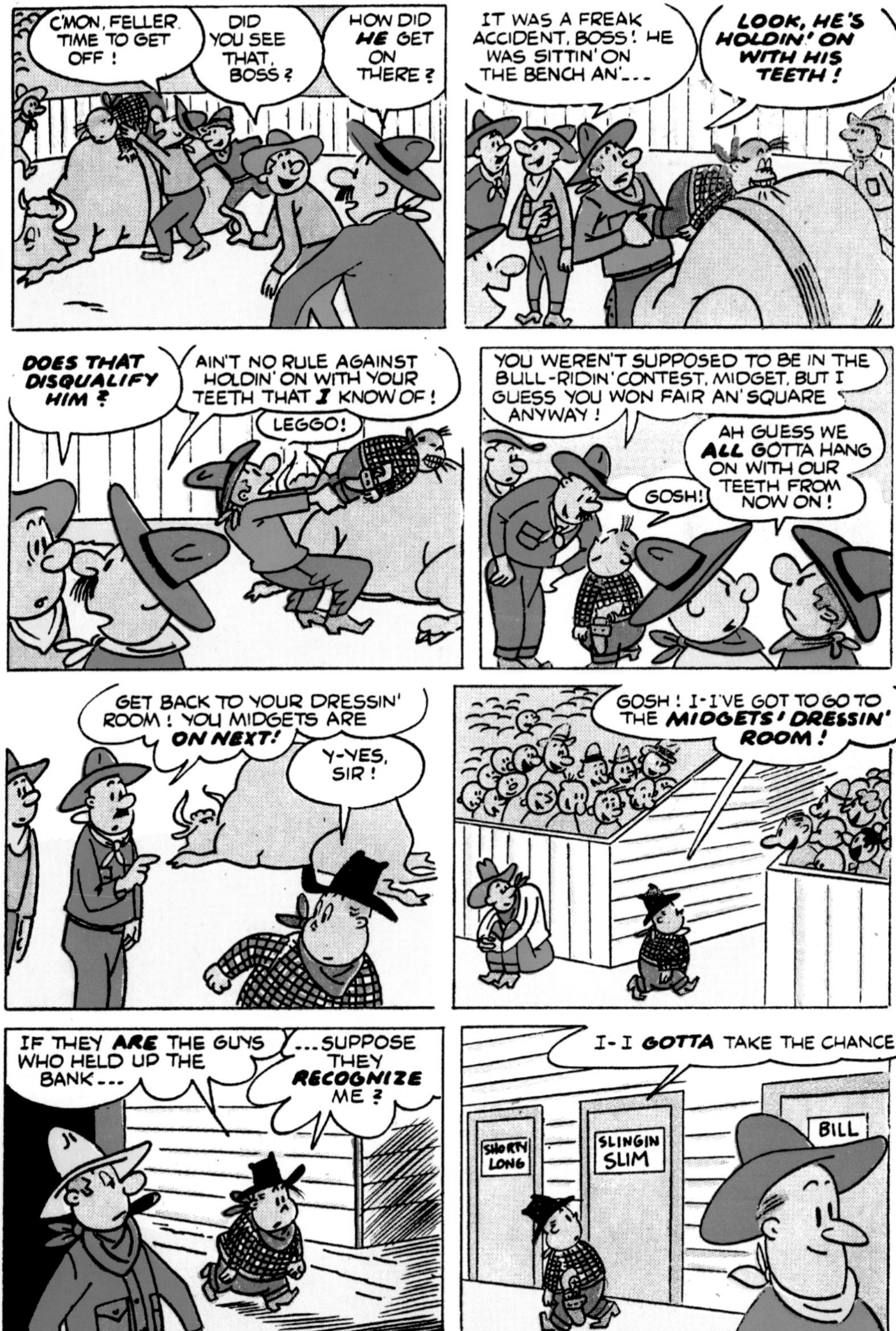
C'MON, FELLER. TIME TO GET OFF!
DID YOU SEE THAT, BOSS?
HOW DID HE GET ON THERE?
IT WAS A FREAK ACCIDENT, BOSS! HE WAS SITTIN' ON THE BENCH AN'...
LOOK, HE'S HOLDIN' ON WITH HIS TEETH!
DOES THAT DISQUALIFY HIM?
AIN'T NO RULE AGAINST HOLDIN' ON WITH YOUR TEETH THAT I KNOW OF!
LEGGO!
YOU WEREN'T SUPPOSED TO BE IN THE BULL-RIDIN' CONTEST, MIDGET, BUT I GUESS YOU WON FAIR AN' SQUARE ANYWAY!
GOSH!
AH GUESS WE ALL GOTTA HANG ON WITH OUR TEETH FROM NOW ON!
GET BACK TO YOUR DRESSIN' ROOM! YOU MIDGETS ARE ON NEXT!
Y-YES, SIR!
GOSH! I-I'VE GOT TO GO TO THE MIDGETS' DRESSIN' ROOM!
IF THEY ARE THE GUYS WHO HELD UP THE BANK...
...SUPPOSE THEY RECOGNIZE ME?
I-I GOTTA TAKE THE CHANCE!
SHORTY LONG
SLINGIN SLIM
BILL

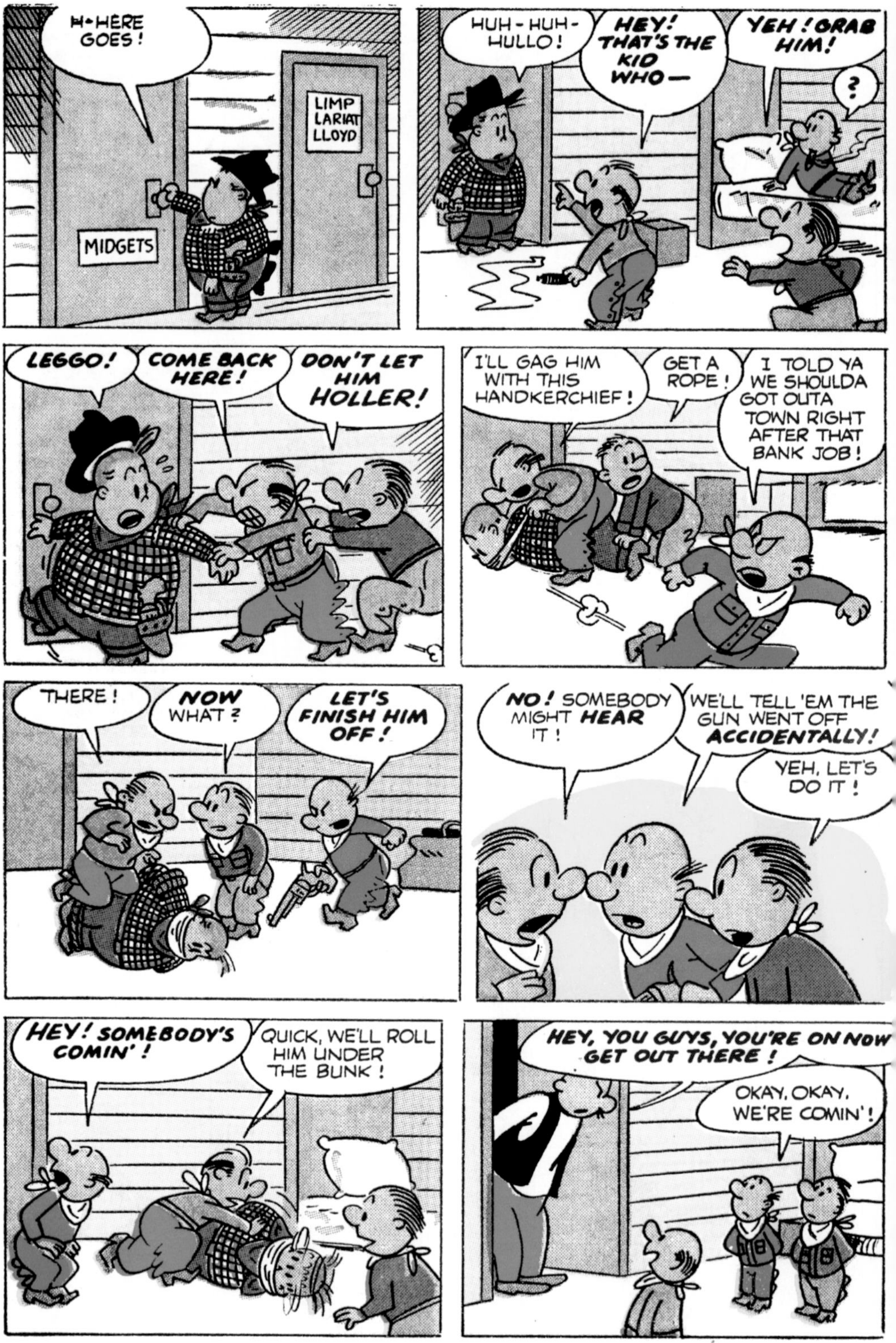

H-HERE GOES!
MIDGETS
LIMP LARIAT LLOYD
HUH-HUH-HULLO!
HEY! THAT'S THE KID WHO—
YEH! GRAB HIM!
?
LEGGO!
COME BACK HERE!
DON'T LET HIM HOLLER!
I'LL GAG HIM WITH THIS HANDKERCHIEF!
GET A ROPE!
I TOLD YA WE SHOULDA GOT OUTA TOWN RIGHT AFTER THAT BANK JOB!
THERE!
NOW WHAT?
LET'S FINISH HIM OFF!
NO! SOMEBODY MIGHT HEAR IT!
WE'LL TELL 'EM THE GUN WENT OFF ACCIDENTALLY!
YEH, LET'S DO IT!
HEY! SOMEBODY'S COMIN'!
QUICK, WE'LL ROLL HIM UNDER THE BUNK!
HEY, YOU GUYS, YOU'RE ON NOW GET OUT THERE!
OKAY, OKAY, WE'RE COMIN'!

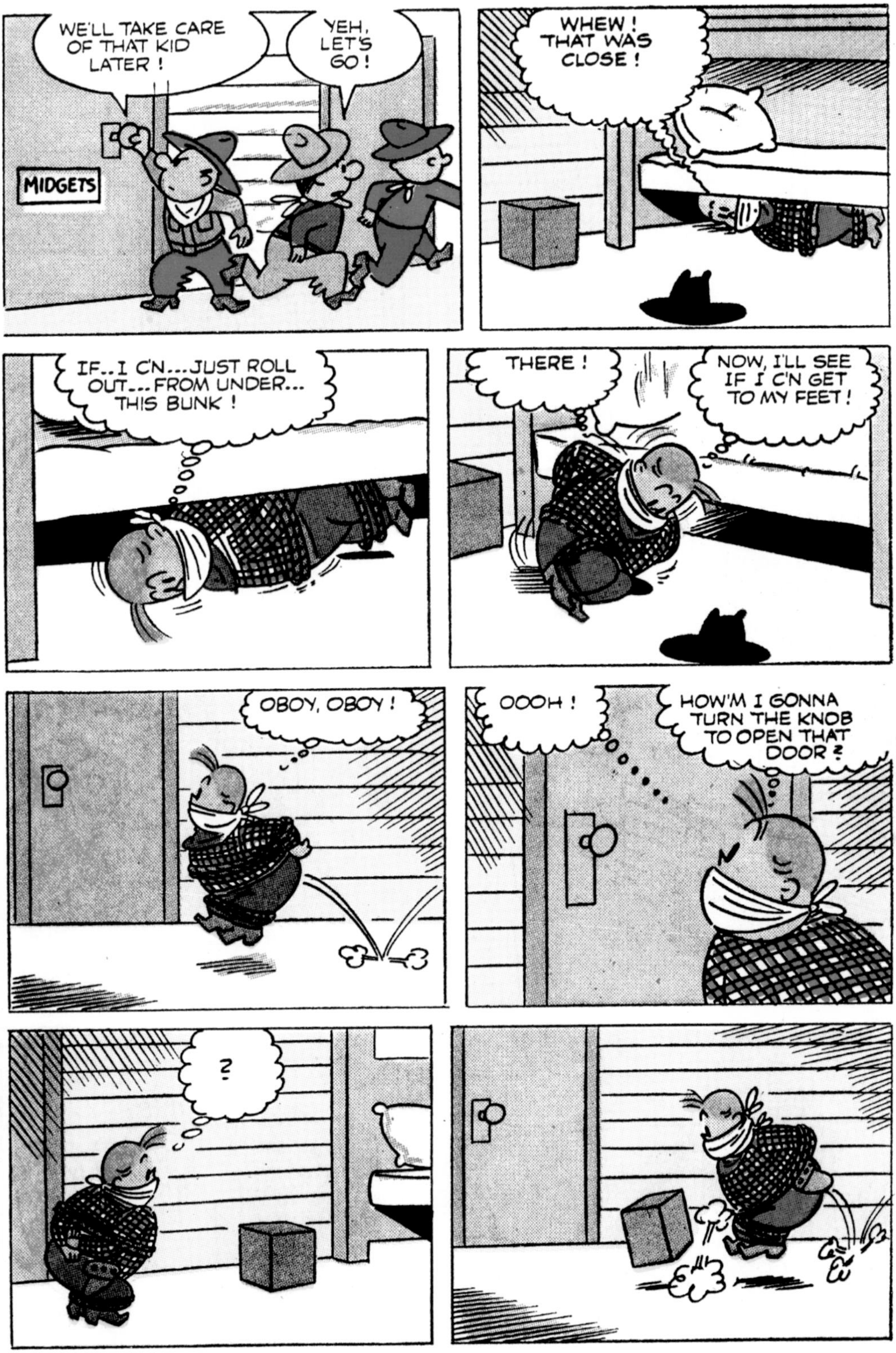
WE'LL TAKE CARE OF THAT KID LATER !
YEH, LET'S GO !
MIDGETS
WHEW ! THAT WAS CLOSE !
IF..I C'N...JUST ROLL OUT...FROM UNDER... THIS BUNK !
THERE !
NOW, I'LL SEE IF I C'N GET TO MY FEET !
OBOY, OBOY !
OOOH !
HOW'M I GONNA TURN THE KNOB TO OPEN THAT DOOR ?
?

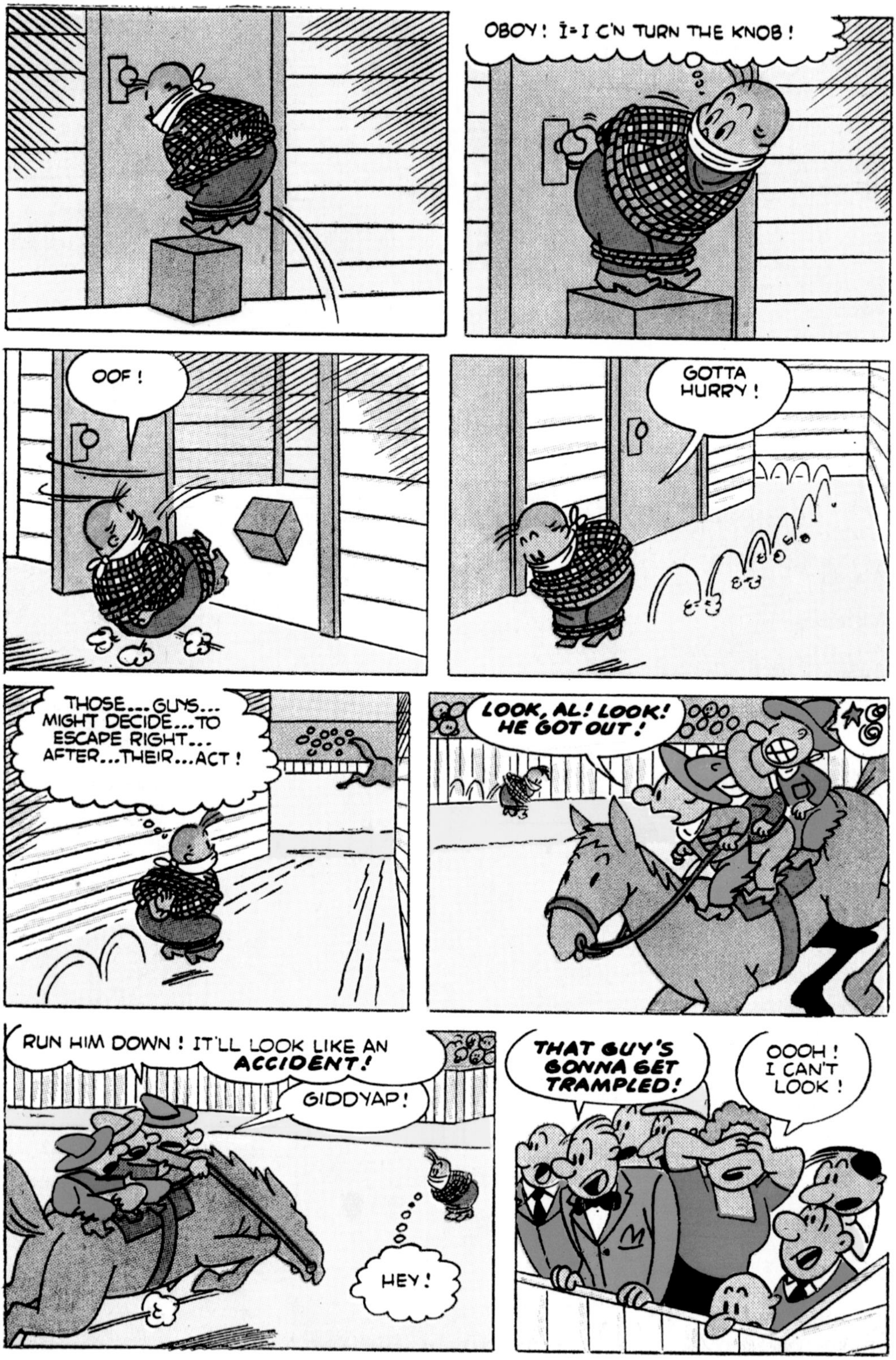
OBOY! I-I C'N TURN THE KNOB!
OOF!
GOTTA HURRY!
THOSE...GUYS... MIGHT DECIDE...TO ESCAPE RIGHT... AFTER...THEIR...ACT!
LOOK, AL! LOOK! HE GOT OUT!
RUN HIM DOWN! IT'LL LOOK LIKE AN ACCIDENT!
GIDDYAP!
HEY!
THAT GUY'S GONNA GET TRAMPLED!
OOOH! I CAN'T LOOK!

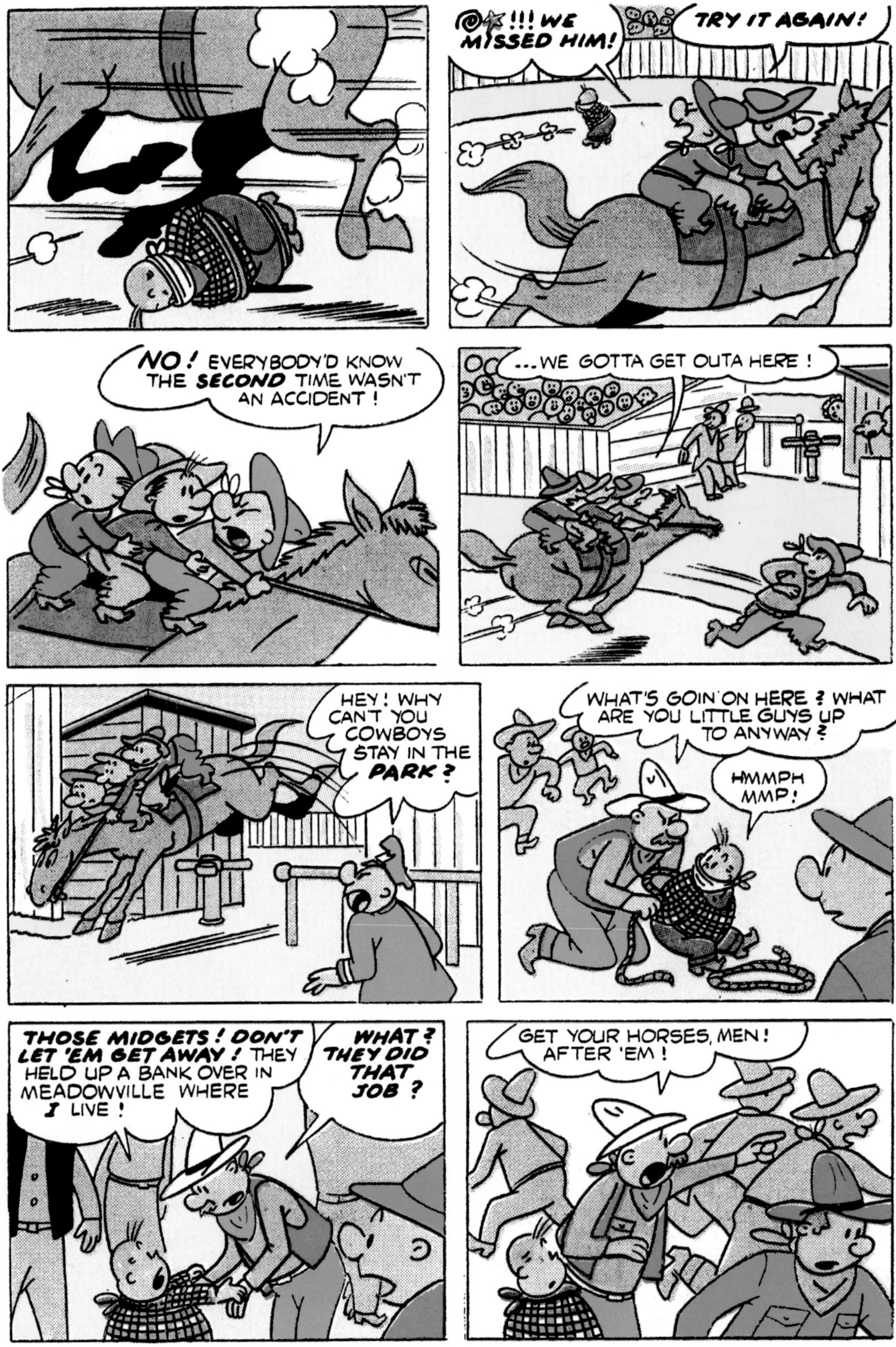

@☆!!! WE MISSED HIM!
TRY IT AGAIN!
NO! EVERYBODY'D KNOW THE SECOND TIME WASN'T AN ACCIDENT!
...WE GOTTA GET OUTA HERE!
HEY! WHY CAN'T YOU COWBOYS STAY IN THE PARK?
WHAT'S GOIN' ON HERE? WHAT ARE YOU LITTLE GUYS UP TO ANYWAY?
HMMPH MMP!
THOSE MIDGETS! DON'T LET 'EM GET AWAY! THEY HELD UP A BANK OVER IN MEADOWVILLE WHERE I LIVE!
WHAT? THEY DID THAT JOB?
GET YOUR HORSES, MEN! AFTER 'EM!

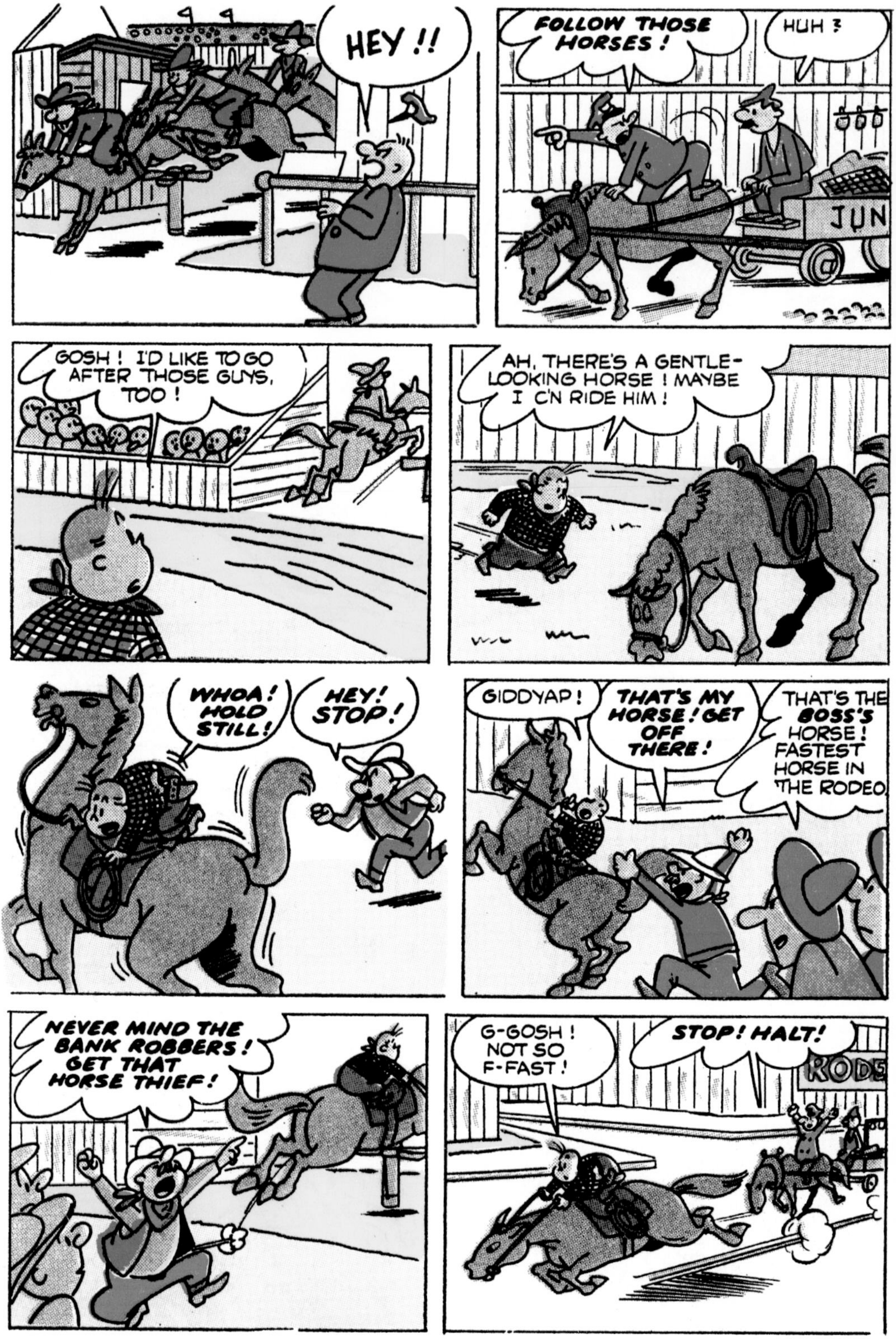
HEY !!
FOLLOW THOSE HORSES !
HUH ?
JUN
GOSH ! I'D LIKE TO GO AFTER THOSE GUYS, TOO !
AH, THERE'S A GENTLE-LOOKING HORSE ! MAYBE I C'N RIDE HIM !
WHOA! HOLD STILL!
HEY! STOP!
GIDDYAP!
THAT'S MY HORSE! GET OFF THERE!
THAT'S THE BOSS'S HORSE! FASTEST HORSE IN THE RODEO
NEVER MIND THE BANK ROBBERS! GET THAT HORSE THIEF!
G-GOSH ! NOT SO F-FAST !
STOP! HALT!
RODE

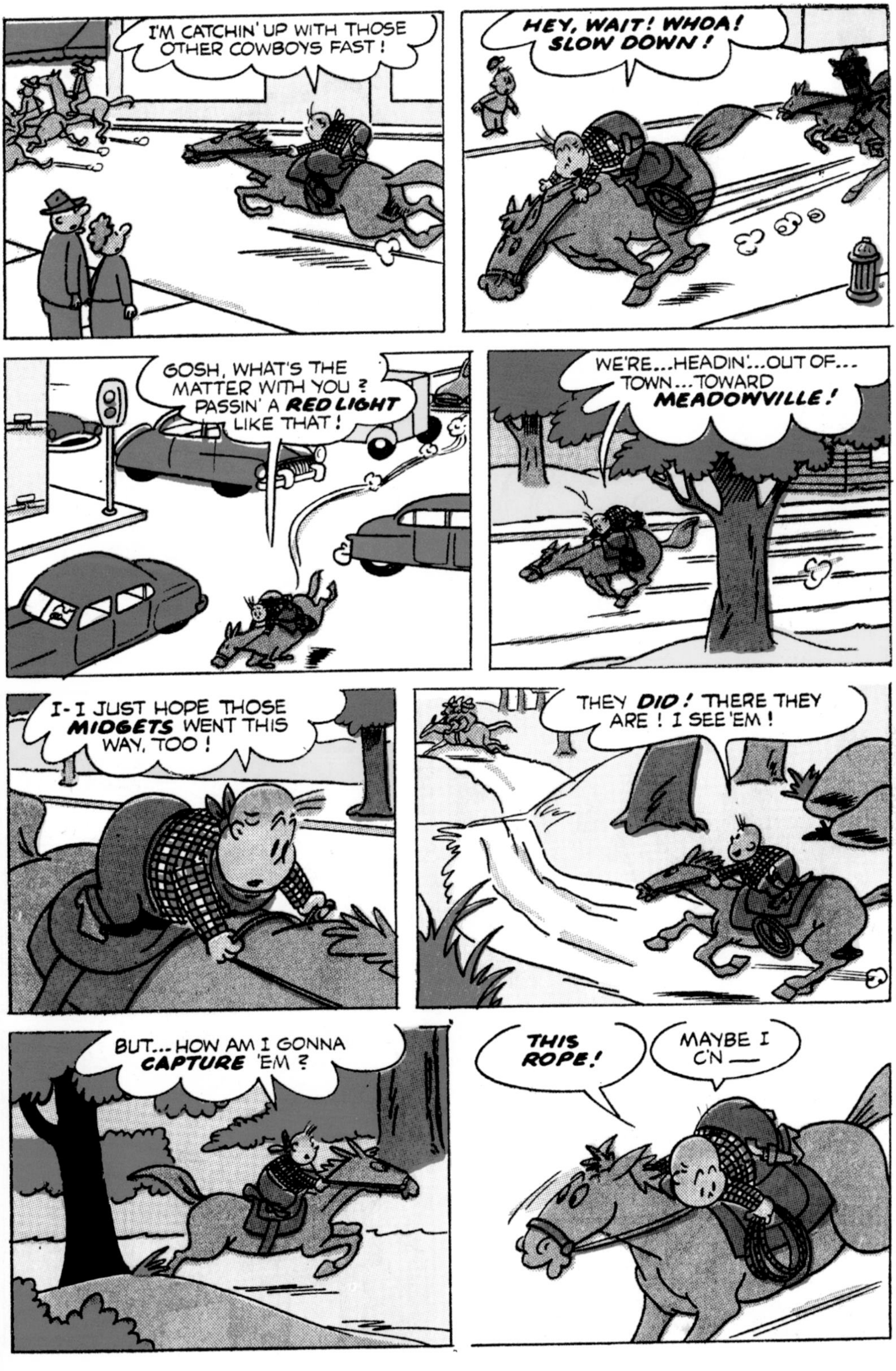
I'M CATCHIN' UP WITH THOSE OTHER COWBOYS FAST!
HEY, WAIT! WHOA! SLOW DOWN!
GOSH, WHAT'S THE MATTER WITH YOU? PASSIN' A RED LIGHT LIKE THAT!
WE'RE...HEADIN'...OUT OF... TOWN...TOWARD MEADOWVILLE!
I-I JUST HOPE THOSE MIDGETS WENT THIS WAY, TOO!
THEY DID! THERE THEY ARE! I SEE 'EM!
BUT... HOW AM I GONNA CAPTURE 'EM?
MAYBE I C'N —
THIS ROPE!

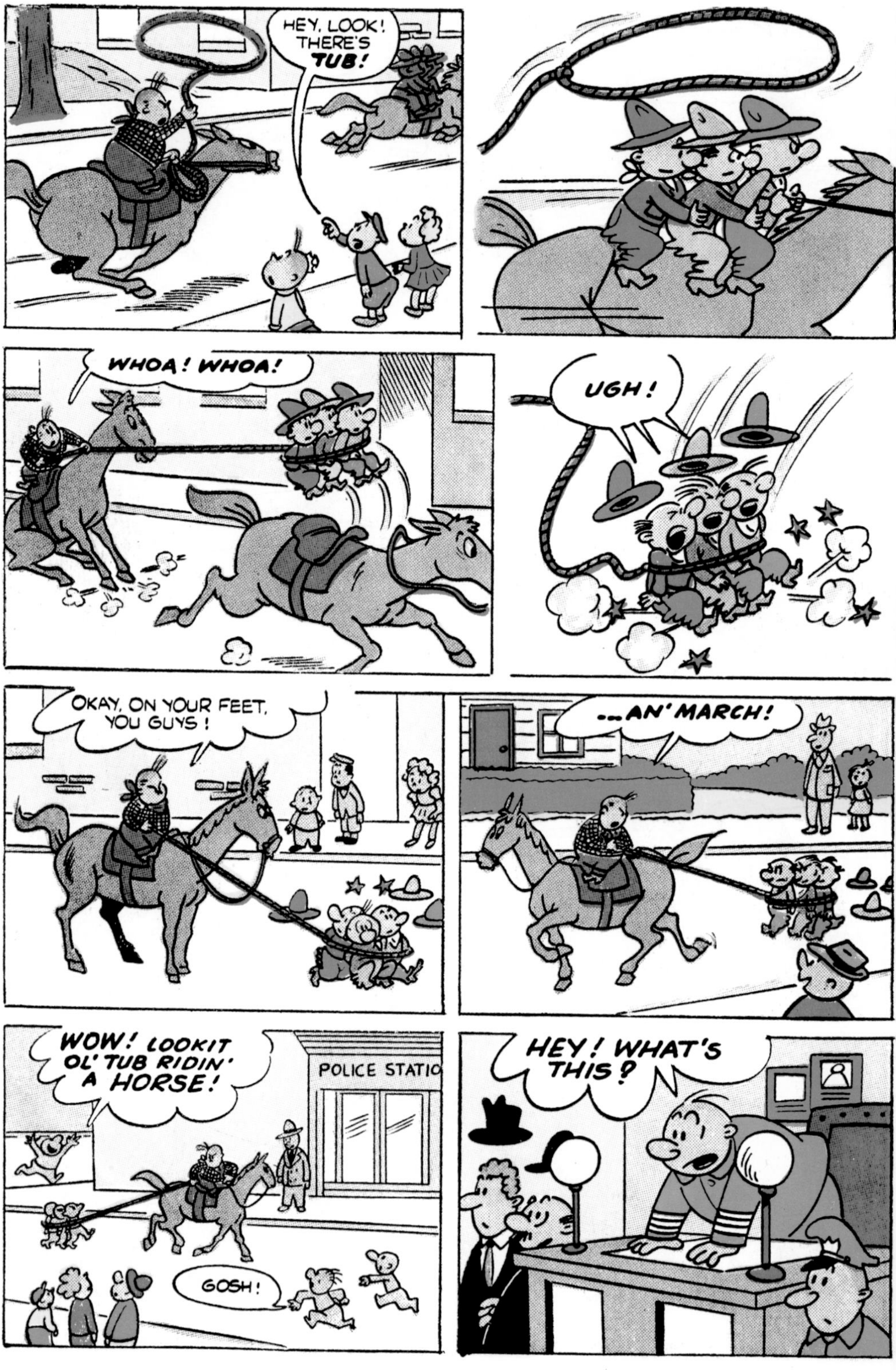
HEY, LOOK! THERE'S TUB!
WHOA! WHOA!
UGH!
OKAY, ON YOUR FEET, YOU GUYS!
...AN' MARCH!
WOW! LOOKIT OL' TUB RIDIN' A HORSE!
POLICE STATIO
GOSH!
HEY! WHAT'S THIS?

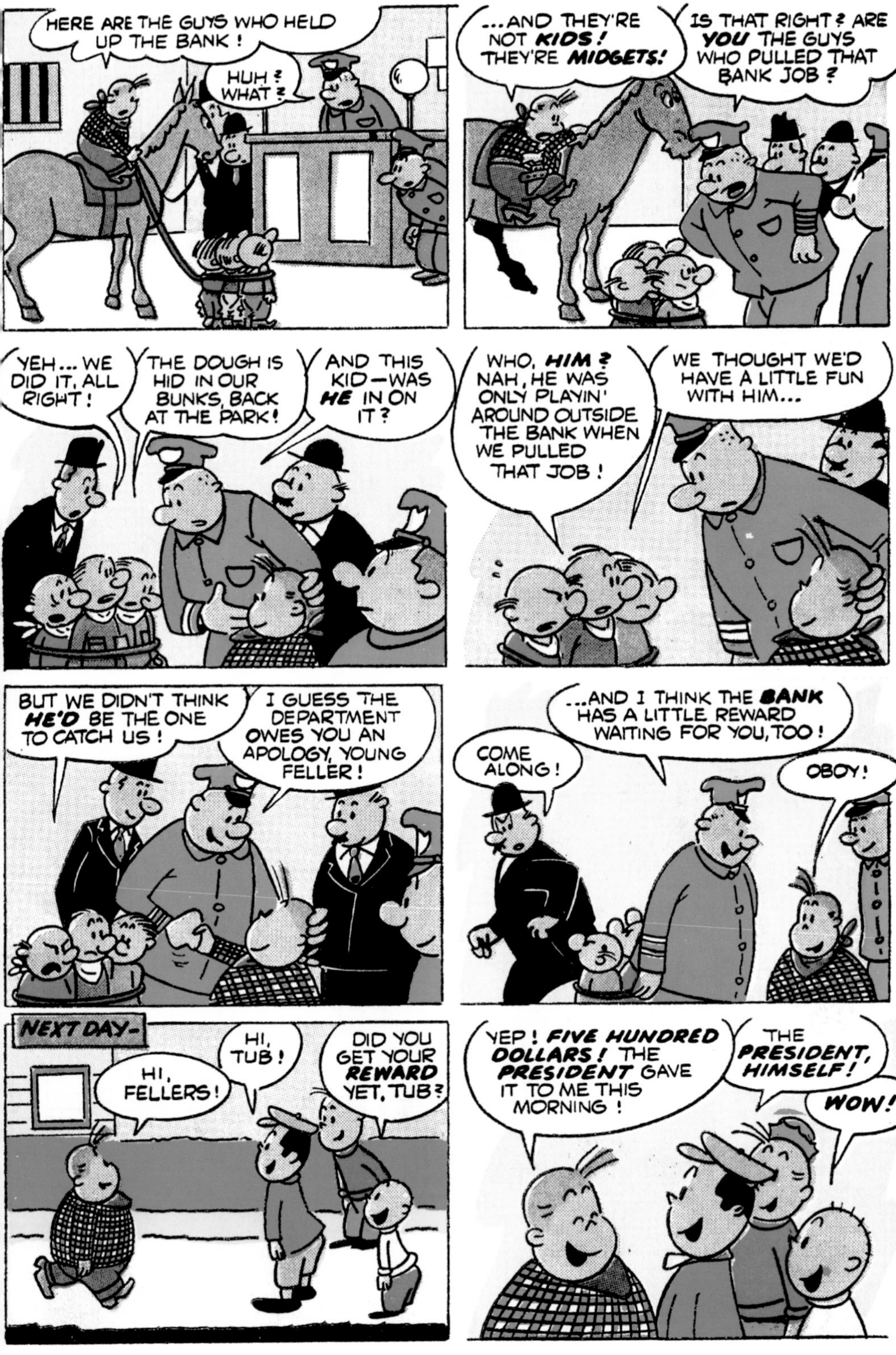
HERE ARE THE GUYS WHO HELD UP THE BANK!
HUH? WHAT?
...AND THEY'RE NOT KIDS! THEY'RE MIDGETS!
IS THAT RIGHT? ARE YOU THE GUYS WHO PULLED THAT BANK JOB?
YEH... WE DID IT, ALL RIGHT!
THE DOUGH IS HID IN OUR BUNKS, BACK AT THE PARK!
AND THIS KID—WAS HE IN ON IT?
WHO, HIM? NAH, HE WAS ONLY PLAYIN' AROUND OUTSIDE THE BANK WHEN WE PULLED THAT JOB!
WE THOUGHT WE'D HAVE A LITTLE FUN WITH HIM...
BUT WE DIDN'T THINK HE'D BE THE ONE TO CATCH US!
I GUESS THE DEPARTMENT OWES YOU AN APOLOGY, YOUNG FELLER!
...AND I THINK THE BANK HAS A LITTLE REWARD WAITING FOR YOU, TOO!
COME ALONG!
OBOY!
NEXT DAY-
HI, FELLERS!
HI, TUB!
DID YOU GET YOUR REWARD YET, TUB?
YEP! FIVE HUNDRED DOLLARS! THE PRESIDENT GAVE IT TO ME THIS MORNING!
THE PRESIDENT, HIMSELF!
WOW!

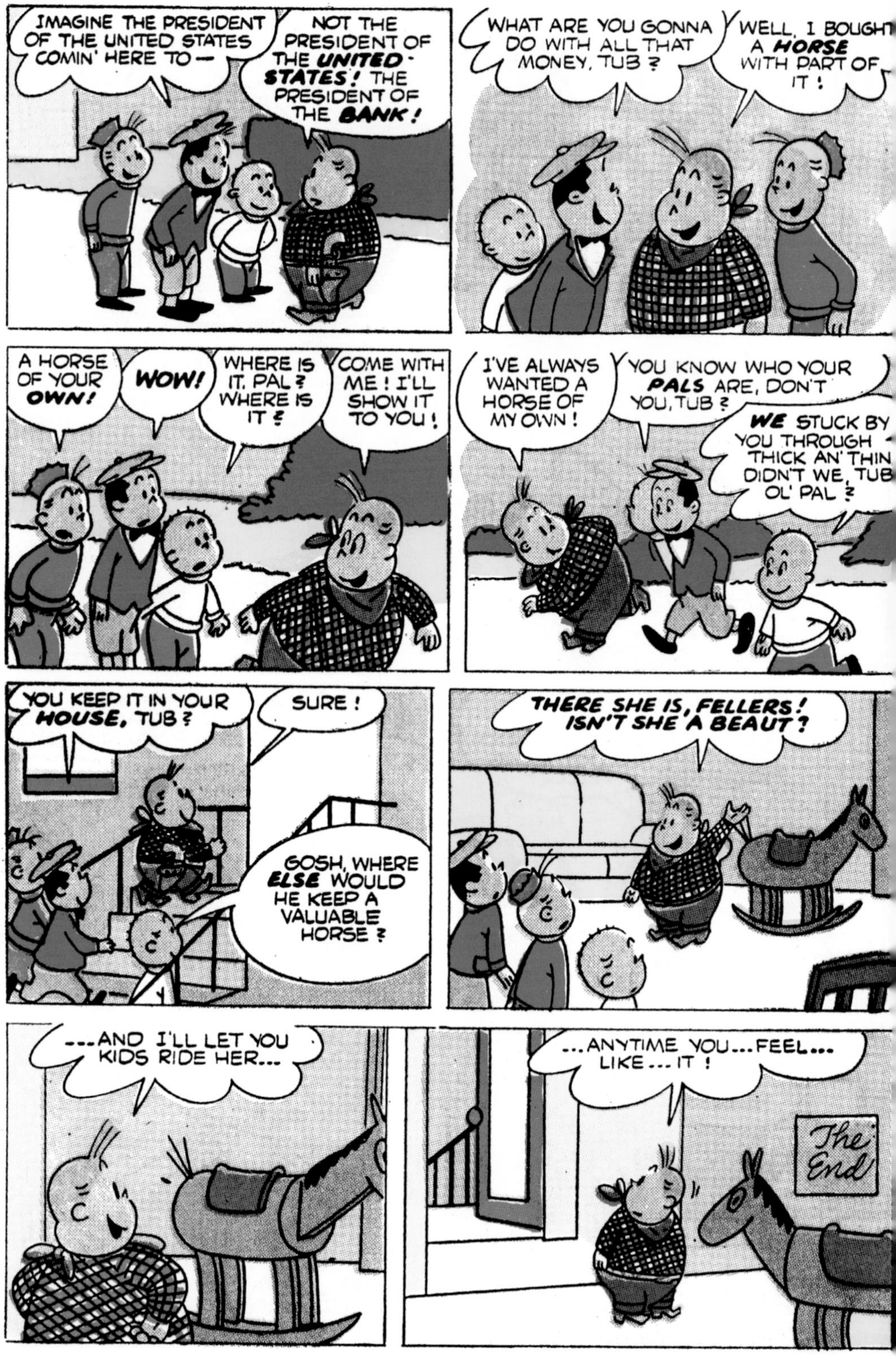
IMAGINE THE PRESIDENT OF THE UNITED STATES COMIN' HERE TO —
NOT THE PRESIDENT OF THE UNITED STATES! THE PRESIDENT OF THE BANK!
WHAT ARE YOU GONNA DO WITH ALL THAT MONEY, TUB?
WELL, I BOUGHT A HORSE WITH PART OF IT!
A HORSE OF YOUR OWN!
WOW!
WHERE IS IT, PAL? WHERE IS IT?
COME WITH ME! I'LL SHOW IT TO YOU!
I'VE ALWAYS WANTED A HORSE OF MY OWN!
YOU KNOW WHO YOUR PALS ARE, DON'T YOU, TUB?
WE STUCK BY YOU THROUGH THICK AN' THIN DIDN'T WE, TUB OL' PAL?
YOU KEEP IT IN YOUR HOUSE, TUB?
SURE!
GOSH, WHERE ELSE WOULD HE KEEP A VALUABLE HORSE?
THERE SHE IS, FELLERS! ISN'T SHE A BEAUT?
...AND I'LL LET YOU KIDS RIDE HER...
...ANYTIME YOU...FEEL... LIKE...IT!
The End

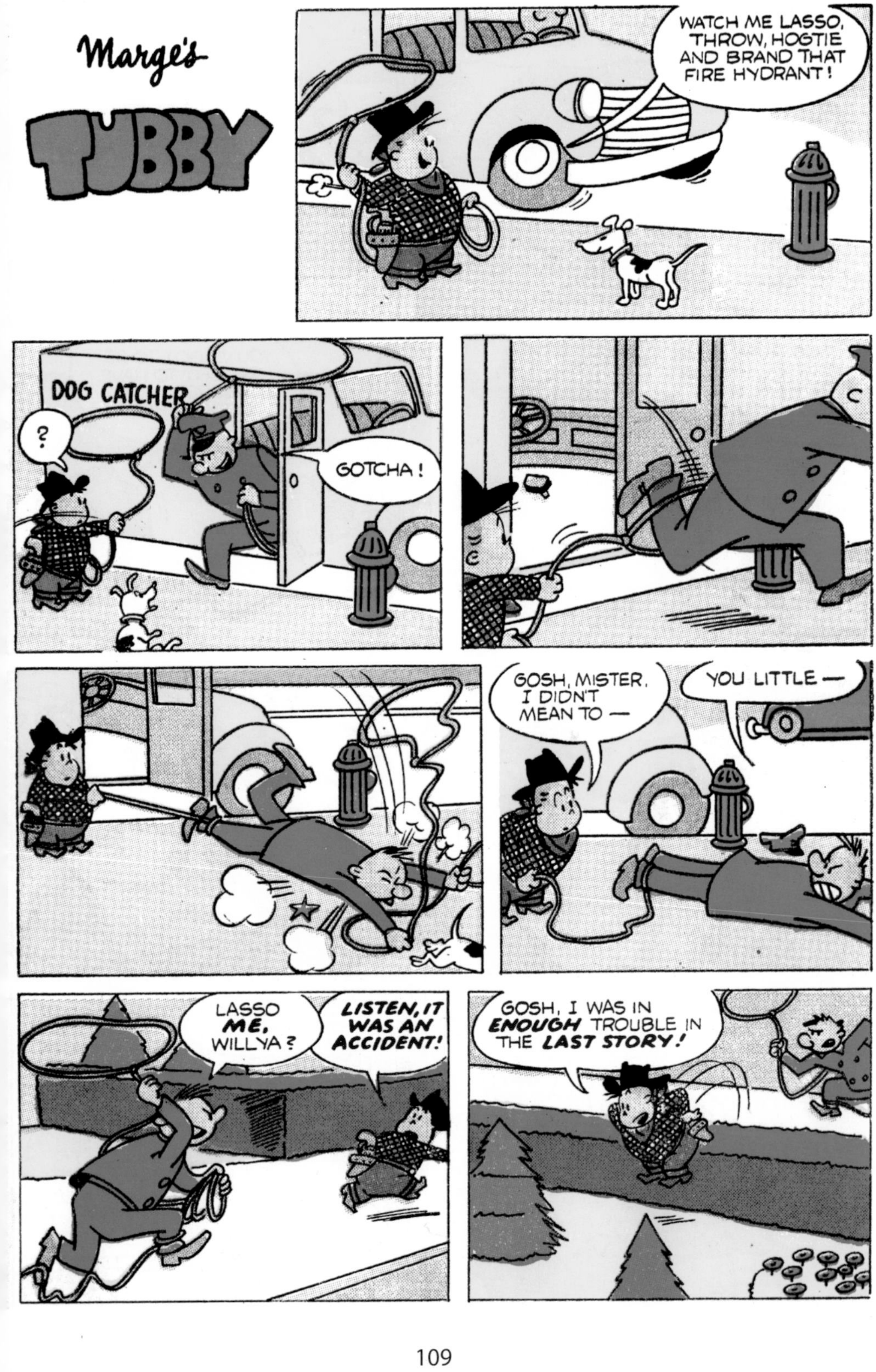
Marge's
TUBBY
WATCH ME LASSO, THROW, HOGTIE AND BRAND THAT FIRE HYDRANT!
DOG CATCHER
?
GOTCHA!
GOSH, MISTER, I DIDN'T MEAN TO —
YOU LITTLE —
LASSO ME, WILLYA?
LISTEN, IT WAS AN ACCIDENT!
GOSH, I WAS IN ENOUGH TROUBLE IN THE LAST STORY!

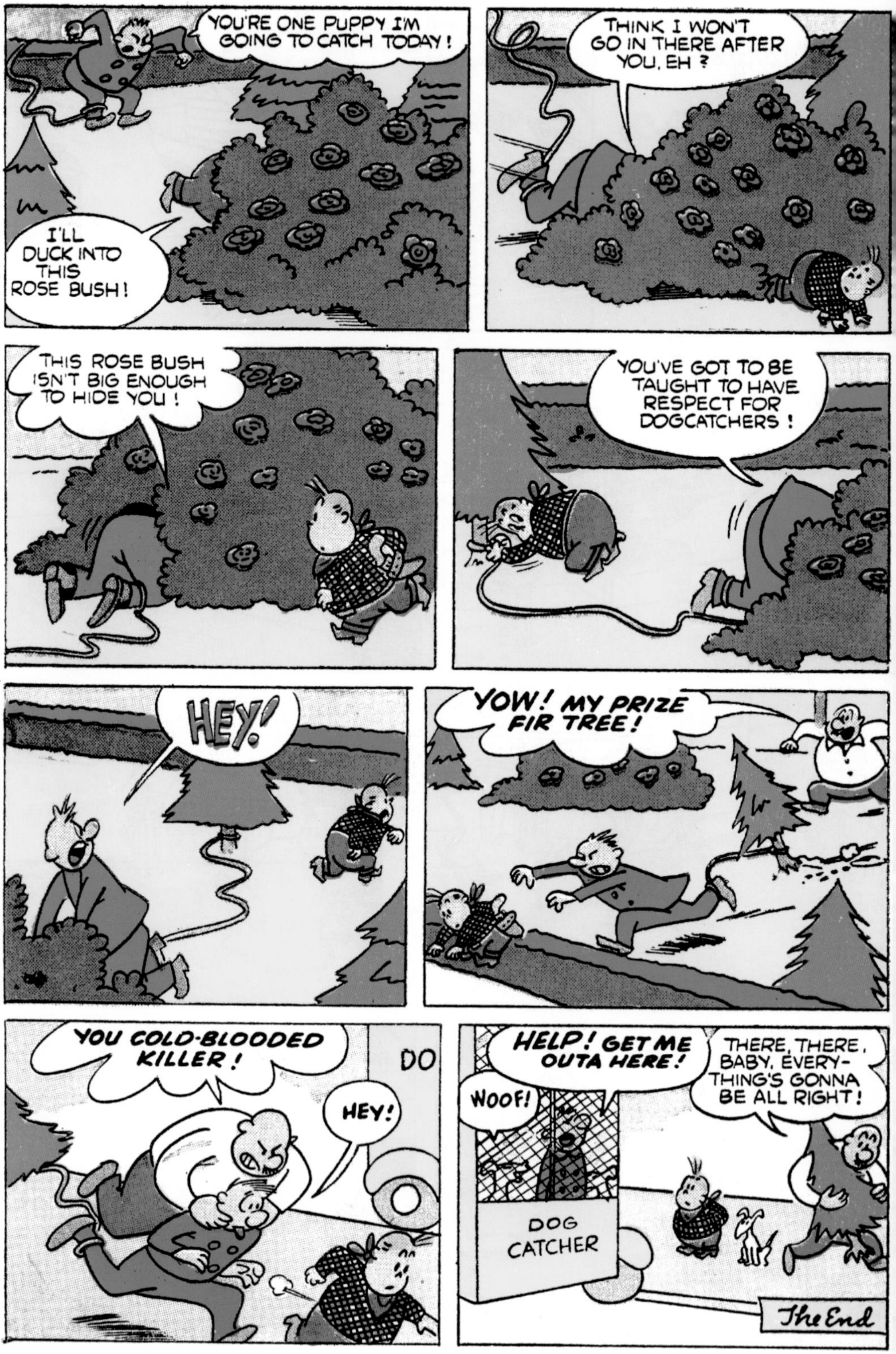
YOU'RE ONE PUPPY I'M GOING TO CATCH TODAY!
I'LL DUCK INTO THIS ROSE BUSH!
THINK I WON'T GO IN THERE AFTER YOU, EH ?
THIS ROSE BUSH ISN'T BIG ENOUGH TO HIDE YOU!
YOU'VE GOT TO BE TAUGHT TO HAVE RESPECT FOR DOGCATCHERS!
HEY!
YOW! MY PRIZE FIR TREE!
YOU COLD-BLOODED KILLER!
DO
HEY!
HELP! GET ME OUTA HERE!
WOOF!
THERE, THERE, BABY, EVERY-THING'S GONNA BE ALL RIGHT!
DOG CATCHER
The End

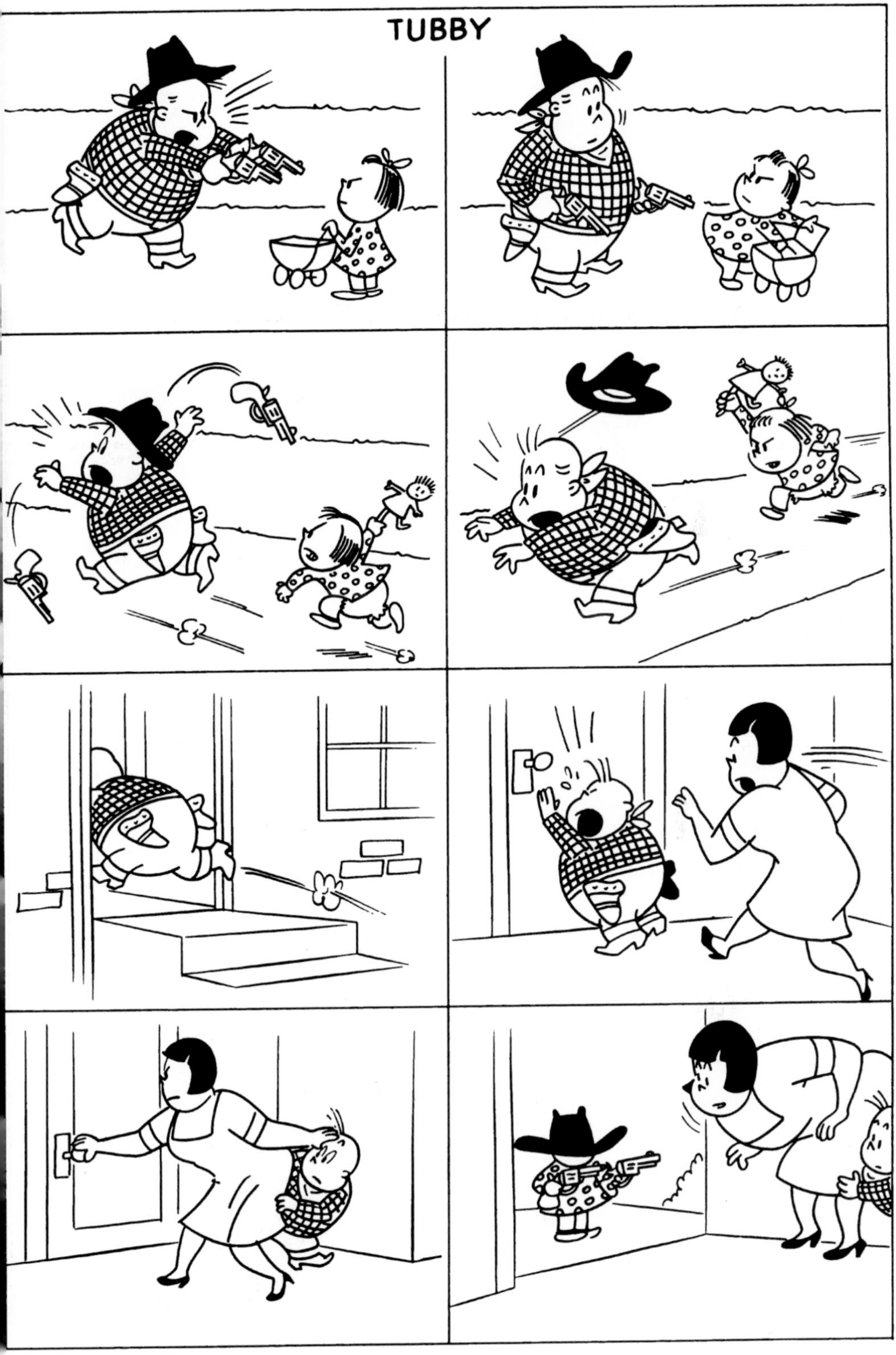
TUBBY

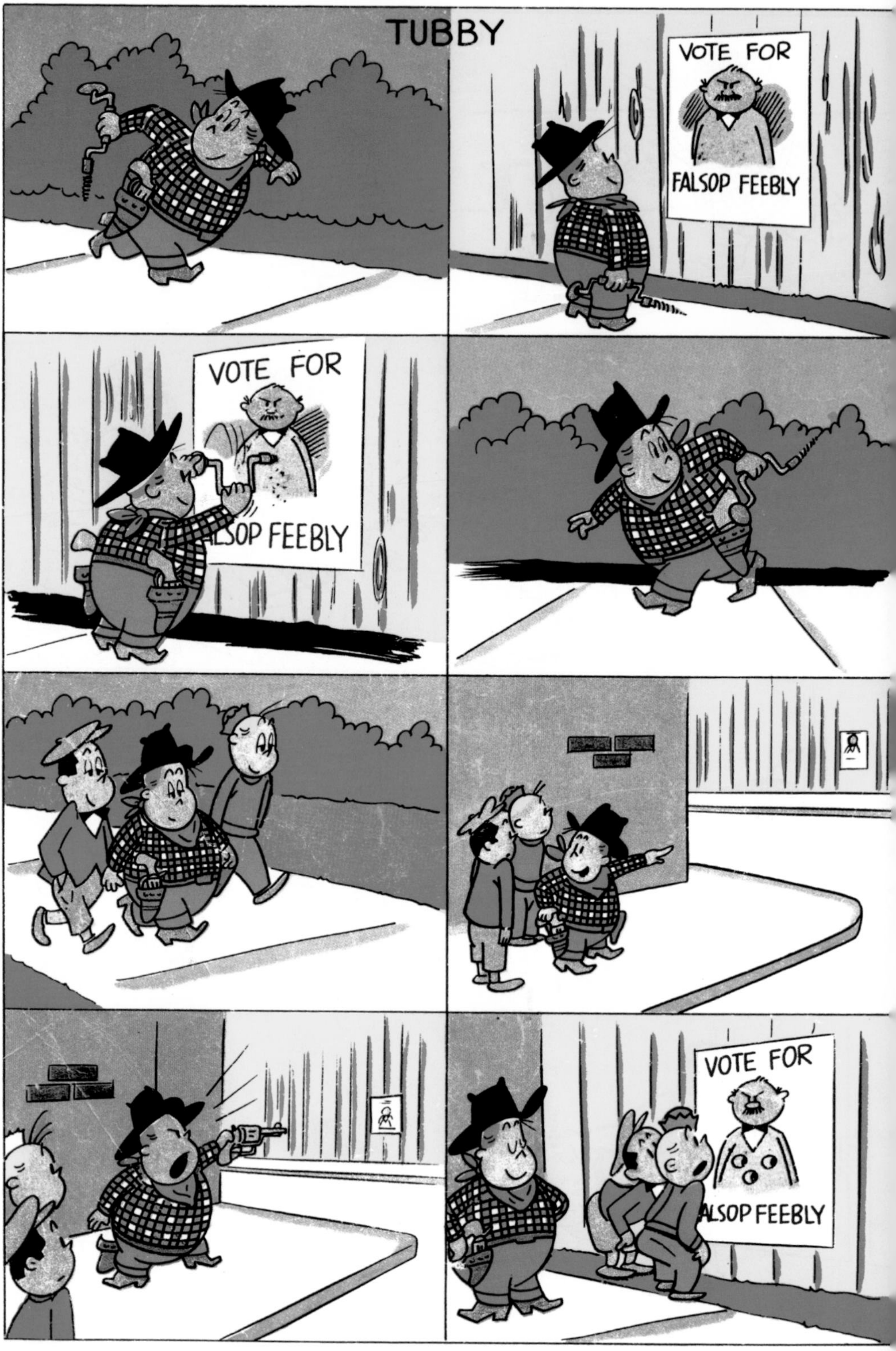
TUBBY
VOTE FOR
FALSOP FEEBLY
VOTE FOR
ALSOP FEEBLY
VOTE FOR
ALSOP FEEBLY

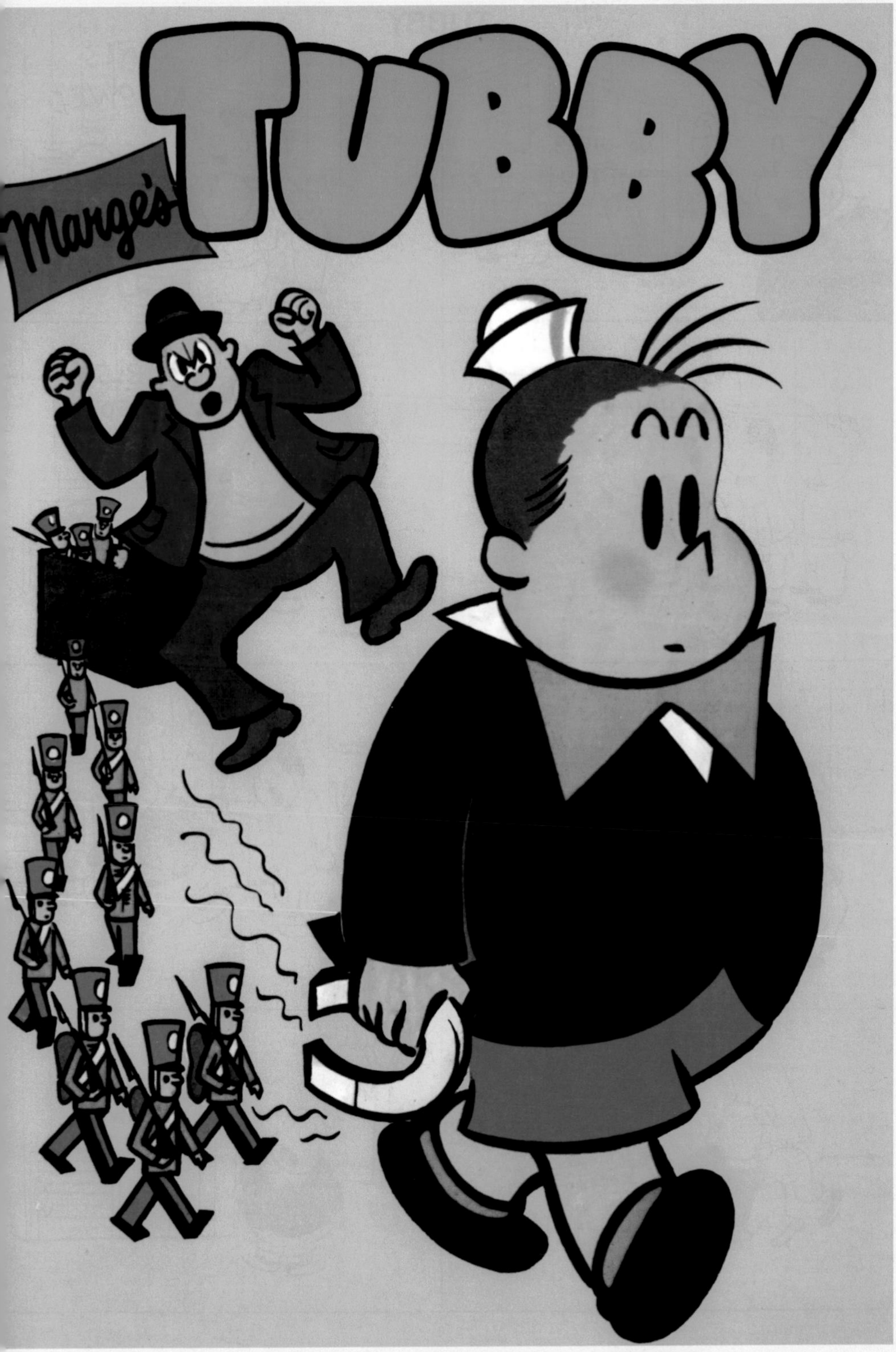
Marge's
TUBBY

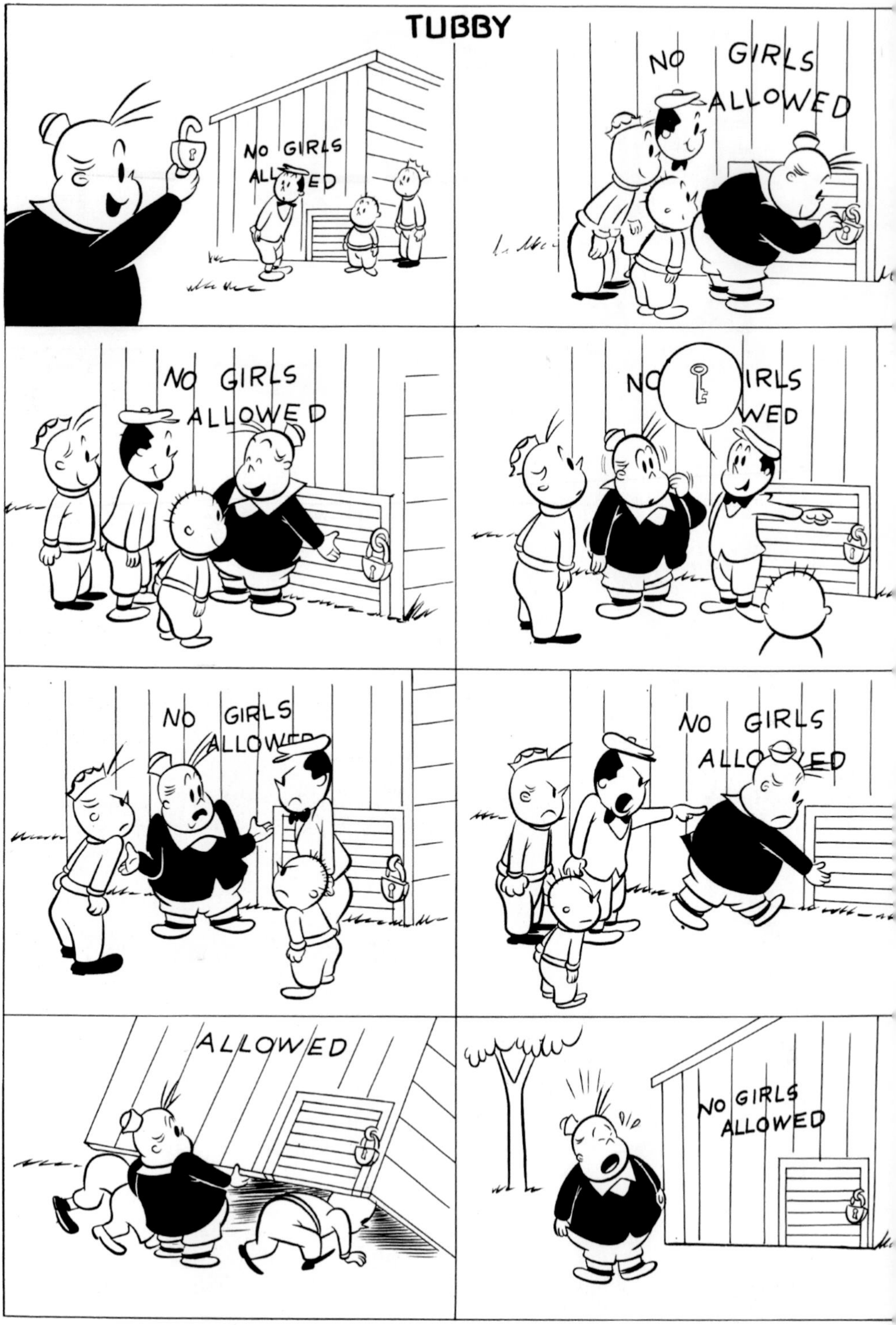
TUBBY
NO GIRLS ALLOWED
NO GIRLS ALLOWED
NO GIRLS ALLOWED
NO GIRLS ALLOWED
ALLOWED
NO GIRLS ALLOWED

marge's TUBBY

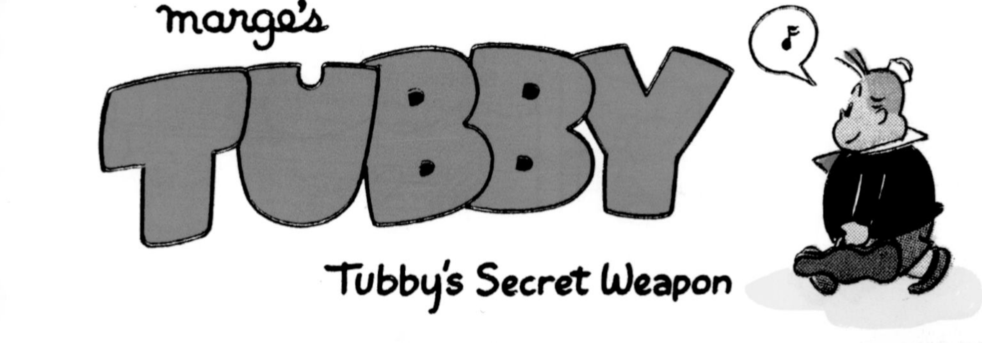

Tubby's Secret Weapon

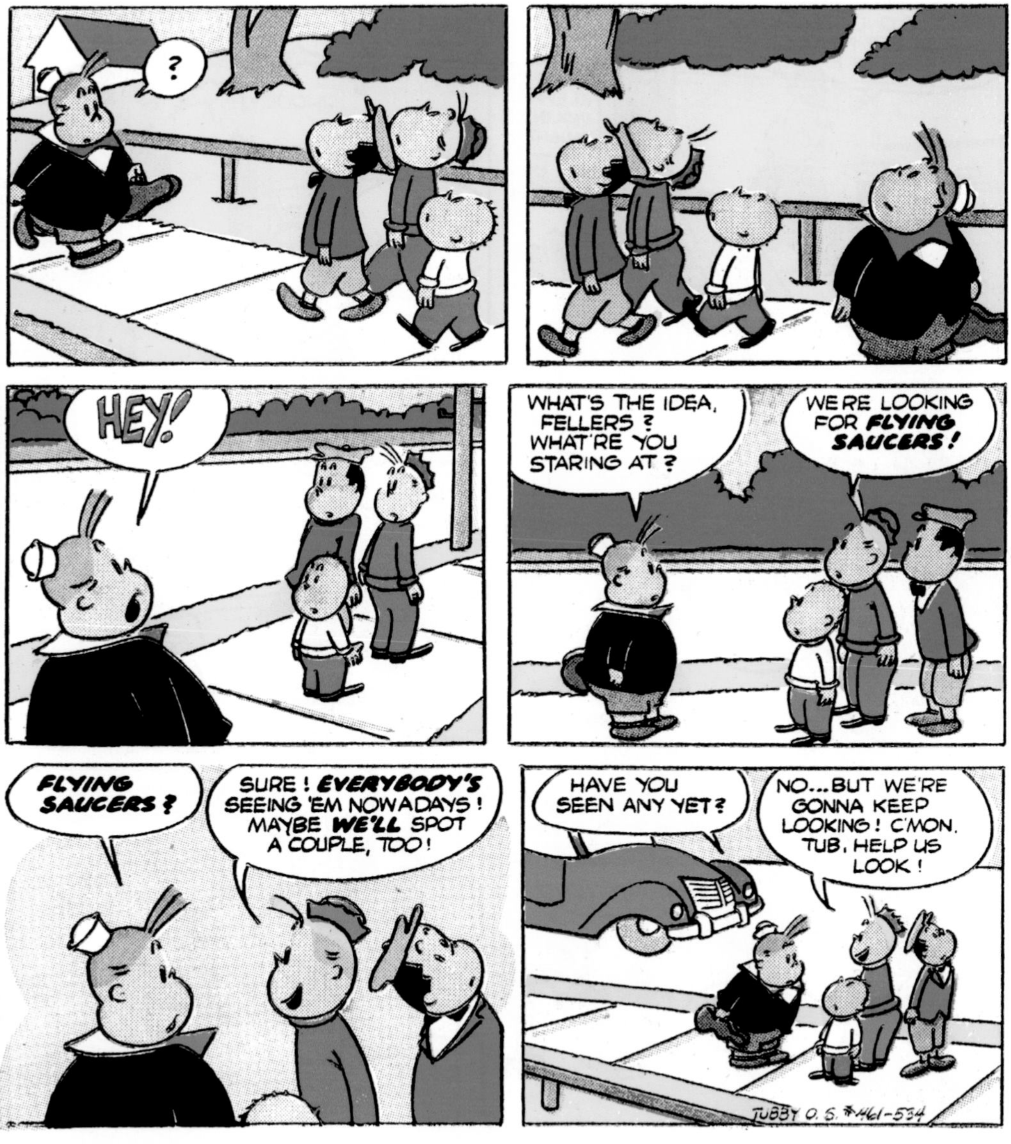
?
HEY!
WHAT'S THE IDEA, FELLERS? WHAT'RE YOU STARING AT?
WE'RE LOOKING FOR **FLYING SAUCERS!**
FLYING SAUCERS?
SURE! **EVERYBODY'S** SEEING 'EM NOWADAYS! MAYBE **WE'LL** SPOT A COUPLE, TOO!
HAVE YOU SEEN ANY YET?
NO...BUT WE'RE GONNA KEEP LOOKING! C'MON, TUB, HELP US LOOK!
TUBBY O.S. #461-534

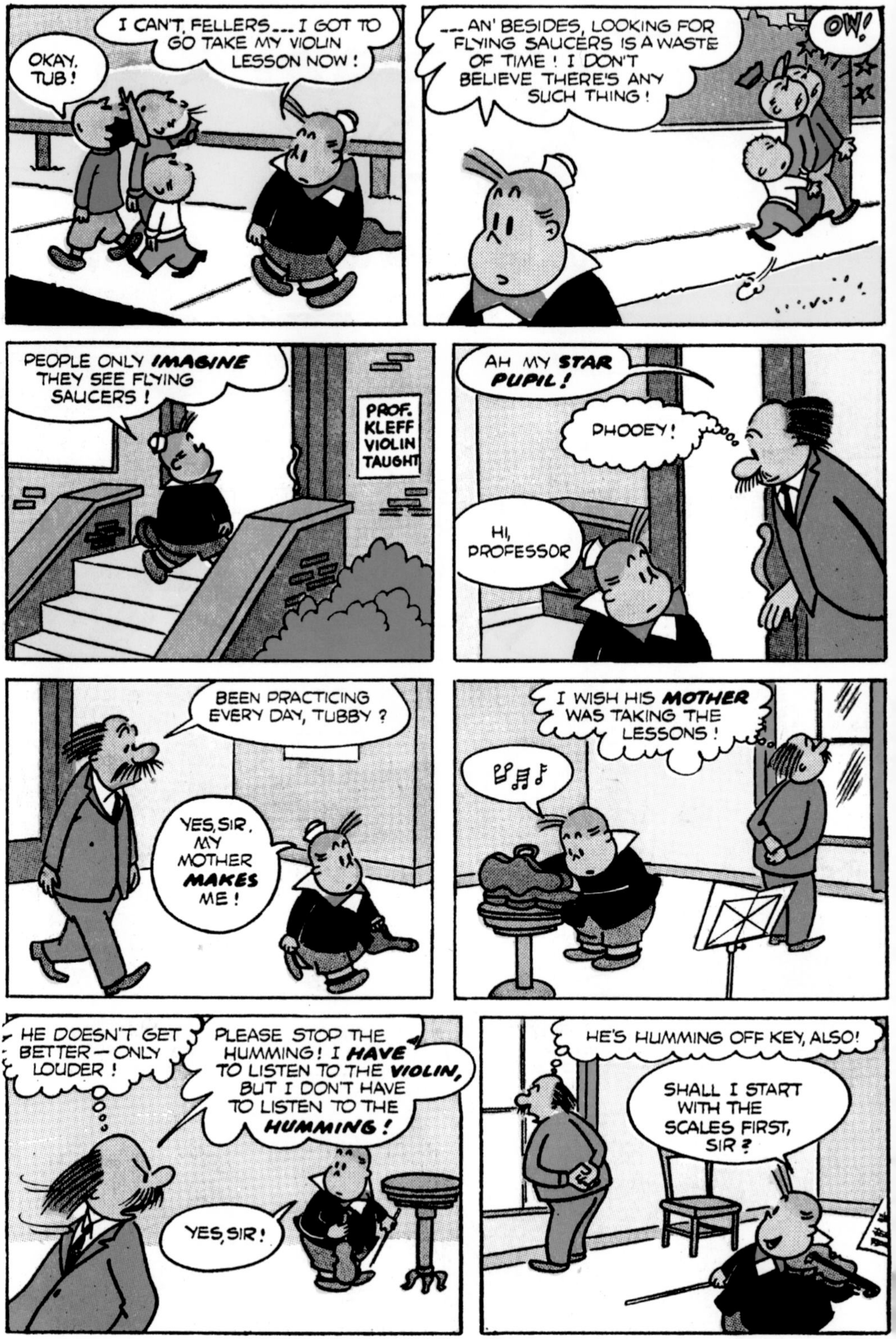

I CAN'T, FELLERS... I GOT TO GO TAKE MY VIOLIN LESSON NOW!
OKAY, TUB!
...AN' BESIDES, LOOKING FOR FLYING SAUCERS IS A WASTE OF TIME! I DON'T BELIEVE THERE'S ANY SUCH THING!
OW!
PEOPLE ONLY IMAGINE THEY SEE FLYING SAUCERS!
PROF. KLEFF VIOLIN TAUGHT
AH MY STAR PUPIL!
PHOOEY!
HI, PROFESSOR
BEEN PRACTICING EVERY DAY, TUBBY?
YES, SIR, MY MOTHER MAKES ME!
I WISH HIS MOTHER WAS TAKING THE LESSONS!
HE DOESN'T GET BETTER—ONLY LOUDER!
PLEASE STOP THE HUMMING! I HAVE TO LISTEN TO THE VIOLIN, BUT I DON'T HAVE TO LISTEN TO THE HUMMING!
YES, SIR!
HE'S HUMMING OFF KEY, ALSO!
SHALL I START WITH THE SCALES FIRST, SIR?

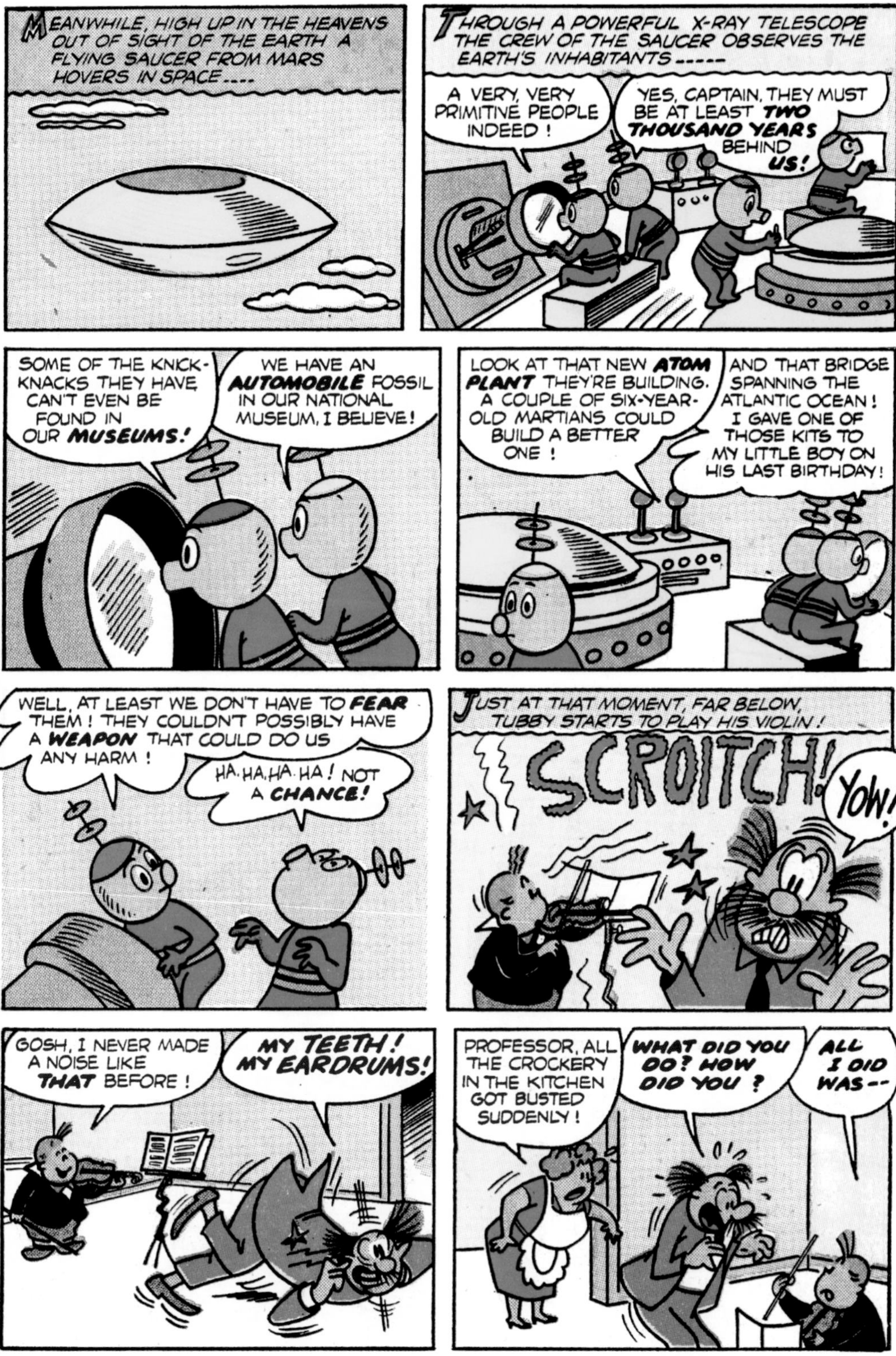
MEANWHILE, HIGH UP IN THE HEAVENS OUT OF SIGHT OF THE EARTH A FLYING SAUCER FROM MARS HOVERS IN SPACE----
THROUGH A POWERFUL X-RAY TELESCOPE THE CREW OF THE SAUCER OBSERVES THE EARTH'S INHABITANTS-----
A VERY, VERY PRIMITIVE PEOPLE INDEED!
YES, CAPTAIN, THEY MUST BE AT LEAST TWO THOUSAND YEARS BEHIND US!
SOME OF THE KNICK-KNACKS THEY HAVE CAN'T EVEN BE FOUND IN OUR MUSEUMS!
WE HAVE AN AUTOMOBILE FOSSIL IN OUR NATIONAL MUSEUM, I BELIEVE!
LOOK AT THAT NEW ATOM PLANT THEY'RE BUILDING. A COUPLE OF SIX-YEAR-OLD MARTIANS COULD BUILD A BETTER ONE!
AND THAT BRIDGE SPANNING THE ATLANTIC OCEAN! I GAVE ONE OF THOSE KITS TO MY LITTLE BOY ON HIS LAST BIRTHDAY!
WELL, AT LEAST WE DON'T HAVE TO FEAR THEM! THEY COULDN'T POSSIBLY HAVE A WEAPON THAT COULD DO US ANY HARM!
HA.HA.HA.HA! NOT A CHANCE!
JUST AT THAT MOMENT, FAR BELOW, TUBBY STARTS TO PLAY HIS VIOLIN!
SCROITCH!
YOW!
GOSH, I NEVER MADE A NOISE LIKE THAT BEFORE!
MY TEETH! MY EARDRUMS!
PROFESSOR, ALL THE CROCKERY IN THE KITCHEN GOT BUSTED SUDDENLY!
WHAT DID YOU DO? HOW DID YOU?
ALL I DID WAS--

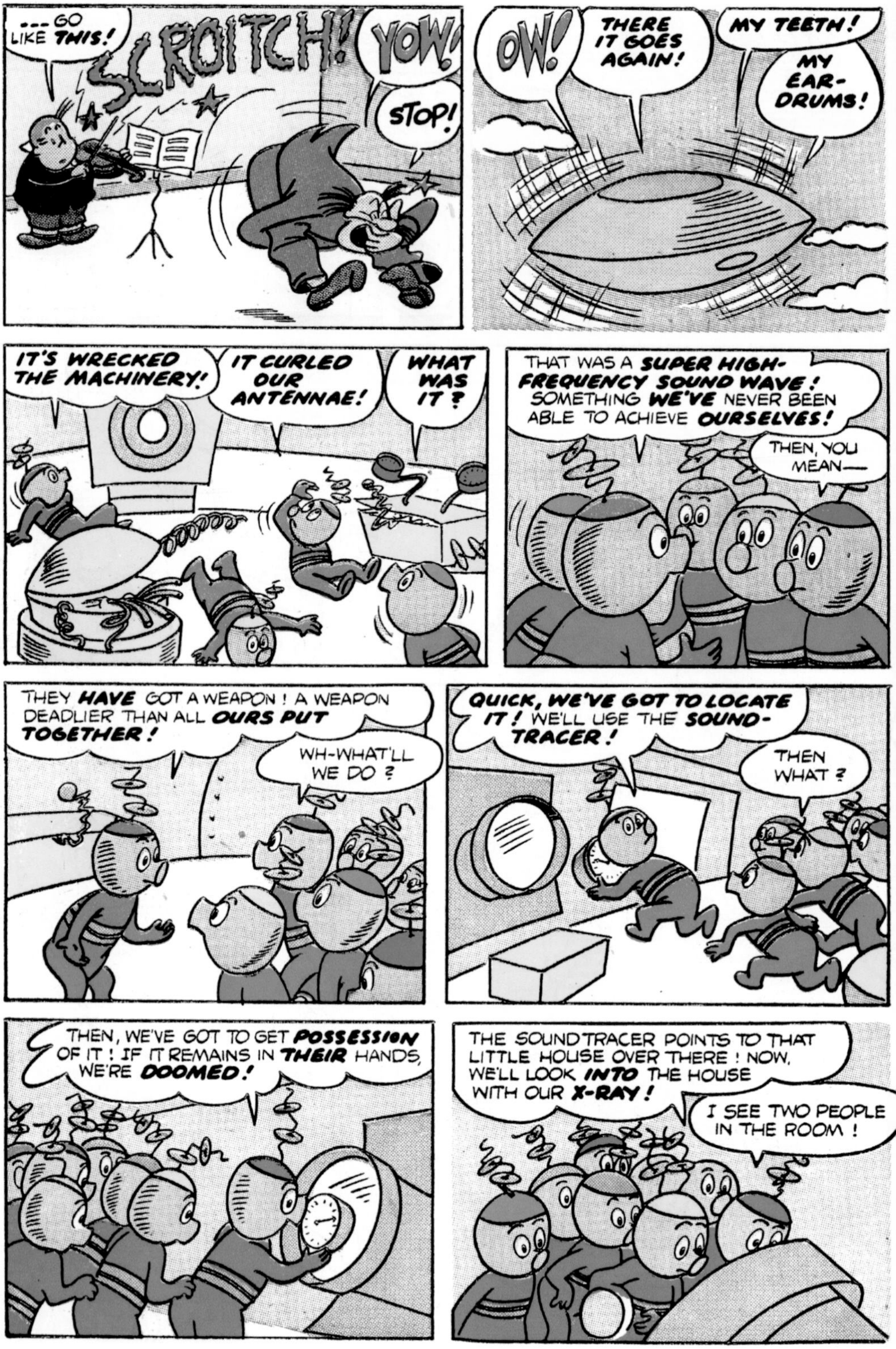

...GO LIKE THIS!
SCROITCH!
YOW!
STOP!
OW!
THERE IT GOES AGAIN!
MY TEETH!
MY EAR-DRUMS!
IT'S WRECKED THE MACHINERY!
IT CURLED OUR ANTENNAE!
WHAT WAS IT?
THAT WAS A SUPER HIGH-FREQUENCY SOUND WAVE! SOMETHING WE'VE NEVER BEEN ABLE TO ACHIEVE OURSELVES!
THEN, YOU MEAN—
THEY HAVE GOT A WEAPON! A WEAPON DEADLIER THAN ALL OURS PUT TOGETHER!
WH-WHAT'LL WE DO?
QUICK, WE'VE GOT TO LOCATE IT! WE'LL USE THE SOUND-TRACER!
THEN WHAT?
THEN, WE'VE GOT TO GET POSSESSION OF IT! IF IT REMAINS IN THEIR HANDS, WE'RE DOOMED!
THE SOUND TRACER POINTS TO THAT LITTLE HOUSE OVER THERE! NOW, WE'LL LOOK INTO THE HOUSE WITH OUR X-RAY!
I SEE TWO PEOPLE IN THE ROOM!

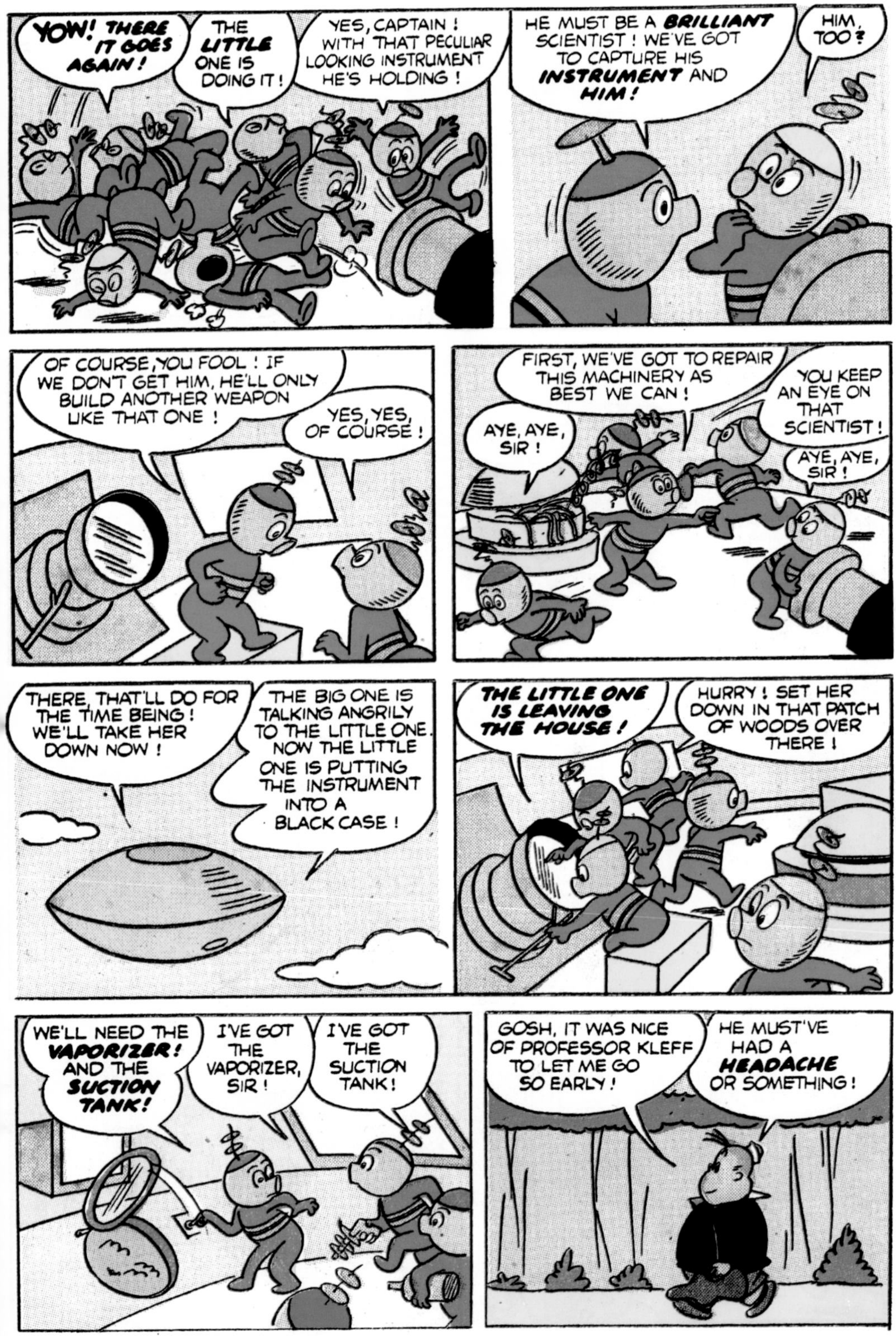
YOW! THERE IT GOES AGAIN!
THE LITTLE ONE IS DOING IT!
YES, CAPTAIN! WITH THAT PECULIAR LOOKING INSTRUMENT HE'S HOLDING!
HE MUST BE A BRILLIANT SCIENTIST! WE'VE GOT TO CAPTURE HIS INSTRUMENT AND HIM!
HIM, TOO?
OF COURSE, YOU FOOL! IF WE DON'T GET HIM, HE'LL ONLY BUILD ANOTHER WEAPON LIKE THAT ONE!
YES, YES, OF COURSE!
FIRST, WE'VE GOT TO REPAIR THIS MACHINERY AS BEST WE CAN!
AYE, AYE, SIR!
YOU KEEP AN EYE ON THAT SCIENTIST!
AYE, AYE, SIR!
THERE, THAT'LL DO FOR THE TIME BEING! WE'LL TAKE HER DOWN NOW!
THE BIG ONE IS TALKING ANGRILY TO THE LITTLE ONE. NOW THE LITTLE ONE IS PUTTING THE INSTRUMENT INTO A BLACK CASE!
THE LITTLE ONE IS LEAVING THE HOUSE!
HURRY! SET HER DOWN IN THAT PATCH OF WOODS OVER THERE!
WE'LL NEED THE VAPORIZER! AND THE SUCTION TANK!
I'VE GOT THE VAPORIZER, SIR!
I'VE GOT THE SUCTION TANK!
GOSH, IT WAS NICE OF PROFESSOR KLEFF TO LET ME GO SO EARLY!
HE MUST'VE HAD A HEADACHE OR SOMETHING!

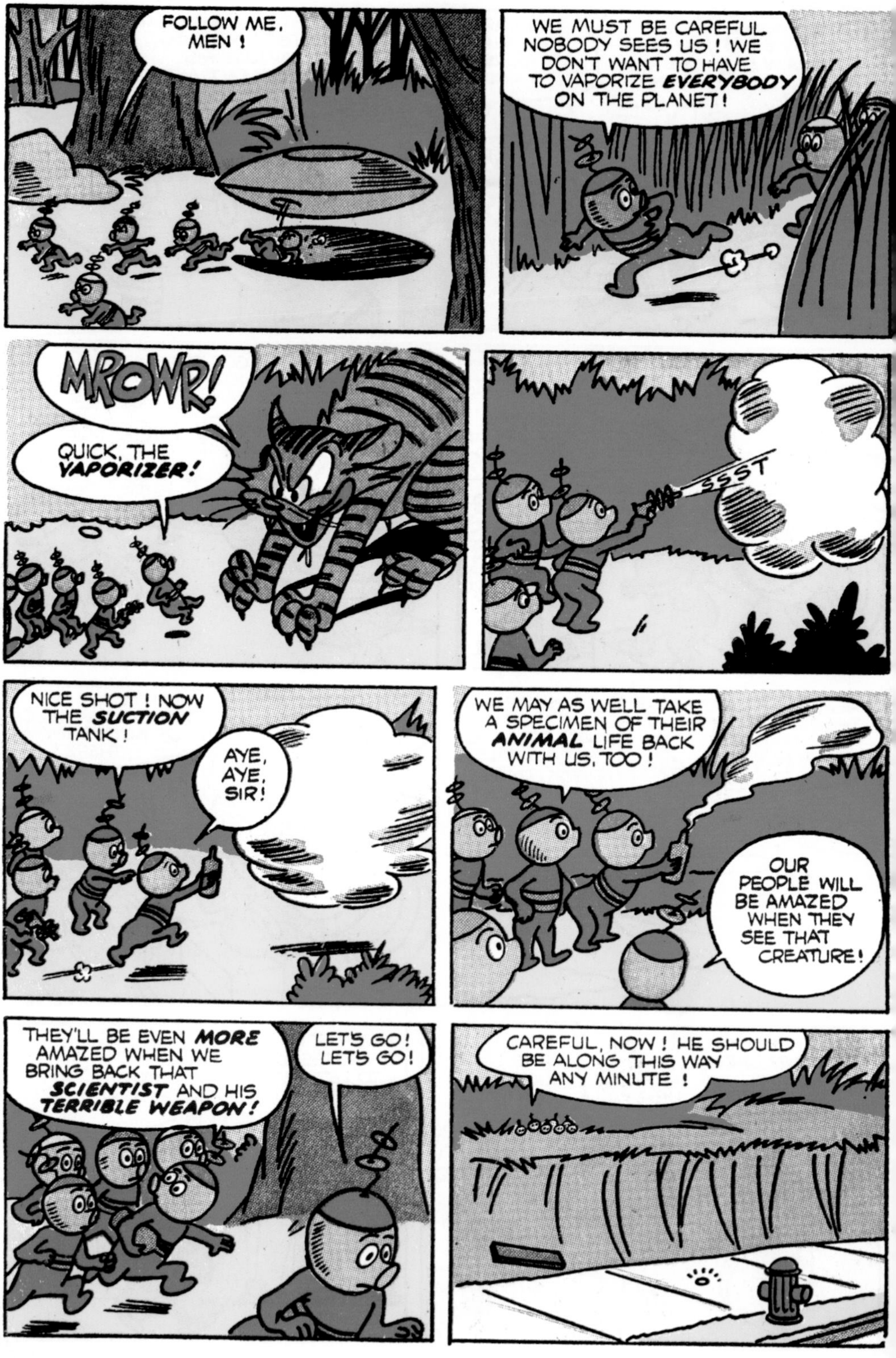
FOLLOW ME, MEN !
WE MUST BE CAREFUL NOBODY SEES US ! WE DON'T WANT TO HAVE TO VAPORIZE EVERYBODY ON THE PLANET !
MROWR!
QUICK, THE VAPORIZER!
SSST
NICE SHOT ! NOW THE SUCTION TANK !
AYE, AYE, SIR!
WE MAY AS WELL TAKE A SPECIMEN OF THEIR ANIMAL LIFE BACK WITH US, TOO !
OUR PEOPLE WILL BE AMAZED WHEN THEY SEE THAT CREATURE!
THEY'LL BE EVEN MORE AMAZED WHEN WE BRING BACK THAT SCIENTIST AND HIS TERRIBLE WEAPON!
LET'S GO! LET'S GO!
CAREFUL, NOW ! HE SHOULD BE ALONG THIS WAY ANY MINUTE !

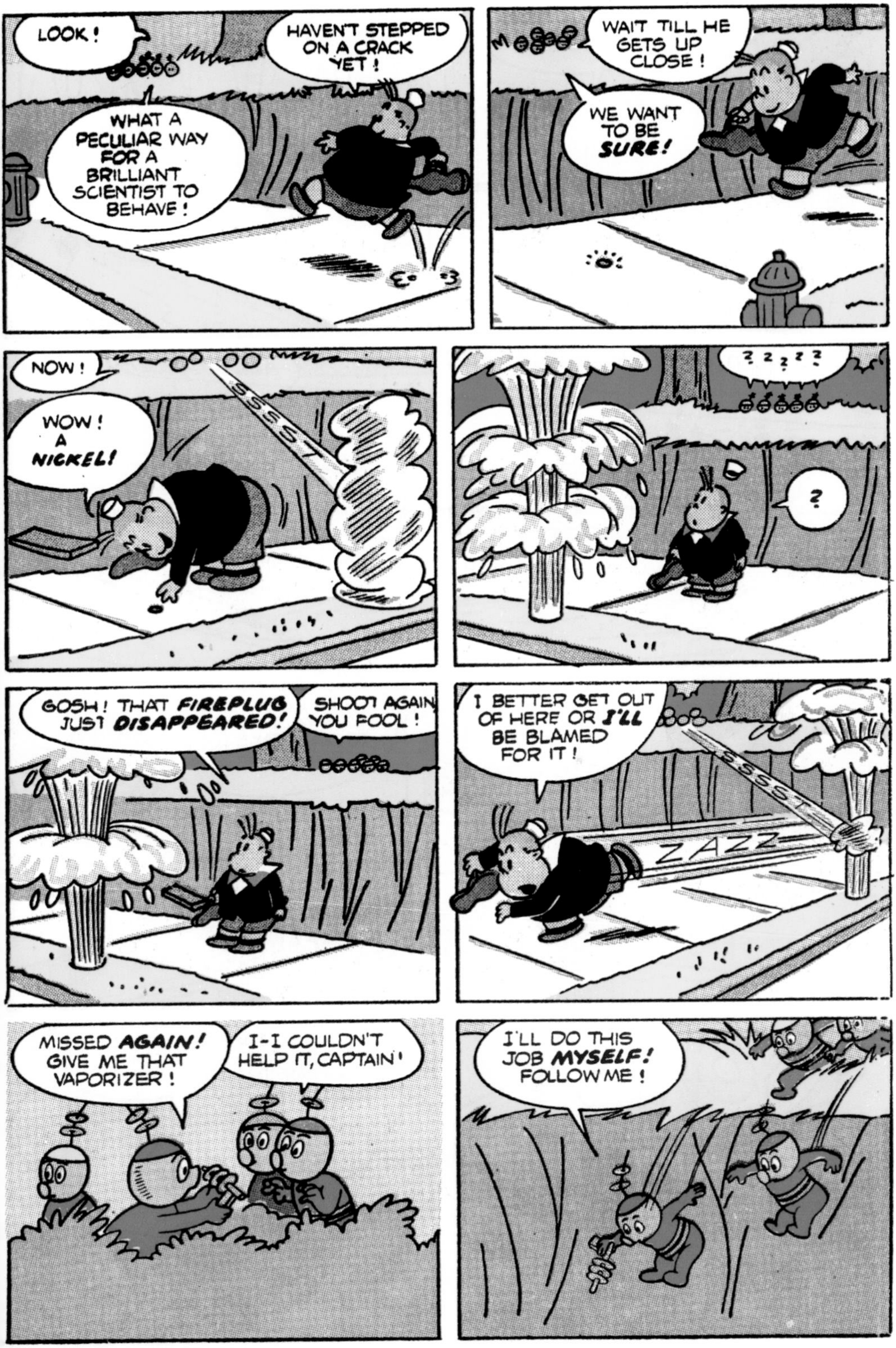
LOOK!
HAVEN'T STEPPED ON A CRACK YET!
WHAT A PECULIAR WAY FOR A BRILLIANT SCIENTIST TO BEHAVE!
WAIT TILL HE GETS UP CLOSE!
WE WANT TO BE SURE!
NOW!
WOW! A NICKEL!
SSSST
?
GOSH! THAT FIREPLUG JUST DISAPPEARED!
SHOOT AGAIN YOU FOOL!
I BETTER GET OUT OF HERE OR I'LL BE BLAMED FOR IT!
SSSST
ZAZZ
MISSED AGAIN! GIVE ME THAT VAPORIZER!
I-I COULDN'T HELP IT, CAPTAIN!
I'LL DO THIS JOB MYSELF! FOLLOW ME!

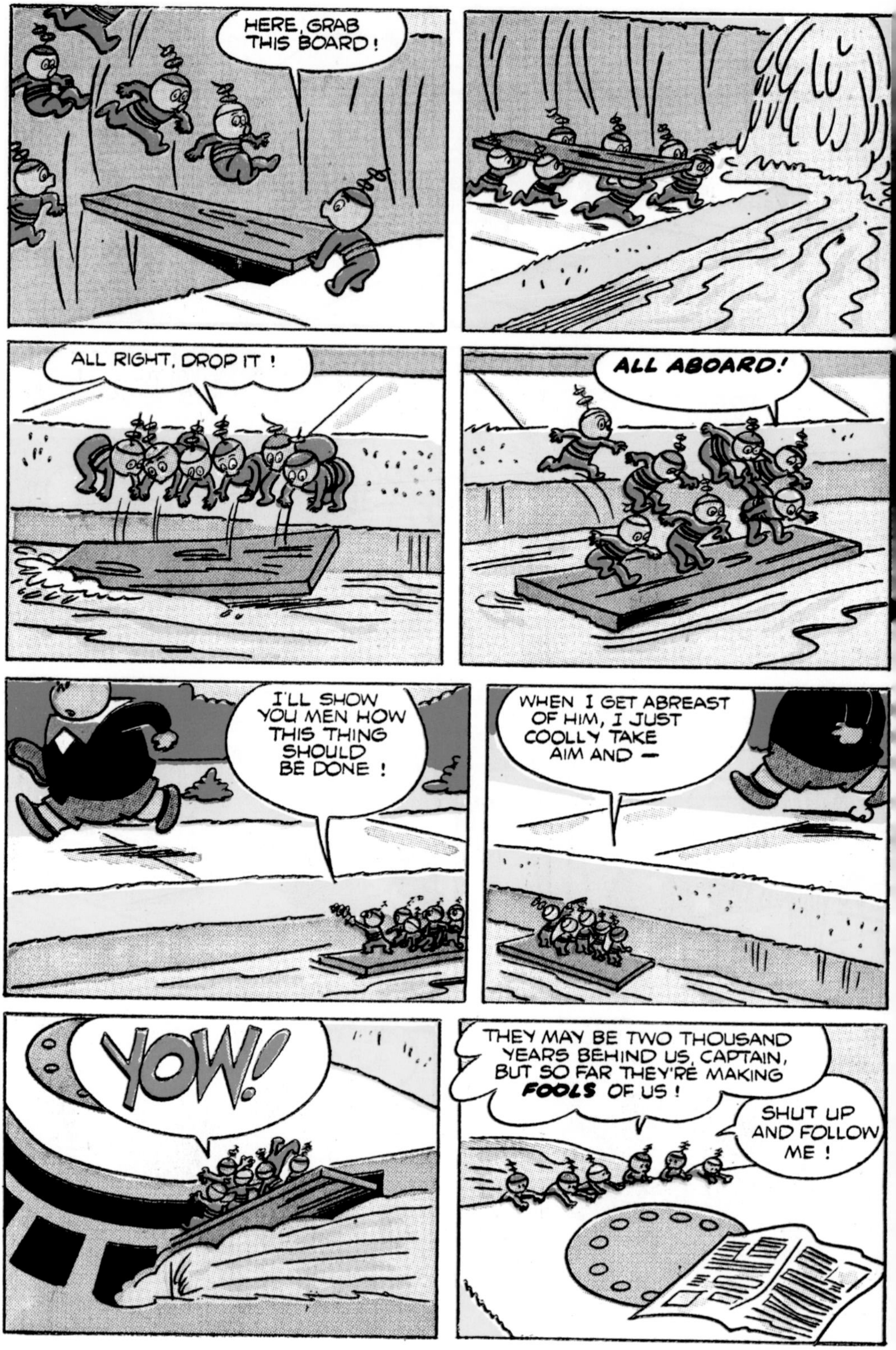
HERE, GRAB THIS BOARD!
ALL RIGHT, DROP IT!
ALL ABOARD!
I'LL SHOW YOU MEN HOW THIS THING SHOULD BE DONE!
WHEN I GET ABREAST OF HIM, I JUST COOLLY TAKE AIM AND —
YOW!
THEY MAY BE TWO THOUSAND YEARS BEHIND US, CAPTAIN, BUT SO FAR THEY'RE MAKING FOOLS OF US!
SHUT UP AND FOLLOW ME!

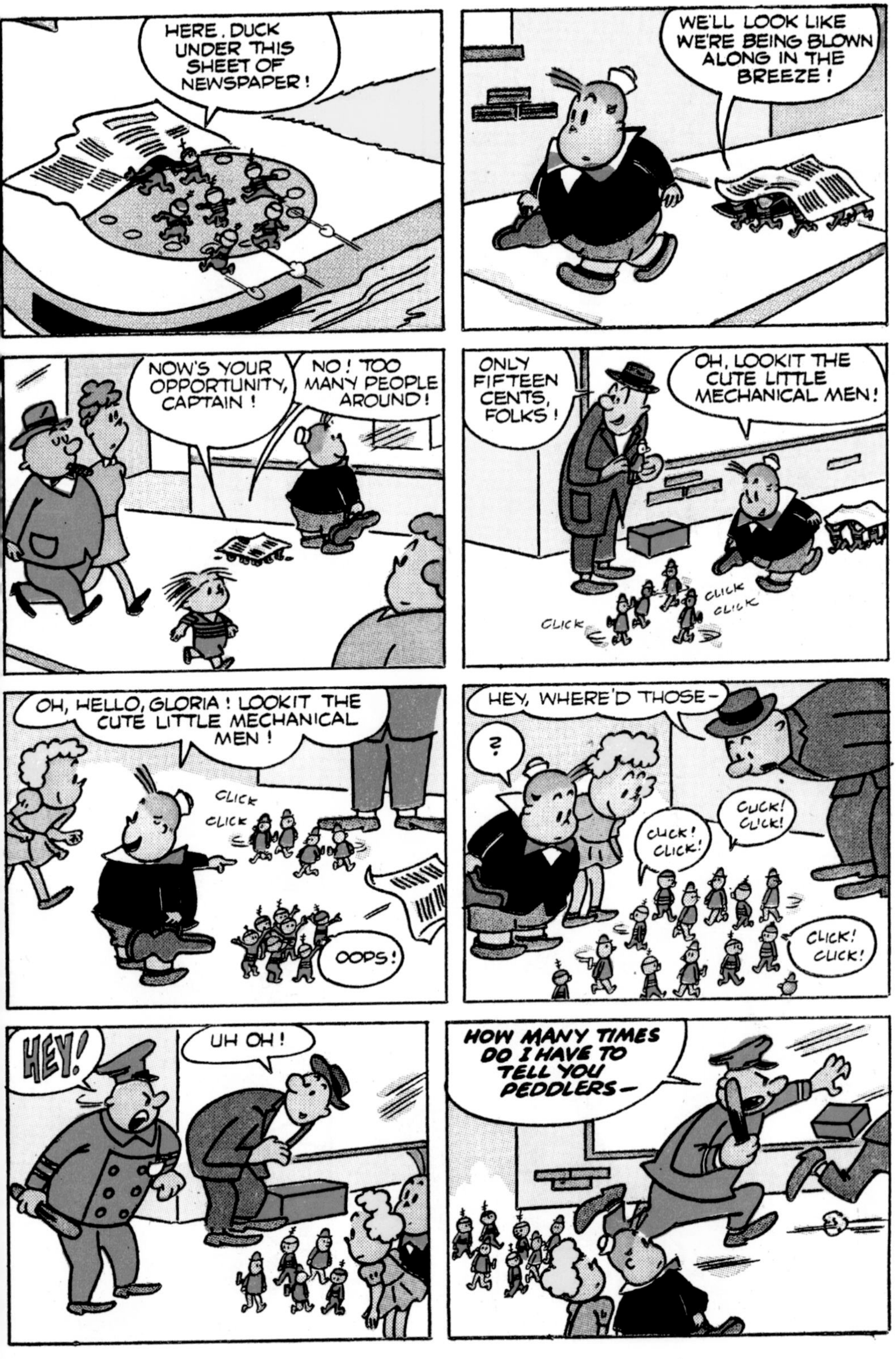
HERE. DUCK UNDER THIS SHEET OF NEWSPAPER!
WE'LL LOOK LIKE WE'RE BEING BLOWN ALONG IN THE BREEZE!
NOW'S YOUR OPPORTUNITY, CAPTAIN!
NO! TOO MANY PEOPLE AROUND!
ONLY FIFTEEN CENTS, FOLKS!
OH, LOOKIT THE CUTE LITTLE MECHANICAL MEN!
CLICK
CLICK
CLICK
OH, HELLO, GLORIA! LOOKIT THE CUTE LITTLE MECHANICAL MEN!
CLICK
CLICK
OOPS!
HEY, WHERE'D THOSE—
?
CLICK! CLICK!
CLICK! CLICK!
CLICK! CLICK!
HEY!
UH OH!
HOW MANY TIMES DO I HAVE TO TELL YOU PEDDLERS—

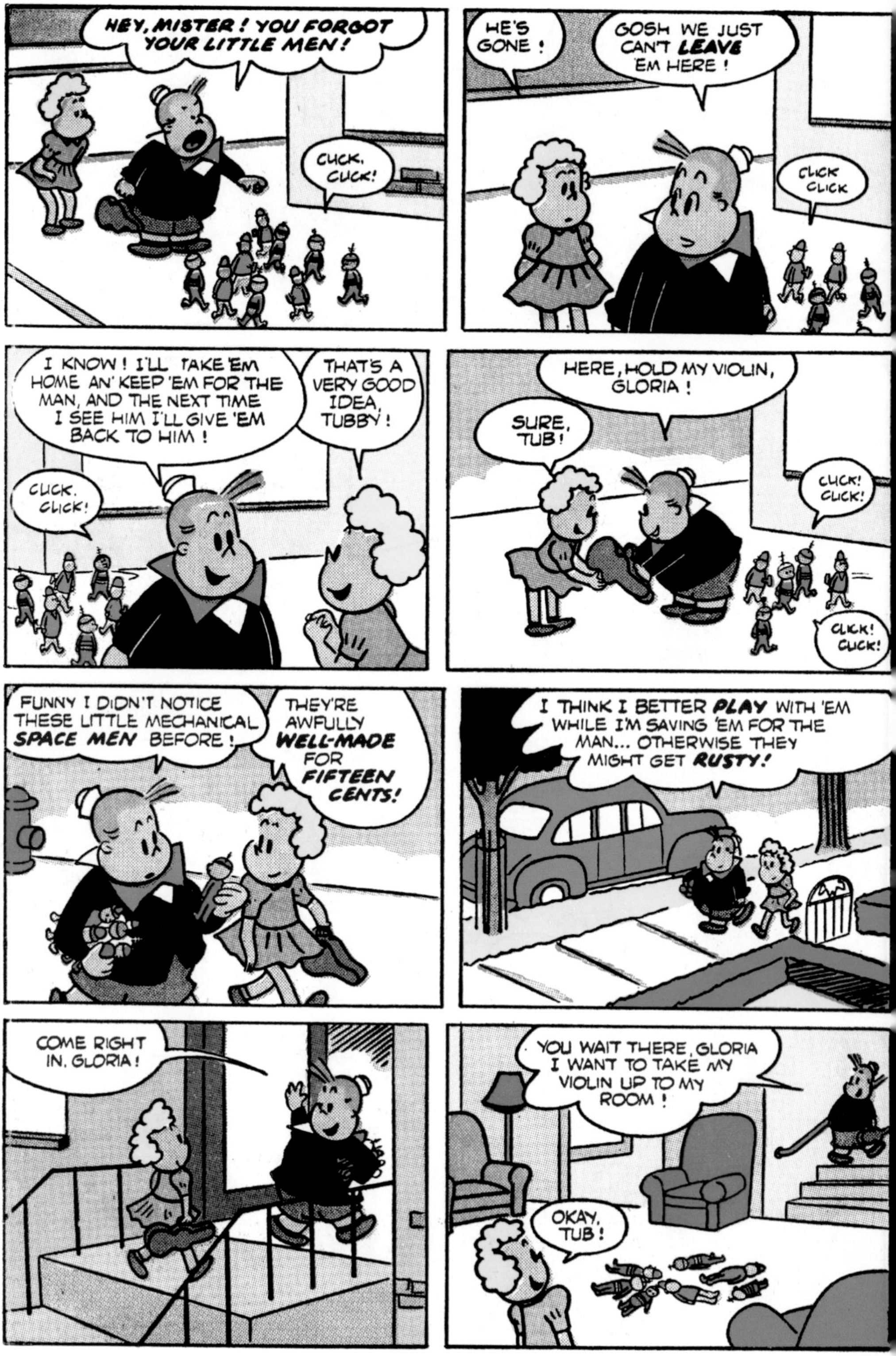
HEY, MISTER! YOU FORGOT YOUR LITTLE MEN!
CLICK, CLICK!
HE'S GONE!
GOSH WE JUST CAN'T LEAVE 'EM HERE!
CLICK CLICK
I KNOW! I'LL TAKE 'EM HOME AN' KEEP 'EM FOR THE MAN, AND THE NEXT TIME I SEE HIM I'LL GIVE 'EM BACK TO HIM!
THAT'S A VERY GOOD IDEA, TUBBY!
CLICK. CLICK!
HERE, HOLD MY VIOLIN, GLORIA!
SURE, TUB!
CLICK! CLICK!
CLICK! CLICK!
FUNNY I DIDN'T NOTICE THESE LITTLE MECHANICAL SPACE MEN BEFORE!
THEY'RE AWFULLY WELL-MADE FOR FIFTEEN CENTS!
I THINK I BETTER PLAY WITH 'EM WHILE I'M SAVING 'EM FOR THE MAN... OTHERWISE THEY MIGHT GET RUSTY!
COME RIGHT IN, GLORIA!
YOU WAIT THERE, GLORIA I WANT TO TAKE MY VIOLIN UP TO MY ROOM!
OKAY, TUB!

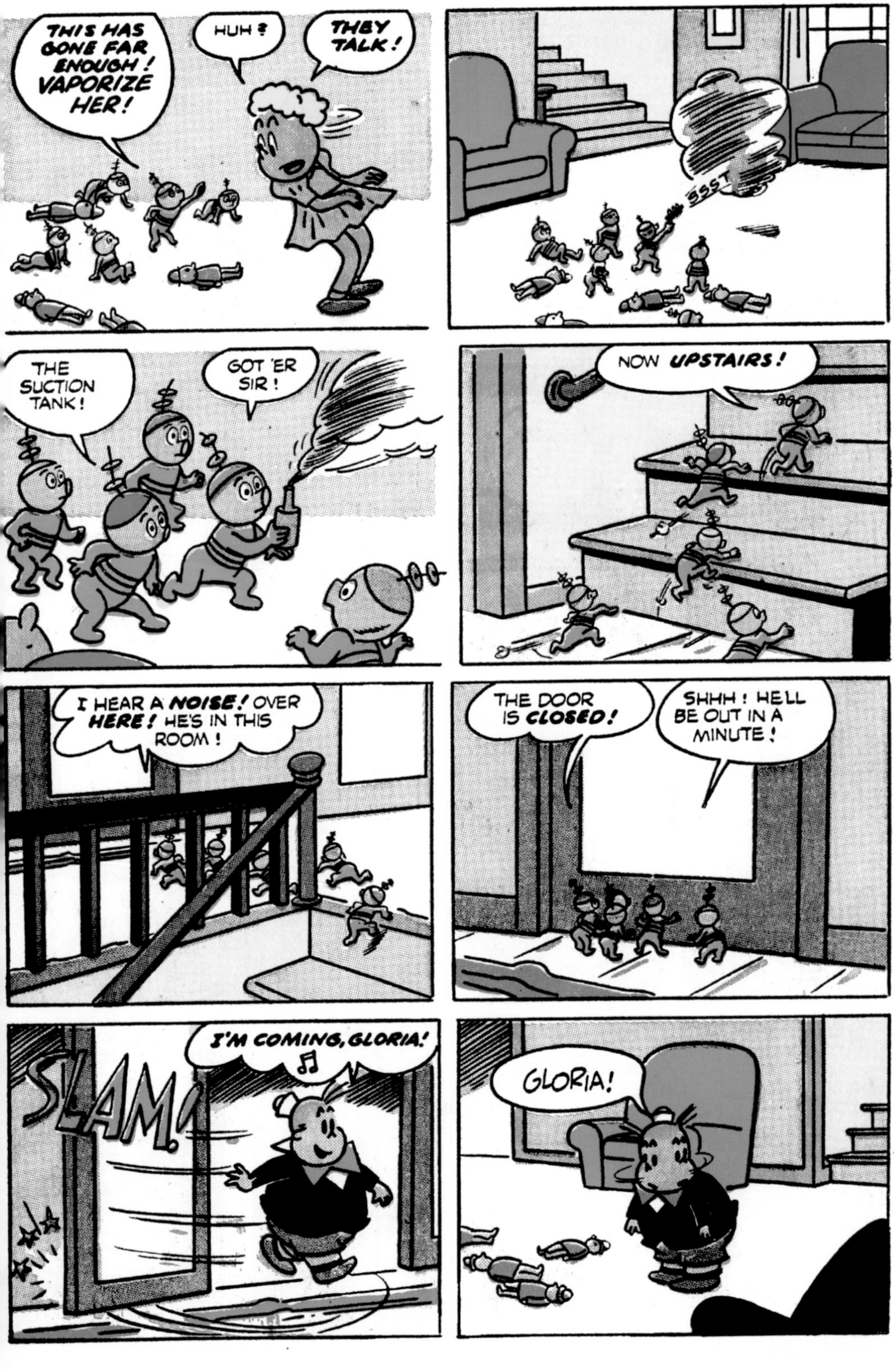
THIS HAS GONE FAR ENOUGH! VAPORIZE HER!
HUH?
THEY TALK!
SSST
THE SUCTION TANK!
GOT 'ER SIR!
NOW UPSTAIRS!
I HEAR A NOISE! OVER HERE! HE'S IN THIS ROOM!
THE DOOR IS CLOSED!
SHHH! HELL BE OUT IN A MINUTE!
SLAM!
I'M COMING, GLORIA!
GLORIA!

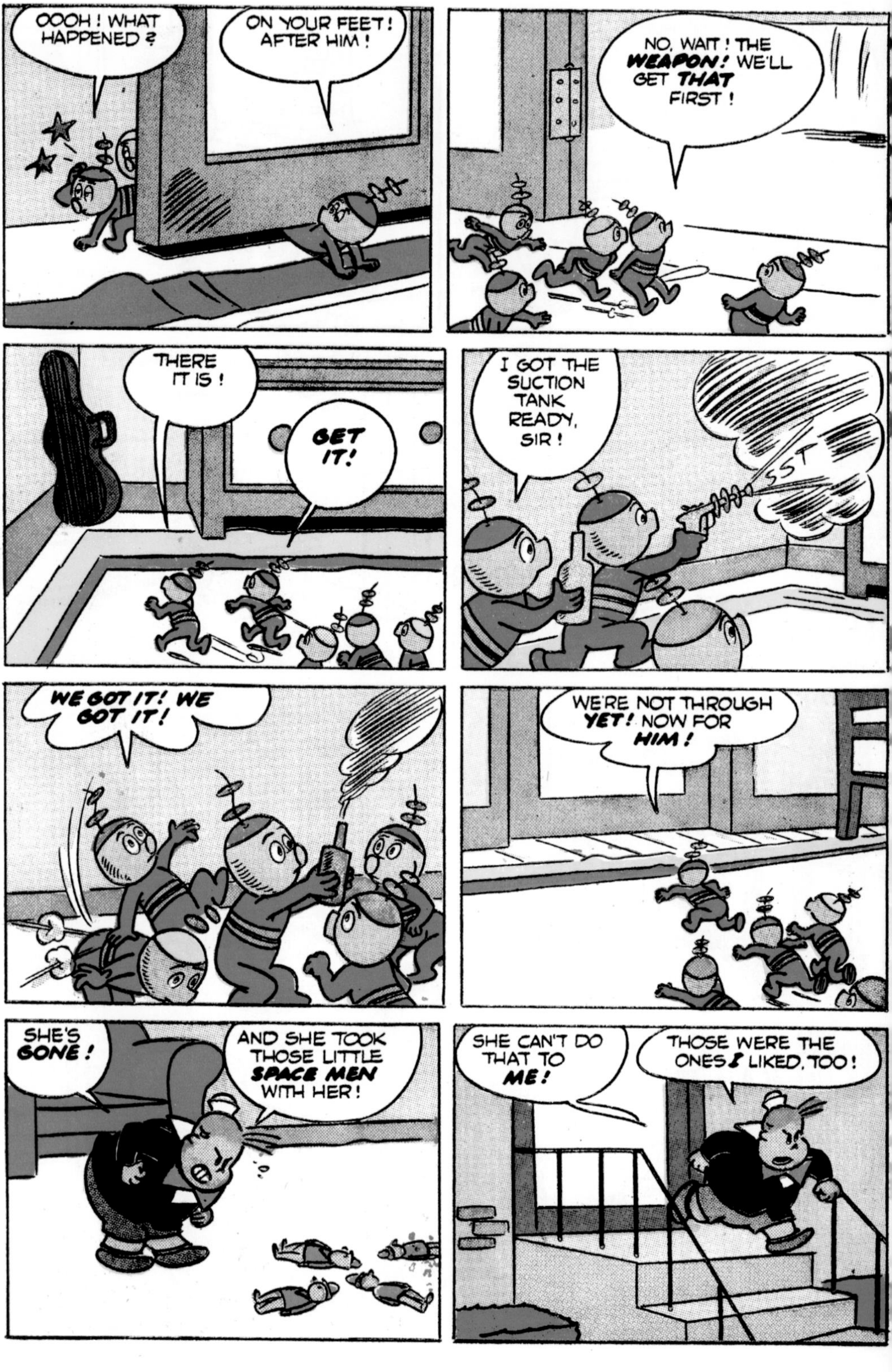
OOOH! WHAT HAPPENED?
ON YOUR FEET! AFTER HIM!
NO, WAIT! THE WEAPON! WE'LL GET THAT FIRST!
THERE IT IS!
GET IT!
I GOT THE SUCTION TANK READY, SIR!
SST
WE GOT IT! WE GOT IT!
WE'RE NOT THROUGH YET! NOW FOR HIM!
SHE'S GONE!
AND SHE TOOK THOSE LITTLE SPACE MEN WITH HER!
SHE CAN'T DO THAT TO ME!
THOSE WERE THE ONES I LIKED, TOO!

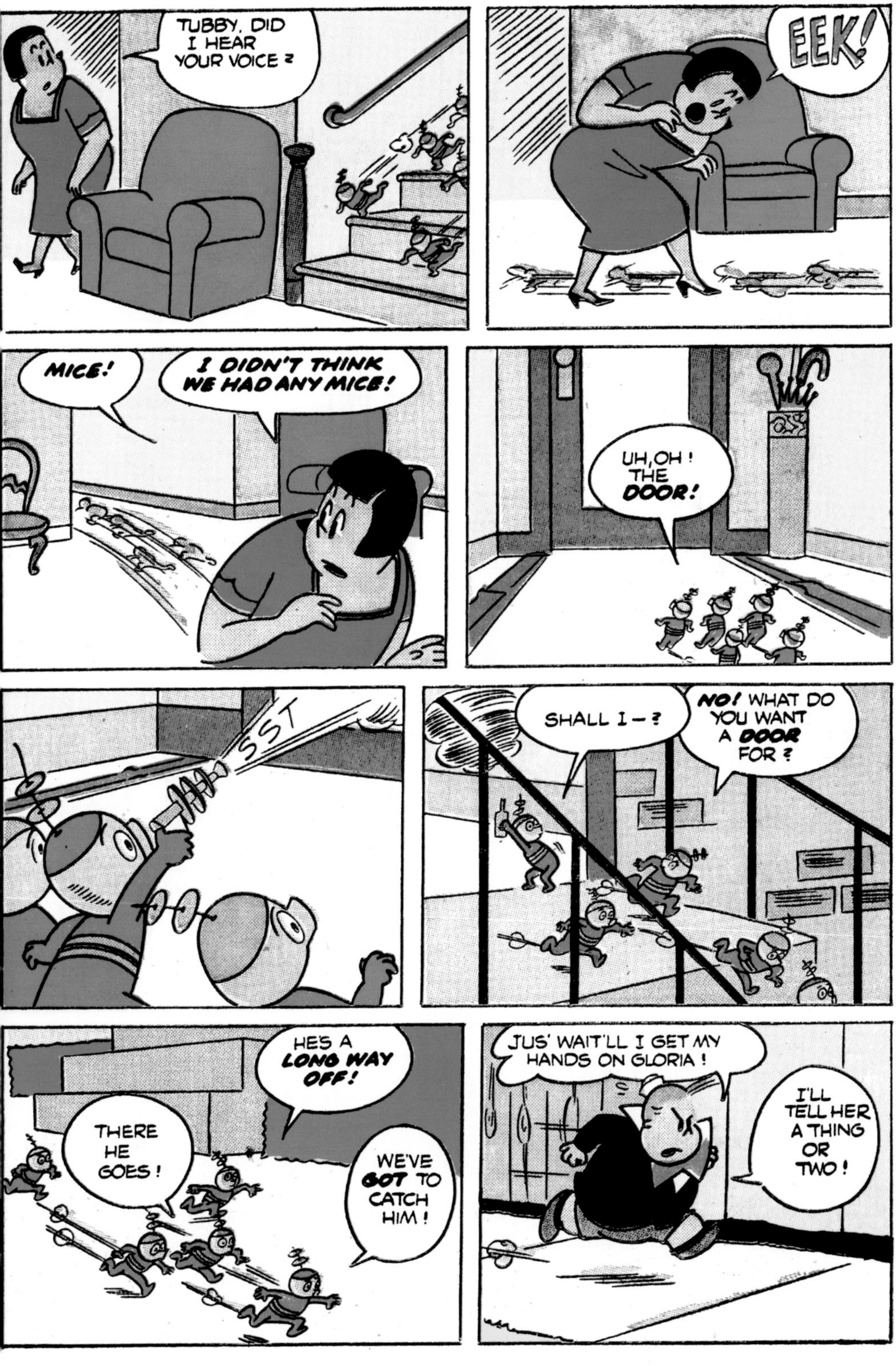
TUBBY, DID I HEAR YOUR VOICE ?
EEK!
MICE!
I DIDN'T THINK WE HAD ANY MICE!
UH, OH! THE DOOR!
SST
SHALL I — ?
NO! WHAT DO YOU WANT A DOOR FOR ?
HE'S A LONG WAY OFF!
THERE HE GOES!
WE'VE GOT TO CATCH HIM!
JUS' WAIT'LL I GET MY HANDS ON GLORIA!
I'LL TELL HER A THING OR TWO!

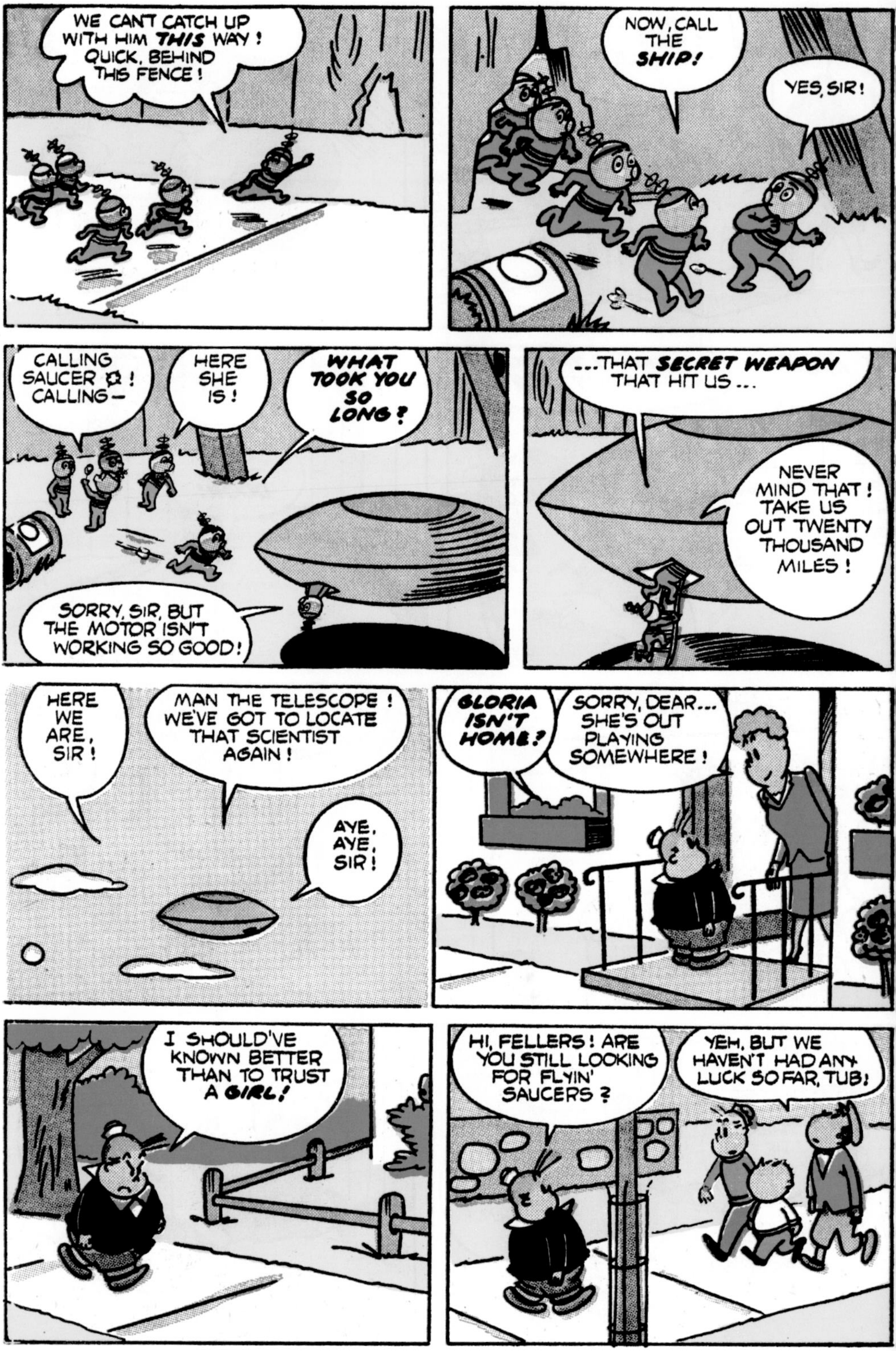
WE CAN'T CATCH UP WITH HIM THIS WAY! QUICK, BEHIND THIS FENCE!
NOW, CALL THE SHIP!
YES, SIR!
CALLING SAUCER ✪! CALLING—
HERE SHE IS!
WHAT TOOK YOU SO LONG?
SORRY, SIR, BUT THE MOTOR ISN'T WORKING SO GOOD!
...THAT SECRET WEAPON THAT HIT US...
NEVER MIND THAT! TAKE US OUT TWENTY THOUSAND MILES!
HERE WE ARE, SIR!
MAN THE TELESCOPE! WE'VE GOT TO LOCATE THAT SCIENTIST AGAIN!
AYE, AYE, SIR!
GLORIA ISN'T HOME?
SORRY, DEAR... SHE'S OUT PLAYING SOMEWHERE!
I SHOULD'VE KNOWN BETTER THAN TO TRUST A GIRL!
HI, FELLERS! ARE YOU STILL LOOKING FOR FLYIN' SAUCERS?
YEH, BUT WE HAVEN'T HAD ANY LUCK SO FAR, TUB!

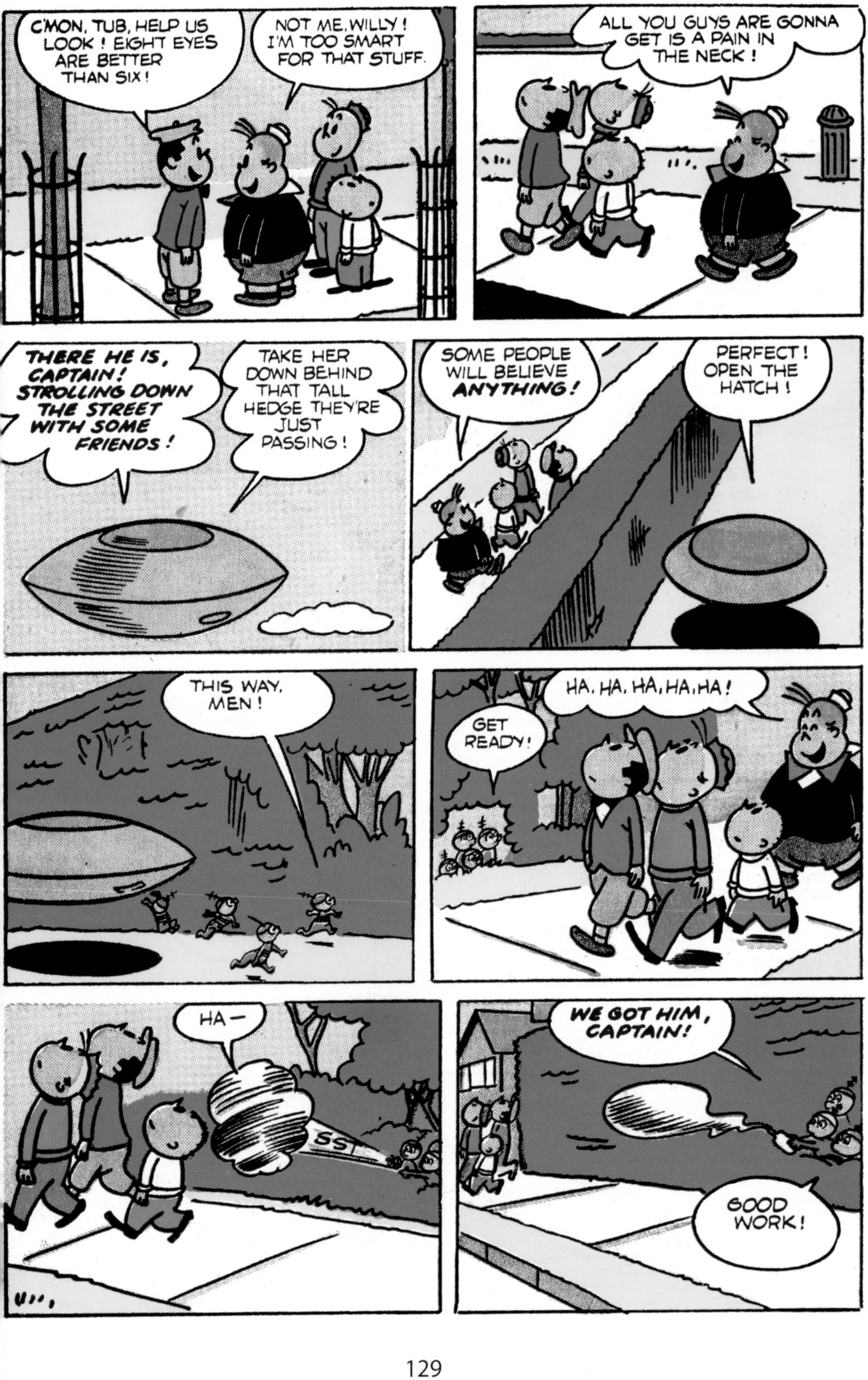
C'MON, TUB, HELP US LOOK! EIGHT EYES ARE BETTER THAN SIX!
NOT ME, WILLY! I'M TOO SMART FOR THAT STUFF.
ALL YOU GUYS ARE GONNA GET IS A PAIN IN THE NECK!
THERE HE IS, CAPTAIN! STROLLING DOWN THE STREET WITH SOME FRIENDS!
TAKE HER DOWN BEHIND THAT TALL HEDGE THEY'RE JUST PASSING!
SOME PEOPLE WILL BELIEVE ANYTHING!
PERFECT! OPEN THE HATCH!
THIS WAY, MEN!
HA, HA, HA, HA, HA!
GET READY!
HA—
SS
WE GOT HIM, CAPTAIN!
GOOD WORK!

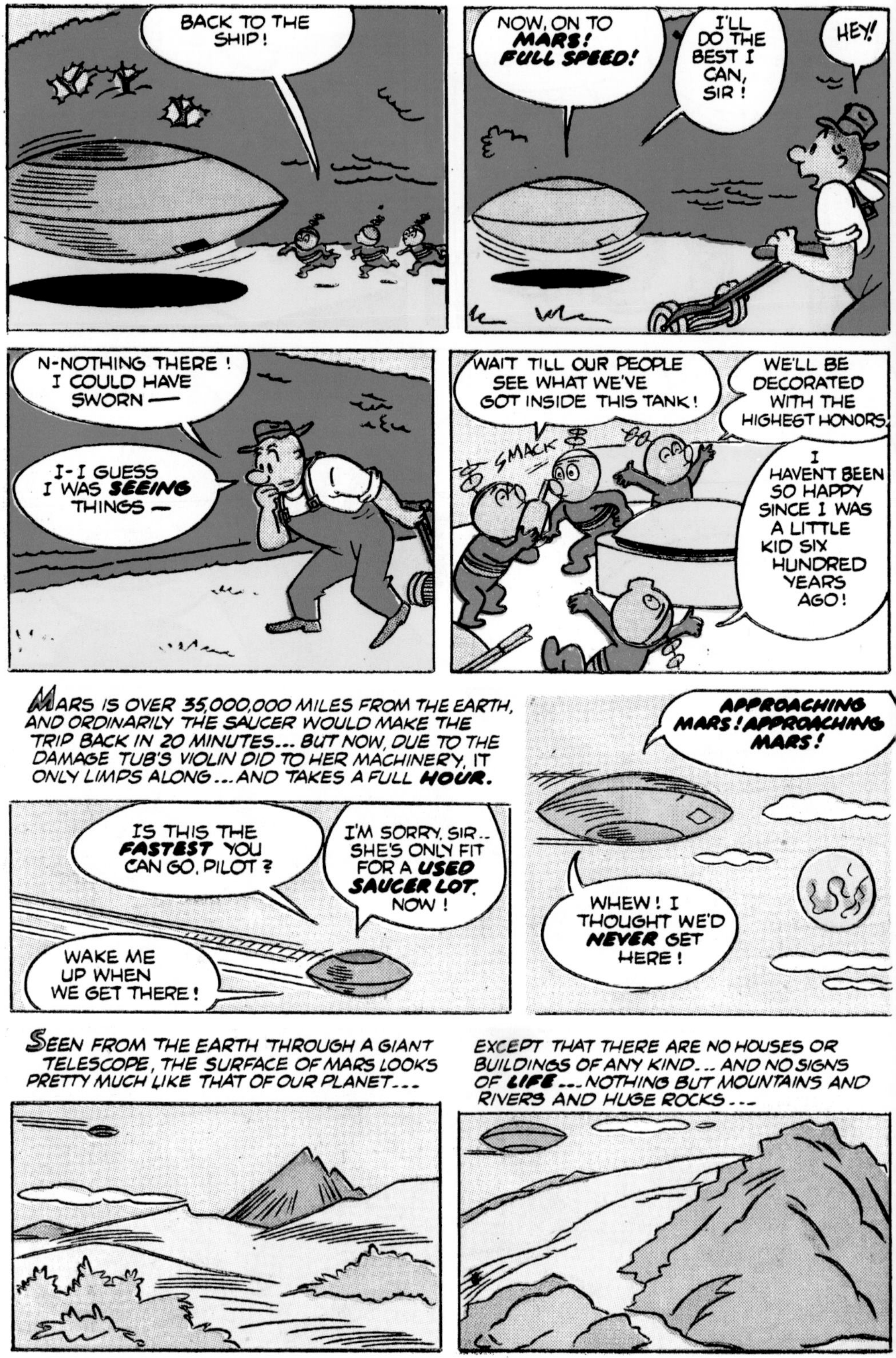
BACK TO THE SHIP!
NOW, ON TO MARS! FULL SPEED!
I'LL DO THE BEST I CAN, SIR!
HEY!
N-NOTHING THERE! I COULD HAVE SWORN —
I-I GUESS I WAS SEEING THINGS —
WAIT TILL OUR PEOPLE SEE WHAT WE'VE GOT INSIDE THIS TANK!
SMACK
WE'LL BE DECORATED WITH THE HIGHEST HONORS!
I HAVEN'T BEEN SO HAPPY SINCE I WAS A LITTLE KID SIX HUNDRED YEARS AGO!
MARS IS OVER 35,000,000 MILES FROM THE EARTH, AND ORDINARILY THE SAUCER WOULD MAKE THE TRIP BACK IN 20 MINUTES... BUT NOW, DUE TO THE DAMAGE TUB'S VIOLIN DID TO HER MACHINERY, IT ONLY LIMPS ALONG... AND TAKES A FULL HOUR.
IS THIS THE FASTEST YOU CAN GO, PILOT?
I'M SORRY, SIR.. SHE'S ONLY FIT FOR A USED SAUCER LOT, NOW!
WAKE ME UP WHEN WE GET THERE!
APPROACHING MARS! APPROACHING MARS!
WHEW! I THOUGHT WE'D NEVER GET HERE!
SEEN FROM THE EARTH THROUGH A GIANT TELESCOPE, THE SURFACE OF MARS LOOKS PRETTY MUCH LIKE THAT OF OUR PLANET...
EXCEPT THAT THERE ARE NO HOUSES OR BUILDINGS OF ANY KIND... AND NO SIGNS OF LIFE... NOTHING BUT MOUNTAINS AND RIVERS AND HUGE ROCKS...

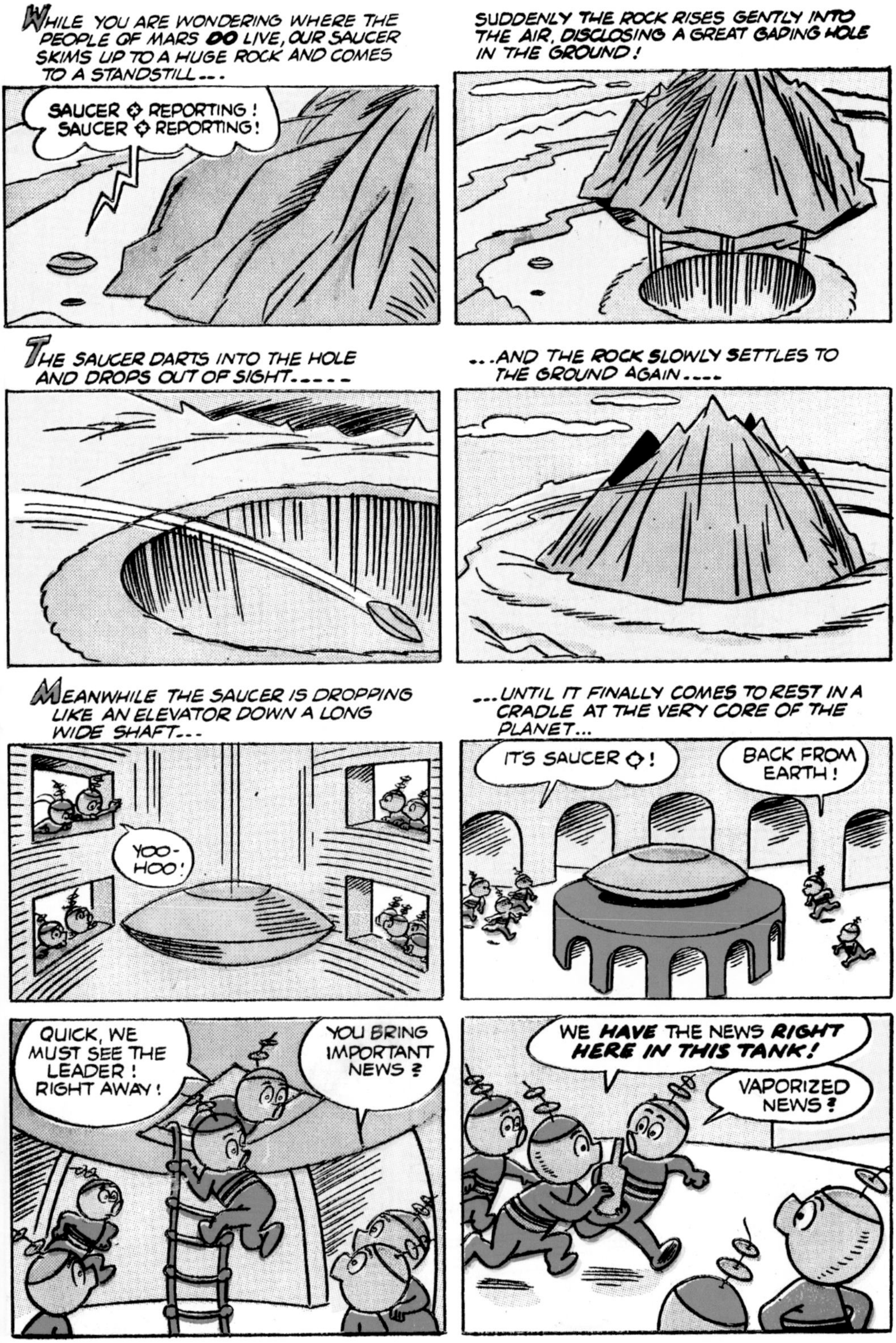
WHILE YOU ARE WONDERING WHERE THE PEOPLE OF MARS DO LIVE, OUR SAUCER SKIMS UP TO A HUGE ROCK AND COMES TO A STANDSTILL...
SAUCER ⊕ REPORTING! SAUCER ⊕ REPORTING!
SUDDENLY THE ROCK RISES GENTLY INTO THE AIR, DISCLOSING A GREAT GAPING HOLE IN THE GROUND!
THE SAUCER DARTS INTO THE HOLE AND DROPS OUT OF SIGHT.....
...AND THE ROCK SLOWLY SETTLES TO THE GROUND AGAIN....
MEANWHILE THE SAUCER IS DROPPING LIKE AN ELEVATOR DOWN A LONG WIDE SHAFT...
YOO-HOO!
...UNTIL IT FINALLY COMES TO REST IN A CRADLE AT THE VERY CORE OF THE PLANET...
IT'S SAUCER ⊕!
BACK FROM EARTH!
QUICK, WE MUST SEE THE LEADER! RIGHT AWAY!
YOU BRING IMPORTANT NEWS?
WE HAVE THE NEWS RIGHT HERE IN THIS TANK!
VAPORIZED NEWS?

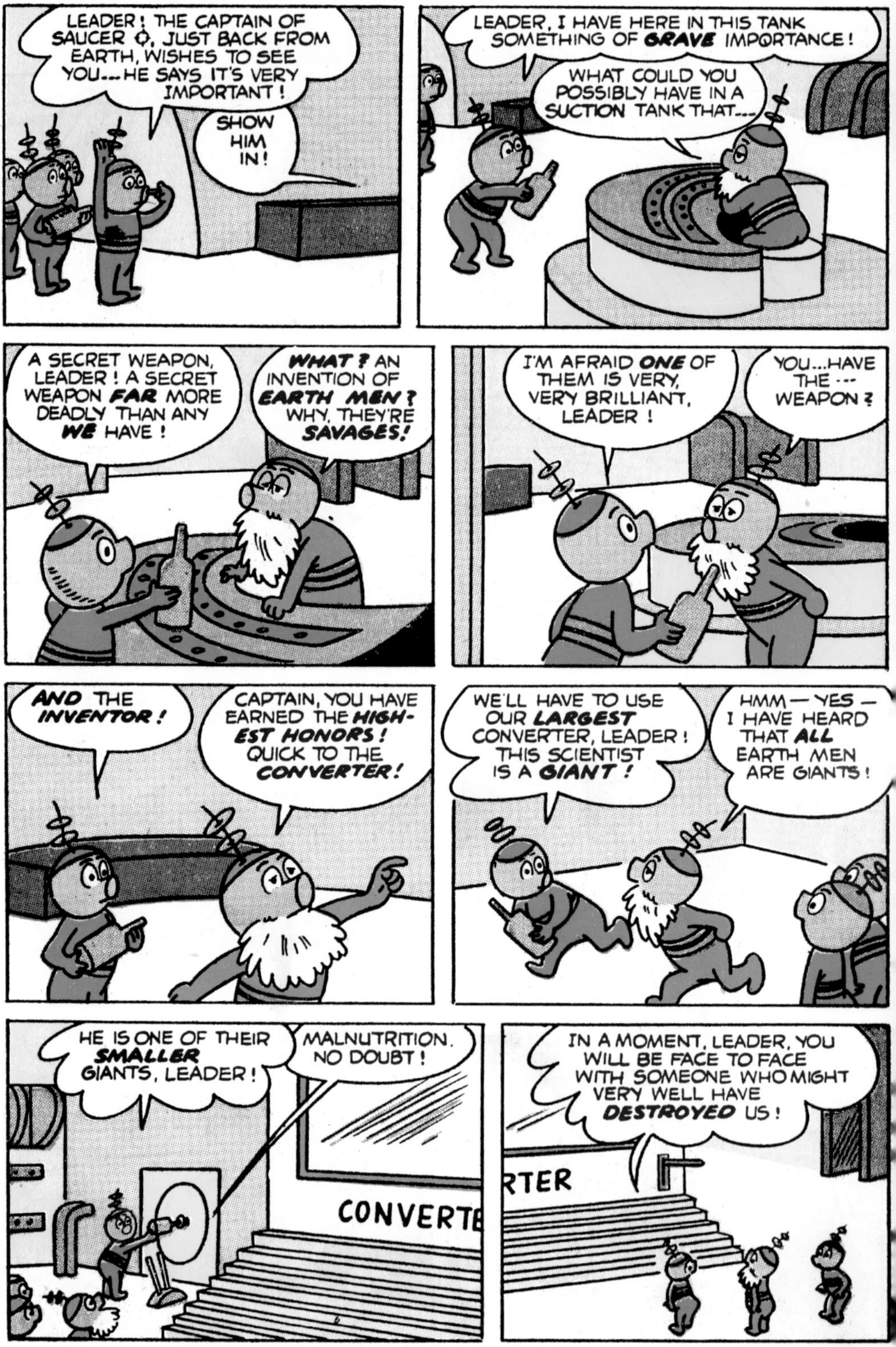
LEADER! THE CAPTAIN OF SAUCER ⊕, JUST BACK FROM EARTH, WISHES TO SEE YOU... HE SAYS IT'S VERY IMPORTANT!
SHOW HIM IN!
LEADER, I HAVE HERE IN THIS TANK SOMETHING OF GRAVE IMPORTANCE!
WHAT COULD YOU POSSIBLY HAVE IN A SUCTION TANK THAT...
A SECRET WEAPON, LEADER! A SECRET WEAPON FAR MORE DEADLY THAN ANY WE HAVE!
WHAT? AN INVENTION OF EARTH MEN? WHY, THEY'RE SAVAGES!
I'M AFRAID ONE OF THEM IS VERY, VERY BRILLIANT, LEADER!
YOU...HAVE THE... WEAPON?
AND THE INVENTOR!
CAPTAIN, YOU HAVE EARNED THE HIGHEST HONORS! QUICK TO THE CONVERTER!
WE'LL HAVE TO USE OUR LARGEST CONVERTER, LEADER! THIS SCIENTIST IS A GIANT!
HMM — YES — I HAVE HEARD THAT ALL EARTH MEN ARE GIANTS!
HE IS ONE OF THEIR SMALLER GIANTS, LEADER!
MALNUTRITION, NO DOUBT!
CONVERTE
IN A MOMENT, LEADER, YOU WILL BE FACE TO FACE WITH SOMEONE WHO MIGHT VERY WELL HAVE DESTROYED US!
RTER

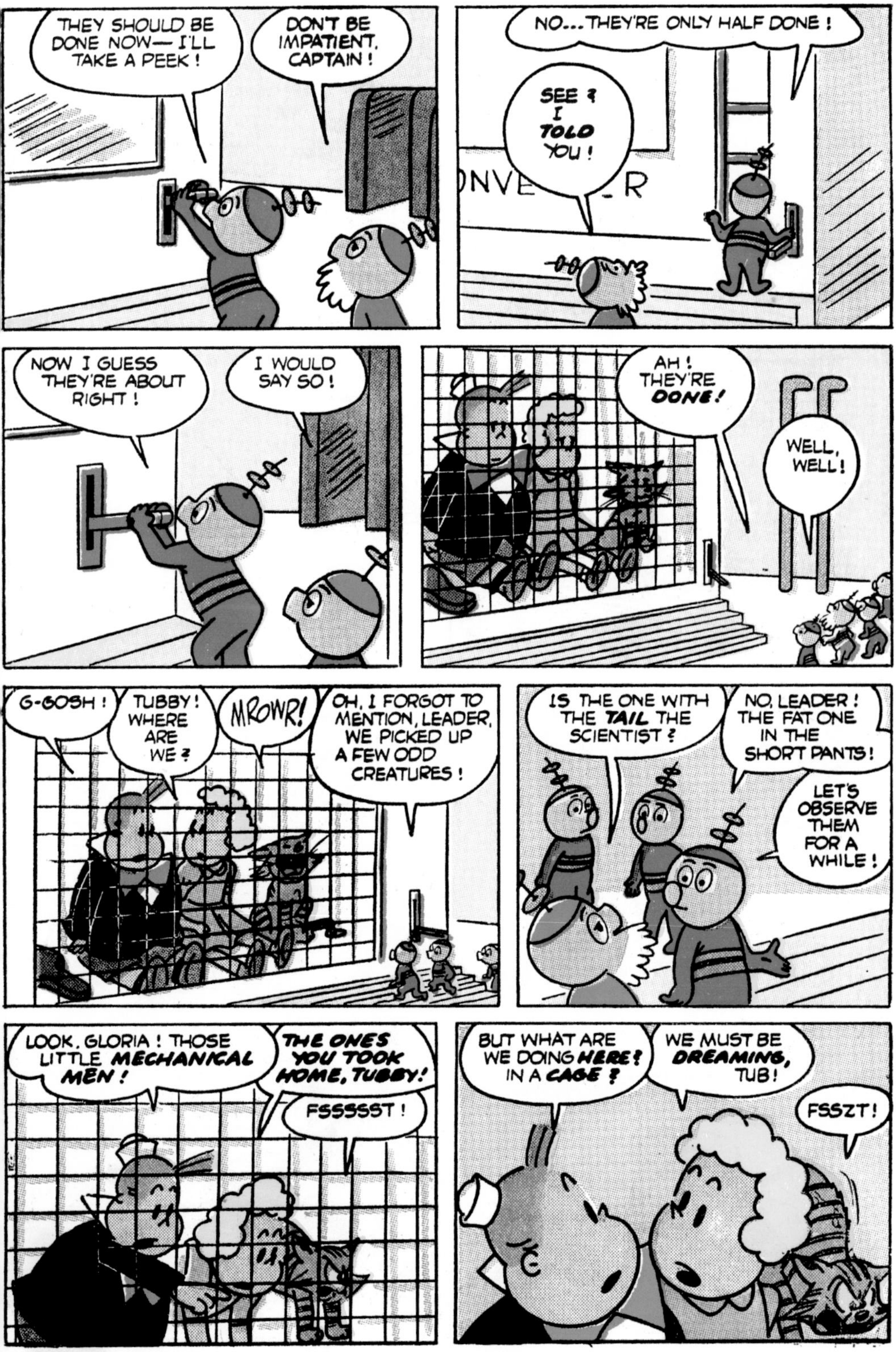
THEY SHOULD BE DONE NOW— I'LL TAKE A PEEK!
DON'T BE IMPATIENT, CAPTAIN!
NO... THEY'RE ONLY HALF DONE!
SEE? I TOLD YOU!
NOW I GUESS THEY'RE ABOUT RIGHT!
I WOULD SAY SO!
AH! THEY'RE DONE!
WELL, WELL!
G-GOSH!
TUBBY! WHERE ARE WE?
MROWR!
OH, I FORGOT TO MENTION, LEADER, WE PICKED UP A FEW ODD CREATURES!
IS THE ONE WITH THE TAIL THE SCIENTIST?
NO, LEADER! THE FAT ONE IN THE SHORT PANTS!
LET'S OBSERVE THEM FOR A WHILE!
LOOK, GLORIA! THOSE LITTLE MECHANICAL MEN!
THE ONES YOU TOOK HOME, TUBBY!
FSSSSST!
BUT WHAT ARE WE DOING HERE? IN A CAGE?
WE MUST BE DREAMING, TUB!
FSSZT!

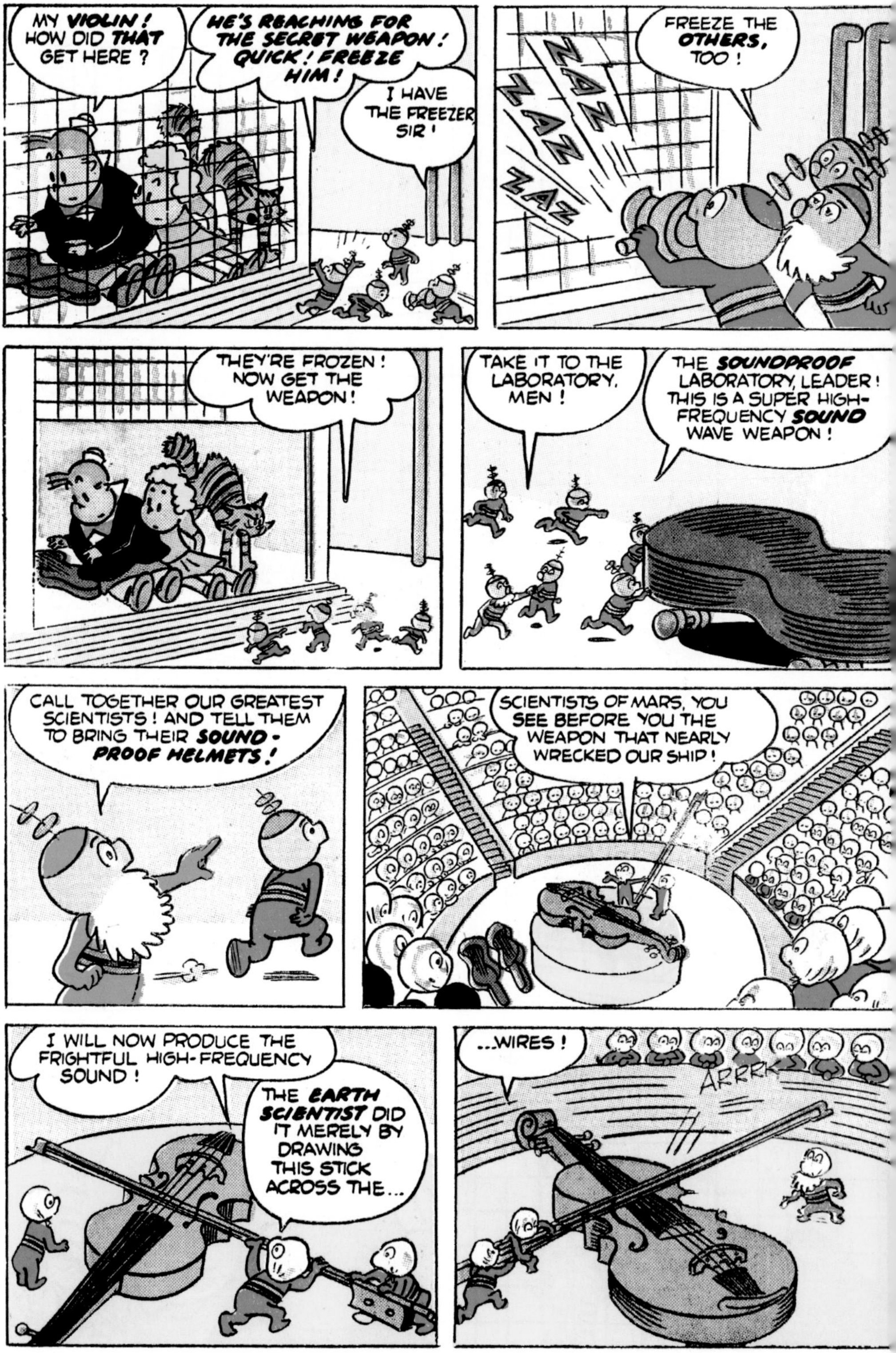
MY VIOLIN! HOW DID THAT GET HERE?
HE'S REACHING FOR THE SECRET WEAPON! QUICK! FREEZE HIM!
I HAVE THE FREEZER, SIR!
FREEZE THE OTHERS, TOO!
ZAZ ZAZ ZAZ ZAZ
THEY'RE FROZEN! NOW GET THE WEAPON!
TAKE IT TO THE LABORATORY, MEN!
THE SOUNDPROOF LABORATORY, LEADER! THIS IS A SUPER HIGH-FREQUENCY SOUND WAVE WEAPON!
CALL TOGETHER OUR GREATEST SCIENTISTS! AND TELL THEM TO BRING THEIR SOUND-PROOF HELMETS!
SCIENTISTS OF MARS, YOU SEE BEFORE YOU THE WEAPON THAT NEARLY WRECKED OUR SHIP!
I WILL NOW PRODUCE THE FRIGHTFUL HIGH-FREQUENCY SOUND!
THE EARTH SCIENTIST DID IT MERELY BY DRAWING THIS STICK ACROSS THE...
...WIRES!
ARRRK

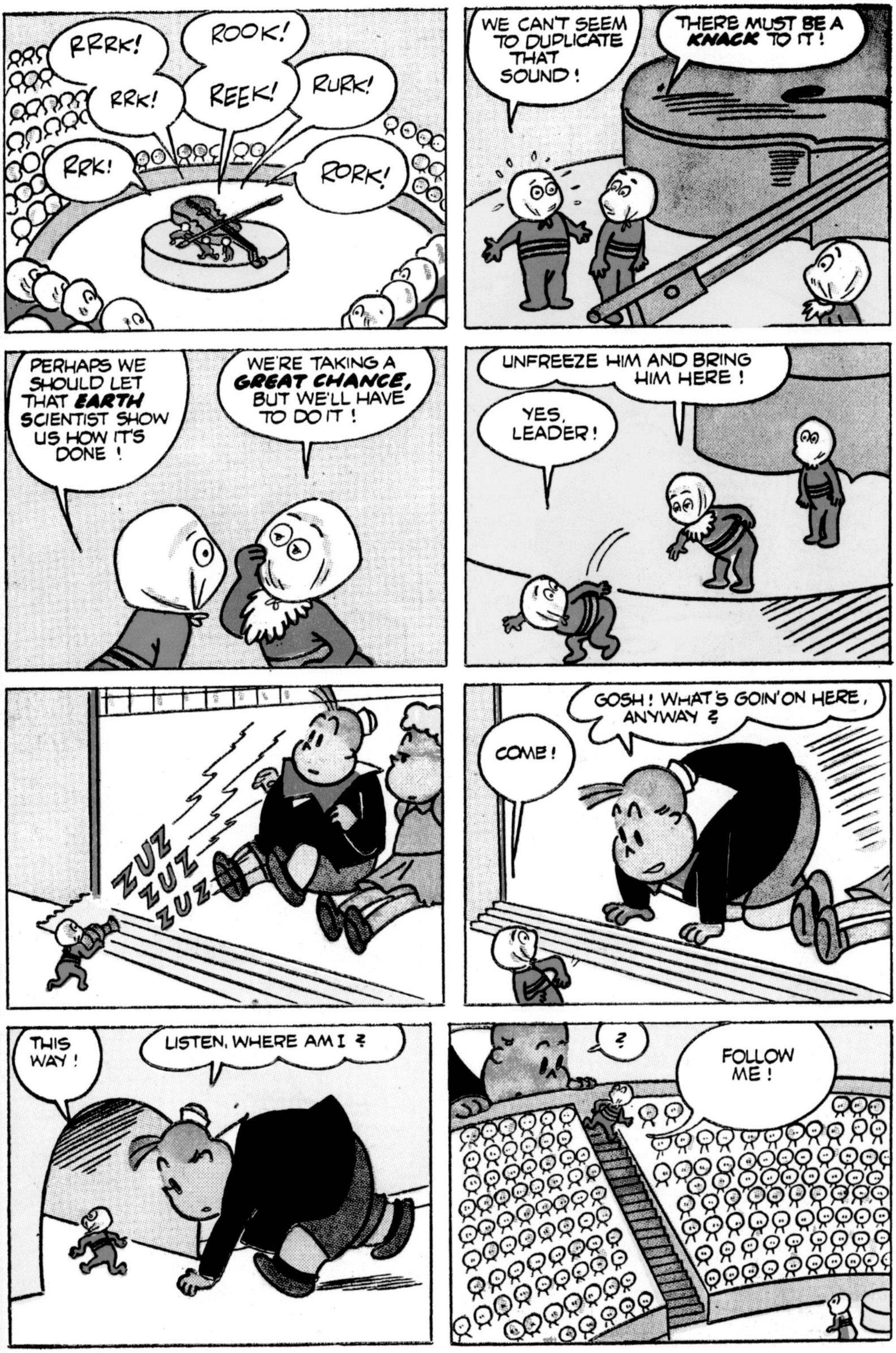
RRRK!
ROOK!
RRK!
REEK!
RURK!
RRK!
RORK!
WE CAN'T SEEM TO DUPLICATE THAT SOUND!
THERE MUST BE A KNACK TO IT!
PERHAPS WE SHOULD LET THAT EARTH SCIENTIST SHOW US HOW IT'S DONE!
WE'RE TAKING A GREAT CHANCE, BUT WE'LL HAVE TO DO IT!
UNFREEZE HIM AND BRING HIM HERE!
YES, LEADER!
ZUZ ZUZ ZUZ
GOSH! WHAT'S GOIN' ON HERE, ANYWAY?
COME!
THIS WAY!
LISTEN, WHERE AM I?
?
FOLLOW ME!

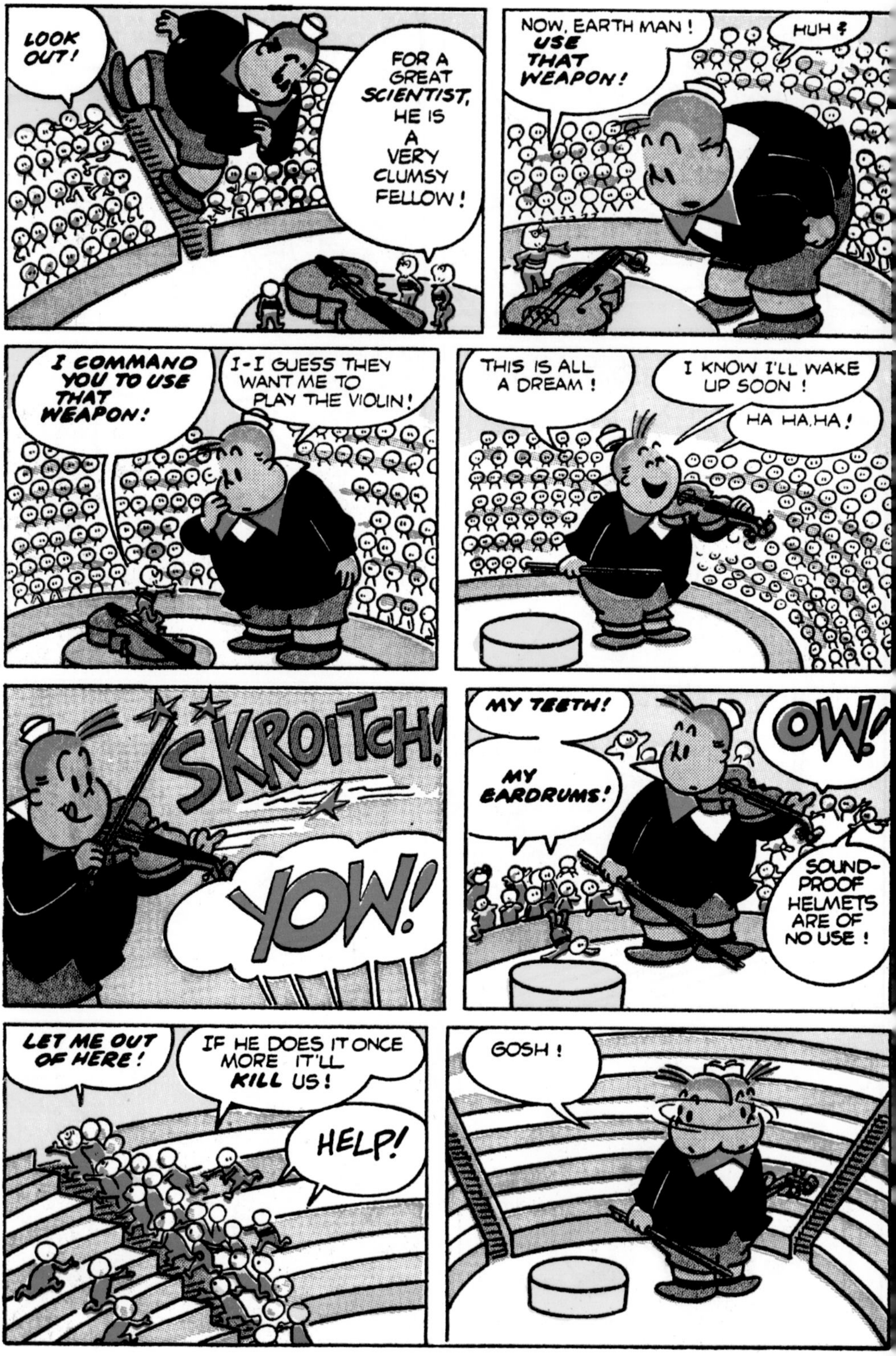
LOOK OUT!
FOR A GREAT SCIENTIST, HE IS A VERY CLUMSY FELLOW!
NOW, EARTH MAN! USE THAT WEAPON!
HUH?
I COMMAND YOU TO USE THAT WEAPON!
I-I GUESS THEY WANT ME TO PLAY THE VIOLIN!
THIS IS ALL A DREAM!
I KNOW I'LL WAKE UP SOON!
HA HA.HA!
SKROITCH!
YOW!
MY TEETH!
OW!
MY EARDRUMS!
SOUND-PROOF HELMETS ARE OF NO USE!
LET ME OUT OF HERE!
IF HE DOES IT ONCE MORE IT'LL KILL US!
HELP!
GOSH!

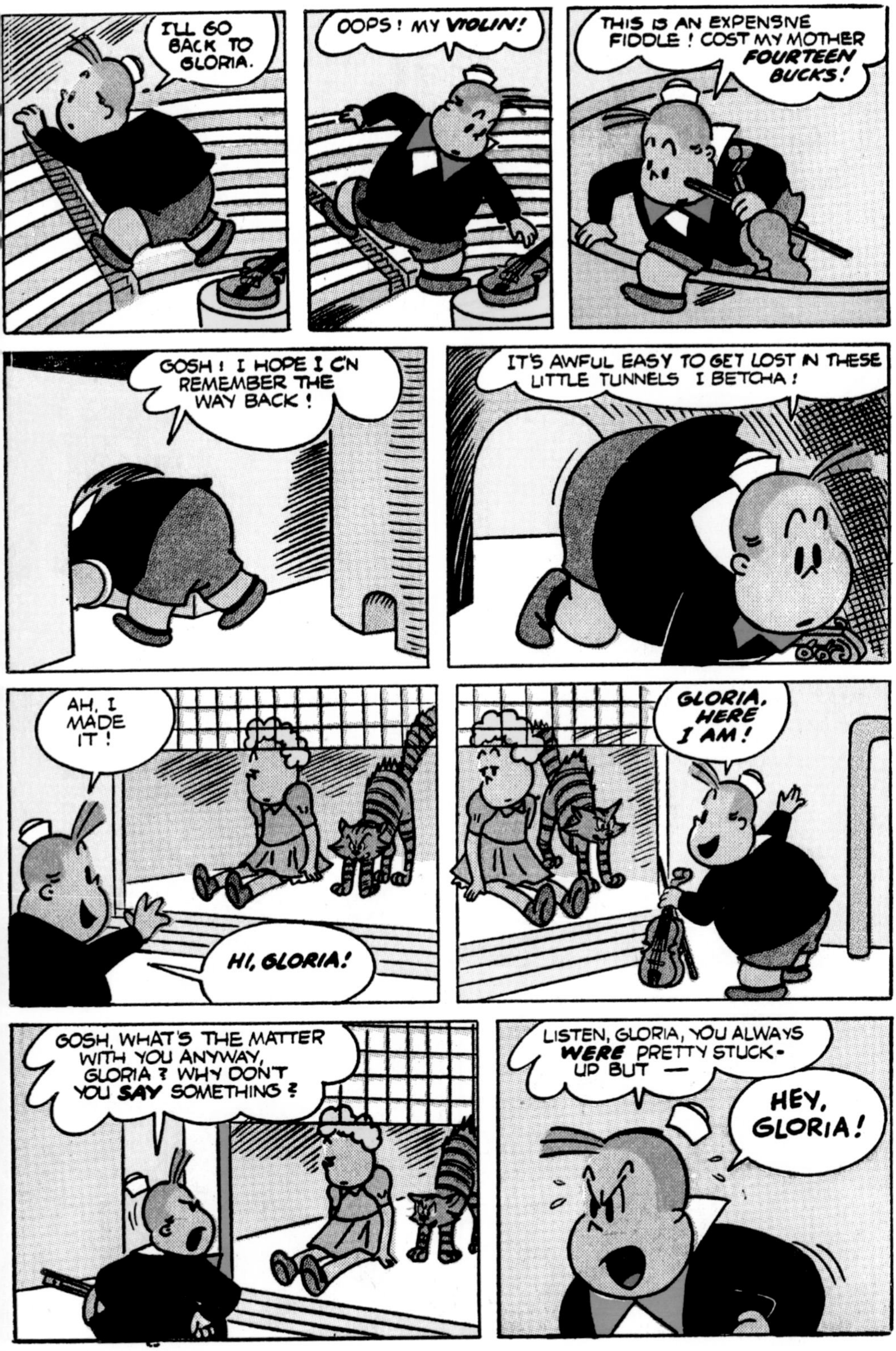
I'LL GO BACK TO GLORIA.
OOPS! MY VIOLIN!
THIS IS AN EXPENSIVE FIDDLE! COST MY MOTHER FOURTEEN BUCKS!
GOSH! I HOPE I C'N REMEMBER THE WAY BACK!
IT'S AWFUL EASY TO GET LOST IN THESE LITTLE TUNNELS I BETCHA!
AH, I MADE IT!
HI, GLORIA!
GLORIA, HERE I AM!
GOSH, WHAT'S THE MATTER WITH YOU ANYWAY, GLORIA? WHY DON'T YOU SAY SOMETHING?
LISTEN, GLORIA, YOU ALWAYS WERE PRETTY STUCK-UP BUT —
HEY, GLORIA!

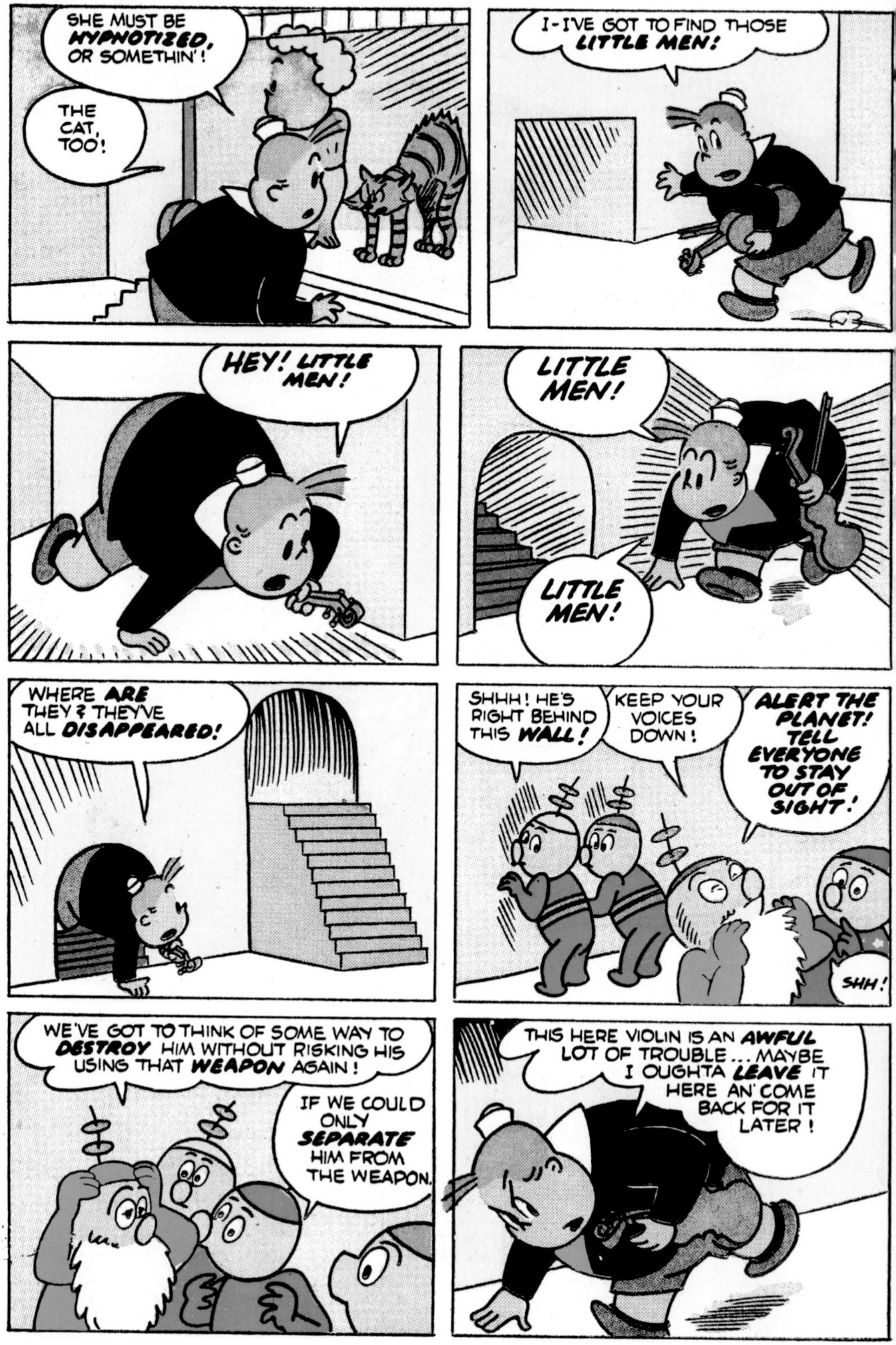
SHE MUST BE HYPNOTIZED, OR SOMETHIN'!
THE CAT, TOO!
I-I'VE GOT TO FIND THOSE LITTLE MEN!
HEY! LITTLE MEN!
LITTLE MEN!
LITTLE MEN!
WHERE ARE THEY? THEY'VE ALL DISAPPEARED!
SHHH! HE'S RIGHT BEHIND THIS WALL!
KEEP YOUR VOICES DOWN!
ALERT THE PLANET! TELL EVERYONE TO STAY OUT OF SIGHT!
SHH!
WE'VE GOT TO THINK OF SOME WAY TO DESTROY HIM WITHOUT RISKING HIS USING THAT WEAPON AGAIN!
IF WE COULD ONLY SEPARATE HIM FROM THE WEAPON.
THIS HERE VIOLIN IS AN AWFUL LOT OF TROUBLE... MAYBE I OUGHTA LEAVE IT HERE AN' COME BACK FOR IT LATER!

NO --- MAYBE I WOULDN'T **FIND** IT AGAIN!

BUT, LEADER, SUPPOSE HE BLUNDERS INTO THE **PLANET CONTROL ROOM**?

DON'T WORRY! DIDN'T WE PUT THE **BUTTON** THAT **OPENS THE DOOR** WAY UP OUT OF REACH!

?

PLANET CONTROL ROOM

STAY OUT! THIS MEANS YOU!

MAYBE SOME OF THOSE LITTLE MEN ARE IN HERE!

UGH! UGH!

CONTR ROOM

STAY THIS N

DOOR WON'T OPEN!

I WONDER WHAT THIS **BUTTON** IS FOR?

PL CON RO

GOSH! THE DOOR IS **OPENING!**

PLANET CONTROL ROOM

STAY OUT! THIS MEANS YOU!

REVERSE

STARTER

A --- **WINDOW!**

THERE ARE THE **PLANETS** AND THE **STARS** OUT THERE!

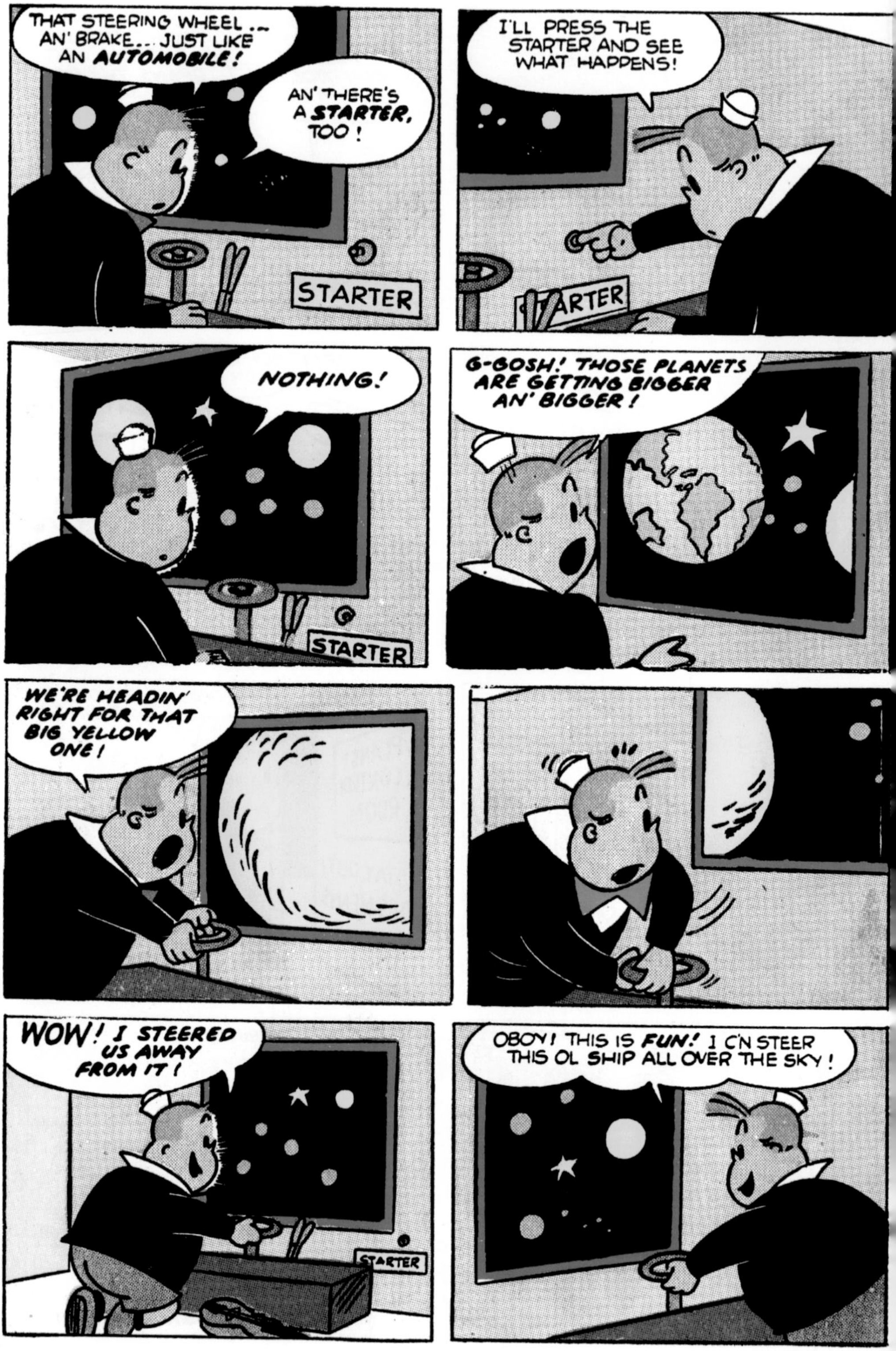
THAT STEERING WHEEL .. AN' BRAKE... JUST LIKE AN AUTOMOBILE!
AN' THERE'S A STARTER, TOO!
STARTER
I'LL PRESS THE STARTER AND SEE WHAT HAPPENS!
NOTHING!
STARTER
G-GOSH! THOSE PLANETS ARE GETTING BIGGER AN' BIGGER!
WE'RE HEADIN' RIGHT FOR THAT BIG YELLOW ONE!
WOW! I STEERED US AWAY FROM IT!
STARTER
OBOY! THIS IS FUN! I C'N STEER THIS OL SHIP ALL OVER THE SKY!

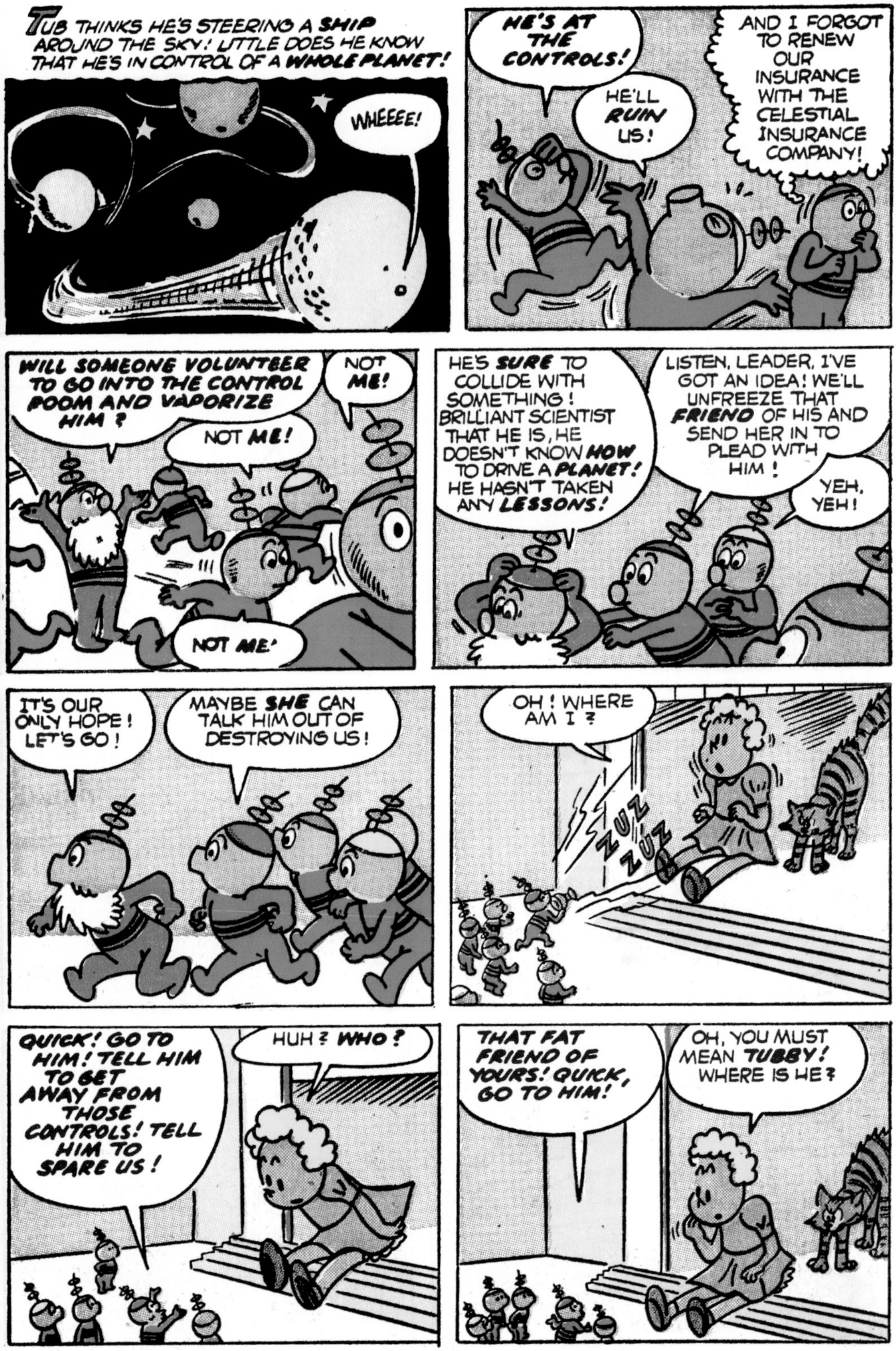
TUB THINKS HE'S STEERING A SHIP AROUND THE SKY! LITTLE DOES HE KNOW THAT HE'S IN CONTROL OF A WHOLE PLANET!
WHEEEE!
HE'S AT THE CONTROLS!
HE'LL RUIN US!
AND I FORGOT TO RENEW OUR INSURANCE WITH THE CELESTIAL INSURANCE COMPANY!
WILL SOMEONE VOLUNTEER TO GO INTO THE CONTROL ROOM AND VAPORIZE HIM?
NOT ME!
NOT ME!
NOT ME!
HE'S SURE TO COLLIDE WITH SOMETHING! BRILLIANT SCIENTIST THAT HE IS, HE DOESN'T KNOW HOW TO DRIVE A PLANET! HE HASN'T TAKEN ANY LESSONS!
LISTEN, LEADER, I'VE GOT AN IDEA! WE'LL UNFREEZE THAT FRIEND OF HIS AND SEND HER IN TO PLEAD WITH HIM!
YEH, YEH!
IT'S OUR ONLY HOPE! LET'S GO!
MAYBE SHE CAN TALK HIM OUT OF DESTROYING US!
OH! WHERE AM I?
ZUZ ZUZ
QUICK! GO TO HIM! TELL HIM TO GET AWAY FROM THOSE CONTROLS! TELL HIM TO SPARE US!
HUH? WHO?
THAT FAT FRIEND OF YOURS! QUICK, GO TO HIM!
OH, YOU MUST MEAN TUBBY! WHERE IS HE?

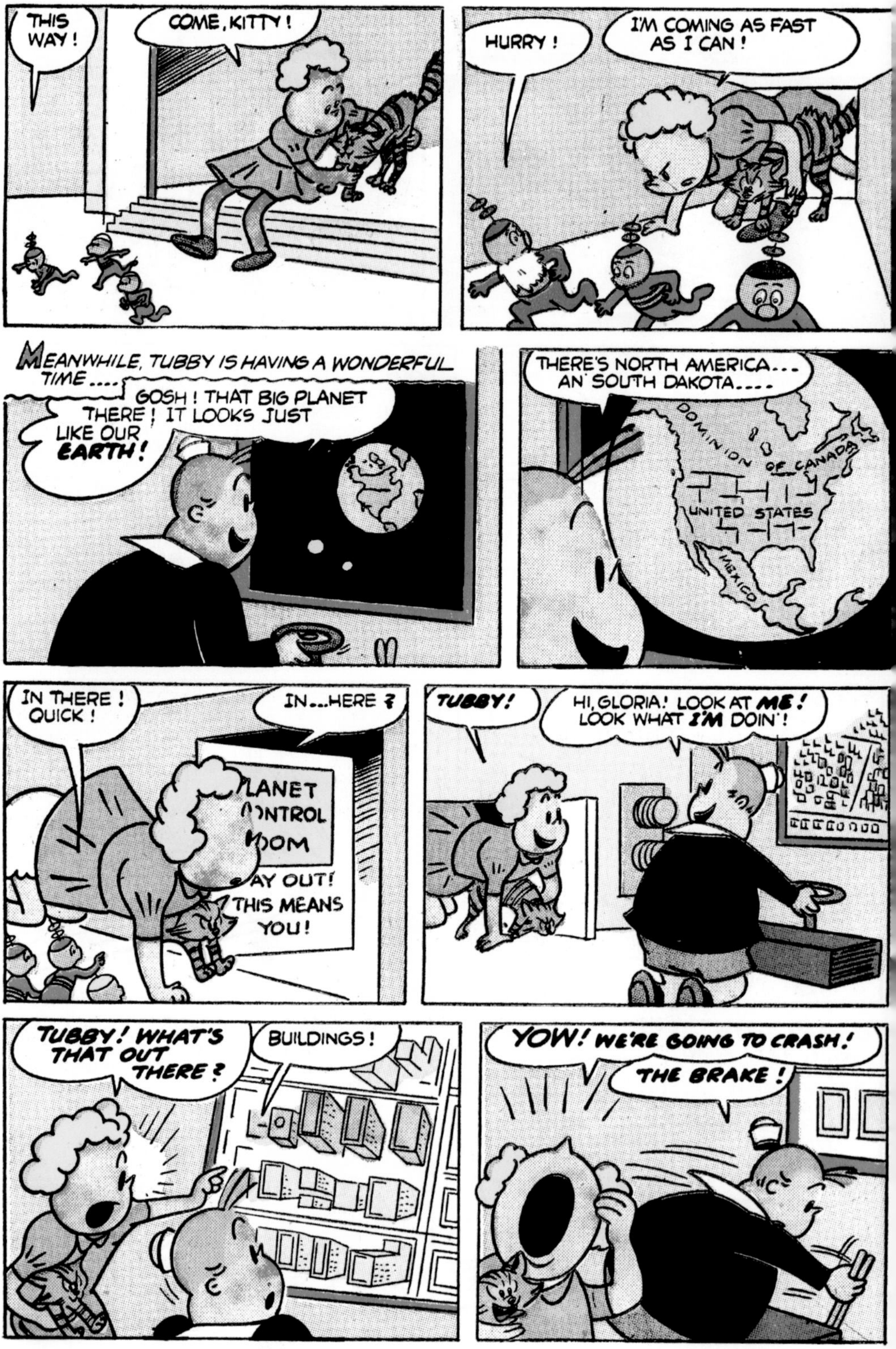
THIS WAY!
COME, KITTY!
HURRY!
I'M COMING AS FAST AS I CAN!
MEANWHILE, TUBBY IS HAVING A WONDERFUL TIME....
GOSH! THAT BIG PLANET THERE! IT LOOKS JUST LIKE OUR EARTH!
THERE'S NORTH AMERICA... AN' SOUTH DAKOTA....
DOMINION OF CANADA
UNITED STATES
MEXICO
IN THERE! QUICK!
IN...HERE?
TUBBY!
HI, GLORIA! LOOK AT ME! LOOK WHAT I'M DOIN'!
TUBBY! WHAT'S THAT OUT THERE?
BUILDINGS!
YOW! WE'RE GOING TO CRASH!
THE BRAKE!

TUB SLAMS ON THE BRAKE AND MARS COMES TO A SCREECHING STOP..... BUT NOT BEFORE THE SPIRE OF A TALL SKYSCRAPER PIERCES HER SIDE....

CRASH!

QUICK! TAKE THE CONTROLS OR ALL IS LOST!

REVERSE!

IN A FEW SECONDS MARS HAS SHOT OFF INTO THE SKY AND BACK TO HER ACCUSTOMED PLACE AMONG THE PLANETS...

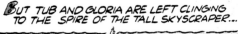

WHAZZ

BUT TUB AND GLORIA ARE LEFT CLINGING TO THE SPIRE OF THE TALL SKYSCRAPER...

HELP! HELP!

HELP!

HELP!

HELP! HELP!

HELP!

HELP!

?

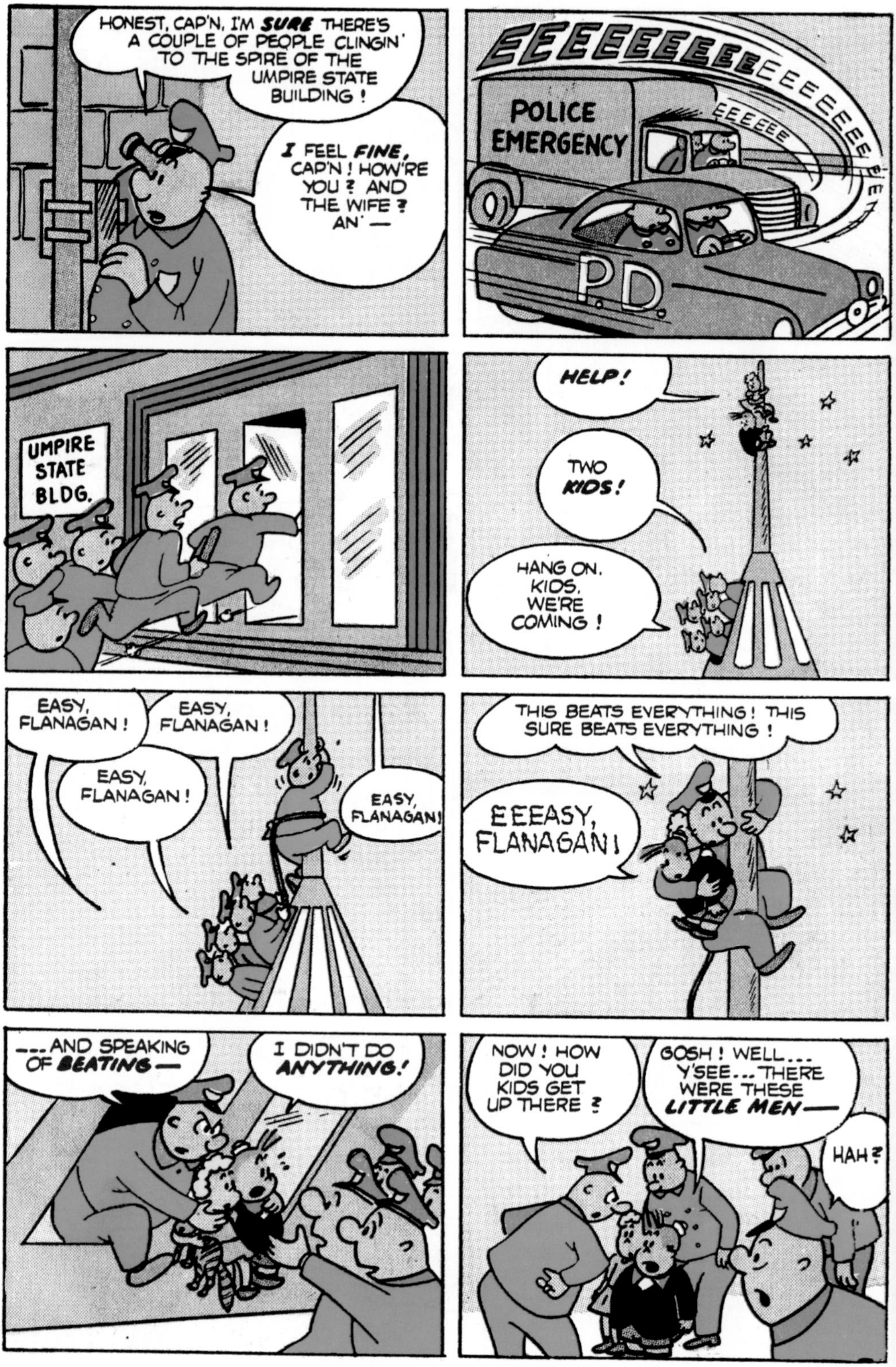
HONEST, CAP'N, I'M SURE THERE'S A COUPLE OF PEOPLE CLINGIN' TO THE SPIRE OF THE UMPIRE STATE BUILDING!
I FEEL FINE, CAP'N! HOW'RE YOU? AND THE WIFE? AN' —
EEEEEEEEEEEEEEEEEEE
POLICE EMERGENCY
P.D.
UMPIRE STATE BLDG.
HELP!
TWO KIDS!
HANG ON, KIDS, WE'RE COMING!
EASY, FLANAGAN!
EASY, FLANAGAN!
EASY, FLANAGAN!
EASY, FLANAGAN!
THIS BEATS EVERYTHING! THIS SURE BEATS EVERYTHING!
EEEASY, FLANAGAN!
---AND SPEAKING OF BEATING —
I DIDN'T DO ANYTHING!
NOW! HOW DID YOU KIDS GET UP THERE?
GOSH! WELL... Y'SEE... THERE WERE THESE LITTLE MEN —
HAH?

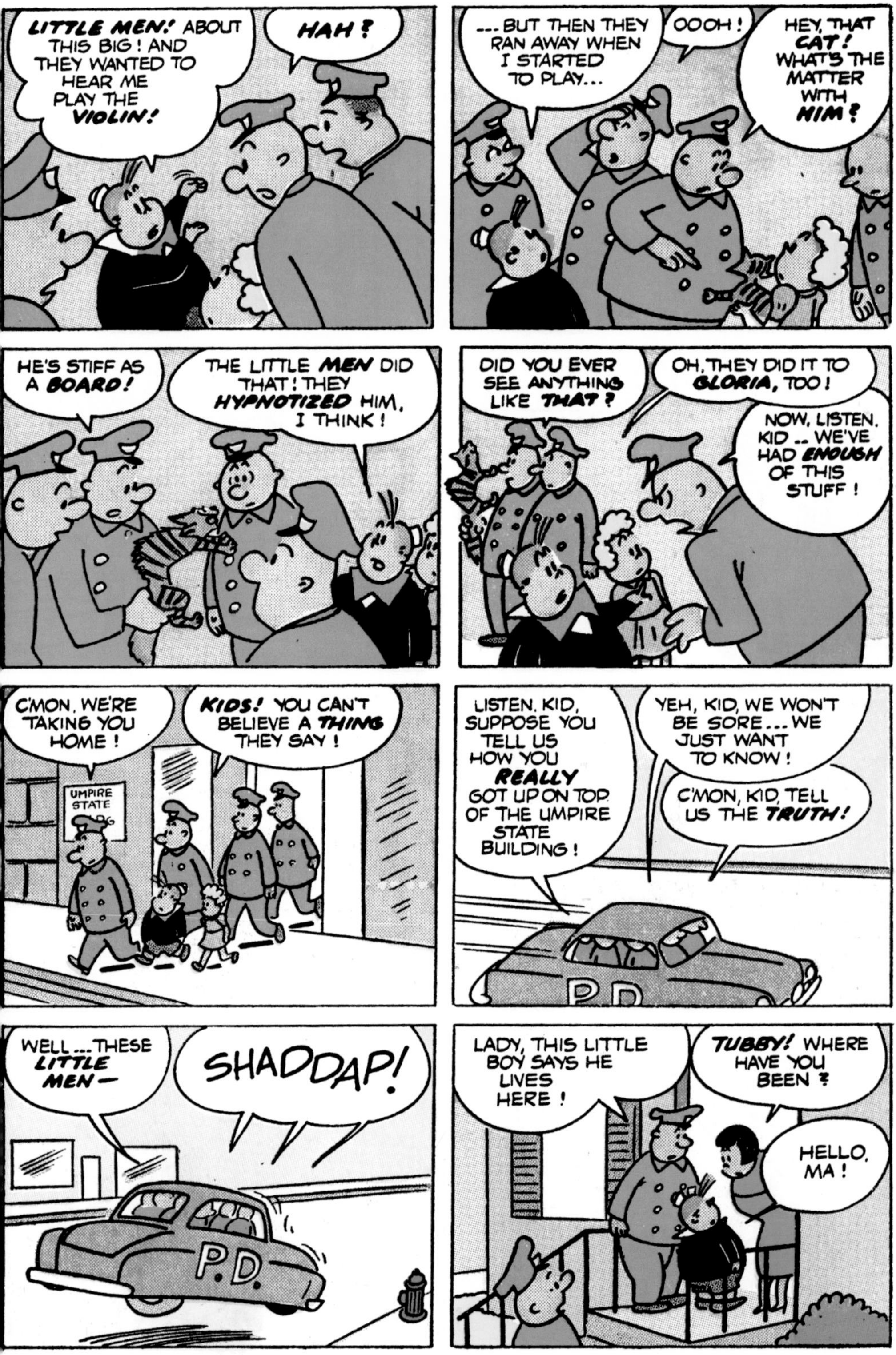
LITTLE MEN! ABOUT THIS BIG! AND THEY WANTED TO HEAR ME PLAY THE VIOLIN!
HAH?
...BUT THEN THEY RAN AWAY WHEN I STARTED TO PLAY...
OOOH!
HEY, THAT CAT! WHAT'S THE MATTER WITH HIM?
HE'S STIFF AS A BOARD!
THE LITTLE MEN DID THAT! THEY HYPNOTIZED HIM, I THINK!
DID YOU EVER SEE ANYTHING LIKE THAT?
OH, THEY DID IT TO GLORIA, TOO!
NOW, LISTEN, KID .. WE'VE HAD ENOUGH OF THIS STUFF!
C'MON, WE'RE TAKING YOU HOME!
KIDS! YOU CAN'T BELIEVE A THING THEY SAY!
UMPIRE STATE
LISTEN, KID, SUPPOSE YOU TELL US HOW YOU REALLY GOT UP ON TOP OF THE UMPIRE STATE BUILDING!
YEH, KID, WE WON'T BE SORE...WE JUST WANT TO KNOW!
C'MON, KID, TELL US THE TRUTH!
P.D.
WELL...THESE LITTLE MEN—
SHADDAP!
P.D.
LADY, THIS LITTLE BOY SAYS HE LIVES HERE!
TUBBY! WHERE HAVE YOU BEEN?
HELLO, MA!

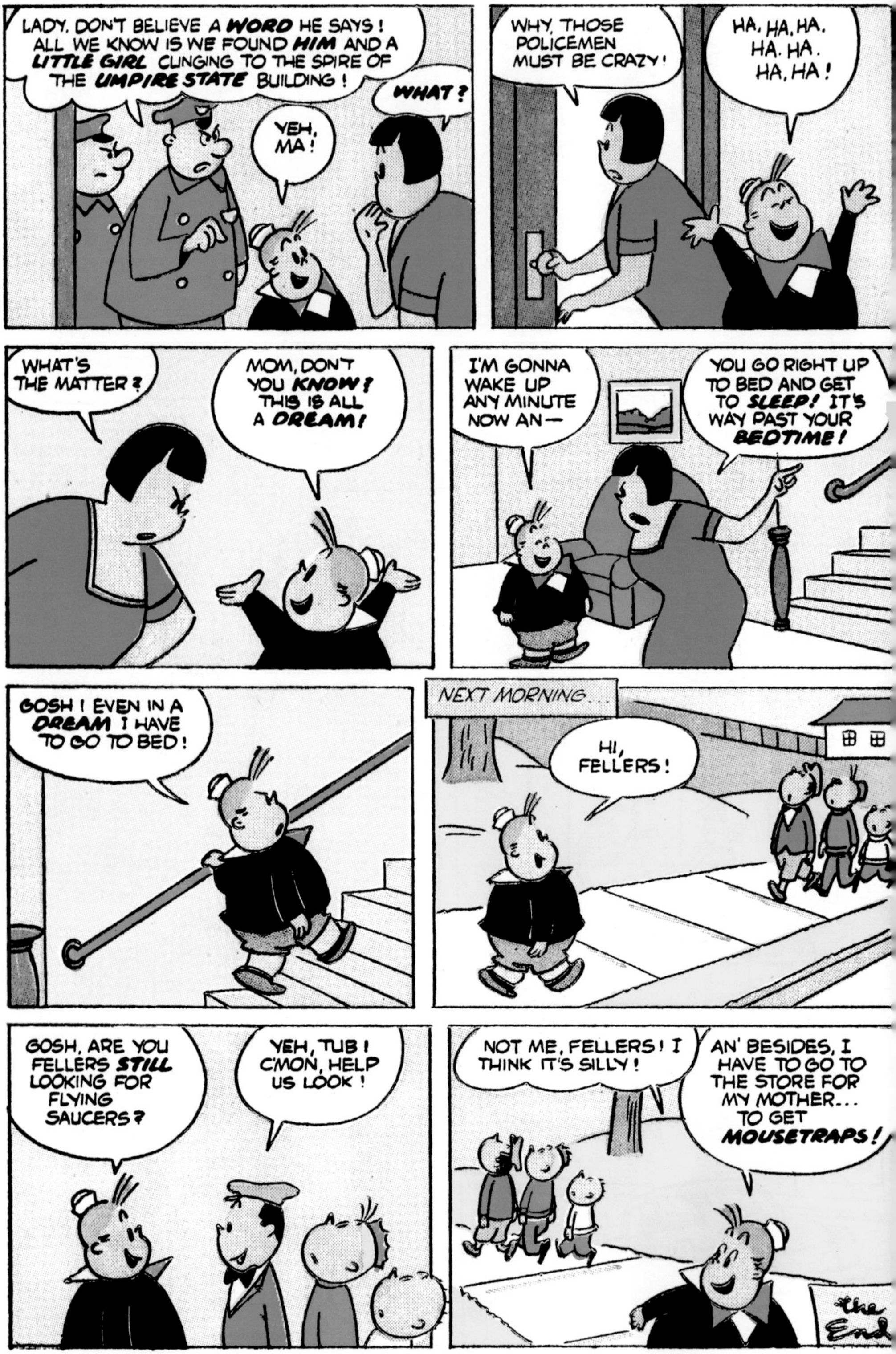
LADY, DON'T BELIEVE A WORD HE SAYS! ALL WE KNOW IS WE FOUND HIM AND A LITTLE GIRL CLINGING TO THE SPIRE OF THE UMPIRE STATE BUILDING!
YEH, MA!
WHAT?
WHY, THOSE POLICEMEN MUST BE CRAZY!
HA, HA, HA, HA, HA, HA, HA!
WHAT'S THE MATTER?
MOM, DON'T YOU KNOW! THIS IS ALL A DREAM!
I'M GONNA WAKE UP ANY MINUTE NOW AN—
YOU GO RIGHT UP TO BED AND GET TO SLEEP! IT'S WAY PAST YOUR BEDTIME!
GOSH! EVEN IN A DREAM I HAVE TO GO TO BED!
NEXT MORNING...
HI, FELLERS!
GOSH, ARE YOU FELLERS STILL LOOKING FOR FLYING SAUCERS?
YEH, TUB! C'MON, HELP US LOOK!
NOT ME, FELLERS! I THINK IT'S SILLY!
AN' BESIDES, I HAVE TO GO TO THE STORE FOR MY MOTHER... TO GET MOUSETRAPS!
the End

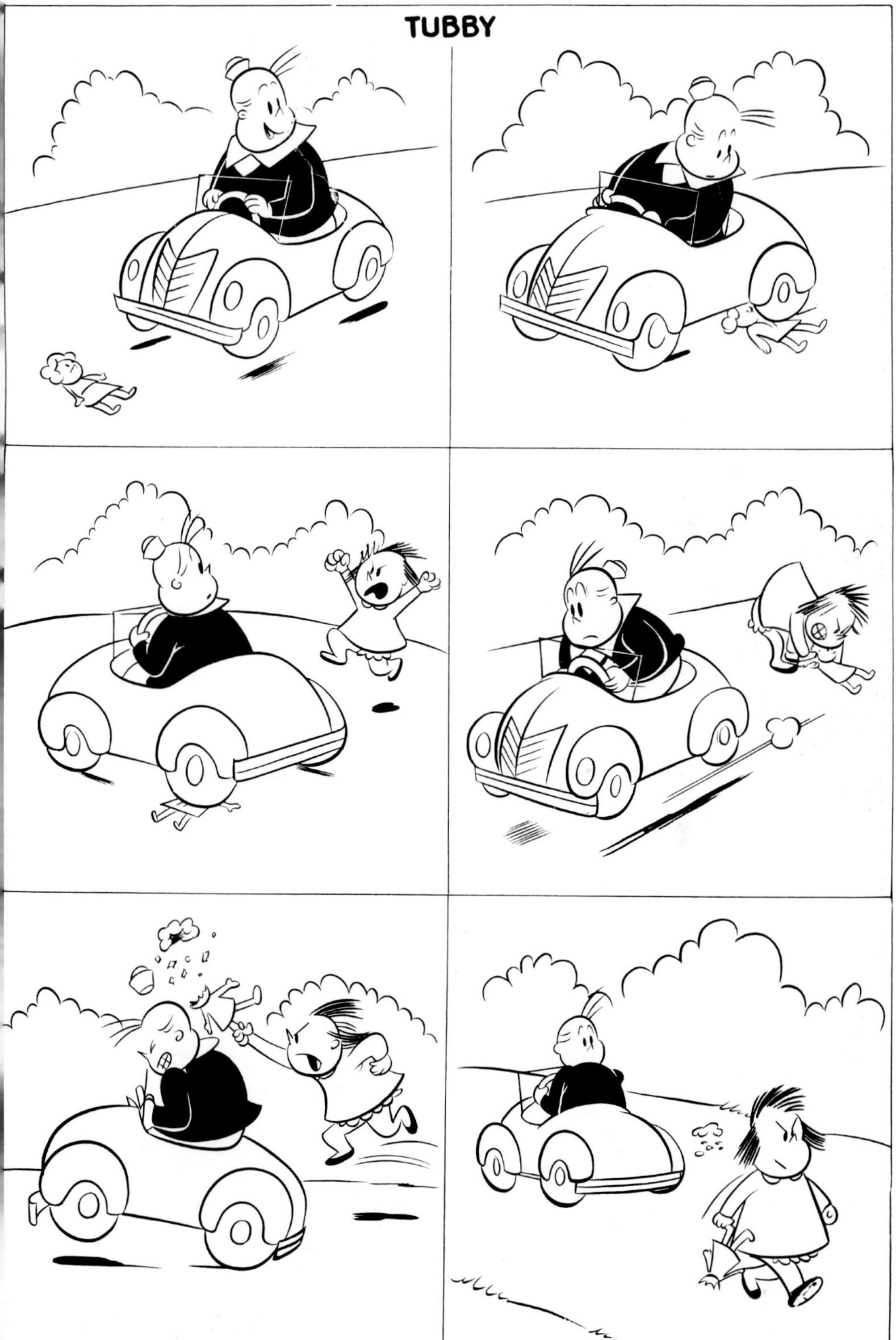
TUBBY

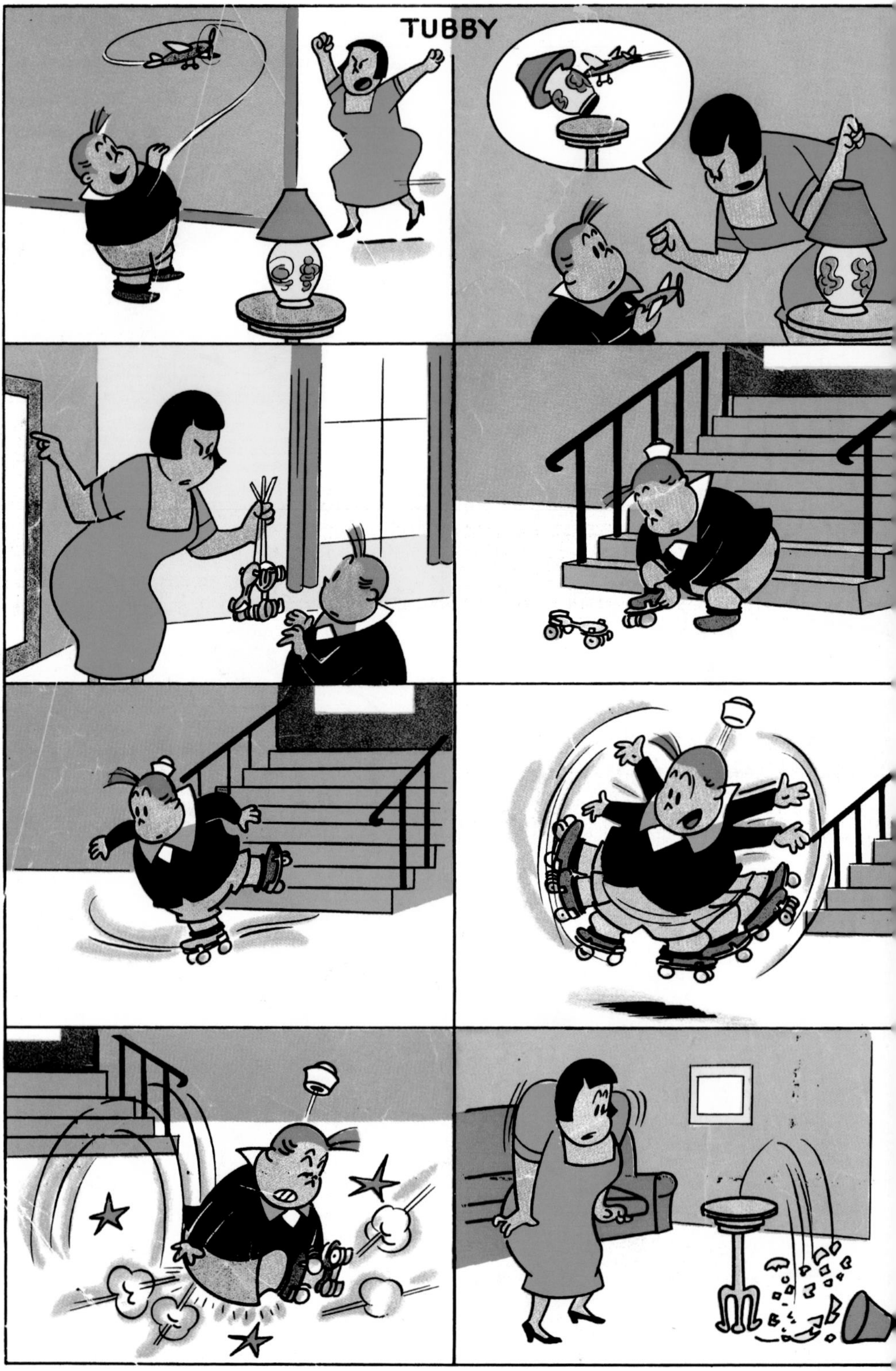
TUBBY

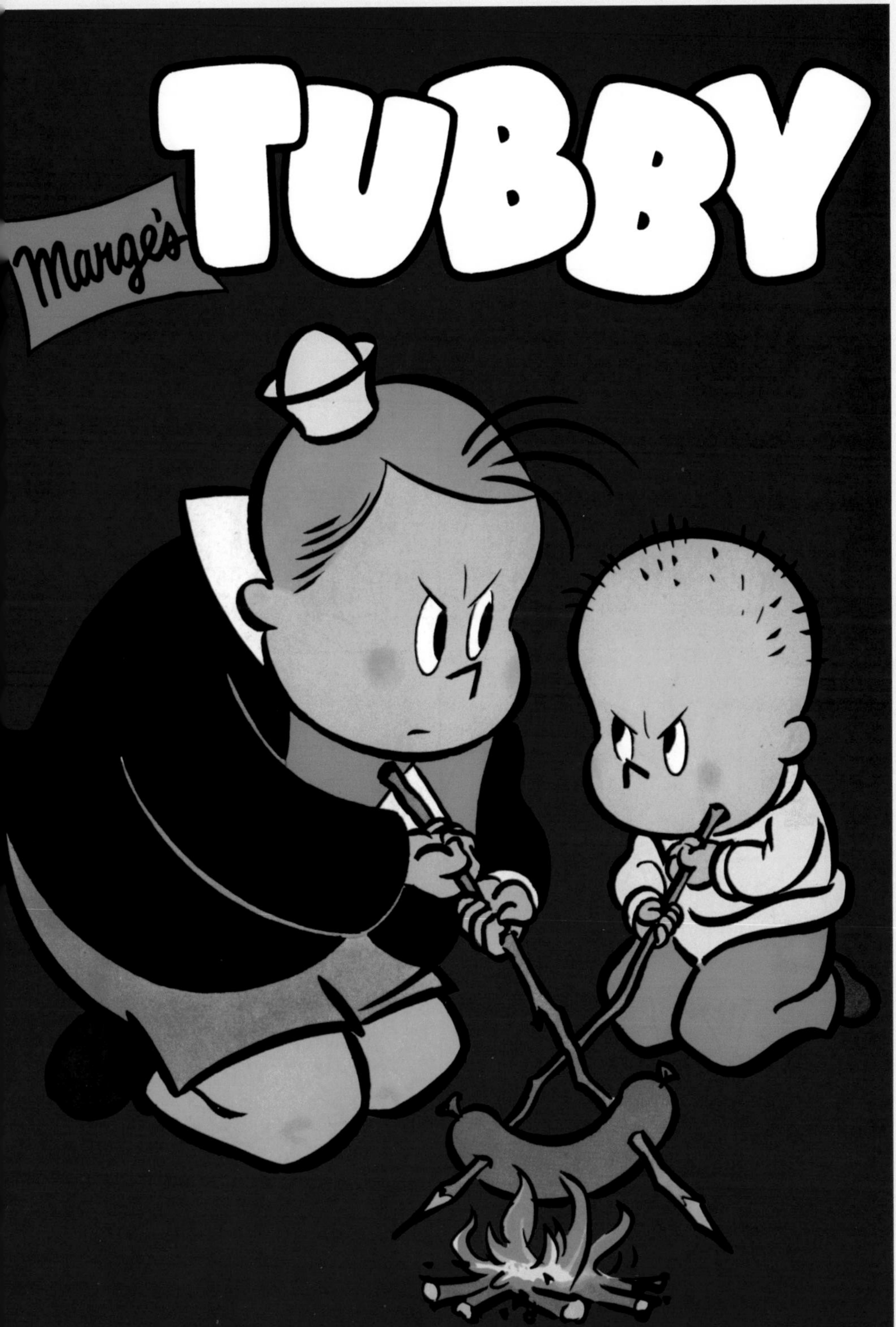
Marge's
TUBBY

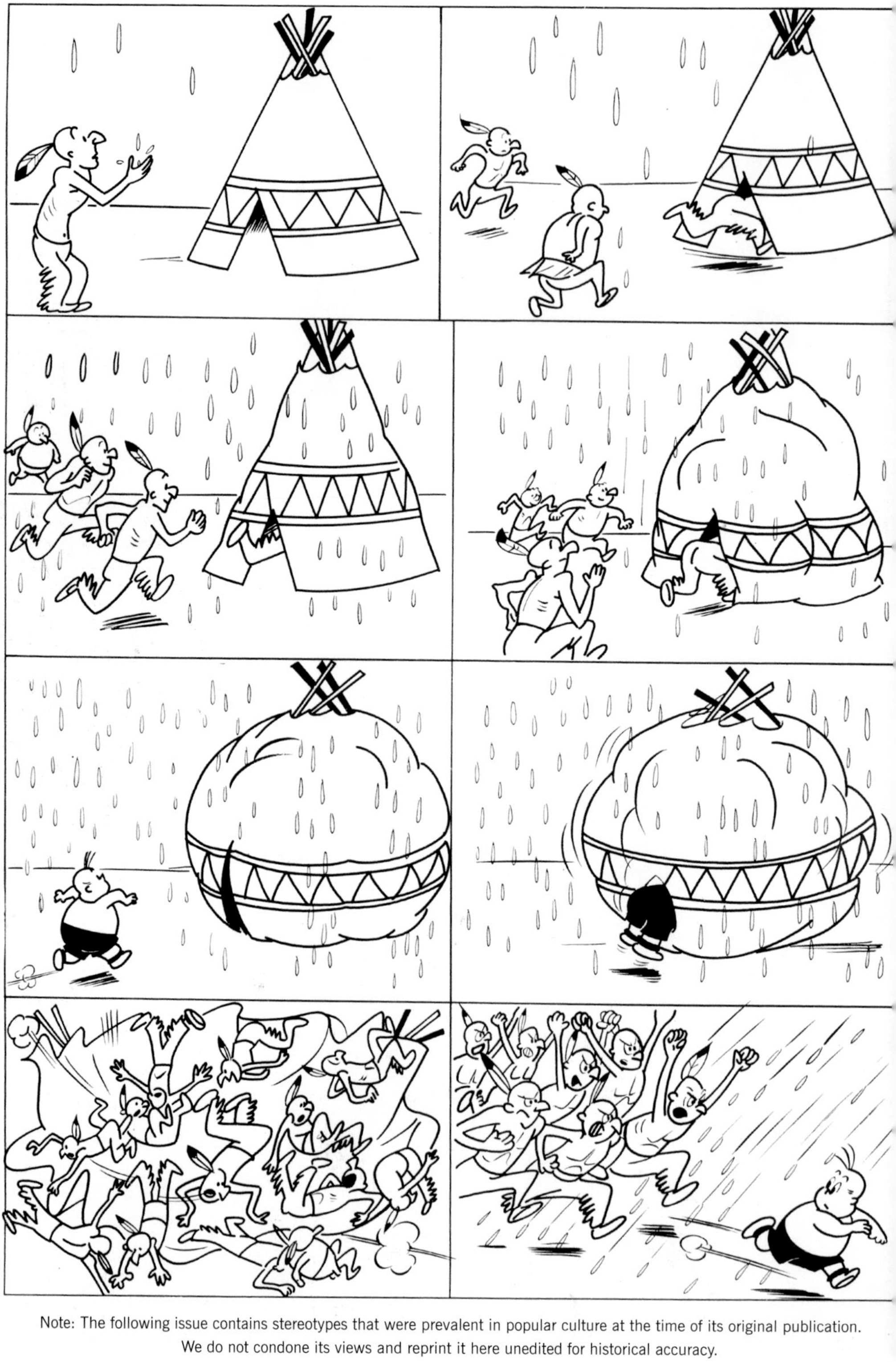

Note: The following issue contains stereotypes that were prevalent in popular culture at the time of its original publication. We do not condone its views and reprint it here unedited for historical accuracy.

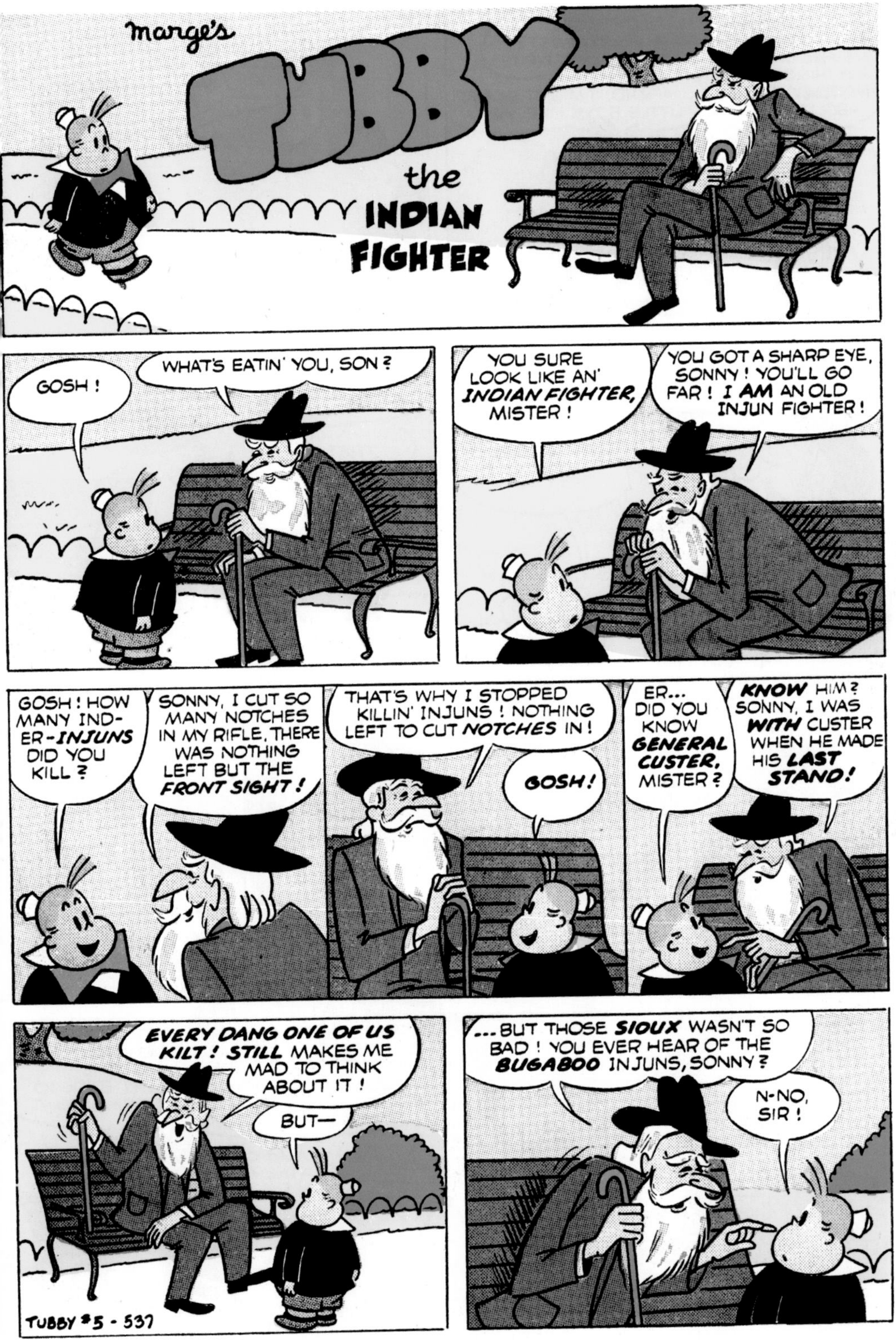
marge's
TUBBY
the INDIAN FIGHTER
GOSH!
WHAT'S EATIN' YOU, SON?
YOU SURE LOOK LIKE AN' INDIAN FIGHTER, MISTER!
YOU GOT A SHARP EYE, SONNY! YOU'LL GO FAR! I AM AN OLD INJUN FIGHTER!
GOSH! HOW MANY IND- ER-INJUNS DID YOU KILL?
SONNY, I CUT SO MANY NOTCHES IN MY RIFLE, THERE WAS NOTHING LEFT BUT THE FRONT SIGHT!
THAT'S WHY I STOPPED KILLIN' INJUNS! NOTHING LEFT TO CUT NOTCHES IN!
GOSH!
ER... DID YOU KNOW GENERAL CUSTER, MISTER?
KNOW HIM? SONNY, I WAS WITH CUSTER WHEN HE MADE HIS LAST STAND!
EVERY DANG ONE OF US KILT! STILL MAKES ME MAD TO THINK ABOUT IT!
BUT—
TUBBY #5 - 537
...BUT THOSE SIOUX WASN'T SO BAD! YOU EVER HEAR OF THE BUGABOO INJUNS, SONNY?
N-NO, SIR!

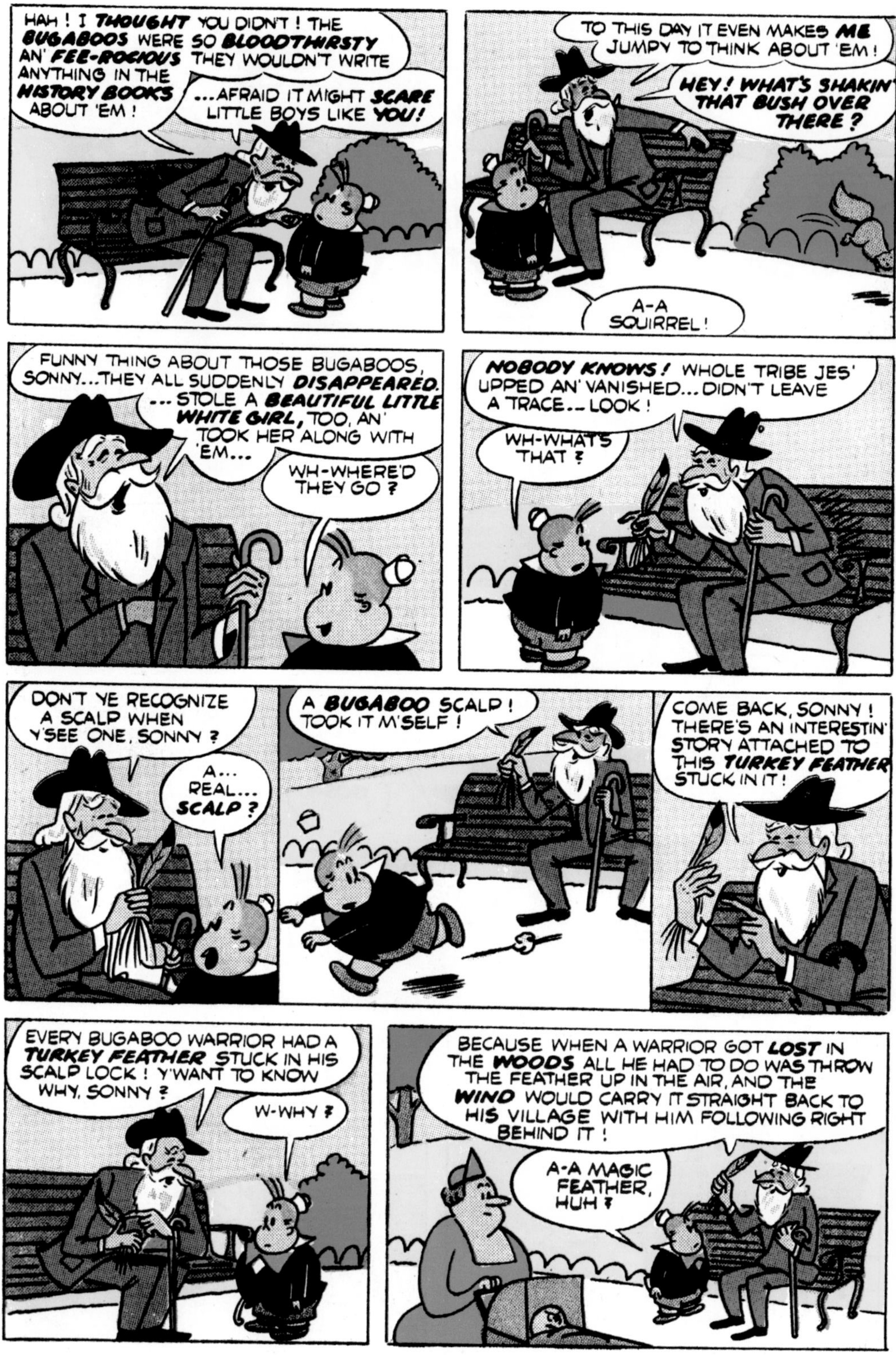
HAH! I THOUGHT YOU DIDN'T! THE BUGABOOS WERE SO BLOODTHIRSTY AN' FEE-ROCIOUS THEY WOULDN'T WRITE ANYTHING IN THE HISTORY BOOKS ABOUT 'EM!
...AFRAID IT MIGHT SCARE LITTLE BOYS LIKE YOU!
TO THIS DAY IT EVEN MAKES ME JUMPY TO THINK ABOUT 'EM!
HEY! WHAT'S SHAKIN' THAT BUSH OVER THERE?
A-A SQUIRREL!
FUNNY THING ABOUT THOSE BUGABOOS, SONNY...THEY ALL SUDDENLY DISAPPEARED. ...STOLE A BEAUTIFUL LITTLE WHITE GIRL, TOO, AN' TOOK HER ALONG WITH 'EM...
WH-WHERE'D THEY GO?
NOBODY KNOWS! WHOLE TRIBE JES' UPPED AN' VANISHED...DIDN'T LEAVE A TRACE...LOOK!
WH-WHAT'S THAT?
DON'T YE RECOGNIZE A SCALP WHEN Y'SEE ONE, SONNY?
A... REAL... SCALP?
A BUGABOO SCALP! TOOK IT M'SELF!
COME BACK, SONNY! THERE'S AN INTERESTIN' STORY ATTACHED TO THIS TURKEY FEATHER STUCK IN IT!
EVERY BUGABOO WARRIOR HAD A TURKEY FEATHER STUCK IN HIS SCALP LOCK! Y'WANT TO KNOW WHY, SONNY?
W-WHY?
BECAUSE WHEN A WARRIOR GOT LOST IN THE WOODS ALL HE HAD TO DO WAS THROW THE FEATHER UP IN THE AIR, AND THE WIND WOULD CARRY IT STRAIGHT BACK TO HIS VILLAGE WITH HIM FOLLOWING RIGHT BEHIND IT!
A-A MAGIC FEATHER, HUH?

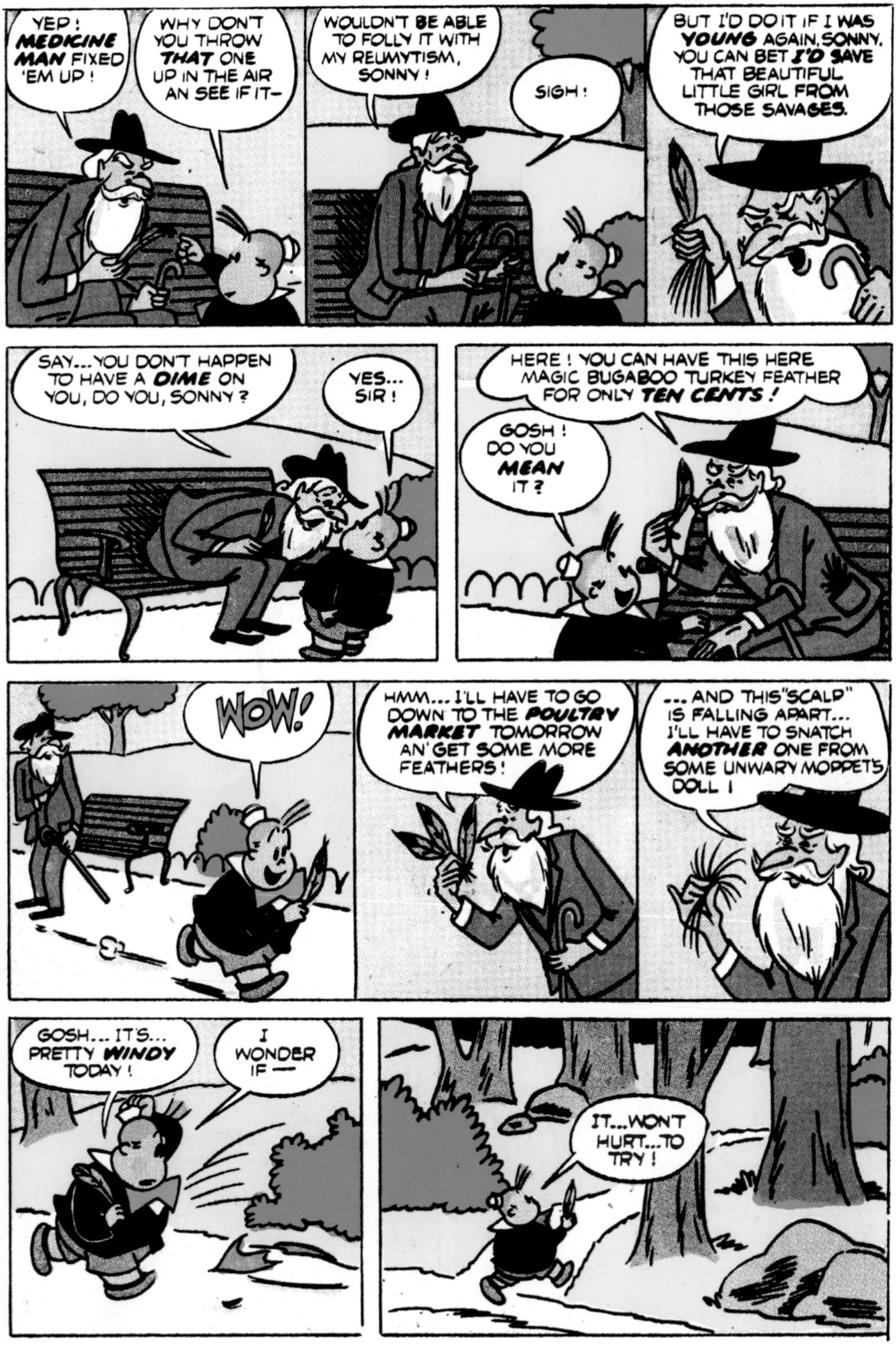
YEP! MEDICINE MAN FIXED 'EM UP!
WHY DON'T YOU THROW THAT ONE UP IN THE AIR AN SEE IF IT—
WOULDN'T BE ABLE TO FOLLY IT WITH MY REUMYTISM, SONNY!
SIGH!
BUT I'D DO IT IF I WAS YOUNG AGAIN, SONNY. YOU CAN BET I'D SAVE THAT BEAUTIFUL LITTLE GIRL FROM THOSE SAVAGES.
SAY... YOU DON'T HAPPEN TO HAVE A DIME ON YOU, DO YOU, SONNY?
YES... SIR!
HERE! YOU CAN HAVE THIS HERE MAGIC BUGABOO TURKEY FEATHER FOR ONLY TEN CENTS!
GOSH! DO YOU MEAN IT?
WOW!
HMM... I'LL HAVE TO GO DOWN TO THE POULTRY MARKET TOMORROW AN' GET SOME MORE FEATHERS!
... AND THIS "SCALP" IS FALLING APART... I'LL HAVE TO SNATCH ANOTHER ONE FROM SOME UNWARY MOPPET'S DOLL!
GOSH... IT'S... PRETTY WINDY TODAY!
I WONDER IF—
IT... WON'T HURT... TO TRY!

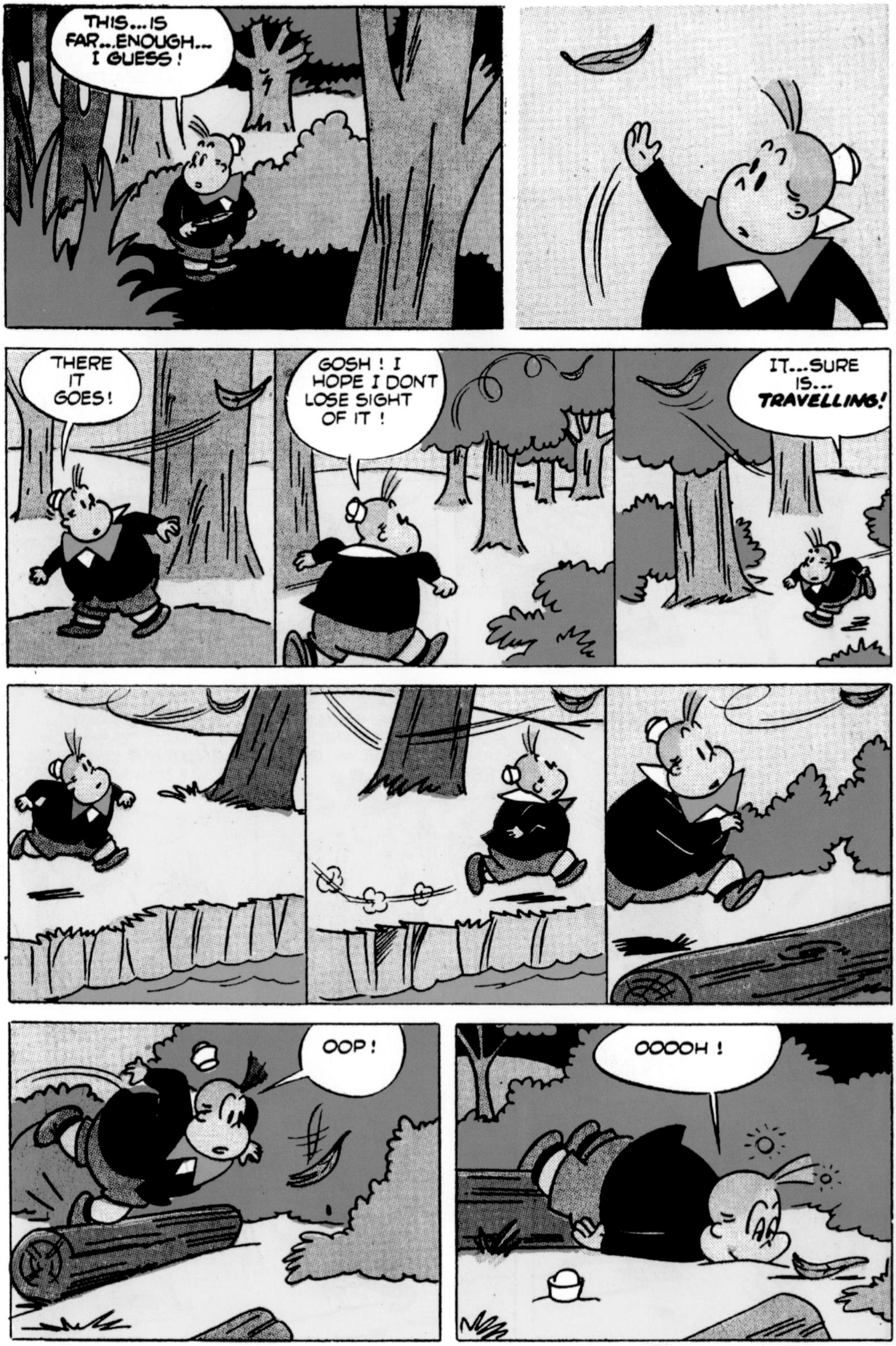
THIS...IS FAR...ENOUGH... I GUESS!
THERE IT GOES!
GOSH! I HOPE I DON'T LOSE SIGHT OF IT!
IT...SURE IS... TRAVELLING!
OOP!
OOOOH!

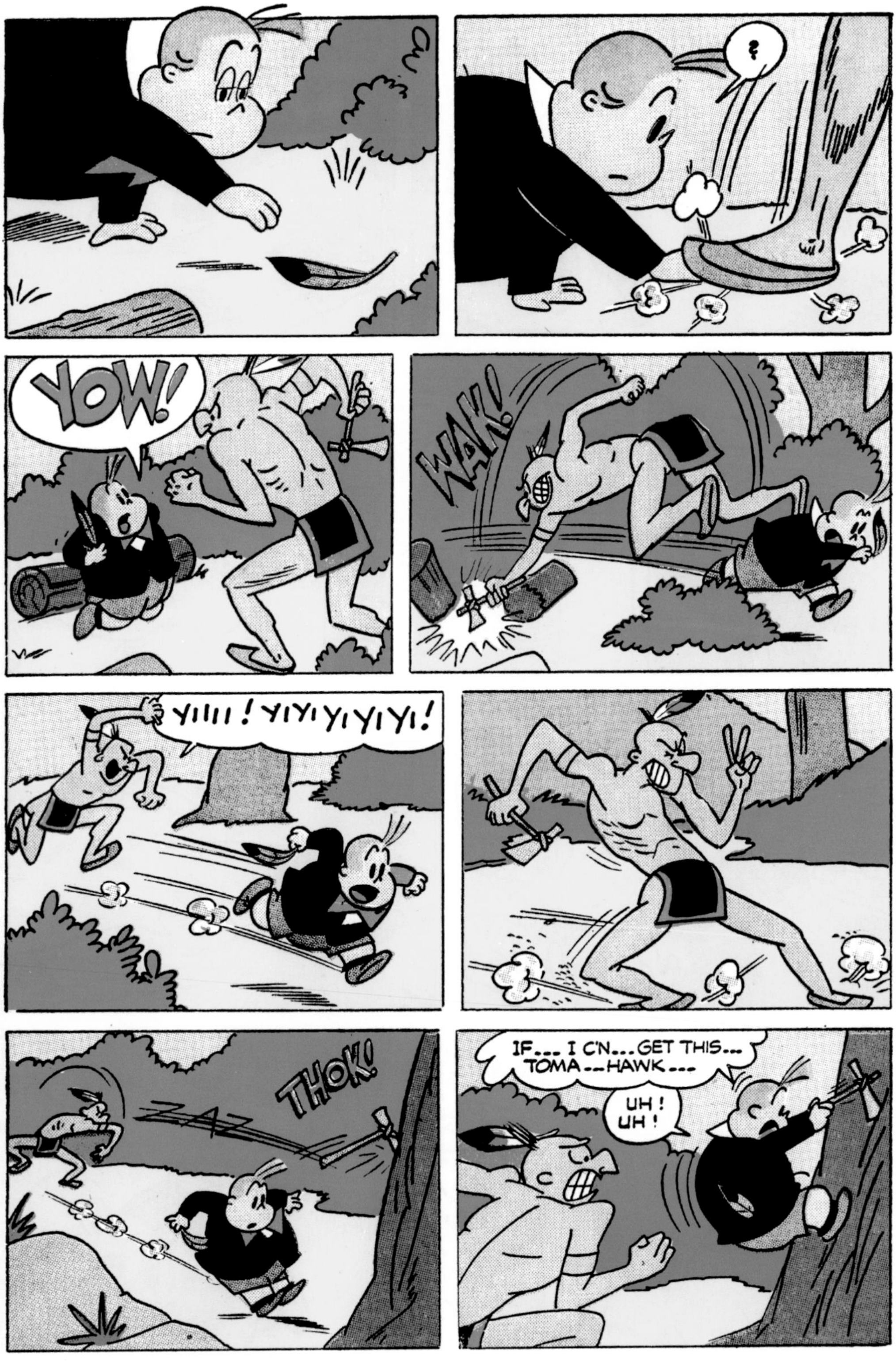
?
YOW!
WAK!
YIIII! YIYIYIYIYI!
THOK!
ZAZ
IF... I C'N... GET THIS... TOMA--HAWK---
UH! UH!

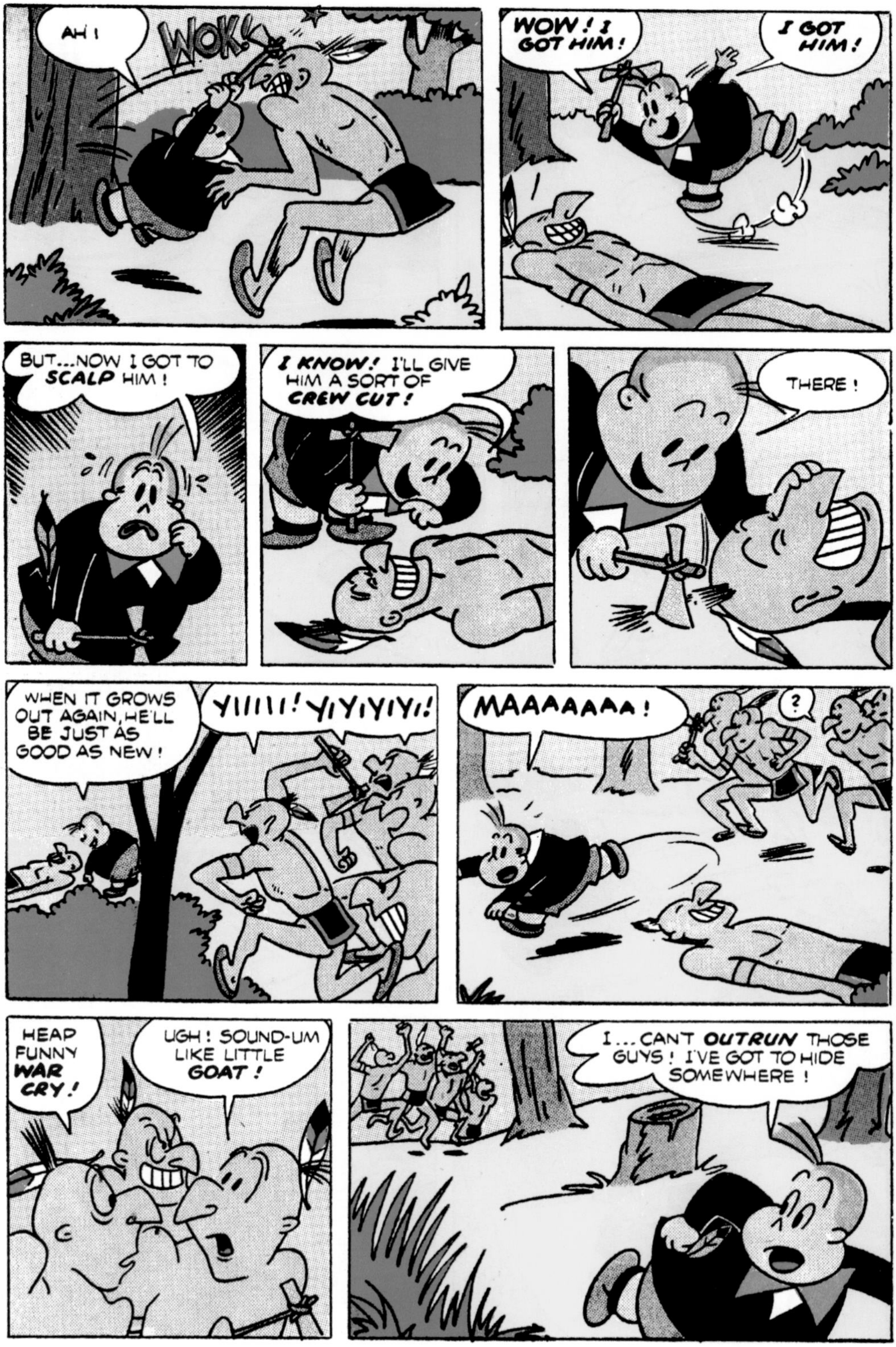
AH!
WOK!
WOW! I GOT HIM!
I GOT HIM!
BUT...NOW I GOT TO SCALP HIM!
I KNOW! I'LL GIVE HIM A SORT OF CREW CUT!
THERE!
WHEN IT GROWS OUT AGAIN, HE'LL BE JUST AS GOOD AS NEW!
YIIIII! YIYIYIYI!
MAAAAAAA!
?
HEAP FUNNY WAR CRY!
UGH! SOUND-UM LIKE LITTLE GOAT!
I...CAN'T OUTRUN THOSE GUYS! I'VE GOT TO HIDE SOMEWHERE!

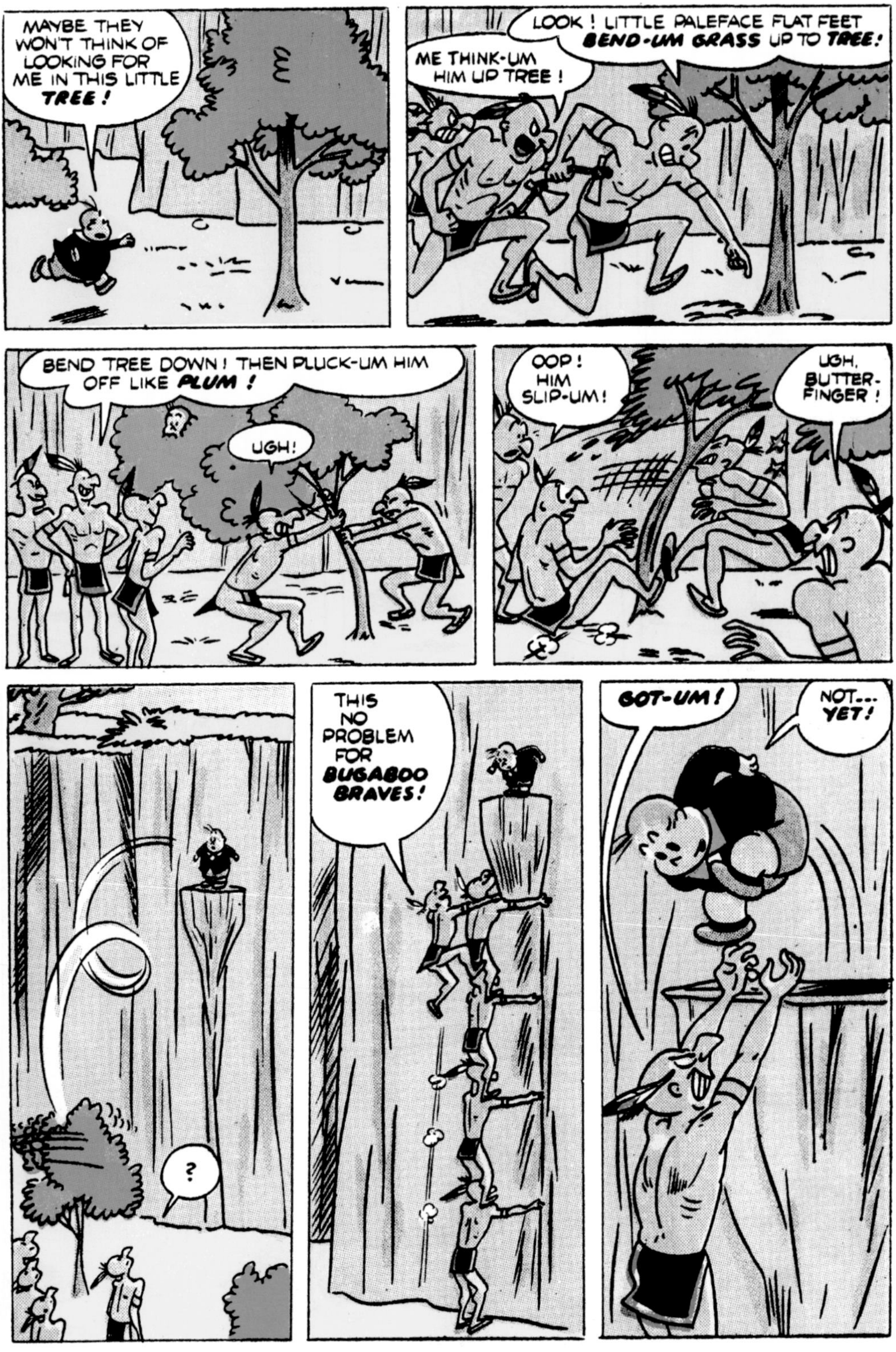
MAYBE THEY WON'T THINK OF LOOKING FOR ME IN THIS LITTLE TREE!
LOOK! LITTLE PALEFACE FLAT FEET BEND-UM GRASS UP TO TREE!
ME THINK-UM HIM UP TREE!
BEND TREE DOWN! THEN PLUCK-UM HIM OFF LIKE PLUM!
UGH!
OOP! HIM SLIP-UM!
UGH, BUTTER-FINGER!
?
THIS NO PROBLEM FOR BUGABOO BRAVES!
GOT-UM!
NOT... YET!

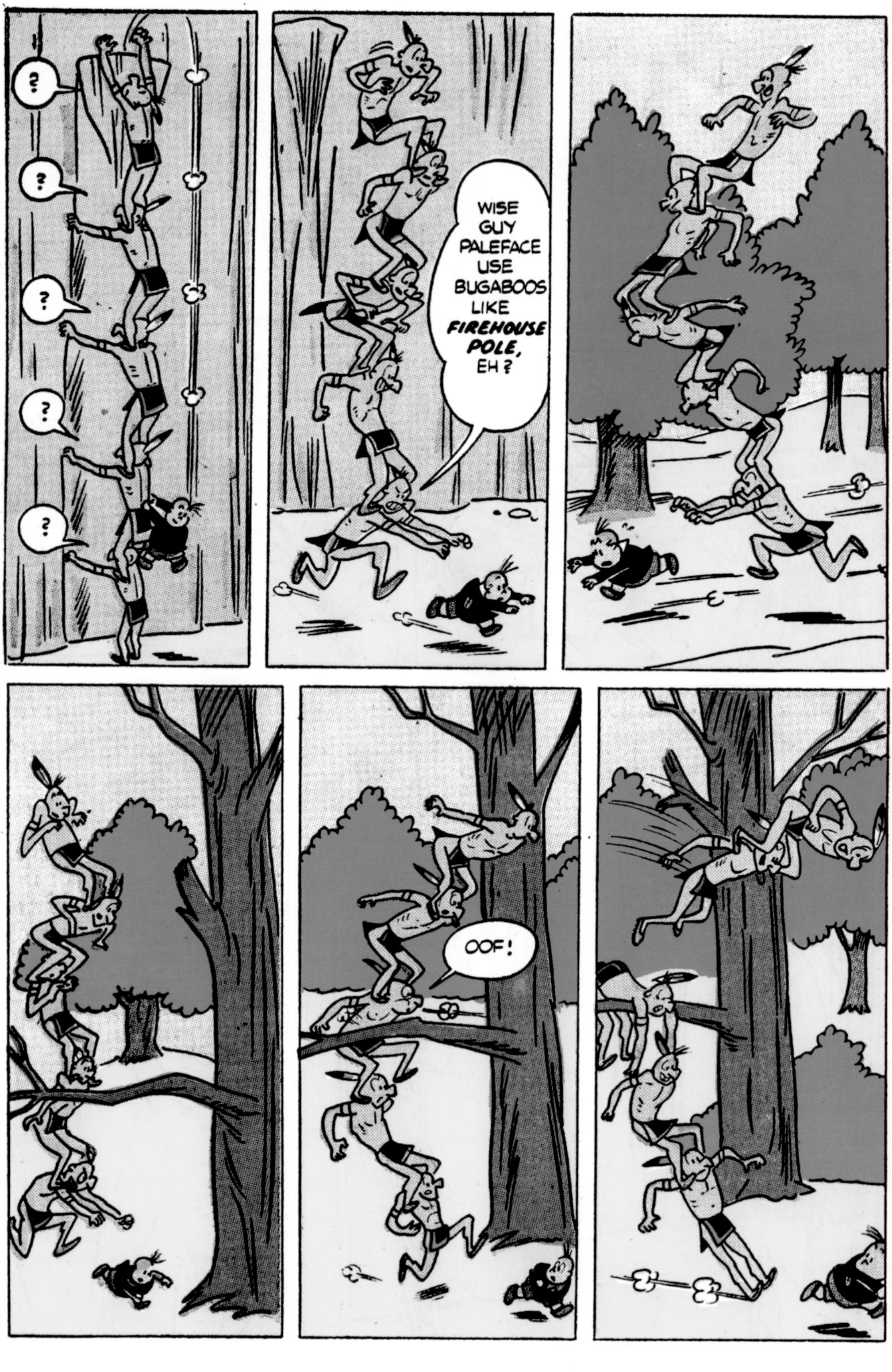
?
?
?
?
?
WISE GUY PALEFACE USE BUGABOOS LIKE FIREHOUSE POLE, EH?
OOF!

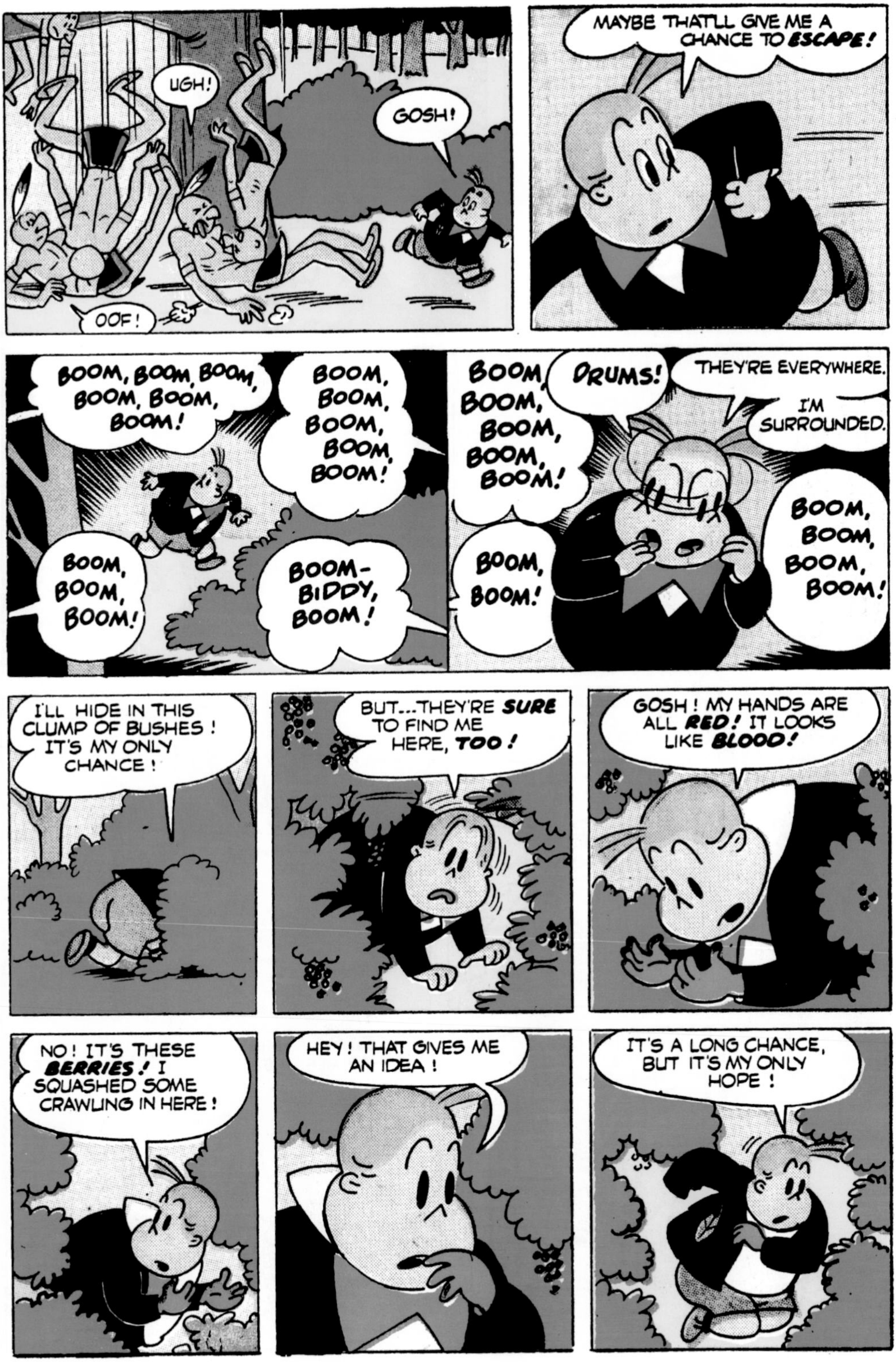
UGH!
GOSH!
OOF!
MAYBE THAT'LL GIVE ME A CHANCE TO ESCAPE!
BOOM, BOOM, BOOM, BOOM, BOOM, BOOM!
BOOM, BOOM, BOOM, BOOM, BOOM!
BOOM, BOOM, BOOM!
BOOM-BIDDY, BOOM!
BOOM, BOOM, BOOM, BOOM, BOOM!
DRUMS!
THEY'RE EVERYWHERE.
I'M SURROUNDED.
BOOM, BOOM!
BOOM, BOOM, BOOM, BOOM!
I'LL HIDE IN THIS CLUMP OF BUSHES! IT'S MY ONLY CHANCE!
BUT...THEY'RE SURE TO FIND ME HERE, TOO!
GOSH! MY HANDS ARE ALL RED! IT LOOKS LIKE BLOOD!
NO! IT'S THESE BERRIES! I SQUASHED SOME CRAWLING IN HERE!
HEY! THAT GIVES ME AN IDEA!
IT'S A LONG CHANCE, BUT IT'S MY ONLY HOPE!

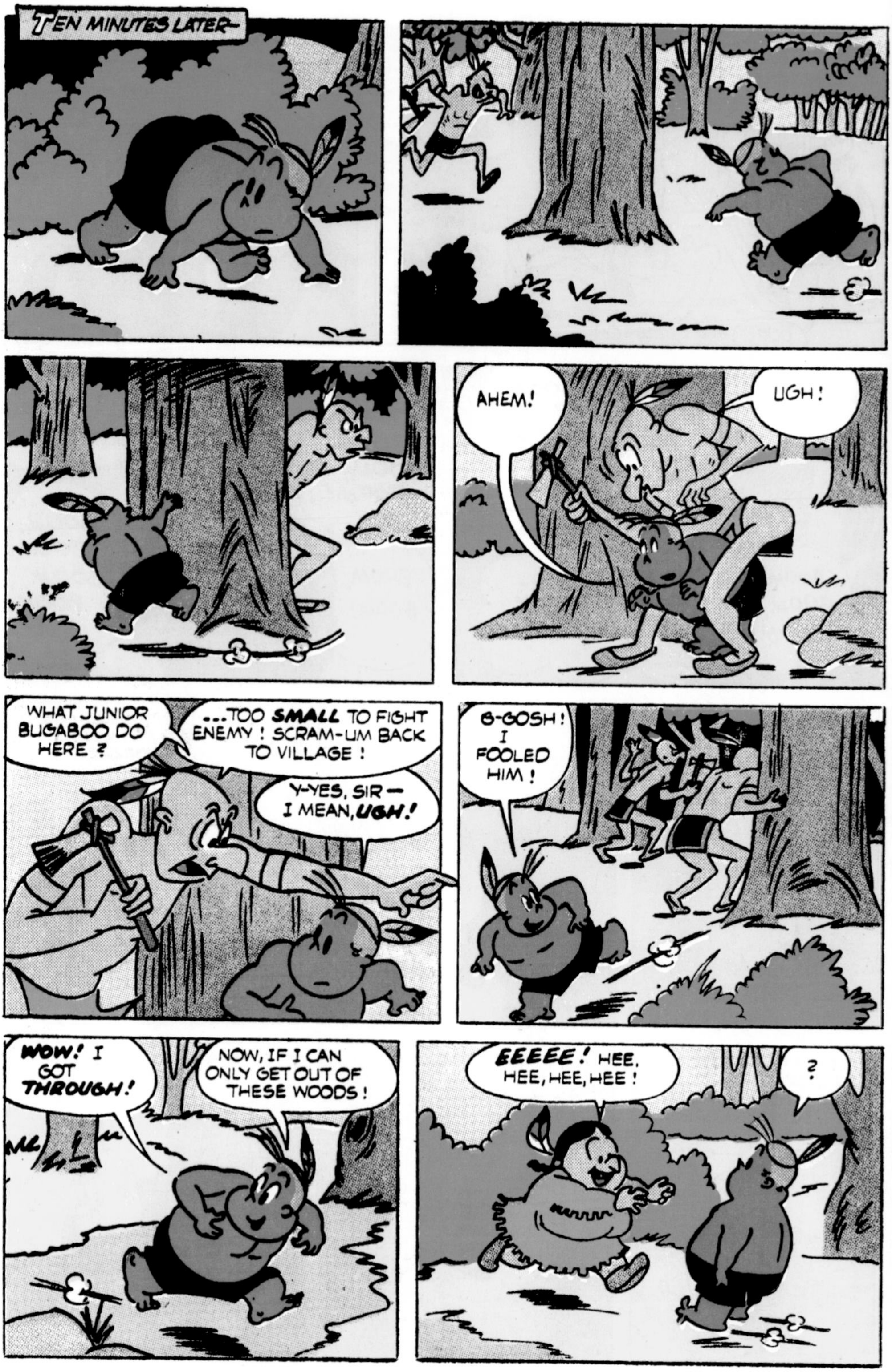
TEN MINUTES LATER—
AHEM!
UGH!
WHAT JUNIOR BUGABOO DO HERE ?
...TOO SMALL TO FIGHT ENEMY ! SCRAM-UM BACK TO VILLAGE !
Y-YES, SIR— I MEAN, UGH!
G-GOSH ! I FOOLED HIM !
WOW! I GOT THROUGH!
NOW, IF I CAN ONLY GET OUT OF THESE WOODS !
EEEEE! HEE, HEE, HEE, HEE !
?

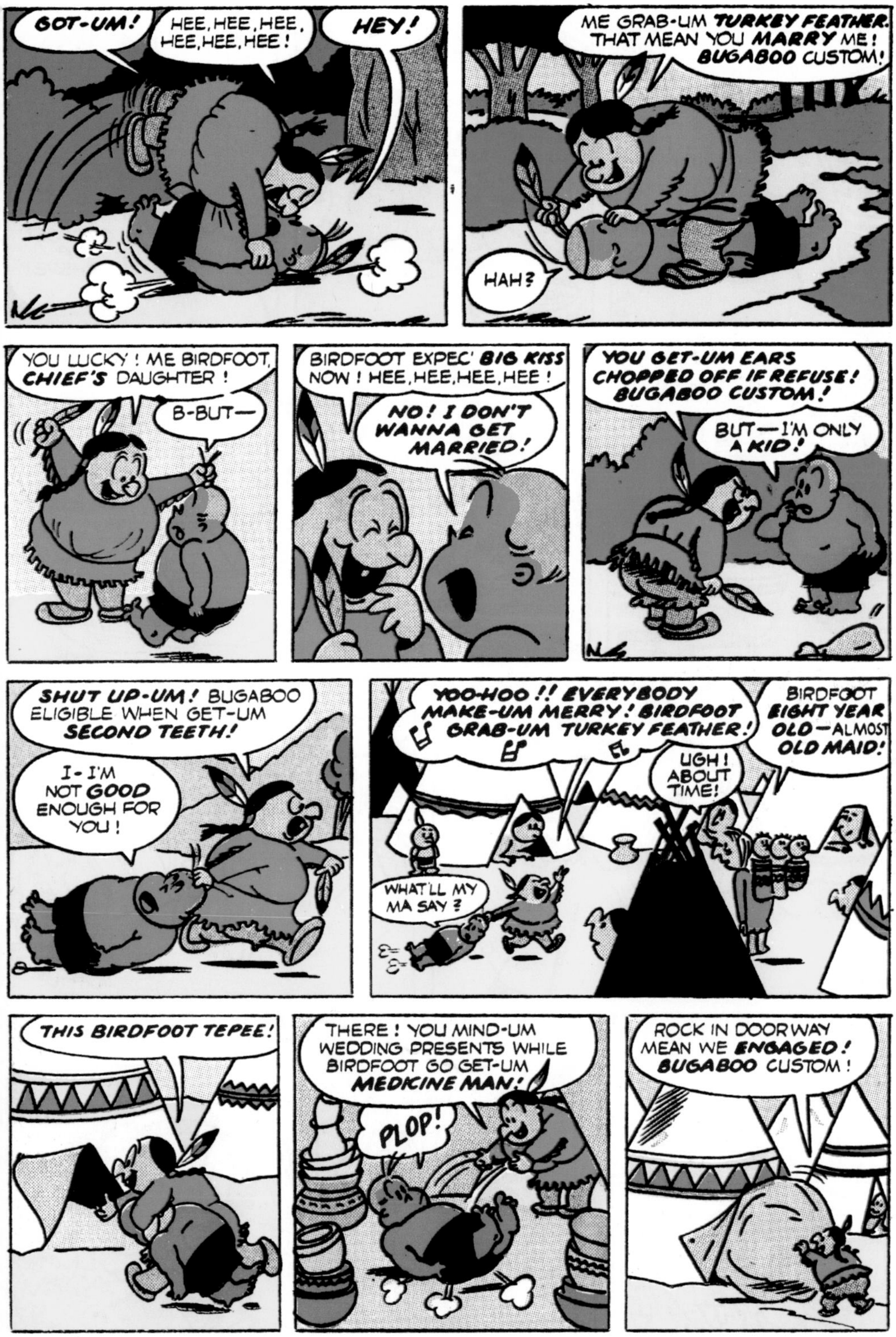
GOT-UM!
HEE, HEE, HEE, HEE, HEE, HEE!
HEY!
ME GRAB-UM TURKEY FEATHER. THAT MEAN YOU MARRY ME! BUGABOO CUSTOM!
HAH?
YOU LUCKY! ME BIRDFOOT, CHIEF'S DAUGHTER!
B-BUT—
BIRDFOOT EXPEC' BIG KISS NOW! HEE, HEE, HEE, HEE!
NO! I DON'T WANNA GET MARRIED!
YOU GET-UM EARS CHOPPED OFF IF REFUSE! BUGABOO CUSTOM!
BUT—I'M ONLY A KID!
SHUT UP-UM! BUGABOO ELIGIBLE WHEN GET-UM SECOND TEETH!
I-I'M NOT GOOD ENOUGH FOR YOU!
YOO-HOO!! EVERYBODY MAKE-UM MERRY! BIRDFOOT GRAB-UM TURKEY FEATHER!
BIRDFOOT EIGHT YEAR OLD—ALMOST OLD MAID!
UGH! ABOUT TIME!
WHAT'LL MY MA SAY?
THIS BIRDFOOT TEPEE!
THERE! YOU MIND-UM WEDDING PRESENTS WHILE BIRDFOOT GO GET-UM MEDICINE MAN!
PLOP!
ROCK IN DOORWAY MEAN WE ENGAGED! BUGABOO CUSTOM!

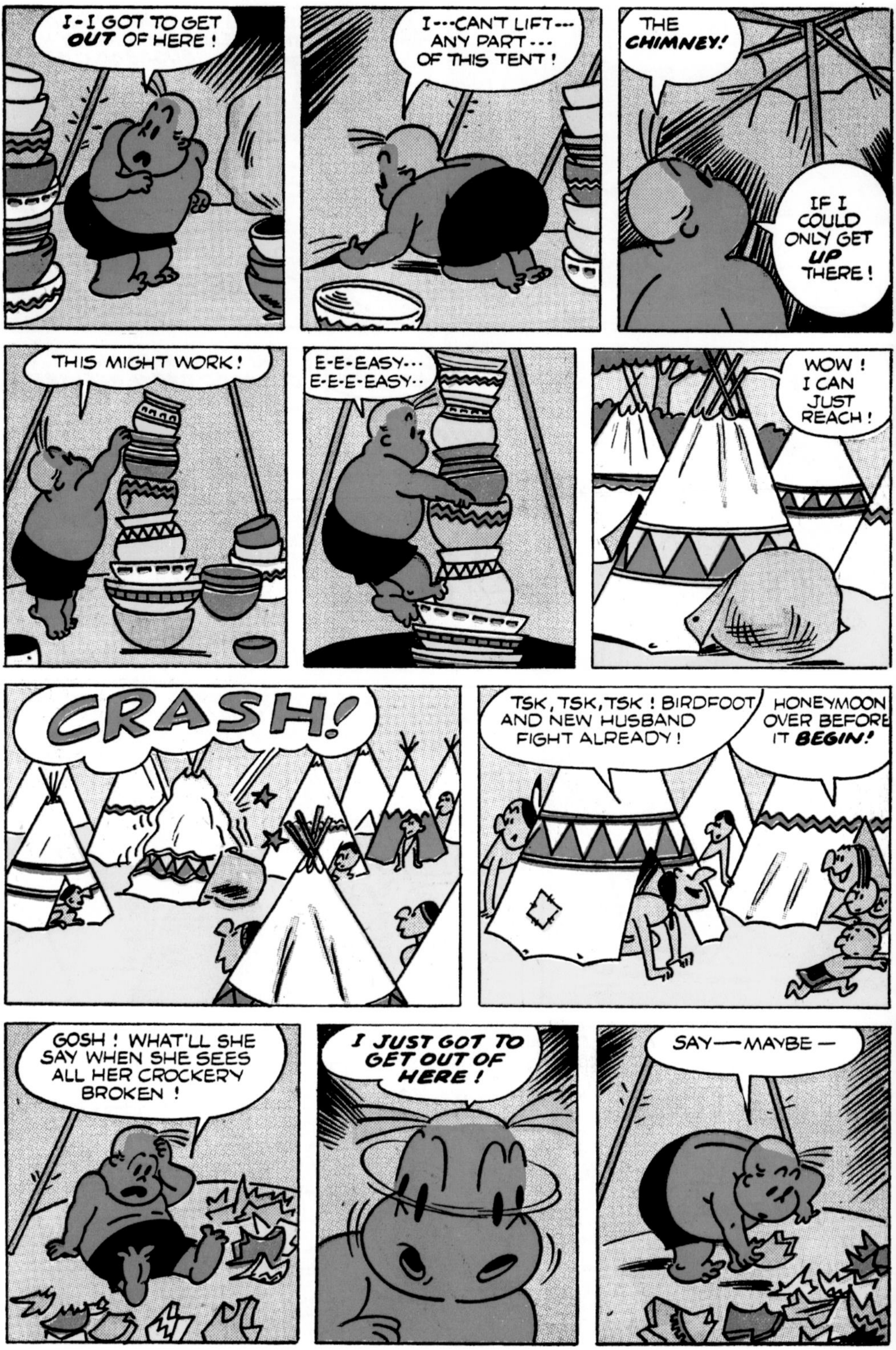
I-I GOT TO GET OUT OF HERE!
I---CAN'T LIFT--- ANY PART--- OF THIS TENT!
THE CHIMNEY!
IF I COULD ONLY GET UP THERE!
THIS MIGHT WORK!
E-E-EASY... E-E-E-EASY..
WOW! I CAN JUST REACH!
CRASH!
TSK, TSK, TSK! BIRDFOOT AND NEW HUSBAND FIGHT ALREADY!
HONEYMOON OVER BEFORE IT BEGIN!
GOSH! WHAT'LL SHE SAY WHEN SHE SEES ALL HER CROCKERY BROKEN!
I JUST GOT TO GET OUT OF HERE!
SAY—MAYBE—

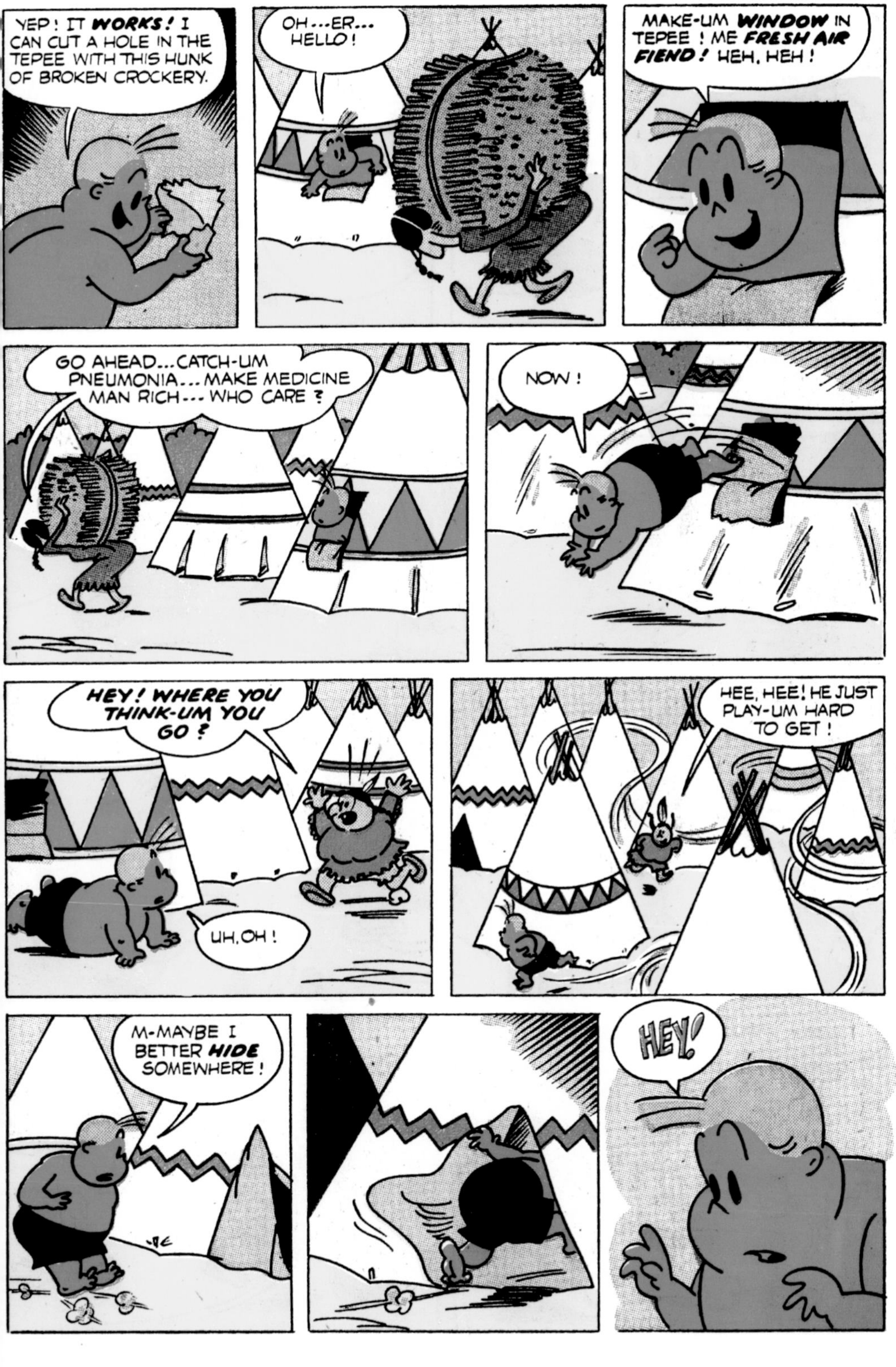

YEP! IT WORKS! I CAN CUT A HOLE IN THE TEPEE WITH THIS HUNK OF BROKEN CROCKERY.
OH...ER... HELLO!
MAKE-UM WINDOW IN TEPEE! ME FRESH AIR FIEND! HEH, HEH!
GO AHEAD...CATCH-UM PNEUMONIA...MAKE MEDICINE MAN RICH...WHO CARE?
NOW!
HEY! WHERE YOU THINK-UM YOU GO?
UH, OH!
HEE, HEE! HE JUST PLAY-UM HARD TO GET!
M-MAYBE I BETTER HIDE SOMEWHERE!
HEY!

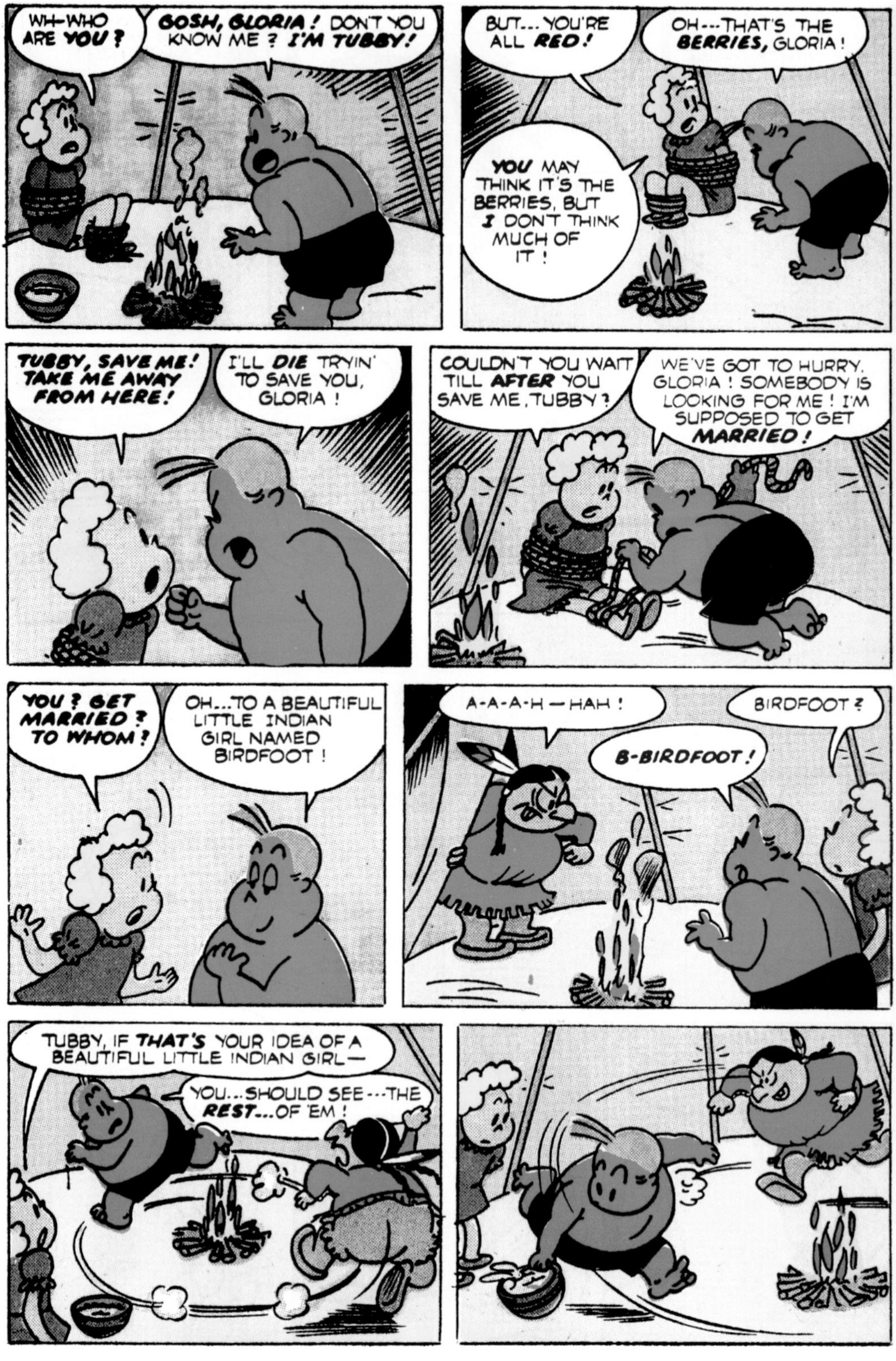

WH-WHO ARE YOU?
GOSH, GLORIA! DON'T YOU KNOW ME? I'M TUBBY!
BUT... YOU'RE ALL RED!
OH---THAT'S THE BERRIES, GLORIA!
YOU MAY THINK IT'S THE BERRIES, BUT I DON'T THINK MUCH OF IT!
TUBBY, SAVE ME! TAKE ME AWAY FROM HERE!
I'LL DIE TRYIN' TO SAVE YOU, GLORIA!
COULDN'T YOU WAIT TILL AFTER YOU SAVE ME, TUBBY?
WE'VE GOT TO HURRY, GLORIA! SOMEBODY IS LOOKING FOR ME! I'M SUPPOSED TO GET MARRIED!
YOU? GET MARRIED? TO WHOM?
OH...TO A BEAUTIFUL LITTLE INDIAN GIRL NAMED BIRDFOOT!
A-A-A-H — HAH!
BIRDFOOT?
B-BIRDFOOT!
TUBBY, IF THAT'S YOUR IDEA OF A BEAUTIFUL LITTLE INDIAN GIRL—
YOU...SHOULD SEE---THE REST...OF 'EM!

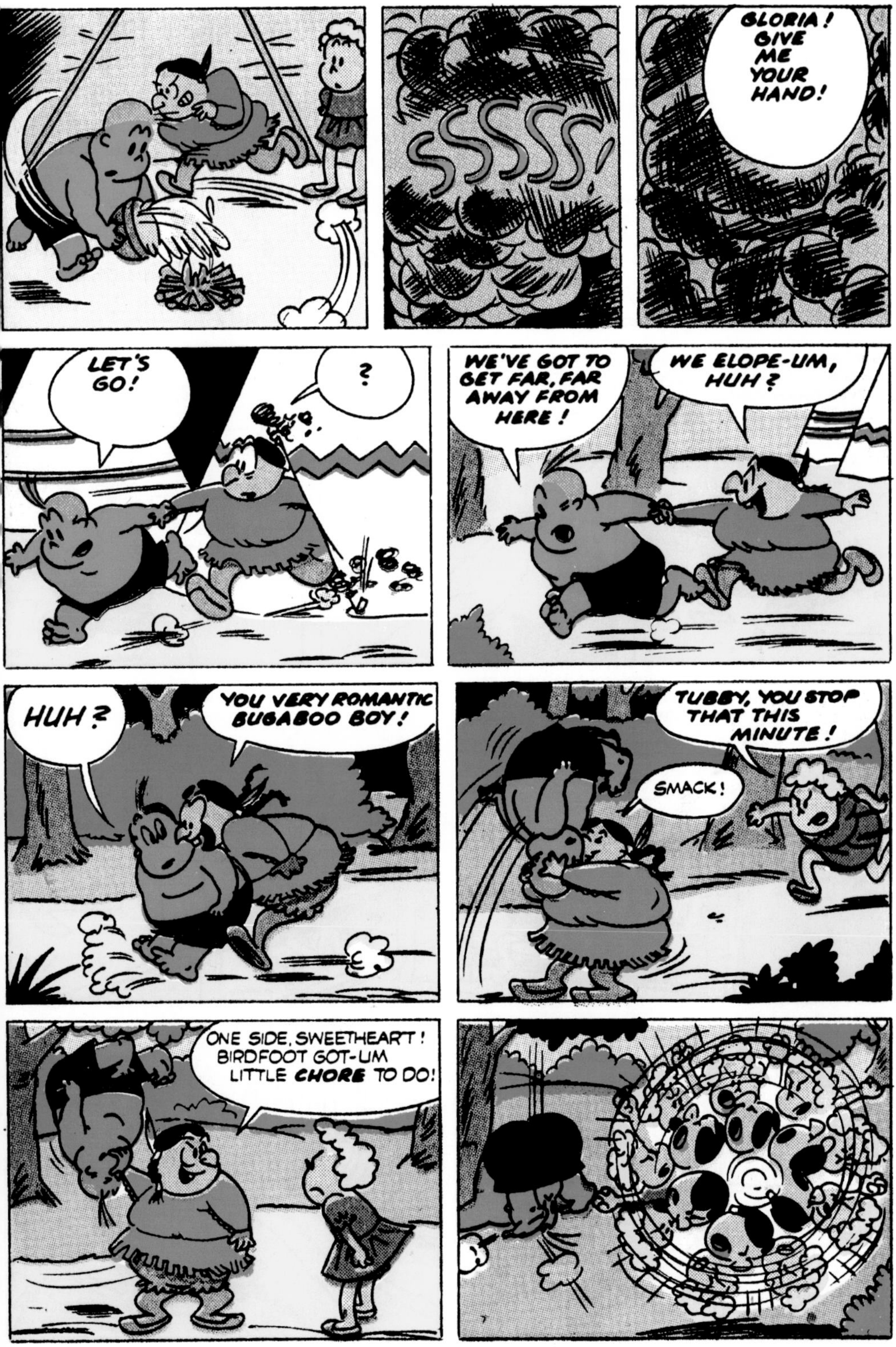
SSSSS!
GLORIA! GIVE ME YOUR HAND!
LET'S GO!
?
WE'VE GOT TO GET FAR, FAR AWAY FROM HERE!
WE ELOPE-UM, HUH?
HUH?
YOU VERY ROMANTIC BUGABOO BOY!
TUBBY, YOU STOP THAT THIS MINUTE!
SMACK!
ONE SIDE, SWEETHEART! BIRDFOOT GOT-UM LITTLE CHORE TO DO!

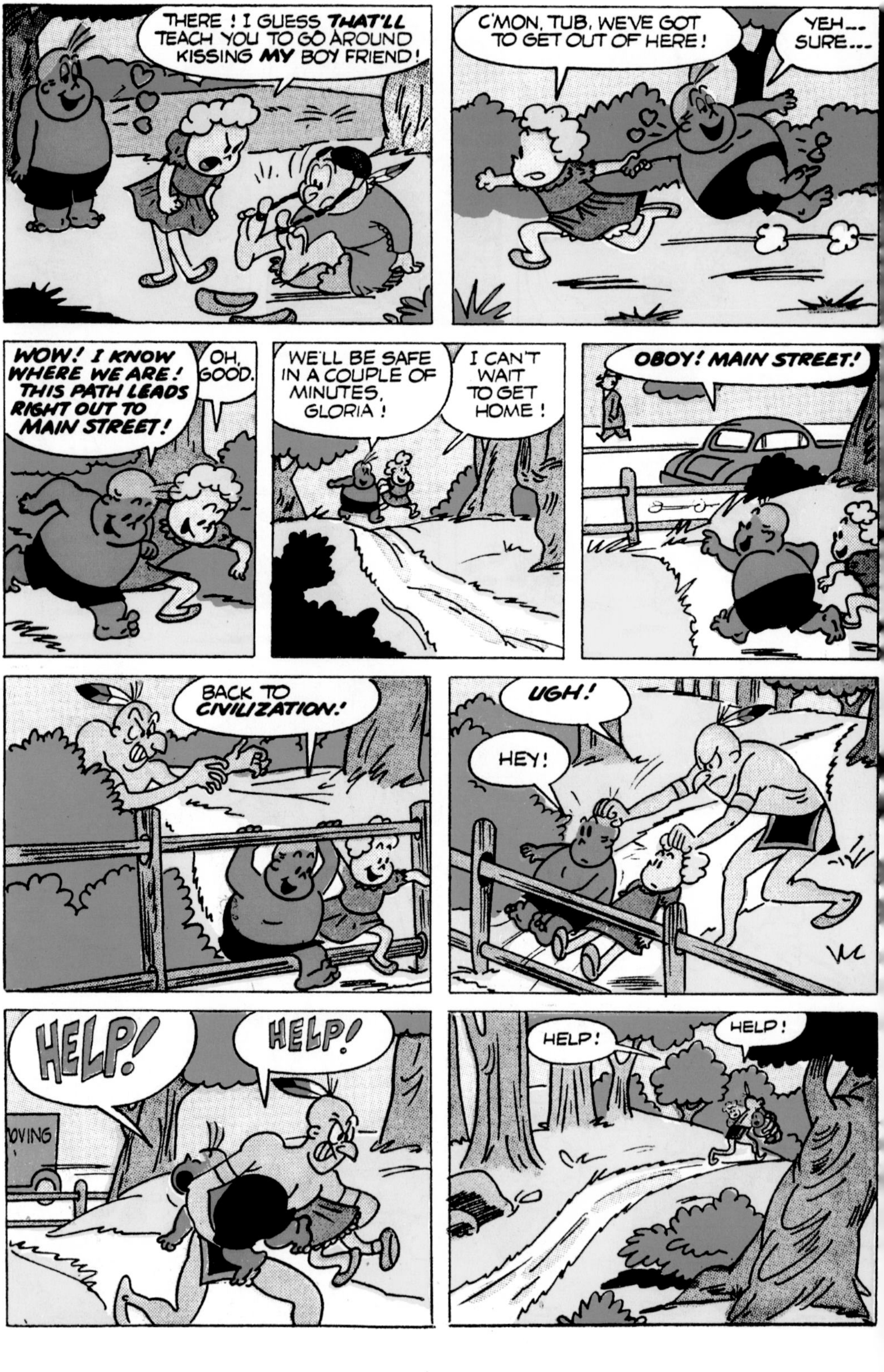
THERE ! I GUESS THAT'LL TEACH YOU TO GO AROUND KISSING MY BOY FRIEND !
C'MON, TUB, WE'VE GOT TO GET OUT OF HERE !
YEH... SURE...
WOW! I KNOW WHERE WE ARE! THIS PATH LEADS RIGHT OUT TO MAIN STREET!
OH, GOOD.
WE'LL BE SAFE IN A COUPLE OF MINUTES, GLORIA !
I CAN'T WAIT TO GET HOME !
OBOY! MAIN STREET!
BACK TO CIVILIZATION!
UGH!
HEY!
HELP!
HELP!
OVING
HELP!
HELP!

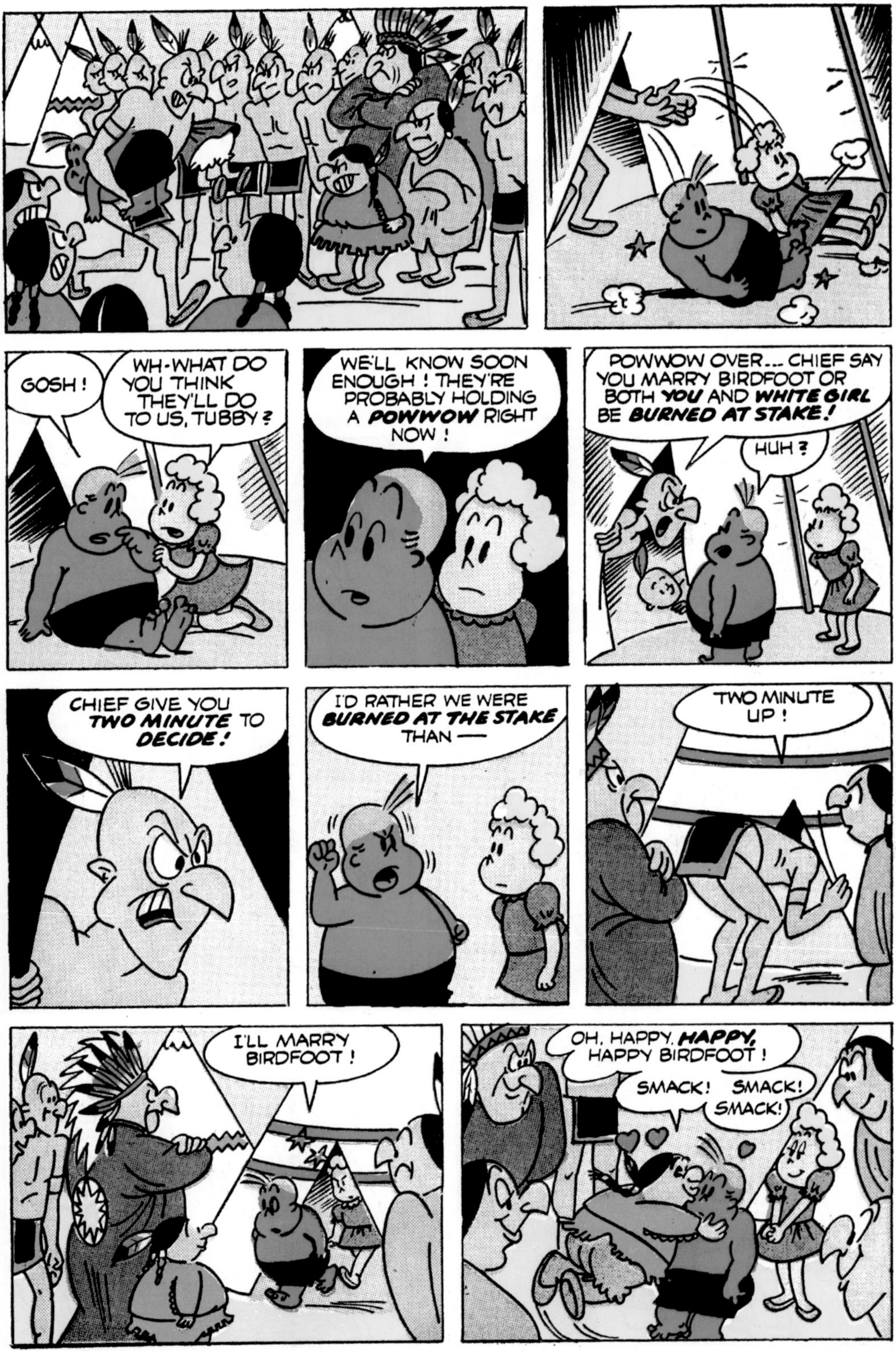
GOSH!
WH-WHAT DO YOU THINK THEY'LL DO TO US, TUBBY?
WE'LL KNOW SOON ENOUGH! THEY'RE PROBABLY HOLDING A POWWOW RIGHT NOW!
POWWOW OVER... CHIEF SAY YOU MARRY BIRDFOOT OR BOTH YOU AND WHITE GIRL BE BURNED AT STAKE!
HUH?
CHIEF GIVE YOU TWO MINUTE TO DECIDE!
I'D RATHER WE WERE BURNED AT THE STAKE THAN —
TWO MINUTE UP!
I'LL MARRY BIRDFOOT!
OH, HAPPY, HAPPY, HAPPY BIRDFOOT!
SMACK! SMACK! SMACK!

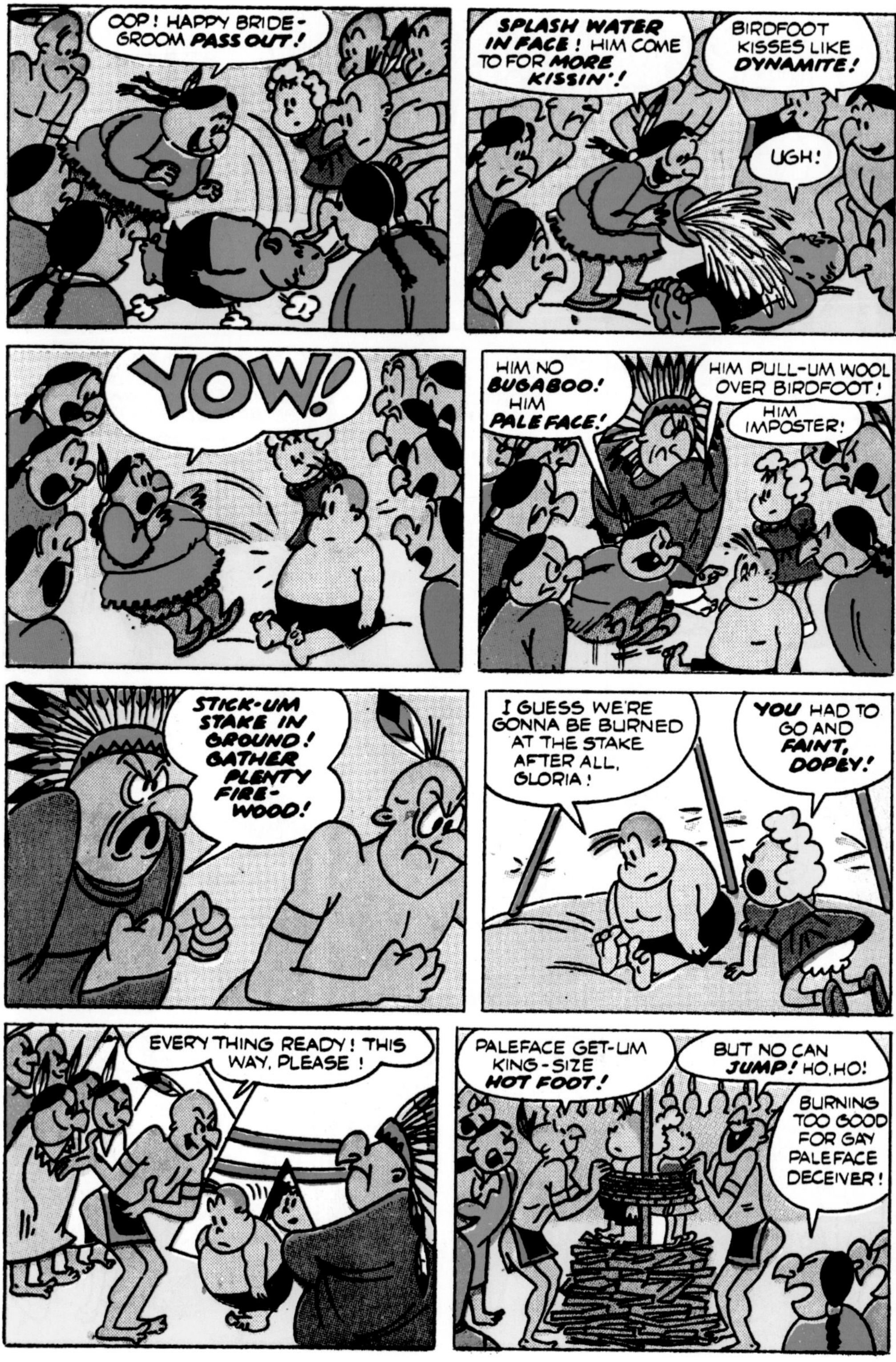
OOP! HAPPY BRIDE-GROOM PASS OUT!
SPLASH WATER IN FACE! HIM COME TO FOR MORE KISSIN'!
BIRDFOOT KISSES LIKE DYNAMITE!
UGH!
YOW!
HIM NO BUGABOO! HIM PALE FACE!
HIM PULL-UM WOOL OVER BIRDFOOT!
HIM IMPOSTER!
STICK-UM STAKE IN GROUND! GATHER PLENTY FIRE-WOOD!
I GUESS WE'RE GONNA BE BURNED AT THE STAKE AFTER ALL, GLORIA!
YOU HAD TO GO AND FAINT, DOPEY!
EVERY THING READY! THIS WAY, PLEASE!
PALEFACE GET-UM KING-SIZE HOT FOOT!
BUT NO CAN JUMP! HO,HO!
BURNING TOO GOOD FOR GAY PALEFACE DECEIVER!

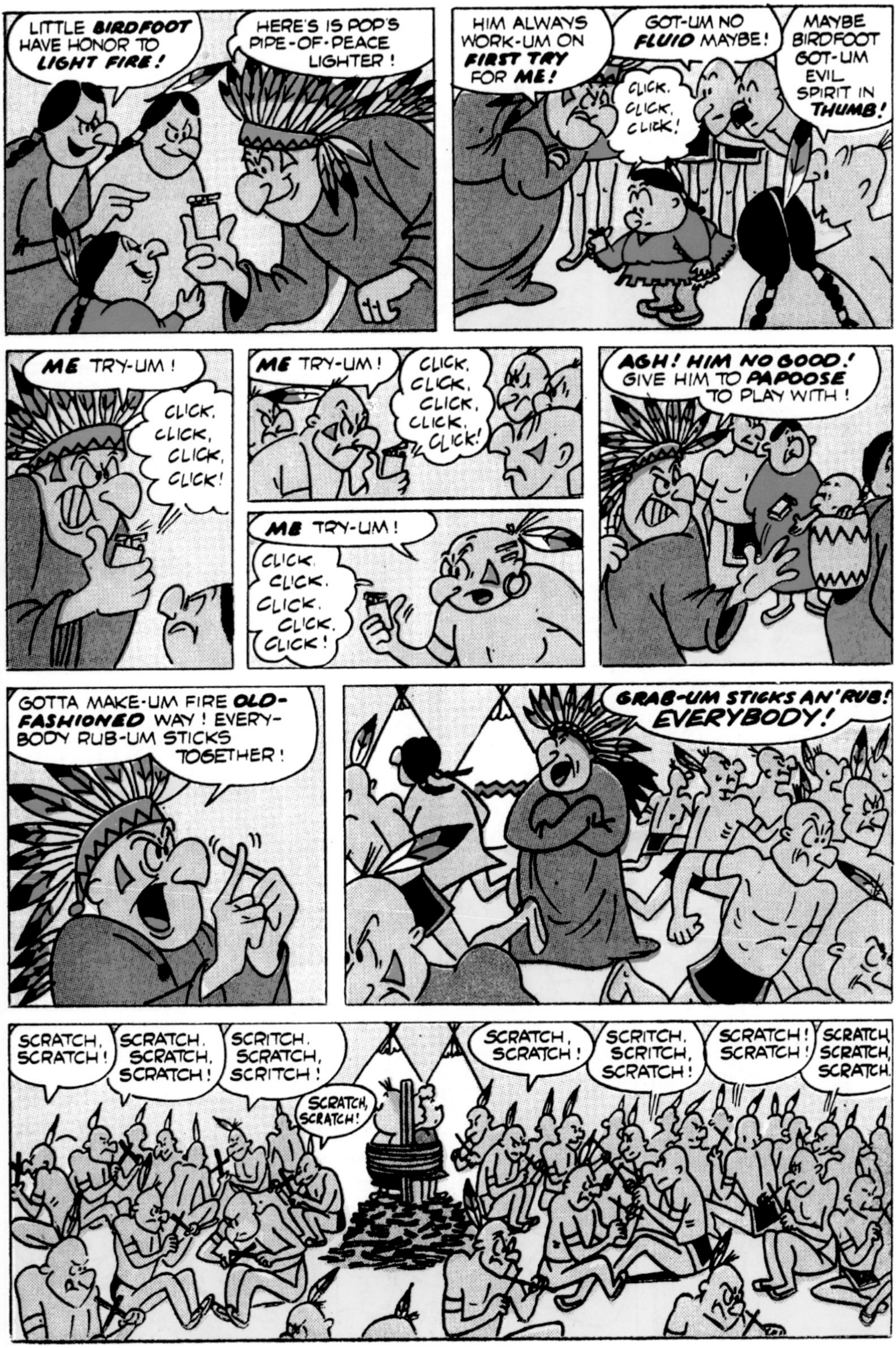

LITTLE BIRDFOOT HAVE HONOR TO LIGHT FIRE!
HERE'S IS POP'S PIPE-OF-PEACE LIGHTER!
HIM ALWAYS WORK-UM ON FIRST TRY FOR ME!
GOT-UM NO FLUID MAYBE!
CLICK. CLICK, CLICK!
MAYBE BIRDFOOT GOT-UM EVIL SPIRIT IN THUMB!
ME TRY-UM!
CLICK. CLICK, CLICK, CLICK!
ME TRY-UM!
CLICK. CLICK. CLICK, CLICK. CLICK!
ME TRY-UM!
CLICK. CLICK. CLICK. CLICK. CLICK!
AGH! HIM NO GOOD! GIVE HIM TO PAPOOSE TO PLAY WITH!
GOTTA MAKE-UM FIRE OLD-FASHIONED WAY! EVERYBODY RUB-UM STICKS TOGETHER!
GRAB-UM STICKS AN' RUB! EVERYBODY!
SCRATCH, SCRATCH!
SCRATCH. SCRATCH, SCRATCH!
SCRITCH. SCRATCH, SCRITCH!
SCRATCH, SCRATCH!
SCRATCH, SCRATCH!
SCRITCH. SCRITCH, SCRATCH!
SCRATCH! SCRATCH!
SCRATCH, SCRATCH, SCRATCH.

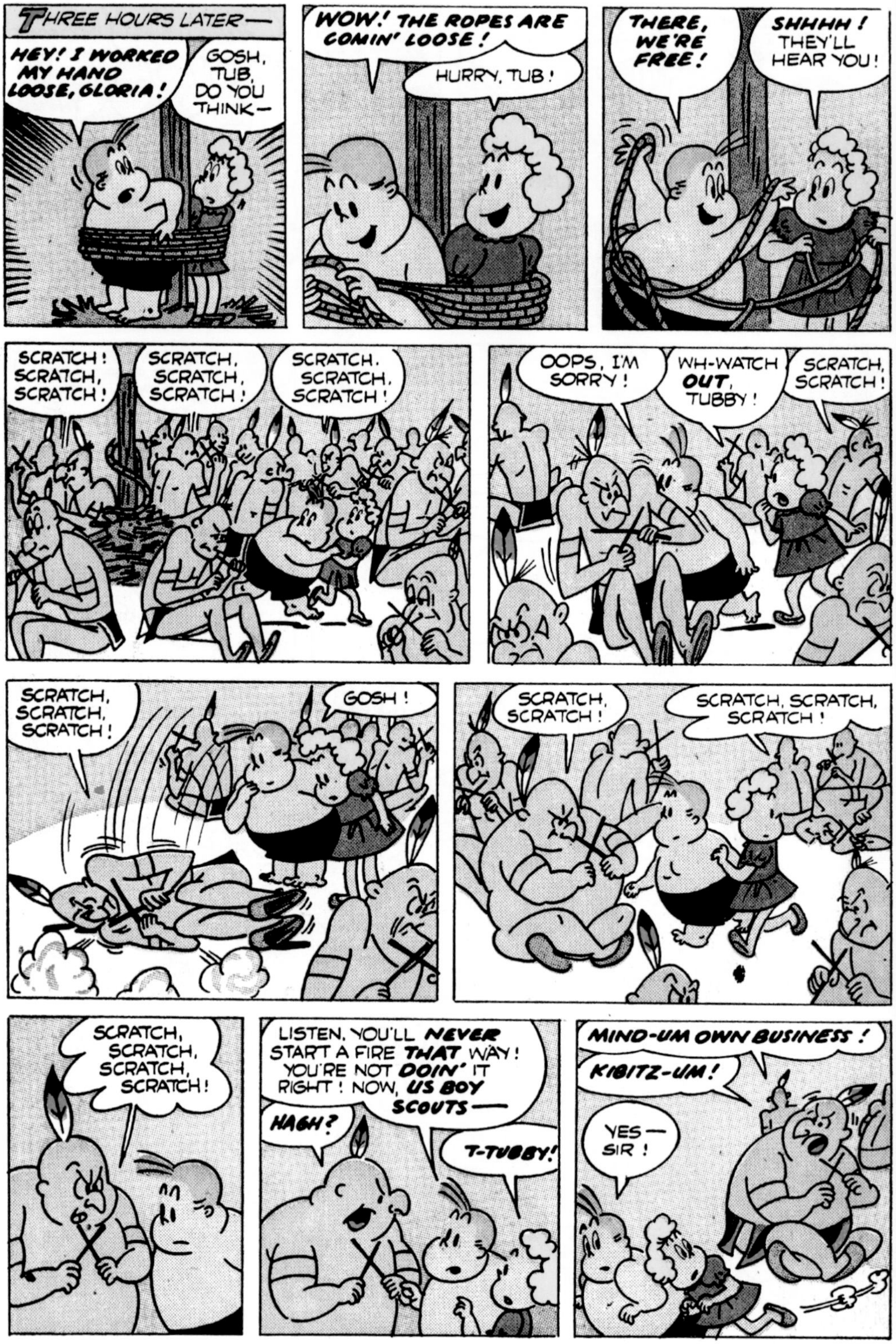
THREE HOURS LATER—
HEY! I WORKED MY HAND LOOSE, GLORIA!
GOSH, TUB, DO YOU THINK—
WOW! THE ROPES ARE COMIN' LOOSE!
HURRY, TUB!
THERE, WE'RE FREE!
SHHHH! THEY'LL HEAR YOU!
SCRATCH! SCRATCH, SCRATCH!
SCRATCH, SCRATCH, SCRATCH!
SCRATCH. SCRATCH, SCRATCH!
OOPS, I'M SORRY!
WH-WATCH OUT, TUBBY!
SCRATCH, SCRATCH!
SCRATCH, SCRATCH, SCRATCH!
GOSH!
SCRATCH, SCRATCH!
SCRATCH, SCRATCH, SCRATCH!
SCRATCH, SCRATCH, SCRATCH, SCRATCH!
LISTEN, YOU'LL NEVER START A FIRE THAT WAY! YOU'RE NOT DOIN' IT RIGHT! NOW, US BOY SCOUTS—
HAGH?
T-TUBBY!
MIND-UM OWN BUSINESS!
KIBITZ-UM!
YES—SIR!

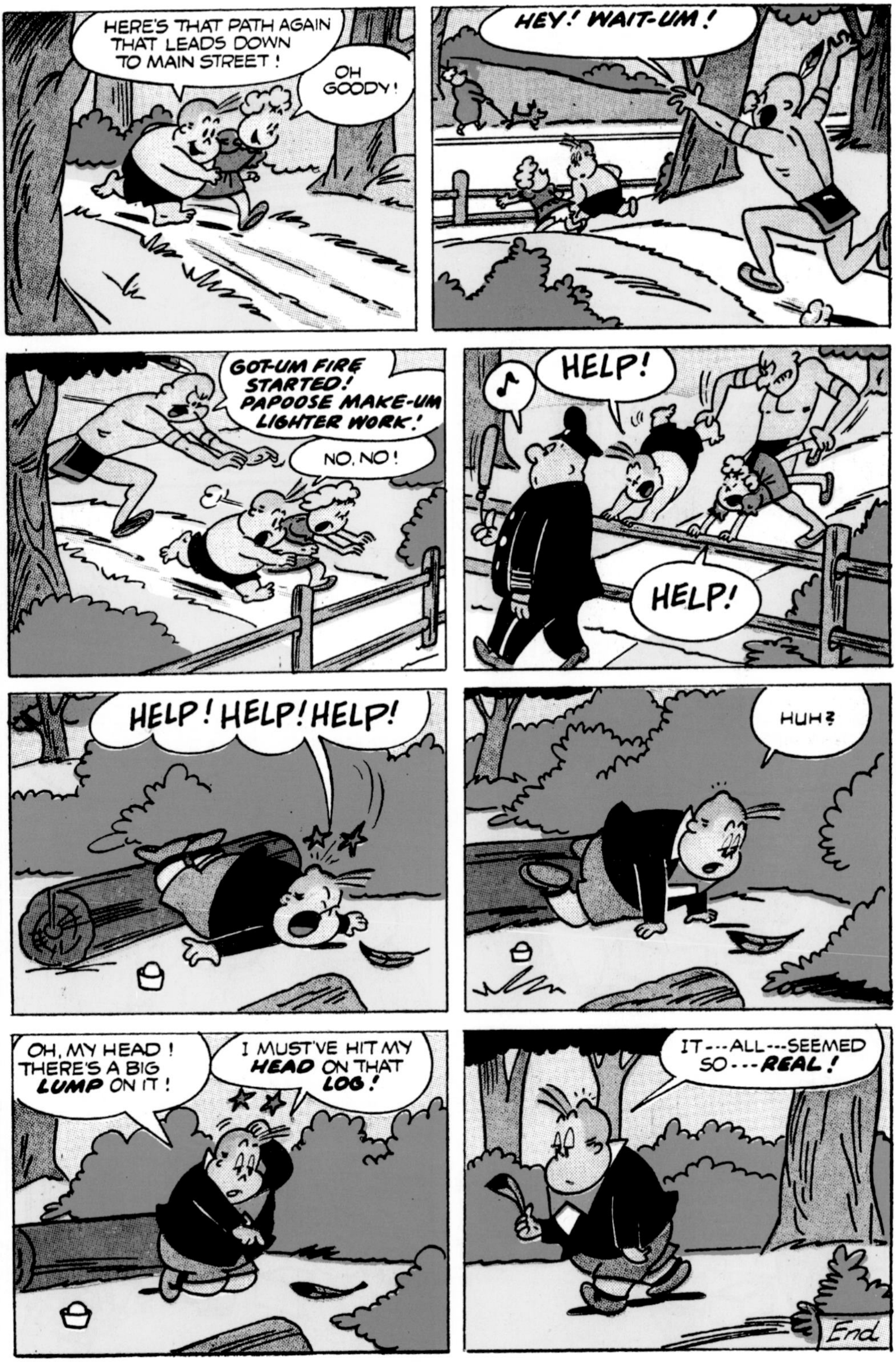
HERE'S THAT PATH AGAIN THAT LEADS DOWN TO MAIN STREET !
OH GOODY !
HEY ! WAIT-UM !
GOT-UM FIRE STARTED! PAPOOSE MAKE-UM LIGHTER WORK!
NO, NO !
HELP!
HELP!
HELP! HELP! HELP!
HUH?
OH, MY HEAD ! THERE'S A BIG LUMP ON IT !
I MUST'VE HIT MY HEAD ON THAT LOG !
IT---ALL---SEEMED SO---REAL !
End

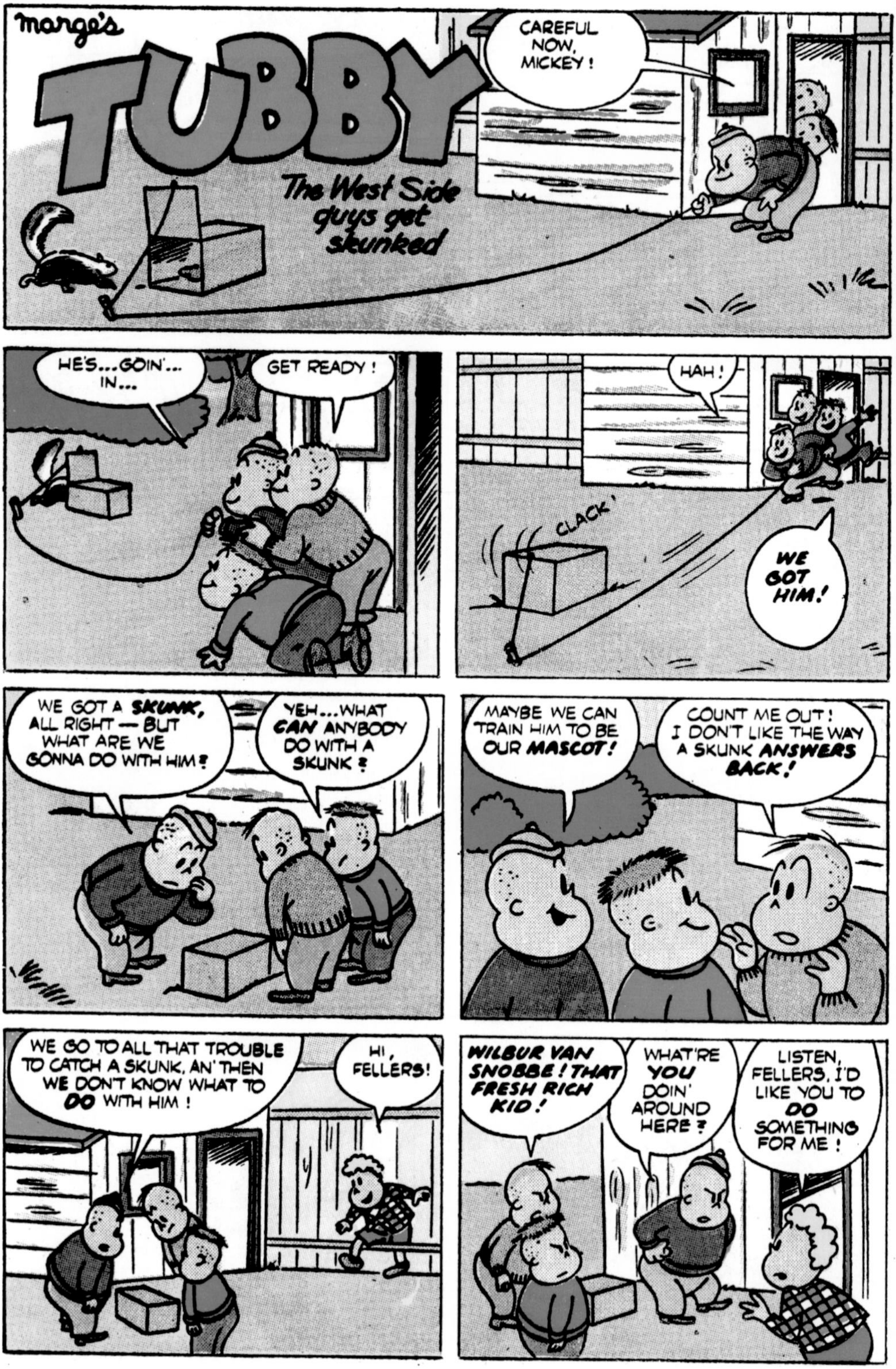
marge's
TUBBY
The West Side guys get skunked
CAREFUL NOW, MICKEY!
HE'S...GOIN'... IN...
GET READY!
HAH!
CLACK
WE GOT HIM!
WE GOT A SKUNK, ALL RIGHT — BUT WHAT ARE WE GONNA DO WITH HIM?
YEH...WHAT CAN ANYBODY DO WITH A SKUNK?
MAYBE WE CAN TRAIN HIM TO BE OUR MASCOT!
COUNT ME OUT! I DON'T LIKE THE WAY A SKUNK ANSWERS BACK!
WE GO TO ALL THAT TROUBLE TO CATCH A SKUNK, AN' THEN WE DON'T KNOW WHAT TO DO WITH HIM!
HI, FELLERS!
WILBUR VAN SNOBBE! THAT FRESH RICH KID!
WHAT'RE YOU DOIN' AROUND HERE?
LISTEN, FELLERS, I'D LIKE YOU TO DO SOMETHING FOR ME!

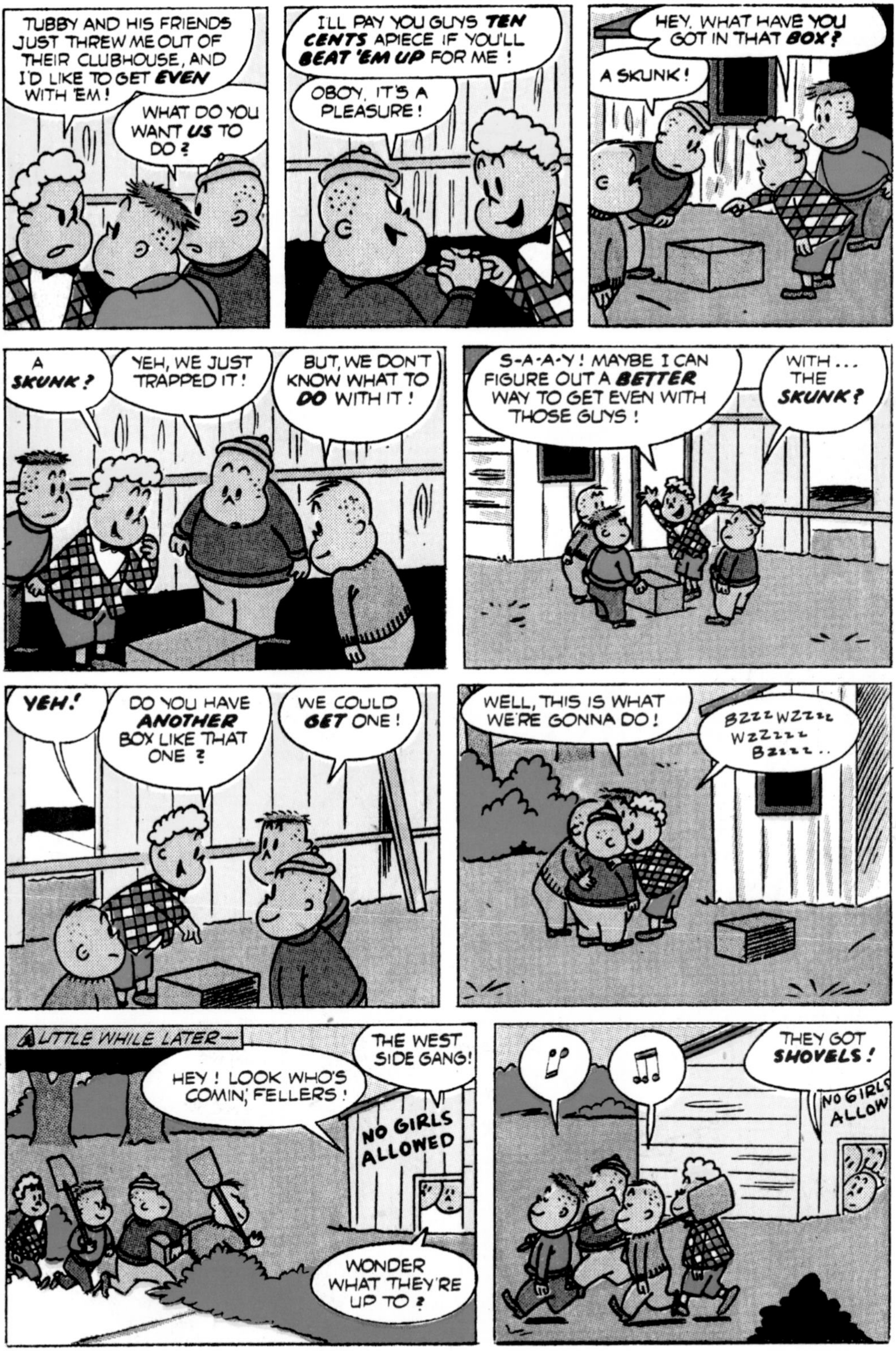
TUBBY AND HIS FRIENDS JUST THREW ME OUT OF THEIR CLUBHOUSE, AND I'D LIKE TO GET EVEN WITH 'EM!
WHAT DO YOU WANT US TO DO?
I'LL PAY YOU GUYS TEN CENTS APIECE IF YOU'LL BEAT 'EM UP FOR ME!
OBOY, IT'S A PLEASURE!
HEY, WHAT HAVE YOU GOT IN THAT BOX?
A SKUNK!
A SKUNK?
YEH, WE JUST TRAPPED IT!
BUT, WE DON'T KNOW WHAT TO DO WITH IT!
S-A-A-Y! MAYBE I CAN FIGURE OUT A BETTER WAY TO GET EVEN WITH THOSE GUYS!
WITH... THE SKUNK?
YEH!
DO YOU HAVE ANOTHER BOX LIKE THAT ONE?
WE COULD GET ONE!
WELL, THIS IS WHAT WE'RE GONNA DO!
BZZZWZZZZ WZZZZZ BZZZZ..
A LITTLE WHILE LATER—
HEY! LOOK WHO'S COMIN', FELLERS!
THE WEST SIDE GANG!
NO GIRLS ALLOWED
WONDER WHAT THEY'RE UP TO?
THEY GOT SHOVELS!
NO GIRLS ALLOW

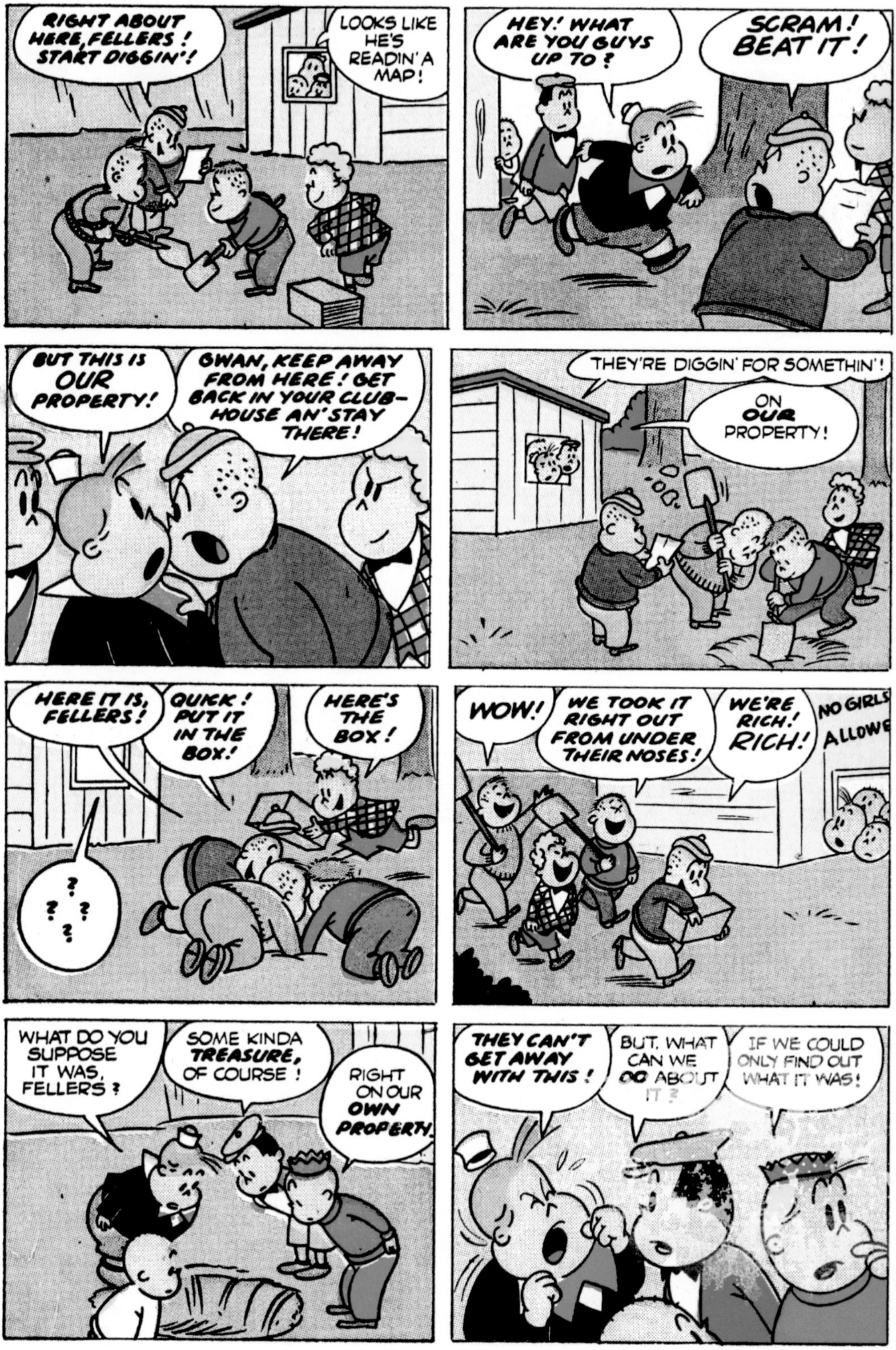
RIGHT ABOUT HERE, FELLERS! START DIGGIN'!
LOOKS LIKE HE'S READIN' A MAP!
HEY! WHAT ARE YOU GUYS UP TO?
SCRAM! BEAT IT!
BUT THIS IS OUR PROPERTY!
GWAN, KEEP AWAY FROM HERE! GET BACK IN YOUR CLUB-HOUSE AN' STAY THERE!
THEY'RE DIGGIN' FOR SOMETHIN'!
ON OUR PROPERTY!
HERE IT IS, FELLERS!
QUICK! PUT IT IN THE BOX!
HERE'S THE BOX!
? ? ? ?
WOW!
WE TOOK IT RIGHT OUT FROM UNDER THEIR NOSES!
WE'RE RICH! RICH!
NO GIRLS ALLOWE
WHAT DO YOU SUPPOSE IT WAS, FELLERS?
SOME KINDA TREASURE, OF COURSE!
RIGHT ON OUR OWN PROPERTY!
THEY CAN'T GET AWAY WITH THIS!
BUT, WHAT CAN WE DO ABOUT IT?
IF WE COULD ONLY FIND OUT WHAT IT WAS!

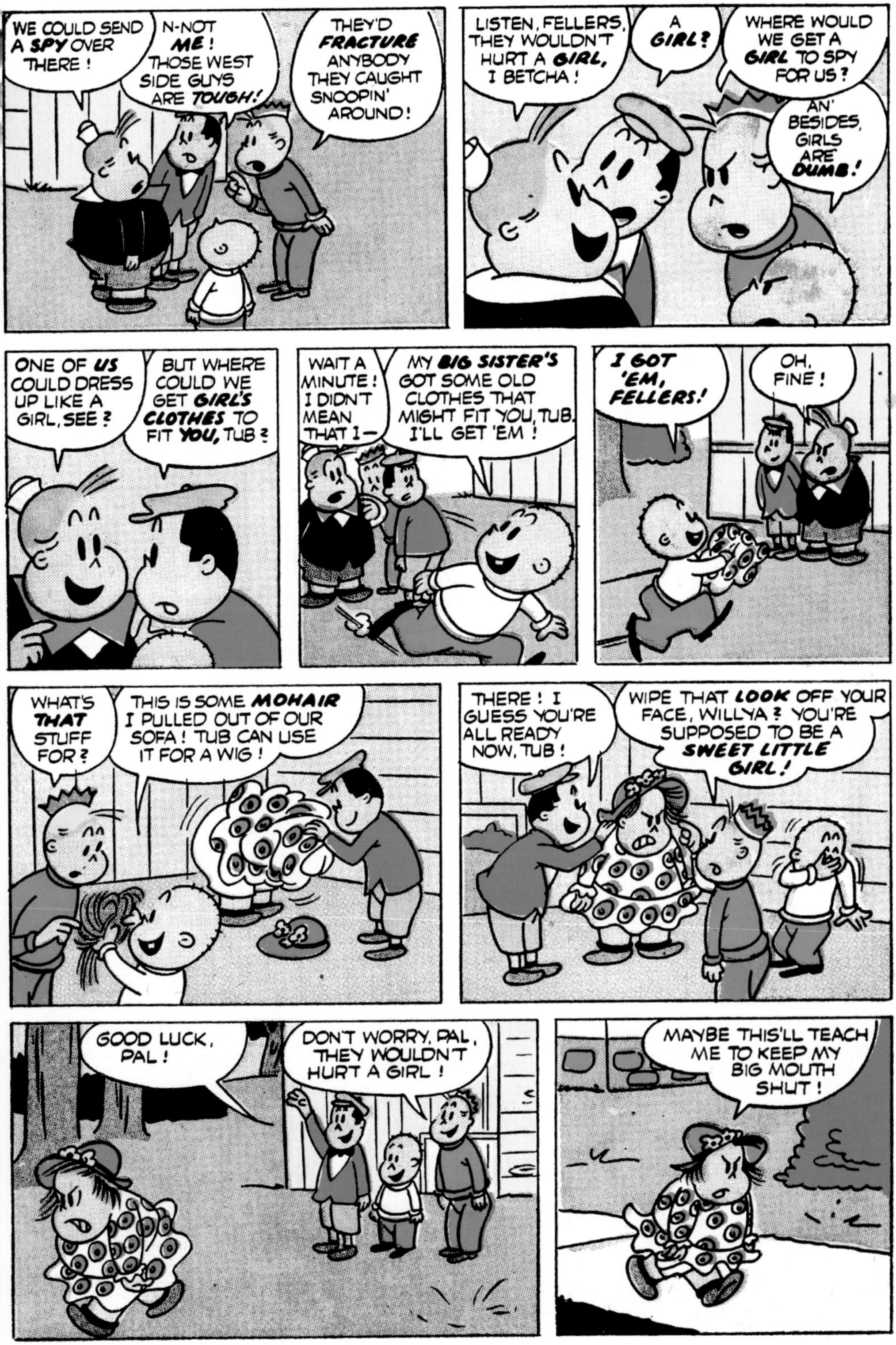

WE COULD SEND A SPY OVER THERE !
N-NOT ME ! THOSE WEST SIDE GUYS ARE TOUGH!
THEY'D FRACTURE ANYBODY THEY CAUGHT SNOOPIN' AROUND!
LISTEN, FELLERS, THEY WOULDN'T HURT A GIRL, I BETCHA !
A GIRL?
WHERE WOULD WE GET A GIRL TO SPY FOR US?
AN' BESIDES, GIRLS ARE DUMB!
ONE OF US COULD DRESS UP LIKE A GIRL, SEE?
BUT WHERE COULD WE GET GIRL'S CLOTHES TO FIT YOU, TUB?
WAIT A MINUTE! I DIDN'T MEAN THAT I—
MY BIG SISTER'S GOT SOME OLD CLOTHES THAT MIGHT FIT YOU, TUB. I'LL GET 'EM !
I GOT 'EM, FELLERS!
OH, FINE !
WHAT'S THAT STUFF FOR?
THIS IS SOME MOHAIR I PULLED OUT OF OUR SOFA ! TUB CAN USE IT FOR A WIG !
THERE ! I GUESS YOU'RE ALL READY NOW, TUB !
WIPE THAT LOOK OFF YOUR FACE, WILLYA? YOU'RE SUPPOSED TO BE A SWEET LITTLE GIRL!
GOOD LUCK, PAL !
DON'T WORRY, PAL, THEY WOULDN'T HURT A GIRL !
MAYBE THIS'LL TEACH ME TO KEEP MY BIG MOUTH SHUT !

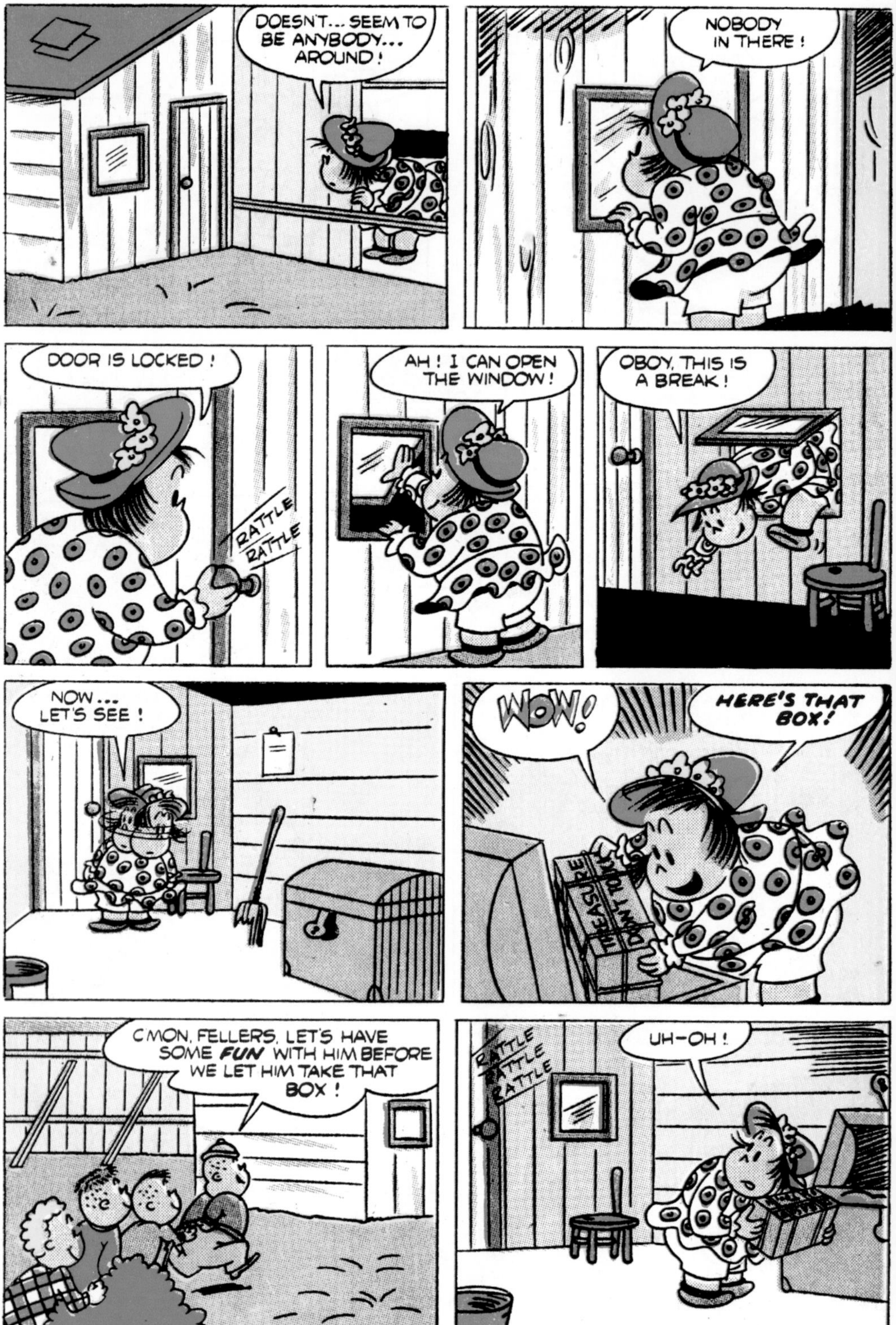
DOESN'T... SEEM TO BE ANYBODY... AROUND!
NOBODY IN THERE!
DOOR IS LOCKED!
RATTLE RATTLE
AH! I CAN OPEN THE WINDOW!
OBOY, THIS IS A BREAK!
NOW... LET'S SEE!
WOW!
HERE'S THAT BOX!
TREASURE
DON'T TOUCH
C'MON, FELLERS, LET'S HAVE SOME FUN WITH HIM BEFORE WE LET HIM TAKE THAT BOX!
RATTLE RATTLE RATTLE
UH-OH!

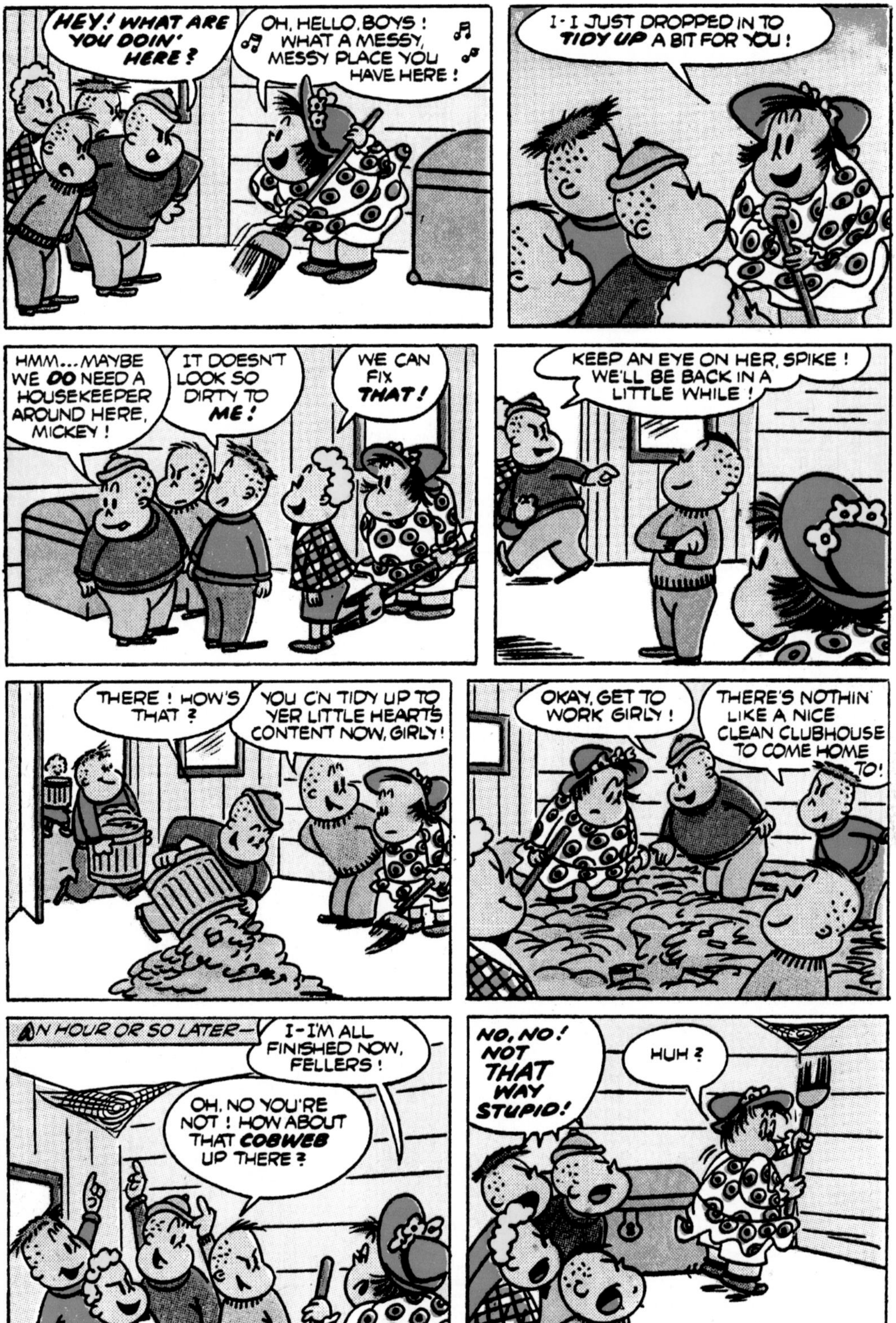
HEY! WHAT ARE YOU DOIN' HERE?
OH, HELLO, BOYS! WHAT A MESSY, MESSY PLACE YOU HAVE HERE!
I-I JUST DROPPED IN TO TIDY UP A BIT FOR YOU!
HMM... MAYBE WE DO NEED A HOUSEKEEPER AROUND HERE, MICKEY!
IT DOESN'T LOOK SO DIRTY TO ME!
WE CAN FIX THAT!
KEEP AN EYE ON HER, SPIKE! WE'LL BE BACK IN A LITTLE WHILE!
THERE! HOW'S THAT?
YOU C'N TIDY UP TO YER LITTLE HEART'S CONTENT NOW, GIRLY!
OKAY, GET TO WORK GIRLY!
THERE'S NOTHIN' LIKE A NICE CLEAN CLUBHOUSE TO COME HOME TO!
AN HOUR OR SO LATER—
I-I'M ALL FINISHED NOW, FELLERS!
OH, NO YOU'RE NOT! HOW ABOUT THAT COBWEB UP THERE?
NO, NO! NOT THAT WAY STUPID!
HUH?

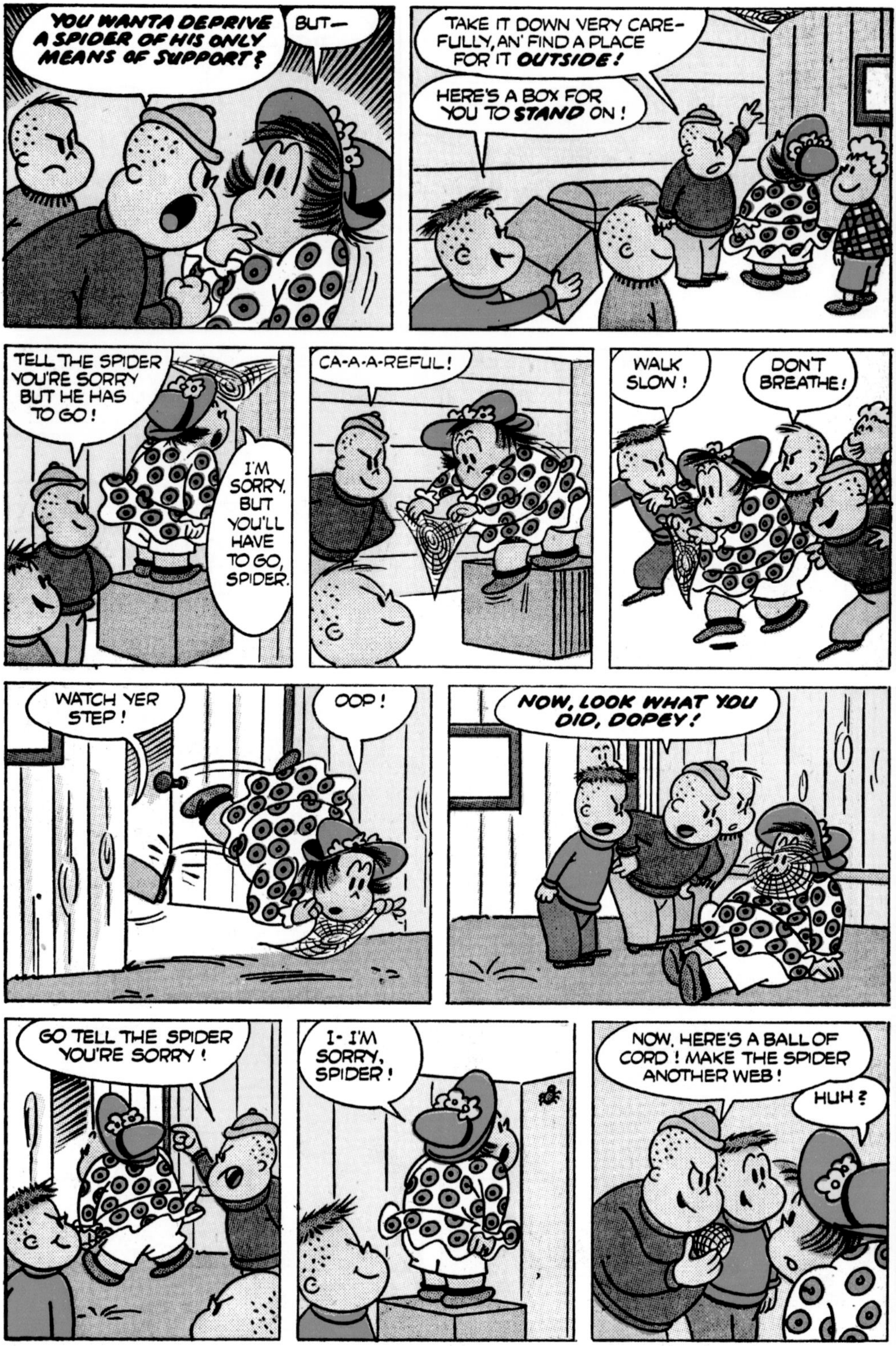
YOU WANTA DEPRIVE A SPIDER OF HIS ONLY MEANS OF SUPPORT?
BUT—
TAKE IT DOWN VERY CARE-FULLY, AN' FIND A PLACE FOR IT OUTSIDE!
HERE'S A BOX FOR YOU TO STAND ON!
TELL THE SPIDER YOU'RE SORRY BUT HE HAS TO GO!
I'M SORRY, BUT YOU'LL HAVE TO GO, SPIDER.
CA-A-A-REFUL!
WALK SLOW!
DON'T BREATHE!
WATCH YER STEP!
OOP!
NOW, LOOK WHAT YOU DID, DOPEY!
GO TELL THE SPIDER YOU'RE SORRY!
I- I'M SORRY, SPIDER!
NOW, HERE'S A BALL OF CORD! MAKE THE SPIDER ANOTHER WEB!
HUH?

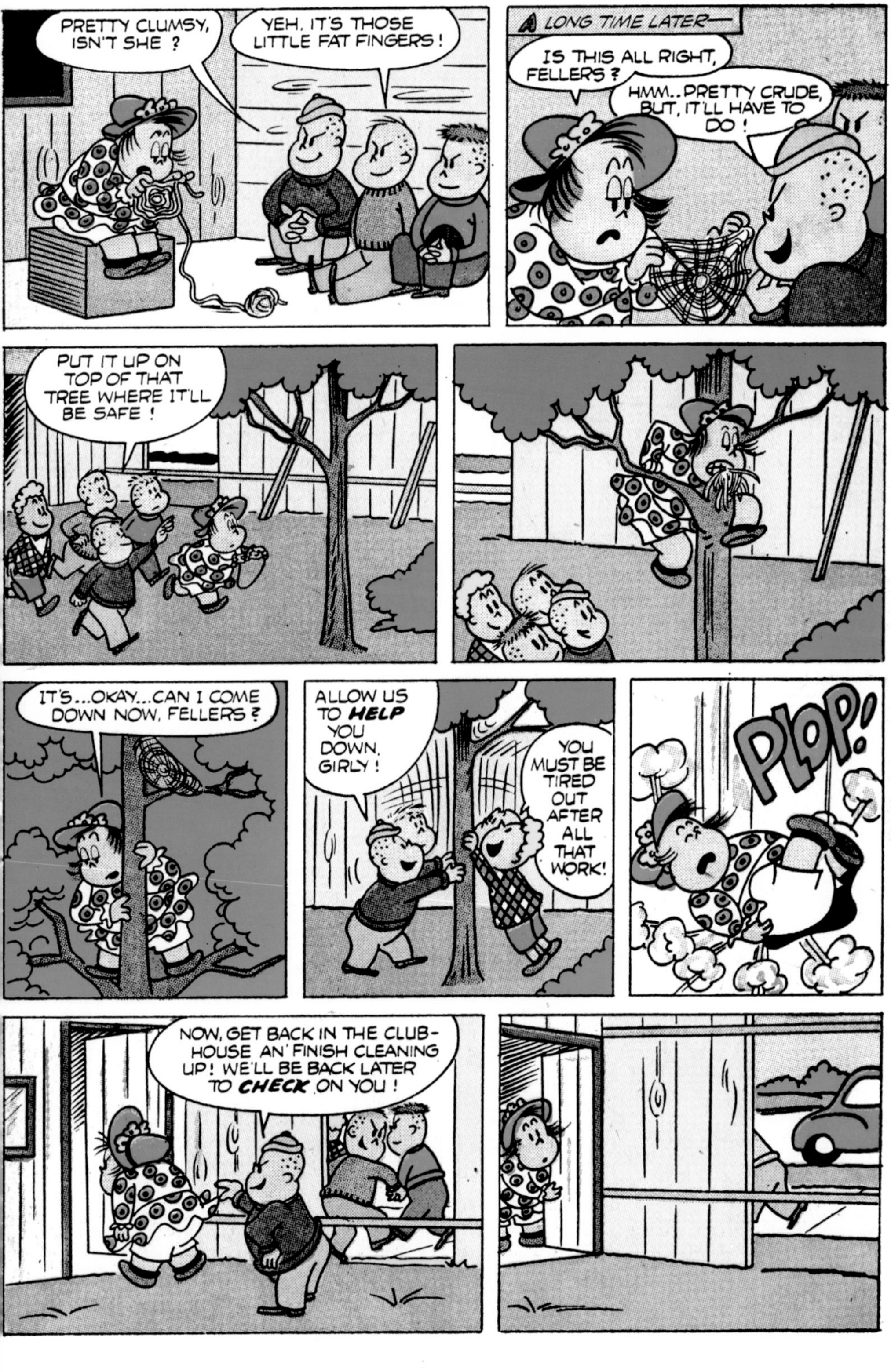
PRETTY CLUMSY, ISN'T SHE ?
YEH, IT'S THOSE LITTLE FAT FINGERS !
A LONG TIME LATER—
IS THIS ALL RIGHT, FELLERS ?
HMM.. PRETTY CRUDE, BUT, IT'LL HAVE TO DO !
PUT IT UP ON TOP OF THAT TREE WHERE IT'LL BE SAFE !
IT'S...OKAY...CAN I COME DOWN NOW, FELLERS ?
ALLOW US TO HELP YOU DOWN, GIRLY !
YOU MUST BE TIRED OUT AFTER ALL THAT WORK!
PLOP!
NOW, GET BACK IN THE CLUB-HOUSE AN' FINISH CLEANING UP! WE'LL BE BACK LATER TO CHECK ON YOU !

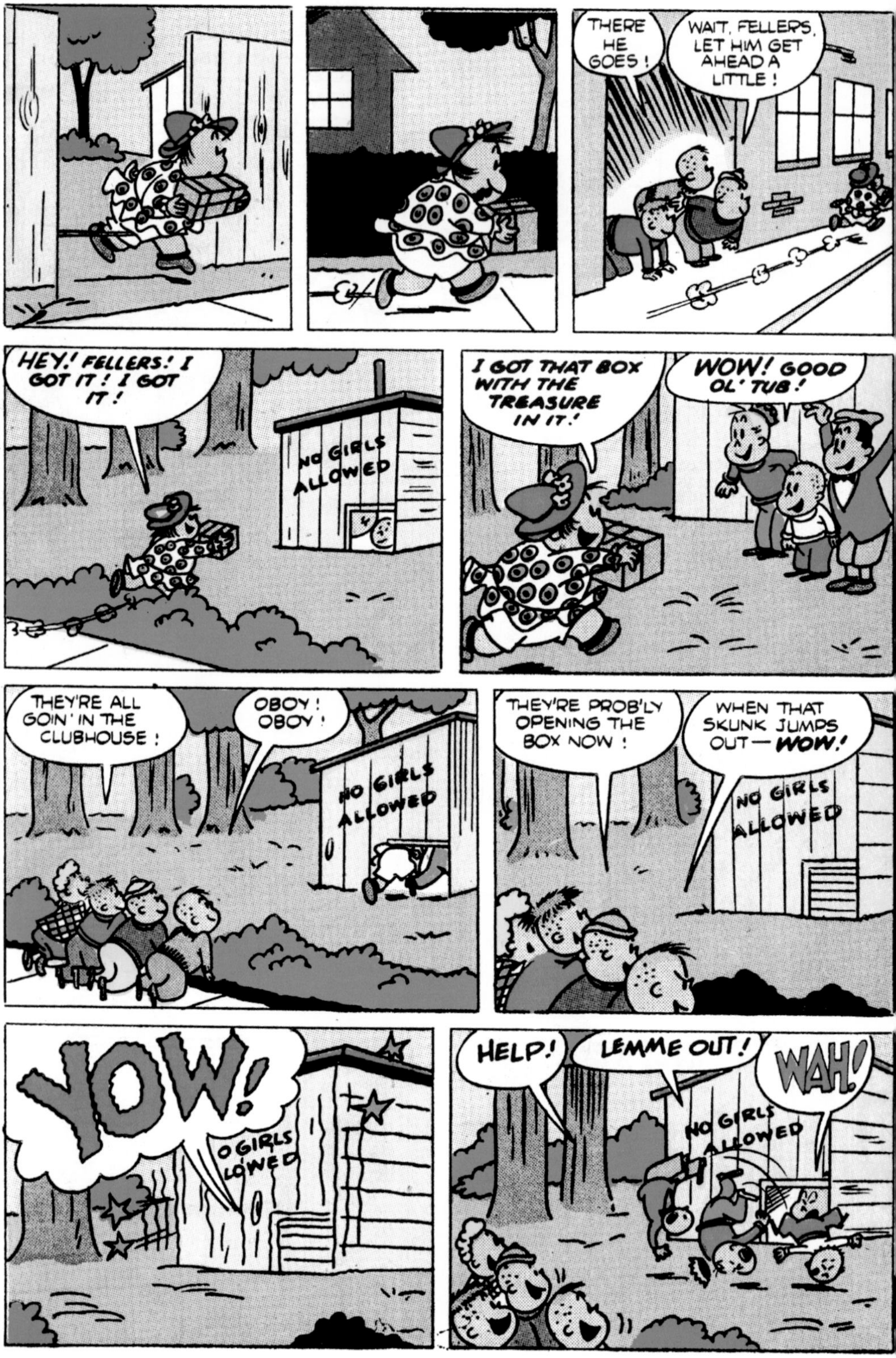
THERE HE GOES!
WAIT, FELLERS, LET HIM GET AHEAD A LITTLE!
HEY! FELLERS! I GOT IT! I GOT IT!
NO GIRLS ALLOWED
I GOT THAT BOX WITH THE TREASURE IN IT!
WOW! GOOD OL' TUB!
THEY'RE ALL GOIN' IN THE CLUBHOUSE!
OBOY! OBOY!
NO GIRLS ALLOWED
THEY'RE PROB'LY OPENING THE BOX NOW!
WHEN THAT SKUNK JUMPS OUT—WOW!
NO GIRLS ALLOWED
YOW!
O GIRLS LOWED
HELP!
LEMME OUT!
WAH!
NO GIRLS ALLOWED

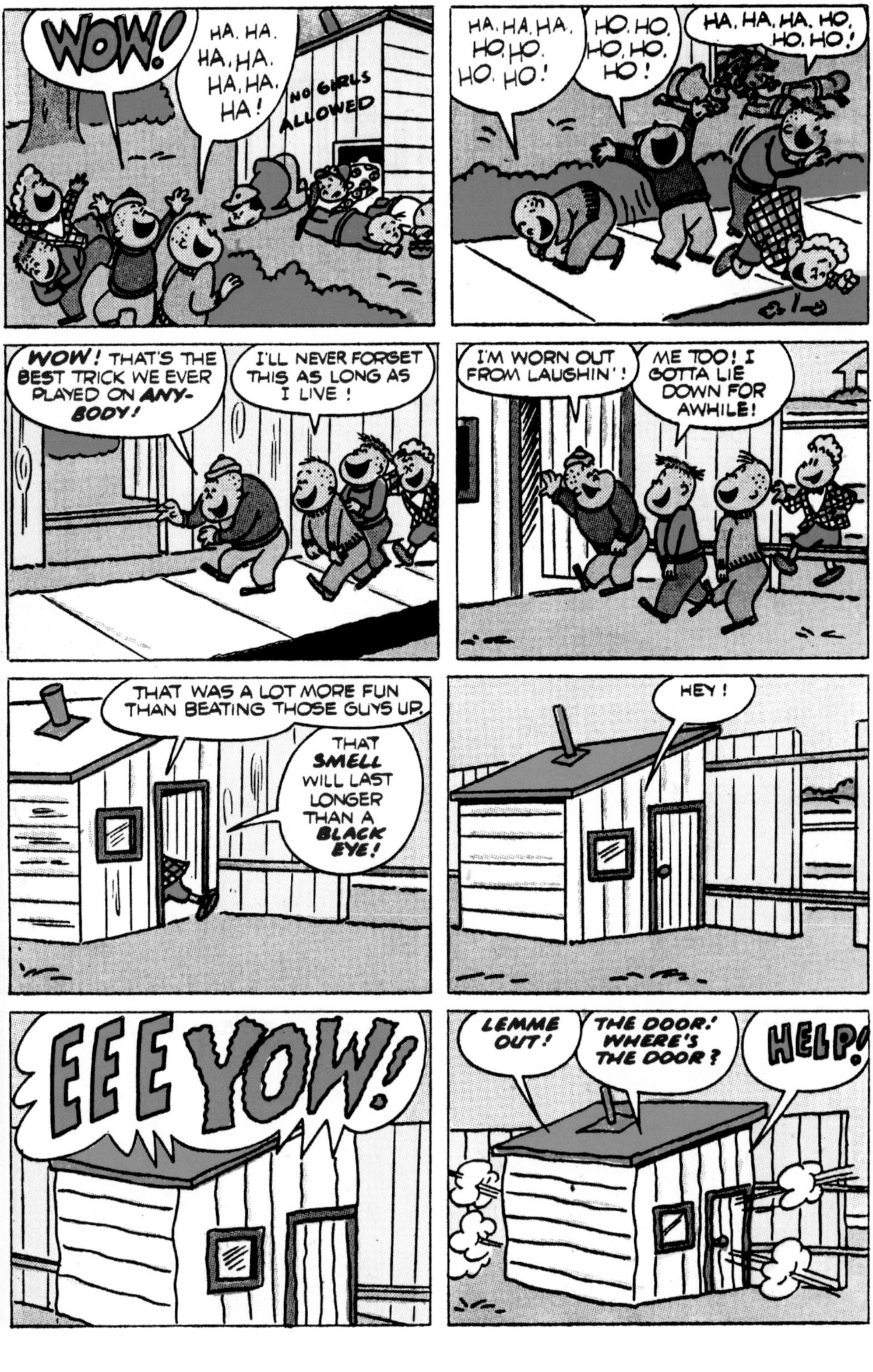
WOW!
HA. HA. HA, HA. HA, HA. HA!
NO GIRLS ALLOWED
HA. HA, HA. HO, HO. HO. HO!
HO. HO. HO, HO. HO!
HA. HA, HA. HO, HO. HO!
WOW! THAT'S THE BEST TRICK WE EVER PLAYED ON ANY-BODY!
I'LL NEVER FORGET THIS AS LONG AS I LIVE!
I'M WORN OUT FROM LAUGHIN'!
ME TOO! I GOTTA LIE DOWN FOR AWHILE!
THAT WAS A LOT MORE FUN THAN BEATING THOSE GUYS UP.
THAT SMELL WILL LAST LONGER THAN A BLACK EYE!
HEY!
EEEYOW!
LEMME OUT!
THE DOOR! WHERE'S THE DOOR?
HELP!

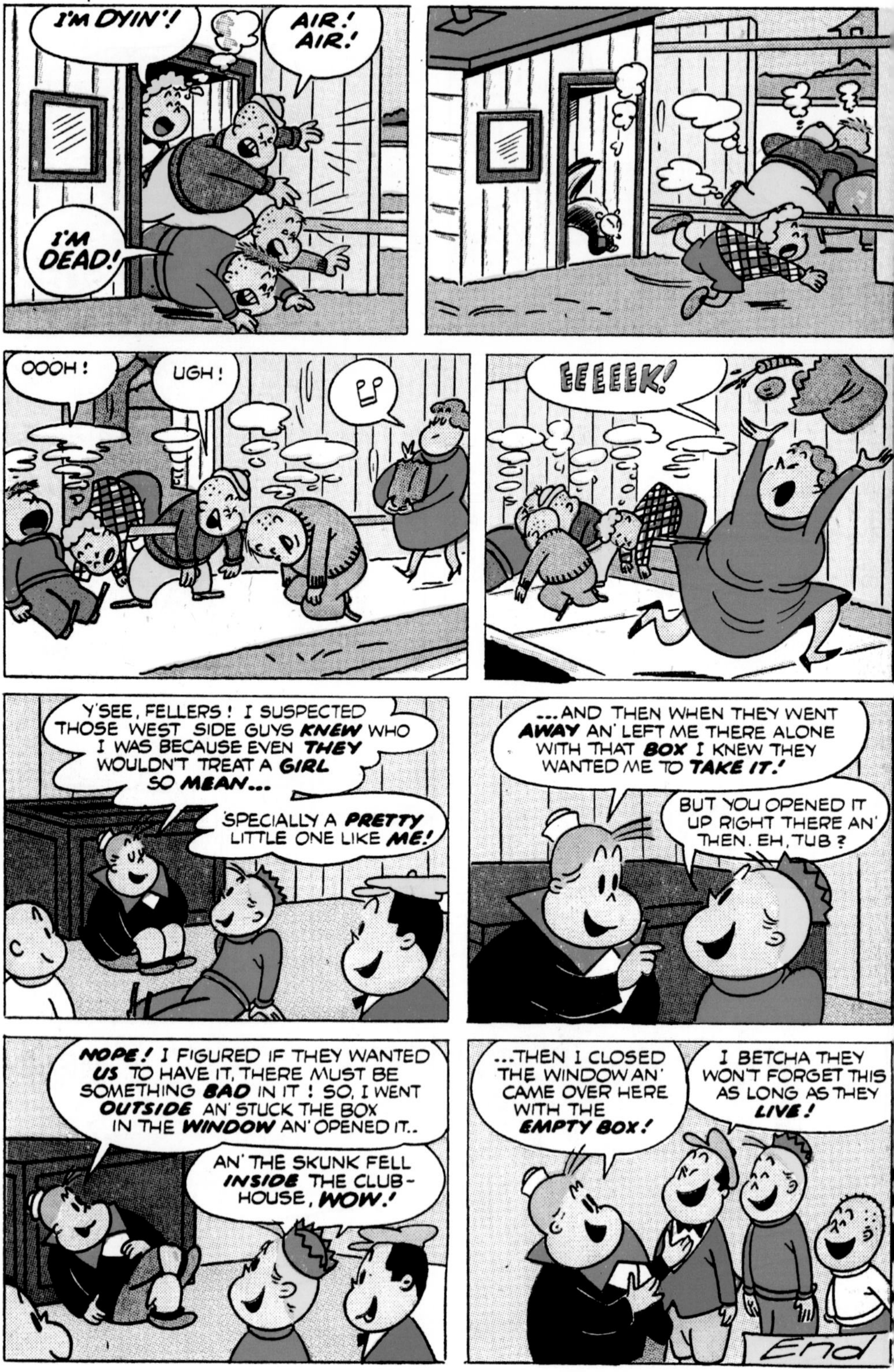
I'M DYIN'!
AIR! AIR!
I'M DEAD!
OOOH!
UGH!
EEEEEK!
Y'SEE, FELLERS! I SUSPECTED THOSE WEST SIDE GUYS KNEW WHO I WAS BECAUSE EVEN THEY WOULDN'T TREAT A GIRL SO MEAN...
'SPECIALLY A PRETTY LITTLE ONE LIKE ME!
...AND THEN WHEN THEY WENT AWAY AN' LEFT ME THERE ALONE WITH THAT BOX I KNEW THEY WANTED ME TO TAKE IT!
BUT YOU OPENED IT UP RIGHT THERE AN' THEN. EH, TUB?
NOPE! I FIGURED IF THEY WANTED US TO HAVE IT, THERE MUST BE SOMETHING BAD IN IT! SO, I WENT OUTSIDE AN' STUCK THE BOX IN THE WINDOW AN' OPENED IT..
AN' THE SKUNK FELL INSIDE THE CLUB-HOUSE, WOW!
...THEN I CLOSED THE WINDOW AN' CAME OVER HERE WITH THE EMPTY BOX!
I BETCHA THEY WON'T FORGET THIS AS LONG AS THEY LIVE!
End

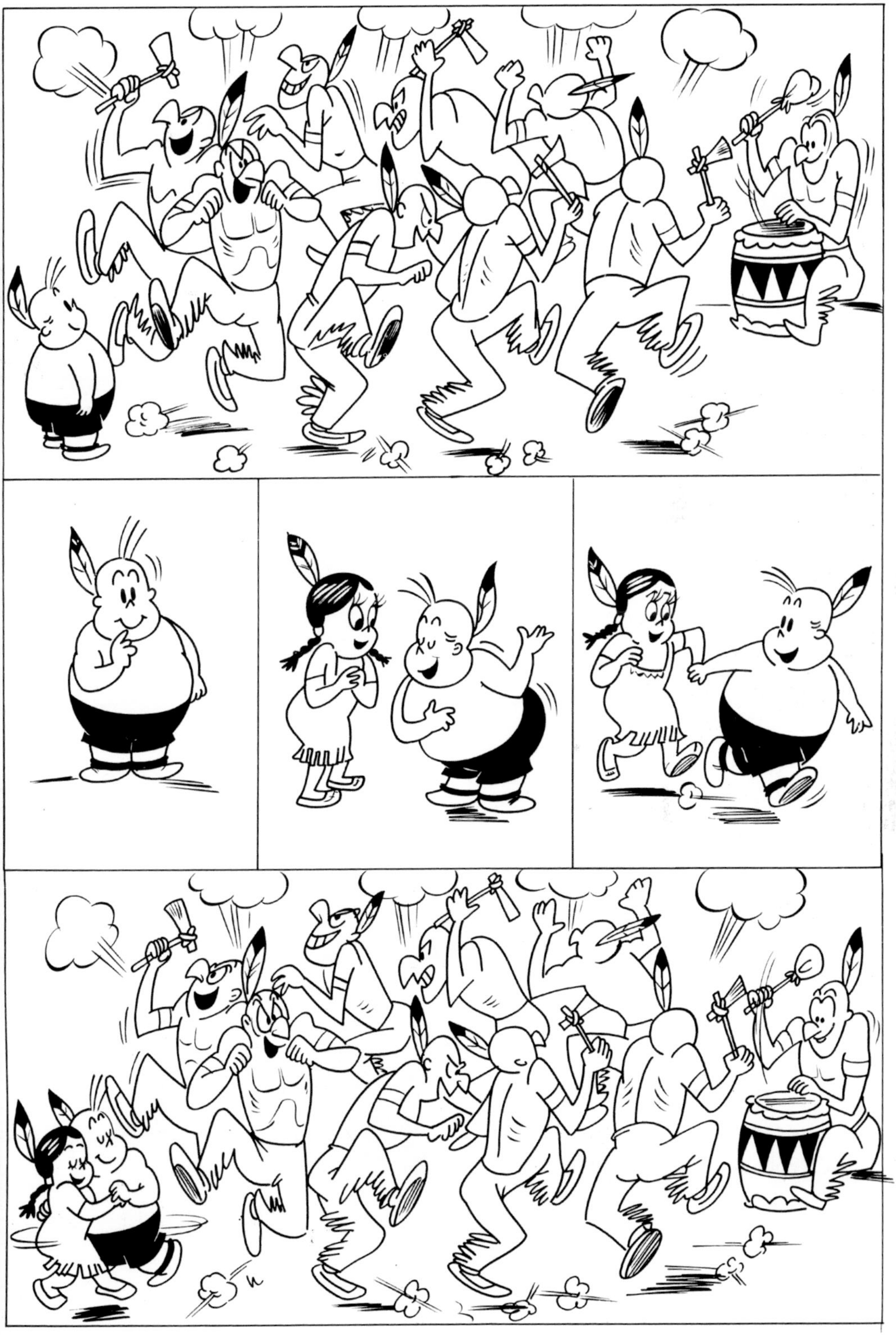

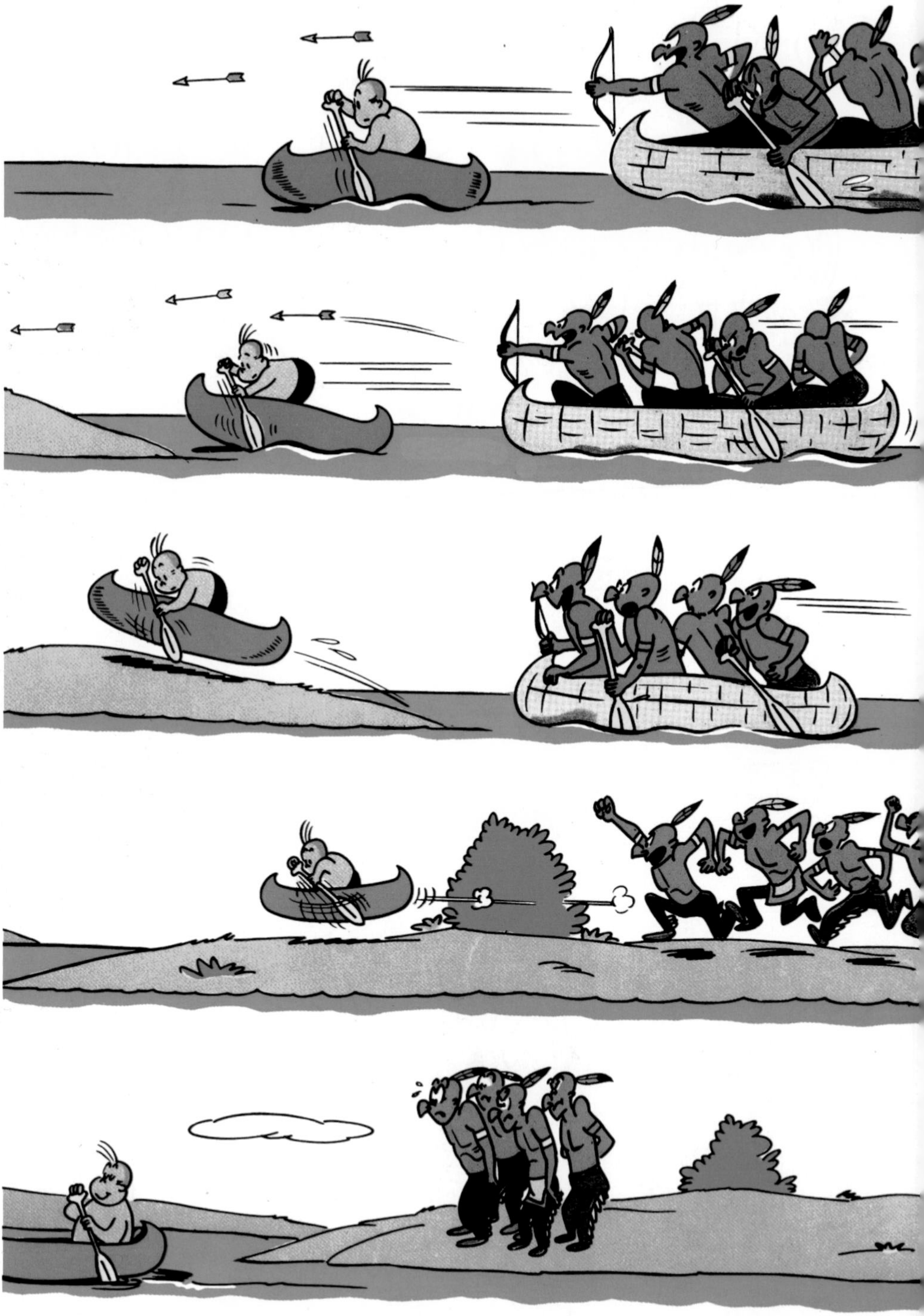

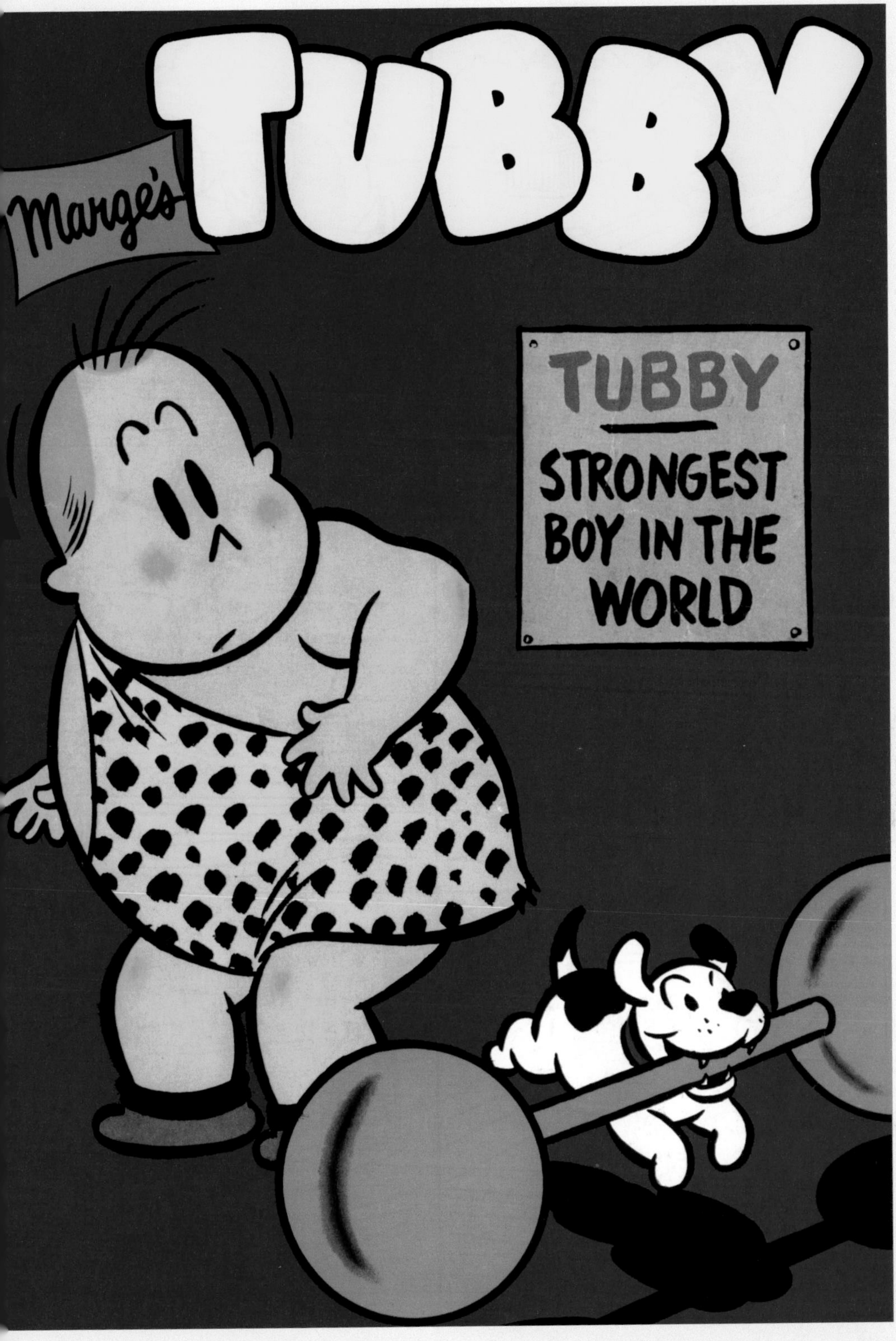
Marge's
TUBBY
TUBBY
STRONGEST BOY IN THE WORLD

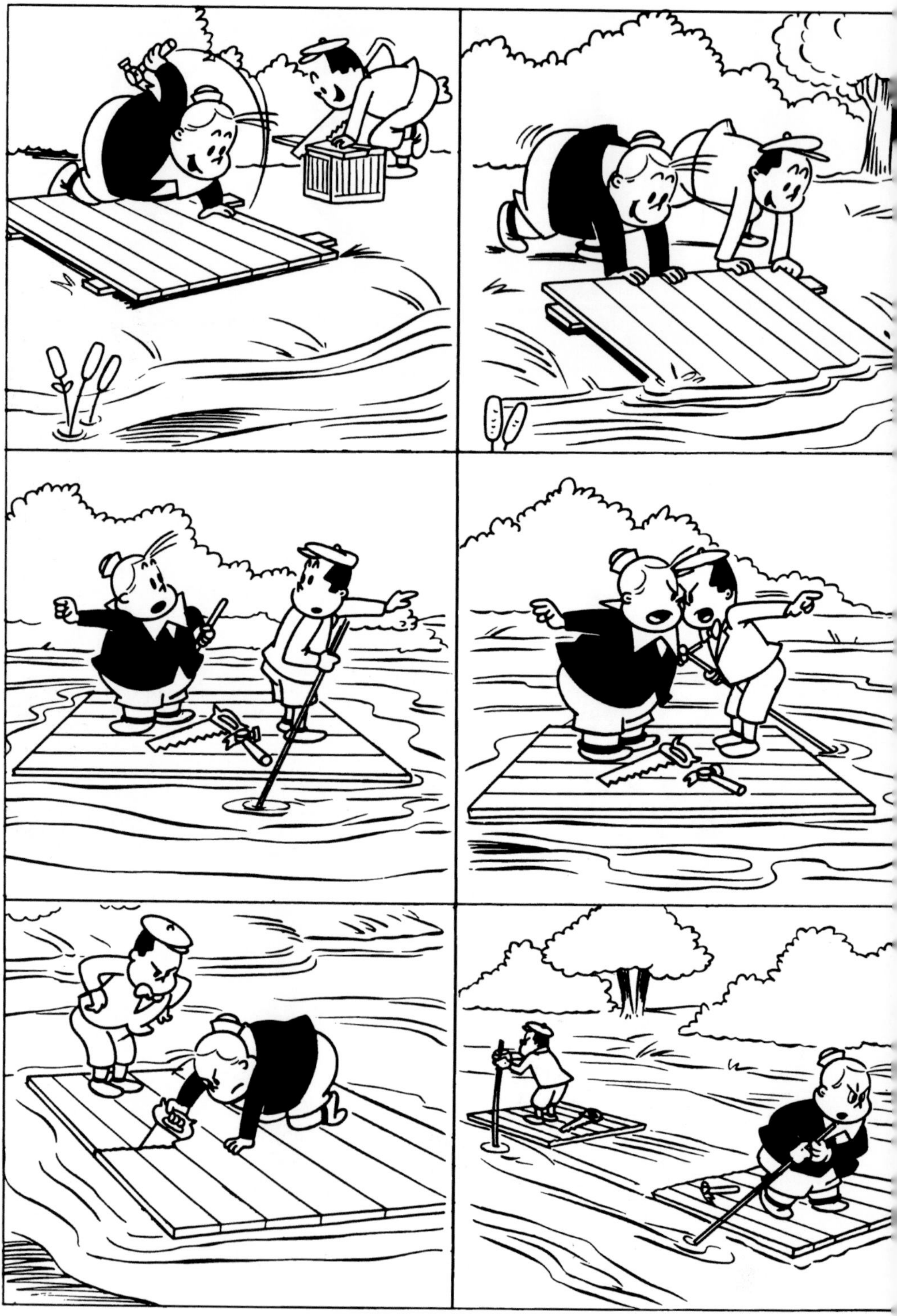

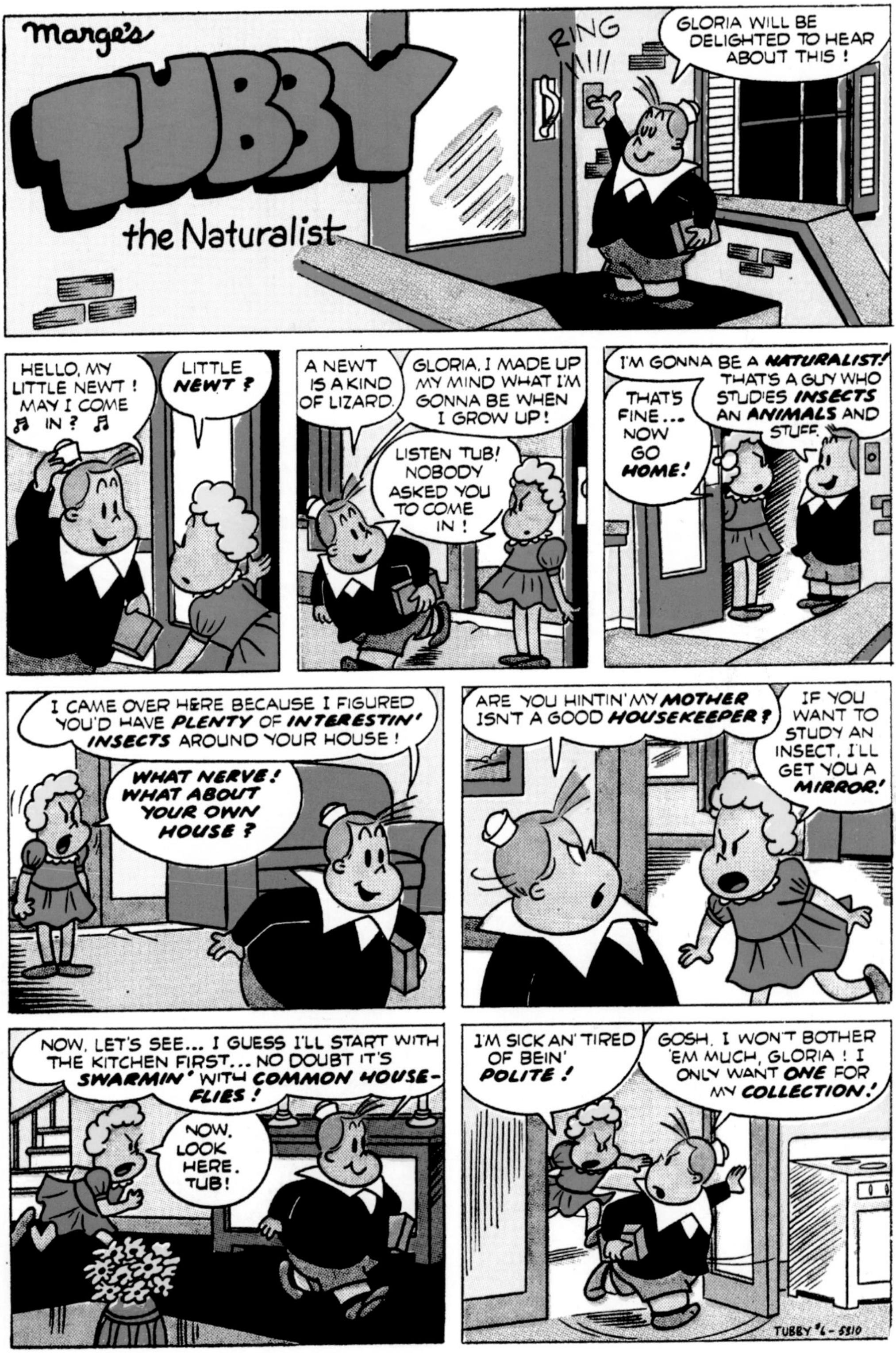

Marge's
TUBBY
the Naturalist
RING
GLORIA WILL BE DELIGHTED TO HEAR ABOUT THIS !
HELLO, MY LITTLE NEWT ! MAY I COME IN ?
LITTLE NEWT ?
A NEWT IS A KIND OF LIZARD.
GLORIA, I MADE UP MY MIND WHAT I'M GONNA BE WHEN I GROW UP!
LISTEN TUB! NOBODY ASKED YOU TO COME IN !
I'M GONNA BE A NATURALIST! THAT'S A GUY WHO STUDIES INSECTS AN ANIMALS AND STUFF.
THAT'S FINE... NOW GO HOME!
I CAME OVER HERE BECAUSE I FIGURED YOU'D HAVE PLENTY OF INTERESTIN' INSECTS AROUND YOUR HOUSE !
WHAT NERVE! WHAT ABOUT YOUR OWN HOUSE ?
ARE YOU HINTIN' MY MOTHER ISN'T A GOOD HOUSEKEEPER ?
IF YOU WANT TO STUDY AN INSECT, I'LL GET YOU A MIRROR!
NOW, LET'S SEE... I GUESS I'LL START WITH THE KITCHEN FIRST... NO DOUBT IT'S SWARMIN' WITH COMMON HOUSE-FLIES !
NOW, LOOK HERE, TUB!
I'M SICK AN' TIRED OF BEIN' POLITE !
GOSH, I WON'T BOTHER 'EM MUCH, GLORIA ! I ONLY WANT ONE FOR MY COLLECTION!
TUBBY #6-5310

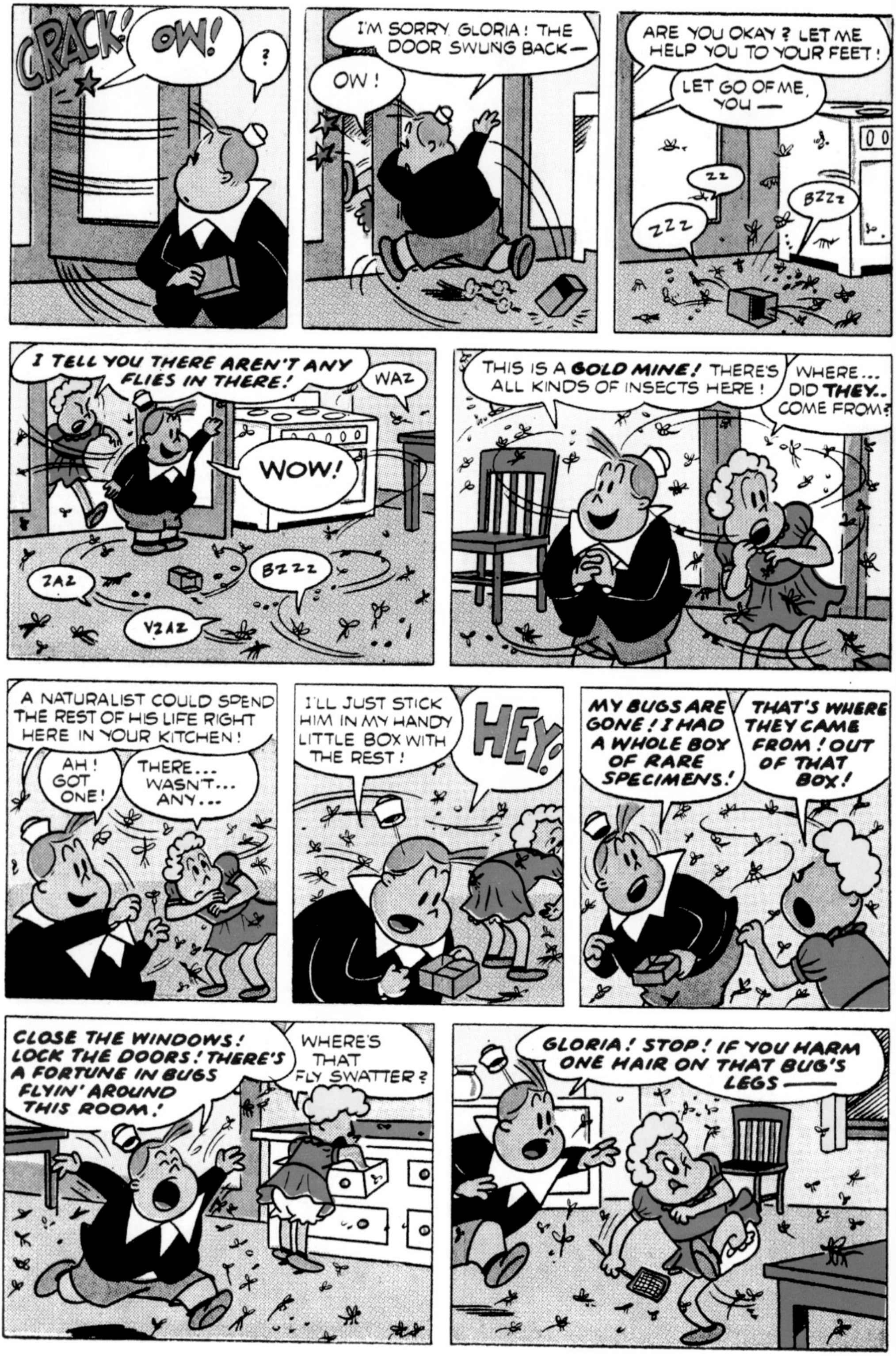
CRACK!
OW!
?
I'M SORRY, GLORIA! THE DOOR SWUNG BACK—
OW!
ARE YOU OKAY? LET ME HELP YOU TO YOUR FEET!
LET GO OF ME, YOU —
ZZ
ZZZ
BZZZ
I TELL YOU THERE AREN'T ANY FLIES IN THERE!
WAZ
WOW!
ZAZ
BZZZ
VZAZ
THIS IS A GOLD MINE! THERE'S ALL KINDS OF INSECTS HERE!
WHERE... DID THEY.. COME FROM?
A NATURALIST COULD SPEND THE REST OF HIS LIFE RIGHT HERE IN YOUR KITCHEN!
AH! GOT ONE!
THERE... WASN'T... ANY...
I'LL JUST STICK HIM IN MY HANDY LITTLE BOX WITH THE REST!
HEY!
MY BUGS ARE GONE! I HAD A WHOLE BOX OF RARE SPECIMENS!
THAT'S WHERE THEY CAME FROM! OUT OF THAT BOX!
CLOSE THE WINDOWS! LOCK THE DOORS! THERE'S A FORTUNE IN BUGS FLYIN' AROUND THIS ROOM!
WHERE'S THAT FLY SWATTER?
GLORIA! STOP! IF YOU HARM ONE HAIR ON THAT BUG'S LEGS —

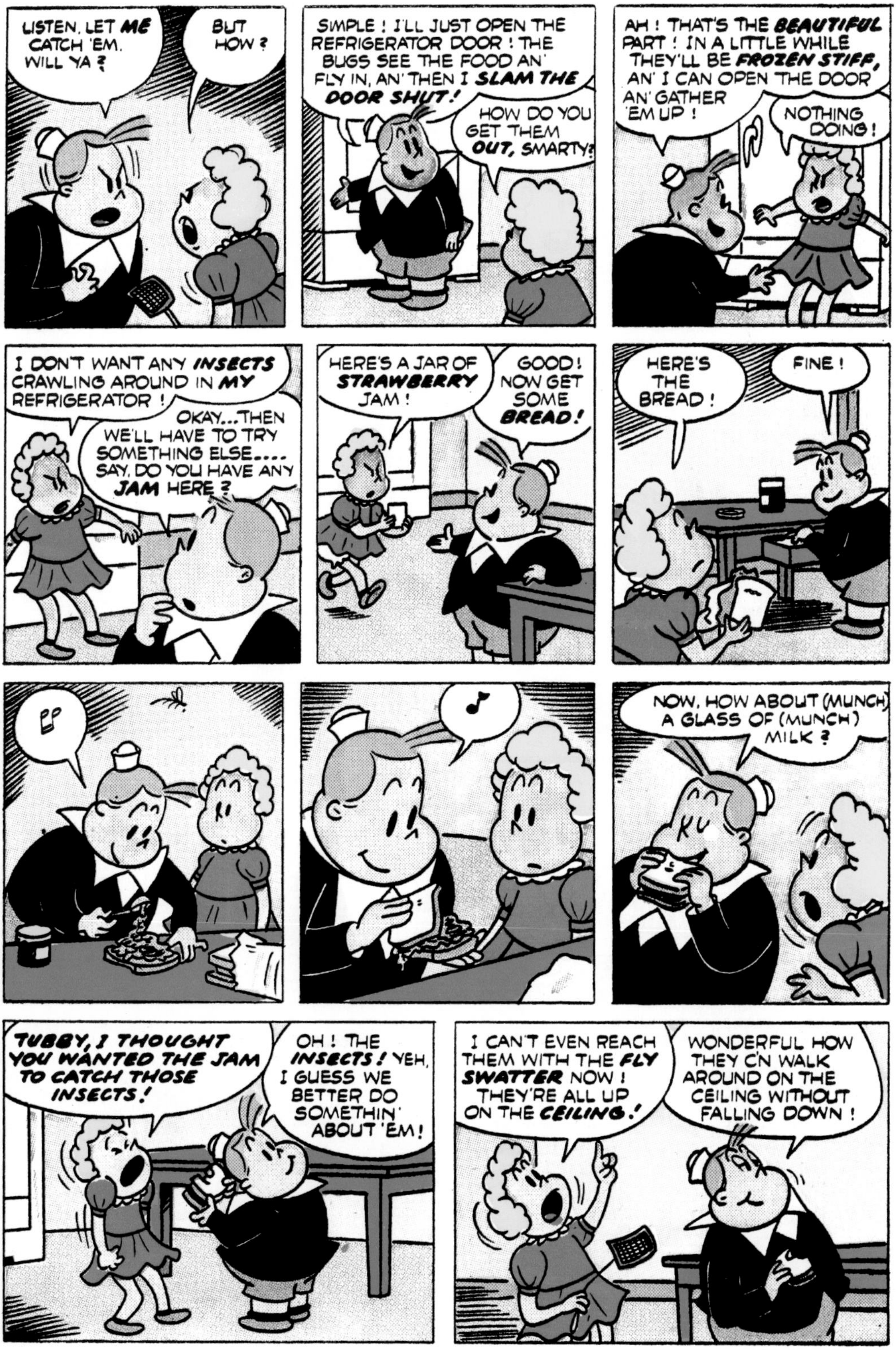
LISTEN, LET ME CATCH 'EM. WILL YA ?
BUT HOW ?
SIMPLE ! I'LL JUST OPEN THE REFRIGERATOR DOOR ! THE BUGS SEE THE FOOD AN' FLY IN, AN' THEN I SLAM THE DOOR SHUT !
HOW DO YOU GET THEM OUT, SMARTY?
AH ! THAT'S THE BEAUTIFUL PART ! IN A LITTLE WHILE THEY'LL BE FROZEN STIFF, AN' I CAN OPEN THE DOOR AN' GATHER 'EM UP !
NOTHING DOING !
I DON'T WANT ANY INSECTS CRAWLING AROUND IN MY REFRIGERATOR !
OKAY... THEN WE'LL HAVE TO TRY SOMETHING ELSE.... SAY, DO YOU HAVE ANY JAM HERE ?
HERE'S A JAR OF STRAWBERRY JAM !
GOOD ! NOW GET SOME BREAD !
HERE'S THE BREAD !
FINE !
NOW, HOW ABOUT (MUNCH) A GLASS OF (MUNCH) MILK ?
TUBBY, I THOUGHT YOU WANTED THE JAM TO CATCH THOSE INSECTS !
OH ! THE INSECTS ! YEH, I GUESS WE BETTER DO SOMETHIN' ABOUT 'EM !
I CAN'T EVEN REACH THEM WITH THE FLY SWATTER NOW ! THEY'RE ALL UP ON THE CEILING !
WONDERFUL HOW THEY C'N WALK AROUND ON THE CEILING WITHOUT FALLING DOWN !

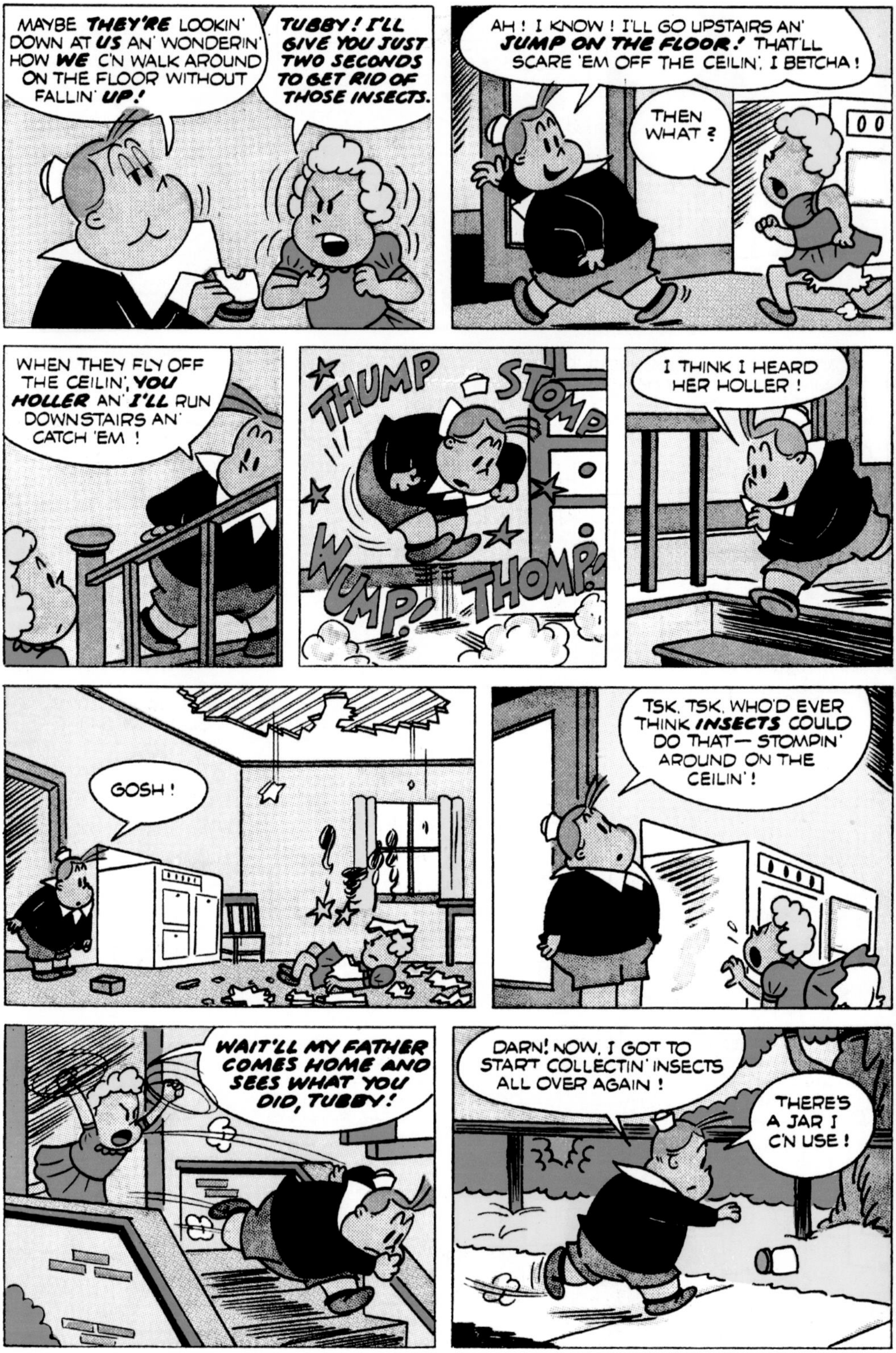
MAYBE THEY'RE LOOKIN' DOWN AT US AN' WONDERIN' HOW WE C'N WALK AROUND ON THE FLOOR WITHOUT FALLIN' UP!
TUBBY! I'LL GIVE YOU JUST TWO SECONDS TO GET RID OF THOSE INSECTS.
AH! I KNOW! I'LL GO UPSTAIRS AN' JUMP ON THE FLOOR! THAT'LL SCARE 'EM OFF THE CEILIN', I BETCHA!
THEN WHAT?
WHEN THEY FLY OFF THE CEILIN', YOU HOLLER AN' I'LL RUN DOWNSTAIRS AN' CATCH 'EM!
THUMP
STOMP
WUMP!
THOMP!
I THINK I HEARD HER HOLLER!
GOSH!
TSK. TSK. WHO'D EVER THINK INSECTS COULD DO THAT— STOMPIN' AROUND ON THE CEILIN'!
WAIT'LL MY FATHER COMES HOME AND SEES WHAT YOU DID, TUBBY!
DARN! NOW, I GOT TO START COLLECTIN' INSECTS ALL OVER AGAIN!
THERE'S A JAR I C'N USE!

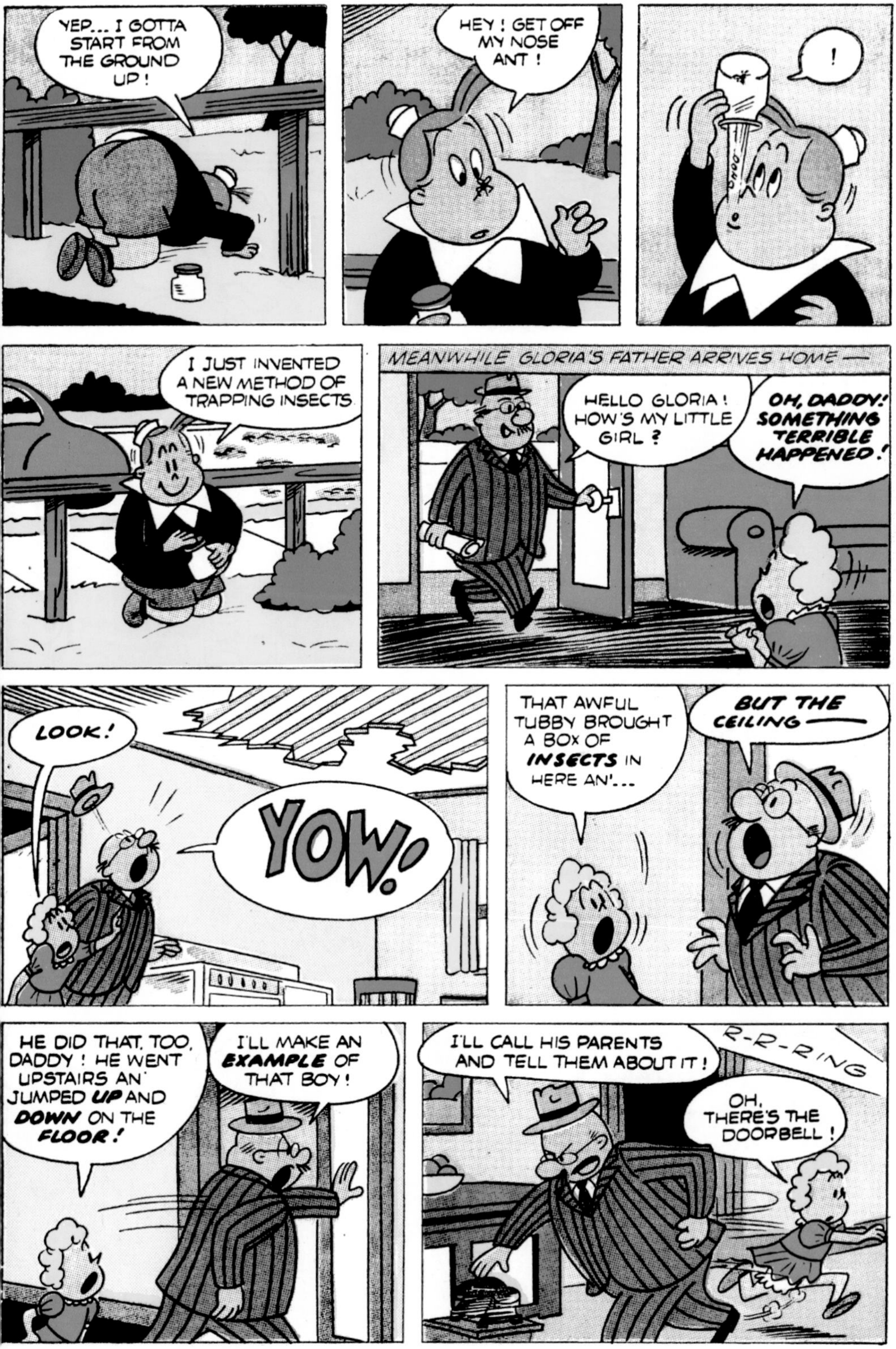
YEP... I GOTTA START FROM THE GROUND UP!
HEY! GET OFF MY NOSE ANT!
!
I JUST INVENTED A NEW METHOD OF TRAPPING INSECTS
MEANWHILE GLORIA'S FATHER ARRIVES HOME —
HELLO GLORIA! HOW'S MY LITTLE GIRL?
OH, DADDY! SOMETHING TERRIBLE HAPPENED!
LOOK!
YOW!
THAT AWFUL TUBBY BROUGHT A BOX OF INSECTS IN HERE AN'...
BUT THE CEILING —
HE DID THAT, TOO, DADDY! HE WENT UPSTAIRS AN' JUMPED UP AND DOWN ON THE FLOOR!
I'LL MAKE AN EXAMPLE OF THAT BOY!
I'LL CALL HIS PARENTS AND TELL THEM ABOUT IT!
R-R-RING
OH, THERE'S THE DOORBELL!

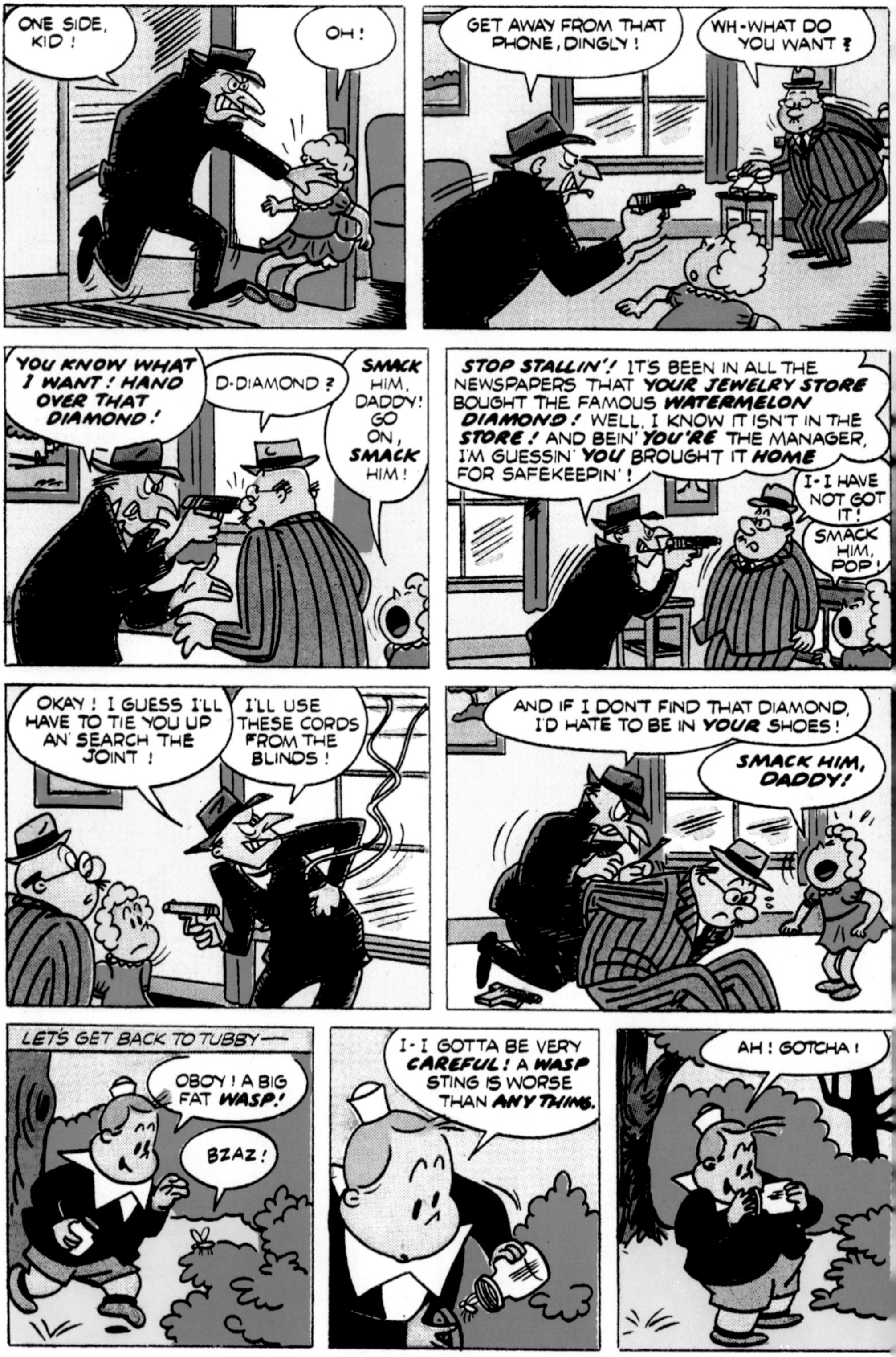

ONE SIDE, KID !
OH !
GET AWAY FROM THAT PHONE, DINGLY !
WH-WHAT DO YOU WANT ?
YOU KNOW WHAT I WANT ! HAND OVER THAT DIAMOND !
D-DIAMOND ?
SMACK HIM, DADDY! GO ON, SMACK HIM !
STOP STALLIN'! IT'S BEEN IN ALL THE NEWSPAPERS THAT YOUR JEWELRY STORE BOUGHT THE FAMOUS WATERMELON DIAMOND ! WELL, I KNOW IT ISN'T IN THE STORE ! AND BEIN' YOU'RE THE MANAGER, I'M GUESSIN' YOU BROUGHT IT HOME FOR SAFEKEEPIN' !
I-I HAVE NOT GOT IT !
SMACK HIM, POP !
OKAY ! I GUESS I'LL HAVE TO TIE YOU UP AN' SEARCH THE JOINT !
I'LL USE THESE CORDS FROM THE BLINDS !
AND IF I DON'T FIND THAT DIAMOND, I'D HATE TO BE IN YOUR SHOES !
SMACK HIM, DADDY!
LET'S GET BACK TO TUBBY—
OBOY ! A BIG FAT WASP!
BZAZ !
I-I GOTTA BE VERY CAREFUL ! A WASP STING IS WORSE THAN ANY THING.
AH ! GOTCHA !

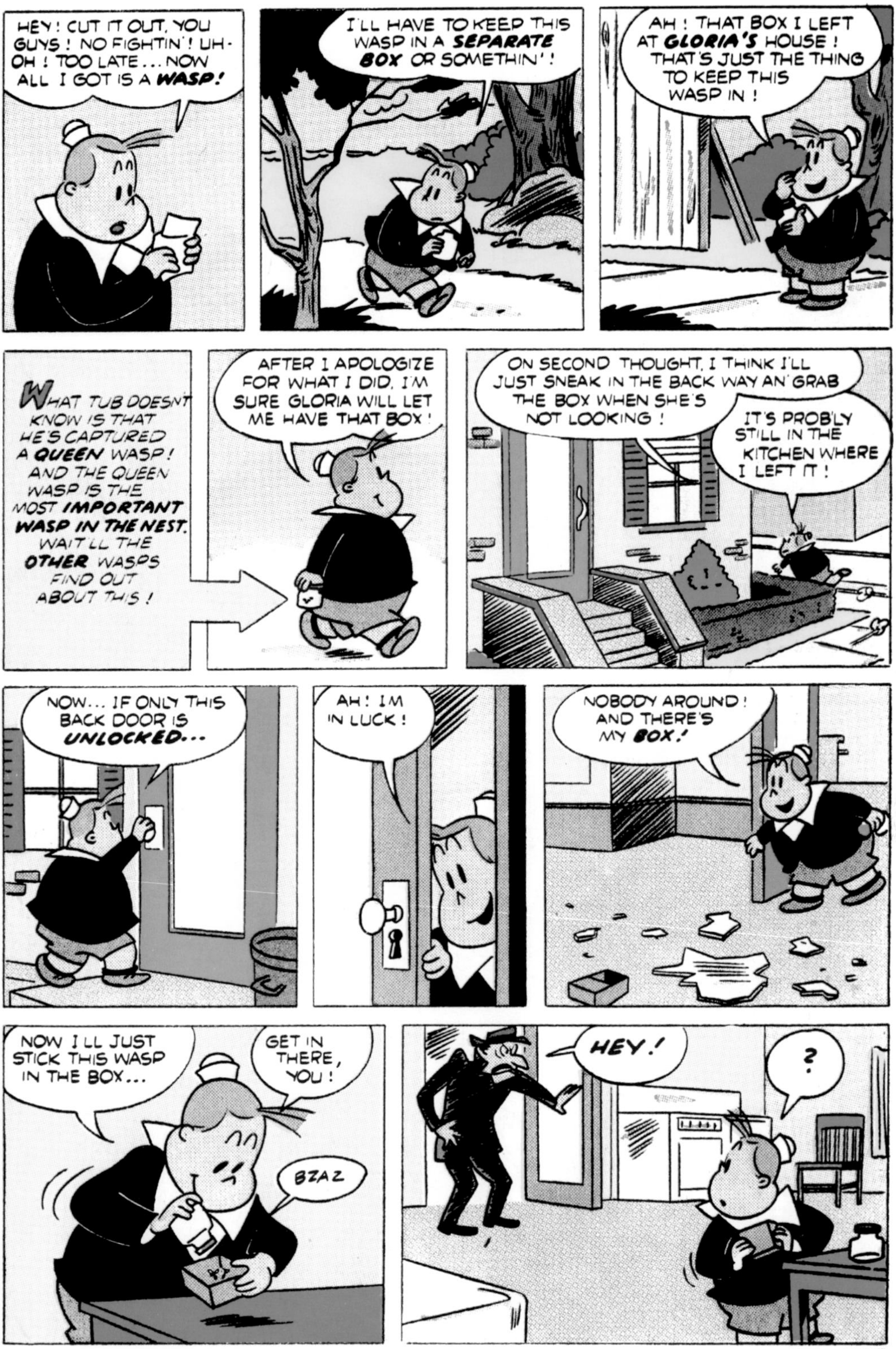
HEY! CUT IT OUT, YOU GUYS! NO FIGHTIN'! UH-OH! TOO LATE... NOW ALL I GOT IS A WASP!
I'LL HAVE TO KEEP THIS WASP IN A SEPARATE BOX OR SOMETHIN'!
AH! THAT BOX I LEFT AT GLORIA'S HOUSE! THAT'S JUST THE THING TO KEEP THIS WASP IN!
WHAT TUB DOESN'T KNOW IS THAT HE'S CAPTURED A QUEEN WASP! AND THE QUEEN WASP IS THE MOST IMPORTANT WASP IN THE NEST. WAIT'LL THE OTHER WASPS FIND OUT ABOUT THIS!
AFTER I APOLOGIZE FOR WHAT I DID, I'M SURE GLORIA WILL LET ME HAVE THAT BOX!
ON SECOND THOUGHT, I THINK I'LL JUST SNEAK IN THE BACK WAY AN' GRAB THE BOX WHEN SHE'S NOT LOOKING!
IT'S PROB'LY STILL IN THE KITCHEN WHERE I LEFT IT!
NOW... IF ONLY THIS BACK DOOR IS UNLOCKED...
AH! I'M IN LUCK!
NOBODY AROUND! AND THERE'S MY BOX!
NOW I'LL JUST STICK THIS WASP IN THE BOX...
GET IN THERE, YOU!
BZAZ
HEY!
?

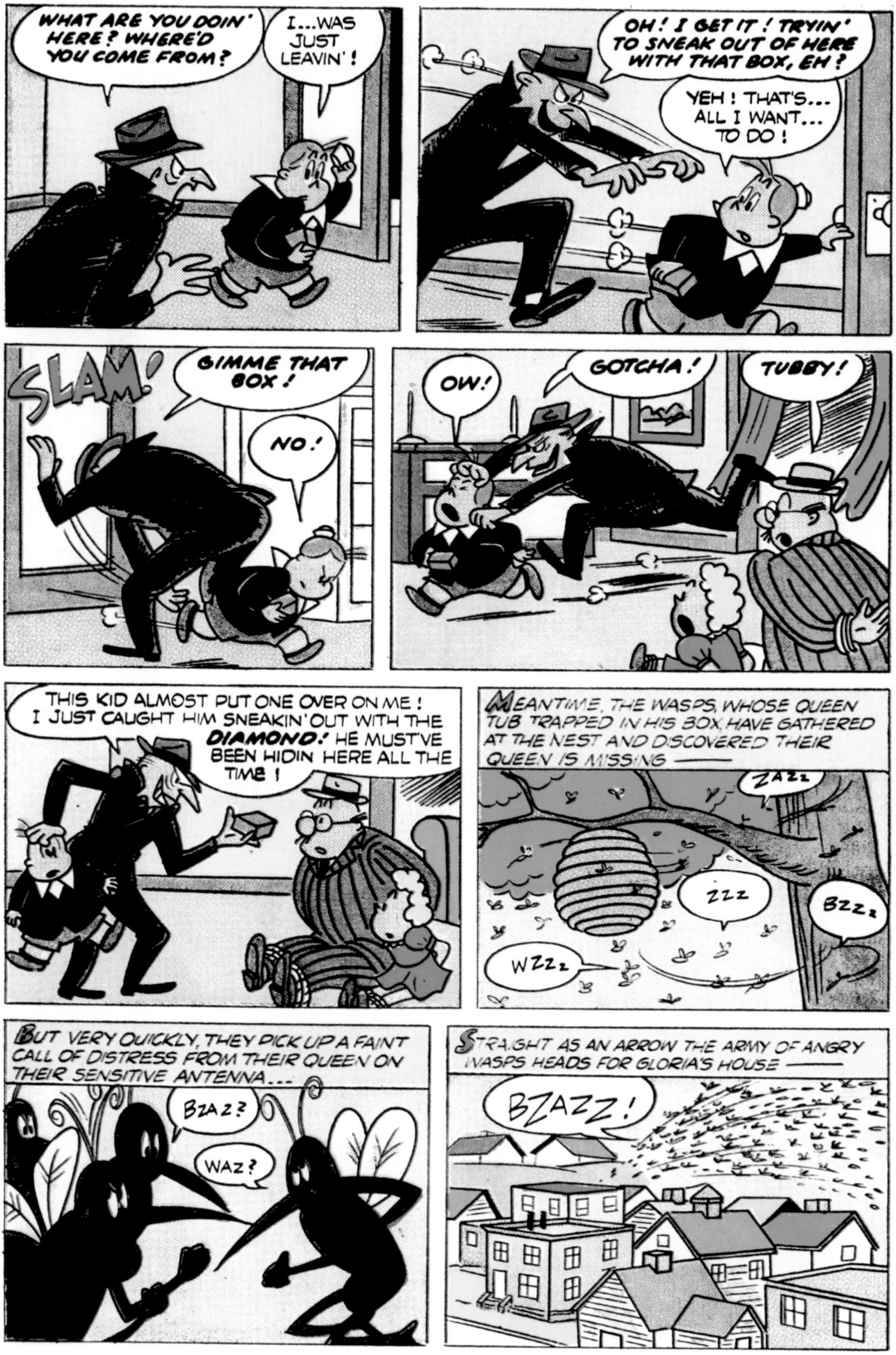

WHAT ARE YOU DOIN' HERE? WHERE'D YOU COME FROM?
I...WAS JUST LEAVIN'!
OH! I GET IT! TRYIN' TO SNEAK OUT OF HERE WITH THAT BOX, EH?
YEH! THAT'S... ALL I WANT... TO DO!
SLAM!
GIMME THAT BOX!
NO!
OW!
GOTCHA!
TUBBY!
THIS KID ALMOST PUT ONE OVER ON ME! I JUST CAUGHT HIM SNEAKIN' OUT WITH THE DIAMOND! HE MUST'VE BEEN HIDIN HERE ALL THE TIME!
MEANTIME, THE WASPS, WHOSE QUEEN TUB TRAPPED IN HIS BOX, HAVE GATHERED AT THE NEST AND DISCOVERED THEIR QUEEN IS MISSING ——
ZAZZ
ZZZ
BZZZ
WZZZ
BUT VERY QUICKLY, THEY PICK UP A FAINT CALL OF DISTRESS FROM THEIR QUEEN ON THEIR SENSITIVE ANTENNA...
BZAZZ?
WAZ?
STRAIGHT AS AN ARROW THE ARMY OF ANGRY WASPS HEADS FOR GLORIA'S HOUSE ——
BZAZZ!

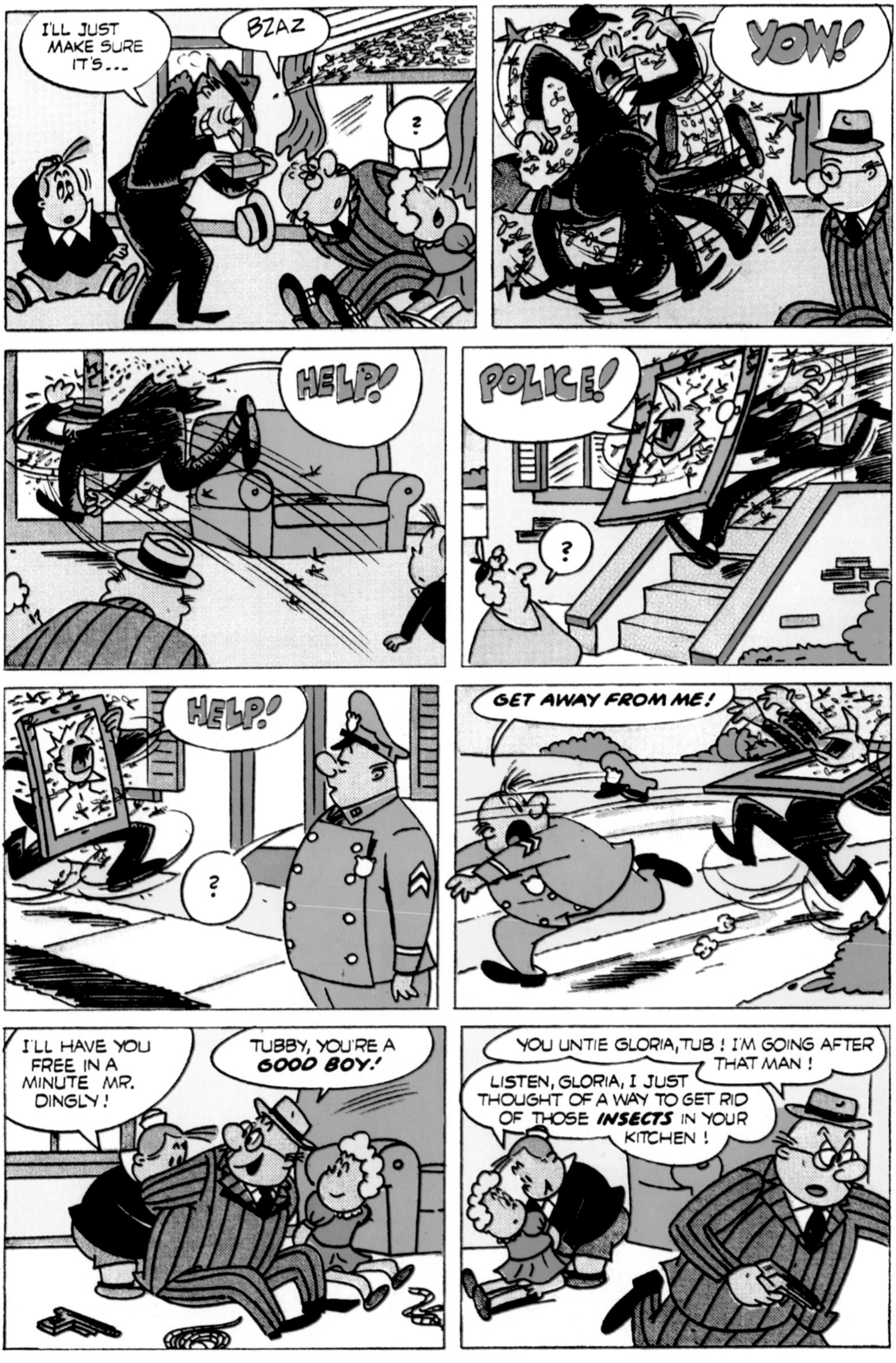
I'LL JUST MAKE SURE IT'S...
BZAZ
?
YOW!
HELP!
POLICE!
?
HELP!
?
GET AWAY FROM ME!
I'LL HAVE YOU FREE IN A MINUTE MR. DINGLY!
TUBBY, YOU'RE A GOOD BOY!
YOU UNTIE GLORIA, TUB! I'M GOING AFTER THAT MAN!
LISTEN, GLORIA, I JUST THOUGHT OF A WAY TO GET RID OF THOSE INSECTS IN YOUR KITCHEN!

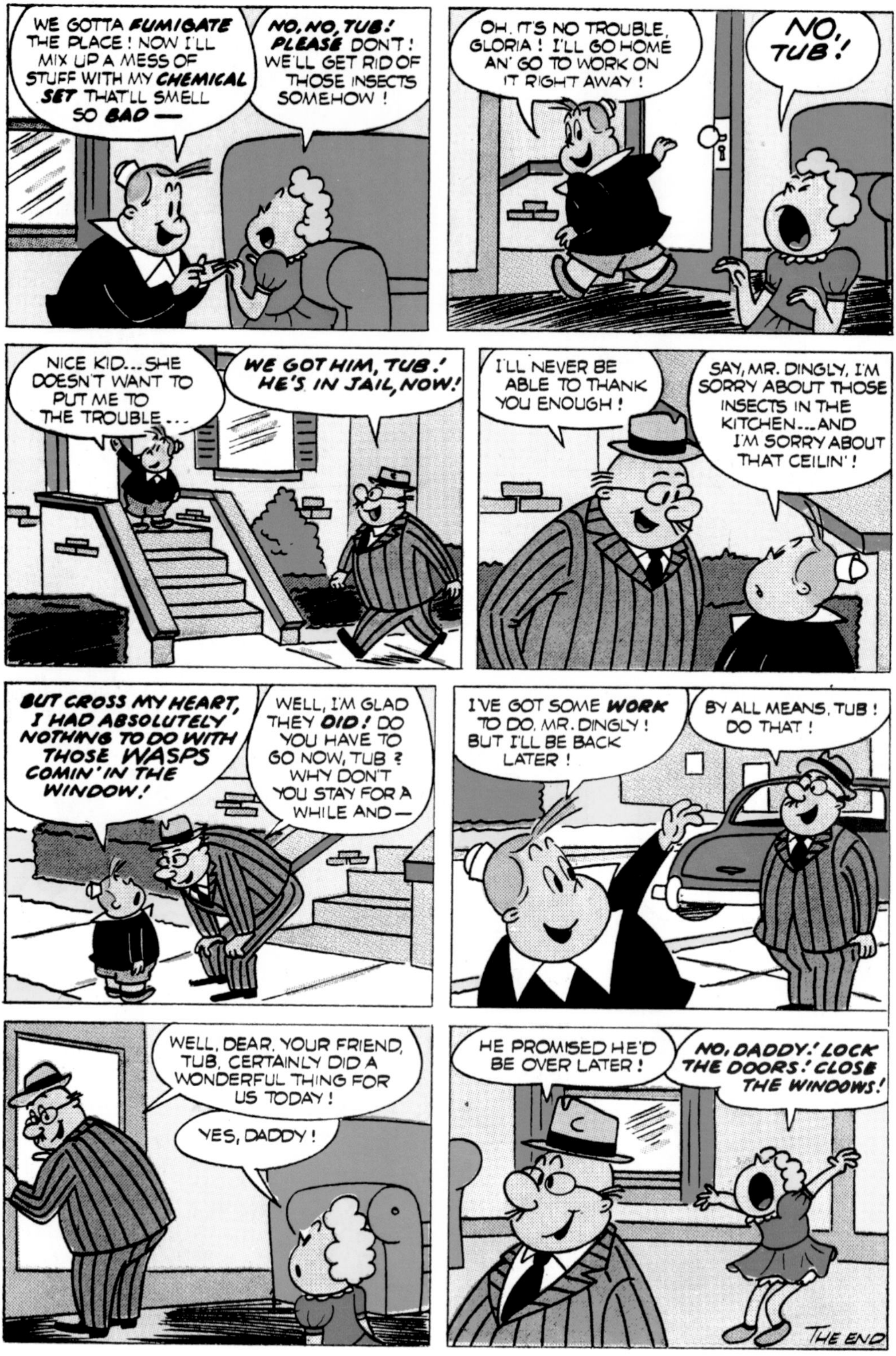
WE GOTTA FUMIGATE THE PLACE! NOW I'LL MIX UP A MESS OF STUFF WITH MY CHEMICAL SET THAT'LL SMELL SO BAD—
NO, NO, TUB! PLEASE DON'T! WE'LL GET RID OF THOSE INSECTS SOMEHOW!
OH, IT'S NO TROUBLE, GLORIA! I'LL GO HOME AN' GO TO WORK ON IT RIGHT AWAY!
NO, TUB!
NICE KID... SHE DOESN'T WANT TO PUT ME TO THE TROUBLE...
WE GOT HIM, TUB! HE'S IN JAIL, NOW!
I'LL NEVER BE ABLE TO THANK YOU ENOUGH!
SAY, MR. DINGLY, I'M SORRY ABOUT THOSE INSECTS IN THE KITCHEN... AND I'M SORRY ABOUT THAT CEILIN'!
BUT CROSS MY HEART, I HAD ABSOLUTELY NOTHING TO DO WITH THOSE WASPS COMIN' IN THE WINDOW!
WELL, I'M GLAD THEY DID! DO YOU HAVE TO GO NOW, TUB? WHY DON'T YOU STAY FOR A WHILE AND—
I'VE GOT SOME WORK TO DO, MR. DINGLY! BUT I'LL BE BACK LATER!
BY ALL MEANS, TUB! DO THAT!
WELL, DEAR, YOUR FRIEND, TUB, CERTAINLY DID A WONDERFUL THING FOR US TODAY!
YES, DADDY!
HE PROMISED HE'D BE OVER LATER!
NO, DADDY! LOCK THE DOORS! CLOSE THE WINDOWS!
THE END

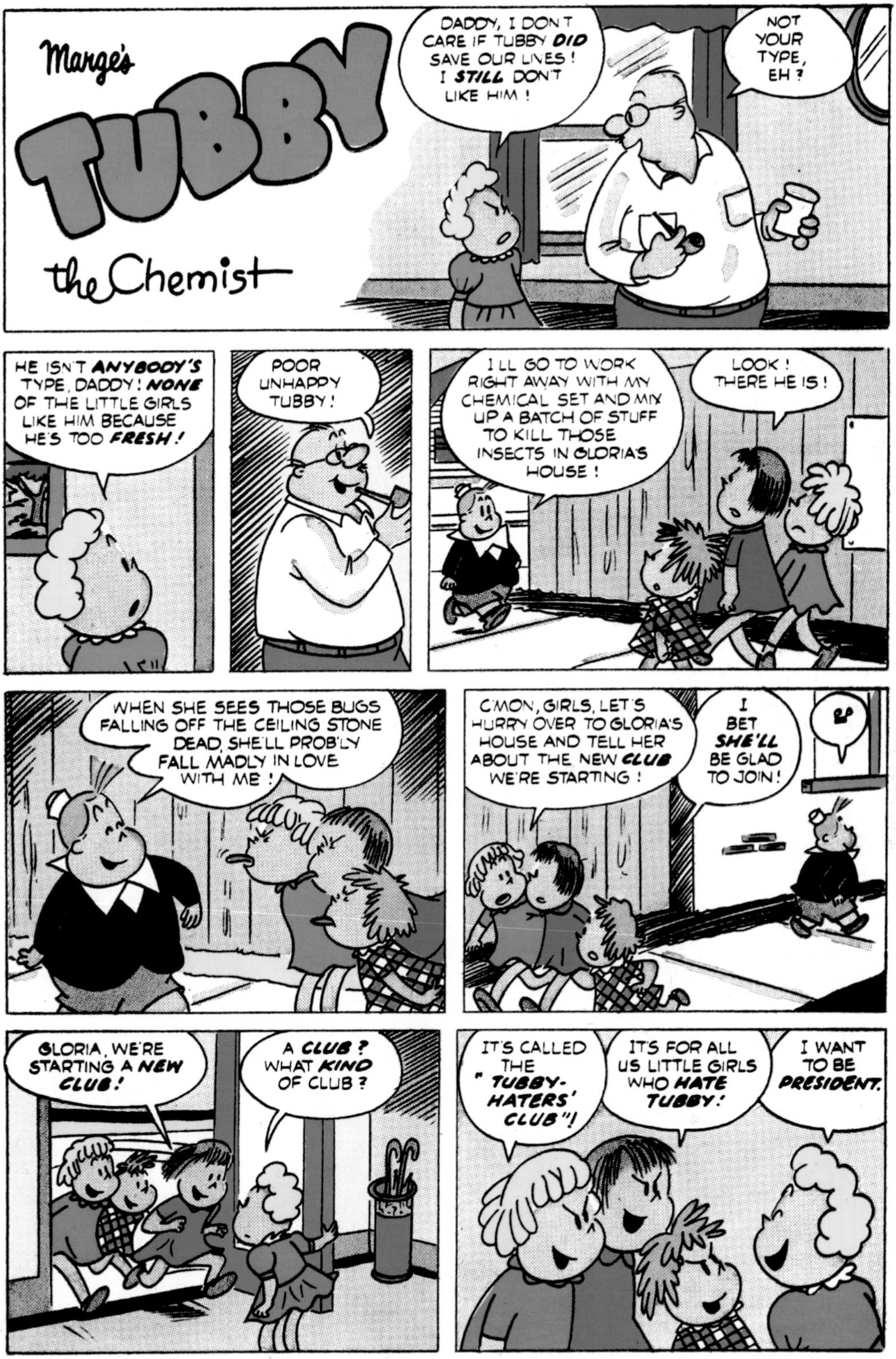
Marge's
TUBBY
the Chemist
DADDY, I DON'T CARE IF TUBBY DID SAVE OUR LIVES! I STILL DON'T LIKE HIM!
NOT YOUR TYPE, EH?
HE ISN'T ANYBODY'S TYPE, DADDY! NONE OF THE LITTLE GIRLS LIKE HIM BECAUSE HE'S TOO FRESH!
POOR UNHAPPY TUBBY!
I'LL GO TO WORK RIGHT AWAY WITH MY CHEMICAL SET AND MIX UP A BATCH OF STUFF TO KILL THOSE INSECTS IN GLORIA'S HOUSE!
LOOK! THERE HE IS!
WHEN SHE SEES THOSE BUGS FALLING OFF THE CEILING STONE DEAD, SHE'LL PROB'LY FALL MADLY IN LOVE WITH ME!
C'MON, GIRLS, LET'S HURRY OVER TO GLORIA'S HOUSE AND TELL HER ABOUT THE NEW CLUB WE'RE STARTING!
I BET SHE'LL BE GLAD TO JOIN!
GLORIA, WE'RE STARTING A NEW CLUB!
A CLUB? WHAT KIND OF CLUB?
IT'S CALLED THE "TUBBY-HATERS' CLUB"!
IT'S FOR ALL US LITTLE GIRLS WHO HATE TUBBY!
I WANT TO BE PRESIDENT.

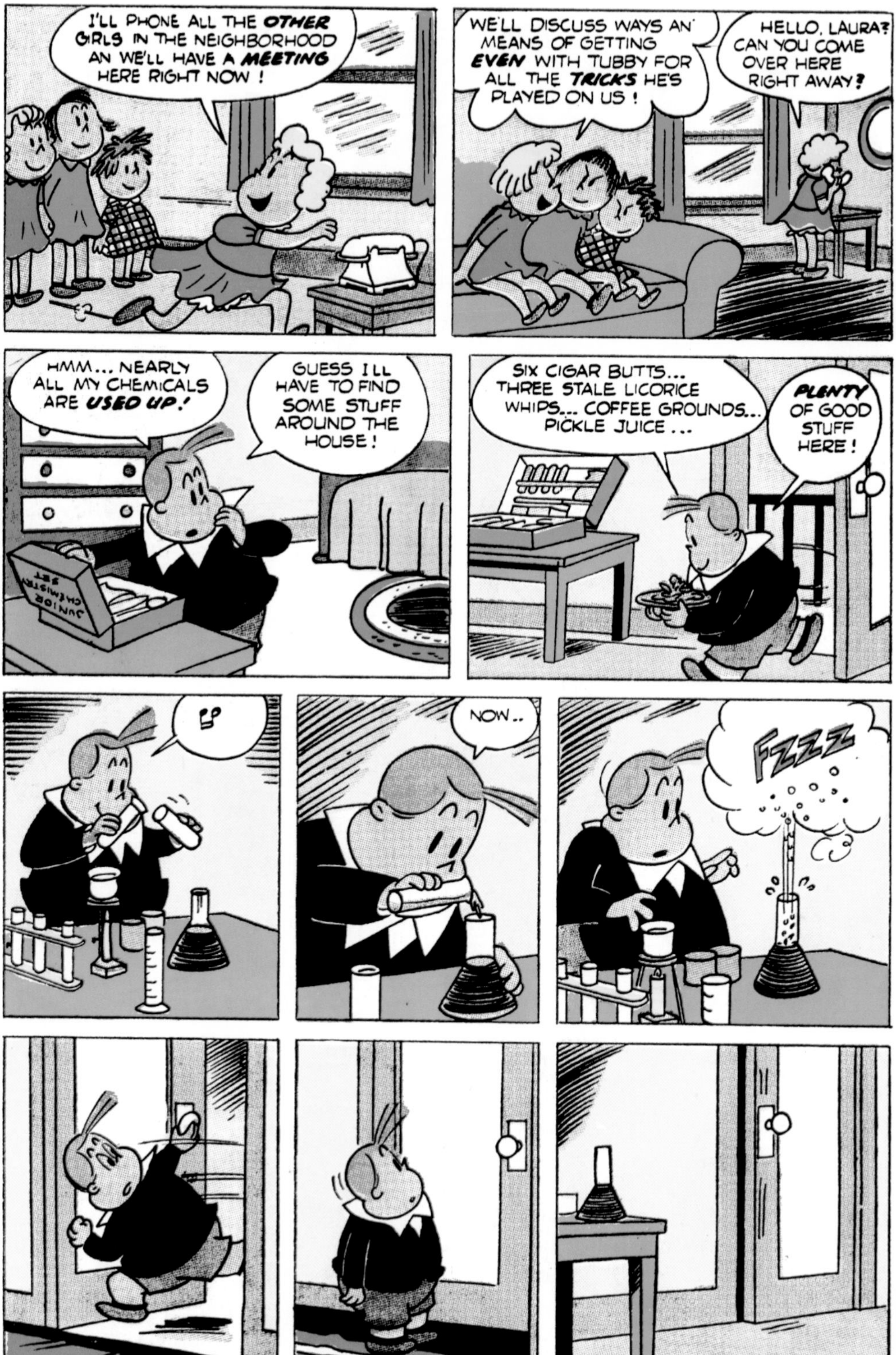
I'LL PHONE ALL THE OTHER GIRLS IN THE NEIGHBORHOOD AN WE'LL HAVE A MEETING HERE RIGHT NOW !
WE'LL DISCUSS WAYS AN' MEANS OF GETTING EVEN WITH TUBBY FOR ALL THE TRICKS HE'S PLAYED ON US !
HELLO, LAURA? CAN YOU COME OVER HERE RIGHT AWAY?
HMM... NEARLY ALL MY CHEMICALS ARE USED UP!
GUESS I'LL HAVE TO FIND SOME STUFF AROUND THE HOUSE!
SIX CIGAR BUTTS... THREE STALE LICORICE WHIPS... COFFEE GROUNDS... PICKLE JUICE...
PLENTY OF GOOD STUFF HERE!
NOW..
FZZZ

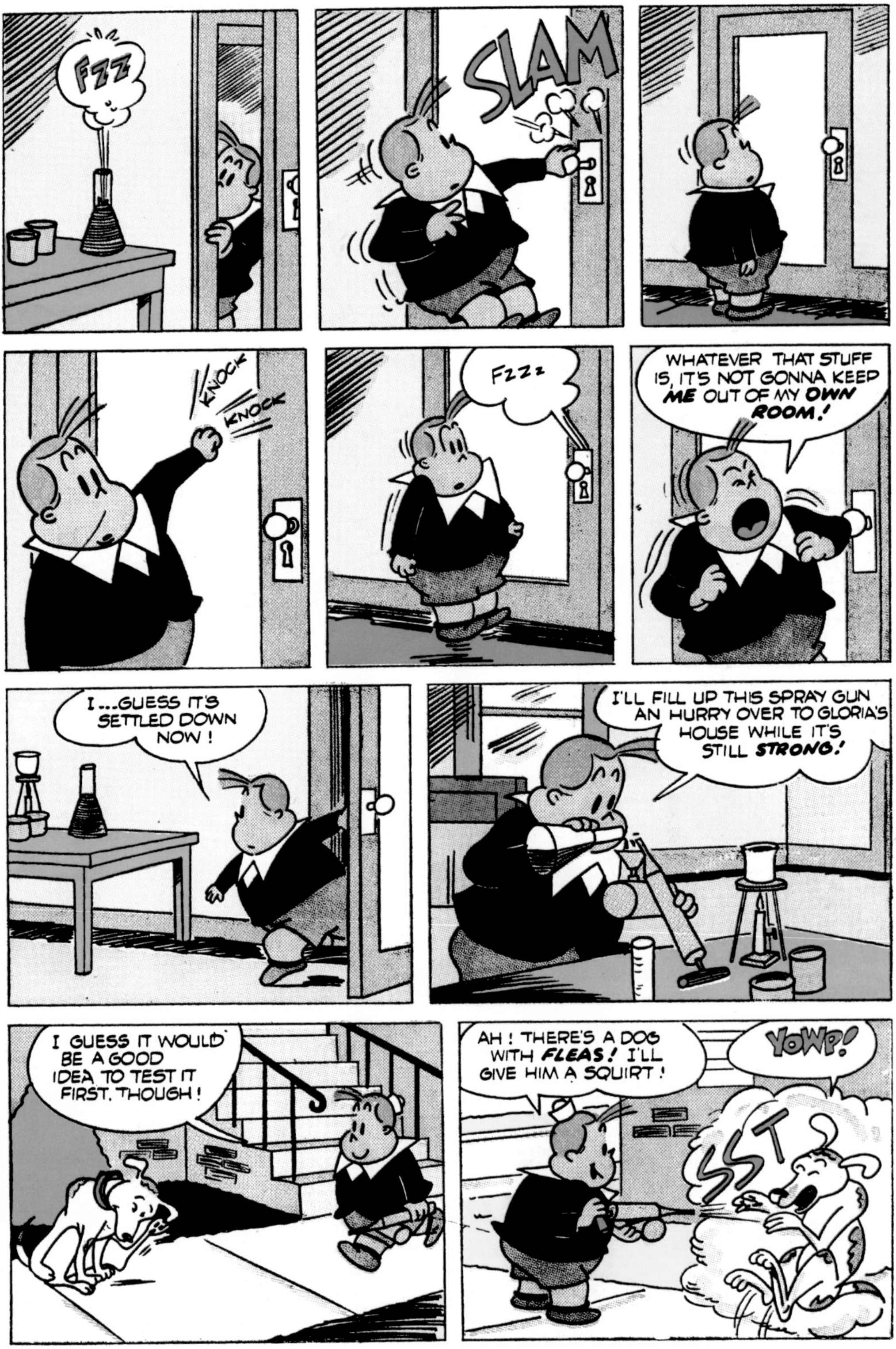
FZZ
SLAM
KNOCK
KNOCK
FZZZ
WHATEVER THAT STUFF IS, IT'S NOT GONNA KEEP ME OUT OF MY OWN ROOM!
I...GUESS IT'S SETTLED DOWN NOW!
I'LL FILL UP THIS SPRAY GUN AN HURRY OVER TO GLORIA'S HOUSE WHILE IT'S STILL STRONG!
I GUESS IT WOULD BE A GOOD IDEA TO TEST IT FIRST, THOUGH!
AH! THERE'S A DOG WITH FLEAS! I'LL GIVE HIM A SQUIRT!
YOWP!
SST

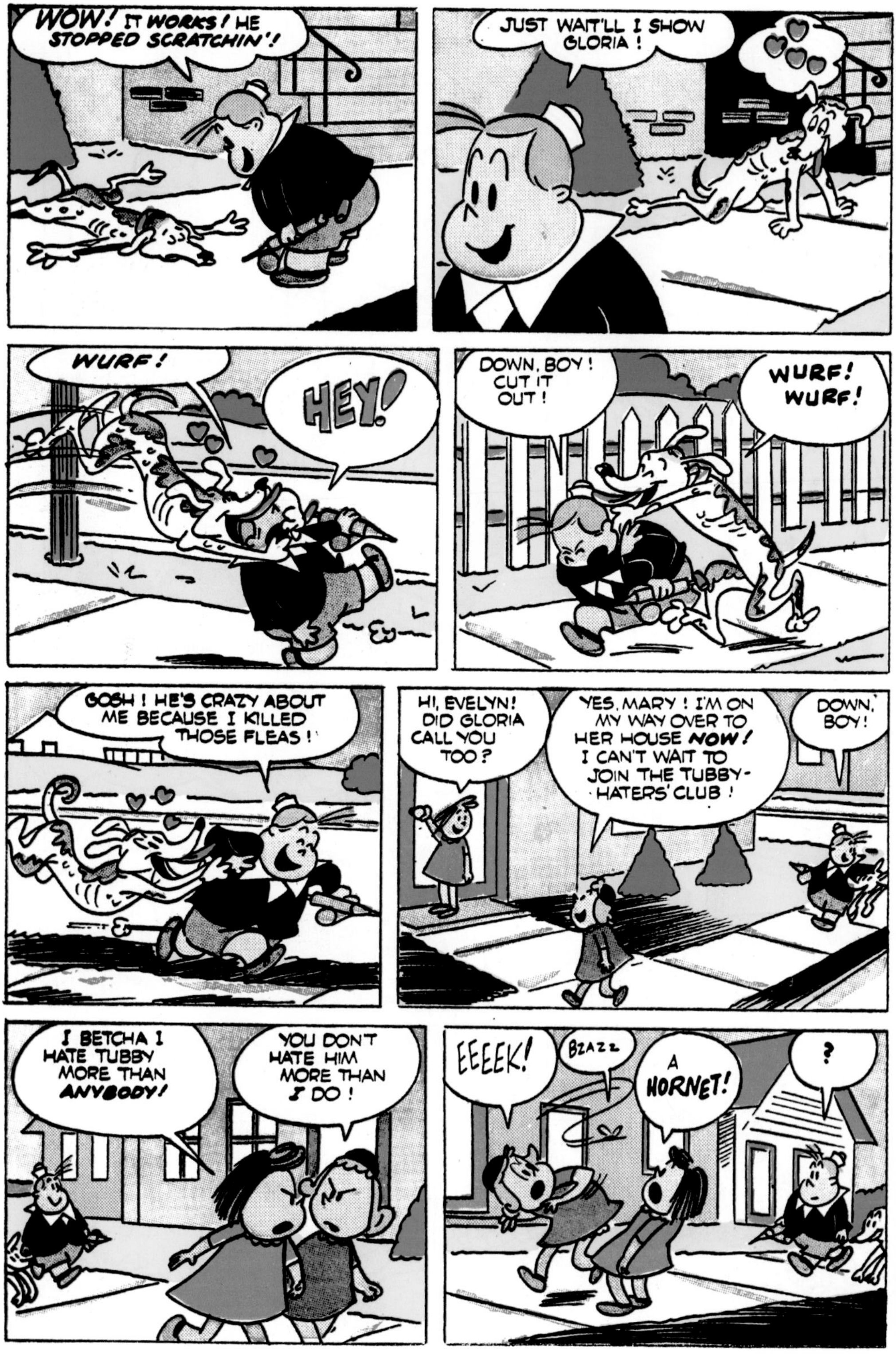
WOW! IT WORKS! HE STOPPED SCRATCHIN'!
JUST WAIT'LL I SHOW GLORIA!
WURF!
HEY!
DOWN, BOY! CUT IT OUT!
WURF! WURF!
GOSH! HE'S CRAZY ABOUT ME BECAUSE I KILLED THOSE FLEAS!
HI, EVELYN! DID GLORIA CALL YOU TOO?
YES, MARY! I'M ON MY WAY OVER TO HER HOUSE NOW! I CAN'T WAIT TO JOIN THE TUBBY-HATERS' CLUB!
DOWN, BOY!
I BETCHA I HATE TUBBY MORE THAN ANYBODY!
YOU DON'T HATE HIM MORE THAN I DO!
EEEEK!
BZAZZ
A HORNET!
?

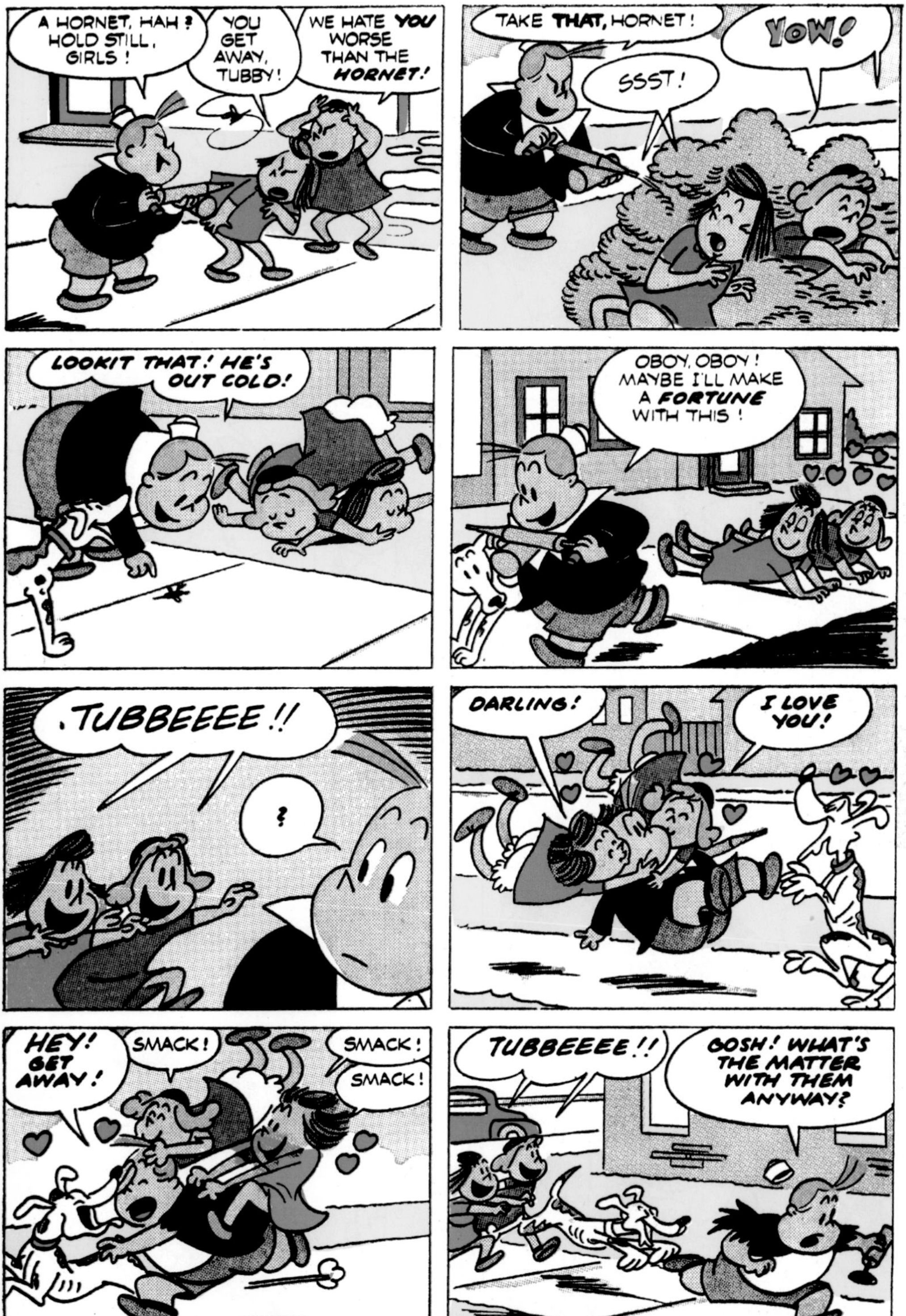
A HORNET, HAH? HOLD STILL, GIRLS!
YOU GET AWAY, TUBBY!
WE HATE YOU WORSE THAN THE HORNET!
TAKE THAT, HORNET!
SSST!
YOW!
LOOKIT THAT! HE'S OUT COLD!
OBOY, OBOY! MAYBE I'LL MAKE A FORTUNE WITH THIS!
TUBBEEEE!!
?
DARLING!
I LOVE YOU!
HEY! GET AWAY!
SMACK!
SMACK!
SMACK!
TUBBEEEE!!
GOSH! WHAT'S THE MATTER WITH THEM ANYWAY?

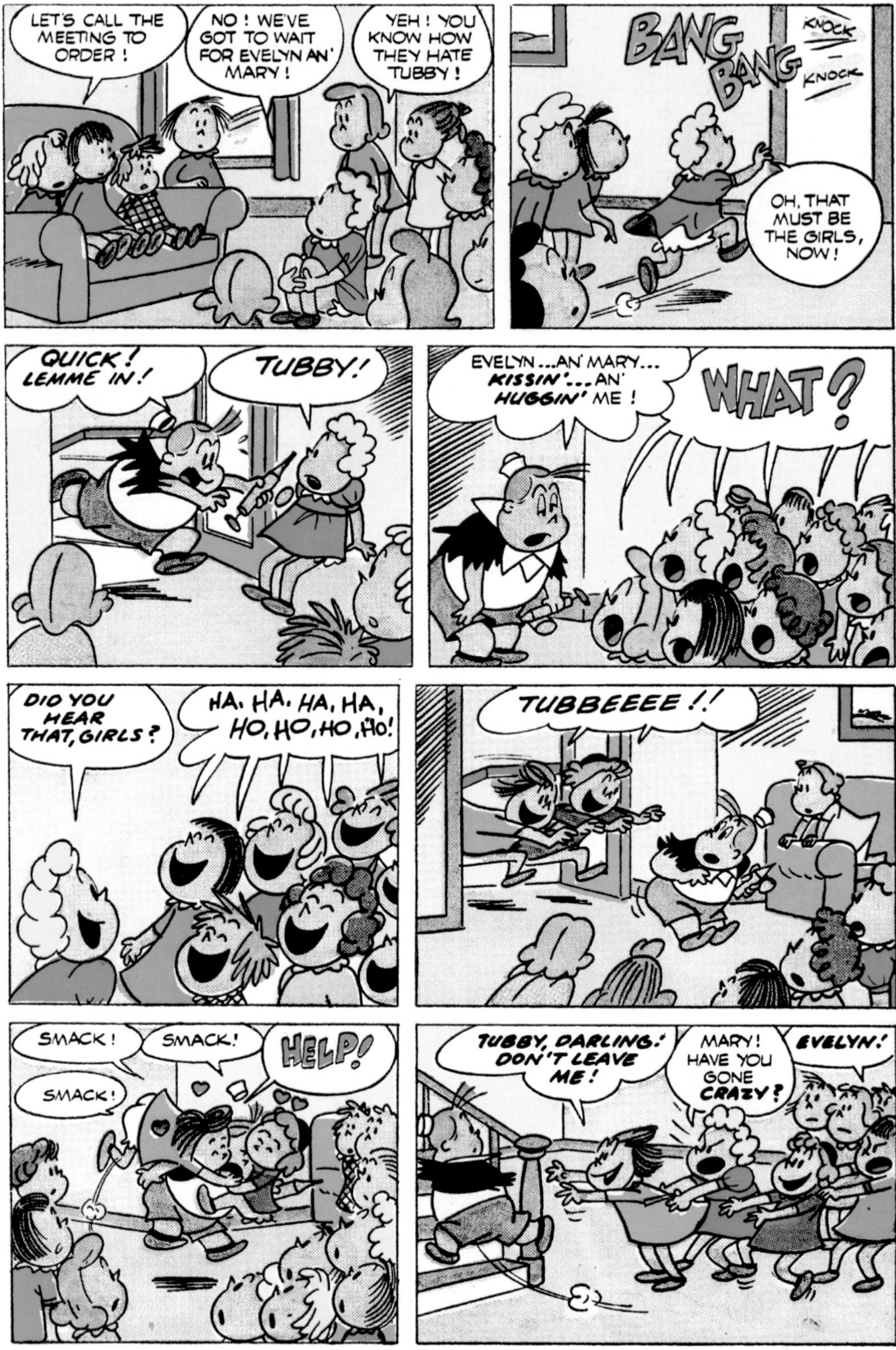

LET'S CALL THE MEETING TO ORDER !
NO ! WE'VE GOT TO WAIT FOR EVELYN AN' MARY !
YEH ! YOU KNOW HOW THEY HATE TUBBY !
BANG BANG
KNOCK KNOCK
OH, THAT MUST BE THE GIRLS, NOW !
QUICK ! LEMME IN !
TUBBY !
EVELYN ...AN' MARY... KISSIN'... AN' HUGGIN' ME !
WHAT ?
DID YOU HEAR THAT, GIRLS ?
HA, HA, HA, HA, HO, HO, HO, HO!
TUBBEEEE !!
SMACK !
SMACK !
SMACK !
HELP !
TUBBY, DARLING ! DON'T LEAVE ME !
MARY ! HAVE YOU GONE CRAZY ?
EVELYN !

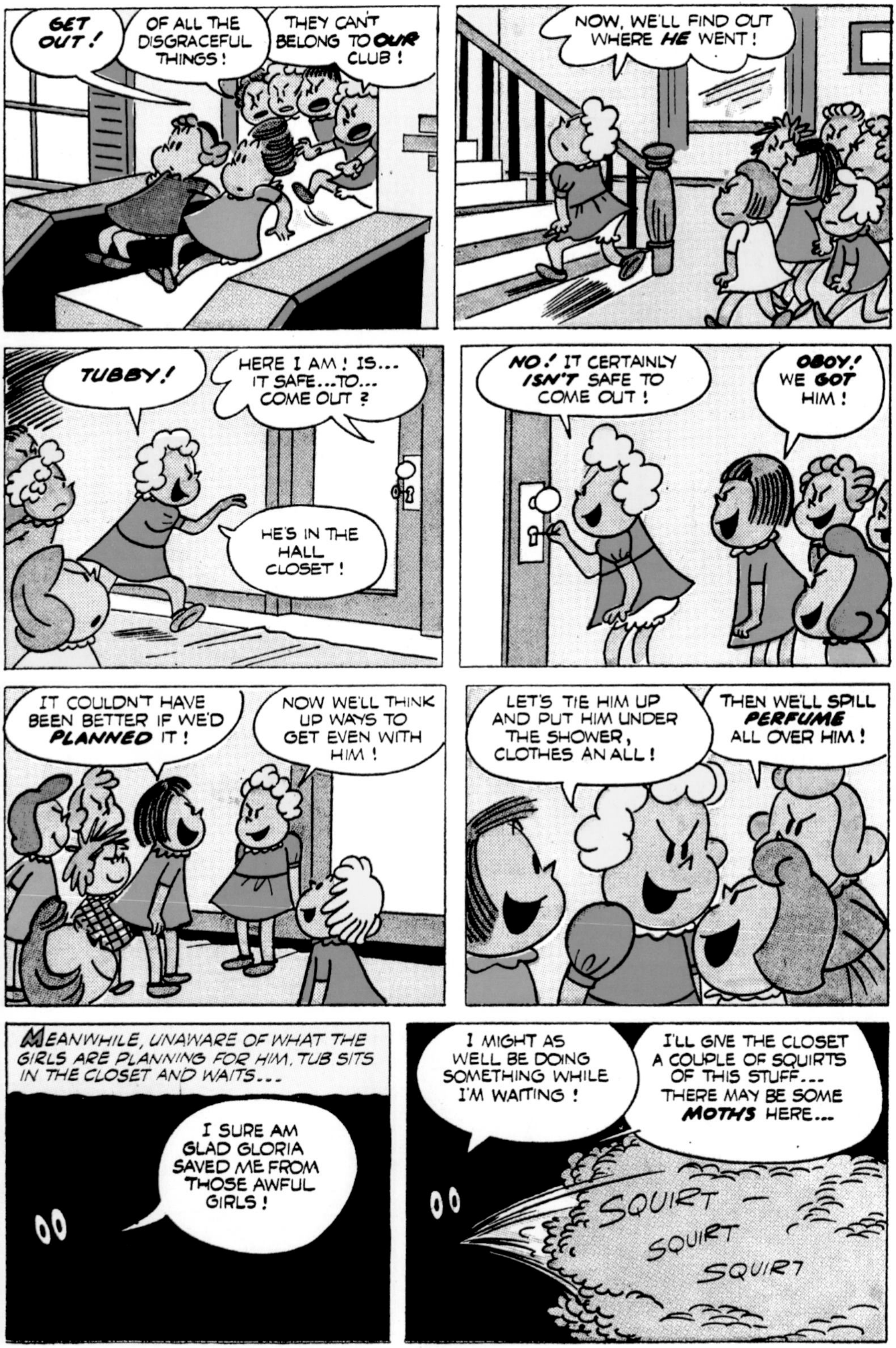

GET OUT!
OF ALL THE DISGRACEFUL THINGS!
THEY CAN'T BELONG TO OUR CLUB!
NOW, WE'LL FIND OUT WHERE HE WENT!
TUBBY!
HERE I AM! IS... IT SAFE...TO... COME OUT?
HE'S IN THE HALL CLOSET!
NO! IT CERTAINLY ISN'T SAFE TO COME OUT!
OBOY! WE GOT HIM!
IT COULDN'T HAVE BEEN BETTER IF WE'D PLANNED IT!
NOW WE'LL THINK UP WAYS TO GET EVEN WITH HIM!
LET'S TIE HIM UP AND PUT HIM UNDER THE SHOWER, CLOTHES AN ALL!
THEN WE'LL SPILL PERFUME ALL OVER HIM!
MEANWHILE, UNAWARE OF WHAT THE GIRLS ARE PLANNING FOR HIM, TUB SITS IN THE CLOSET AND WAITS...
I SURE AM GLAD GLORIA SAVED ME FROM THOSE AWFUL GIRLS!
I MIGHT AS WELL BE DOING SOMETHING WHILE I'M WAITING!
I'LL GIVE THE CLOSET A COUPLE OF SQUIRTS OF THIS STUFF... THERE MAY BE SOME MOTHS HERE...
SQUIRT
SQUIRT
SQUIRT

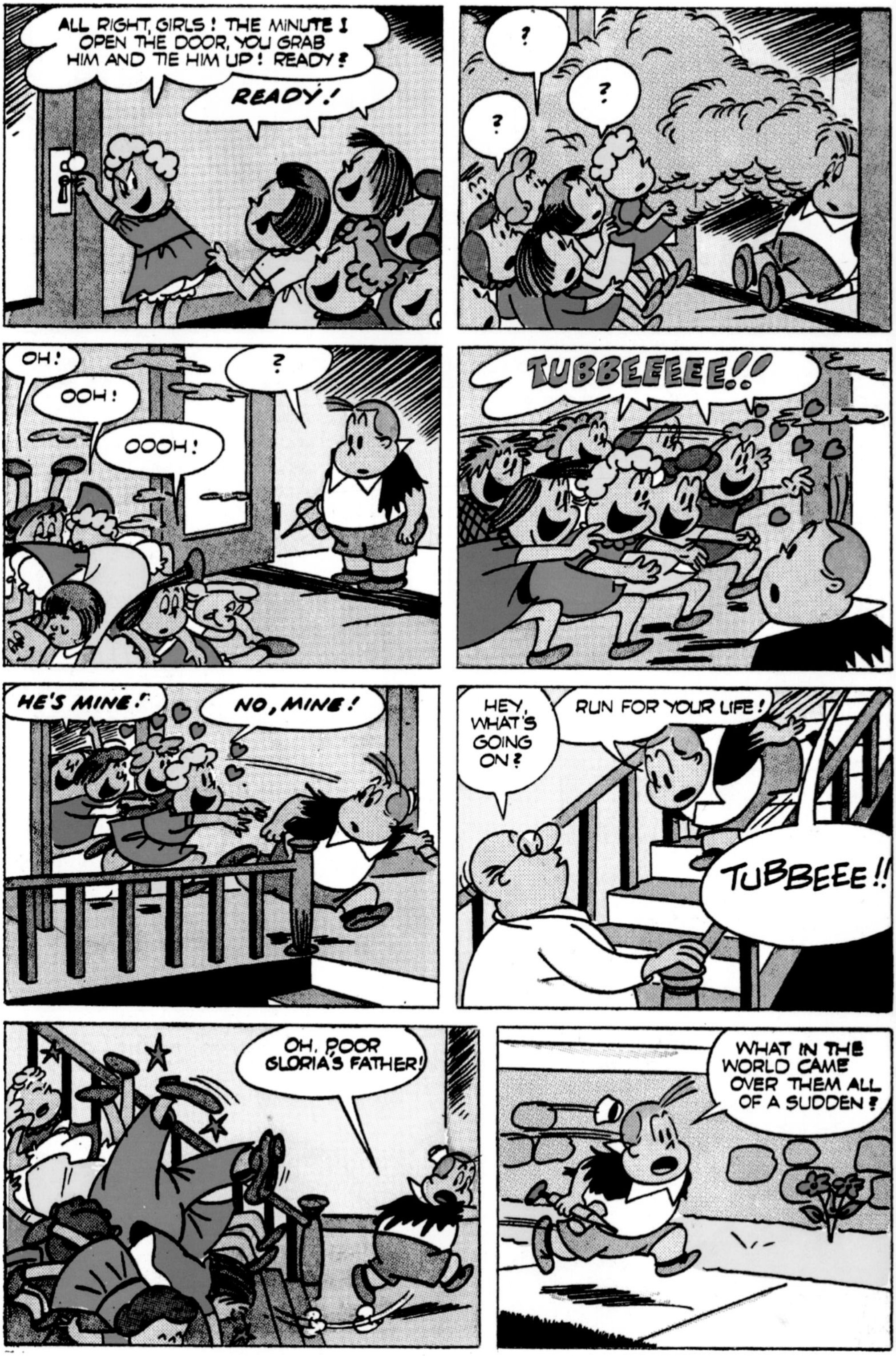
ALL RIGHT, GIRLS! THE MINUTE I OPEN THE DOOR, YOU GRAB HIM AND TIE HIM UP! READY?
READY!
?
?
?
OH!
OOH!
OOOH!
?
TUBBEEEEEE!!
HE'S MINE!
NO, MINE!
HEY, WHAT'S GOING ON?
RUN FOR YOUR LIFE!
TUBBEEE!!
OH, POOR GLORIA'S FATHER!
WHAT IN THE WORLD CAME OVER THEM ALL OF A SUDDEN?

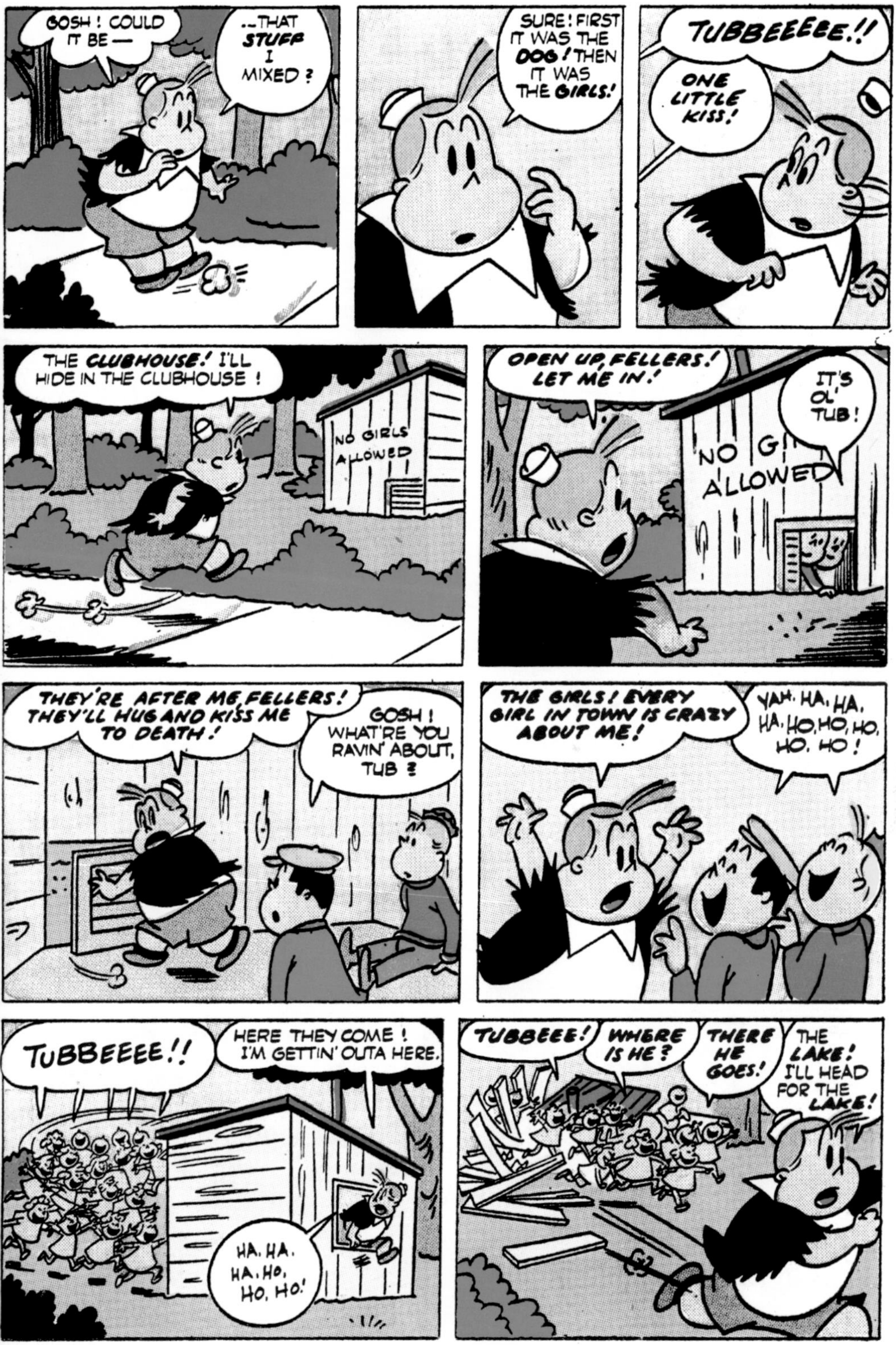

GOSH! COULD IT BE —
..THAT STUFF I MIXED?
SURE! FIRST IT WAS THE DOG! THEN IT WAS THE GIRLS!
TUBBEEEEE!!
ONE LITTLE KISS!
THE CLUBHOUSE! I'LL HIDE IN THE CLUBHOUSE!
NO GIRLS ALLOWED
OPEN UP, FELLERS! LET ME IN!
IT'S OL' TUB!
NO G ALLOWED
THEY'RE AFTER ME, FELLERS! THEY'LL HUG AND KISS ME TO DEATH!
GOSH! WHAT'RE YOU RAVIN' ABOUT, TUB?
THE GIRLS! EVERY GIRL IN TOWN IS CRAZY ABOUT ME!
YAH. HA. HA. HA. HO, HO, HO, HO. HO!
TUBBEEEE!!
HERE THEY COME! I'M GETTIN' OUTA HERE.
HA. HA. HA. HO, HO, HO!
TUBBEEE!
WHERE IS HE?
THERE HE GOES!
THE LAKE! I'LL HEAD FOR THE LAKE!

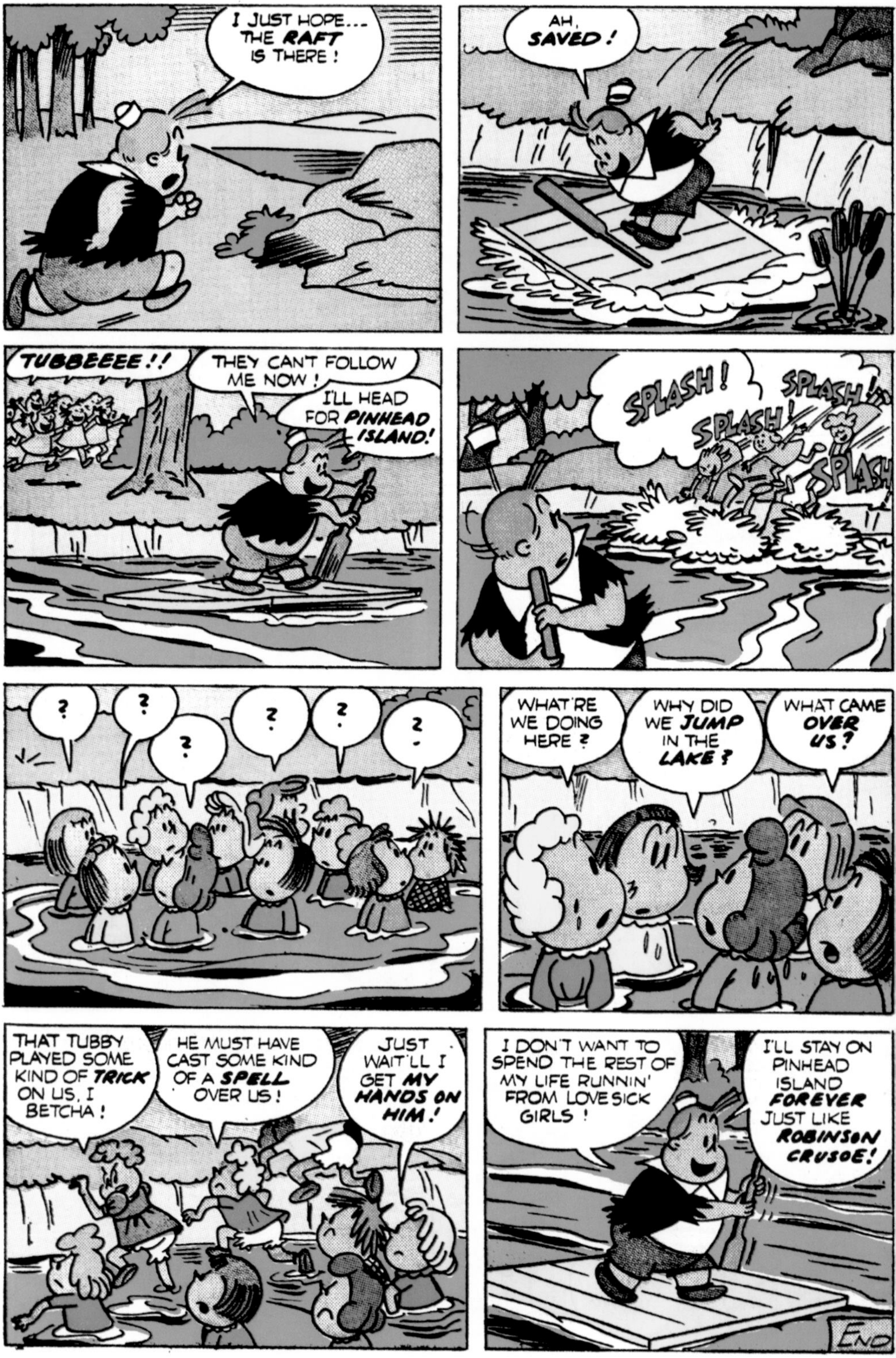
I JUST HOPE... THE RAFT IS THERE!
AH, SAVED!
TUBBEEEE!!
THEY CAN'T FOLLOW ME NOW!
I'LL HEAD FOR PINHEAD ISLAND!
SPLASH!
SPLASH!!
SPLASH!
SPLASH
?
?
?
?
?
?
WHAT'RE WE DOING HERE?
WHY DID WE JUMP IN THE LAKE?
WHAT CAME OVER US?
THAT TUBBY PLAYED SOME KIND OF TRICK ON US, I BETCHA!
HE MUST HAVE CAST SOME KIND OF A SPELL OVER US!
JUST WAIT'LL I GET MY HANDS ON HIM!
I DON'T WANT TO SPEND THE REST OF MY LIFE RUNNIN' FROM LOVESICK GIRLS!
I'LL STAY ON PINHEAD ISLAND FOREVER JUST LIKE ROBINSON CRUSOE!
END

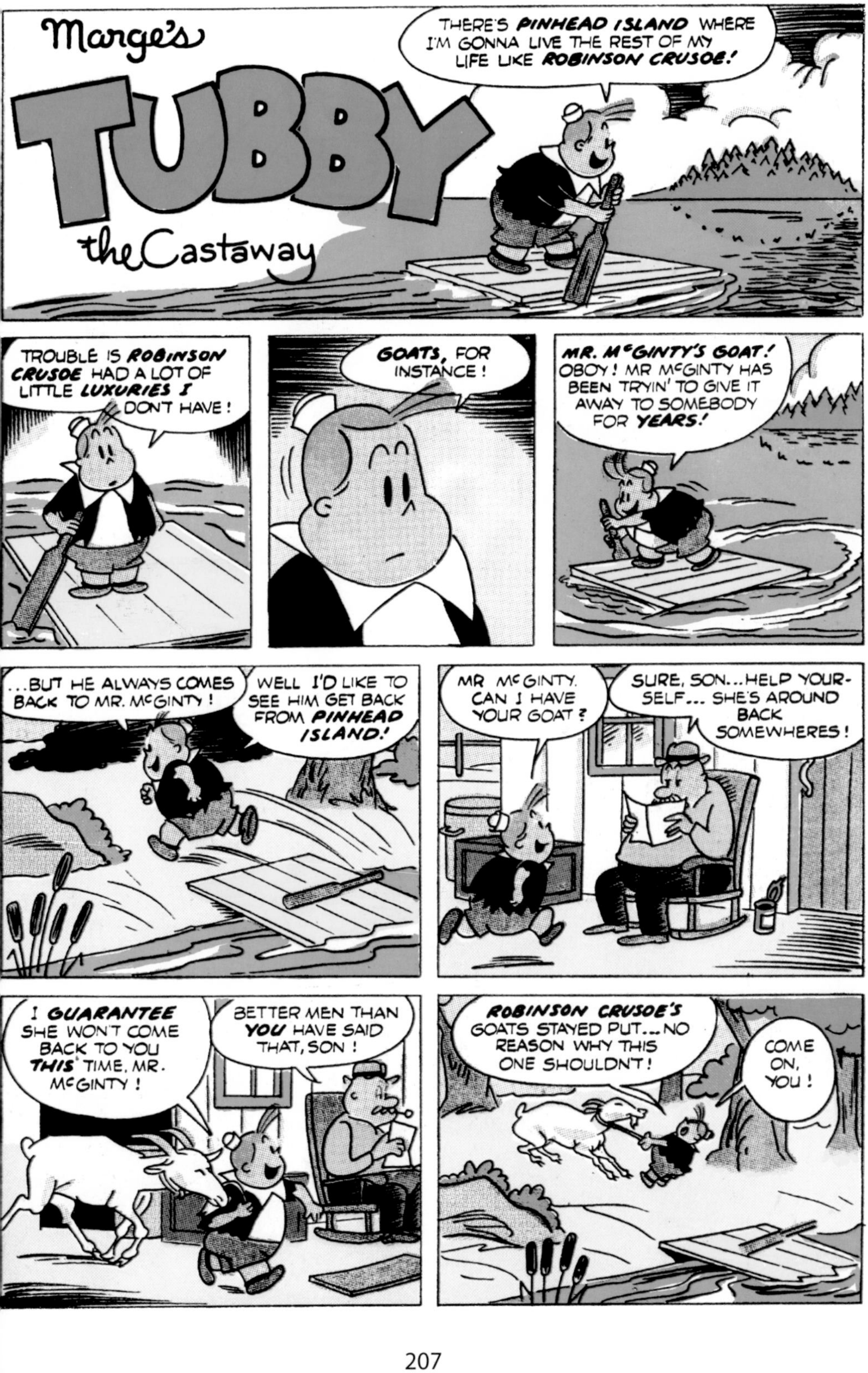
Marge's
TUBBY
the Castaway
THERE'S PINHEAD ISLAND WHERE I'M GONNA LIVE THE REST OF MY LIFE LIKE ROBINSON CRUSOE!
TROUBLE IS ROBINSON CRUSOE HAD A LOT OF LITTLE LUXURIES I DON'T HAVE!
GOATS, FOR INSTANCE!
MR. McGINTY'S GOAT! OBOY! MR McGINTY HAS BEEN TRYIN' TO GIVE IT AWAY TO SOMEBODY FOR YEARS!
...BUT HE ALWAYS COMES BACK TO MR. McGINTY!
WELL I'D LIKE TO SEE HIM GET BACK FROM PINHEAD ISLAND!
MR McGINTY. CAN I HAVE YOUR GOAT?
SURE, SON...HELP YOURSELF... SHE'S AROUND BACK SOMEWHERES!
I GUARANTEE SHE WON'T COME BACK TO YOU THIS TIME, MR. McGINTY!
BETTER MEN THAN YOU HAVE SAID THAT, SON!
ROBINSON CRUSOE'S GOATS STAYED PUT... NO REASON WHY THIS ONE SHOULDN'T!
COME ON, YOU!

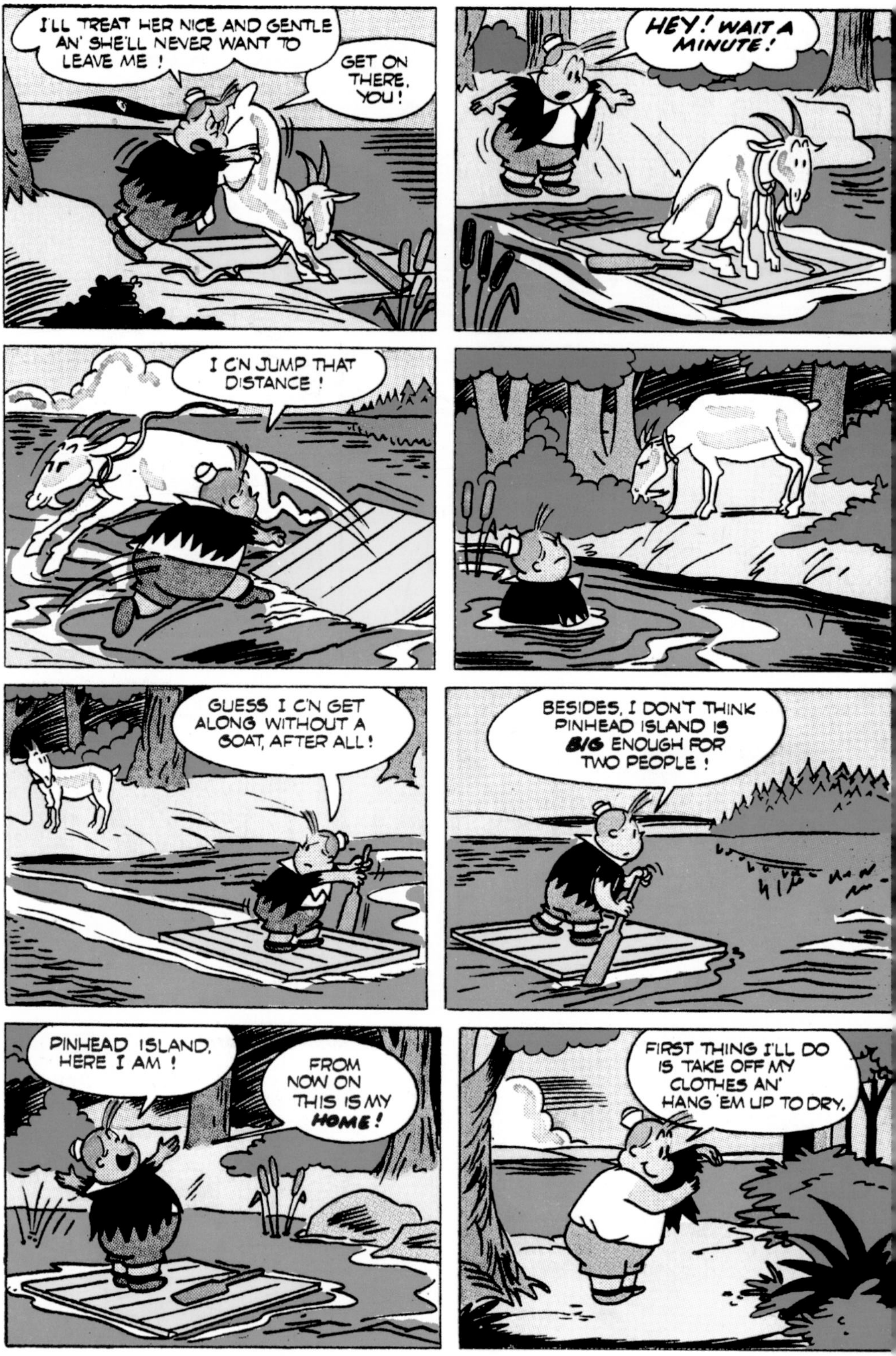

I'LL TREAT HER NICE AND GENTLE AN' SHE'LL NEVER WANT TO LEAVE ME !
GET ON THERE, YOU !
HEY! WAIT A MINUTE!
I C'N JUMP THAT DISTANCE !
GUESS I C'N GET ALONG WITHOUT A GOAT, AFTER ALL !
BESIDES, I DON'T THINK PINHEAD ISLAND IS **BIG** ENOUGH FOR TWO PEOPLE !
PINHEAD ISLAND, HERE I AM !
FROM NOW ON THIS IS MY **HOME** !
FIRST THING I'LL DO IS TAKE OFF MY CLOTHES AN' HANG 'EM UP TO DRY.

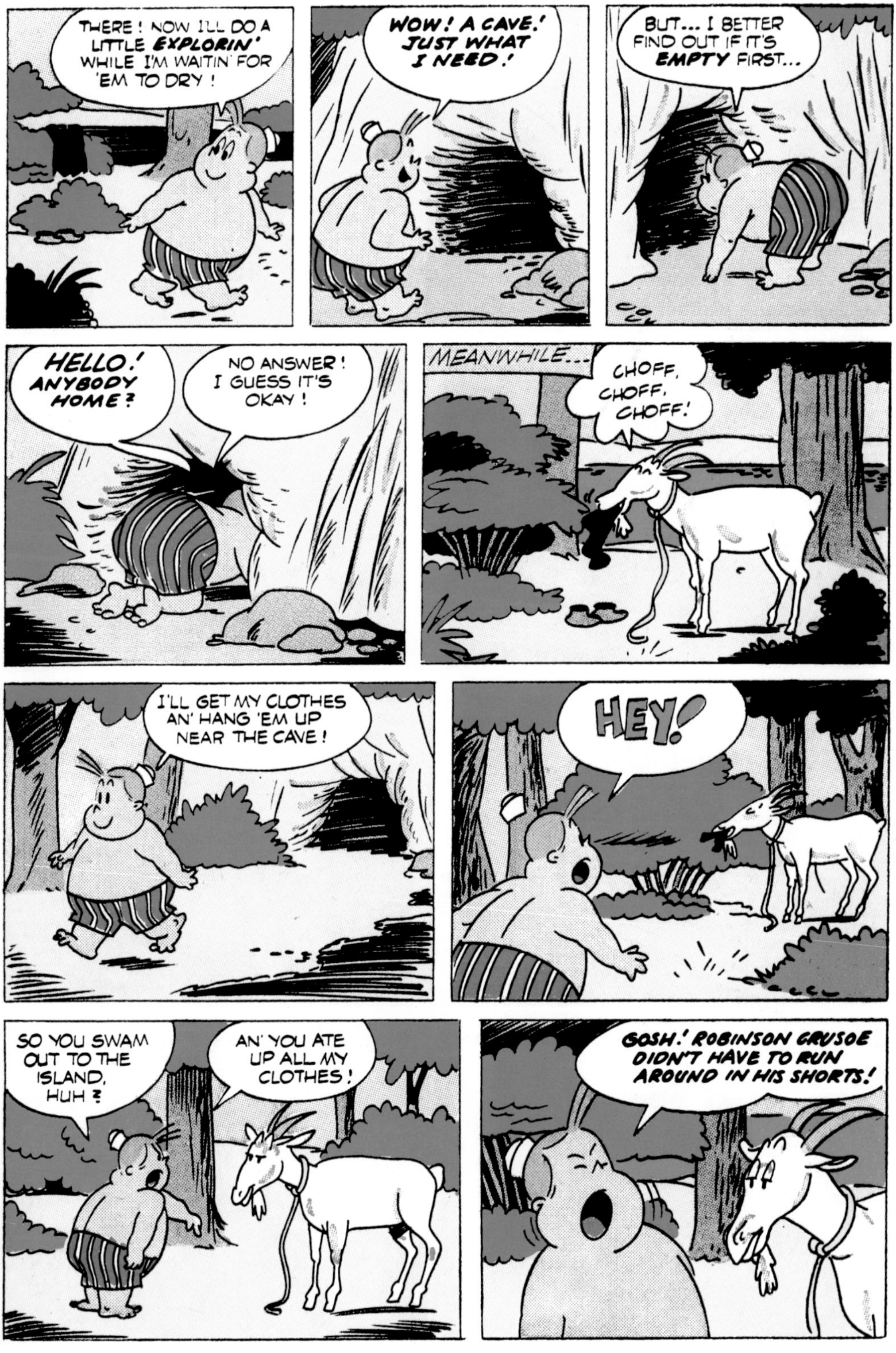
THERE! NOW I'LL DO A LITTLE EXPLORIN' WHILE I'M WAITIN' FOR 'EM TO DRY!
WOW! A CAVE! JUST WHAT I NEED!
BUT... I BETTER FIND OUT IF IT'S EMPTY FIRST...
HELLO! ANYBODY HOME?
NO ANSWER! I GUESS IT'S OKAY!
MEANWHILE...
CHOFF, CHOFF, CHOFF!
I'LL GET MY CLOTHES AN' HANG 'EM UP NEAR THE CAVE!
HEY!
SO YOU SWAM OUT TO THE ISLAND, HUH?
AN' YOU ATE UP ALL MY CLOTHES!
GOSH! ROBINSON CRUSOE DIDN'T HAVE TO RUN AROUND IN HIS SHORTS!

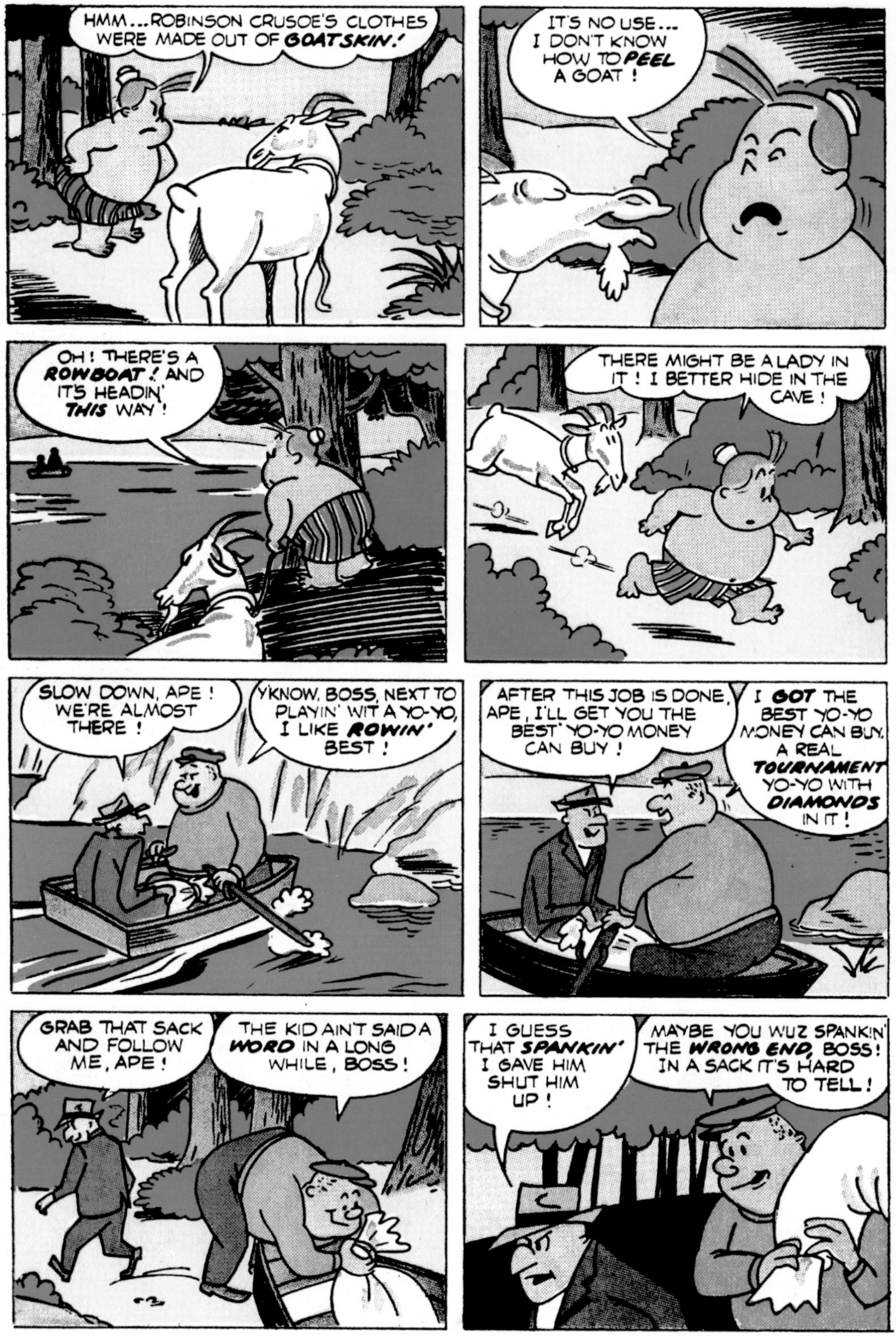
HMM... ROBINSON CRUSOE'S CLOTHES WERE MADE OUT OF GOATSKIN!
IT'S NO USE... I DON'T KNOW HOW TO PEEL A GOAT!
OH! THERE'S A ROWBOAT! AND IT'S HEADIN' THIS WAY!
THERE MIGHT BE A LADY IN IT! I BETTER HIDE IN THE CAVE!
SLOW DOWN, APE! WE'RE ALMOST THERE!
Y'KNOW, BOSS, NEXT TO PLAYIN' WIT A YO-YO, I LIKE ROWIN' BEST!
AFTER THIS JOB IS DONE, APE, I'LL GET YOU THE BEST YO-YO MONEY CAN BUY!
I GOT THE BEST YO-YO MONEY CAN BUY. A REAL TOURNAMENT YO-YO WITH DIAMONDS IN IT!
GRAB THAT SACK AND FOLLOW ME, APE!
THE KID AIN'T SAID A WORD IN A LONG WHILE, BOSS!
I GUESS THAT SPANKIN' I GAVE HIM SHUT HIM UP!
MAYBE YOU WUZ SPANKIN' THE WRONG END, BOSS! IN A SACK IT'S HARD TO TELL!

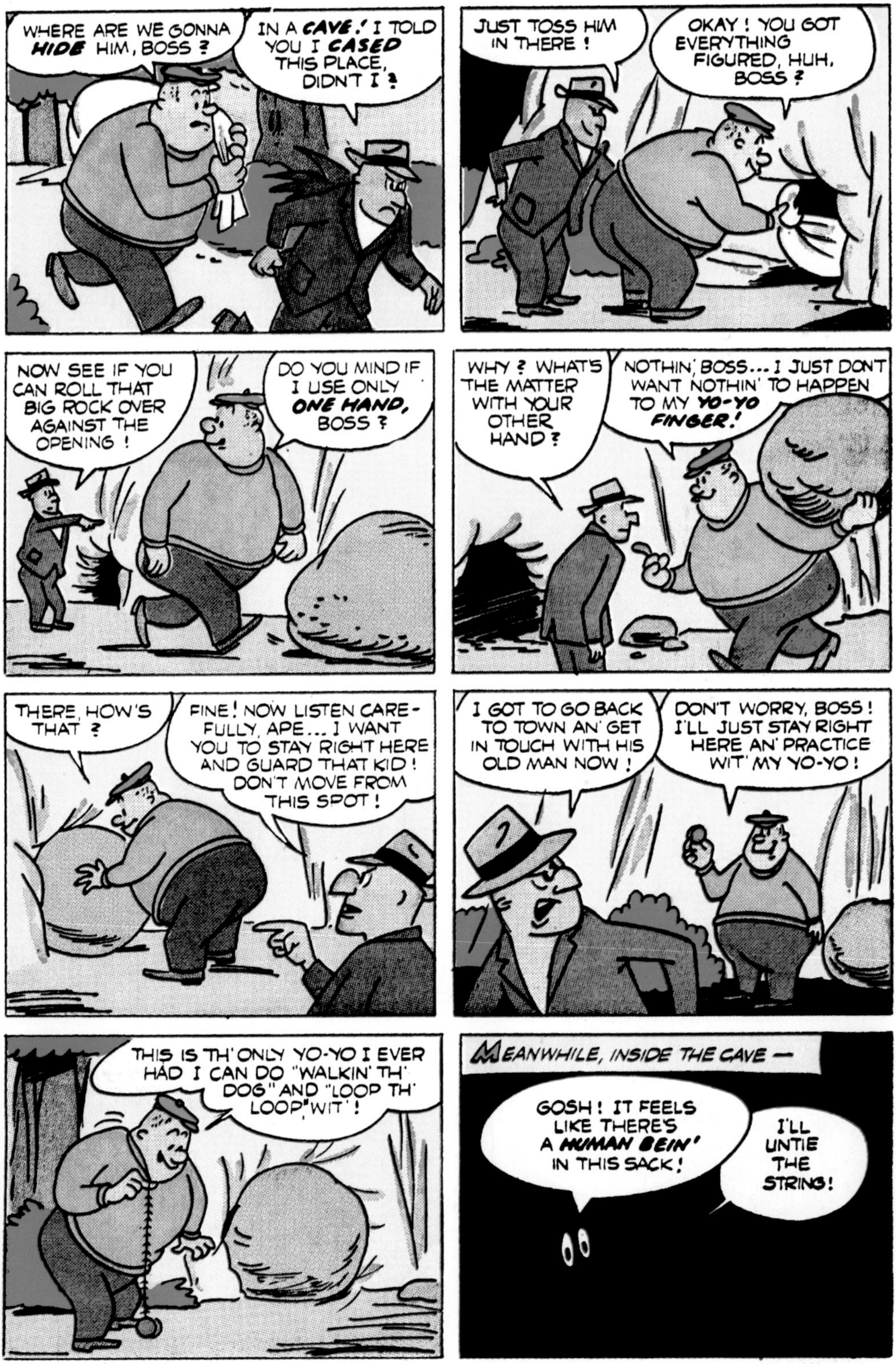

WHERE ARE WE GONNA HIDE HIM, BOSS ?
IN A CAVE ! I TOLD YOU I CASED THIS PLACE, DIDN'T I ?
JUST TOSS HIM IN THERE !
OKAY ! YOU GOT EVERYTHING FIGURED, HUH, BOSS ?
NOW SEE IF YOU CAN ROLL THAT BIG ROCK OVER AGAINST THE OPENING !
DO YOU MIND IF I USE ONLY ONE HAND, BOSS ?
WHY ? WHAT'S THE MATTER WITH YOUR OTHER HAND ?
NOTHIN', BOSS... I JUST DON'T WANT NOTHIN' TO HAPPEN TO MY YO-YO FINGER !
THERE, HOW'S THAT ?
FINE ! NOW LISTEN CAREFULLY, APE... I WANT YOU TO STAY RIGHT HERE AND GUARD THAT KID ! DON'T MOVE FROM THIS SPOT !
I GOT TO GO BACK TO TOWN AN' GET IN TOUCH WITH HIS OLD MAN NOW !
DON'T WORRY, BOSS ! I'LL JUST STAY RIGHT HERE AN' PRACTICE WIT' MY YO-YO !
THIS IS TH' ONLY YO-YO I EVER HAD I CAN DO "WALKIN' TH' DOG" AND "LOOP TH' LOOP" WIT' !
MEANWHILE, INSIDE THE CAVE —
GOSH ! IT FEELS LIKE THERE'S A HUMAN BEIN' IN THIS SACK !
I'LL UNTIE THE STRING !

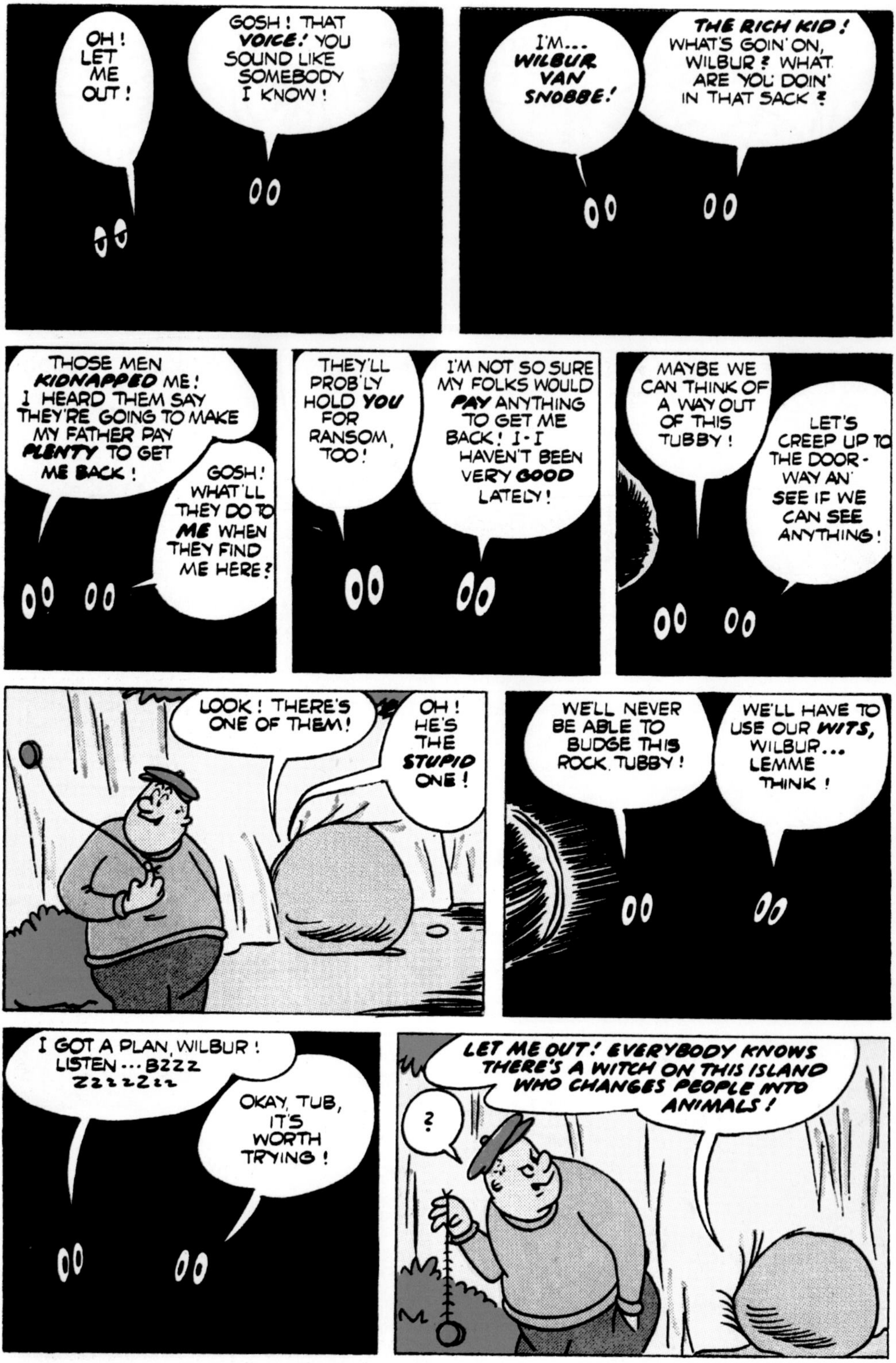

OH! LET ME OUT!
GOSH! THAT VOICE! YOU SOUND LIKE SOMEBODY I KNOW!
I'M... WILBUR VAN SNOBBE!
THE RICH KID! WHAT'S GOIN' ON, WILBUR? WHAT ARE YOU DOIN' IN THAT SACK?
THOSE MEN KIDNAPPED ME! I HEARD THEM SAY THEY'RE GOING TO MAKE MY FATHER PAY PLENTY TO GET ME BACK!
GOSH! WHAT'LL THEY DO TO ME WHEN THEY FIND ME HERE?
THEY'LL PROB'LY HOLD YOU FOR RANSOM, TOO!
I'M NOT SO SURE MY FOLKS WOULD PAY ANYTHING TO GET ME BACK! I-I HAVEN'T BEEN VERY GOOD LATELY!
MAYBE WE CAN THINK OF A WAY OUT OF THIS TUBBY!
LET'S CREEP UP TO THE DOOR-WAY AN' SEE IF WE CAN SEE ANYTHING!
LOOK! THERE'S ONE OF THEM!
OH! HE'S THE STUPID ONE!
WE'LL NEVER BE ABLE TO BUDGE THIS ROCK, TUBBY!
WE'LL HAVE TO USE OUR WITS, WILBUR... LEMME THINK!
I GOT A PLAN, WILBUR! LISTEN... BZZZ ZZZZZZZ
OKAY, TUB, IT'S WORTH TRYING!
LET ME OUT! EVERYBODY KNOWS THERE'S A WITCH ON THIS ISLAND WHO CHANGES PEOPLE INTO ANIMALS!
?

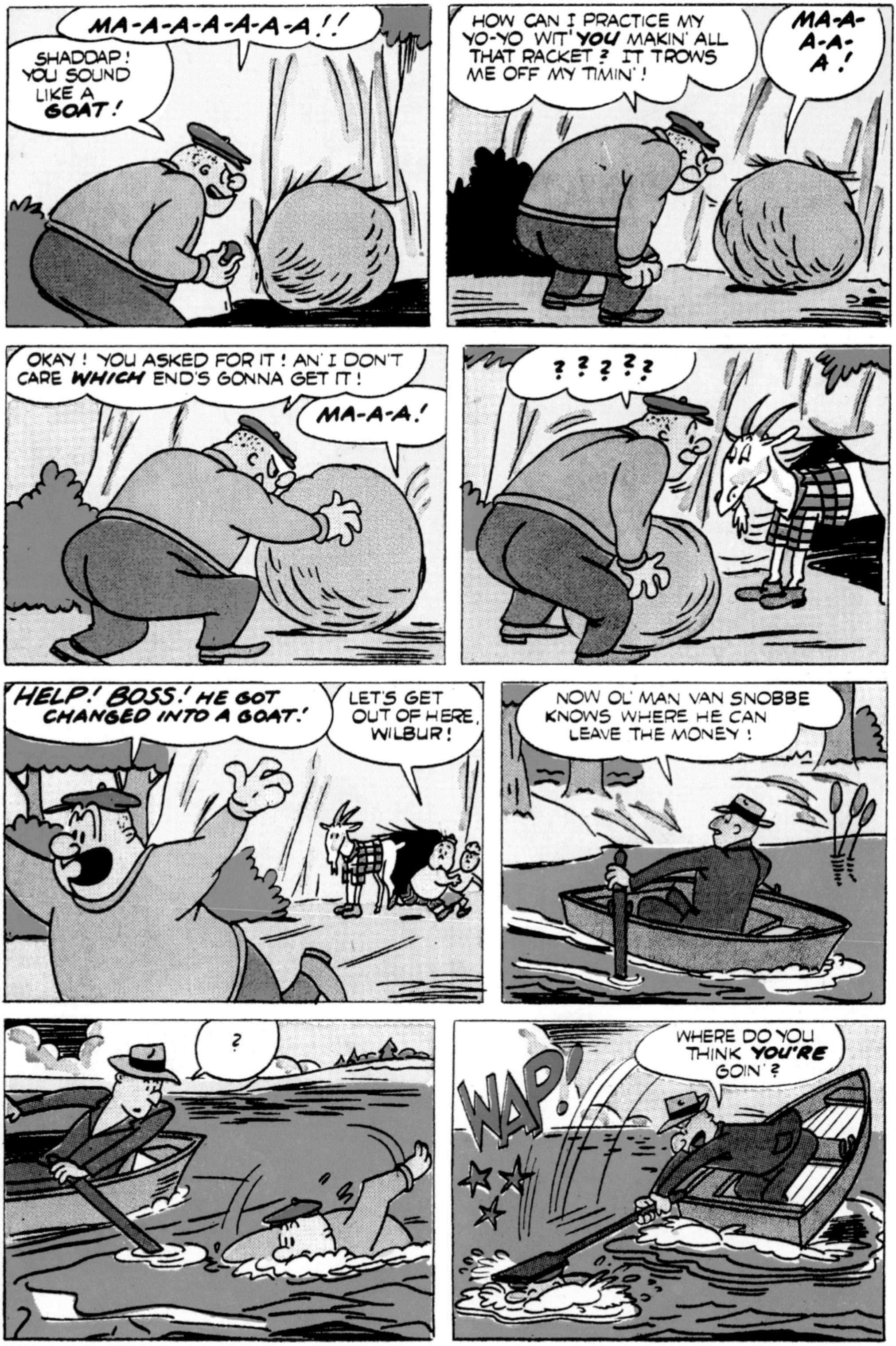
MA-A-A-A-A-A-A!!
SHADDAP! YOU SOUND LIKE A GOAT!
HOW CAN I PRACTICE MY YO-YO WIT' YOU MAKIN' ALL THAT RACKET? IT TROWS ME OFF MY TIMIN'!
MA-A-A-A-A!
OKAY! YOU ASKED FOR IT! AN' I DON'T CARE WHICH END'S GONNA GET IT!
MA-A-A!
?????
HELP! BOSS! HE GOT CHANGED INTO A GOAT!
LET'S GET OUT OF HERE, WILBUR!
NOW OL' MAN VAN SNOBBE KNOWS WHERE HE CAN LEAVE THE MONEY!
?
WAP!
WHERE DO YOU THINK YOU'RE GOIN'?

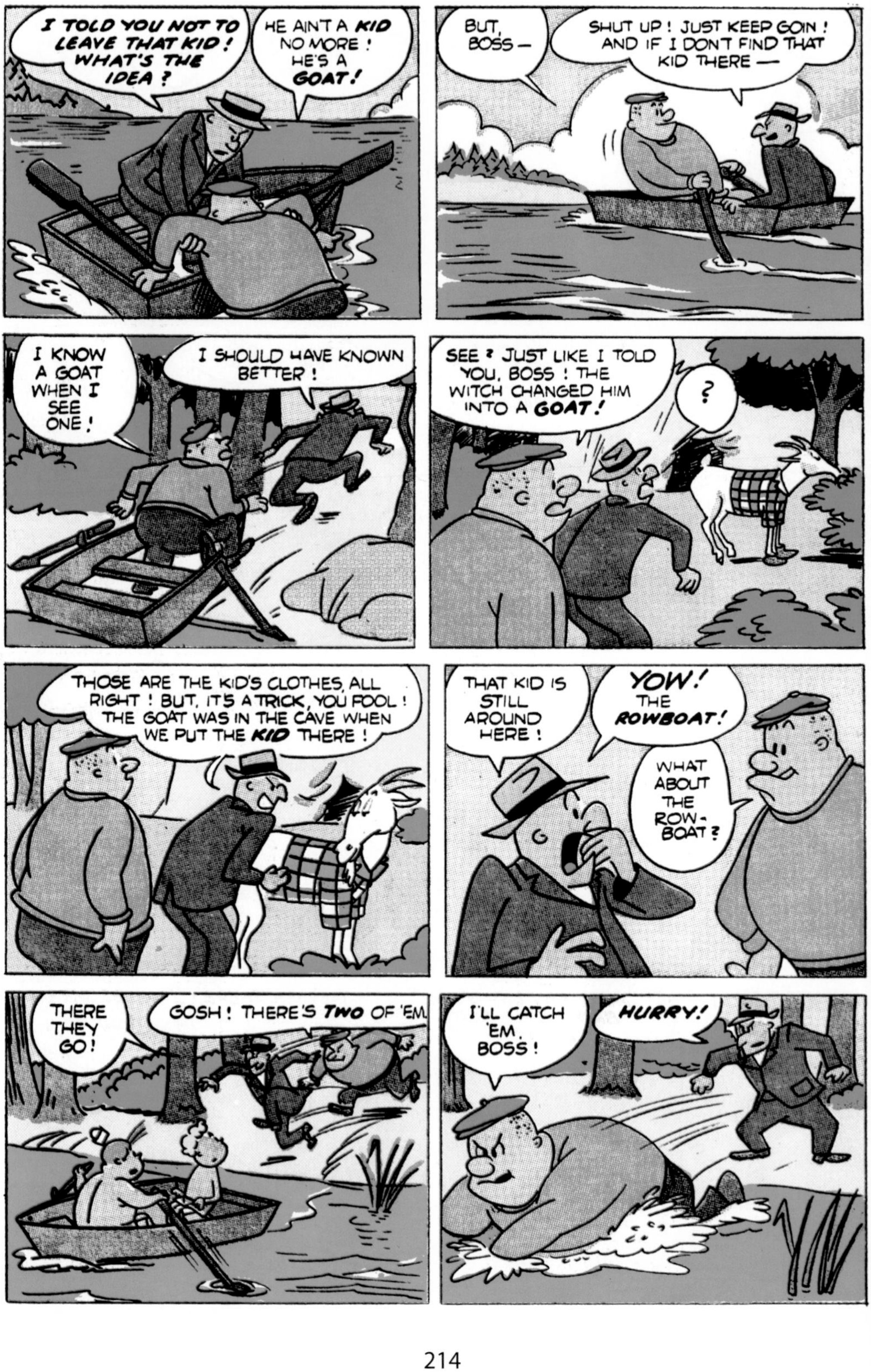
I TOLD YOU NOT TO LEAVE THAT KID! WHAT'S THE IDEA?
HE AIN'T A KID NO MORE! HE'S A GOAT!
BUT, BOSS —
SHUT UP! JUST KEEP GOIN! AND IF I DON'T FIND THAT KID THERE —
I KNOW A GOAT WHEN I SEE ONE!
I SHOULD HAVE KNOWN BETTER!
SEE? JUST LIKE I TOLD YOU, BOSS! THE WITCH CHANGED HIM INTO A GOAT!
?
THOSE ARE THE KID'S CLOTHES, ALL RIGHT! BUT, IT'S A TRICK, YOU FOOL! THE GOAT WAS IN THE CAVE WHEN WE PUT THE KID THERE!
THAT KID IS STILL AROUND HERE!
YOW! THE ROWBOAT!
WHAT ABOUT THE ROW-BOAT?
THERE THEY GO!
GOSH! THERE'S TWO OF 'EM
I'LL CATCH 'EM, BOSS!
HURRY!

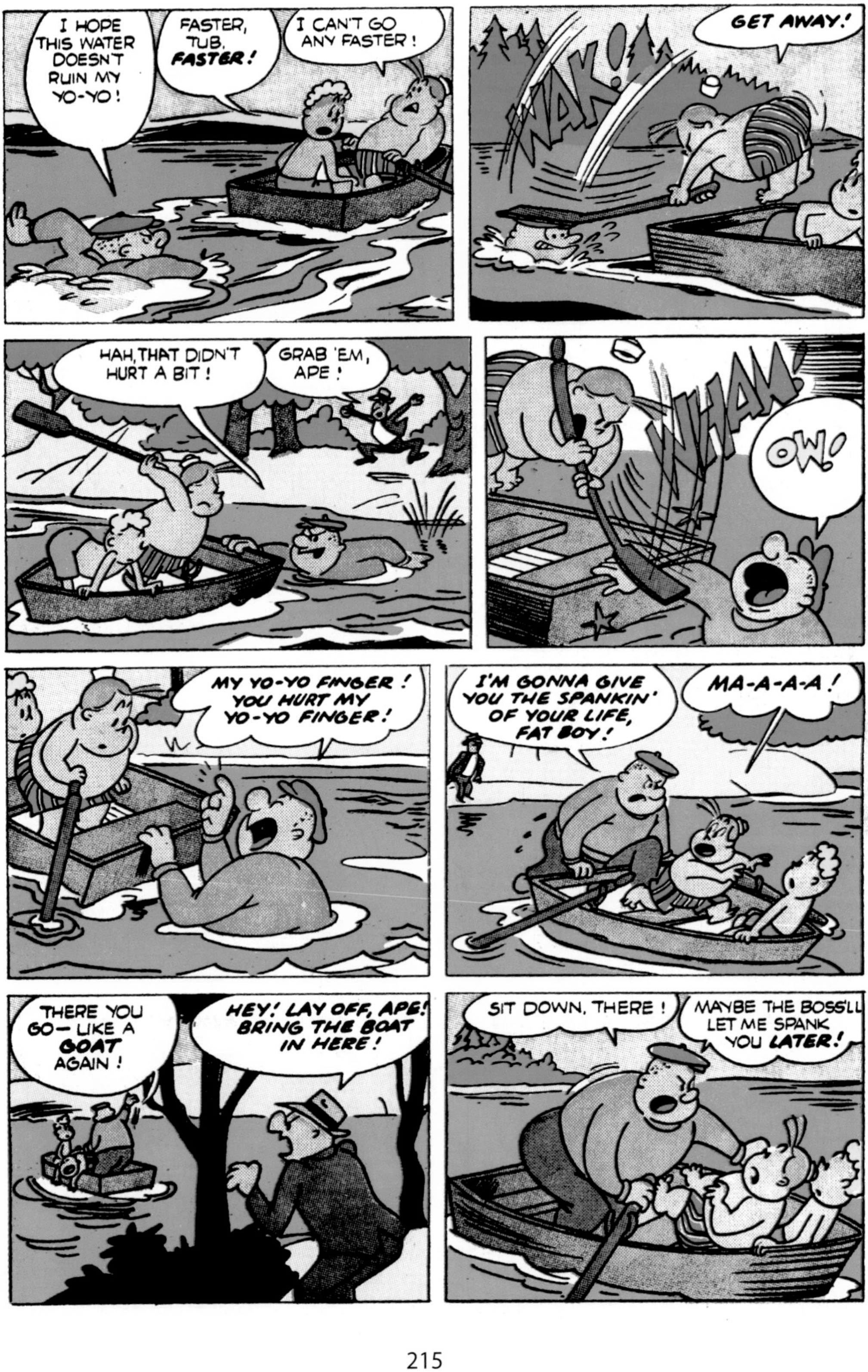

I HOPE THIS WATER DOESN'T RUIN MY YO-YO!
FASTER, TUB, FASTER!
I CAN'T GO ANY FASTER!
WAK!
GET AWAY!
HAH, THAT DIDN'T HURT A BIT!
GRAB 'EM, APE!
WHAM!
OW!
MY YO-YO FINGER! YOU HURT MY YO-YO FINGER!
I'M GONNA GIVE YOU THE SPANKIN' OF YOUR LIFE, FAT BOY!
MA-A-A-A!
THERE YOU GO— LIKE A GOAT AGAIN!
HEY! LAY OFF, APE! BRING THE BOAT IN HERE!
SIT DOWN, THERE!
MAYBE THE BOSS'LL LET ME SPANK YOU LATER!

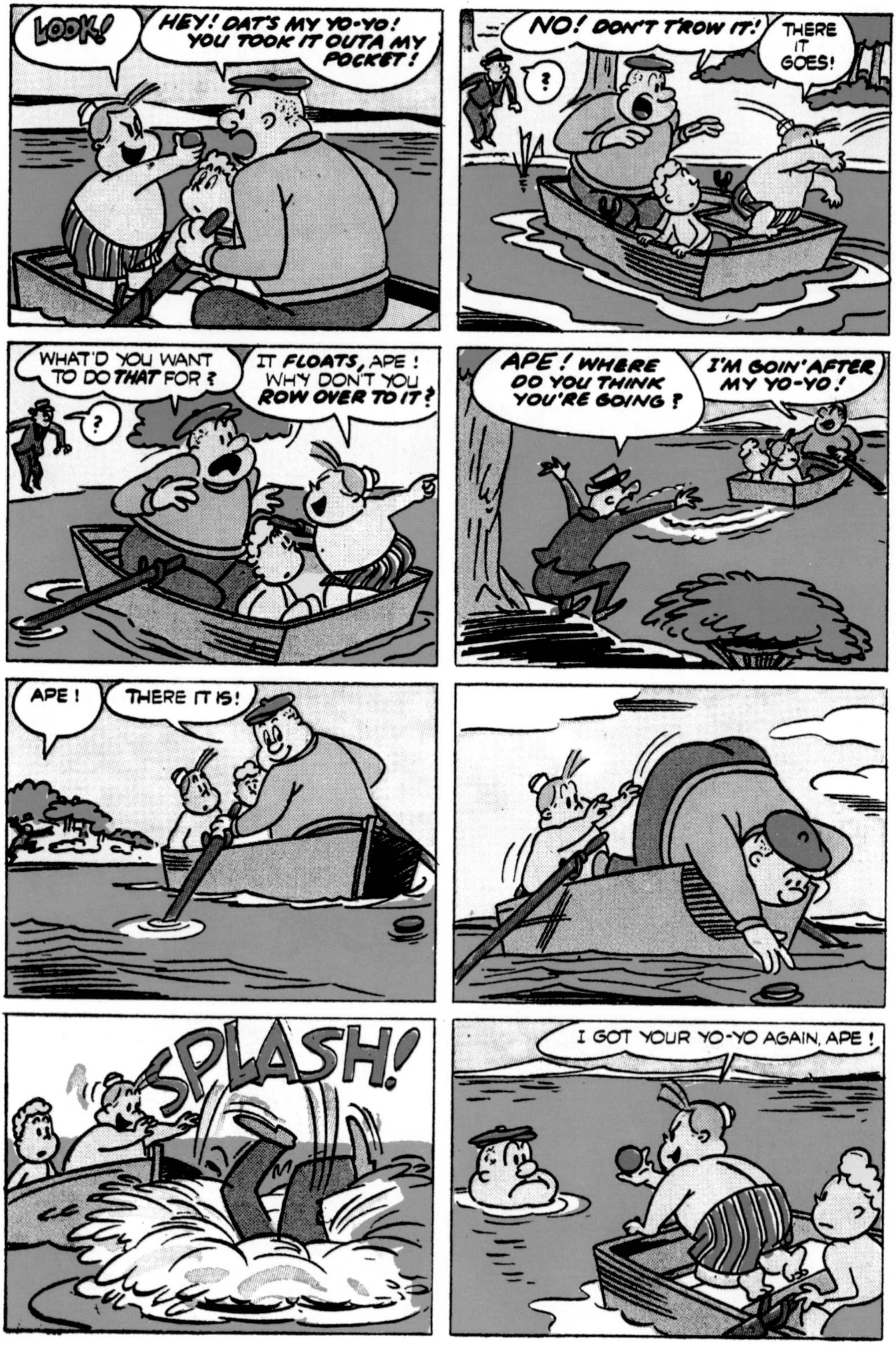
LOOK!
HEY! DAT'S MY YO-YO! YOU TOOK IT OUTA MY POCKET!
NO! DON'T T'ROW IT!
THERE IT GOES!
?
WHAT'D YOU WANT TO DO THAT FOR?
IT FLOATS, APE! WHY DON'T YOU ROW OVER TO IT?
?
APE! WHERE DO YOU THINK YOU'RE GOING?
I'M GOIN' AFTER MY YO-YO!
APE!
THERE IT IS!
SPLASH!
I GOT YOUR YO-YO AGAIN, APE!

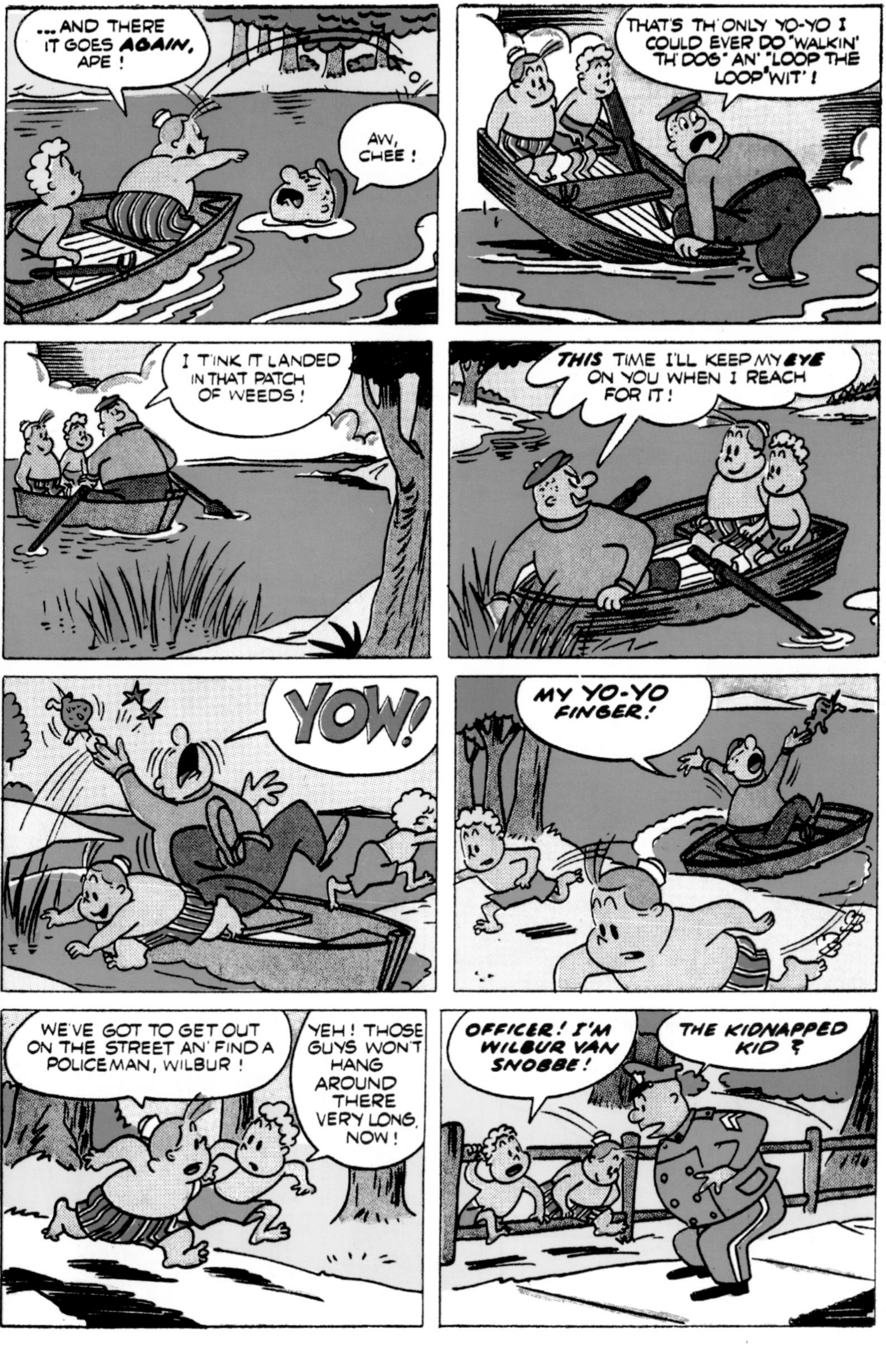
...AND THERE IT GOES AGAIN, APE !
AW, CHEE !
THAT'S TH' ONLY YO-YO I COULD EVER DO "WALKIN' TH' DOG" AN' "LOOP THE LOOP" WIT' !
I T'INK IT LANDED IN THAT PATCH OF WEEDS !
THIS TIME I'LL KEEP MY EYE ON YOU WHEN I REACH FOR IT !
YOW!
MY YO-YO FINGER!
WE'VE GOT TO GET OUT ON THE STREET AN' FIND A POLICEMAN, WILBUR !
YEH ! THOSE GUYS WON'T HANG AROUND THERE VERY LONG, NOW !
OFFICER! I'M WILBUR VAN SNOBBE!
THE KIDNAPPED KID ?

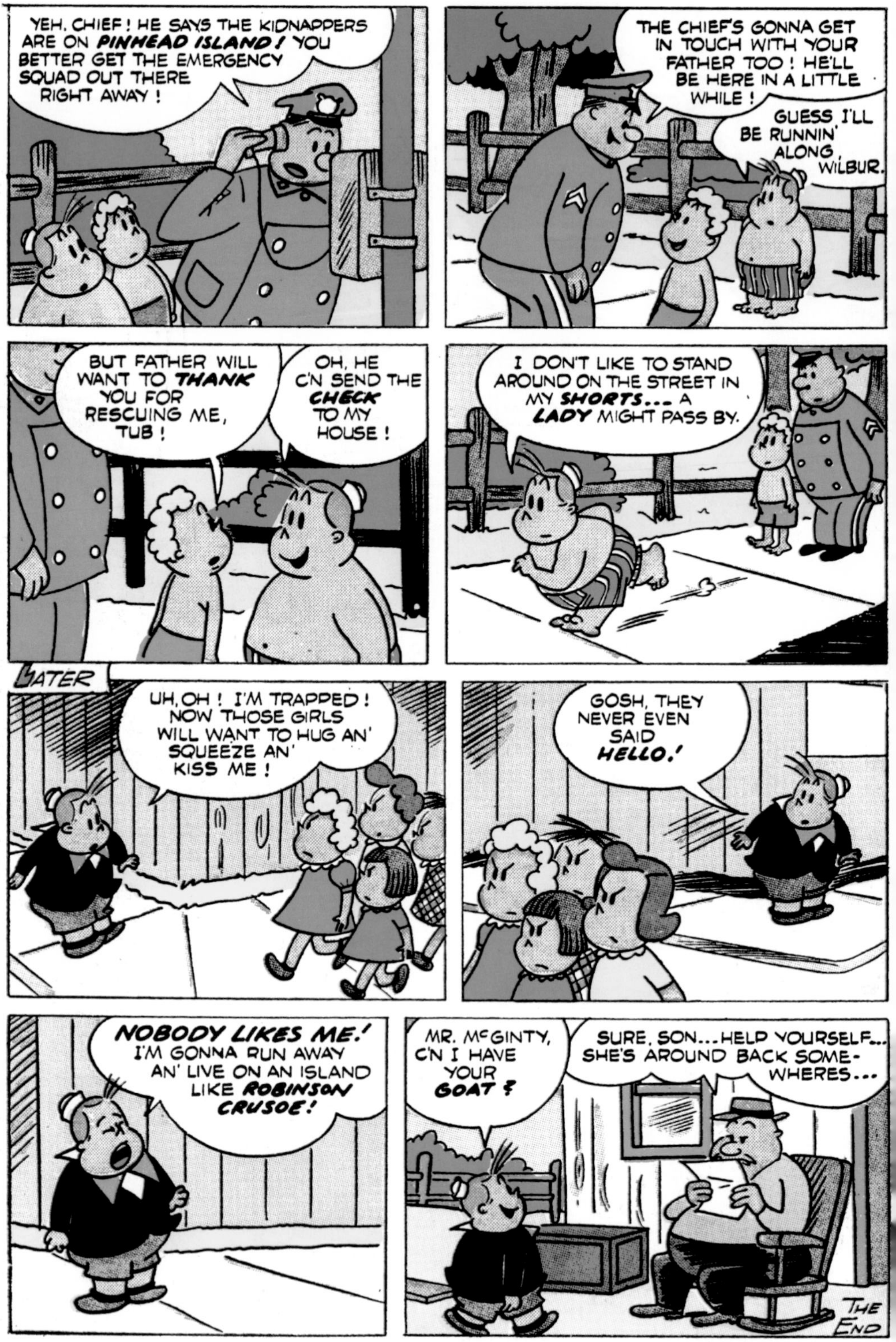
YEH, CHIEF! HE SAYS THE KIDNAPPERS ARE ON PINHEAD ISLAND! YOU BETTER GET THE EMERGENCY SQUAD OUT THERE RIGHT AWAY!
THE CHIEF'S GONNA GET IN TOUCH WITH YOUR FATHER TOO! HE'LL BE HERE IN A LITTLE WHILE!
GUESS I'LL BE RUNNIN' ALONG, WILBUR.
BUT FATHER WILL WANT TO THANK YOU FOR RESCUING ME, TUB!
OH, HE C'N SEND THE CHECK TO MY HOUSE!
I DON'T LIKE TO STAND AROUND ON THE STREET IN MY SHORTS... A LADY MIGHT PASS BY.
LATER
UH, OH! I'M TRAPPED! NOW THOSE GIRLS WILL WANT TO HUG AN' SQUEEZE AN' KISS ME!
GOSH, THEY NEVER EVEN SAID HELLO!
NOBODY LIKES ME! I'M GONNA RUN AWAY AN' LIVE ON AN ISLAND LIKE ROBINSON CRUSOE!
MR. McGINTY, C'N I HAVE YOUR GOAT?
SURE, SON... HELP YOURSELF... SHE'S AROUND BACK SOMEWHERES...
THE END

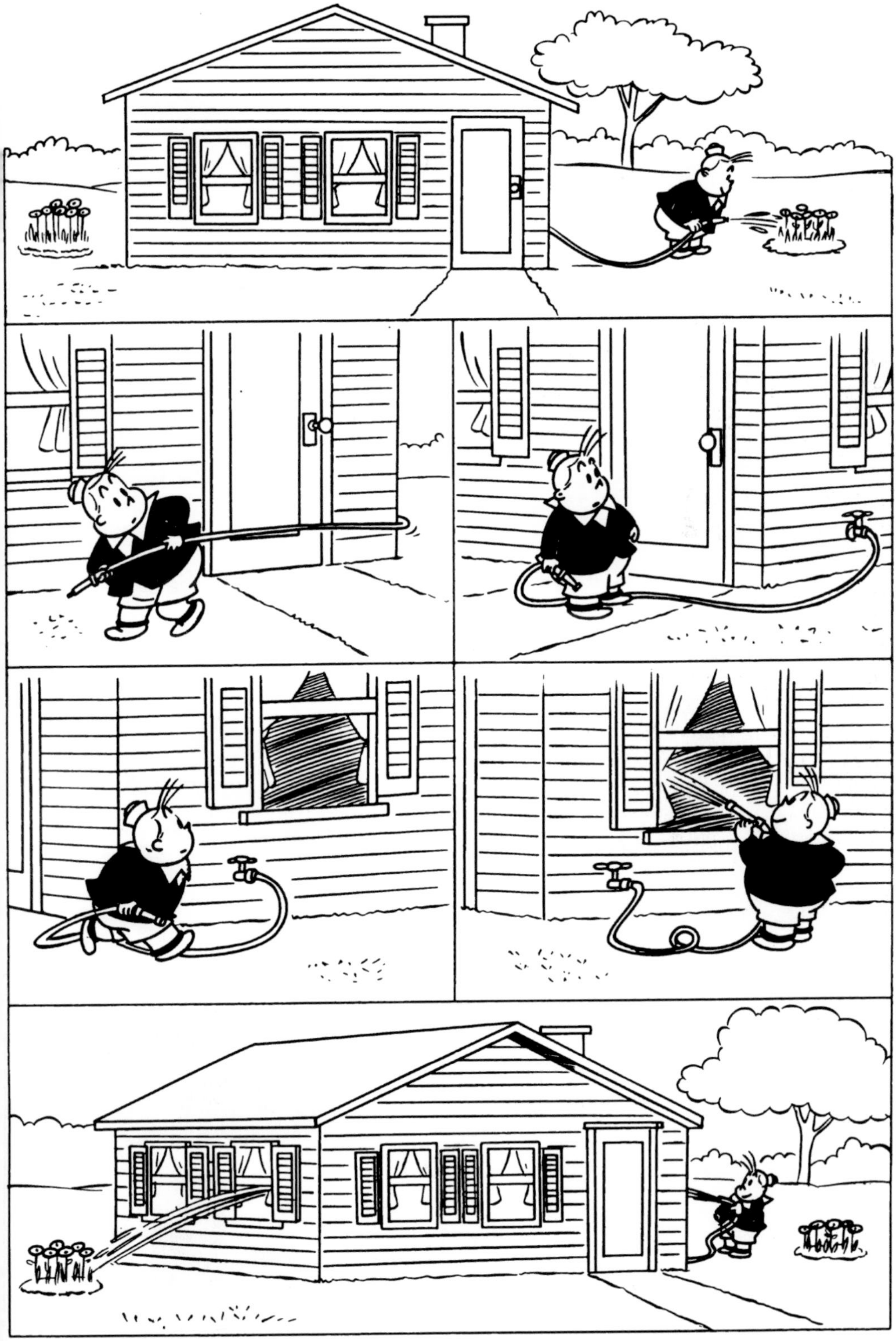

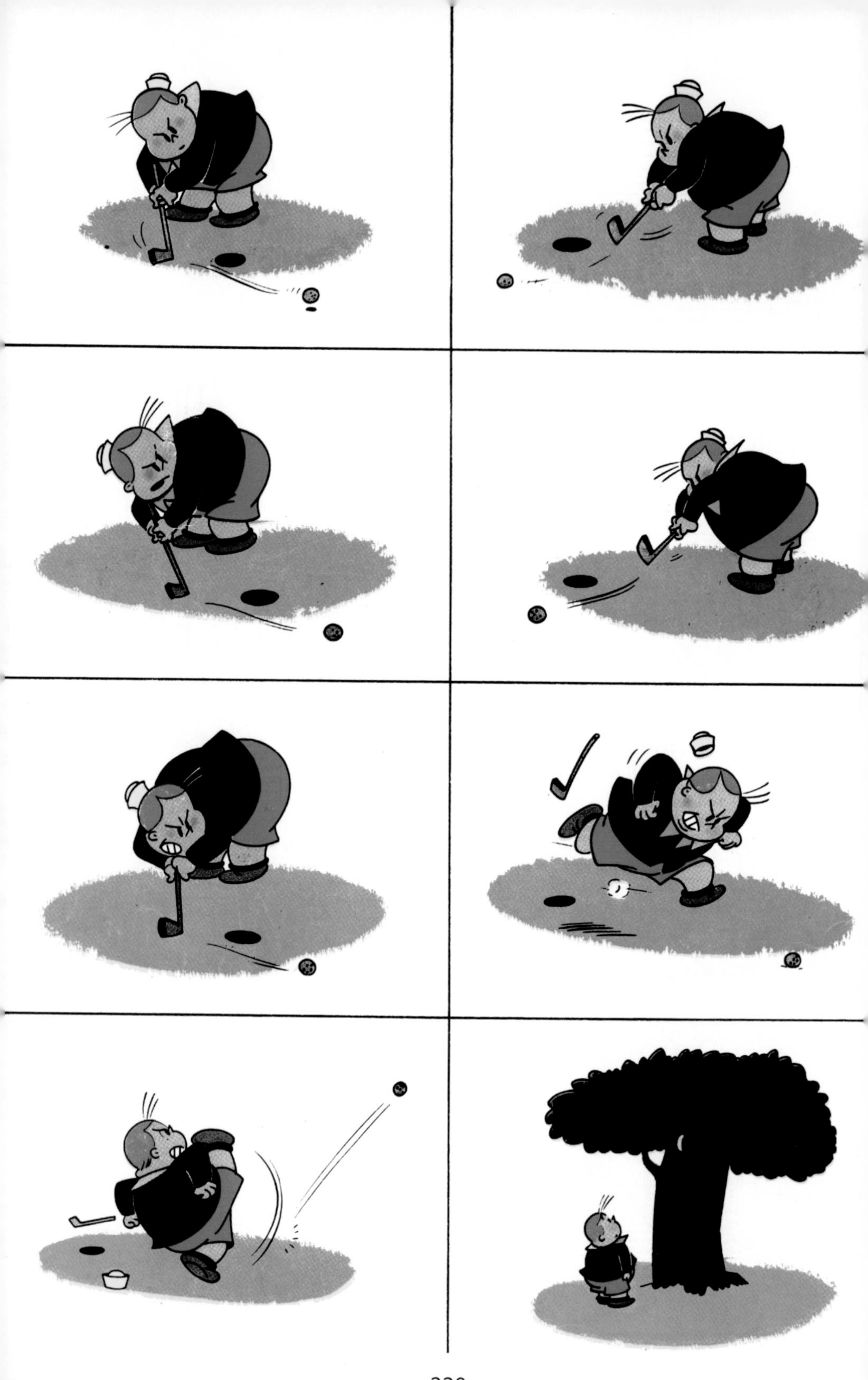

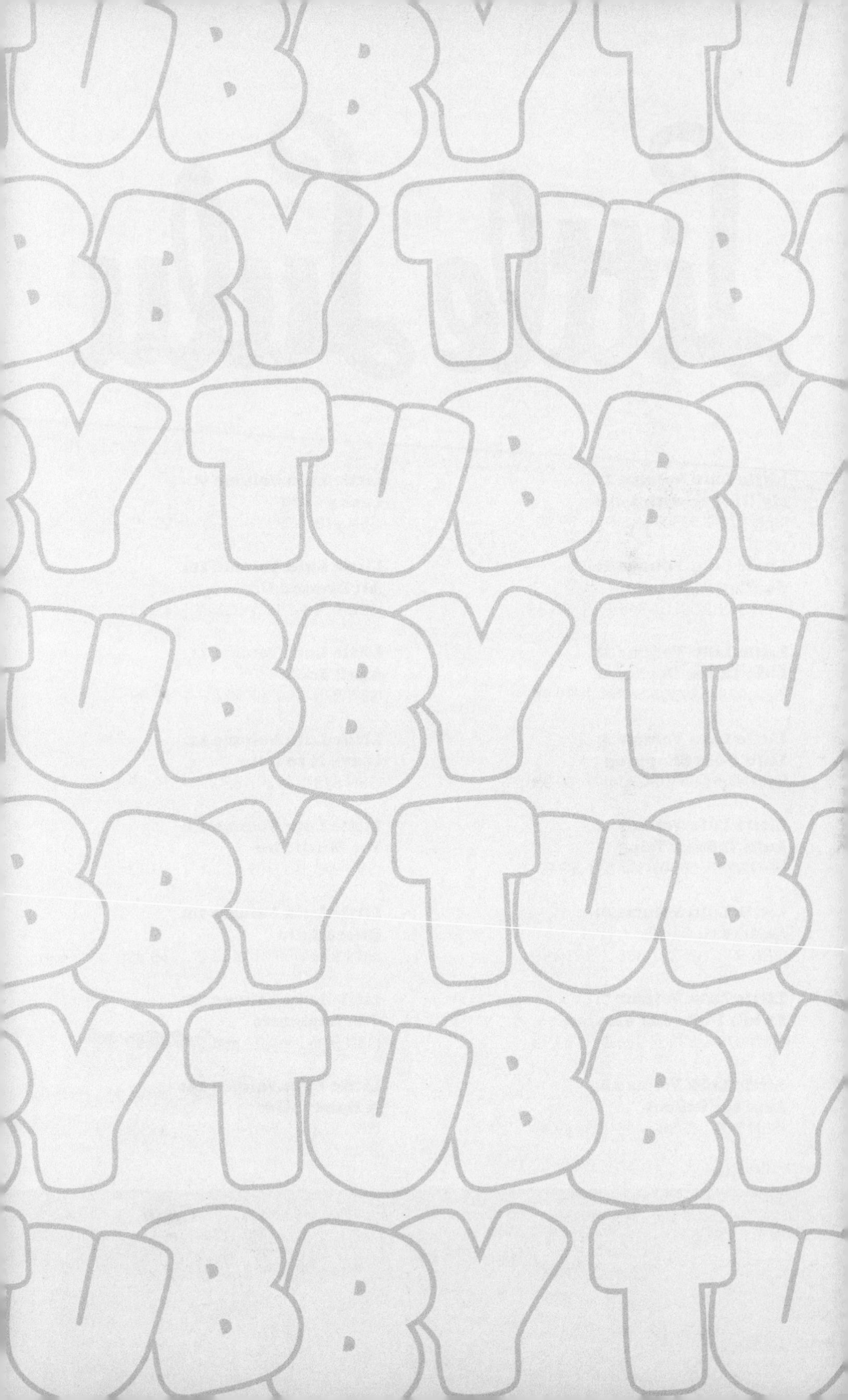
TUBBY

Little Lulu®

Little Lulu Volume 1:
My Dinner with Lulu
ISBN 978-1-59307-318-3 | $9.99

Little Lulu Volume 2:
Sunday Afternoon
ISBN 978-1-59307-345-9 | $9.99

Little Lulu Volume 3:
Lulu in the Doghouse
ISBN 978-1-59307-346-6 | $9.99

Little Lulu Volume 4:
Lulu Goes Shopping
ISBN 978-1-59307-270-4 | $9.99

Little Lulu Volume 5:
Lulu Takes a Trip
ISBN 978-1-59307-317-6 | $9.99

Little Lulu Volume 6:
Letters to Santa
ISBN 978-1-59307-386-2 | $9.99

Little Lulu Volume 7:
Lulu's Umbrella Service
ISBN 978-1-59307-399-2 | $9.99

Little Lulu Volume 8:
Late for School
ISBN 978-1-59307-453-1 | $9.99

Little Lulu Volume 9:
Lucky Lulu
ISBN 978-1-59307-471-5 | $9.99

Little Lulu Volume 10:
All Dressed Up
ISBN 978-1-59307-534-7 | $9.99

Little Lulu Volume 11:
April Fools
ISBN 978-1-59307-557-6 | $9.99

Little Lulu Volume 12:
Leave It to Lulu
ISBN 978-1-59307-620-7 | $9.99

Little Lulu Volume 13:
Too Much Fun
ISBN 978-1-59307-621-4 | $9.99

Little Lulu Volume 14:
Queen Lulu
ISBN 978-1-59307-683-2 | $9.99

Little Lulu Volume 15:
The Explorers
ISBN 978-1-59307-684-9 | $9.99

Little Lulu Volume 16:
A Handy Kid
ISBN 978-1-59307-685-6 | $10.99

Little Lulu Volume 17:
The Valentine
ISBN 978-1-59307-686-3 | $10.99

Little Lulu Volume 18:
The Expert
ISBN 978-1-59307-687-0 | $10.99

Giant Size Little Lulu
Volume 1
ISBN 978-1-59582-502-5 | $24.99

Giant Size Little Lulu
Volume 2
ISBN 978-1-59582-540-7 | $24.99

FULL COLOR VOLUMES!

Little Lulu Volume 19:
The Alamo and Other Stories
ISBN 978-1-59582-293-2 | $14.99

Little Lulu Volume 20:
The Bawlplayers and Other Stories
ISBN 978-1-59582-364-9 | $14.99

Little Lulu Volume 21:
Miss Feeny's Folly and Other Stories
ISBN 978-1-59582-365-6 | $14.99

Little Lulu Volume 22:
The Big Dipper Club and Other Stories
ISBN 978-1-59582-420-2 | $14.99

Little Lulu Volume 23:
The Bogey Snowman and Other Stories
978-1-59582-474-5 | $14.99

Little Lulu Volume 24:
The Space Dolly and Other Stories
978-1-59582-475-2 | $14.99

Little Lulu Color Special
978-1-59307-613-9 | $13.99

Tubby Volume 1:
The Castaway and Other Stories
978-1-59582-421-9 | $15.99

Looking for something new to read?

CHECK OUT THESE HARVEY CLASSICS TITLES FROM DARK HORSE BOOKS!

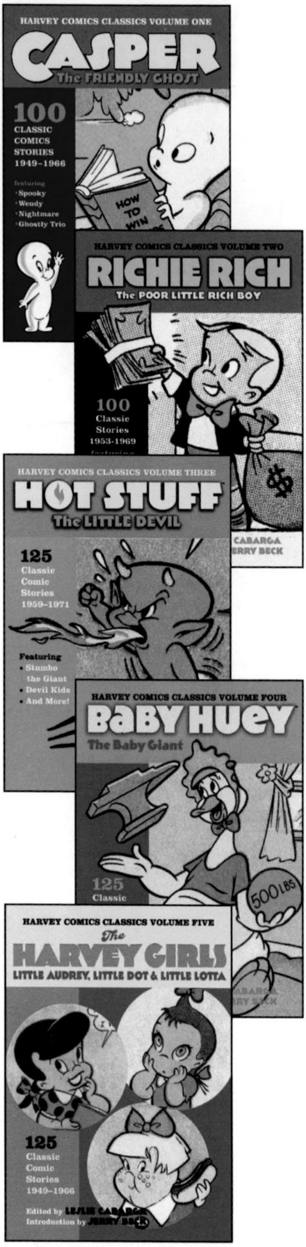
HARVEY COMICS CLASSICS VOLUME ONE
CASPER
The FRIENDLY GHOST
100 CLASSIC COMICS STORIES 1949–1966
featuring
• Spooky
• Wendy
• Nightmare
• Ghostly Trio
HARVEY COMICS CLASSICS VOLUME TWO
RICHIE RICH
The POOR LITTLE RICH BOY
100 Classic Stories 1953–1969
HARVEY COMICS CLASSICS VOLUME THREE
HOT STUFF
The LITTLE DEVIL
125 Classic Comic Stories 1959–1971
Featuring
• Stumbo the Giant
• Devil Kids
• And More!
HARVEY COMICS CLASSICS VOLUME FOUR
BABY HUEY
The Baby Giant
125 Classic
500 LBS
HARVEY COMICS CLASSICS VOLUME FIVE
The HARVEY GIRLS
LITTLE AUDREY, LITTLE DOT & LITTLE LOTTA
125 Classic Comic Stories 1949–1966

HARVEY CLASSICS VOLUME 1: CASPER

It's amazing how many comics fans who grew up admiring Spider-Man, Batman, and Nick Fury still retain warm places in their hearts for Casper the Friendly Ghost. Now Dark Horse is delighted to participate in the revival of Casper, who remains among the most beloved of cartoon and comic-book icons. *Harvey Comics Classics Volume 1: Casper* contains over one hundred of Casper's best stories.

ISBN 978-1-59307-781-5

HARVEY CLASSICS VOLUME 2: RICHIE RICH

Move over, Uncle Scrooge! The richest character in comic-book history is about to get his due. This megacompilation of the essential Richie Rich collects his earliest and most substantial stories for the first time ever.

ISBN 978-1-59307-848-5

HARVEY CLASSICS VOLUME 3: HOT STUFF

Who's the hotheaded little devil with a tail as pointed as his personality? It's Hot Stuff! This adorably mischievous imp has delighted comics fans since the 1950s. This volume collects over one hundred of the funniest (and hottest!) classic cartoons featuring Hot Stuff and his pals.

ISBN 978-1-59307-914-7

HARVEY CLASSICS VOLUME 4: BABY HUEY

Oversized, oblivious, and oh-so-good-natured duckling Baby Huey first delighted audiences in 1949, but quickly lumbered his way into the bigger world of cartoons and his own comic-book series! Join Baby Huey, his baffled parents, and his duckling pals in this jumbo collection of classic stories.

ISBN 978-1-59307-977-2

HARVEY CLASSICS VOLUME 5: THE HARVEY GIRLS

They're cute, they're clever, and they're obsessive! Some of Harvey Comics' biggest stars were three "little" girls with large dreams, enormous hearts, and king-size laughs: Little Audrey, Little Dot, and Little Lotta. This book includes 125 classic tales of three amazing girls!

ISBN 978-1-59582-171-3

$19.99 each!

Find out more about these and other great Dark Horse all-ages titles at darkhorse.com!